CALIFORNIA

Environmental
Law AND Policy

Publisher's Note

Before you rely on the information

in this book, be sure you are aware

that some changes in the statutes or

case law may have gone into effect

since the date of publication. The book,

moreover, provides general information

about the law. Readers should consult

their own attorneys before relying

on the representations found herein.

CALIFORNIA

Environmental
Law AND Policy

A PRACTICAL GUIDE

Albert I. Herson

Gary A. Lucks

CALIFORNIA

Environmental Law AND Policy

A PRACTICAL GUIDE

Copyright © 2008 by
Albert I. Herson and Gary A. Lucks

Solano Press Books
Post Office Box 773
Point Arena, California 95468

tel: 800 931-9373
fax: 707 884-4109
email: spbooks@solano.com

Cover and book design by
        Julie Shell and Pat Shell

Index by Daniel McNaughton,
        Chicago, Illinois

ISBN 978-0-923956-60-8

Notice

This book is designed to assist you in
understanding environmental law and
policy. It is necessarily general in nature
and does not discuss all exceptions and
variations to general rules. Also, it may
not reflect the latest changes in the law.
It is not intended as legal advice and
should not be relied on to address legal
problems. You should always consult
an attorney for advice regarding your
specific factual situation.

California Environmental Law and
Policy is printed on stock comprised
of ten percent post-consumer fiber
with soy-based ink formulated for
minimally low VOC emissions.

Dedication

Al Herson dedicates this book to his wife Laurie Warner Herson,
who gave generous support and understanding, as always,
during the writing. And to his wonderful daughters Allie
and Michelle Herson; may they live on a sustainable planet.

Gary A. Lucks dedicates this book to his wife, Lisa Marie Gibson,
for her patience and support as he endeavored to complete
the project after the birth of their baby, Dylan Gibson Lucks.

Chapters at a Glance

Contents

PART ONE

Introduction and Environmental/ Land Use Planning

CHAPTER 1

Introduction / 3

Contents

Contents

Contents

Contents

Contents

Contents

Contents

Contents

Contents

Contents

Contents

Contents

Contents

Contents

List of Tables

Contents

Preface

Book Overview

The field of California environmental law is vast and ever-changing. Planners, project applicants, developers, landowners, regulatory agency staff, consultants, attorneys, environmental managers, interested citizens, and students need a survey of California environmental law written for a general, non-technical audience. This book was written to serve that need.

Guide to California Environmental Law is the only book that covers the entire field of California environmental, land use, and natural resources law in a concise, user-friendly format. Written in non-technical language, the book comprehensively surveys the most important California environmental statutes and regulatory programs, as well as relevant federal environmental statutes and regulatory programs. It highlights landmark court cases and current policy issues, and provides practical tips on getting through the regulatory process successfully.

Guide to California Environmental Law is completely up-to-date, incorporating changes to statutes and regulatory programs through 2007. To assist in more in-depth research, the book identifies sources of further information for each major program, as well as regulatory agency contacts and websites.

The legal citations in the book are selective, to promote readability. Because this book is intended for a generalist non-technical audience, procedural topics such as administrative appeals, litigation, enforcement, and remedies are addressed only briefly. Attorneys seeking more comprehensive legal citations and expanded coverage of specific topics should refer to other excellent publications identified in this book, including Solano Press titles, and the Matthew Bender treatise, *California Environmental Law and Land Use Practice*. This book is not intended to give legal advice, for which an attorney should be consulted.

Book Objectives, Scope, and Format

Objectives

The specific objectives of this book are to provide readers with:

- A comprehensive, user-friendly, concise review of California and related federal environmental law in non-technical language
- Focused information on what practicing planners, project applicants, attorneys, and other audiences need to know
- References to key publications and websites for further research

Scope

The book is divided into four major parts:

- **Part One** starts with an introduction (chapter 1), reviewing the basic framework of California environmental law. It then covers the broadest environmental programs, those related to environmental and land use planning. It includes chapters on the California Environmental Quality Act or CEQA (chapter 2), local land use planning (chapter 3), and state and regional land use controls (chapter 4).
- **Part Two** covers specific pollution control programs. It includes chapters on air quality (chapter 5), noise (chapter 6), hazardous materials and toxic substances (chapter 7), hazardous wastes (chapter 8), solid waste (chapter 9), water quality (chapter 10), and drinking water (chapter 11).
- **Part Three** covers programs regulating the state's natural resources. It includes chapters on agriculture (chapter 12), water resources (chapter 13), fish and wildlife (chapter 14), wetlands (chapter 15), forestry (chapter 16), and surface mining (chapter 17).
- **Part Four** presents two practical guides for environmental compliance. Chapter 18 is a permitting guide designed to help project applicants navigate the complexities of environmental, land use, and natural resource permitting in California. Chapter 19 is an environmental auditing guide designed to help facility managers plan environmental compliance audits.

Format

The book's chapters covering individual land use or environmental regulatory programs (chapters 2 through 17) follow a common internal organization:

- Identification of key laws and agencies
- Summaries of major regulatory programs
- A glossary of terms used in the chapter (major permits and approvals are indicated by an asterisk)
- Acronyms used in the chapter
- References to key publications and websites

Acknowledgments

The authors wish to thank the following individuals, who reviewed and provided suggestions on early drafts of various chapters:

- Mark Beuhler, Assistant General Manager, Coachella Valley Water District

- Robert A. Bray, Director, The Elm Consulting Group International LLC

- Matt Haber, Deputy Director, Air Division, Environmental Protection Agency Region 9

- Jennifer Harder, Esq., Downey Brand

- Sara Hilbrich, Esq.

- B. Demar Hooper, Esq., Law Offices of B. Demar Hooper

- Gary Liss, President, Gary Liss and Associates, Zero Waste Consultant

- Jon B. Marshack, D.Env., Staff Environmental Scientist, California Regional Water Quality Control Board, Central Valley Region

- Mike McCoy, Co-Director, University of California Davis Information Center for the Environment

- Dave Stein, PE, CH2MHill

- Michael J. Steel, Esq., Pillsbury, Winthrop, Shaw, and Pittman LLP

- James Stettler, California Department of Toxic Substances Control

- Lynette Stetler, Esq., Beyond Compliance LLC

- Terry Trumbull, Esq., Trumbull Law Firm
  and Professor at San Jose State University

- Paul Wack, Associate Professor, California
  Polytechnic University, San Luis Obispo

In addition, the authors wish to thank Theresa Schultz and Julie Shell for their important roles in editing the text and designing the book, respectively. The authors also wish to thank Erin Sullivan, JD, who completed legal research and analysis and validated regulatory citations. Also, the authors appreciate the creative efforts of Tom Wyatt, who prepared illustrations to help convey the book's ideas in easy-to-understand graphic form.

About the Authors

Albert I. Herson, J.D., FAICP, is a planner and attorney who has practiced, taught, and written about California environmental law for 30 years. He has been an environmental consultant since 1979. He currently is Principal and Environmental Planning Practice Leader with SWCA Environmental Consultants, a 500-person environmental science and planning firm, where he helps private and public clients with environmental compliance and training.

Mr. Herson has devoted much of his career to making CEQA, NEPA, and natural resource laws understandable and accessible to California planners and attorneys. He is a frequent speaker and writer on California environmental law topics and on several occasions advised state agencies on revisions to the CEQA Guidelines to make them more practical and user-friendly.

Mr. Herson is co-author of *The NEPA Book* (2000) and the *CEQA Deskbook* (second edition, 1999) published by Solano Press. He is co-author of the CEQA and wetlands regulation chapters in *California Environmental Law and Land Use Practice* (Matthew Bender), and a contributing editor and regular writer for *California Environmental Law Reporter.*

Mr. Herson is a member of the State Bar, Fellow of the American Institute of Certified Planners (AICP), as well as 2007–2008 President of the California Planning Roundtable. He is Past-President of the California Chapter, American Planning Association, which awarded him the Distinguished Leadership Award for a Professional Planner in 1996. He also has served on the California State Bar Environmental Law Section Executive Committee. Mr. Herson received a J.D. from the University of the Pacific McGeorge School of Law, where he was class valedictorian, and an M.A. in Urban Planning from the University of California, Los Angeles, where he graduated *summa cum laude.*

Gary A. Lucks J.D., CPEA, is a principal attorney and scientist with Beyond Compliance LLC where he advises clients on environmental compliance matters, sustainability, and environmental management systems (EMS). He is a Certified Professional Environmental Auditor (CPEA) with more than 20 years of environmental regulatory compliance and sustainability experience. Mr. Lucks specializes in environmental compliance auditing, compliance management systems (CMS), compliance counseling, EMS, environmental training, and environmental permitting.

Mr. Lucks is also a co-founder of the Sustainable Earth Initiative, a nonprofit organization specializing in EMS and dedicated to helping public agencies improve their environmental performance.

Mr. Lucks has written extensively on environmental law, legislation, and policy. He authored the environmental auditing chapter for the *California Environmental Law and Land Use Practice* treatise (Matthew Bender), and contributed to the chapter on Hazardous Materials and Toxic Substances. He has also written more than a dozen lead articles in the *California Environmental Law Reporter*.

Mr. Lucks is a frequent speaker on environmental law, auditing, legislation, and sustainability and teaches numerous environmental courses at the University of California Extension (Berkeley, Davis, and Santa Cruz campuses) ranging from hazardous waste management and air quality to environmental auditing. He currently serves on the California State Bar Environmental Legislation Committee and is the West Coast Chair of The Auditing Roundtable.

Mr. Lucks earned his B.S. in Environmental Biology from Tulane University and his law degree from the University of the Pacific McGeorge School of Law. He is licensed to practice law in California.

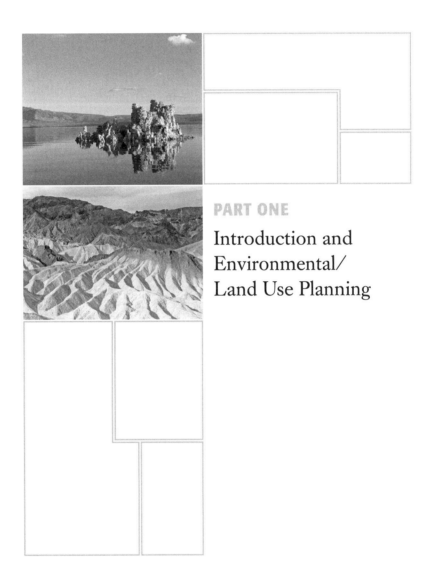

PART ONE

Introduction and Environmental/ Land Use Planning

Introduction

This chapter reviews —

- Basic framework of California environmental law
- Sources of California environmental law: federal and state statutes and regulations, environmental common law, public trust doctrine
- California environmental agencies and their roles
- Environmental law terminology and principles

Glossary

CALFED—a consortium of federal and state agencies overseeing Bay–Delta water management, superseded by the Bay–Delta Authority.

Common law—system of law derived from judges' decisions, rather than statutes or constitutions.

Environmental indicator—an objective measure of environmental quality used to assess the effectiveness of environmental programs.

Environmental justice—a program to ensure that environmental programs and enforcement fairly treat people of all races, cultures, and incomes, especially minority and low-income populations.

Negligence—the failure to exercise the degree of care considered reasonable, resulting in unintended injury to another party.

Nuisance—a condition or activity interfering with the free use and enjoyment of property or the exercise of certain public rights.

Police power—the power of state and local governments to enact legislation to protect public health, safety, and welfare.

Public trust doctrine—enforceable doctrine by which certain natural resources are held in trust by the government for the use and enjoyment of the public.

Sovereign lands—submerged lands, tidelands, and the beds of navigable rivers.

Statute of limitations—time limit for filing a lawsuit.

Strict liability—for certain activities, *e.g.,* ultrahazardous activities, a defendant is liable even if the activity is carried out with all reasonable care.

Submerged lands—includes state-owned lands between the tidelands and the three-mile limit of offshore waters subject to state jurisdiction, as well as lands underlying navigable waters.

Tidelands—lands over which the tide ebbs and flows.

Trespass—an unauthorized and wrongful entry or intrusion onto land.

CHAPTER 1

Introduction

Introduction

The purpose of this chapter is to give the reader a basic understanding of the foundations of California environmental law. It first reviews the various sources of California and related federal environmental law: federal and state constitutions, statutes, and regulations; common (judge-made) law; and the public trust doctrine. It then describes the numerous California agencies responsible for environmental and resource protection, and how they are organized. The chapter concludes with a review of basic environmental law terminology and principles.

Federal and State Environmental Law

Federal Law

Federal constitution. The federal constitution defines the powers of the executive, legislative, and judicial branches of government. Constitutional requirements particularly relevant to environmental law include the Commerce Clause, the Fifth Amendment, and the Supremacy Clause.

The Commerce Clause (Art. I, Sec. 8, Clause 3) gives the federal government the authority to regulate interstate commerce and is the constitutional basis for many federal environmental laws. The Fifth Amendment bans the taking of private property without just compensation and has been the basis for "regulatory taking" legal challenges to overly harsh environmental and land use regulations. Under the Supremacy Clause (Art. 6, Para. 2), federal law must be followed if there is conflicting state law. A conflict exists either when compliance

The Commerce Clause gives the federal government the authority to regulate interstate commerce and is the constitutional basis for many federal environmental laws.

5

with both federal and state law is impossible, or when a state law is an obstacle to achieving the execution of Congress' full purposes. *See Edgar v. Mite Corp.* (1982) 457 U.S. 624.

Federal statutes. For most California environmental programs, federal statutes and regulations are implemented in an integrated fashion with California laws. Federal statutes are enacted by Congress and signed by the President. A description of this process can be found at the Library of Congress website (http://thomas.loc.gov/home/lawsmade.toc.html). Once enacted, laws are compiled into United States Codes (USC) organized by title and subject matter. U.S. Codes are available on the Government Printing Office (GPO) website (www.gpoaccess.gov/uscode/index.html).

CFR = Code of Federal Regulations
GPO = Government Printing Office
USC = United States Code

Federal regulations. Federal agency regulations implementing environmental statutes may be found in the Code of Federal Regulations (CFR). The CFR is divided into titles that represent broad areas subject to federal regulation. Each volume of the CFR is updated once each calendar year and is issued on a quarterly basis. The CFR is available on the GPO website (www.gpoaccess.gov/uscode/index.html). Federal agency regulations and decisionmaking must comply with requirements established by the Administrative Procedures Act (5 USC 511 *et seq.*).

An executive order is a Presidential declaration that has the force of law, usually based on existing statutory powers, and requires no action by Congress.

Executive orders. An executive order is a Presidential declaration that has the force of law, usually based on existing statutory powers, and requires no action by Congress. Examples of executive orders related to environmental law include those on wetlands (Executive Order 11990), floodplains (Executive Order 11988), and environmental justice (Executive Order 12898). Executive orders are effective during the Presidential term in which they were issued unless adopted by successor Presidents.

Judicial decisions. Federal courts play an important role in the implementation of environmental law in California through reviewing the constitutionality of state environmental statutes and regulations, as well as interpreting federal environmental statutes and regulations. Federal environmental cases in California are typically first brought to the relevant federal district court: Northern District, Central District, Southern District, or Eastern District. Decisions issued by these courts may be appealed to the Ninth Circuit Court of Appeals and ultimately the U.S. Supreme Court. In case citations, district court decisions are abbreviated as "Fed. Supp.," Court of Appeals decisions are abbreviated as "Fed. Rptr.," and Supreme Court decisions are abbreviated as "U.S."

State Law

All state statutes, state regulations, and local ordinances must be consistent with the California Constitution.

State constitution. The California Constitution sets forth the fundamental laws by which the state is governed. Amendments to the California Constitution require a vote of the people. All state statutes, state regulations, and local

Figure 1-1

How a Bill Becomes a Law

IDEA

- Ideas come from anyone.
- Process begins when someone persuades legislator to author bill.

↓

AUTHOR

- Legislator sends idea and bill language to Legislative Counsel, who drafts into actual bill.
- Bill returned to legislator for introduction.

↓

FIRST READING

- Clerk reads bill number, author name, and bill title.
- Bill sent to Office of State printing.
- Bill must be in print 30 days before acted upon.

↓

COMMITTEE HEARINGS

- Bill goes to Senate or Assembly Rules Committee, where it is assigned to appropriate policy committee for first hearing.
- During hearing, author presents bill, supporters and opponents testify, and committee acts on bill.
- Committee may either pass, pass as amended, or defeat bill.
- Bills requiring money must also be heard in Senate or Assembly Appropriations Committee.

↓

SECOND AND THIRD READING

- Bill read second time in house of origin, then placed in Daily File for third reading.
- In third reading, author explains bill, legislators discuss, and vote via roll call.
- Bills requiring money or urgency bills require 27 votes in Senate or 64 in Assembly.
- All other bills require 21 and 41 votes, respectively.

↓

REPEAT PROCESS IN OTHER HOUSE

- Once bill approved by house of origin, it proceeds to other house, where procedure is repeated.

↓

RESOLUTION OF DIFFERENCES

- If bill amended in second house, it goes back to house of origin for concurrence.
- If agreement not reached, bill moves to two-house conference committee to resolve differences.
- If compromise reached, conference report voted upon in both houses.

↓

GOVERNOR

- Bill goes to Governor, who may sign into law, allow to become law without signature, or veto.
- Veto may be overridden by two-thirds vote in both houses.
- Urgency bills take effect immediately upon Governor's signing.
- Other bills go into effect January 1 of next year.

Source: Adapted from California Senate. 2000. The Legislative Process: A Citizen's Guide to Participation

Most regulatory programs described in this book were established by state legislation.

ordinances must be consistent with the California Constitution. The California Constitution (Art. XI, Sec. 7) establishes the police power under which a city or county may enact ordinances to protect public health, safety, and welfare. Also, the public trust doctrine, derived in part from the California Constitution, has been influential in the development of California environmental law and is reviewed separately below.

State statutes. Most of the regulatory programs described in this book are established by state statute. The legislative process by which a bill becomes law is reviewed briefly below and is illustrated in Figure 1-1.

The California Legislature is comprised of two houses: the Senate with 40 Senators and the Assembly with 80 Assembly Members. The Legislature, which is full time, meets in two-year sessions.

A legislator sends the idea for a new bill to the Legislative Counsel's office, which drafts the bill language. The bill is returned to the legislator for introduction in either the Senate or Assembly (house of origin). The Rules Committee of the house of origin then assigns the bill to the appropriate policy committee for its first hearing. Bills are assigned to policy committees according to subject matter of the bill. Committees typically addressing environmental programs include the following:

- **Assembly.** Environmental Safety and Toxic Materials; Natural Resources; Water, Parks and Wildlife
- **Senate.** Environmental Quality; Natural Resources and Water

The policy committee votes to pass the bill, to pass the bill as amended, or to defeat the bill. Bills passed by committees then are voted on by the house of origin. Once the bill has been approved by the house of origin, the bill proceeds to the other house where the procedure is repeated. If a bill is amended in the second house, it must return to the house of origin for concurrence (agreement on the amendments). If agreement cannot be reached, the bill is referred to a two-house conference committee to resolve differences. If a compromise is reached, the bill is returned to both houses for a vote.

If both houses approve, the bill then goes to the Governor. The Governor can sign the bill into law, allow it to become law without signature, or veto it. A Governor's veto can be overridden by a two-thirds vote in both houses. Almost all bills go into effect on the first day of January of the next year. Urgency measures, which require a two-thirds vote in both houses, take effect immediately after they are signed or allowed to become law without signature.

Bills passed by the Legislature and approved by the Governor are assigned a chapter number by the Secretary of State. These chaptered bills (also referred to as Statutes of the year they were enacted) then become part of the California Codes. The California Codes are a comprehensive collection of laws grouped by subject matter. For example, the California Public Resources Code compiles statutes such as the California Environmental Quality Act (CEQA), state fish and wildlife laws, and state forestry laws. California codes are available at the Legislative Counsel's website (www.leginfo.ca.gov/calaw.html).

State regulations. Agencies responsible for statutory programs typically adopt detailed regulations describing the law's implementation. The state Office of Administrative Law (OAL) is responsible for reviewing regulations for compliance with the standards set forth in California's Administrative Procedure Act (Gov. Code 11340 *et seq., see* OAL 2005), for transmitting these regulations to the Secretary of State, and for publishing regulations in the California Code of Regulations (CCR).

The CCR is divided into numeric titles grouping regulations by subject matter. For example, Title 14 contains regulations governing resources, and Title 22 contains regulations governing hazardous waste. The CCR is available at the Westlaw website (http://government.westlaw.com/linkedslice/default.asp?SP=CCR-1000).

Executive orders. A Governor's executive order is a declaration that has the force of law, usually based on existing statutory powers, and requires no action by the Legislature. Examples of executive orders related to environmental law include those on global climate change (Exec. Order S-3-05) and repair of levees in the Sacramento–San Joaquin Delta (Exec. Order S-01-06).

Initiative and referendum. California has a long tradition of direct democracy, giving voters the power to enact laws without relying on the Legislature or local government. An initiative is a vehicle empowering the voters to propose and adopt state statutes and constitutional amendments (authorized by Art. II, Sec. 8(a) of the California Constitution), and to propose and adopt local legislation (authorized by Art. II, Sec. 11). A referendum similarly gives voters the power to approve or reject certain types of statutes (authorized by Art. II, Sec. 9).

The 1972 California Coastal Initiative, which established a state system for coastal zone management, was a particularly powerful use of the initiative process to enact environmental policy. At the local government level, initiatives or referenda on land use controls are common (*see* chapter 3).

Local ordinances. Ordinances are local laws passed by local agencies such as city councils and county boards of supervisors. Environmental and land use ordinances usually are based on the police power. Local agencies have individualized methods of enacting land use and environmental ordinances; the content of these ordinances often is influenced or controlled by state or federal legislation.

Judicial decisions. California courts are responsible for interpreting state and local statutes and regulations. They also establish and interpret environmental

CCR = California Code of Regulations

CEQA = California Environmental Quality Act

OAL = Office of Administrative Law

An initiative is a vehicle empowering the voters to propose and adopt state statutes and constitutional amendments, and to propose and adopt local legislation.

What Citizens Need to Know to Enforce Environmental Laws

- Which specific environmental issues are involved?

- Who are the key players? Who is in charge of decisions affecting the environmental issues of concern? What are their authorities?

- Which environmental laws apply? Which laws apply to the environmental issues, what do they require, and which provide the best tools to address the issues?

- What are the key deadlines? What are the agency decisionmaking schedules and the opportunities for citizen input? Failure to participate in the administrative process often results in the loss of the right to take later legal action.

- What are the sources of relevant information? Which agencies and online information sources are available to learn more about the environmental issues of concern?

Source: Adapted from Environmental Law Institute (2002)

Common law doctrines applicable to environmental claims include nuisance, trespass, negligence, and strict liability.

common law (*see* below). Environmental cases in California are typically first brought to one of the state's 58 trial courts, one for each county. Trial court decisions may be appealed to the appropriate Court of Appeal (there are six district courts of appeal) and ultimately to the California Supreme Court. Court of Appeal decisions are cited as "Cal. App." and Supreme Court decisions are cited as "Cal."

Private Enforcement of Environmental Laws

Citizen enforcement. Citizens and citizen groups play a vital role in the enforcement of federal and state environmental laws. Most of these laws have citizen suit provisions, allowing citizens to sue agencies for taking actions inconsistent with statutes, regulations, and ordinances. For example, citizens having environmental concerns about a development project can make their concerns known through taking advantage of public notice and comment provisions, or filing citizen lawsuits.

Citizen enforcement of environmental laws is challenging, because many environmental laws and agencies may be involved for a particular project or environmental approval. To get started with enforcement, citizens can do initial research to address the questions listed in the sidebar.

Unfair competition statute. Business and Professions Code 17200 *et seq.* creates a private right of action for "unfair competition," defined to include "any unlawful, unfair or fraudulent business act or practice." By referring to unlawful acts and practices, these sections create a right to sue under environmental statutes even if the statutes themselves do not allow private enforcement. Suits may be filed on behalf of others (representative suits), but as a result of proposition 64 approved by the voters in 2004, representatives must have suffered injury and lost money or property because of unfair competition (Bus. and Prof. Code 17203, 17205, 17535).

Environmental Common Law

Common law is a system of law derived from judges' decisions arising from the judicial branch of government, rather than statutes or constitutions derived from the legislative branch of government. Common law is an alternative legal pathway to seek relief for those injured by environmental harms.

Common law doctrines applicable to environmental claims include nuisance, trespass, negligence, and strict liability. The term "toxic torts" means use of one of these theories of liability to remedy various types of toxic and environmental exposures. (A tort is defined as a civil wrong creating liability that does not arise from a statute or contract.)

Nuisance

Nuisance defined and types of nuisances. A nuisance is a condition or activity interfering with the free use and enjoyment of property or the exercise of certain public rights (Civ. Code 3479, which codifies common law), for which injunctive and damages remedies are authorized (Code Civ. Proc. 731). Examples of environmental nuisances include air and water pollution, hazardous waste contamination, noise, odors, and violation of land use regulations. Also, certain actions are defined as nuisances either by state statute or local ordinance.

Two types of nuisances exist. Public nuisances affect an entire community, neighborhood, or population; only government attorneys may bring a public nuisance lawsuit. Private nuisances consist of all non-public nuisances; parties must own a property interest that is damaged in order to bring a private nuisance lawsuit. The classification of a nuisance as public or private may determine whether certain defenses apply and what remedies are available.

Also, nuisances are classified as permanent or continuing. A permanent nuisance is a single completed act or condition that cannot be abated, causing permanent damages that can be assessed at one time. A continuing nuisance is an ongoing act or condition that is capable of being stopped (*i.e.,* abatable). The classification of a nuisance as permanent or continuing may determine whether a plaintiff's claim is time-barred by a statute of limitations and what remedies are available.

Defenses. To prove a nuisance, the plaintiff must show that a condition or activity resulted in substantial harm and that the use of property causing the condition or activity is unreasonable. Several defenses exist to a nuisance claim, including:

To prove a nuisance, the plaintiff must show that a condition or activity resulted in substantial harm and that the use of property causing the condition or activity is unreasonable.

- An activity is not a nuisance if the utility of the defendant's conduct outweighs the environmental damage caused.

- Acts authorized by statute, agricultural activities, and certain other activities are declared by statute not to be nuisances. Civ. Code 3482, 3482.5.

- A plaintiff who consents to maintenance of a nuisance may not file a private nuisance lawsuit.

- An injunction may not be granted for a nuisance lawsuit against a legally permitted commercial or industrial use unless it employs unnecessary or injurious methods of operation.

However, the following are not valid defenses: a continuing nuisance was maintained by a prior landowner, the defendant's activity occurred first and the plaintiff "came to the nuisance," the defendant complied with relevant government regulations, or the defendant is a government agency.

Remedies. The remedies for a nuisance are injunctions and money damages. Courts can issue injunctions to abate a nuisance, both to stop the nuisance activity (mandatory injunction) or to prevent it from occurring in the future

The remedies for a nuisance are injunctions and money damages.

(prohibitory injunction). Money damages may consist of lost property values for a permanent nuisance, or costs of abatement for a continuing nuisance. Punitive damages are available for malicious or fraudulent acts.

Trespass

A trespass is an unauthorized and wrongful entry or intrusion onto land. Examples of environmental types of trespass include depositing wastes onto land, airplane overflights, and groundwater contamination or removal by neighboring landowners.

Trespass is an alternative legal theory to nuisance for environmental harms. Like nuisances, trespasses can be either permanent or continuing depending on whether they can be abated; this classification determines the statute of limitations for bringing a lawsuit. However, trespass has more limitations than nuisance as a legal theory. Only those who actually possess property that has been damaged may file a trespass lawsuit. Also, a trespass requires an actual physical intrusion on the plaintiff's property, so intangible intrusions such as odor and noise are not actionable.

Like nuisance actions, trespass also may allow the plaintiff to obtain injunctions or money damages. Injunctions are available to prevent a continuing or threatened nuisance. Damages typically are measured by loss of property value due to the trespass, or by the cost of restoring the property plus its rental value when it could not be used.

Negligence

Negligence is the failure to exercise the degree of care considered reasonable under the circumstances, resulting in an unintended injury to another party. Environmental harms may be remedied through a negligence lawsuit. To prove negligence, the plaintiff must show the following: the defendant had a legal duty of care to the plaintiff, the defendant breached that duty of care, the breach was a cause of the resulting injury, and actual damages resulted from the injury. Examples of negligence claims for environmental harm include improper storage, treatment, or disposal of hazardous waste, or a property owner failing to warn purchasers of property contamination.

The doctrine of "negligence per se" is often useful in environmental cases; it creates a presumption of negligence if a plaintiff violates a regulatory requirement, the violation causes personal injury or property damage, and the plaintiff is within the class of persons the regulatory requirement is intended to protect. A long-established environmental statute commonly used to impose negligence per se states that "[n]o person shall discharge…waste…in any manner which will result in contamination, pollution, or a nuisance" (Health and Safety Code 5411). The presumption of negligence may be rebutted by the defendant proving it did what might be expected of a person of ordinary prudence, acting under similar circumstances, with a desire to comply with the law.

Strict Liability

Under California common law, certain uncommon activities are so inherently dangerous that they are classified as ultrahazardous (also referred to as "abnormally dangerous" activities). Defendants that conduct ultrahazardous activities, and know or should know that they could cause injury, are held strictly liable for the injury. Strict liability means that the defendant is liable even if the activity is carried out with all reasonable care.

Certain environmentally risky activities may create strict liability because they are ultrahazardous; examples include aerial application of herbicides, use of chemicals in transformers, and use of explosives near residential areas. Defenses to a strict liability lawsuit include the defendant's comparative fault (negligence), the defendant's assumption of risk, and a three-year statute of limitations for injury to real property.

Strict products liability is a related strict liability legal theory. Strict products liability applies when a product is defective due to the product's design or manufacture, or when the manufacturer fails to give appropriate warnings. Examples where this doctrine may apply include manufacture of pesticides or pollution control equipment.

Cropdusting is an example of an ultrahazardous activity.

Statutes of Limitations

In any civil action for personal injury or wrongful death due to exposure to a hazardous material or toxic substance, the action must be brought within two years from either the date of the injury or the date the plaintiff should reasonably have been aware of the injury, the physical cause of the injury, and the wrongful acts leading to the injury (Code Civ. Proc. 340.8). For releases of contaminants from facilities regulated by the Comprehensive Environmental Response, Compensation, and Liability Act (CERCLA), a delayed discovery rule applies, and the statute of limitations begins to run only when the plaintiff knew or reasonably should have known both the existence and the cause of the injury.

For real property damages due to contamination, the statute of limitations is three years from the contamination or when the plaintiff should reasonably have been aware of the contamination (Code Civ. Proc. 338(b)).

CERCLA = Comprehensive Environmental Response, Compensation, and Liability Act

Origins of the Public Trust Doctrine

The public trust doctrine's origins are in the work of Emperor Justinian (Institutes of Justinian 2.1.1), whose statement of Roman law included the following: "[b]y law the nature of these things are common to mankind—the air, running water, the sea and consequently the shores of the sea." The state was to hold these resources in trust for the benefit of the people and to preserve their rights for commerce, fishing, and navigation.

The public trust was recognized in English common law, which formed the basis of common law in the United States. In the landmark case of *Arnold v. Mundy* (1821) 6 N.J.L. 1, a New Jersey state court found the public right to take oysters from beneath navigable waters of a coastal bay. The court held that certain types of property are unique and should not be privately owned, and that the state holds these types of properties for the benefit of all the people, but that the state may dispose of (*e.g.,* sell or lease) portions of trust property if it furthers the public interest.

Relying on this decision, in another oyster fishing case, the U.S. Supreme Court in *Martin v. Lessee of Waddell* (1852) 41 US 367 found that the state of New Jersey owned the beds of navigable waters in its sovereign capacity, to be held as a public trust for the benefit of the people and freely used by all for navigation and fishing. These principles were further interpreted in the *Illinois Central* case cited in the text. The Supreme Court in *Illinois Central* emphasized that the state may not dispose of trust lands except for public purposes.

In California, the landmark public trust case is *People v. California Fish Co.* (1913) 166 Cal. 576. In that case, the California Supreme Court ruled that state conveyance of state tideland, swamp, and overflowed lands remained subject to the public trust interest, retained by the state for the benefit of the people. The court left open the possibility of invalidating legislation that would cause the destruction of public trust uses.

In *Marks v. Whitney* (1971) 6 Cal. 3d 251, the Supreme Court expanded the public trust beyond the traditional purposes of commerce, fishing, and navigation, to include environmental and aesthetic uses. Finally, in *National Audubon Society v. Superior Court* (1983) 33 Cal. 3d 419, the Supreme Court expanded the application of the public trust doctrine to non-navigable streams and to state grants of water rights. ▪

Public Trust Doctrine

Origins of the Public Trust Doctrine

The public trust doctrine, originated by ancient Roman law, derives from both the California Constitution and California common law. It has become a powerful tool for citizens seeking to develop a comprehensive legal approach to resource management issues (*see* Sax 1970).

The public trust doctrine states that certain natural resources, even those in private ownership, must be held in trust by the government for use and enjoyment by the people of the state. Constitutional provisions related to the public trust include a ban on the sale of state tidelands within two miles of an unincorporated city (Art. X, Sec. 3), the guarantee of public access to navigable waters of the state (Art. X, Sec. 4), and the right of the public to fish on public lands, including public lands sold into private ownership (Art. I, Sec. 25).

California public trust case law is based on a federal Supreme Court case, *Illinois Central Railroad Co. v. Illinois* (1892) 146 U.S. 307. In that case, the Supreme Court upheld the Illinois Legislature's repeal of its earlier granting of the Chicago waterfront to a private railroad. The court held that the grant substantially impaired the public from exercising its trust rights to lands underlying navigable waters.

Scope of the Public Trust Doctrine

Public uses protected by the public trust. Public uses protected by the public trust include commerce, navigation, fishing, recreation, and environmental preservation. In administering the public trust, agencies attempt to accommodate multiple uses, but have the discretion to promote one use over another.

Resources subject to the public trust. The public trust doctrine applies to the following resources:

- Tidelands and submerged lands: tidelands are lands over which the tide ebbs and flows. Submerged lands include state-owned lands between the tidelands and the three-mile limit of offshore waters subject to state jurisdiction, as well as lands underlying navigable waters.

- Navigable waters: the beds of inland navigable waters, as defined by federal law (*see* chapter 15), and lakes are subject to the public trust doctrine.

- Non-navigable waters and water rights: the landmark case of *National Audubon Society v. Superior Court* (1983) 33 Cal. 3d 419 extended the public trust to non-navigable waters and to water rights. *See* chapter 13.

- Fish and wildlife: California's fish and wildlife resources are publicly owned in trust for the benefit of the public.

Mono Lake water rights were the subject of the landmark *National Audubon Society* public trust case.

Agencies administering the public trust. The agencies administering the public trust in California include:

- State Lands Commission: has primary jurisdiction to act as trustee for public trust lands.

- Department of Fish and Game: administers the public trust doctrine for fish and wildlife resources.

- State Water Resources Control Board: applies the public trust doctrine to water rights decisions. See chapter 13 for a detailed discussion of the application of the doctrine to water rights.

- Local agencies: have been granted state sovereign lands in trust (in some cases, by the Legislature) for purposes such as port development.

These agencies have an affirmative duty to protect trust resources and have limited ability to transfer public trust resources into private ownership (*see City of Long Beach v. Mansell* (1970) 3 Cal. 3d 462).

California Environmental Agencies

The Legislature has given numerous agencies the authority to regulate and protect the state's environment and natural resources. This discussion provides an overview of state environmental agencies. Subsequent chapters discuss in more detail the roles of these agencies, as well as federal, regional, and local agencies, in implementing specific environmental programs.

Figure 1-2
**Cal/EPA
Organization**

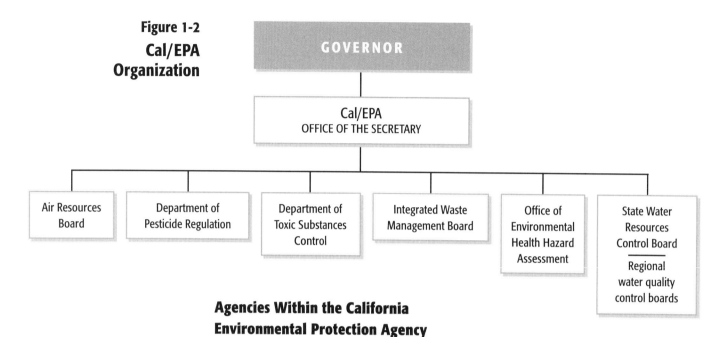

Figure 1-2
**Cal/EPA
Organization**

Agencies Within the California Environmental Protection Agency

Cal/EPA = California Environmental
Protection Agency

DTSC = Department of Toxic
Substances Control

The California Environmental Protection Agency (Cal/EPA) was created in 1991 by an executive order. Several boards, departments, and the office of the Secretary of Cal/EPA were placed within the Cal/EPA umbrella to create a cabinet-level voice for environmental protection and to assure coordinated administration of environmental programs. Cal/EPA's mission is to "restore, protect and enhance the environment, to ensure public health, environmental quality and economic vitality."

Boards, departments, and offices. Boards, departments, and offices within Cal/EPA (*see* Figure 1-2) are the:

- **Air Resources Board.** Regulates air pollution sources, including greenhouse gases contributing to global climate change
- **State Water Resources Control Board and Regional Water Quality Control Boards.** Regulate water pollution sources and (State Water Resources Control Board only) water rights
- **Integrated Waste Management Board.** Regulates solid waste disposal and recycling
- **Department of Toxic Substances Control (DTSC).** Regulates hazardous waste and hazardous waste cleanup
- **Office of Environmental Health Hazard Assessment.** Provides information on adverse health effects of environmental exposures to non-infectious agents
- **Department of Pesticide Regulation.** Regulates registration, sale, and use of pesticides

Office of the Secretary. The Office of the Secretary heads Cal/EPA and is responsible for overseeing and coordinating the activities of all Cal/EPA agencies. The Secretary does not direct policies and decisions of Cal/EPA agencies. Specific Office of the Secretary functions include budget review, review of personnel management, enforcement coordination, information management coordination, strategic planning, and pollution prevention.

In addition to these agency duties, the Legislature has given the Office of the Secretary several specific programmatic responsibilities. These include the Environmental Justice (EJ) program and the Environmental Protection Indicators for California (EPIC) program.

DPH = California Department of Public Health
EJ = Environmental justice
EPIC = Environmental Protection Indicators for California
PRC = Public Resources Code

Environmental justice (EJ) program. Cal/EPA's EJ program was created by Public Resources Code (PRC) 71110 *et seq*. The Legislature charged Cal/EPA with conducting its programs and enforcing environmental laws in a manner that ensures the fair treatment of people of all races, cultures, and income levels, including minority and low-income populations. Among other things, Cal/EPA was required to:

- Develop a model environmental justice mission statement for Cal/EPA agencies
- Convene an interagency working group composed of state agency heads, assisted by an advisory group, to develop an EJ strategy to be implemented by Cal/EPA agencies
- Ensure greater public participation in the development, adoption, and implementation of environmental regulations and policies
- Improve research and data collection on EJ issues
- Develop an agency-wide strategy for addressing gaps in existing programs or policies impeding the achievement of EJ

In 2004, Cal/EPA issued its environmental justice strategy (Cal/EPA 2004a), with the following goals:

- Ensure meaningful public participation and promote capacity-building so all communities can effectively participate in environmental decisionmaking processes
- Integrate EJ into the development, adoption, implementation, and enforcement of environmental laws, regulations, and policies
- Improve research and data collection to promote and address EJ issues related to the health and environment of communities of color and low-income populations
- Ensure effective cross-media coordination and accountability in addressing EJ issues

Also in 2004, the interagency working group issued an EJ Action Plan (Cal/EPA 2004b) describing short-term activities to implement these goals.

Environmental Protection Indicators for California program. The EPIC program is a collaborative effort of Cal/EPA, the Resources Agency, the Department of Public Health (DPH) (formerly the Department of Health Services), and an external advisory group consisting of representatives from business, public interest groups, academia, and local government. The program, led by the

OEHHA = Office of Environmental
Health Hazard Assessment

Office of Environmental Health Hazard Assessment (OEHHA), is responsible for developing and maintaining a set of environmental indicators for California.

Environmental indicators are objective measures of environmental quality used to assess the effectiveness of environmental programs. The indicators are scientifically based measures that convey complex information on environmental status and trends in an easily understood format.

OEHHA's first environmental indicators report was published in 2002 (Cal/EPA 2002) and updated in 2004 (Cal/EPA 2004c) and 2005 (Cal/EPA 2005). OEHHA set forth environmental indicators for:

- Air quality
- Water
- Land, waste, and materials management
- Pesticides
- Transboundary issues
- Environmental exposure impacts upon human health
- Ecosystem health

Agencies Within the Resources Agency

The Resources Agency is a second cabinet-level umbrella agency for agencies with authority to protect and manage natural resources.

Boards, commissions, departments, and conservancies. The Resources Agency is a second cabinet-level umbrella agency for agencies with authority to protect and manage natural resources. The Resources Agency consists of seventeen boards and commissions and eight departments, as well as nine regional conservancies. The Resources Agency mission is to "restore, protect and manage the state's natural, historical and cultural resources for current and future generations using creative approaches and solutions based on science, collaboration and respect for all the communities and interests involved."

Boards and commissions within the Resources Agency are the:

- **California Coastal Commission.** Plans and regulates land use within the coastal zone
- **California Energy Commission.** Implements the state's energy policy and programs, and administers the energy facility licensing program
- **California State Lands Commission.** Manages state sovereign lands, and energy and minerals leasing on state lands
- **San Francisco Bay Conservation and Development Commission.** Plans and regulates land use within San Francisco Bay, Suisun Marsh, and adjacent areas
- **Delta Protection Commission.** Plans land use within the Sacramento–San Joaquin Delta region
- **Colorado River Board of California.** Protects California's rights and interests in the Colorado River, and represents California in negotiations regarding the Colorado River

- **Central Valley Flood Protection Agency (formerly State Reclamation Board).** Manages levees and flood control along the Sacramento and San Joaquin Rivers
- **Board of Forestry.** Regulates forest practices and oversees California Department of Forestry and Fire Protection programs
- **Fish and Game Commission.** Regulates hunting and fishing
- **Mining and Geology Board.** Represents the state's interests in geology, geologic and seismologic hazards, conservation of mineral resources, and surface mining reclamation
- **Native American Heritage Commission.** Protects Native American burials from vandalism and inadvertent destruction, and provides for notification of most likely descendants regarding the discovery of Native American remains
- **Parks and Recreation Commission.** Approves general plans for units of the state park system, establishes general policies for the system, and recommends comprehensive recreation policies for the state
- **State Historical Resources Commission.** Reviews applications for listing historic and archaeological resources on the National Register of Historic Places and the California Register of Historical Resources
- **State Off-Highway Motor Vehicle Recreation Commission.** Provides policy guidance for the state's off-highway motor vehicle program
- **California Water Commission.** Provides policy input to the Department of Water Resources
- **California Boating and Waterways Commission.** Provides policy input to the Department of Boating and Waterways
- **Wildlife Conservation Board.** Administers a capital outlay program for wildlife conservation and related public recreation

Departments within the Resources Agency are:

- **Department of Boating and Waterways.** Enforces the state's boating laws and helps construct state boating facilities
- **Department of Conservation.** Implement programs on beverage container recycling, mine reclamation, energy leasing, and agricultural land resource protection
- **CALFED Bay–Delta Program.** Develops and implements a long-term comprehensive plan to restore ecological health and improve water management
- **Department of Fish and Game.** Regulates the state's fish and wildlife resources
- **Department of Forestry and Fire Protection.** Regulates the state's forest resources and provides fire protection and emergency response services
- **Department of Parks and Recreation.** Manages the state's park resources
- **Department of Water Resources.** Manages the state's water resources and operates the State Water Project
- **California Conservation Corps.** Implements a youth workforce development program that includes work in environmental conservation, fire protection, and emergency response

CALFED = Consortium of federal and state agencies overseeing Bay–Delta water management, superseded by the Bay–Delta Authority

*The Legislature has created nine conser-
vancies within the Resources Agency whose
mission is to acquire and manage open
space and conservation lands.*

The Legislature has created nine conservancies within the Resources Agency whose mission is to acquire and manage open space and conservation lands. These are:

- Baldwin Hills Conservancy
- California Tahoe Conservancy
- Coachella Valley Mountains Conservancy
- San Diego River Conservancy
- San Gabriel and Lower Los Angeles Rivers & Mountains Conservancy
- San Joaquin River Conservancy
- Santa Monica Mountains Conservancy
- Sierra Nevada Conservancy
- State Coastal Conservancy

Office of the Secretary. The Office of the Secretary for Resources serves as the Governor's spokesperson for resources policy and implements a number of programs established by either the Legislature or the Governor. These include the following:

- **California Environmental Quality Act.** The Resources Agency adopts the CEQA Guidelines and certifies state environmental regulatory programs as CEQA functional equivalents. *See* chapter 2.

- **California Biodiversity Council.** The Council coordinates the efforts of federal, state, and local agencies to develop strategies and policies for conserving biodiversity. *See* below.

CERES = California Environmental
Resources Evaluation System

- **California Environmental Resources Evaluation System (CERES).** CERES is a statewide information system that facilitates access to a variety of electronic data describing California's environment.

- **California Ocean Resources Management Program.** The Resources Agency develops and maintains an ocean resources planning and management program to promote coordinated management of federal and state resources, and to ensure coordination with adjacent states.

Other Agencies

Governor's Office of Planning and Research. OPR is the statewide planning agency and also oversees CEQA implementation. *See* chapter 2 for OPR's CEQA responsibilities. OPR is responsible for the following activities:

- Formulating long-range goals and policies for land use, population growth and distribution, urban expansion, land development, resource preservation, and other factors affecting statewide development patterns

- Assisting in the preparation of functional plans by state agencies and departments that relate to protection and enhancement of the state's environment

- Ensuring that all state policies and programs conform to the state's adopted land use planning goals and programs
- Preparing the state's environmental goals and policy report every four years
- Developing and adopts guidelines for the preparation of city and county general plans
- Providing general planning assistance to local governments, including publishing the Planners' Book of Lists (*see* sidebar)
- Providing guidelines for local agency formation commission (LAFCO) boundary adjustments

California Biodiversity Council. The CBC was formed in 1991 to improve coordination and cooperation between the numerous resource management and environmental protection organizations at federal, state, and local government levels. Its purpose is to discuss, coordinate, and assist in developing strategies and complementary policies for conserving biodiversity. The Council has 40 members, including ten regional agencies or associations, 16 state agencies, 12 federal agencies, the University of California, and the California Association of Resource Conservation Districts.

Department of Public Health. DPH administers a broad range of public and clinical health programs. The DPH's Environmental Health Investigations Branch controls environmental factors harmful to human health through conducting health and exposure investigations, monitoring trends in environmental exposures and health indicators, and providing public health oversight, technical assistance, and training. DPH's Drinking Water Program is responsible for the enforcement of the federal and California Safe Drinking Water Acts, and the regulatory oversight of public water systems to assure the delivery of safe drinking water; within this program, the Recycled Water Unit is responsible for developing water recycling criteria and regulations and evaluating water recycling projects. DPH also certifies state laboratories.

Department of Pesticide Regulation. DPR regulates the registration, sale, and use of pesticides (Food and Agric. Code 11501 *et seq.*). DPR must evaluate and register pesticides before they may be sold or used in the state. DPR is also responsible for fostering reduced-risk pest management.

City and district attorneys' offices. Local law enforcement agencies play an important role in prosecuting violations of state and local environmental laws. Local prosecutors are particularly active in enforcing air pollution and hazardous waste laws. The Hazardous Waste Enforcement Unit within the DTSC provides information, training, and assistance for local law agencies enforcing hazardous waste laws.

Planners' Book of Lists

Every year, OPR conducts a local government planning survey to compile the latest information on local planning activities and issues. The results, together with other reference information, are published in the *California Planners' Book of Lists* (OPR 2007). The publication includes:

- Directories of city and county planning agencies
- Directories of councils of government, LAFCOs, CEQA judges, and selected federal agencies
- The status of every city and county local general plan
- Jurisdictions that have adopted plans and programs that can serve as models for other planning agencies

This publication is available from the California Planners Information Network website (www.calpin.ca.gov).

CBC = California Biodiversity Council
DPR = Department of Pesticide Regulation
LAFCO = Local agency formation commission

CUPA = Certified unified
program agency
NO$_X$ = Oxides of nitrogen

Other regional and local agencies. Numerous regional and local agencies are responsible for implementing or enforcing environmental law in California. These include regional or county air pollution control districts responsible for implementing federal and state clean air programs at the local level (*see* chapter 5). Also, certified unified program agencies (CUPAs) are designated local agencies responsible for consolidated implementation of six hazardous materials programs (*see* chapter 7).

Environmental Law and Regulation Terminology and Principles

Many environmental regulatory programs are comprised of four common components: applicability criteria, key definitions, substantive standards, and procedural requirements.

Many environmental regulatory programs are comprised of four common components: applicability criteria, key definitions, substantive standards, and procedural requirements. This section describes components and is intended to provide a framework for the discussions of individual programs in subsequent chapters.

Applicability Criteria

Applicability criteria define the types of activities that are regulated. Environmental regulatory programs typically apply to specified activities (*e.g.,* filling wetlands), specified types of industries (*e.g.,* semiconductor or aerospace manufacturing), or specified facility types (*e.g.,* facility, owner, operator, or major source). Substantive standards will apply to these regulated categories unless they enjoy an exemption or exclusion.

Air quality programs are an example of the complexity of applicability criteria (*see* chapter 5). Certain air quality permits are required for "major" sources of air pollutants, which are distinguished from non-regulated "minor" air emissions sources. A major source is defined differently under several air quality programs. Also, a major source under the non-attainment new source review program is defined differently depending on where a regulated facility is located. For those facilities emitting oxides of nitrogen (NO$_X$) in the Sacramento Metropolitan Air Quality Management District, a major source emits 25 tons per year, whereas in the San Diego Air Pollution Control District, a major source emits 50 tons per year. Further, different definitions of "major source" are used in the Prevention of Significant Deterioration and Operating Permits programs.

Key Definitions

It is critically important to read and understand the definitions of specific regulated activities or pollutants. Each regulatory definition is a term of art, usually having a different meaning from the same term found in Webster's dictionary. For example, although the following terms appear similar, California environmental regulations create important legal distinctions among a "hazardous waste," "toxic waste," "hazardous material," and "hazardous substance." Other terms that sound familiar at first glance, such as "ignitable," "flammable," and "combustible," also have specific regulatory definitions.

Substantive Standards

Environmental regulatory programs typically establish a number of substantive standards governing regulated activities. Examples of substantive standards are emissions limitations expressed in mass loadings (*e.g.,* pounds per day and tons per year) or concentrations (*e.g.,* parts per million). Substantive requirements also include specified emissions controls designed to meet emissions limits. For example, a regulated air emissions source may be required to use the best available control technology (BACT) that may require use of selective catalytic reduction for certain pollutant emissions.

Environmental regulatory programs typically establish a number of substantive standards governing regulated activities.

BACT = Best available
control technology

Procedural Requirements

Environmental regulatory programs typically specify a variety of compliance procedures. These may include:

- Permit applications and approvals
- Compliance with permit conditions (which may be substantive or procedural)
- Monitoring
- Recordkeeping
- Payment of fees or penalties
- Notifications (*e.g.,* accidents or spills)
- Inspections
- Design requirements
- Training
- Preparation of plans (*e.g.,* spill prevention and emergency response plans)

For more information...

Publications

Cal/EPA. 2004b. Cal/EPA Environmental Justice Action Plan

Cal/EPA. 2002. Environmental Protection Indicators for California

Cal/EPA. 2004c. Environmental Protection Indicators for California: 2004 Update

Cal/EPA. 2005. Environmental Protection Indicators for California: 2005 Addendum to 2004 Update

Cal/EPA. 2004a. Interagency Environmental Justice Strategy

California Senate. 2000. The Legislative Process: A Citizen's Guide to Participation

Environmental Law Institute. 2002. A Citizen's Guide to Using Federal Environmental Laws to Secure Environmental Justice. Washington, D.C.

Governor's Office of Planning and Research. 2007. California Planners' Book of Lists

Hsiao, P. and D.R. Black. 2004. California Environmental and Natural Resources Law Handbook, 12th edition. Government Institutes. Rockville, Md.

Manaster, K.A. and D.P. Selmi (eds). ND. Chapters 1, 2, 3, 10, and 12 of California Environmental Law and Land Use Practice. Matthew Bender. San Francisco, Calif.

Office of Administrative Law. 2005. California Rulemaking Law

Sax, J. 1970. The Public Trust Doctrine in Natural Resource Law: Effective Judicial Intervention. 68 Michigan Law Review 471

Websites

California Biodiversity Council
http://ceres.ca.gov/biodiv

California Code of Regulations
http://government.westlaw.com/linkedslice/default.asp?SP=CCR-1000

California Codes
www.leginfo.ca.gov/calaw.html

California Environmental Resources Evaluation System
www.ceres.ca.gov

California EPA
www.calepa.ca.gov/About/default.htm

California EPA, Environmental Justice Program
www.calepa.ca.gov/EnvJustice

California Legislative Information
www.leginfo.ca.gov

California Ocean Resources Management Program
http://resources.ca.gov/ocean

California Planners' Book of Lists
www.calpin.ca.gov

Code of Federal Regulations
www.gpoaccess.gov/cfr/index.html

Department of Pesticide Regulation
www.cdpr.ca.gov

Governor's Office of Planning and Research
www.opr.ca.gov/index.html

Library of Congress, Federal Legislative Process Description
http://thomas.loc.gov/home/lawsmade.toc.html

Office of Administrative Law
www.oal.ca.gov

Resources Agency
http://resources.ca.gov/index.html

U.S. Codes
www.gpoaccess.gov/uscode/index.html

California Environmental Quality Act

This chapter reviews—

- CEQA's legal basis and implementing agencies
- The process for preparing CEQA documents
- Contents of CEQA documents: Initial Studies, Negative Declarations, and EIRs
- How CEQA can be integrated with other environmental laws
- CEQA enforcement

Related Solano Press titles—

CEQA Deskbook
Ronald E. Bass, Albert I. Herson, and Kenneth M. Bogdan
1999 with 2001 Update

The NEPA Book
Ronald E. Bass, Albert I Herson, and Kenneth M. Bogdan. 2000

Guide to the California Environmental Quality Act
Michael H. Remy *et al.* 2006

Glossary

Baseline–the starting point for determining a proposed project's significant effects, normally the same as the existing environmental setting.

Categorical exemption–CEQA exemptions for classes of projects that the Resources Agency has determined do not have a significant environmental effect.

Cumulative impacts–two or more individual impacts that, when considered together, are considerable or that compound other environmental impacts.

Environmental assessment*–brief preliminary analysis by a federal lead agency to determine whether an EIS should be prepared.

Environmental impact report*–a detailed statement prepared by a state or local lead agency describing a proposed project, its significant environmental effects, mitigation measures, and alternatives.

Environmental impact statement*–a detailed statement prepared by a federal lead agency describing a proposed action, its significant environmental effects, mitigation measures, and alternatives.

Environmental setting–the physical environmental conditions in the project vicinity.

Feasible–capable of being accomplished successfully within a reasonable period of time, taking into account economic, environmental, legal, social, and technological factors.

Findings–written conclusions prepared by a lead agency at the end of the EIR process explaining the disposition of each significant environmental effect.

Guidelines–state CEQA Guidelines.

Initial study–preliminary analysis to determine whether a negative declaration or EIR should be prepared.

Lead agency–public agency having the principal responsibility for carrying out or approving a project.

Mitigated negative declaration*–brief written statement prepared by a state or local lead agency explaining why a proposed project will not have a significant environmental effect, and therefore will not require an EIR, because the project's significant environmental effects have been mitigated.

Mitigation measure–avoiding, minimizing, rectifying, reducing, or compensating for an environmental impact.

Negative declaration*–brief written statement prepared by a state or local lead agency explaining why a proposed project will not have a significant environmental effect, and therefore will not require an EIR.

Notice of determination–notice filed after project approval, once a negative declaration or EIR has been prepared.

Notice of exemption–optional notice filed after project approval, indicating a CEQA exemption applies.

Notice of preparation–brief notice indicating a lead agency intends to prepare an EIR.

Project–the whole of an action with the potential for a direct or indirect physical environmental impact.

Responsible agency–public agency that uses a lead agency environmental document to carry out or approve a project.

Significant effect–a substantial or potentially substantial change in the physical environment.

Statement of overriding considerations–written explanation prepared at the end of the EIR process explaining why a lead agency approved a project notwithstanding its significant environmental effects.

Statutory exemption–an exemption created by the state Legislature.

Substantial evidence–enough relevant information and inferences that a fair argument can be made to support a conclusion. Includes facts, and reasonable assumptions and expert opinion supported by facts.

Tiering–coverage of general matters in broader environmental documents, and project-specific matters in subsequent project-specific environmental documents.

Trustee agency–state agency with jurisdiction over natural resources held in trust for the people of the state.

Writ of mandamus–a judicial command to an official to perform a ministerial act that the law recognizes as an absolute duty and not discretionary.

* equals permit or approval

CHAPTER 2

California Environmental Quality Act

Introduction

The California Environmental Quality Act (CEQA) (Public Resources Code 21000 *et seq.*) is California's broadest-reaching environmental law. CEQA is not a substantive law establishing environmental standards for a particular regulated activity or medium. Rather, it sets broad environmental policies for the state, and it requires state and local agencies that carry out or approve discretionary projects to evaluate, mitigate, and publicly disclose the environmental effects of those projects before taking action. CEQA does not grant state or local agencies new powers to mitigate environmental effects of proposed projects. However, agencies may use powers granted by other laws, typically the police power, to require project mitigation or deny projects with significant adverse environmental effects.

CEQA's main objectives are to:

*   Disclose to decisionmakers and the public the environmental effects of proposed projects

*   Identify ways to avoid or reduce environmental damage

*   Prevent environmental damage by requiring implementation of feasible alternatives or mitigation measures

*   Disclose to the public the reasons for agency approval of projects with significant adverse environmental effects

*   Foster interagency coordination in project review

*   Enhance public participation in the planning process

This chapter reviews the key laws and agencies involved in implementing CEQA, the process for preparing CEQA documents, their contents, CEQA integration with other environmental laws, and CEQA enforcement.

CEQA = California Environmental Quality Act

CEQA does not grant state or local agencies new powers to mitigate environmental effects of proposed projects.

Key Laws and Agencies

State Statute and Guidelines

CEQA requirements are established by the CEQA statute (Public Resources Code (PRC) 21000 *et seq.*) and the CEQA Guidelines (Guidelines, 14 California Code of Regulations (CCR) 15000 *et seq.*). CEQA originally was enacted in 1970 and was modeled after the National Environmental Policy Act (NEPA), which had been enacted a year earlier. The statute has been amended frequently, and is the subject of frequent litigation.

The CEQA Guidelines are the official administrative interpretation of CEQA, and are relied upon heavily by both agencies implementing CEQA and by courts interpreting the law. The Guidelines also are amended frequently in response to new developments in case law and CEQA practice. The Governor's Office of Planning and Research (OPR) drafts amendments to the Guidelines that ultimately are adopted by the Resources Agency after public review.

This chapter cites the CEQA Guidelines for authority because the Guidelines are the most commonly-used CEQA reference.

Resources Agency

The Resources Agency is a cabinet-level agency that oversees state natural resources policy and agencies.

The Resources Agency is a cabinet-level agency that oversees state natural resources policy and agencies. Its CEQA responsibilities include formal rule-making and adoption of CEQA Guidelines amendments, and certification of state regulatory programs as CEQA equivalents (*see* below).

The Resources Agency also maintains the California Environmental Resource Evaluation System (www.ceres.ca.gov). CERES is an information system that facilitates access to a variety of electronic data describing California's environment. An invaluable website located within CERES (www.ceres.ca.gov/ceqa) includes an interactive CEQA flow chart, and links to the CEQA statute, CEQA Guidelines, and CEQA case law.

Governor's Office of Planning and Research

OPR's major CEQA responsibilities include recommending changes to the CEQA Guidelines, operating the State Clearinghouse, publishing CEQA notices, publishing technical advisories on CEQA compliance, and maintaining the CEQAnet database (www.ceqanet.ca.gov) to assist agencies in CEQA implementation. OPR's CEQA technical advisories cover topics such as: public notice and review, master environmental impact reports (EIRs), and mitigated negative declarations. The State Clearinghouse is the single point of contact in the state government that coordinates state agency review of CEQA and NEPA documents.

Other State and Local Agencies

Every state and local agency in California must adopt CEQA implementation procedures consistent with CEQA and the CEQA Guidelines. Typically, a state or local agency plays one of two roles in CEQA implementation–lead agency or responsible agency.

A lead agency has the principal responsibility for carrying out or approving a project, and therefore has the lead responsibility for preparing the CEQA document for that project. For private projects requiring multiple governmental approvals, the agency with general governmental powers (city or county) is typically the lead agency. 14 CCR 15050, 15051.

A responsible agency is an agency other than the lead agency with responsibility for carrying out or approving a project. For example, if a development project requires a Department of Fish and Game (DFG) lake or streambed alteration agreement, a city may be the lead agency and DFG the responsible agency. A responsible agency must participate in the lead agency's CEQA process and must use the lead agency's CEQA document in its decisionmaking. 14 CCR 15096.

CEQA also requires lead agencies to consult with relevant trustee agencies and "agencies with jurisdiction by law" when preparing CEQA documents. Trustee agencies, such as the DFG, have jurisdiction over resources held in trust for California. Lead agencies must also consult with agencies exercising authority over the resources affected by a project. 14 CCR 15086, 15386.

A lead agency has the principal responsibility for carrying out or approving a project. A responsible agency is an agency other than the lead agency with responsibility for carrying out or approving a project.

DFG = Department of Fish and Game

CEQA also requires lead agencies to consult with relevant trustee agencies and "agencies with jurisdiction by law" when preparing CEQA documents.

Overview of the CEQA Process

The CEQA process consists of three phases:

- Preliminary review to determine whether a project is subject to CEQA or exempt from CEQA

- If a project is subject to CEQA, preparation of an initial study to determine whether the project may have a significant environmental effect

- Preparation of an EIR if the project may have a significant environmental effect, or a negative declaration or mitigated negative declaration if no significant effect will occur

The CEQA process is illustrated in Figure 2-1.

Preliminary Review

Is the Activity a Project?

During preliminary review, the lead agency determines whether an activity is a "project" under CEQA, and if so, whether a statutory or categorical exemption may apply. A "project" includes (14 CCR 15378):

Figure 2-1
CEQA Process Flow Chart

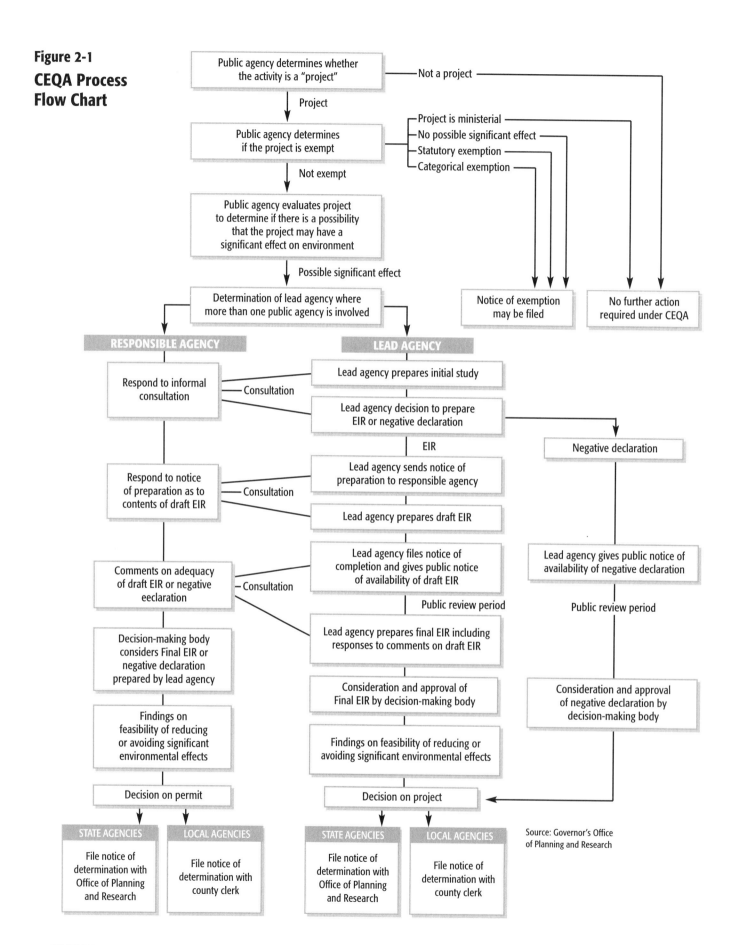

Source: Governor's Office of Planning and Research

- An activity directly undertaken by a public agency, such as a public works project or enactment of ordinances or general plans

- An activity supported by a public agency through contracts, financial assistance, or other assistance

- A public or private activity involving the issuance of a public agency permit or other entitlement, *e.g.,* a rezoning or conditional use permit for a development project

A project includes the whole of an action with the potential for direct or indirect environmental effects. An agency generally is not allowed to piecemeal a large project into smaller pieces to evade environmental review. For example, in the landmark case *Laurel Heights Improvement Association v. Regents of the University of California* (1988) 47 Cal. App. 3d 376, the Supreme Court held that future development phases of a single building must be evaluated in the EIR prepared for the first phase of development, because the future phases were reasonably foreseeable and could be meaningfully evaluated.

A project includes the whole of an action with the potential for direct or indirect environmental effects. An agency generally is not allowed to piecemeal a large project into smaller pieces to evade environmental review.

Is the Project Exempt?

CEQA has four main categories of exemptions: statutory exemptions, categorical exemptions, the "common sense" exemption, and certified regulatory programs.

Statutory exemptions. Statutory exemptions are created by the Legislature; if a project is statutorily exempt, no CEQA compliance is needed. Common statutory exemptions include ministerial projects, emergency projects, and feasibility or planning studies for possible future actions. 14 CCR 15260 *et seq.*

The most common statutory exemption is for ministerial projects—those requiring little exercise of judgment by the decisionmaker, such as final subdivision map approval. CEQA applies only to discretionary projects—those that require the exercise of judgment or deliberation when a decision is made. 14 CCR 15268.

Categorical exemptions. Categorical exemptions are adopted by the Resources Agency and found in the CEQA Guidelines. 14 CCR 15300 *et seq.* The most commonly applied categorical exemptions include those for existing facilities and for construction of new, small facilities.

Categorical exemptions represent activities that the Resources Agency has determined generally do not result in significant environmental effects. However, certain exceptions to a categorical exemption may make the exemption inapplicable to an activity. 14 CCR 15300.2. For example, a categorical exemption does not apply if, due to "unusual circumstances," there is a reasonable possibility of a significant project-level or cumulative impact.

Firefighting is an emergency activity that is statutorily exempt from CEQA.

So, a minor alteration of an existing facility, which would normally qualify for a Class 1 exemption (14 CCR 15301), would not qualify for the exemption if it involved disturbance of a listed endangered species habitat.

Common sense exemption. An activity is exempt from CEQA when it can be seen with certainty that there is no possibility that the activity may have a significant environmental effect. 14 CCR 15061(b)(3). This exemption has also been termed the "common sense" exemption. Although disfavored for many years because of its strict language, this exemption may now be used more often as a result of the Supreme Court's decision in *Muzzi Ranch Co. v. Solano County Airport Land Use Commission* (2007) 41 Cal. 4th 372. In that case, the court upheld the use of the common sense exemption for a county airport land use commission's adoption of policies restricting development to currently permitted levels.

Certified regulatory programs. The Resources Agency has certified certain state regulatory programs, exempting them from CEQA's requirement to prepare EIRs and Negative Declarations. A certified program must still comply with other CEQA policies, and preparation of a substitute document that is the functional equivalent of a Negative Declaration or EIR is required. Common state-certified regulatory programs include Coastal Commission certification of local coastal programs and the Energy Commission's energy facility licensing program. 14 CCR 15250 *et seq.*

Integration of the California Environmental Quality Act and the Permit Streamlining Act

During preliminary review, the lead agency must determine if the project is subject to the Permit Streamlining Act (PSA). Gov. Code 65920 *et seq.* The PSA, which applies to certain private development projects requiring government approval, sets forth certain time limits for determining completeness of an application, for completion of environmental documents, and for project approval. *See* chapter 3 for a further discussion of the PSA.

PSA time limits include the following (extensions are possible for some of these time limits):

- Acceptance of application as complete–30 days from submittal of a development project application. 14 CCR 15060

- Completion of Negative Declaration–180 days from acceptance of application as complete. 14 CCR 15107

- Completion of EIR–one year from acceptance of application as complete. 14 CCR 15108

- Project approval–60 days from exemption decision or adoption of Negative Declaration; 180 days from date of EIR certification. Gov. Code 65950 (EIR certification is a step before project approval, as described later in this chapter)

Preparing the Initial Study and Negative Declaration

Initial Study

If an activity is a project subject to CEQA and no exemptions apply, the lead agency generally prepares an initial study to determine whether to prepare an EIR or a negative declaration. A lead agency has the discretion to decide to prepare an EIR without first preparing an initial study.

An initial study is a short document containing a project description, environmental setting, potential environmental impacts, and mitigation measures for any significant effects. If the initial study concludes that the project will not have a significant effect, the lead agency adopts a negative declaration. If mitigation is needed to reduce any significant effects to less than significant levels, the lead agency adopts a mitigated negative declaration. If the initial study shows that the project may have a significant environmental effect that cannot be mitigated, then the lead agency must prepare an EIR. 14 CCR 15063.

The initial study generally uses a checklist format modeled after Appendix G of the CEQA Guidelines. Each checklist answer requires a fact-based explanation to support conclusions, particularly conclusions that an impact is not significant.

An initial study is a short document containing a project description, environmental setting, potential environmental impacts, and mitigation measures for any significant effects.

Decision to Prepare a Negative Declaration versus an EIR

An EIR must be prepared when the lead agency determines that it can be "fairly argued," based on "substantial evidence," that a project may have a significant environmental effect. This "fair argument" standard means that if project opponents have substantial evidence that a project may have a significant environmental effect, an EIR must be prepared, even if the lead agency's substantial evidence indicates lack of significant environmental effect. Thus, a low threshold exists for EIR preparation. 14 CCR 15064.

"Substantial evidence" includes facts, fact-based assumptions, and expert opinion. It does not include argument, speculation, or unsubstantiated opinion. Public controversy about a project is not considered substantial evidence, but may be used to require an EIR in marginal cases when it is unclear that substantial evidence of a significant environmental impact exists. 14 CCR 15384.

An EIR must be prepared when the lead agency determines that it can be "fairly argued," based on "substantial evidence," that a project may have a significant environmental effect.

Determining Whether Environmental Effects Are Significant

An ironclad definition of significant effect is not possible. Instead, CEQA practice uses several tools for determining whether an environmental effect is significant: the initial study checklist (CEQA Guidelines Appendix G); mandatory findings of significance; and agency thresholds of significance.

CEQA Guidelines Appendix G sets forth criteria or thresholds for each environmental topic (*e.g.*, aesthetics, biological resources) to determine whether a project's environmental effects are potentially significant. A project may still have a significant environmental effect even if it does not trigger an Appendix G threshold.

The Guidelines set forth several mandatory findings of significance, requiring an EIR to be prepared when these findings are made.

The Guidelines set forth several mandatory findings of significance, requiring an EIR to be prepared when these findings are made. 14 CCR 15065. Mandatory findings of significance include substantially reducing the habitat of a fish or wildlife species, substantially reducing the number or restricting the range of an endangered or threatened species, or causing cumulatively considerable effects.

The CEQA Guidelines encourage lead agencies to voluntarily adopt thresholds of significance. 14 CCR 15064.7. A threshold of significance is an identifiable quantitative, qualitative, or performance level of a particular environmental effect that normally would be significant. Thresholds must be adopted through a public review process and supported by substantial evidence. OPR has compiled examples of thresholds used by representative jurisdictions (http://ceres.ca.gov/planning/ceqa/thresholds.html). CEQA requires that both direct and indirect (secondary) impacts of a project be evaluated for significance. An economic or social impact is not considered a significant environmental effect, but an economic or social impact related to a physical impact may be used to determine whether the physical impact is significant. 14 CCR 15064(c), (f).

Negative Declaration Process

A negative declaration documents the decision not to prepare an EIR. It includes a brief project description and a proposed finding of no significant impact, with the initial study as an attachment.

A negative declaration documents the decision not to prepare an EIR. It includes a brief project description and a proposed finding of no significant impact, with the initial study as an attachment. 14 CCR 15371. Mitigated negative declarations also must describe mitigation measures included in the project to avoid significant effects. OPR guidance on mitigated negative declarations is available on the OPR website (http://ceres.ca.gov/topic/env_law/ceqa/more/tas/mit_neg_dec/index.html).

Public notice of a proposed negative declaration starts a 20- or 30-day public review period; the 30-day review period is required if a project requires State Clearinghouse review. 14 CCR 15073. State Clearinghouse review is required if a state agency is a lead, responsible, or trustee agency, or an agency with jurisdiction by law, or if the project is of "statewide, regional, or areawide significance," as defined by 14 CCR 15206. The State Clearinghouse, located within OPR, is responsible for sending the draft negative declaration to relevant state agencies and sending collated state agency comments to the lead agency. OPR guidance on circulation and notice of both negative declarations and EIRs is available on the OPR website (http://ceres.ca.gov/planning/ceqa/circulation).

The lead agency must consider comments received on the proposed negative declaration before adopting it and approving the project, but need not respond to comments in writing. For a mitigated negative declaration, the lead agency may substitute equally or more effective mitigation measures, provided this substitution is considered at a public hearing. If a negative declaration is "substantially revised" after public review, the lead agency must recirculate it for an additional round of public review. 14 CCR 15073.5, 15074, 15074.1.

When approving a mitigated negative declaration, the lead agency also must adopt a mitigation monitoring and reporting program (*see* description under EIR section). After approving a negative declaration, the lead agency files a notice of determination (NOD) with OPR or the county clerk, and pays applicable DFG environmental review fees. 14 CCR 15075. Following adoption of a negative declaration, if circumstances change and the lead agency still has discretionary authority over the project, a subsequent negative declaration may be required. *See* rules for subsequent and supplemental EIRs below.

EIS = Environmental impact statement

NOD = Notice of determination

Preparing the EIR

Types of Environmental Impact Reports and Tiering

An EIR must be prepared if a project may have a significant environmental effect that cannot be reduced to less than significant levels through a mitigated negative declaration. The CEQA Guidelines recognized several types of EIRs:

- For specific projects: project EIR, joint EIR/environmental impact statement (EIR/EIS), focused EIR, staged EIR

- First-tier EIRs for plans and policies: tiered EIR, program EIR, master EIR, general plan EIR

- Following EIR certification: supplemental EIR, subsequent EIR

An EIR must be prepared if a project may have a significant environmental effect that cannot be reduced to less than significant levels through a mitigated negative declaration.

Tiering refers to preparation of environmental documents using a multi-layered approach. In tiering, a first-tier EIR examines broad alternatives, mitigation criteria, and cumulative impacts, and a second-tier EIR or negative declaration can be focused on project-specific impacts, alternatives, and mitigation measures. For example, a first-tier general plan EIR can analyze jurisdiction-wide alternatives, and regional impacts and mitigation measures. A second-tier EIR prepared for approval of a specific plan and rezoning can then be limited to project-specific alternatives and impacts and can incorporate by reference the general plan EIR's treatment of broader alternatives and impacts. 14 CCR 15152. Further, under CEQA streamlining procedures (14 CCR 15183), a project consistent with general plan development policies for which an EIR was certified does not require additional environmental review, unless needed to examine site-specific impacts that are "peculiar to the parcel or site."

Several types of EIRs facilitate the tiering process, as described in Appendix J of the CEQA Guidelines. The program EIR is the most common type of first-tier EIR. 14 CCR 15168. Following preparation of the program EIR, if a subsequent activity has effects that are within the its scope, no new CEQA document is required. If the subsequent activity's effects are not within its scope, a new negative declaration or EIR must be prepared that focuses on project- or site-specific impacts. The master EIR process functions similarly, but is procedurally more complex, with a negative declaration or focused EIR prepared for subsequent activities outside the master EIR's scope. 14 CCR 15175 *et seq*. OPR guidance on master EIR preparation is available on the OPR website (http://ceres.ca.gov/topic/env_law/ceqa/more/tas/master/Master_EIR.html).

Environmental Impact Report Process

Scoping. The EIR process starts with scoping, which is a process to determine the scope of environmental impacts and alternatives to be examined in the EIR. Scoping includes a scoping meeting (required for projects of statewide, regional, or areawide significance) and the notice of preparation (NOP) process. The NOP describes the proposed project and requests comments from reviewing agencies and the public. Comments responding to the NOP must be sent to the lead agency within 30 days of issuance, and the lead agency must consider these comments when preparing the EIR. 14 CCR 15082.

Draft environmental impact report. An administrative draft EIR then is prepared for internal lead agency review, followed by publication and distribution of the public draft EIR. The draft EIR may be prepared by lead agency staff, another public or private entity, the project applicant, or a consultant hired by the lead agency or applicant. The lead agency is ultimately responsible for EIR content and must independently review the document prior to release. 14 CCR 15084.

Public notice of availability of the draft EIR starts a 30- or 45-day public review period–the 45-day review period is required if a project requires State Clearinghouse review. The lead agency files a notice of completion with the State Clearinghouse at the same time it provides public notice of draft EIR availability. Many lead agencies hold a public hearing on the draft EIR to receive public comments, although CEQA does not require a public hearing. 14 CCR 15085–15087.

Final environmental impact report. Following receipt of comments on the draft EIR, the lead agency proceeds to prepare a final EIR. The final EIR contains comments on the draft EIR, responses to comments, and any necessary revisions to the draft EIR. 14 CCR 15089. If significant new information (as defined by Guidelines 15088.5(a)) is added to a draft EIR, the lead agency must recirculate the draft EIR and provide a second public review period.

Decisionmaking process. The lead agency must review and consider the Final EIR before acting on the proposed project. Before approving the project, in a step called EIR certification, the lead agency must certify that the final EIR complies with CEQA, was reviewed by the decisionmaking body, and represents the

NOP = Notice of preparation

The draft EIR may be prepared by lead agency staff, another public or private entity, the project applicant, or a consultant hired by the lead agency or applicant.

The final EIR contains comments on the draft EIR, responses to comments, and any necessary revisions to the draft EIR.

lead agency's independent judgment. The lead agency's decisionmaking body may either certify the final EIR or delegate this responsibility to an advisory body or staff. 14 CCR 15090.

The lead agency may disapprove a project with significant environmental effects, or approve a project with significant environmental effects provided it adopts a statement of overriding considerations (*see* below). If the lead agency wishes to impose mitigation measures to reduce a project's significant environmental effects, it must possess the legal authority to do so independent of CEQA, and must act consistently with the constitutional prohibition on "takings" of private property. 14 CCR 15040 *et seq. See* chapter 3.

The lead agency may disapprove a project with significant environmental effects, or approve a project with significant environmental effects provided it adopts a statement of overriding considerations.

CEQA requires a unique set of findings, supported by substantial evidence, to be adopted prior to project approval. 14 CCR 15191. For each significant impact disclosed in the final EIR, the lead agency must find one of the following:

- Changes in the project have been made (through mitigation or alternatives) to avoid or substantially lessen the impact.

- Changes to the project are within another agency's jurisdiction and have been or should be adopted.

- Specific economic, social, legal, technical, or other considerations make mitigation measures or alternatives infeasible.

If the lead agency cannot make one of the first two findings, it still may approve the project, provided it adopts a statement of overriding considerations. The statement, which must be supported by substantial evidence, must set forth the specific overriding social, economic, legal, or technical benefits overriding the project's significant environmental effects. The statement of overriding considerations allows the decisionmaker to balance the benefits of a proposed project against its unavoidable environmental impacts. This process is designed to assure political accountability. Typically, increases in jobs, housing, and tax revenues are used as project benefits to override significant adverse environmental impacts. 14 CCR 15093. When adopting CEQA findings on the final EIR, the lead agency also must adopt a mitigation monitoring and reporting program. After project approval, the lead agency files a notice of determination with OPR or the county clerk, and pays applicable Department of Fish and Game environmental review fees. 14 CCR 15094, 15097.

Subsequent or supplemental environmental impact reports. Following project approval, if circumstances change and the lead agency still has discretionary authority over the project, a subsequent or supplemental EIR may be required. These documents are required if:

Following project approval, if circumstances change and the lead agency still has discretionary authority over the project, a subsequent or supplemental EIR may be required.

- Substantial changes in the project cause new or substantially increased significant impacts.

- Substantial changes in project circumstances cause new or substantially increased significant impacts.

California Environmental Quality Act and Wal-Mart

Does a shopping center project description need to identify Wal-Mart as a project tenant and analyze Wal-Mart's urban blight impacts on existing commercial development? Wal-Mart is a controversial tenant for both environmental and non-environmental reasons. CEQA preparers should be concerned about a shopping center tenant's identity only if the tenant causes unique environmental impacts.

In *Maintain Our Desert Environment v. Town of Apple Valley* (2004) 120 Cal. App. 4th 396, the court ruled that a Negative Declaration for a commercial development did not need to identify a Wal-Mart distribution center as a project tenant because there was nothing Wal-Mart did to cause unique environmental effects. This ruling is similar to *Friends of Davis v. City of Davis* (2000) 83 Cal. App. 4th 1004, in which a shopping center EIR did not need to identify Borders as a project tenant.

On the other hand, in *Bakersfield Citizens for Local Control v. City of Bakersfield* (2004) 125 Cal. App. 4th 1184, the court ruled that EIRs prepared for two shopping centers including Wal-Mart did need to identify Wal-Mart's identity as a project tenant, because of the unique environmental impacts (*e.g.*, hours of operation, truck traffic) associated with Wal-Mart's operations. The court further ruled that the EIRs were inadequate because they did not address urban blight impacts of the proposed projects. Another case, *American Canyon Community United for Responsible Growth v. City of American Canyon* (2006) 145 Cal. App. 4th 1062,

rejected a Wal-Mart EIR because the urban blight analysis did not extend to existing commercial development located outside a city's boundaries.

A similar challenge to urban blight analysis, with a different result, was made in *Anderson First Coalition v. City of Anderson* (2005) 130 Cal. App. 4th 1173, which involved a challenge to an EIR for a retail shopping area that included a Wal-Mart. As in the *Bakersfield* case, project opponents submitted studies alleging that the project would cause urban decay in the city's central business district (CBD). The EIR concluded that no urban blight impacts in the CBD would occur, but supported this conclusion by including in the EIR detailed economic analyses prepared by experts.

Another question decided by the courts is whether CEQA review is required when a local government adopts a zoning ordinance prohibiting big-box commercial developments like Wal-Mart Supercenters. In *Wal-Mart Stores Inc. v. City of Turlock* (2006) 138 Cal. App. 4th 273, the court upheld a city ordinance prohibiting construction of retail stores exceeding 100,000 square feet that contain full-service groceries. The court ruled that under CEQA streamlining procedures (14 CCR 15183), CEQA review of the ordinance was not required because the zoning changes were consistent with the city's general plan, and its impacts were covered adequately by the prior general plan EIR. The court also ruled that the ordinance was a proper use of the city's police power and served the public's general welfare. ▪

- New information of substantial importance shows the project will have a new or substantially increased significant impact, or mitigation measures or alternatives that were unknown or thought to be infeasible are now feasible, and the project proponent declines to adopt them.

A subsequent EIR must be prepared if the previous EIR requires substantial changes, whereas a supplemental EIR may be prepared if changes are not major. If changed circumstances do not require a subsequent or supplemental EIR, the lead agency should prepare an EIR addendum, an internal agency document explaining the minor technical EIR changes. 14 CCR 15162, 15163, 15164.

EIR Contents

General rules. Key EIR contents include a summary, a project description, an environmental setting, significant environmental impacts, alternatives, and mitigation measures. The lead agency may present these and other required contents in any format. Although the CEQA Guidelines encourage EIRs to be written in plain language, to be between 150 to 300 pages long, and to emphasize the project's significant effects, in practice these suggestions often are not followed. The EIR's summary should be no longer than 15 pages; should summarize the project's significant effects, mitigation measures, and alternatives; and should identify areas of controversy and unresolved issues. 14 CCR 15120 *et seq.*

Project description. The project description must include the project objectives, project location, and project characteristics. It also must include a list of required project approvals, and related environmental review and consultation requirements. When an individual project is required for action on a larger project or commits the lead agency to a larger project, the project description must address the larger project. 14 CCR 15124. Generally, the project description need not disclose the identity of the project proponent, unless the proponent's identity creates unique environmental impacts. *See* sidebar on page 38.

Environmental setting. The EIR must describe the physical environmental conditions in the project vicinity, from both local and regional perspectives, at the time of NOP publication. The setting also must describe inconsistencies between the proposed project and applicable general and regional plans. 14 CCR 15125.

The environmental setting normally constitutes the baseline by which the lead agency determines whether an impact is significant. The CEQA Guidelines encourage the environmental setting to be no longer than necessary to support analysis of the proposed project's significant environmental effects, though in practice environmental settings are unnecessarily long.

Significant environmental impacts. CEQA requires EIRs to evaluate several types of impacts (14 CCR 15126.2):

- **Direct impacts.** Impacts caused by the project that occur at the same time and place
- **Indirect impacts.** Caused by the project, but that may occur later in time or some distance away
- **Irreversible environmental changes.** For example, use of nonrenewable resources
- **Growth-inducing impacts.** The extent to which the project directly or indirectly fosters growth, removes an obstacle to growth, taxes community services and facilities, or facilitates other activities causing significant environmental effects
- **Cumulative impacts.** Incremental impacts of the proposed project when added to other closely related past, present, or reasonably foreseeable future projects

Cumulative impact analysis is one of the most difficult tasks in CEQA document preparation. Two methods can be used for cumulative impact analysis. 14 CCR 15130. In the list approach, the lead agency identifies related projects that could add to the proposed project's environmental impacts. In the projection, or plan, approach, the lead agency relies on projections contained in an adopted planning document (*e.g.*, a general plan EIR) or prior environmental document. A particularly challenging cumulative impact topic is a proposed project's cumulative contribution to global climate change. *See* sidebar on page 40. CEQA sets forth special rules for analyzing impacts on particular resources:

GHG = Greenhouse gas

Legislature Requires CEQA Documents to Analyze Climate Change Impacts

Global climate change is the world's most critical environmental problem, but until 2006 was seldom considered in CEQA documents. CEQA does not require that lead agencies "foresee the unforeseeable" or consider impacts that are too speculative to evaluate. 14 CCR 15144, 15145. Global climate change, and a project's impacts on global climate change, were generally thought to be too speculative to evaluate.

In 2006, AB 32 (The Global Warming Solutions Act, *see* chapter 5) was enacted, and soon afterwards scientific consensus was achieved that global climate change was accelerating due to increasing emissions of greenhouse gases (GHGs) caused by human activities. In 2006 and 2007 Attorney General Jerry Brown wrote EIR comment letters and filed lawsuits arguing that in order to not impair achievement of AB 32's goals, CEQA documents should quantify and mitigate a project's GHG emissions.

These Attorney General initiatives were highly controversial; some groups believed that AB 32's regulatory scheme precluded the requirement for independent CEQA climate change analysis, and that it was not technically feasible to conduct CEQA climate change analyses. The controversy was ultimately resolved by the Attorney General settling two climate change challenges filed against San Bernardino County and ConocoPhillips, and by the simultaneous enactment of SB 97 (Statutes of 2007, Chapter 185). SB 97 definitively establishes that CEQA documents are intended to address climate change impacts.

SB 97 (PRC 21083.05, 21097) requires that the Resources Agency adopt, by January 1, 2010, guidelines for analyzing and mitigating a project's contribution to global climate change, as well as the impacts of global climate change on a project; it also con-ditionally exempts certain state bond-funded infrastructure projects from CEQA climate change analysis until adoption of Agency guidance in 2010. The guidelines are to be periodically revised to incorporate new information developed pursuant to AB 32 regulations. Until the 2010 guidelines are issued, however, considerable uncertainty will exist on how best to conduct CEQA climate change analysis. The Governor's Office of Planning and Research in June 2008 issued a technical advisory presenting alternative approaches to CEQA climate change analysis. ▪

- **Economic and social effects.** Must be related to a physical environmental change. 14 CCR 15358(b)

- **Historical resources.** A significant impact occurs if the resource is historically significant and the project would cause a substantial adverse change in the significance of the resource. 14 CCR 15064.5(a)

- **Public water system impacts.** For certain large projects, a water supply assessment, which analyzes whether sufficient reliable water supplies will be available to serve the proposed project, must be incorporated into the draft EIR. 14 CCR 15155

Alternatives. An EIR must describe a reasonable range of alternatives that could feasibly attain most of the basic project objectives and that would avoid or substantially lessen the proposed project's significant effects. An alternative or mitigation measure is feasible when it is capable of being accomplished successfully within a reasonable time, taking into account economic, environmental, legal, social, and technological factors. The EIR must include enough information about each alternative to allow meaningful evaluation, analysis, and comparison, with quantitative analyses preferred. 14 CCR 15126.6.

The EIR must describe and evaluate the "no-project alternative" and identify an alternative other than the no-project alternative that is environmentally superior. The no-project alternative allows decisionmakers to compare the impacts of approving versus not approving the proposed project. When the proposed project is a development project at a specific location, the no-project alternative is usually the property remaining in its existing state, unless future uses of the land are predictable. When the proposed project is a revision to a plan or ongoing operation, the no-project alternative is continuation of the existing plan or operation. 14 CCR 15152.6(e).

Alternative project sites need to be evaluated when they are feasible and would avoid or substantially lessen the proposed project's significant environmental effects. In the landmark case *Citizens of Goleta*

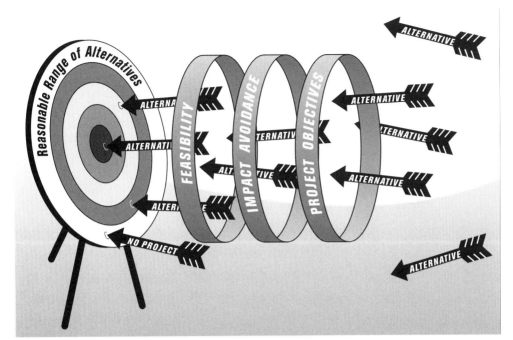

Source: Bass, R.E. *et al.* 1999. *CEQA Deskbook.* Solano Press. Reprinted with permission

Figure 2-2

Developing a Reasonable Range of Alternatives

Valley v. Board of Supervisors (1990) 52 Cal. 3d 553, the Supreme Court articulated several factors for determining whether off-site alternatives are feasible, including site suitability, economic viability, infrastructure availability, general plan consistency, regulatory limitations, jurisdictional boundaries, and the applicant's control over alternative sites. Adopted regional and local plans should be used to guide the selection of feasible alternative sites. 14 CCR 15126(f).

Alternatives analysis in an EIR is typically a two-step process. First, the lead agency screens a set of preliminary alternatives to determine which alternatives meet most of the project objectives, are feasible, and reduce significant impacts. The lead agency documents the reasons for rejecting alternatives based on one or more of these factors. Second, the remaining "reasonable range" of alternatives is evaluated for environmental impacts, and these impacts are compared to proposed project impacts. Figure 2-2 illustrates the alternatives selection process.

Mitigation measures. The EIR must discuss feasible mitigation measures for each significant environmental effect that avoid the impact, minimize the impact, rectify the impact over time, reduce the impact over time, or compensate for the impact by providing substitute resources. The EIR must identify responsibilities for implementing each mitigation measure, disclose any significant side effects of implementing a mitigation measure, and explain why a particular mitigation measure was selected when several were available. 14 CCR 15126.4(a).

Mitigation measures cannot be improperly deferred to the results of future studies or regulatory agency actions. However, mitigation measures may specify performance standards that would mitigate a significant effect and that can be accomplished in several alternative ways. Figure 2-3 provides examples of

Mitigation measures cannot be improperly deferred to the results of future studies or regulatory agency actions.

Figure 2-3
Mitigation Measure Adequacy

Adequate ✓	Questionable ?	Inadequate ⊗
• Avoid	• Provide funding for	• Consult with
• Minimize	• Hire staff	• Submit for review
• Rectify	• Monitor or report	• Coordinate with
• Reduce over time	• Comply with existing regulations or ordinances	• Study further
• Compensate	• Preserve already existing natural area	• Inform
		• Encourage/discourage
		• Facilitate
		• Strive to

Source: Bass, R.E. *et al.* 1999. *CEQA Deskbook.* Solano Press. Reprinted with permission

CEQA does not give lead agencies new authorities to require mitigation, so lead agencies must use other regulatory authorities such as the police power.

CEQ = Council on Environmental Quality
EIS = Environmental impact statement
FONSI = Finding of no significant impact
NOE = Notice of exemption
USC = United States Code

State legislation limits the amount of school impact fees that can be imposed as CEQA mitigation.

mitigation measures that are adequate, inadequate, or questionable, based on the CEQA Guidelines and case law.

CEQA does not give lead agencies new authorities to require mitigation, so lead agencies must use other regulatory authorities such as the police power. To avoid "regulatory taking" challenges, there must be a clear nexus between an impact and a mitigation measure, and rough proportionality between the extent of the impact and the mitigation measure imposed. 14 CCR 15126.4.

CEQA and other statutes set forth specific limitations on mitigation measures that can be used for impacts on specific resources:

- **Historical and archeological resources.** CEQA establishes cost limitations on fees, and the CEQA Guidelines define examples of adequate mitigation. PRC 21082.2, 14 CCR 15126.4(b)

- **Schools.** Lead agencies may not impose fees higher than those designated by statute. Gov. Code 65995

- **Housing.** Lead agencies may not reduce housing density as a mitigation measure unless the project has a significant impact on health or safety, and there are no feasible alternative mitigation measures. Gov. Code 65589.5

Public universities have argued over the years that they are not subject to CEQA's requirement to mitigate off-site impacts when feasible. However, Supreme Court and Court of Appeal decisions in 2006 clearly established that public universities are required to adopt feasible mitigation measures for significant off-site impacts. *See* sidebar.

Mitigation monitoring or reporting programs. When making findings on significant effects identified in an EIR, the lead agency must adopt a monitoring or reporting program setting forth roles and responsibilities to assure mitigation measures are implemented; this program is often included in the draft EIR. Monitoring refers to oversight of project implementation for complex mitigation measures such as wetland restoration or cultural resources recovery. Reporting refs to written mitigation measure compliance reviews. Lead agencies use their non-CEQA authorities, *e.g.*, the police power, to enforce mitigation measure implementation. 14 CCR 15097.

Final environmental impact report contents. The final EIR, prepared after public review of the draft EIR, includes the draft EIR, any revisions to the draft EIR, draft EIR public comments or comment summaries, and lead agency responses to public comments. The responses must demonstrate good faith and be well reasoned, and may not be conclusory. 14 CCR 15132.

Judicial review of EIR adequacy. Courts typically apply a "rule of reason" when reviewing the adequacy of EIRs. Courts require that all required contents are included in an EIR and that the EIR shows an objective, good-faith attempt at full disclosure. The scope of judicial review does not extend to the correctness of an EIR's conclusion, but only the EIR's sufficiency as an informative document for decisionmakers and the public. Disagreement among experts regarding conclusions in an EIR is acceptable, as long as the lead agency recognizes the disagreement and explains its choice of conclusions. 14 CCR 15003(i), 15151.

Integrating CEQA with the National Environmental Policy Act

NEPA Overview

The National Environmental Policy Act (NEPA, 42 United States Code (USC) 4321 *et seq.*) is similar to CEQA, but applies only to federal agencies. For details about NEPA implementation, *see* Bass *et al.* 2000.

NEPA authorizes federal agencies to carry out their activities consistent with NEPA's environmental protection policies. Its "action-forcing mechanism" is the requirement for federal agencies to prepare an environmental impact statement for major federal actions significantly affecting the quality of the human environment. The President's Council on Environmental Quality (CEQ) regulations (40 Code of Federal Regulations

Universities Must Mitigate Off-Site Impacts

Two 2006 decisions ruled that CEQA requires public universities to mitigate their off-campus traffic impacts (*City of Marina v. Board of Trustees of the California State University* (2006) 39 Cal. 4th 341; *County of San Diego v. Grossmont-Cuyamaca Community College District* (2006) 141 Cal. App. 4th 86 (2006)).

In *City of Marina,* the California State University Board of Trustees certified an EIR for the Master Plan for its Monterey Bay campus at Fort Ord. After Fort Ord closed in the early 1990s, the Legislature created the Fort Ord Reuse Authority (FORA) to finance and construct new public facilities for new land uses on the base. FORA adopted a development plan that included improvements for traffic, fire protection, water, and wastewater to be financed through "fair share" funding of future base developments, based on their impacts on infrastructure.

The EIR for the CSU Master Plan identified significant off-site impacts to traffic, water, sewer, and fire safety. However, the EIR found that FORA's "fair share" fees were infeasible because these off-site improvements could only be completed by FORA, and because CSU was not legally permitted to fund such improvements. The Supreme Court rejected both arguments, finding nothing in state law that prohibited the University of California from paying mitigation fees for off-site traffic impacts.

In the *County of San Diego* case, a community college district adopted a master plan that identified major construction projects needed to accommodate a burgeoning student enrollment, and certified an EIR for this project. The EIR identified several off-campus roadways that would experience significant impacts. However, the district's CEQA findings stated that it was legally infeasible for the District to mitigate for off-campus traffic impacts. The court rejected this argument, finding nothing in state law that prohibited a community college district from constructing or contributing fees to construct off-site traffic improvements. The district also claimed the off-site traffic improvements were economically infeasible, but the court found no substantial evidence in the record to support this finding. ∎

Figure 2-4
CEQA and NEPA Processes Compared

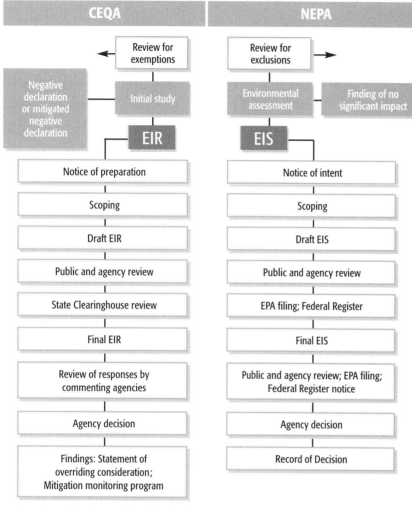

Source: Bass, R.E. *et al.* 1999. *CEQA Deskbook.* Solano Press. Reprinted with permission

CEQA	NEPA
Proposed project	Proposed action
Exemptions	Categorical exclusions
Notice of preparation	Notice of intent
Initial study	Environmental assessment
Negative declaration	Finding of no significant impact (FONSI)
Environmental impact report	Environmental impact statement
Findings	Record of Decision
Responsible agency	Cooperating agency

(CFR) 1500.1 *et seq.*) provide the basic framework for NEPA implementation.

Although federal agencies are normally responsible for NEPA implementation, for federally-funded surface transportation projects, in 2007 the Federal Highway Administration (FHWA) delegated full NEPA implementation responsibilities to the California Department of Transportation (Caltrans). This innovative five-year pilot program was authorized by a federal transportation bill enacted in 2005. 23 USC 327.

Comparing CEQA and NEPA

CEQA and NEPA have parallel three-step environmental review processes, as shown in Figure 2-4. CEQA and NEPA terminology differ somewhat.

A major difference between the two laws is their "substantive effect." CEQA requires state and local agencies to avoid or mitigate significant environmental impacts when feasible. 14 CCR 15021, 15091. NEPA does not require impact avoidance or mitigation (unless mitigation is required to support a FONSI), but rather is essentially procedural; its requirements are satisfied when an EIS contains a good-faith disclosure of a proposed action's impacts and alternatives. *See Robertson v. Methow Valley* (1989) 490 U.S. 332.

Another major difference between the laws is the treatment of alternatives. Under CEQA, alternatives included in an EIR may be described and evaluated in less detail than the proposed project impact. Under NEPA, alternatives included in an EIS must be described and evaluated at an equivalent level of detail. 14 CCR 15126.6, 40 CFR 1502.14.

Integrating CEQA and NEPA

Lead agencies are required to integrate CEQA with other federal, state, and local environmental review requirements, of which NEPA is the most notable. 14 CCR 15124(d). State and local agencies are encouraged to prepare joint environmental documents; when CEQA and NEPA requirements differ, the most stringent requirement of the two laws should be followed. Further, procedures exist for using a NEPA document to satisfy CEQA requirements, provided CEQA public notice and review requirements are met. 14 CCR 15221, 15222.

Enforcing CEQA

CEQA is enforced mainly through lawsuits filed by citizens, environmental and other organizations, or public agencies. The California Attorney General also has discretionary authority to file CEQA lawsuits.

The courts have played a major role in interpreting CEQA's requirements, and judicial interpretations periodically are integrated in updates of the CEQA Guidelines. CEQA has become the main vehicle for project opponents to challenge land use approvals and public agency projects, in large part because the "fair argument" standard of review applied to negative declaration decisions favors CEQA petitioners more than the deferential "substantial evidence" standard typically applied to agency decisionmaking.

Under the fair argument standard, if project opponents have substantial evidence that a project may have a significant environmental effect, an EIR must be prepared, even if the lead agency's substantial evidence indicates lack of significant environmental effect. Under the "substantial evidence" test, which is more typically applied to other agency decisionmaking, a lead agency decision will be upheld as long as it is procedurally correct and supported by substantial evidence, even if project opponents have substantial evidence that would lead to a different decision.

CEQA lawsuits challenging infill and affordable housing projects have become particularly controversial. *See* sidebar.

Typical CEQA Challenges

Typical grounds for CEQA lawsuits include:

CEQA Challenges to Infill and Affordable Housing Cause Backlash

Housing advocates and planners over the past few years increasingly have become concerned about project opponents using CEQA lawsuits to stop infill and affordable housing projects thought to be both socially desirable and environmentally superior to greenfield development in suburban and rural areas.

These concerns have led to the development of narrow statutory (PRC 21159.24) exemptions for infill housing projects. The use of the statutory exemption for infill housing for a multi-family project across from Balboa Park in San Diego was upheld in *Banker's Hill, et al. v. City of San Diego* (2006) 139 Cal. App. 4th 249.

However, the statutory infill housing exemptions are relatively narrow, and a UCLA study found they are seldom used (Elkind and Stone 2005). The study found that local planners seldom grant statutory exemptions for urban infill for one of the following reasons:

- Projects are inconsistent with the general plan (making them ineligible for the exemptions).
- Developers are reluctant to ask for CEQA exemptions.
- Counties cannot use the exemptions for incorporated land.
- The exemptions are too narrow in scope to cover certain affordable housing projects.

Given California's worsening housing affordability problems, continued efforts to amend CEQA to broaden the statutory exemptions for infill and affordable housing projects are likely. In the meantime, CEQA also has a categorical exemption for infill development that is being used more frequently than the statutory exemptions. 14 CCR 15332. ▪

- Procedural violations in environmental document preparation, such as failure to prepare an EIR when one is required, or failure to provide required public notice and review
- Procedural violations in decisionmaking, such as an inappropriate finding that mitigation is infeasible, or a statement of overriding considerations not supported by substantial evidence
- Inadequate or incomplete project description
- Technical inadequacies in environmental documents, such as failure to include an adequate urban blight, water supply, or cumulative impact analysis

Barriers to Judicial Review

CEQA has unusually short statutes of limitation. 14 CCR 15112(c). A CEQA lawsuit must be filed within:

- 35 days after filing and posting of a notice of exemption (NOE)
- 30 days after filing and posting of a notice of determination for either a negative declaration or an EIR
- 180 days after the decision to carry out, approve, or start project, if no NOE or NOD has been filed

Standing refers to a petitioner's eligibility to file a lawsuit; CEQA has liberal standing rules. Most petitioners are entitled to file CEQA lawsuits, provided they exhaust their remedies by raising their CEQA objections before the close of the public hearing on the project. PRC 21177(b).

Remedies

A successful CEQA challenge results in a writ of mandamus (a judicial command to an official to perform a ministerial act that the law recognizes as an absolute duty and not discretionary). A court finding a CEQA violation may void the agency action, enjoin project implementation until CEQA compliance is achieved, or order the agency to comply with CEQA by preparing new environmental documents. PRC 21168.9. Civil or criminal penalties are not available for CEQA violations.

For more information...

Publications

Barbour, E. and M. Teitz. 1995. CEQA Reform: Issues and Options. Public Policy Institute of California

Bass, R., A. Herson, and K. Bogdan. 1999 with 2001 Update. CEQA Deskbook. Solano Press. Point Arena, Calif.

Bass, R., A. Herson, and K. Bogdan. 2000. The NEPA Book. Solano Press. Point Arena, Calif.

Elkind, E. and E. Stone. 2005. CEQA and Affordable Housing Exemptions: A Policy Analysis. UCLA Law School Public Policy Clinic

Governor's Office of Planning and Research. Circulation and Notice under the California Environmental Quality Act

Governor's Office of Planning and Research. Focusing on Master EIRs

Governor's Office of Planning and Research. Mitigated Negative Declarations

Governor's Office of Planning and Research. State Clearinghouse Handbook

Governor's Office of Planning and Research. Technical Advisory: CEQA and Climate Change

Manaster, K.A. and D.P. Selmi (eds.). ND. Chapters 20–23 of California Environmental Law and Land Use Practice. Matthew Bender. San Francisco, Calif.

Remy, M.H, T.A. Thomas, J.G. Moose, and W.F. Manley. 2006. Guide to the California Environmental Quality Act (CEQA). Solano Press. Point Arena, Calif.

Websites

CEQA Guidelines
http://ceres.ca.gov/topic/env_law/ceqa/guidelines

CEQA Home Page
http://ceres.ca.gov/ceqa

CEQA Process Flow Chart
http://ceres.ca.gov/topic/env_law/ceqa/flowchart/index.html

CEQA Map (CEQA documents online)
www.ceqamap.com

CEQAnet (an electronic database of CEQA documents filed with the State Clearinghouse)
www.ceqanet.ca.gov

Governor's Office of Planning and Research, State Clearinghouse
www.opr.ca.gov/clearinghouse/Clearinghouse.html

NEPAnet
www.nepa.gov

The Resources Agency
http://resources.ca.gov

Thresholds of Significance, Examples
http://ceres.ca.gov/planning/ceqa/thresholds.html

Local Land Use Planning and Regulation

This chapter reviews –

- Key laws and agencies involved in local land use planning and regulation
- General plans, specific plans, and redevelopment plans
- Zoning and subdivisions
- Permit Streamlining Act
- Historic preservation
- Takings, exactions, and development agreements
- Growth management and boundary changes
- Enforcement of land use regulations

Related Solano Press titles–

Ballot Box Navigator
Michael P. Durkee *et al.* 2003

Curtin's California Land Use and Planning Law. Cecily T. Talbert. 2008

Eminent Domain.
Richard G. Rypinski. 2002

Exactions and Impact Fees in California
William W. Abbott *et al.* 2001 with 2002 Supplement

Guide to California Planning
William E. Fulton and Paul Shigley. 2005

Putting Transfer of Development Rights to Work in California. Rick Pruetz. 1993

Redevelopment in California
David F. Beatty *et al.* 2004

Subdivision Map Act Manual
Daniel J. Curtin and Robert E. Merritt. 2003

Understanding Development Regulations
Robert E. Merritt and Ann R. Danforth (eds.). 1994

Glossary

Affordable housing—housing capable of being purchased or rented by a household with very low, low, or moderate income.

Annexation—incorporating land into an existing city or special district.

Blight—physical and economic conditions within an area that causes a reduction of, or lack of, proper utilization of that area.

California Register of Historic Places—a register of historic places meeting criteria established by state law.

Charter city—a city that has been incorporated under its own charter rather than under the general laws of the state.

Conditional use permit*—pursuant to a zoning ordinance, this permit authorizes uses not routinely allowed on a particular site.

Dedication*—offering by an applicant, and acceptance by the government, of private land for public use, typically imposed as a condition of development approval.

Density bonus—permission to increase a project's housing density, typically in return for production of low income housing units.

Development agreement*—a legally binding agreement between a city or county and a developer that typically prevents future changes in land use regulations from affecting a given project, in return for developer concessions.

Easement—the right to use property owned by another for specific purposes.

Eminent domain—the taking of private property by a government unit for public use.

Exaction*—land dedication or impact fee required as a condition of development approval or construction.

Final subdivision map*—map of an approved subdivision filed in the county recorder's office.

General plan—a statement of development policies, including diagrams and text, setting forth objectives, principles, standards, and plan proposals, for the future development of a city or county.

Growth management—local government use of a variety of measures to influence the amount, type, and location of growth.

Impact fee*—also known as a development fee, a monetary exaction to defray costs of public facilities related to a development project.

Initiative—a legislative measure that has been placed on the election ballot as a result of voter signatures.

Local agency formation commission—a countywide commission that reviews and approves city and special district boundary changes.

National Register of Historic Places—historic properties meeting eligibility criteria established by the Advisory Council on Historic Preservation.

New urbanism—closely related to smart growth, a planning doctrine that emphasizes restoration of existing urban centers within coherent metropolitan regions, reconfiguration of sprawling suburbs into communities of real neighborhoods, conservation of natural environments, and preservation of the built environment.

Nexus—for purposes of this chapter, a reasonable relationship between a land use regulation and the impacts of a proposed action.

Nonconforming use—land use that was lawful before a zoning ordinance was adopted, but does not conform to the new zoning ordinance.

Overlay zone—a set of zoning requirements that is superimposed on a base zone, e.g., an historic preservation district.

Planned unit development*—a master-planned development within a zoning district that allows multiple uses (e.g., residential, commercial, industrial).

Police power—the power of state and local governments to enact legislation to protect public health, safety, and welfare.

Quasi-judicial decision—a quasi-judicial decision is one that applies policy based on factual determinations, rather than sets policy.

Redevelopment—the legally authorized process of rehabilitating or rebuilding a deteriorated section of a city.

Redevelopment plan—legal framework for revitalization activities in a redevelopment project area.

Referendum—a ballot measure challenging a legislative action of a city or county.

Smart growth—closely related to new urbanism, a planning doctrine that discourages urban sprawl and emphasizes compact, transit-accessible, pedestrian-oriented, mixed use development patterns, and land reuse.

Specific plan*—a plan addressing land use distribution, open space availability, and infrastructure for a portion of a community.

Sphere of influence—the physical boundary and service area that a local government is expected to ultimately serve, as adopted by the LAFCO.

Subdivision—the process of dividing a larger parcel of land into smaller lots.

Taking—the appropriation by government of private land for public use, requiring just compensation under the U.S. Constitution.

Tentative subdivision map*—a map illustrating a subdivision proposal. A subdivision is complete only when conditions imposed on the tentative map have been satisfied and a final map has been certified and recorded.

Variance*—a limited waiver from the property development standards of a zoning ordinance.

Vested right—a right to develop that cannot be changed by subsequent changes in regulations.

Zoning*—a local code dividing a city or county into land use zones and specifying allowable uses in each zone.

* equals permit or approval

CHAPTER 3

Local Land Use Planning and Regulation

Introduction

This chapter reviews local government land use planning and regulation. City and county land use plans and regulations can play a critical role in protecting and preserving environmental quality. Following a review of key laws and agencies, this chapter reviews general plans, specific plans, and redevelopment plans; zoning law; subdivision law; the Permit Streamlining Act; historic preservation programs; takings, exactions, and development agreements; and growth management and boundary changes. State agencies such as the Coastal Commission, and regional planning agencies such as councils of government (COGs) also play an important role in land use planning and regulation. These agencies and their programs are reviewed in chapter 4 (State and Regional Land Use Controls).

COG = Council of government

Key Laws and Agencies

Key Laws

Police power. The police power is the legal basis for local governments (*i.e.,* cities and counties) to regulate land use to protect public health, safety, and welfare within their boundaries. The sources of the police power are:

The police power is the legal basis for local governments to regulate land use to protect public health, safety, and welfare within their boundaries.

- The powers retained by the states (reserved powers), pursuant to the U.S. Constitution (10th Amendment)
- The California Constitution (Art. XI, Sec. 7), which authorizes a city or county to make and enforce within its limits all local and police ordinances and regulations not in conflict with general law

State legislation. Numerous state laws create the legal framework for local government land use planning and regulation. The most important of these are:

- General plan and specific plan requirements. Gov. Code 65100 *et seq.*
- Zoning regulations. Gov. Code 65300 *et seq.*
- California Redevelopment Law. Health and Safety Code 33000 *et seq.*
- Subdivision Map Act. Gov. Code 66410 *et seq.*
- Permit Streamlining Act. Gov. Code 65920 *et seq.*
- The authorization of development agreements. Gov. Code 65864 *et seq.*

Key Agencies

Local governments. City councils and county boards of supervisors are the local government land use decisionmaking bodies. Some of their functions may be assigned to planning commissions, or to design or architectural review boards. Typically, some planning commission decisions, such as general plan amendments, are recommendations to the city council or county board of supervisors, whereas other decisions are final unless appealed, such as subdivisions and zoning variances.

OPR = Governor's Office of Planning and Research

Governor's Office of Planning and Research. State agencies play a limited role in local land use planning and regulation. Instead, the Governor's Office of Planning and Research (OPR) issues General Plan Guidelines that are frequently revised to reflect statutory changes. OPR also periodically issues other land use guidance, *e.g.*, guidelines for Native American tribal consultation, and advice on how to prepare specific plans. These publications are available on the OPR website (www.opr.ca.gov), and many are listed as sources of further information at the end of this chapter.

General Plans, Specific Plans, and Redevelopment Plans

General Plans

Cities and counties are required to prepare general plans, which serve as the blueprints, or constitutions, for all future developments within their jurisdiction.

Overview. Cities and counties are required to prepare general plans, which serve as the blueprints, or constitutions, for all future developments within their jurisdiction. Prior to 1971, the general plan was considered an advisory document, but in 1971, legislation passed requiring zoning and subdivision approvals to be consistent with an adopted general plan. Gov. Code 65860; *see* discussion of consistency requirement below.

The general plan must be a comprehensive, long-term plan for the physical development of the city or county. The general plan must include a statement of development policies, including diagrams and text, setting forth objectives, principles, standards, and plan proposals. Gov. Code 65302. The general plan also must contain seven elements: land use, circulation, housing, conservation, open space, noise, and safety. Gov. Code 65302(a)–(g). Table 3-1 depicts the environmental and other issues that must be addressed in each required element.

Table 3-1. General Plan Issues and Elements

Issue	Element						
	Land Use	Circulation	Housing	Conservation	Open Space	Noise	Safety
Agriculture	X			(X)	X		
Air quality					X		
Airports	(X)	(X)			(X)	X	
Density	X		X				
Education	X						
Fire					X		X
Fisheries				(X)	X		
Flooding	X			X	X		X
Forests/Timber	X			X	X		
Housing	(X)		X				
Industrial uses	X					X	
Land reclamation				X			
Land use	X	X	(X)	X	(X)	X	(X)
Minerals				X	X		
Noise contours	(X)					X	
Public buildings	X						
Railways/Yards		(X)				X	
Recreation	X				X		
Scenic resources	X				X		
Seismic hazards					X		X
Soil conservation				X	X		
Soil instability							X
Transportation routes		X			X*	X	X
Transportation terminals		X					
Utilities/Easements		X			X		
Waste facilities	X		X**				
Water quality				X	X		
Water supply	(X)		X**	X	X		
Watersheds				X	X		
Waterways/Water bodies				X	X		
Wildlife				X	X		

X   topic identified in statutes
(X) topic closely related to
     relevant statutory requirements

* Trail systems
** Factors affecting adequate inventory of sites

Source: Governor's Office of Planning and Research. General Plan Guidelines

A city or county also may choose to adopt additional elements, *e.g.*, agriculture, urban design, air quality, energy, or water supply.

If a general plan does not have all the mandatory elements, if the elements do not meet statutory criteria, or if the elements are inconsistent (*see below*), then a land use decision related to the plan deficiency can be declared invalid.

For example, the issuance of a conditional use permit may be beyond a county's authority if the noise element of the county's general plan does not meet the statutory criteria. *Neighborhood Action Group v. City of Calaveras* (1984) 156 Cal. App. 3d 1176. However, a city or county with an inadequate general plan may apply to OPR for a two-year extension to correct the inadequacy, during which time the city's or county's land use decisions cannot be challenged as inconsistent with the general plan. Gov. Code 65361.

A general plan must be integrated and internally consistent, both across elements and within each element.

Internal consistency. A general plan must be integrated and internally consistent, both across elements and within each element. Gov. Code 95300.5. For example, the land use and circulation elements must be based on the same population growth projections, and general plan diagrams of land use or circulation systems must be internally consistent with written policies and programs in the land use and circulation elements.

Consistency of land use decisions. Generally, all land use decisions must be consistent with the general plan. However, a charter city, other than the charter city of Los Angeles, is exempt from the requirement for zoning to be consistent with the general plan unless it adopts a consistency rule. Gov. Code 55803. (In a charter city, the legal authority for the city's acts originates with a city charter, rather than from state laws. About one-fifth of California's cities are charter cities.)

A land use decision is consistent with the general plan if, considering all its aspects, it will further the objectives and policies of the general plan and not obstruct their attainment.

A land use decision, such as a rezoning or subdivision map approval, is consistent with the general plan if, considering all its aspects, it will further the objectives and policies of the general plan and not obstruct their attainment. Courts generally defer to a city's or county's interpretation of its own general plan when reviewing consistency determinations. *See, e.g., City of Irvine v. Irvine Citizens against Overdevelopment* (1994) 25 Cal. App. 4th 868.

General plan adoption and amendment process. The process for general plan adoption and amendment is set forth in Government Code 63530 *et seq.* The planning commission must hold a public hearing before taking action on the general plan proposal, and then the city council or county board of supervisors must likewise hold at least one public hearing before taking action on the general plan proposal and the planning commission recommendation. A CEQA document must be prepared for the general plan proposal and considered at these hearings.

LAFCO = Local agency formation commission

State law encourages intergovernmental coordination in general plan preparation. The general plan proposal should be referred to any county or city within or adjacent to the area covered by the proposal, to any special district that may be significantly affected by the proposal, to any school district within the area covered by the proposal, to the local agency formation commission (LAFCO), and to any affected regional planning or federal agencies. These agencies generally have 45 days to comment. Gov. Code 65301, 65302.

Under recent legislation (Senate Bill (SB) 18 of 2004; Gov. Code 65092, 65352 *et seq.*), cities and counties must send their general plan and specific plan proposals to those California Native American Tribes that are on the Native American Heritage Commission contact list and have traditional lands located within the city's or county's jurisdiction. Cities and counties also must consult with these tribes prior to adopting or amending their general plans or specific plans. OPR (2005b) has issued detailed guidelines for SB 18 consultation.

Housing element. Local governments must prepare housing elements consistent with the State Housing Element Guidelines prepared by the Department of Housing and Community Development (HCD). Gov. Code 65585(a). HCD is responsible for determining regional housing needs for all income groups, and COGs (or HCD where no COG exists) are responsible for adopting a regional housing need plan that allocates a "fair share" of the regional housing need to each city and county. Gov. Code 65584.06.

Local government housing elements must meet these fair share requirements. Local governments must submit draft housing elements and proposed amendments to HCD for review and comment. They must also submit adopted housing elements and amendments to HCD. Additionally, local governments must update their housing elements every five years and submit an annual report to OPR and HCD on the status of the general plan and housing element implementation. Gov. Code 65400(b), 65588(b).

Flood management. Legislation enacted in 2007 (AB 162, Statutes of 2007, Chapter 369) established new requirements for general plans to consider flood management. The land use element is now required to identify and annually review areas subject to flooding, as identified on floodplain maps prepared by the Federal Emergency Management Agency (FEMA) or the Department of Water Resources (DWR). The conservation element must now identify land and water resources that can accommodate floodwater for purposes of groundwater recharge and storm water management. The safety element must identify flood hazard zones, and establish policies to protect the community from unreasonable risks of flooding. In Central Valley cities and counties, the revised safety element must be submitted to the Central Valley Flood Protection Board for review and comment, and local agencies must make formal findings if they reject any of the board's recommendations. The conservation element and safety element revisions are required no later than the agency's next revision to the housing element, starting on January 1, 2009.

SB 70 of 2007 (Statutes of 2007, Chapter 367) provides local governments with additional incentives to keep development out of the floodplains in their general plans. It requires local governments, under some circumstances, to pay their fair share of flood damages, to the extent they increase the state's exposure

DWR = Department of Water Resources

FEMA = Federal Emergency Management Agency

HCD = Department of Housing and Community Development

SB = Senate Bill

Local governments must prepare housing elements consistent with the State Housing Element Guidelines prepared by HCD.

Legislation enacted in 2007 required general plans to strengthen flood management policies.

to liability for property damage by unreasonably approving new development in a previously undeveloped area protected by a state flood control project. *See* chapter 4.

Amendments and updates. Cities and counties must periodically review and revise the general plan. A mandatory element of the general plan may be amended only four times a year. The housing element must be updated at least every five years (Gov. Code 65588(b)), but there is no statutory update requirement for the other elements.

Legal challenges to general plan adequacy. When general plan adequacy is challenged, courts generally use a deferential standard of review, considering whether adoption or amendment of the general plan was arbitrary, capricious, or lacking in evidentiary support. Code Civ. Proc. 1085; *see, e.g., Garrick Development Company v. Hayward Unified School District* (1992) 3 Cal. App. 4th 320. The court determines whether the plan substantially complies with the statutory criteria. The housing element gets closer judicial scrutiny because it has more detailed statutory requirements.

The statute of limitations for challenging a decision to adopt or amend a general plan (or specific plan) is generally 90 days. Gov. Code 65009(c). If a general plan is found to be deficient, the court may order one or more of the following measures until the general plan deficiency has been corrected (Gov. Code 65755):

- Suspending authority to issue building permits and other permits
- Suspending authority to issue variances
- Suspending authority to issue subdivision approvals
- Mandating approval of certain permits for housing, and certain subdivision maps, when the city's or county's ability to implement an adequate housing element will not be impaired

Specific Plans

A specific plan implements a general plan within a smaller geographic area. Land use controls, such as zoning ordinances and subdivision regulations, must be consistent with adopted specific plans, as are public works projects and development agreements. Gov. Code 65450 *et seq.* A specific plan includes text and diagrams covering the following topics (Gov. Code 65454(a)):

- Distribution, location, and extent of land uses
- Distribution, location, extent, and intensity of infrastructure
- Standards by which development will proceed and natural resources will be managed

- Implementation measures such as regulations, public works projects, and financing measures

A specific plan must be consistent with the general plan. It is adopted using essentially the same procedures as for adoption of a general plan. Unlike general plan amendments, there is no annual limit on the number of specific plan amendments. OPR (2001) has issued guidance on specific plan preparation.

Some cities and counties also prepare community plans or area plans that often cover larger areas than specific plans. A community plan supplements the general plan by focusing on issues relevant to a particular community. For example, the City of Los Angeles has prepared community plans for 35 specific community plan areas.

Redevelopment Plans and Eminent Domain

A redevelopment plan provides the legal framework for revitalization activities in a redevelopment project area. Redevelopment is a tool created by state law to assist local governments in eliminating blight, as well as to achieve the goals of development, reconstruction, and rehabilitation of residential, commercial, industrial, and retail districts. Blight is the physical and economic conditions within an area that causes a reduction in, or lack of, proper utilization of that area. Gov. Code 33301.

Redevelopment plans are prepared and implemented by redevelopment agencies. A redevelopment agency is a separate public body that reports to the city council or county board of supervisors. In most communities, the local governing body also serves as the redevelopment agency board. Gov. Code 33100 *et seq.*

The redevelopment plan must be consistent with the city or county general plan. A redevelopment plan generally contains the following (Gov. Code 33324):

- A legal description of the project area and a description of land uses
- Descriptions of the proposed actions by the redevelopment agency and landowners
- Authority and limitations for financing the proposed actions

Redevelopment plans are often implemented using the power of eminent domain, in which the redevelopment agency takes private property for a public use and pays the landowner just compensation. The use of eminent domain for redevelopment became

2006 Laws Limit Eminent Domain

In response to the *Kelo* decision, the following laws limiting eminent domain were enacted in 2006:

- SB 53 (Chapter 591, Statutes of 2006) requires an agency to make additional findings of blight if it wishes to extend the time limits on its authorization for eminent domain actions. This bill also requires a redevelopment agency, in its redevelopment plan, to specify where, when, and how the agency is authorized to use the power of eminent domain.

- SB 1206 (Chapter 595, Statutes of 2006) narrows the statutory blight definition; increases state oversight over redevelopment by the Attorney General, Department of Finance, and the Department of Housing and Community Development; and makes it easier to challenge redevelopment decisions.

- SB 1210 (Chapter 594, Statutes of 2006) limits the ability of government to possess land prior to an eminent domain judgment, and requires a public entity seeking to use eminent domain to pay the reasonable costs of an independent appraisal, up to $5,000. The bill also prohibits a redevelopment agency from exercising eminent domain more than 12 years after adoption of the redevelopment plan, unless substantial blight exists that cannot be eliminated without eminent domain.

- SB 1650 (Chapter 602, Statutes of 2006) prohibits a public entity from using a property for any use other than the public use stated in its adopted resolution of necessity, unless the entity first adopts a new resolution that finds the public interest and necessity of using the property for a new stated public use.

- SB 1809 (Chapter 603, Statutes of 2006) requires a redevelopment agency to record with the county recorder a statement describing any land situated in a redevelopment project area within 60 days of any action adopting or amending a redevelopment plan. The bill also prohibits a redevelopment agency from commencing an eminent domain action under an adopted redevelopment plan before the required statement is recorded.

controversial nationally after the Supreme Court decision in *Kelo v. City of New London* (2005) 545 U.S. 469, in which the court upheld a Connecticut city's use of eminent domain to acquire 15 homes in order for a private developer to build a commercial development.

The *Kelo* decision did not fundamentally change the law in California, which generally permitted the use of eminent domain for economic development only if it is for the removal of blight. The use of eminent domain in California was further limited by a series of laws enacted in 2006. *See* sidebar.

Zoning and Subdivisions

Zoning

Overview. Whereas the general plan is a long-range policy document focusing on the future, a zoning ordinance describes the immediate allowable uses on each piece of property within the city or county. Zoning divides a city or county into districts or zones, such as single-family residential, multi-family residential, commercial, industrial, and open space. Zoning regulations regulate both building standards (*e.g.,* building heights and setbacks) and the allowable uses of buildings in each of these zones.

Zoning divides a city or county into districts or zones, such as single-family residential, multi-family residential, commercial, industrial, and open space.

In addition to zoning applied to specific parcels, many cities or counties use overlay zones to further regulate development to address special concerns. For example, overlay zones may apply to floodplains or historic districts.

Zoning authority. Zoning authority originates from city and county police powers and from the state's Planning and Zoning Law. Gov. Code 65000 *et seq.* This law sets minimum zoning standards for counties and general law cities (non-charter cities). Certain sections of the Planning and Zoning Law, *e.g.,* procedures for zoning hearings, also apply to charter cities. Zoning ordinances are subject to initiatives and referenda. *See* below.

Consistency with general plans and specific plans. A zoning ordinance must be consistent with the general plan and applicable specific plans. However, a charter city, other than Los Angeles, is exempt from the requirement of zoning being consistent with the general plan unless the charter city adopts a consistency rule. A zoning ordinance is consistent with an adopted general or specific plan if the land uses authorized by the ordinance are compatible with the plan objectives, policies, general land uses, and programs.

Zoning ordinance amendments. Most zoning ordinance amendments are subject to minimum due process requirements of notice and hearing. To enact a zoning amendment, the planning commission must hold a noticed public hearing and make its recommendation to the city council or county board of supervisors, which in turn adopts the amendment after a second noticed public hearing.

Variances and conditional use permits. Variances and conditional use permits (CUPs) provide flexibility in the application of zoning ordinances, and some cities or counties have a zoning adjustment board to grant these permits. OPR Guidance on variances and CUPs is available on the OPR website (http://ceres.ca.gov/planning/var/variance.htm; http://ceres.ca.gov/planning/cup/condition.htm). For counties and general law cities, state law governs the issuance of variances and conditional use permits. Gov. Code 65901 *et seq.* Charter cities may adopt different procedures.

A zoning variance is a limited exception to the usual requirements of local zoning. Gov. Code 65906. When a city or county is asked to approve development on an unusual property, the variance gives flexibility to the usual standards of the zoning ordinance. Approval of a variance allows the property owner to use property in a manner basically consistent with the zoning ordinance, with minor variations, *e.g.*, a change in building setback requirements. Restrictions on a zoning variance must be imposed to ensure the variance will not grant special privilege to a particular landowner. For a variance to be granted, the local government must find all of the following (*Topanga Association for a Scenic Community v. County of Los Angeles* (1974) 11 Cal. 3d 506):

Approval of a variance allows the property owner to use property in a manner basically consistent with the zoning ordinance, with minor variations, e.g., a change in building setback requirements.

- There are unique physical constraints on the property
- Deprivation or hardship would result without relief
- There are disparities between the applicant's parcel and neighboring land

A conditional use permit, sometimes called a special use permit, is issued for specified uses that are not permitted by right by a zoning ordinance, but which may still be appropriate under certain circumstances. Examples of uses requiring a conditional use permit include community facilities, public buildings, liquor stores, churches, and landfills. Some local zoning ordinances have special requirements for approval of certain conditional use permits, such as approval of neighborhood owners, or standards for proximity to sensitive uses such as schools or churches. Conditional use permits typically are granted with special conditions; however, state law prohibits conditions requiring either the dedication of land or the posting of a bond for public improvements not reasonably related to the conditional use. Gov. Code 65909.

A conditional use permit, sometimes called a special use permit, is issued for specified uses that are not permitted by right by a zoning ordinance, but which may still be appropriate under certain circumstances.

Nonconforming uses and their termination. A nonconforming use is a land use that was lawful before a zoning ordinance was adopted, but does not conform to the new zoning ordinance. *See Hill v. City of Manhattan Beach* (1971) 6 Cal. 3d 279. The concept of nonconforming uses includes nonconforming activities on undeveloped land and within structures, as well as nonconforming structures. Like a variance or conditional use permit, a legal nonconforming use is an exception from the strict application of a local zoning ordinance.

A nonconforming use is a land use that was lawful before a zoning ordinance was adopted, but does not conform to the new zoning ordinance.

Zoning ordinances typically prohibit the expansion of a nonconforming use, starting a new nonconforming use of the property, or making the nonconforming use more permanent through structural alterations. Zoning ordinances may terminate nonconforming uses after a reasonable time period that allows the landowner to amortize his or her investment in the nonconforming use; the amortization period is proportional to the landowner's investment and the nature of the use. *See City of Los Angeles v. Gage* (1954) 127 Cal. App. 2d 577.

PUD = Planned unit development

Planned unit developments. A planned unit development (PUD) is a master-planned development within a zoning district that allows multiple uses (*e.g.*, residential, commercial, industrial). PUDs typically consist of individually owned lots and areas owned in common (*e.g.*, greenbelts, streets) by all lot owners. A PUD permits flexibility in site planning and location of structures. The concept of a PUD is not expressly recognized by state law, but has been approved by the courts. *See, e.g.*, *Orinda Homeowners Committee v. Board of Supervisors* (1970) 11 Cal. App. 3d 768.

Inclusionary housing programs, typically implemented through zoning, require residential developers to set aside a certain percentage of new units for low-income households.

Inclusionary zoning and affordable housing requirements. Inclusionary housing programs, typically implemented through zoning, require residential developers to set aside a certain percentage of new units for low-income households. Inclusionary zoning also can include density bonuses, reduced development standards, or fees to fund affordable housing production.

The state has enacted a number of statutes to prevent local governments from using zoning and land use controls to discourage affordable housing, and instead to encourage the production of affordable housing through incentives. For example, density bonuses (permission to increase project housing density) may be used as incentives for production of low-income housing units. Gov. Code 65915(a) *et seq*. Also, cities and counties are prohibited from disapproving affordable housing projects unless they make certain overriding findings. Gov. Code 65598.5. Incentives for affordable housing are part of the state's housing policy (Gov. Code 65915 *et seq.*), and are described in detail on the Department of Housing and Community Development's housing policy website (www.hcd.ca.gov/hpd).

Legal challenges to zoning ordinances. Adoption of a zoning ordinance is a legislative act, to which the courts typically defer, and a zoning ordinance is presumed to be constitutional. A zoning ordinance is valid if it is reasonably related to the public welfare. The California Supreme Court established the following test for determining whether a land use regulation such as a zoning ordinance is reasonably related to the public welfare (*Associated Homebuilders, Inc. v. City of Livermore* (1982) 18 Cal. 3d 582):

A zoning ordinance is valid if it is reasonably related to the public welfare.

- What is the probable effect and duration of the land use restriction?

- What are the competing interests (*e.g.*, affordable housing) affected by the land use restriction?

- Does the regulation, considering its probable effect, represent a reasonable accommodation of the competing interests?

A zoning ordinance is sometimes challenged on the grounds that it is too vague, thereby violating due process rights of those to which it applies. However, courts have permitted a substantial amount of vagueness in zoning ordinances. Also, zoning and other land use controls can be challenged as regulatory "takings" of private property, in violation of the Fifth Amendment to the U.S. Constitution (as is discussed later in this chapter).

First Amendment challenges to zoning ordinances. The application of zoning ordinances to adult business (*e.g.*, adult bookstores or movie theaters), billboards, and religious land uses has generated much litigation. A zoning ordinance regulating adult businesses will be upheld as not violating the First Amendment's free speech clause, if it is content-neutral, designed to serve a substantial government interest, and allows reasonable alternative avenues of communication. *City of Renton v. Playtime Theaters, Inc.* (1986) 475 U.S. 41. The leading case on billboard regulation is *Metromedia, Inc. v. San Diego* (1981) 453 U.S. 490, in which the Supreme Court ruled that commercial interests are entitled to less freedom of speech protections than non-commercial interests, but rejected the city's billboard ordinance because it selectively banned billboards based on content.

Land use regulation of religious uses is governed not only by the First Amendment, but also by the Religious Land Use and Institutionalized Persons Act of 2000 (RLUIPA, 42 United States Code (USC) 2000cc). Under RLUIPA, a city or county land use regulation may not impose a "substantial burden" on religious exercise unless the regulation furthers a "compelling government interest" and is the least restrictive means to further that interest. To be successfully challenged, the regulation must do more than regulate a religious institution's land use–it must actually impose a burden on religious exercise. *See, e.g.*, *San Jose Christian College v. City of Morgan Hill* (2004) 360 F. 3d 1024, in which a city's denial of a religious college's application to rezone property from hospital use to a place of religious education did not impose a substantial burden on the exercise of religion.

RLUIPA = Religious Land Use and Institutionalized Persons Act of 2000

USC = United States Code

Subdivisions

Overview. Dividing land for sale, lease, or financing is regulated by local ordinances based on the Subdivision Map Act (Gov. Code 66410 *et seq.*). The Act's main goals are to encourage orderly development, ensure areas dedicated for public purposes will be properly improved, and protect public and land purchasers from fraud. The Act is implemented through local governments adopting a local subdivision ordinance. The local subdivision ordinance, together with the general plan and zoning, govern a subdivision's design, lot size, and infrastructure such as streets, water service, sewer service, and drainage facilities.

The Subdivision Map Act's main goals are to encourage orderly development, ensure areas dedicated for public purposes will be properly improved, and protect public and land purchasers from fraud.

Certain property divisions are exempt from the Subdivision Map Act. These include lot line adjustments, granny or second units, conveyance to or from public agencies, and condominium conversions. Gov. Code 66412.

Typically, cities and counties impose conditions–fees or exactions–on a subdivision to meet increased public services demands caused by the subdivision's future residents. The fees or exactions are subject to constitutional and statutory limits, discussed later in this chapter. Two basic types of subdivisions exist. A parcel map is limited (with some exceptions) to divisions resulting in fewer than five lots. A subdivision map, also called a tract map, applies to subdivisions resulting in five or more lots. Gov. Code 66426.

Subdivision processing. A city or county first approves a tentative tract map (for subdivisions of five lots or greater) after ensuring it meets the requirements of the local general plan, zoning ordinance, and subdivision ordinance, and after holding a public hearing. The applicant then typically has two years to install required infrastructure or post a bond as security, following which the city or county approves a final subdivision map, which allows the subdivision to be recorded. Gov. Code 66424.5 *et seq.*

Subdivision approvals and other local land use approvals that are considered administrative are subject to application procedures and time limits established by the Permit Streamlining Act (Gov. Code 65920 *et seq.*). The Act's requirements are reviewed later in this chapter.

Approval of a parcel map or final map does not confer a vested right to develop. A vested right to develop occurs when actual building occurs or permits for buildings have been granted, and substantial work was performed in reliance on those permits. *Avco Community Developers, Inc. v. South Coast Regional Commission* (1976) 17 Cal. 3d 785. In 1986, the Legislature created a new form of tentative map, called the vesting tentative map, that generally confers a vested right to develop in substantial compliance with those land use polices and regulations that were in effect at the time the subdivision application is completed. Gov. Code 66498.1 *et seq.*

Enforcement. The Subdivision Map Act prohibits the sale, lease, or financing of parcels for which a subdivision map is required. Grantees or buyers may void land transactions within one year of discovering a violation of the Act. A city or county may enforce the Subdivision Map Act through seeking an injunction against a violation, or by withholding permits and approvals needed to develop a property divided in violation of the Act. Gov. Code 66499.31 *et seq.*

Permit Streamlining Act

Purpose and Applicability

PSA = Permit Streamlining Act

The Permit Streamlining Act (PSA, Gov. Code 65920 *et seq.*) was passed by the California Legislature in 1977. It is intended to streamline the numerous requirements related to development projects and to expedite decisions related to such projects. The PSA requires all public agencies to follow uniform time limits and procedures for approving development projects. Although the PSA is reviewed in this chapter because it is most often encountered in local land use decision-making, it also applies to state agency approvals of development projects.

Development projects subject to the PSA include those projects requiring the issuance of "quasi-judicial" environmental and land use permits. Development projects do not include ministerial projects (non-discretionary projects requiring little judgment by the decisionmaker) such as building permits, nor do they include legislative acts such as rezoning or general plan amendments. Gov. Code 65928.

Review of Permit Applications for Completeness

Under the PSA, public agencies must compile one or more lists detailing the information required from any applicant for a development project. However, accepting an application as complete does not limit the permitting agency's authority to require the applicant to submit additional information for environmental evaluation of the project under CEQA. 14 California Code of Regulations (CCR) 15060.

Accepting an application as complete does not limit the permitting agency's authority to require the applicant to submit additional information for environmental evaluation of the project under CEQA.

Once an applicant submits an application for a development project, public agencies have 30 days to determine in writing whether the application is complete enough for processing. If the agency fails to notify the applicant of the application's completeness or incompleteness within the 30-day review period, the application is automatically deemed complete. Gov. Code 65943.

CCR	= California Code of Regulations
CEQA	= California Environmental Quality Act
EIR	= Environmental impact report
ND	= Negative declaration

If the agency determines that an application is incomplete, the applicant may resubmit the application. If the application is again determined incomplete, the applicant may appeal the decision, in which case the agency must issue a final written determination within 60 days. Again, failure to notify the applicant within this time frame constitutes acceptance of the application. Gov. Code 65943.

Time Limits for CEQA Documents and Project Approvals

PSA time limitations are closely integrated with CEQA time limitations. Once an application is accepted as complete, the following time limits apply:

- CEQA documents (14 CCR 15100 *et seq.*):
  - Thirty days from application acceptance as complete: lead agency must decide whether to prepare negative declaration (ND) or environmental impact report (EIR)
  - Forty-five days from decision to prepare ND or EIR: lead agency must execute consultant contract (this time limit is seldom enforced)
  - One hundred and eighty days from application acceptance as complete: lead agency must complete ND
  - One year from application acceptance as complete: lead agency must certify EIR

- Project approval (Gov. Code 65950 *et seq.*):
  - Lead agency must approve project within 60 days after an exemption decision or adoption of an ND
  - Lead agency must approve project within six months after EIR certification
  - Responsible agency must approve project within 180 days after responsible agency accepts application as complete, or after lead agency decision, whichever is later

The PSA allows for a one-time limited extension of most of these time limits with mutual consent of the project applicant and permitting agency. Gov. Code 65957. The PSA disallows any other extensions or waivers of time limits. A seldom-used provision of the PSA states that a project may be deemed approved if the permitting agency fails to act within the time limits for project approval, provided public notice requirements have been met. Gov. Code 65956(b).

Historic Preservation

Preservation of historic resources is governed by federal, state, and local laws and regulations.

National Historic Preservation Act

The National Historic Preservation Act protects National Register-listed historic properties.

ACHP = Advisory Council on Historic Preservation
CFR = Code of Federal Regulations
SHPO = State Historic Preservation Officer

The National Historic Preservation Act (NHPA, 16 USC 470 *et seq.*) established the National Register of Historic Places, created the Advisory Council on Historic Preservation, and established the Section 106 consultation process. The Section 106 review process (36 Code of Federal Regulations (CFR) 800 *et seq.*) applies to federal agencies taking actions, including permitting and funding actions, that may affect National Register listed or eligible properties.

Federal agencies taking such actions are required to consult with the Advisory Council on Historic Preservation (ACHP), State Historic Preservation Officer (SHPO), local agencies, and Indian tribes, and avoid or mitigate adverse effects on National Register listed or eligible properties. For example, if the U.S. Army Corps of Engineers issues a Section 404 permit (*see* chapter 15) allowing filling of wetlands on a project site with historic significance, the Corps would need to initiate Section 106 consultation with the ACHP, SHPO, local agencies, and affected tribes.

Other Federal Laws

The following federal laws provide more direct protection to archeological sites:

- **Antiquities Act of 1906.** Regulates excavation of archeological sites and imposes penalties for removal or damage to archeological resources. 16 USC 431 *et seq.*
- **Archeological Recovery Act.** Protects significant historical or archeological finds discovered during construction. 16 USC 469 *et seq.*
- **Archeological Resources Protection Act.** Requires permits for excavation and removal of archeological resources on Indian or public lands. 16 USC 670
- **Section 4(f) of the Department of Transportation Act.** Prohibits the Department of Transportation from approving or funding a transportation project requiring the "use" of specified historic sites unless there is no prudent and feasible alternative, and the project includes all possible mitigation measures. 49 USC 303

State Laws

California has two main laws affecting historic preservation. First, Public Resources Code 5020 *et seq.* establishes the California Register of Historic Resources, which is to be used by local governments in their historic preservation efforts. Second, CEQA (*see* chapter 2) sets forth a detailed statutory process for protection of historic resources. 14 CCR 15064.5(a). An historic resource under CEQA includes California Register listed and eligible properties, as well as locally designated historic resources. A project that causes a substantial adverse change to an historic resource creates a significant impact under CEQA, requiring mitigation when feasible. 14 CCR 15064(b).

Local Laws

Local governments have authority under their general police power to protect historic properties. Cities and counties are authorized to place conditions on development approvals to protect historic and aesthetic values. Gov. Code 25373, 37361. Typically, local governments establish a historic preservation zone or district and require property owners to seek approval before changing affected properties. Local preservation commissions often are used to administer local historic preservation regulations.

Cities and counties are authorized to place conditions on development approvals to protect historic and aesthetic values.

Takings, Exactions, and Development Agreements

Takings

Overly restrictive land use regulations may be considered a "taking" of property without just compensation, which is prohibited by the Fifth Amendment to the U.S. Constitution. The prohibition against takings applies not just to physical appropriation of land by the government, but also to overly restrictive local, state, and federal land use or environmental regulations (sometimes termed regulatory takings).

Overly restrictive land use regulations may be considered a "taking" of property without just compensation, which is prohibited by the Fifth Amendment to the U.S. Constitution.

The U.S. and California Supreme Courts have evolved their interpretations of regulatory takings in a long and convoluted series of cases. *See* Curtin's Guide to California Land Use, Talbert (2008), chapter 12. In general, a land use regulation becomes a taking if it does not substantially advance a legitimate government purpose, or if it deprives a landowner of all economically viable use of his or her land. *Lingle v. Chevron* (2005) 544 U.S. 528. Also, a nexus (reasonable relationship) and rough proportionality must exist between the land use regulation and the impacts of a proposed development.

Nollan v. California Coastal Commission, (1987) 483 US 825, established the nexus requirement. In that case, the Supreme Court found a regulatory taking when the Coastal Commission imposed a condition on a permit allowing the landowner's dedication of a lateral public access easement across a property's beachfront but requiring demolition and reconstruction of an existing house; a nexus did not exist between the impacts of the project and the requirement for demolition and reconstruction. *Dolan v. City of Tigard,* (1994) 512 US 374, established the rough proportionality requirement. In that case, the Supreme Court found a regulatory taking when a city imposed a condition on a permit allowing redevelopment of a commercial property but requiring dedication of a floodway and bicycle path; the impacts of the project alone did not justify the dedication of floodway and bicycle path facilities serving regional needs.

Landowner remedies for regulatory takings include both money damages and invalidation of the unconstitutional regulation. Once a court determines that a regulatory taking has occurred, the city or county may be liable for temporary taking during the period that the regulation was in effect. *See First English Lutheran Church of Glendale v. Los Angeles County* (1987) 482 US 304.

The term regulatory takings is also sometimes applied to any government regulation that has the potential to reduce property values, even if the regulation passes constitutional muster. In 2006, California voters defeated Proposition 90, which would have imposed government liability for potential losses in property value caused by routine land use and environmental regulations. However, a similar initiative qualified for the 2008 ballot. *See* sidebar on facing page.

Exactions

An exaction is a local government requirement to dedicate land or pay fees as a condition of development approval or construction.

An exaction is a local government requirement to dedicate land or pay fees as a condition of development approval or construction. Exactions are designed to mitigate the impacts of a project's population and employment growth on public services and facilities. The general police power authorizes local governments to impose exactions, but overly restrictive exactions may be challenged as a regulatory taking. The nexus and rough proportionality standards apply not only to exactions involving land dedication, but also to the discretionary exaction of project-specific development fees. *See Ehrlich v. City of Culver City* (1996) 12 Cal. 4th 854.

In California, the Mitigation Fee Act (Gov. Code 66000) regulates local government imposition of impact fees. Among other things, it requires local agencies imposing impact fees to identify the purpose of the fee and how it will be used, and show a reasonable relationship between the purpose and amount of the fee and the proposed project's impact on public facilities. The Mitigation Fee Act does not apply to development agreements (*see* below).

Also, special statutory limitations apply to the imposition of school impact fees. SB 50 of 1998, Gov. Code 65995. Under this legislation, statutory caps are placed on the amount of school fees that a school district can impose on new residential development.

Development Agreements

If land use regulations change following project approval, a developer has no vested right to develop land for the approved use until the developer has obtained a building permit and performed substantial work in reliance on the permit. *Avco Community Developers, Inc. v. South Coast Regional Commission* (1976) 17 Cal. 3d 785. Development agreement legislation (Gov. Code 65864 *et seq.*) is designed to give developers greater certainty against changes following project approval that might interfere with a property's development.

Under this legislation, a local government may enter into development agreements that freeze land use regulations applicable to a project and provide guidance for issuance of future project approvals. In return, the local government can negotiate exactions higher than those allowed under the Mitigation Fee Act, as well as commitments for public facility and infrastructure financing.

Growth Management, Smart Growth, and Climate Change

Growth management refers to local government use of a variety of measures to influence the amount, type, and location of growth. Growth management measures are often undertaken to achieve smart growth sustainability objectives in order to limit urban sprawl. New urbanism is another growth management doctrine closely related to smart growth. *See* sidebar on page 69.

Growth can be managed by using the basic regulatory tools described earlier in this chapter, such as general plans, specific plans, zoning, and subdivision regulation. In addition, some local governments have imposed moratoria on growth to prevent overtaxing of public services and facilities, or created urban limit lines to control urban sprawl. Growth moratoria and

Proposition 90 Defeated

In 2006, voters rejected Proposition 90 by a 52 to 48 percent margin. Proposition 90 would have placed additional limits on government use of eminent domain, but also would have created potential government liability when a land use or environmental regulation reduces property values. Proponents of Proposition 90 vowed to again place the initiative on future ballots. Proposition 90 and similar eminent domain reform initiatives in other states were sparked by the Supreme Court's decision in *Kelo v. City of New London* (2005) 545 U.S. 469 (*see* text).

Proposition 90 was opposed by the Governor and a broad coalition of taxpayer, business, civic, and environmental groups. Agencies would have had to either pay claims for potential lost property values due to new regulations, or refrain from adopting new regulations. If Proposition 90 had passed, many environmental and land use regulatory programs would have been affected, for example:

- CEQA mitigation measures
- Local land use controls
- Conservation easements
- Wetlands protection
- Endangered species protections

GHG = Greenhouse gas
VMT = Vehicle miles travelled

Smart Growth

The smart growth movement has become very influential in guiding local land use planning and regulation to discourage urban sprawl. The hallmarks of smart growth are compact, transit-accessible, pedestrian-oriented, mixed use development patterns, and land reuse. According to the American Planning Association's policy guide on smart growth:

> Smart Growth means using comprehensive planning to guide, design, develop, revitalize, and build communities for all that:
>
> • Have a unique sense of community and place
>
> • Preserve and enhance valuable natural and cultural resources
>
> • Equitably distribute the costs and benefits of development
>
> • Expand the range of transportation, employment and housing choices in a fiscally responsible manner
>
> • Value long-range, regional considerations of sustainability over short term incremental geographically isolated actions; and
>
> • Promotes public health and healthy communities

In contrast to prevalent development practices, Smart Growth refocuses a larger share of regional growth within central cities, urbanized areas, inner suburbs, and areas that are already served by infrastructure. Smart Growth reduces the share of growth that occurs on newly urbanizing land, existing farmlands, and in environmentally sensitive areas. In areas with intense growth pressure, development in newly urbanizing areas should be planned and developed according to Smart Growth principles.

urban limit lines can be imposed by voter initiative or be approved by voter referendum.

After enactment of California's climate change legislation (AB 32 of 2006, *see* chapter 5), growth management and smart growth strategies received renewed interest by policymakers seeking to reduce greenhouse gas (GHG) emissions caused by conventional development patterns. For example:

- The California Energy Commission (CEC 2007) released a staff report recommending that regional and local agencies adopt land use policies that reduce vehicle miles travelled (VMT), thereby reducing tailpipe emissions of GHGs.

- The Urban Land Institute (ULI 2007) issued a policy paper summarizing research showing that compact development can dramatically reduce VMT and GHG emissions. VMT reductions of 20–40 percent can be achieved compared to conventional development on the outer suburban edge.

- Many California mayors have signed the U.S. Mayors Climate Protection Agreement, which calls for cities to achieve a 7 percent reduction in GHG emissions by 2012. A handbook for implementing the agreement describes smart growth, transportation, and other strategies to achieve this goal. ICLEI *et al*. 2006.

Local Agency Boundary Changes

Project applicants seeking to develop or provide services to their properties must sometimes seek to include their properties within city or special district boundaries. Such boundary changes require approval by the appropriate local agency formation commission. In addition to annexations, other boundary changes approved by LAFCOs include detachment from a city or special district, incorporation of a city, or formation of a special district. Many requirements governing LAFCOs can be found in the Local Government Reorganization Act of 2000 (Gov. Code 56000 *et seq.*).

A key planning tool used by LAFCOs is adoption of a sphere of influence, which is the physical boundary and service area that a local government is expected to ultimately serve. Gov. Code 56076. The sphere of influence requirement promotes orderly development and extension of public services. A change in a sphere of influence must be accompanied by a study called a municipal service review; OPR (2003b) has issued guidelines on the preparation of municipal service reviews.

Enforcement

In general, cities and counties have a variety of administrative and judicial remedies available when an applicant fails to comply with a permit condition or violates a local land use ordinance. Administrative procedures include infraction or citation processes. The most common judicial remedy sought is a judicial order requiring the applicant to comply with the permit condition or ordinance.

For example, the City of Oakland zoning ordinance has the following enforcement provisions:

- Infractions: any violation of the zoning regulations is an infraction, with separate infractions for each day of violation.
- Public nuisance: in addition, any violation of the zoning regulations is a public nuisance and may be abated as such by the city.
- Injunction: any violation of the zoning is declared to be contrary to the pubic interest and, at the city's discretion, creates a cause of action for injunctive relief.
- Penalties: an infraction is punishable to the maximum permitted under state law. Any violation beyond the third conviction may be prosecuted as a misdemeanor, also punishable by a fine or imprisonment to the maximum permitted under state law.
- Liability for expenses: in addition to the above, a violator is liable for costs and expenses incurred by the city in correction, abatement, and prosecution of the violation.

Oakland Municipal Code 17.152

New Urbanism

New urbanism is a planning doctrine closely related to smart growth. Created by the Congress for the New Urbanism, the Charter for the New Urbanism (www.cnu.org/aboutcnu/index.cfm?formaction=charter) includes the following preamble:

The Congress for the New Urbanism views disinvestment in central cities, the spread of placeless sprawl, increasing separation by race and income, environmental deterioration, loss of agricultural lands and wilderness, and the erosion of society's built heritage as one interrelated community-building challenge.

We stand for the restoration of existing urban centers and towns within coherent metropolitan regions, the reconfiguration of sprawling suburbs into communities of real neighborhoods and diverse districts, the conservation of natural environments, and the preservation of our built legacy.

We recognize that physical solutions by themselves will not solve social and economic problems, but neither can economic vitality, community stability, and environmental health be sustained without a coherent and supportive physical framework.

We advocate the restructuring of public policy and development practices to support the following principles: neighborhoods should be diverse in use and population; communities should be designed for the pedestrian and transit as well as the car; cities and towns should be shaped by physically defined and universally accessible public spaces and community institutions; urban places should be framed by architecture and landscape design that celebrate local history, climate, ecology, and building practice.

For more information...

Publications

Abbott, W.W. *et al*. 2000 (with 2002 Supplement). Exactions and Impact Fees in California. Solano Press. Point Arena, Calif.

Beatty, D.F. *et al*. 2004. Redevelopment in California. Solano Press. Point Arena, Calif.

California Energy Commission. 2007. Final Staff Report: The Role of Land Use in Meeting California's Climate Change and Energy Goals. CEC 600-2007-008–SF

Curtin, D.J. and R.E. Merritt. 2003. Subdivision Map Act Manual. Solano Press. Point Arena, Calif.

Daniels, T. and K. Daniels. 2003. The Environmental Planning Handbook for Sustainable Communities and Regions. Planners Press. Chicago, Ill.

Durkee, M.P. *et al*. 2003. Ballot Box Navigator. Solano Press. Point Arena, Calif.

Fulton, W.E. and P. Shigley. 2005. Guide to California Planning Solano Press. Point Arena, Calif.

Governor's Office of Planning and Research. A Citizen's Guide to Planning

Governor's Office of Planning and Research. General Plan Guidelines

Governor's Office of Planning and Research. Local Agency Formation Commission Municipal Service Review Guidelines

Governor's Office of Planning and Research. Planning, Zoning and Development Laws

Governor's Office of Planning and Research. The Planner's Guide to Specific Plans

Governor's Office of Planning and Research. Tribal Consultation Guidelines

Hoch, C. *et al*. (eds.). 2000. The Practice of Local Government Planning (3rd ed.). International City/County Management Association. Washington, D.C.

ICLEI-Local Governments for Sustainability, City of Seattle, and U.S. Conference of Mayors. 2006. U.S. Mayors' Climate Protection Agreement Climate Action Handbook

Lindgren, A. and S. Mattas (eds.). 2006. California Land Use Practice. University of California, Continuing Education of the Bar. San Francisco, Calif.

Manaster, K.A. and D.P. Selmi (eds.). ND. Chapters 60–65, 71, 73, 74, and 75 of California Environmental Law and Land Use Practice. Matthew Bender. San Francisco, Calif.

Mandelker, D.L. 2003. Land Use Law (5th ed.). Matthew Bender. Newark, N.J.

Merritt, R.E. and A.R. Danforth (eds.). 1994. Understanding Development Regulations. Solano Press. Point Arena, Calif.

Pruetz, R. 1993. Putting Transfer of Development Rights to Work in California. Solano Press. Point Arena, Calif.

Rypinski, R.G. 2002. Eminent Domain: A Step-by-Step Guide to the Acquisition of Real Property. Solano Press. Point Arena, Calif.

Talbert, C.T. 2008. Curtin's California Land Use and Planning Law. Solano Press. Point Arena, Calif.

Urban Land Institute. 2007. Growing Cooler: Evidence on Urban Development and Climate Change

Websites

American Planning Association
www.planning.org

American Planning Association, California Chapter
www.calapa.org

California Land Use Planning Information Network
www.ceres.ca.gov/planning

California Redevelopment Association
www.calredevelop.org

California State Association of Counties
www.csca.counties.org

Congress for the New Urbanism
www.cnu.org

Department of Housing and Community Development
www.hcd.ca.gov/hpd

Governor's Office of Planning and Research
www.opr.ca.gov

League of California Cities
www.cacities.org

Local Government Commission
www.lgc.com

Office of Historic Preservation
http://ohp.parks.ca.gov

Smart Growth Network
www.smartgrowth.org

Urban Land Institute
www.uli.org

State and Regional Land Use Controls

This chapter reviews —

- Coastal zone management
- Programs regulating regional natural hazards: floodplains, earthquakes, and fires
- State Lands Commission leases
- California Energy Commission power plant certification program
- Regional planning agencies: Councils of government and specific planning agencies for the San Francisco Bay, Tahoe Basin, and Sacramento–San Joaquin Delta regions

Related Solano Press titles —

Curtin's California Land Use and Planning Law
Cecily T. Talbert. 2008

Guide to California Planning
William E. Fulton and Paul Shigley. 2005

Glossary

Application for certification*—an application filed by an energy facility developer seeking CEC certification of a proposed project with 50 MW or more of generating capacity.

Certificate of Public Convenience and Necessity*—a certificate issued by the PUC to a public utility for construction of electricity facilities such as power plants and transmission lines.

Coastal development permit*—a permit for development in the coastal zone issued by a local government or the Coastal Commission.

Coastal zone—an area extending seaward to the state's outer limit of jurisdiction and inland to boundaries designated by the Legislature.

Fault trace—the line formed by the intersection of a fault and the earth's surface.

Ground shaking—ground movement resulting from the transmission of seismic waves during an earthquake.

Land use lease*—a State Lands Commission lease to use state-owned sovereign lands.

Liquefaction—a process by which water-saturated granular solids transform from a solid to a liquid state during strong ground shaking.

Local coastal program—a combination of a local government's land use plans, zoning ordinances, and other implementing actions that meet the requirements of the California Coastal Act.

State responsibility area—an area where fire protection is primarily a state responsibility.

* equals permits and approvals

CHAPTER 4

State and Regional Land Use Controls

Introduction

State and regional land use controls play an important role in California environmental protection and regulation. Although the Legislature has left land use planning and regulation largely in the control of cities and counties, over time it has adopted individual land use programs for sensitive areas (*e.g.*, the coastal zone) or special project types (*e.g.*, electrical energy facilities). In addition, cities and counties voluntarily have created regional councils of government (COGs) that have important planning responsibilities. This chapter reviews California's most important state and regional land use planning and regulatory programs.

COG = Council of government
CZMA = Coastal Zone Management Act
NOAA = National Oceanographic and Atmospheric Administration
USC = United States Code

Coastal Zone Management

Key Laws and Agencies

Key laws. The key federal law is the Coastal Zone Management Act (CZMA) of 1972 (16 United States Code (USC) 451 *et seq.*). Administered by the National Oceanographic and Atmospheric Administration (NOAA), the CZMA's basic purpose is to preserve coastal zones, consisting of coastal waters and adjacent coastal lands. The CZMA established a grant program to help states develop coastal programs consistent with the CZMA; NOAA must approve these programs.

California's coastal zone management started with voter approval of the 1972 Coastal Initiative, which adopted the California Coastal Zone Conservation Act of 1972. This law was superseded by the California Coastal Act of 1976 (PRC 30000 *et seq.*). The Coastal Act defines statewide planning and management policies for the zone and establishes planning and permit programs to implement these policies. Statewide policies cover:

- Expanding public access to the coast
- Increasing coastal recreation opportunities
- Protecting the marine environment
- Protecting environmentally sensitive and agricultural lands
- Implementing standards for coastal development related to location, scenic and visual qualities, public access, and minimizing adverse effects
- Implementing standards for industrial facilities such as energy facilities

California Coastal Commission. The California Coastal Commission administers the Coastal Act and has responsibility for certifying local coastal programs and for issuing and enforcing coastal permits. The California Coastal Commission has issued detailed regulations for Coastal Act administration. California Code of Regulations (CCR) Title 14, Division 5.5.

Regulation under the Coastal Act is limited to the coastal zone (Public Resources Code (PRC) 30103), defined as extending seaward to the state's outer limit of jurisdiction (three miles) and inland to boundaries designated by the Legislature. For important natural resource areas, inland boundaries extend to the first major ridgeline or five miles from the mean high tide line, whichever is less. In developed areas, the coastal zone is much narrower, sometimes just a few blocks.

The Coastal Act empowers the Coastal Commission to protect the marine environment.

State Coastal Conservancy. The State Coastal Conservancy is responsible for land acquisition and restoration, consistent with Coastal Act policies. PRC 31100. Coastal Conservancy programs include construction of trails and other public access facilities, restoration and enhancement of wetlands and other wildlife habitat, restoration of public piers and urban waterfronts, and farmland preservation.

Local Coastal Programs

The Coastal Act gives the 74 cities and counties with land in the coastal zone the responsibility of preparing local coastal programs (LCPs) consistent with Coastal Act policies. LCPs consist of a land use plan and an implementation plan, including zoning ordinances. PRC 30108.4, 30108.5. LCP adoption is exempt from the California Environmental Quality Act (CEQA). PRC 21080.9. However, local governments usually prepare CEQA documents when adopting LCPs because they usually make other discretionary decisions, such as general plan and zoning ordinance amendments that are subject to CEQA.

The Act also requires certain ports (Hueneme, Long Beach, Los Angeles, and San Diego) to prepare comprehensive port master plans consistent with Coastal Act policies, including policies in the Act that encourage port development. PRC 30515 *et seq.* Local governments and ports can amend LCPs and port master plans by following the same procedures as when originally adopted.

The California Coastal Commission is responsible for certifying both LCPs and port master plans as being consistent with Coastal Act policies. PRC 30511 *et seq.* LCP certification is subject to CEQA, but also is a certified regulatory program. This means that LCP certification is exempt from CEQA's requirement to prepare a negative declaration or an environmental impact report (EIR), but not exempt from CEQA's policy directives, *e.g.*, to mitigate significant impacts when feasible (*see* chapter 2).

EIR = Environmental impact report

Many of the 74 coastal cities and counties have elected to divide their coastal zone jurisdictions into separate geographic segments, resulting in 126 separate LCPs. According to the California Coastal Commission website (www.coastal.ca.gov/lcps.html), as of 2002, approximately 70 percent of the LCP segments had been certified, representing close to 90 percent of the geographic area of the coastal zone.

Coastal Permits

The Coastal Act gives local governments the responsibility of issuing coastal development permits for developments that are consistent with LCPs. PRC 306000 *et seq.* Local coastal development permits can be appealed administratively to the California Coastal Commission. PRC 30603(a) *et seq.* Permit decisions by the California Coastal Commission, local governments, and ports are judicially reviewable.

The Coastal Act gives local governments the responsibility of issuing coastal development permits for developments that are consistent with LCPs.

Permits are required for the following types of activities in the coastal zone (PRC 30106):

- Placement of any solid material or structure
- Change in land use density or intensity (including any land division)
- Change in the intensity of water use or access to water
- Removal of major vegetation

Coastal permits are subject to the time limitations established by the Permit Streamlining Act (*see* chapter 2) and require CEQA compliance. The Coastal Act sets forth special procedures for processing emergency permits and small projects such as single-family dwellings. PRC 30604(c), 30624(a). Certain activities, such as minor improvements to single-family residences, are exempt from permit requirements. PRC 30610(a).

For those areas without a certified LCP, the California Coastal Commission is responsible for issuing coastal development permits. In addition, the California Coastal Commission retains primary permitting authority for issuing

For those areas without a certified LCP, the California Coastal Commission is responsible for issuing coastal development permits.

coastal development permits for certain project types: those located on tidelands, submerged lands, or public trust lands; major public works projects; and major energy facilities. PRC 30519(b).

Federal Agency Consistency

CFR = Code of Federal Regulations
FEMA = Federal Emergency Management Agency
NFIP = National Flood Insurance Program
USACE = U.S. Army Corps of Engineers

Under the CZMA, federal agencies conducting or supporting activities or development projects directly affecting the coastal zone must ensure that their activities and projects are consistent with the approved state coastal program. Also, applicants for federal licenses or permits must certify in their applications that their proposed activity complies with and will be carried out consistent with the state coastal program. 16 USC 1456(c); 15 Code of Federal Regulations (CFR) 930 *et seq.*

The California Coastal Commission reviews the federal agency's consistency determination. If the Commission determines that the federal agency's action would not be consistent with the state's coastal program "to the maximum extent practicable," the Commission must describe alternative measures to allow the activity to be consistent. If the Commission and federal agency continue to disagree, the Secretary of Commerce may mediate the dispute, or as a last resort the state may sue in federal court to enjoin the federal activity. 15 CFR 930.42(a) *et seq.*

Special consistency requirements apply to applicants for offshore oil and gas leases under the Outer Continental Shelf Lands Act. 43 USC 1331 *et seq.* The Coastal Act gives special recognition to the need for oil and gas (and other coastal dependent industrial) development; the Act allows these projects to be permitted even if inconsistent with certain Coastal Act policies, provided there are no feasible less damaging alternatives, and adverse environmental impacts are mitigated to the maximum extent feasible. PRC 30260.

Enforcement

For violations of the Coastal Act, the Commission can issue cease-and-desist or restoration orders for activities undertaken without a required coastal permit or in violation of an existing permit.

For violations of the Coastal Act, the Commission can issue cease-and-desist or restoration orders for activities undertaken without a required coastal permit or in violation of an existing permit. The Commission cannot administratively order civil penalties. Rather, the Commission refers cases involving significant resource damage to the attorney general for judicial enforcement. Violation of any provision of the Coastal Act can result in civil fines, for example, up to $15,000 per day for knowing and intentional violations. PRC 30800 *et seq.*, 14 CCR 13171 *et seq.*

Regulating Regional Natural Hazards: Floodplains, Earthquakes, and Fires

The local general plan safety element, and its implementing regulations, is the primary local government basis for protecting development against risks from flood, earthquakes, and fires.

The local general plan safety element, and its implementing regulations, is the primary local government basis for protecting development against risks from flood, earthquakes, and fires. Key state and federal programs that influence local hazard-protection requirements are described below.

Flood Management

Key laws and agencies. Many urban areas in California are located in historic floodplains. To reduce risks of loss of life and property, the federal and state governments have implemented a number of programs. Key agencies involved in flood control include:

- **U.S. Army Corps of Engineers (USACE).** Constructs and operates federal flood control projects

- **U.S. Bureau of Reclamation.** Operates several water resources projects that include flood control as a project purpose

- **National Weather Service.** Issues weather forecasts and flood warnings, and provides technical assistance to local governments

- **Federal Emergency Management Agency (FEMA).** Administers the National Flood Insurance Program (NFIP), and disaster planning and recovery programs

- **Department of Water Resources, Floodplain Management Branch.** Operates several water resources projects that include flood control as a project purpose, runs the state–federal flood operations center, carries out state floodplain management laws, conducts floodplain mapping, and coordinates implementation of the NFIP

- **Central Valley Flood Protection Agency (formerly State Reclamation Board).** Coordinates with the USACE in planning, constructing, operating, and maintaining flood control projects in California's Central Valley, issues encroachment permits for development near levees

- **California Governor's Office of Emergency Services.** Provides financial assistance for disaster recovery, and administers FEMA's hazard mitigation program in California

National Flood Insurance Program. A voluntary, incentive-based program, the NFIP requires that new or replacement buildings in flood hazard areas be constructed to limit future flood damage. FEMA, which implements the NFIP, has published a useful guide to the program. FEMA 2005. Local governments must regulate development in designated floodplains through the adoption of floodplain management ordinances meeting minimum NFIP requirements. Residents of participating communities meeting NFIP requirements are eligible to receive federally subsidized flood insurance. For each participating community, flood insurance rate maps are prepared that delineate areas of special flood hazards and insurance premium zones. FEMA 2005.

Colbey–Alquist Floodplain Management Act. When a federal flood control project report designates floodway boundaries, this law (PRC 8400 *et seq.*) provides that the state will not appropriate money to support the

Report Finds Central Valley Flood Control Crisis

A 2005 DWR report found that California's Central Valley flood control system is deteriorating, and in some places is literally washing away. Although rapid urban development has placed more people and structures in flood prone areas, funding to maintain and upgrade flood protection infrastructure has declined.

The report recommends the following strategies to better protect the Central Valley from flood damage:

- Ensure the integrity of existing flood project infrastructure through improved maintenance programs

- Evaluate the integrity and capability of existing flood control projects and prepare an economically viable rehabilitation plan

- Improve the effectiveness of emergency response programs

- Create a sustainable fund to support flood management programs

- Update floodplain maps and provide better education on flood risks to the public and agencies authorizing development in floodplains

- Where feasible, implement a multi-objective approach to floodplains that includes ecosystem restoration and farmland protection, as well as flood protection

- Evaluate potential policies that may determine the state's capacity to fund levee maintenance, infrastructure improvements, and emergency response in the Sacramento–San Joaquin Delta

The report's recommendations are being implemented through legislation and DWR's "Floodsafe California" program. ▩

Weakening Sacramento River levees need repairs to provide urban levels of flood protection.

DWR = Department of Water Resources

project unless affected local governments have enacted floodplain regulations meeting certain minimum requirements.

Central Valley flood management. A 2005 DWR report explained that a flood control crisis in California's Central Valley has developed due to weakening Sacramento/San Joaquin delta levees, and continued local government approval of development in floodplains (*see* sidebar on page 77). In response, in the 2005–2006 session, the Legislature considered but failed to pass comprehensive flood management legislation. However, in 2006, voters did approve Proposition 1E, which authorized $4.1 billion in flood control bonds.

2007 legislation. In 2007, several major flood management bills were enacted. Senate Bill 5 (Statutes of 2007, Chapter 364) focuses on Central Valley flood protection. It requires DWR to prepare updated maps of 100-year and 200-year floodplains by 2008, establishes a 200-year standard for Central Valley urban areas, and requires adoption of building standards for construction within 200-year floodplains by 2009. The bill requires that the Central Valley Flood Protection Board prepare a Central Valley flood control plan by 2012. Local governments must amend their general plans by 2014 and their land use regulations by 2015 to be consistent with the state plan, following which they may not approve inconsistent development projects unless "adequate progress" is being made towards achieving 200-year protection.

Assembly Bill 70 (Statutes of 2007, Chapter 367) requires local governments to pay their fair share of flood damages, to the extent they increase the state's exposure to liability for property damage by unreasonably approving new development in a previously undeveloped area protected by a state flood control project. This payment is not required once local governments amend their general plans and land use regulations, pursuant to SB 5, to be consistent with the Central Valley flood control plan. Other major flood management bills enacted in 2007 include the following:

- AB 156 (Statutes of 2007, Chapter 368): directs DWR and the Central Valley Flood Protection Board to perform a number of duties integral to the state flood protection plan under SB 5

- AB 162 (Statutes of 2007, Chapter 369): requires revisions of several general plan elements starting in 2009 to address flood protection concerns (*see* chapter 3)

- SB 17 (Statutes of 2007, Chapter 365): makes numerous changes to the Reclamation Board composition and responsibilities, including renaming it to the Central Valley Flood Protection Board

Seismic Safety

Three major laws govern seismic safety in California. The Alquist–Priolo Earthquake Fault Zoning Act (PRC 2621 *et seq.*) restricts development on the surface traces of known active earthquake faults. The Act requires a geological investigation before a local government can approve development projects near known earthquake faults.

The Seismic Hazards Mapping Act (PRC 2690 *et seq.*) directs the state geologist to map potential hazard areas for ground shaking, liquefaction, and earthquake-triggered landslides. Local governments must inform the public about locations of all designated earthquake fault zones.

Lastly, the Unreinforced Masonry Law (PRC 9975 *et seq.*) requires local governments within a certain seismic zone (Zone 4) to identify hazardous unreinforced masonry buildings and to consider regulations to abate dangerous buildings through retrofitting or demolition.

The above laws are administered through regulations adopted by the State Mining and Geology Board, an independent board that operates within the Department of Conservation. The California Seismic Safety Commission is responsible for disseminating public information on earthquake hazards to decisionmakers and the public.

Fire Hazards

Pursuant to PRC 4125 *et seq.*, commonly known as the State Fire Responsibility Act, the State Board of Forestry classifies all lands within the state to determine those areas for which the financial responsibility of preventing and suppressing fires is primarily a state responsibility–these areas are referred to as state responsibility areas (SRAs). The prevention and suppression of fires in non-SRA areas is primarily the responsibility of either local or federal agencies.

SLC = State Lands Commission
SRA = State responsibility area

The State Board of Forestry has issued fire safe regulations (14 CCR 1270 *et seq.*) for local governments to reduce pre-fire fuel loads. These regulations include road and signage standards, minimum water supply reserves for emergency fire use, and fuel breaks around structures and subdivisions. Also, the California Department of Forestry and Fire Protection has developed fire hazard severity zoning information for use by local governments. Gov. Code 51175 *et seq.*

State Lands Commission Leases

The State Lands Commission (SLC) may lease or otherwise manage the use of sovereign tidelands, submerged lands, and beds of navigable waters under its jurisdiction. The SLC also manages state-owned school lands and regulates marine terminals in state waters to control oil spills. The SLC's regulatory programs are established by PRC 6000 *et seq.* and 2 CCR 1900 *et seq.*

The State Lands Commission may lease or otherwise manage the use of sovereign tidelands, submerged lands, and beds of navigable waters under its jurisdiction.

Those proposing to use state-owned sovereign lands must obtain a land use lease. PRC 6501.1. Special SLC authorization is needed for dredging, mining, and oil, gas, or geothermal development. The SLC evaluates applications for land use leases to determine whether the proposed activity:

- Is consistent with the trusts under which the lands are held
- Is environmentally acceptable
- Will affect the value of state lands
- Will be in the best interests of the people of California

The SLC may charge rental fees, royalties, or other fees for the use of state lands. Fees may be based on a percentage of the property's appraised value, percentage of gross income, or volume of minerals extracted. PRC 6503.5.

California Energy Commission Power Plant Certification Program

CEC = California Energy Commission
DOE = Department of Energy
FERC = Federal Energy Regulatory Commission
LNG = Liquefied natural gas
MW = Megawatt

The analysis below focuses on land use aspects of state energy regulation, the most prominent of which are the Warren–Alquist Act and the California Energy Commission (CEC) energy facility licensing program.

Key Laws and Agencies

Energy Policy Act of 2005. At the federal level, the Energy Policy Act of 2005 (PL 109-58) contains a number of provisions related to the siting of energy facilities. The Act clarifies the federal government's role in siting of liquefied natural gas (LNG) facilities. Also, to expedite transmission line and gas pipeline permitting, the Act requires the Department of Energy (DOE), working with federal land management agencies, to designate energy corridors across the western U.S. after preparation of a programmatic environmental impact statement.

Federal Energy Regulatory Commission. Among other responsibilities, the Federal Energy Regulatory Commission (FERC) licenses hydropower projects and approves the siting of interstate natural gas facilities, including pipelines, storage facilities, and liquefied natural gas.

Warren–Alquist Act. Enacted in 1975, the Warren–Alquist Act (PRC 21000 *et seq.*) establishes a streamlined "one-stop" permitting process for power plants with at least 50 megawatts (mw) of generating capacity. The Act is intended to consolidate the state's responsibility for energy resources, including research and development, and the regulation of electrical generating and related transmission facilities. The Act's policies recognize that it is the state's responsibility to ensure a reliable electrical energy supply consistent with protecting public health, safety, and welfare, and environmental quality.

Two provisions of the Warren–Alquist Act restrict the ability to construct new nuclear power plants in California. PRC 25524.2, 25524.1. Construction of new nuclear power plants is prohibited until a satisfactory method of nuclear waste disposal has been developed. Also required is a case-by-case review of the adequacy of a proposed plant's nuclear waste storage capacity.

California Energy Commission. The Warren–Alquist Act created the CEC, which was charged with the following responsibilities (PRC 25216):

- Processing applications for the licensing of thermal power plants of at least 50 MW generating capacity, and related transmission lines
- Implementing measures to reduce wasteful and inefficient use of energy
- Collecting and analyzing information on alternative ways to conserve, generate, and supply energy
- Predicting future energy demands and keeping historical data
- Developing energy technologies and encouraging renewable energy programs
- Supporting energy efficiency through appliance and building standards

Public Utilities Commission. If the CEC issues a power plant or transmission line license to a public utility, the Public Utilities Commission (PUC) must issue a certificate of public convenience and necessity, authorizing construction of the licensed facility. Also, the PUC has exclusive jurisdiction over approving, through issuing a certificate of public convenience and necessity, the siting of all transmission lines not under CEC's jurisdiction. The majority of the state's transmission lines are under PUC jurisdiction. Public Utilities Code 1001.

Legislation enacted in 2006 gave both the PUC and the CEC new authority to require "green" power (*see* sidebar on page 82).

California Energy Commission Licensing Process

Overview. The CEC has exclusive certification jurisdiction over (PRC 25120):

- Thermal power plants with a generating capacity of 50 MW or more
- Modifications that result in a generating capacity of 50 MW or more
- Transmission lines carrying the electricity from a power plant with a generating capacity of 50 MW or more to the interconnected grid

Construction of new nuclear power plants in California is prohibited until a satisfactory method of nuclear waste disposal is developed.

PUC = Public Utilities Commission

AFC = Application for certification
LORS = Laws, ordinances, regulations, and standards
NOI = Notice of intention
RPS = Renewable Portfolio Standard
SPPE = Small power plant exemption

The CEC's jurisdiction supersedes the permit authority of other state agencies and local government land use authorities, although as discussed below, the CEC must consider state and local government policies and regulations in making siting decisions. PRC 25500. Also, the CEC certification process has been determined to be a CEQA-certified regulatory program PRC 21080.5 (*see* chapter 2). The CEC's staff assessment (*see* below) serves as the functional equivalent of an EIR.

The certification process is described in CEC regulations. 20 CCR 1701 *et seq.* Useful guidance on the licensing process also can be found in a draft CEC report for energy facility developers. CEC 2000.

Consultation with other agencies. Although the CEC has exclusive jurisdiction over licensing thermal power plants of 50 MW or more in generating capacity and related facilities, the CEC is required to consult with all interested agencies regarding applicable laws, ordinances, regulations, and standards (LORS). Typically, these issues arise in the context of local government land use requirements, 20 CCR 1752(k), 1755(b). The CEC must make findings on whether a proposed facility complies with LORS. The CEC is directed to consult with agencies to eliminate any non-compliance with LORS, and may not certify a non-complying project unless it finds via an "override" that the project is needed for public convenience and necessity, and that there are no more prudent feasible means to meet these needs. PRC 25527.

Types of licensing proceedings. An applicant initiates the certification process by filing either a small power plant exemption (SPPE) or an application for certification (AFC). A notice of intention (NOI) also is available, and is intended to preliminarily evaluate alternative sites for complex projects such as nuclear power plants. However, NOIs have not been used recently because recent proposed projects have been exempt from the NOI requirement. PRC 25540.6.

Small power plant exemption. The SPPE is available for projects between 50 MW and 100 MW, provided the proposed project does not create an unmitigated significant impact on environmental resources. The CEC completes an initial study and, if approved by the CEC, the project developer is responsible for securing local, state, and federal permits to construct and operate the facility. The CEC strives to complete the SPPE review in 135 days. PRC 25541, 20 CCR 1936.

Application for certification. The standard AFC process is required to be completed within 12 months of an approved AFC, but some controversial projects take longer. The AFC is a detailed description of the proposed facilities, their environmental impacts, and their compliance with LORS. When the AFC is "data adequate" (*i.e.*, deemed complete), the CEC appoints a siting committee to oversee its processing. The staff recommendation on data adequacy must be made within 30 days of AFC filing, and the CEC must act on this recommendation within 45 days of filing. If the AFC is incomplete, the applicant is provided a written list of inadequacies to be corrected in a supplemental filing that the CEC must evaluate for adequacy within 30 days of receipt. 20 CCR 1704.

Staff assessment. After acceptance of the AFC, the CEC staff then prepares a preliminary and final staff assessment analyzing the environmental impacts of the proposed facilities and their compliance with the LORS. The staff assessment serves as the staff written testimony for the AFC hearing (*see* below), as well as the CEQA functional equivalent document. 20 CCR 1742 *et seq.*

Evidentiary hearing and decision. The CEC siting committee conducts an evidentiary hearing on the AFC in which the applicant has the burden of presenting sufficient evidence to support the findings required for project certification. In addition to the applicant, testimony is provided by the staff of the CEC, staff of other agencies, interveners, and the public–the CEC has a public advisor who advises the public on how to participate in CEC proceedings. After the hearing, the siting committee's presiding member prepares a proposed decision for public review and comment. 20 CCR 1748, 1749.

The CEC then either approves or denies the AFC, making findings on implementation of feasible mitigation measures, compliance with the LORS, and feasible alternatives. Special restrictions apply to CEC approval of sites in the coastal zone, sites within San Francisco Bay Conservation and Development Commission (BCDC) jurisdiction, and sites with recreational or environmental values such as wildlife preserves or parks. PRC 25526, 25527.

BCDC = San Francisco Bay Conservation and Development Commission

COC = Condition of certification

If the AFC is approved, the CEC adopts conditions of certification (COCs) that cover topics such as implementation of mitigation measures and compliance with federal, state, and local requirements. The Commission also adopts a compliance plan, which describes the procedures for post-certification monitoring of compliance with the COCs. PRC 25532, 20 CCR 1770.

Roles of other agencies in the certification process. State agencies such as the California Independent System Operator and the Air Resources Board, and federal agencies such as the Environmental Protection Agency and the U.S. Fish and Wildlife Service, often review and comment on the AFC. For facilities in the coastal zone, the Coastal Commission must comment on the AFC in a report, and the CEC must follow the report's findings and recommendations. PRC 25531(c). Special procedures exist to assure that proposed facilities comply with the regulatory requirements of local air pollution control districts as well. 20 CCR 1744.5.

Judicial review of siting decisions. A CEC project certification can be reviewed only by filing a petition for review with California Supreme Court. PRC 25531. These petitions for review have seldom been granted.

Regional Planning Agencies

Several types of regional planning agencies exist in California, with different levels of regulatory authority over land use and environmental quality.

Several types of regional planning agencies exist in California, with different levels of regulatory authority over land use and environmental quality. Councils of Government are joint powers agencies established by local governments. The BCDC, Tahoe Regional Planning Agency (TRPA), and Delta Protection Commission (DPC) are regional planning and regulatory agencies established by state statute.

Councils of Governments

DPC = Delta Protection Commission

TRPA = Tahoe Regional Planning Agency

COGs are joint powers agencies established pursuant to the Joint Powers Act (Gov. Code 6500 *et seq.*) that conduct regional planning activities in most of the state. COGs do not have the authority to regulate land use or environmental quality, but are influential in establishing regional planning frameworks and guiding federal funding for transportation and housing.

A main purpose of COGs is to serve as metropolitan planning organizations to meet federal transportation planning requirements. This role involves preparation of long-range regional transportation plans and adoption of transportation improvement programs that allocate state and federal funds for highway, transit, and other surface transportation projects. In the San Francisco Bay Area, regional transportation planning is done by the Metropolitan Transportation Commission, which is a statutory planning agency. Gov. Code 66502.

COGs also allocate "fair share" regional housing needs to all cities and counties within their boundaries. *See* chapter 3. Many COGs undertake planning for growth management and air quality management as well.

San Francisco Bay Conservation and Development Commission

Overview. The San Francisco Bay Conservation and Development Commission is a state agency with land use planning and regulatory authority over San Francisco Bay, Suisun Marsh, and adjacent areas. A part of the Resources Agency, BCDC was created in 1965 by the McAteer–Petris Act (Gov. Code 66600 *et seq.*) in response to growing public concerns about the filling of San Francisco Bay. BCDC's Suisun March responsibilities were established by the Suisun Marsh Preservation Act of 1977. PRC 29000 *et seq.*

BCDC's responsibilities include (Gov. Code 66630 *et seq.*):

- Regulating all filling and dredging of San Francisco Bay
- Regulating new development within the first 100 feet inland from the Bay
- Protecting Suisun Marsh by administering the Suisun Marsh Preservation Act in cooperation with local governments
- Administering the CZMA within the San Francisco Bay segment of the California Coast
- Pursuing an active planning program to study Bay issues

Regulatory program. San Francisco Bay development permits may be issued only if consistent with bay fill and public access policies in the Bay Plan adopted by BCDC. Gov. Code 66632. Similarly, Suisun Marsh development permits may be issued only if consistent with protection policies established by the Suisun Marsh Protection Plan and certified local protection programs adopted by local governments with jurisdiction over the marsh. PRC 29500.

BCDC's regulatory program is a CEQA certified regulatory program. *See* chapter 2. CEQA's policies apply to BCDC permit decisions, but BCDC is not required to prepare CEQA environmental documents such as negative declarations and EIRs. 14 CCR 11500 *et seq.*

BCDC regulates filling of San Francisco Bay and new development 100 feet inland.

BCDC issues several types of permits (Gov. Code 66632):

- An administrative permit is issued for minor repair or improvement activities
- A major permit is issued for larger fills or substantial changes in use
- A regionwide permit is issued for certain activities that BCDC has determined will have no substantial impact, such as routine maintenance work
- An emergency permit is issued for an activity necessary to avoid an immediate danger to life, health, or property

BCDC may enforce permit requirements through a permit revocation, a cease-and-desist order, or a penalty order. Gov. Code 66637, 66641.6. BCDC may impose a penalty of $1,000–$2,000 per day of violation, up to a maximum of $30,000. Alternatively, injunctive relief and civil misdemeanor penalties may be sought from the courts. Gov. Code 66632(j).

Tahoe Regional Planning Agency

Overview. The Tahoe Regional Planning Agency was established in 1969 by an interstate compact between the states of California and Nevada, approved by Congress. Public Law 91-148. The compact was substantially amended in 1980. Public Law 96-551; Gov. Code 66800 *et seq.* Through the compact, the California, Nevada, and the U.S. Congress recognized Lake Tahoe's unique environmental qualities, as well as the substantial threats to Tahoe's environment posed by development and recreation activities.

The DPC has adopted a regional plan to implement the Delta Protection Act; local governments within the "primary zone" of the Delta Region are required to amend their general plans to be consistent with the regional plan.

EIS = Environmental impact statement
NEPA = National Environmental Policy Act

Responsibilities. TRPA has the following major responsibilities (Gov. Code 66801 *et seq.*):

- Establish environmental threshold carrying capacities for the Tahoe Region (whose boundaries are generally the hydrologic boundaries of the Lake Tahoe Basin).

- Prepare a regional plan to achieve and maintain the thresholds. Key features of the plan include regional goals and policies, and a land use element.

- Adopt the TRPA regulatory code, which sets forth regulations needed to implement the regional plan.

- Prepare plan area statements and community plans for specific areas within the Tahoe Basin.

- Review and approve those development projects consistent with the regional plan and TRPA regulatory code.

- Prepare environmental impact statements (EISs) for projects that will have a significant impact on the environment. TRPA EISs are patterned after National Environmental Policy Act (NEPA) EISs, but NEPA's requirements do not apply to TRPA since it is not a federal agency.

- Implement an environmental improvement program, consisting of numerous projects to improve Lake Tahoe water clarity and environmental quality.

TRPA's strict land use regulations have been the subject of a number of "takings" lawsuits. *See* sidebar.

Delta Protection Commission

The Delta Protection Act (PRC 29700 *et seq.*) established the Delta Protection Commission (DPC) to protect the natural resources of the Sacramento–San Joaquin Delta. The DPC has adopted a regional plan to implement the Act; local governments within the "primary zone" of the Delta Region are required to amend their general plans to be consistent with the regional plan. The primary zone of the Sacramento–San Joaquin Delta includes approximately 500,000 acres of waterways, levees, and farmed lands extending over portions of five counties: Solano, Yolo, Sacramento, San Joaquin, and Contra Costa. The DPC implementing regulations can be found at 14 CCR 20300 *et seq.*

For more information...

Publications

California Coastal Commission. 1999. Questions and Answers about the California Coastal Act

California Department of Water Resources. 2005. Flood Warnings–Responding to California's Flood Crisis

California Energy Commission. 2000. Energy Facility Licensing Process–Developers Guide of Practices and Procedures (draft report)

Federal Emergency Management Agency. 2005. Flood Management Requirements–A Study Guide and Desk Reference for Local Officials. Report Number 480

Fulton, W.E. and P. Shigley. 2005. Guide to California Planning Solano Press. Point Arena, Calif.

Manaster, K.A. and D.P. Selmi (eds). ND. Chapters 1, 2, 3, 10, and 12 of California Environmental Law and Land Use Practice. Matthew Bender. San Francisco, Calif.

Talbert, C.T. 2008. Curtin's California Land Use and Planning Law. Solano Press. Point Arena, Calif.

Water Education Foundation. 2004. Layperson's Guide to Flood Management. Sacramento, Calif.

Websites

California Association of Councils of Government
www.calcog.org

California Coastal Commission
www.coastal.ca.gov

California Coastal Conservancy
www.coastalconservancy.ca.gov

California Department of Forestry and Fire Protection
www.fire.ca.gov/index.php

California Department of Water Resources, Division of Flood Management
www.dfm.water.ca.gov/pubs/pubs.cfm

California Energy Commission, Licensing Program
www.energy.ca.gov/sitingcases/index.html

California Seismic Safety Commission
www.seismic.ca.gov

California State Mining and Geology Board
www.conservation.ca.gov/smgb/index.htm

Delta Protection Commission
www.delta.ca.gov

Federal Emergency Management Agency, National Flood Insurance Program
www.floodsmart.gov/floodsmart/pages/index.jsp

Federal Emergency Management Agency, Region IX
www.fema.gov/regions/ix/r9_nfip.shtm

Federal Energy Regulatory Commission
www.ferc.gov

San Francisco Bay Conservation and Development Commission
www.bcdc.ca.gov

State Lands Commission
www.slc.ca.gov

Tahoe Regional Planning Agency
www.trpa.org

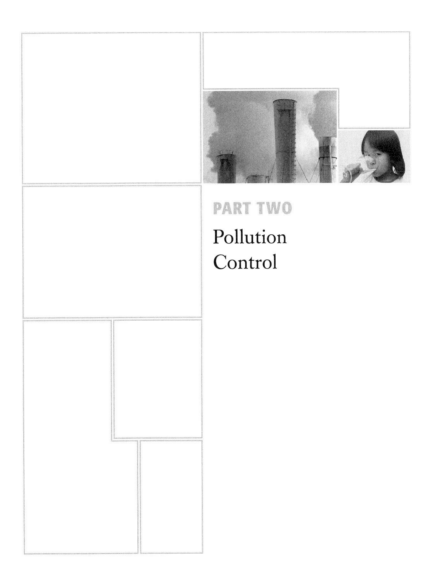

PART TWO

Pollution Control

Air Quality

This chapter reviews —

- Key laws and agencies involved in regulating California air quality
- Ambient air quality standards and air quality planning
- Stationary source programs
- Stratospheric ozone protection
- Acid rain
- Air toxics
- Transportation controls (including mobile source regulation)
- Enforcement

Related Solano Press title—

Transportation Law in California: A Guide to Federal, State, and Regional Requirements. Jeremy G. March. 2000

Glossary

Acid rain–a category of air emissions involving two criteria pollutants (NO_X and SO_X) that chemically react with moisture in the atmosphere to create nitric acid and sulfuric acid. Most acid rain is produced from the burning of high sulfur coal (generating SO_X) and boiler systems (generating NO_X).

Air pollution control district–a local agency responsible for monitoring air pollution.

Air quality management district–a multi-county area that administers guidelines on state and federal Clean Air Acts.

Air toxics inventory*–a "comprehensive characterization of the full range of hazardous materials that are released, or that may be released to the surrounding air from" a regulated facility.

Ambient air quality standards–allowable concentrations of atmospheric pollutants. Federal standards are adopted by EPA; state standards are adopted by the Air Resources Board.

Authority-to-construct permit*– permit to construct a new or modified stationary source of air pollution, issued by a local air pollution control district or an air quality management district.

Best available control technology– under the federal PSD program an emissions limitation based on the maximum degree of reduction for each pollutant on a case-by-case basis, taking into account energy, environmental, and economic impacts, and other costs. Under California's new source review, best available control technology is equivalent to lowest achievable emission rate under the federal nonattainment new source review program

Best demonstrated available control technology– an emissions reduction applicable to industrial source categories, based on emission standards or operational standards (where numerical limitations are infeasible) that considers cost, environmental impacts, and energy requirements.

California ambient air quality standards– ambient standards for criteria pollutants that generally are health-based. California ambient air quality standards are often more strict than national ambient air quality standards.

CAM rule–requires that properly designed and adequate control measures for emission limitations are implemented and properly operated and maintained.

Conformity process*–the process by which transportation agencies show that their activities conform to the state implementation plan.

Criteria pollutant–a category of pollutant for which ambient air quality standards have been established based on the effect upon health and property.

District attainment plan–contains a discussion of California ambient air quality standards data and trends; a baseline emissions inventory; future-year projection of emissions, that include growth projections and adopted air emission control measures; a comprehensive control strategy of additional measures needed to reach attainment; an attainment demonstration that generally involves complex modeling; and contingency measures.

Emissions offsets–the reduction of emissions from other sources to mitigate the effect of any emissions from a proposed new or modified source.

Federal implementation plan–a plan to achieve attainment of air quality standards, used when a state is unable to develop an adequate plan.

Generally available control technology– hazardous air pollution control under National Emission Standards for Hazardous Air Pollutants (NESHAP) imposed on sources too small to qualify as major sources.

Greenhouse gas–a gas, principally carbon dioxide, that allows sunlight to enter the atmosphere freely. When sunlight strikes the earth's surface, some of it is reflected back toward space as infrared radiation (heat). Greenhouse gases absorb this infrared radiation and trap the heat in the atmosphere.

Hazardous air pollutant–an air pollutant that poses an adverse effect and threat to human health or the environment.

Lowest achievable emission rate–a technology-forcing standard that may not be less stringent than any applicable new source performance standards. LAER is an emissions rate specific to each type of emissions unit, including fugitive emissions sources.

Major modification–a change to a major stationary source of emissions with respect to Prevention of Significant Deterioration and New Source Review under the Clean Air Act.

Maximum achievable control technology– a technology-based standard under the federal NESHAP that requires the maximum degree of reduction in emissions of hazardous air pollutants, and that EPA determines is chievable or not, after considering costs and other environmental impacts.

Methyl tertiary butyl ether–a chemical compound produced by a chemical reaction between methanol and isobutylene.

Mobile source–any non-stationary source of air pollution, such as an automobile or locomotive.

Modification–any physical or operational change in an existing facility that would increase emission of any air pollutant.

National ambient air quality standards– ambient standards for six criteria pollutants that are widespread and considered harmful to public health and the environment.

New source performance standards– emissions limitations for industrial source categories, adopted by EPA.

New source review rules–rules guiding authority-to-construct permits, requiring application of best available control technology and emissions offsets to new or modified major sources.

Non-attainment area—a geographic area in which the level of an air pollutant is higher than an ambient air quality standard.

Non-attainment area plan—a local air district plan for attainment and maintenance of ambient air quality standards.

Non-attainment new source review—requires stationary sources of air pollution to obtain permits before they start construction. New source review is also referred to as construction permitting or pre-construction permitting.

Ozone-depleting chemical—a compound that aggressively reacts and destroys ozone molecules in the upper stratosphere. Examples include freons, chlorofluorocarbons, and other halogenated compounds.

Particulate matter—a mixture of extremely small particles and liquid droplets that can include acids (such as nitrates and sulfates), organic chemicals, metals, and soil or dust particles. Also known as particle pollution. The size of particles is linked directly to the potential for causing health problems.

Permit by rule*—a permit in which the applicant submits a notice of intent to comply with pre-set permit conditions that are not site-specific.

Permit to operate*—an operational permit issued by an air district to a stationary air emissions source.

Potential to emit—the maximum amount of a specific pollutant that is capable of being released into the air and must be considered in equipment design.

Prevention of significant deterioration permit*—a permit for a major source of a criteria pollutant, to assure that clean air

areas meeting national ambient air quality standards remain clean.

Reasonably available control technology—the lowest emissions limit that a particular existing source is capable of meeting by applying control technology that is reasonably available and technologically and economically feasible.

Reconstruction—involves replacement of one or more components where the cost of the new component(s) exceeds 50 percent of the cost of constructing a comparable new facility.

Reformulated gasoline—specially refined gasoline with low levels of smog-forming volatile organic compounds and low levels of hazardous air pollutants.

Risk management plan*—facilities that manufacture, process, use, store, or handle "highly hazardous chemicals" in excess of threshold quantities may be required to develop a plan that evaluates the risk of an unplanned chemical release. The risk management plan may be required to include a hazard assessment, an off-site consequence analysis, a prevention plan, and an emergency response plan.

State implementation plan—a detailed plan prepared by the Air Resources Board that describes the program the state will use to attain national ambient air quality standards. A state implementation plan is required by the federal Clean Air Act for areas with unhealthy levels of ozone, carbon monoxide, nitrogen dioxide, sulfur dioxide, and inhalable particulate matter.

Stationary source—any building, structure, facility, or installation that emits or may emit any air pollutant subject to regulation under the Clean Air Act.

Title V operating permit*—all encompassing permit including relevant conditions for all regulated stationary source permits at a "major facility." The permit is effective for five years.

Permit holders must submit compliance reports every six months that must be certified by a responsible official.

Toxic air contaminant—an air pollutant, under California law, that may cause or contribute to an increase in mortality or in serious illness, or that may pose a present or potential hazard to human health. Toxic air contaminants include substances listed as hazardous air pollutants.

Transportation control measures—strategies to reduce vehicle trips, vehicle use, and vehicle miles traveled.

Transportation improvement plan—a program for transportation projects for a specific period of time, developed by a metropolitan planning organization in conjunction with a state.

Volatile organic compound—any organic compound reacting with atmospheric photochemicals except those designated by the Environmental Protection Agency or a local air pollution control district or air quality management district as having a small photochemical reactivity. Examples include gasoline, dry cleaning solvents, and paint solvents.

* equals permits and approvals

CHAPTER 5

Air Quality

Introduction

Air quality regulation in California is based on both the federal Clean Air Act (CAA) and several state regulatory programs that implement and go further than the CAA. Key regulatory agencies include the U.S. Environmental Protection Agency (EPA), the California Air Resources Board (ARB), and 35 regional and local air quality management districts. Federal and state air quality laws create different regulatory programs for two major types of air pollution sources—stationary sources (*e.g.*, an industrial facility like a power plant or refinery) and mobile sources (*e.g.*, automobiles and trucks). This chapter reviews key laws and agencies involved in air quality regulation and standards; air quality planning to attain and maintain those standards; regulatory programs for stationary sources, ozone protection, acid rain, "criteria" pollutants, air toxics, greenhouse gases (GHGs), and mobile sources; and enforcement of air quality regulations.

ARB = Air Resources Board
CAA = Clean Air Act
EPA = U.S. Environmental Protection Agency
GHG = Greenhouse gas
NAAQS = National ambient air quality standards
SIP = State implementation plan

Key Laws and Agencies

Federal Laws and Agencies

Clean Air Act. The CAA (42 USC 7401 *et seq.*) requires states to develop air quality plans and regulatory programs to attain and maintain federal air quality standards. Enacted in 1963, the Act was amended comprehensively in 1970, 1977, and 1990. The CAA requires the following:

- EPA must establish and enforce national ambient air quality standards (NAAQS) for criteria pollutants.

- States must prepare state implementation plans (SIPs), approved by EPA, to attain NAAQS.

The CAA requires states to develop air quality plans and regulatory programs to attain and maintain federal air quality standards.

CAAQS = California ambient
air quality standards

CCR = California Code of Regulations

HSC = Health and Safety Code

NESHAP = National Emission Standards
for Hazardous Air Pollutants

NSPS = New source
performance standards

NSR = New source review

ODC = Ozone-depleting chemical

PSD = Prevention of
significant deterioration

TAC = Toxic air contaminant

- States must establish regulatory programs to attain and maintain NAAQS
- States must conduct new source review (NSR) permitting of "major sources" of air pollution in regions of the country that exceed one or more NAAQS
- EPA must administer a prevention of significant deterioration (PSD) permitting program for "major sources" of criteria pollutants to assure that clean air areas meeting NAAQS remain clean
- EPA must establish new source performance standards (NSPS) for stationary sources that fall within specified industrial categories
- EPA must administer the National Emission Standards for Hazardous Air Pollutants (NESHAP) program, which imposes rigorous emission controls on hazardous air pollutants
- EPA must regulate mobile source emissions through regulations on motor vehicles, fuel, service station vapor recovery, tailpipe emissions, and clean fuel vehicles
- EPA must regulate sources of acid rain
- EPA must protect the stratosphere by prohibiting the production of chemicals that deplete the upper layer of ozone
- EPA must administer a post-construction permitting program governing air quality permits for "major sources"
- EPA must regulate sources responsible for significant visibility impairment
- EPA must consider whether to regulate GHGs

Environmental Protection Agency. EPA is principally responsible for implementing and enforcing the provisions of the CAA discussed above.

State Laws and Agencies

Health and Safety Code and California Code of Regulations. California's air quality regulatory programs are authorized primarily by the state's:

- Health and Safety Code. HSC 39000 *et seq.*
- California Code of Regulations, Title 17, Division 3. CCR 60000 *et seq.*

The HSC establishes a broad range of rigorous state air quality regulatory programs that govern criteria pollutants, air toxics, ozone-depleting chemicals (ODCs), GHGs, and acid rain, requiring the ARB to:

- Adopt and enforce California ambient air quality standards (CAAQS) for California criteria pollutants
- Designate each air basin in California as either "attainment" for a given pollutant (meeting or surpassing the CAAQS for that pollutant) or "non-attainment" (failing CAAQS for a particular criteria pollutant)
- Prepare the California SIP
- Establish programs for controlling toxic air contaminants (TACs)
- Undertake a number of research and monitoring programs
- Oversee regulatory activities of regional and local air districts

- Monitor consumer products to reduce emitted volatile organic compounds (VOCs)

APCD = Air pollution control district
AQMD = Air quality management district
Cal/EPA = California Environmental Protection Agency
PUC = Public Utilities Commission
VOC = Volatile organic compound

California Clean Air Act. The Legislature enacted the California CAA in 1988. It added an ambitious regulatory layer on top of the existing state and federal criteria pollutant programs in an effort to meet CAAQS by 2010.

Air Resources Board. The ARB is the state agency charged with regulating air pollution and implementing the CAA. It is part of the California Environmental Protection Agency (Cal/EPA) and is led by an 11-member board of directors.

Climate Action Team. The Climate Action Team is composed of representatives from Cal/EPA, the Business, Transportation and Housing Agency, the Department of Food and Agriculture, ARB, and the PUC. The team was established to meet the GHG emissions reduction targets set by the Governor's Executive Order on climate change, Executive Order S-03-05.

Local Laws and Agencies

Local air districts. Several types of local air districts operate in California, including:

- Countywide air pollution control districts (APCDs), such as San Diego APCD
- Multi-county unified air pollution control districts, such as San Joaquin Valley Unified APCD (includes eight Central Valley counties)
- Multi-county air quality management districts (AQMDs), such as South Coast AQMD and Bay Area AQMD

Though the types of air districts have different funding and governing board compositions, their powers and duties are similar, with the exception of the South Coast AQMD and Bay Area AQMD, which have more specific powers and duties specified in the state Health and Safety Code. California's 35 air districts and their respective boundaries are shown in Figure 5-1.

Local air districts are responsible for:

- Permitting and enforcing stationary sources
- Preparing regional and local air quality attainment or maintenance plans
- Regulating toxic air contaminants

Although the local air districts and ARB share responsibility for implementing the CAA, local air districts provide most of the regulatory interface in California.

Ambient Air Quality Standards and Air Quality Planning

Air Pollution Principles

The Earth's atmosphere is comprised of approximately 78 percent nitrogen and 21 percent oxygen, with the balance comprised of trace concentrations of argon, carbon dioxide, methane, and other gases. Air pollutants are divided into

Figure 5-1
California's Air Districts and Their Boundaries

AIR DISTRICTS	
1 North Coast Unified	16 Placer
2 Siskiyou	17 Sacramento Metro
3 Modoc	18 El Dorado
4 Shasta	19 Amador
5 Lassen	20 Bay Area
6 Tehama	21 Calaveras
7 Northern Sierra	22 Tuolumne
8 Mendocino	23 Mariposa
9 Glenn	24 Monterey Bay Unified
10 Butte	25 San Joaquin Valley Unified
11 Lake	26 Great Basin Unified
12 Colusa	27 San Luis Obispo
13 Feather River	28 Kern
14 Northern Sonoma	29 Santa Barbara
15 Yolo-Solano	30 Ventura
	31 Antelope Valley
	32 Mojave Desert
	33 South Coast
	34 San Diego
	35 Imperial

Source: California Air Resources Board

☐ Air District Boundaries
- - - - - County Boundaries

0   50   100 miles

the following general categories: criteria pollutants, air toxics, ozone-depleting chemicals, and GHGs. The CAA has established one or more regulatory programs to address each category of air pollutants, except for GHGs.

Criteria pollutants. A criteria pollutant is a pollutant that has had an ambient air quality standard established for it, based on the adverse effect the pollutant has on public health and welfare. Criteria pollutants are chemicals commonly emitted in high volumes from industrial and mobile sources. Federal and state agencies regulate the criteria pollutants listed in Table 5-1.

Many criteria pollutants are generated as products of incomplete combustion (PICs) or from the oxidation of impurities bound up in fossil fuels. Complete combustion of a fossil fuel (or wood) primarily produces carbon dioxide and water, and no PICs. Since complete combustion very rarely occurs, stationary and mobile sources that generate these pollutants may be required to use emissions controls (such as catalysts and scrubbers) to abate the PICs (either before or after the combustion process).

While many criteria pollutants are generated from incomplete combustion, others are generated from escaping gases (such as gasoline escaping from a pipe or seam, or during fueling). Smog–the most heavily regulated criteria pollutant–typically is generated by a photochemical reaction involving NO_X (oxides of nitrogen, such as NO) and VOCs (volatile organic compounds or gases). NO_X–which is a PIC–reacts with VOCs in the presence of sunlight to create ground-level ozone. Ozone, which is present at or below the troposphere (from ground level to approximately 5–9 miles high), can cause respiratory illnesses such as aggravated asthma in children and the elderly. Ground-level ozone is managed by regulating its precursor chemicals– NO_X and VOCs. NO_X is regulated both as a precursor pollutant to ozone and as a stand-alone criteria pollutant.

Other chemicals in the particulate form (either a solid or a mist) are regulated as particulate matter (PM), which is another criteria pollutant. PM (which includes suspended dust, soot, and more) can become imbedded deeply within the lungs and cause premature death, chronic bronchitis, and aggravated asthma. As with health problems linked to ozone, children, and the elderly are most at risk. Diesel PM also is an air toxic due to the presence of nickel and arsenic, along with polycyclic aromatic hydrocarbons, which are suspected carcinogens.

Acid rain is another phenomenon involving two criteria pollutants. Atmospheric NO_X and SO_X chemically react with moisture in the atmosphere to create nitric acid and sulfuric acid. Most acid rain is produced from the burning of high sulfur coal (generating SO_X) and from boiler systems (generating NO_X).

Air toxics. The air toxics category of pollutants includes heavy metals, organic chemicals, pesticides, and radionuclides. Gaseous air toxics (*e.g.*, benzene) are VOCs (a precursor chemical that forms ground-level ozone). Air toxics can cause acute and chronic illness ranging from birth defects to cancer.

NO_X = Oxides of nitrogen
PIC = Products of incomplete combustion
PM = Particulate matter
SO_X = Oxides of sulfur

Air quality in the South Coast Basin has improved dramatically, but ozone standards are still being violated.

Ambient Air Quality Standards

Pollutant	Averaging Time	California Standards [1]		Federal Standards [2]		
		Concentration [3]	Method [4]	Primary [3,5]	Secondary [3,6]	Method [7]
Ozone (O_3)	1 Hour	0.09 ppm (180 $\mu g/m^3$)	Ultraviolet Photometry	—	Same as Primary Standard	Ultraviolet Photometry
	8 Hour	0.070 ppm (137 $\mu g/m^3$)		0.075 ppm (147 $\mu g/m^3$)		
Respirable Particulate Matter (PM10)	24 Hour	50 $\mu g/m^3$	Gravimetric or Beta Attenuation	150 $\mu g/m^3$	Same as Primary Standard	Inertial Separation and Gravimetric Analysis
	Annual Arithmetic Mean	20 $\mu g/m^3$		—		
Fine Particulate Matter (PM2.5)	24 Hour	No Separate State Standard		35 $\mu g/m^3$	Same as Primary Standard	Inertial Separation and Gravimetric Analysis
	Annual Arithmetic Mean	12 $\mu g/m^3$	Gravimetric or Beta Attenuation	15 $\mu g/m^3$		
Carbon Monoxide (CO)	8 Hour	9.0 ppm (10mg/m^3)	Non-Dispersive Infrared Photometry (NDIR)	9 ppm (10 mg/m^3)	None	Non-Dispersive Infrared Photometry (NDIR)
	1 Hour	20 ppm (23 mg/m^3)		35 ppm (40 mg/m^3)		
	8 Hour (Lake Tahoe)	6 ppm (7 mg/m^3)		—	—	—
Nitrogen Dioxide (NO_2)	Annual Arithmetic Mean	0.030 ppm (57 $\mu g/m3$)	Gas Phase Chemiluminescence	0.053 ppm (100 $\mu g/m^3$)	Same as Primary Standard	Gas Phase Chemiluminescence
	1 Hour	0.18 ppm (339 $\mu g/m^3$)		—		
Sulfur Dioxide (SO_2)	Annual Arithmetic Mean	—	Ultraviolet Fluorescence	0.030 ppm (80 $\mu g/m^3$)	—	Spectrophotometry (Pararosaniline Method)
	24 Hour	0.04 ppm (105 $\mu g/m^3$)		0.14 ppm (365 $\mu g/m^3$)	—	
	3 Hour	—		—	0.5 ppm (1300 $\mu g/m^3$)	
	1 Hour	0.25 ppm (655 $\mu g/m^3$)		—	—	—
Lead[8]	30 Day Average	1.5 $\mu g/m^3$	Atomic Absorption	—	—	—
	Calendar Quarter	—		1.5 $\mu g/m^3$	Same as Primary Standard	High Volume Sampler and Atomic Absorption
Visibility Reducing Particles	8 Hour	Extinction coefficient of 0.23 per kilometer — visibility of ten miles or more (0.07 — 30 miles or more for Lake Tahoe) due to particles when relative humidity is less than 70 percent. Method: Beta Attenuation and Transmittance through Filter Tape.		No		
Sulfates	24 Hour	25 $\mu g/m^3$	Ion Chromatography		Federal	
Hydrogen Sulfide	1 Hour	0.03 ppm (42 $\mu g/m^3$)	Ultraviolet Fluorescence			
Vinyl Chloride[8]	24 Hour	0.01 ppm (26 $\mu g/m^3$)	Gas Chromatography		Standards	

See Notes for Table 5-1 on facing page.

Source: California Air Resources Board

Ozone-depleting chemicals. The upper stratosphere (approximately seven miles above ground to 25 to 31 miles high) is comprised of a gaseous layer of protective ozone molecules that screen out the sun's ultraviolet light. Millions of chemical refrigerants (such as freon, chlorofluorocarbons, and other halogenated compounds) have escaped over the last half century into the stratosphere. These highly reactive chemicals have depleted the protective layer of ozone significantly at the South Pole and other weak spots around the globe, resulting in increases in skin cancer and cataracts.

Greenhouse gases. First postulated by a Swedish chemist in 1896, the theory of global warming suggests that increased levels of carbon dioxide and other gases released into the atmosphere as a result of human industrial activity are increasing atmospheric temperature. Gases that contribute to global warming are known as greenhouse gases. The increase in atmospheric temperature associated with global warming has the potentially devastating effects of disrupting natural weather cycles and increasing global sea levels, thus increasing the risk, range, and strength of natural disasters worldwide. Since 1990, the theory of global warming has received an international consensus among scientists for both its potential effects, as well as its anthropogenic source based largely on burning fossil fuels. However, a year after the decision, still EPA had not determined whether to regulate GHGs under the CAA; the California Attorney General, joined by seventeen other states and several environmental groups, then filed suit in the District of Columbia Court of Appeals, asking the court to order EPA to release its determination within 60 days.

Air Quality Standards

Local air districts must develop plans to attain and maintain both NAAQS and CAAQS. HSC 40001. The CAAQS are often more strict than the NAAQS, and also establish ambient standards for three additional criteria pollutants. *See* Table 5-1. The CAA establishes two sets of NAAQS—primary standards (to protect human health) and secondary standards (to protect public welfare, which includes non-health considerations such as aesthetics and property). CAAQS are also generally health-based (except for visibility-reducing particles).

The CAA and the California CAA (discussed below) contain specific deadlines for non-attainment areas to achieve primary NAAQS and CAAQS, respectively. The NAAQS and the CAAQS are not permitting programs—instead, they directly influence a

Notes for Table 5-1

1. California standards for ozone, carbon monoxide (except Lake Tahoe), sulfur dioxide (one and 24 hour), nitrogen dioxide, suspended particulate matter—PM_{10}, $PM_{2.5}$, and visibility reducing particles, are values that are not to be exceeded. All others are not to be equaled or exceeded. California ambient air quality standards are listed in the Table of Standards in Section 70200 of Title 17 of the California Code of Regulations.

2. National standards (other than ozone, particulate matter, and those based on annual averages or annual arithmetic mean) are not to be exceeded more than once a year. The ozone standard is attained when the fourth highest eight hour concentration in a year, averaged over three years, is equal to or less than the standard. For PM_{10}, the 24-hour standard is attained when the expected number of days per calendar year with a 24-hour average concentration above 150 $\mu g/m3$ is equal to or less than one. For $PM_{2.5}$, the 24-hour standard is attained when 98 percent of the daily concentrations, averaged over three years, are equal to or less than the standard. Contact U.S. EPA for further clarification and current federal policies.

3. Concentration expressed first in units in which it was promulgated. Equivalent units given in parentheses are based upon a reference temperature of 25°C and a reference pressure of 760 torr. Most measurements of air quality are to be corrected to a reference temperature of 25°C and a reference pressure of 760 torr; ppm in this table refers to ppm by volume, or micromoles of pollutant per mole of gas.

4. Any equivalent procedure which can be shown to the satisfaction of the ARB to give equivalent results at or near the level of the air quality standard may be used.

5. National Primary Standards: The levels of air quality necessary, with an adequate margin of safety to protect the public health.

6. National Secondary Standards: The levels of air quality necessary to protect the public welfare from any known or anticipated adverse effects of a pollutant.

7. Reference method as described by the EPA. An "equivalent method" of measurement may be used but must have a "consistent relationship to the reference method" and must be approved by the EPA.

8. The ARB has identified lead and vinyl chloride as "toxic air contaminants" with no threshold level of exposure for adverse health effects determined. These actions allow for the implementation of control measures at levels below the ambient concentrations specified for these pollutants.

number of federal, state, and local permitting programs that regulate criteria pollutants to attain and maintain these ambient air quality standards.

Attainment Status

The federal CAA program and its 1990 amendments classify non-attainment air districts as marginal, moderate, serious, severe, or extreme, for the six criteria pollutants. Air districts in more severely non-attainment regions must impose stricter air quality permitting requirements on smaller stationary sources.

The state CAA program, similar to but different than the federal program, classifies non-attainment air districts as moderate, serious, severe, or extreme, through the ARB. Under the state CAA (HSC 40910 *et seq.*), a local air district that is non-attainment for ozone, CO, SO_2, or NO_2 is required to prepare a plan to achieve attainment and maintenance of the CAAQS as expeditiously as practicable. These district attainment plans establish or modify stationary source permitting and transportation control programs to ultimately reach CAAQS attainment. Like the federal program, the stationary source and transportation control planning requirements become increasingly more strict for the more severely non-attainment air districts.

In general, local air district attainment plans discuss:

- CAAQS data and trends
- A baseline emissions inventory
- Future-year projections of emissions, which include growth projections and adopted air emission control measures
- A comprehensive control strategy of additional measures needed to reach attainment
- An attainment demonstration, which generally involves complex modeling
- Contingency measures

Plans also may include interim milestones for progress toward attainment.

State Implementation Plan

The federal CAA requires a SIP to include:

- Enforceable emissions limitations and other control measures, such as economic incentives
- Timetables for compliance
- Air quality monitoring programs
- Stationary source regulatory programs
- Assurance of implementation capability
- Non-attainment area plans

The SIP, maintained by the ARB, is not a formal planning document. Rather, the California SIP is a compilation of new and previously submitted plans and programs (such as those for monitoring, modeling, permitting, air district rules, state regulations, and federal controls). Many of California's SIP elements rely on the same core set of federal control strategies, including motor vehicle emission standards and fuel regulations.

Local air districts and other agencies, such as the Bureau of Automotive Repair, prepare SIP elements and submit them to ARB for review and approval. ARB forwards SIP revisions to EPA for approval and publication in the Federal Register. 40 CFR 52.220 *et seq.* Many California submittals are pending EPA approval.

If the EPA finds a SIP or SIP revision inadequate, the EPA is authorized to prepare a federal implementation plan (FIP) on behalf of the state, or to impose sanctions on a state's federal transportation funding. However, the EPA has never promulgated a FIP in response to California's inadequate SIP preparation, because the state either revised its SIP before EPA took action or because legislation was passed that changed the requirements.

FIP = Federal implementation plan

Federal Criteria Pollutant Programs

Definition of Stationary Source

The CAA defines a stationary source as any building, structure, facility, or installation that emits or may emit any air pollutant subject to regulation under the CAA. Wooley and Morss 2001. A "building, structure, facility, or installation" is on one or more contiguous or adjacent properties under common ownership or control and belongs to a common industrial grouping (Standard Industrial Classification). An emissions unit is any part of a stationary source that emits or has the potential to emit regulated air pollutants. EPA 1990.

Stationary sources are regulated by both federal and state air quality laws.

New Source Performance Standards

The new source performance standards apply to "new," "modified," and "reconstructed" stationary sources. A "new" source is one that is constructed after the most recent version of the NSPS for the industrial category in question. If the source was constructed prior to a given NSPS, the source is grandfathered and not subject to the standards. A "modified" source is any physical or operational change in an existing source that increases emissions. A "reconstructed" source involves a replacement of a component where the cost of the replacement exceeds 50 percent of the cost of constructing a comparable new facility. 40 CFR 60.14 *et seq.*, 40 CFR 60.2, 40 CFR 63.41.

The NSPS varies according to the type of industrial facility. The CAA regulates over 60 types of industrial facilities (such as oil refineries, coke ovens, fossil fuel burning sources, and electric utility steam generating units) that contribute significantly to air pollution. 40 CFR 60 *et seq.*

NSPS requires that an owner or operator of specified stationary industrial sources listed in 40 CFR 60 must meet specified emissions limitations and operating standards for the criteria pollutant or pollutants that it emits, regardless of whether the source is within an attainment or non-attainment area. Stationary industrial sources must comply with emission limitations by applying the best demonstrated available control technology (BDACT). Cost, environmental impacts, and energy considerations can be considered when determining BDACT for a given industry type. BDACT includes operational standards where numerical emissions limitations are infeasible. Other air quality programs (discussed below) impose more rigorous emission control standards that give little or no consideration to costs and energy consumption.

NSPS also include notification requirements, testing procedures, monitoring, and reporting obligations.

An industrial stationary source may be subject to other federal or state air quality permitting programs, in addition to NSPS, that govern toxic or other pollutants. This can result in a stationary source having several federal and state air permits with layers of controls and operating conditions. Most NSPS sources have permits to operate a given source (operating permits) and to construct new sources or modify existing sources (new source review permits).

EPA may delegate to states the authority to implement and enforce the NSPS, but maintains concurrent enforcement authority. Many California air districts have received EPA delegation. Some air districts adopt the NSPS program and add stringent requirements for one or more industrial sources.

New Source Review

In the 1970 version of the CAA, a new source review permitting program was established for major sources of criteria pollutants in non-attainment areas (known as the non-attainment NSR program). The permitting program initially focused on improving the air quality in air basins designated non-attainment for one or more criteria air pollutants. Then, in 1972, the Sierra Club successfully challenged the federal NSR program because the program failed to consider regulating major sources of criteria pollutants in cleaner, attainment areas. *Sierra Club v. Ruckelshaus* (1972) 344 F. Supp. 253. This lawsuit spawned the prevention of significant deterioration permitting program. Both the PSD and non-attainment NSR programs were expanded further in major amendments to the CAA in 1977 and 1990, as a result of more litigation brought in the 1970s and 1980s. The PSD program and the non-attainment NSR program are discussed separately

BDACT = Best demonstrated available control technology

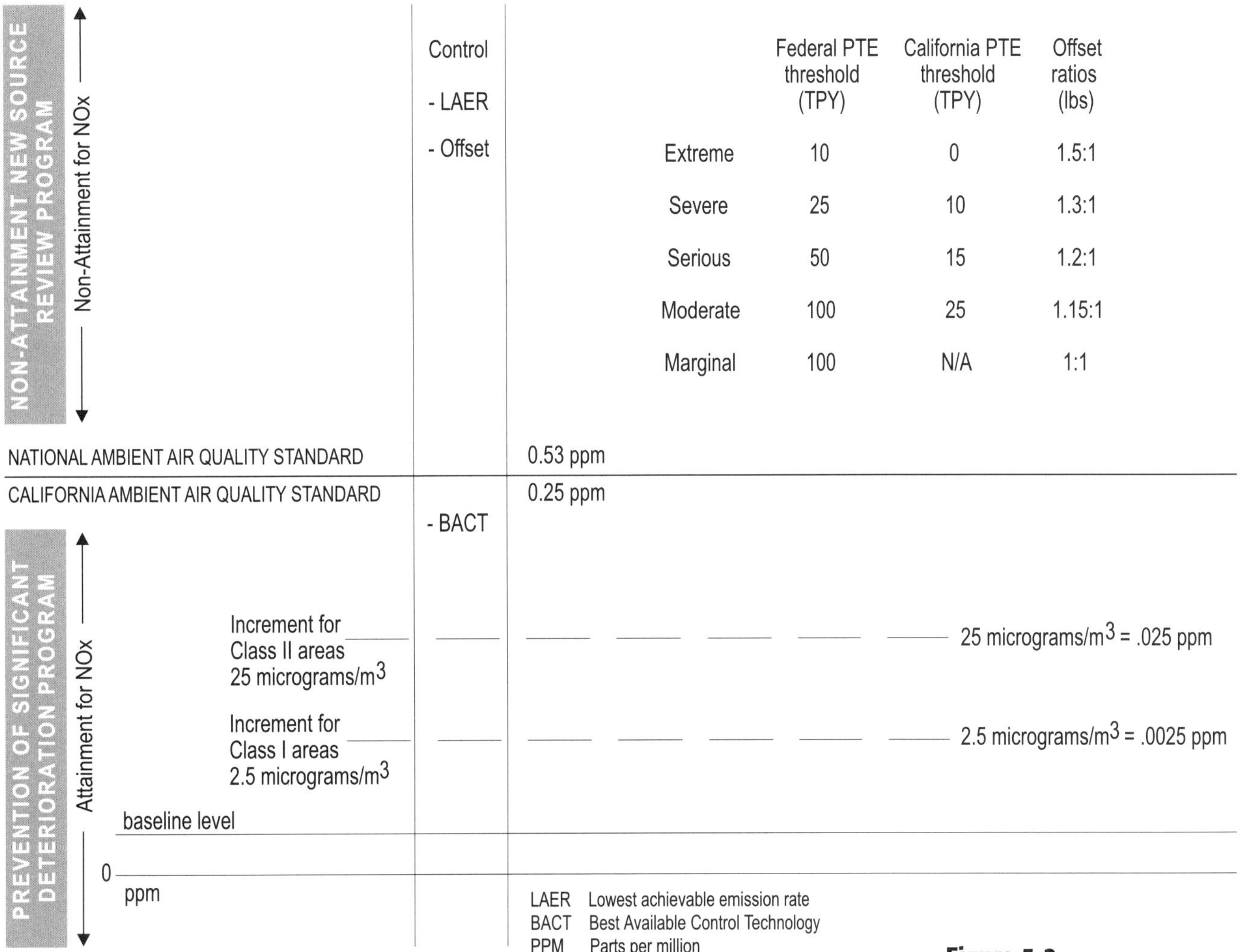
NON-ATTAINMENT NEW SOURCE REVIEW PROGRAM
Non-Attainment for NOx
Control
- LAER
- Offset
	Federal PTE threshold (TPY)	California PTE threshold (TPY)	Offset ratios (lbs)
Extreme	10	0	1.5:1
Severe	25	10	1.3:1
Serious	50	15	1.2:1
Moderate	100	25	1.15:1
Marginal	100	N/A	1:1
NATIONAL AMBIENT AIR QUALITY STANDARD
0.53 ppm
CALIFORNIA AMBIENT AIR QUALITY STANDARD
0.25 ppm
- BACT
PREVENTION OF SIGNIFICANT DETERIORATION PROGRAM
Attainment for NOx
Increment for Class II areas 25 micrograms/m3
25 micrograms/m3 = .025 ppm
Increment for Class I areas 2.5 micrograms/m3
2.5 micrograms/m3 = .0025 ppm
baseline level
0
ppm

LAER Lowest achievable emission rate
BACT Best Available Control Technology
PPM Parts per million
TPY Tons per year
PTE Potential to emit
Class 1 Federal lands include National Parks, National Wilderness Areas, and National Monuments

Figure 5-2

New Source Review Guide – NO_X Example

below. The relationship between the various programs regulating major sources is shown in Figure 5-2.

Prevention of Significant Deterioration Program

The PSD program (40 CFR 52.01 *et seq.*) applies to attainment areas, and is designed to allow a level of economic growth that is consistent with preserving existing clean air resources. In addition, the PSD program is structured to preserve, protect, and enhance the air quality in national parks, national wilderness areas, national monuments, national seashores, and other areas of special national or regional natural, recreational, scenic, or historic value. 42 USC 7470.

The PSD program applies to attainment areas, and is designed to allow a level of economic growth that is consistent with preserving existing clean air resources.

Program applicability. A stationary source subject to the PSD program is required to obtain a PSD permit that may include technology-oriented and operational conditions. This requirement is for a stationary source that is deemed a new major source or a major modification. The definitions of major source and major modification depend on the amount of a criteria pollutant that *potentially* can be emitted (not *actually* is emitted).

The potential to emit (PTE) is the maximum capacity of a stationary source to emit a pollutant under its physical and operational design. The following federal PTE restrictions are enforceable (EPA 1990):

- Requirements to install and operate air pollution control equipment at prescribed efficiencies
- Restrictions on design capacity utilization
- Restrictions on hours of operation
- Restrictions on the types or amount of material processed, combusted, or stored

A new stationary source is considered a major source for PSD permitting if the source is on the list of 28 industrial source categories (Table 5-2) and has a PTE threshold of 100 tons per year (TPY) of any regulated pollutant. Other new stationary sources (not on the list of 28 industrial source categories) are considered major sources for PSD permitting if the sources have a PTE of 250 TPY for any regulated pollutant. New major sources exceeding these thresholds are subject to PSD review and permitting, as are major modifications to existing major sources if modifications cause emissions of criteria pollutants to equal or exceed "significant emission rates." Major modifications are discussed further below.

Major modifications and netting out. As mentioned previously, major modifications to existing major sources are subject to PSD permitting, if modifications cause emissions of criteria pollutants to equal or exceed significant net emission rates (Table 5-3). A modification means a physical change or a change in the method of operation of the major source. In some air districts, a modification means any new equipment, even the replacement of existing equipment. A significant net emissions rate is the net PTE increase, after combining source increases and decreases. Thus, a PSD applicant may be able to "net out" of PSD review by accounting for prior emissions reductions to avoid the major modification classification.

Best available control technology requirements. Once a stationary source is subject to PSD review, the source must meet best available control technology (BACT) requirements. 42 USC 165(a)(4), 40 CFR 52.210. BACT requirements are specific to each type of stationary source. However, determining BACT is far from straightforward. BACT results in maximum reduction for a pollutant while taking into account energy, environmental, and economic impacts, and other costs. EPA 1990. BACT is determined case-by-case using a top-down approach, where the most effective control technology feasible for the source is considered before turning to less effective control options. Each technology is evaluated for feasibility, cost-effectiveness, and other energy or environmental impacts. BACT can include a certain type of control technology, equipment design, equipment type, work practice, or operational standard. An example of a non-high-tech BACT is using paints low in VOCs to minimize the generation of ozone precursor emissions.

Prevention of significant deterioration increments. Increments of allowable air quality degradation have been established to ensure NAAQS will not be exceeded in attainment areas. Each NAAQS maximum concentration is an air quality ceiling; increments are maximum allowable fractional increases (measured in concentrations) above the existing background concentration for the attainment area. A stationary source may not be permitted if it would exceed NAAQS or completely consume the remaining increment for the attainment area.

Allowable increments vary depending on whether the proposed new or modified source is to be located in a Class I, II, or III area. *See* Table 5-4. Class I areas are assigned the highest degree of protection from air quality degradation. These areas include national wilderness areas, national memorial parks, and national parks. Class I areas have small increment levels, and thus new industrial growth is limited in or near these areas. *See* Figure 5-3. Class II areas include virtually all other areas of the country. Class II areas have increments that allow reasonable, well-managed industrial growth. Class III areas have the highest increments, but EPA has not proposed to designate any areas as such.

Air quality impact analysis. In addition to meeting BACT, a PSD applicant must complete an air quality impact analysis (AQIA) demonstrating that the stationary source will not cause or contribute to a violation of NAAQS or PSD increments. This analysis considers construction, operation impacts, secondary emissions, and emissions after application of BACT. If the NAAQS or PSD increment is exceeded, a PSD permit cannot be issued.

Table 5-2. Prevention of Significant Deterioration "Major Source" Industrial Source Categories and Their Potential to Emit Thresholds

Industrial source category	PTE in tons per year
Any (except the sources below)	250
Fossil fuel-fired steam electric plants of more than 250 million Btu/hr heat input	100
Coal cleaning plants with thermal dryers	100
Kraft pulp mills	100
Portland cement plants	100
Primary zinc smelters	100
Iron and steel mill plants	100
Primary aluminum ore reduction plants	100
Primary copper smelters	100
Municipal incinerators capable of charging more than 250 tons of refuse per day	100
Hydrofluoric acid plants	100
Sulfuric acid plants	100
Nitric acid plants	100
Petroleum refineries	100
Lime plants	100
Phosphate rock processing plants	100
Coke oven batteries	100
Sulfur recovery plants	100
Carbon black plants (furnace plants)	100
Primary lead smelters	100
Fuel conversion plants	100
Sintering plants	100
Secondary metal production plants	100
Chemical process plants	100
Fossil fuel boilers (or combinations thereof) totaling more than 250 million Btu/hr heat input	100
Petroleum storage and transfer units with a total storage capacity exceeding 300,000 barrels	100
Taconite ore processing plants	100
Glass fiber processing plants	100
Charcoal production plants	100

Source: EPA. 1990

Table 5-3. Significant Net Emission Rates Regulated under the Clean Air Act	
Criteria pollutant	Tons per year
CO	$\geq$ 100
NO_X	$\geq$ 40
SO_2	$\geq$ 40
Particulate matter	$\geq$ 25
PM_{10}	$\geq$ 15
Ozone	$\geq$ 40
Lead	$\geq$ 0.6

Source: 40 CFR 52.21 *et seq.*

Table 5-4. Prevention of Significant Deterioration Increments			
Class I, II, and III			
Pollutant	Class I	Class II	Class III
SO_2, annual	2	20	40
SO_2, 24-hour	5	91	182
SO_2, 3-hour	25	512	700
PM_{10}, annual	4	17	34
PM_{10}, 24-hour	8	30	60
NO_2, annual	2.5	25	50

Units: micrograms/meter^3 Source: 40 CFR 52.21(58)(c)

LAER = Lowest achievable emission rate
RACT = Reasonably available control technology

The AQIA evaluates the existing ambient air quality level, together with the projected increased concentrations from the major new or modified source. Specifically, the AQIA uses a computer-based model to postulate the PTE from the new or modified source and adds these levels to the measured background concentrations from all existing sources in the air basin.

Non-attainment New Source Review Program

The objective of non-attainment NSR is to achieve continuing improvement in air quality while allowing reasonable growth. The non-attainment NSR program is similar to the PSD program, and only the principal differences regarding program applicability, control technology, and offsets are addressed in this section. Unlike the PSD permitting program, which allows sources to emit pollutants up to an increment of a given NAAQS, major new sources or modifications in non-attainment areas are subject to more rigorous permitting standards. The key differences between a non-attainment NSR permit and a PSD permit are (42 USC 7503(a)(5)):

- The definition of major source

- Imposing reasonably available control technology (RACT) retrofits for existing sources with PTE of 100 TPY of ozone precursors in non-attainment areas

- Requiring the most stringent criteria pollutant control technologies available, using the lowest achievable emission rate (LAER)

- Requiring emission offsets (described below) for new or modified major sources

- The need for applicants to certify that all major stationary sources they own or operate in the state are in compliance with CAA regulations

- The need for applicants to analyze alternative sites, sizes, production processes, and environmental control techniques demonstrating that the benefits of the proposed new source "significantly outweigh the environmental and social costs imposed as a result of its location, construction or modification"

A major new source or a modification to an existing major source could involve simultaneous PSD and NSR permits.

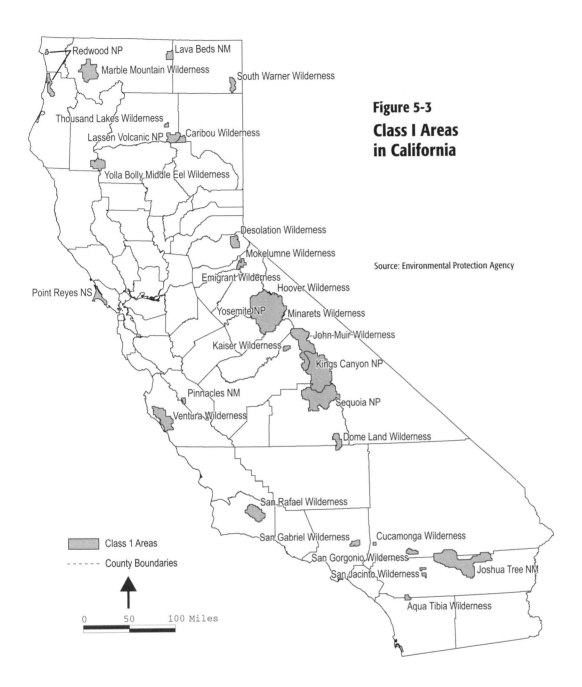

Figure 5-3
Class I Areas in California

Source: Environmental Protection Agency

Redwood NP
Lava Beds NM
Marble Mountain Wilderness
South Warner Wilderness
Thousand Lakes Wilderness
Lassen Volcanic NP
Caribou Wilderness
Yolla Bolly Middle Eel Wilderness
Desolation Wilderness
Mokelumne Wilderness
Emigrant Wilderness
Hoover Wilderness
Point Reyes NS
Yosemite NP
Minarets Wilderness
John Muir Wilderness
Kaiser Wilderness
Kings Canyon NP
Pinnacles NM
Sequoia NP
Ventura Wilderness
Dome Land Wilderness
San Rafael Wilderness
Cucamonga Wilderness
San Gabriel Wilderness
San Gorgonio Wilderness
Joshua Tree NM
San Jacinto Wilderness
Aqua Tibia Wilderness

Class 1 Areas
County Boundaries

0   50   100 Miles

Program applicability. Non-attainment NSR permitting requirements apply to the non-attainment pollutants from new or modified major sources. With the advent of the 1990 federal CAA Amendments, the non-attainment NSR permitting program now applies to increasingly smaller new or modified major sources. The definition of "major source" depends on the severity of an air basin's air pollution problems. Thus, a source emitting 10 TPY of NO_X or VOC is a major source in the South Coast Basin (an extreme ozone non-attainment area), but is a non-major or minor source in the San Francisco Bay Area (a marginal ozone non-attainment area). Table 5-5 presents the federal PTE thresholds and offset ratios for ozone in non-attainment air districts.

Non-attainment NSR permitting requirements apply to the non-attainment pollutants from new or modified major sources.

Non-attainment classification	Federal PTE threshold—in tons per year	Offset ratio
Marginal	100	1.1 to 1
Moderate	100	1.15 to 1
Serious	50	1.2 to 1
Severe	25	1.3 to 1
Extreme	10	1.5 to 1

Source: 42 USC 7511

ERC = Emission reduction credit
SNEI = Significant net emissions increase

The emissions offsets program is one of the most stringent controls for criteria pollutants emitted from major sources or major modifications.

As with PSD permitting, when a major non-attainment source has a significant net emissions increase (SNEI) of a non-attainment pollutant, then non-attainment NSR permitting is triggered. The SNEI thresholds for ozone, PM_{10}, NO_2, SO_2, and CO appear in Table 5-6.

Lowest achievable emission rate. LAER is the most stringent emissions limitation and is often a technology-forcing standard. Like BACT under the PSD program, LAER is specific to each type of stationary source, including fugitive emissions sources. It may not be less stringent than any applicable NSPS. LAER is determined by one of the following (whichever is more stringent) (EPA 1990):

- The most stringent emission limitation in the SIP of any state, by any source in the same industrial category (unless shown to be unachievable). In practice, LAER is set by the South Coast AQMD, which typically has the most stringent SIP requirements in the country.
- The most stringent emission control achieved, by any source in the same industrial category. 42 USC 7501(3), HSC 40405(b).

Air districts determine whether a single measure or a combination of measures will be used to meet the LAER emissions limitation, on a case-by-case basis for a given source, without regard to cost, energy, or other environmental factors. Measures used to control emissions may consist of:

- A change in the raw materials processed
- A process modification
- Add-on controls

Emissions offsets. The emissions offsets program is one of the most stringent controls for criteria pollutants emitted from major sources or major modifications. A proposed emissions increase by a major non-attainment source must be offset by an emissions decrease by existing sources within the area for the same criteria pollutant. The specific ratio of required offsets to emission increases is greater in more severe non-attainment areas, as illustrated in Table 5-5.

The units of replaced air emissions are referred to as offsets or emission reduction credits (ERCs). For example, in a marginal ozone non-attainment area, if a major new source proposes to generate 100 new TPY of NO_X (after installing LAER), the source would need to provide at least 110 TPY of NO_X

Table 5-6. Federal Significant Net Emissions Increase Thresholds for Major Non-attainment Pollutants

Non-attainment classification	SNEI for ozone* (PTE in tons per year)	SNEI for PM₁₀ (PTE in tons per year)	SNEI for NO₂ (PTE in tons per year)	SNEI for SO₂ (PTE in tons per year)	SNEI for CO (PTE in tons per year)
Marginal	40	—	40	40	100
Moderate	40	15	40	40	100
Serious	25	15	40	40	100
Severe	25**	—	40	40	100
Extreme	Any increase at an emission unit	—	40	40	100

* Including volatile organic compounds and NO_X as ozone precursors   ** Please refer to statute for detailed explanation   Source: 42 USC 7501 *et seq.*

reductions from an existing source in the area. This can be accomplished in one of three ways:

- Pay an existing stationary source of non-attainment criteria pollutants to shut down
- Pay an existing stationary source to better control existing emissions of non-attainment criteria pollutants
- Purchase offsets from an emissions bank (an emissions bank is an entity that holds emissions offsets "deposited" by stationary sources that shut down or installed better performing emission controls; offsets can be purchased and used later by other stationary sources)

Typical emission reductions that qualify for offsets include those that result from a source doing one or more of the following:

- Installing a control device that results in emissions control greater than required by regulation
- Agreeing to further limit actual emissions below levels required by permit or regulation
- Switching to a fuel that results in lower emissions

Offsets must be pollutant-specific, quantifiable, surplus, permanent, federally enforceable, and voluntary. Emissions reductions that result from other regulatory action do not qualify as offsets.

Federal Title V Operating Permits Program

Prior to the enactment of the 1990 CAA Amendments, many state and local jurisdictions across the country did not require that a stationary source receive a permit to operate (PTO); an authority-to-construct (ATC) permit was all that was needed (these permits are discussed below). In these states, no mechanism existed to ensure that air emissions from a source under an ATC permit did not

ATC = Authority to construct
PTO = Permit to operate

exceed emission limitations. To rectify this, the 1990 CAA Amendments established the Title V Operating Permits program (42 USC 7661 *et seq.*), which is an expanded version of California's PTO program.

Under the Title V program, each state is obligated to adopt a federally enforceable operating permits program meeting specified minimum standards.

Under the Title V program, each state was obligated to adopt a federally enforceable operating permits program meeting specified minimum standards. 40 CFR 70. Title V consolidated all applicable federally enforceable requirements into one document for facilities meeting the definition of a major source under the Title V program. For example, a Title V operating permit serves as an umbrella document covering all relevant permit conditions for an oil refinery that hosts hundreds of stationary sources subject to a variety of permits (*e.g.*, federal non-attainment NSR, PSD, NSPS, and NESHAP).

Local air districts implement the Title V program. Although the Title V program does not create new substantive performance standards, Title V operating permits obligate responsible officials to assure compliance at all permitted emission points.

Program Applicability

CAM = Compliance assurance monitoring
HAP = Hazardous air pollutant

The following stationary sources are considered major under Title V and thus are subject to Title V operating permit requirements:

- Sources that emit or have the potential to emit more than 100 TPY of any air pollutant
- A major source of hazardous air pollutants (includes sources with the potential to emit 10 TPY of a single hazardous air pollutant (HAP) or 25 TPY of two or more HAPs, and facilities considered area sources under the NESHAP program)
- New or modified sources required to obtain a PSD or non-attainment NSR permit
- Facilities subject to NSPS
- Power plants and other facilities subject to the acid rain program (Title IV of the 1990 CAA Amendments)

Operating Permit Features

Key elements of a Title V operating permit include the permit application shield, operational flexibility, and compliance assurance monitoring.

Key elements of a Title V operating permit include the permit application shield, operational flexibility, and compliance assurance monitoring (CAM).

A permit application shield is available for applicants who submit applications that are complete and timely. 42 USC 7661c. Because the applicant may operate without a permit until the air district processes the application, the applicant may avoid (or be shielded from) additional or changed regulatory requirements not identified in the permit application.

Operational flexibility allows applicants to avoid the expense and uncertainty of a permit modification. A permit holder may modify operations with seven days notice to the regulating agency provided that both of the following are met (42 USC 7661(a)):

- The modification falls within an alternative operating scenario previously identified in the permit application and approved in the permit. For example, a permit for a boiler system intended to burn natural gas could switch to fuel oil if the latter was approved as an alternative operating scenario.

- The emissions do not exceed the limitations established in the Title V operating permit.

Finally, the CAM rule (40 CFR 64.3) is intended to ensure that permit holders properly design and implement adequate control measures. The CAM rule is designed to ensure that control devices provide a reasonable assurance of compliance with emission limitations or standards for the anticipated range of operations at a facility.

Permit Applications and Renewals

New facilities must submit an initial application for an operating permit within 12 months after the source becomes subject to Title V. Generally, applications for Title V operating permits must include the following:

- Description of processes and products
- SIC code
- Description of equipment
- Description of exempt sources
- Citations of all air requirements applicable to the source(s)
- Summary of annual emissions
- Description of compliance status of all source(s)
- Compliance statement
- Compliance certification (including a statement that all fees are paid) signed by a responsible official

Title V operating permits are effective for five years. Permit renewal applications must be submitted at least six months before permit expiration. Local air districts have the discretionary authority to require renewal applications up to 18 months before permit expiration. Facilities subject to Title V operating permits must submit reports of any required monitoring every six months, certified by the responsible official.

California Clean Air Act Programs

Prior to the enactment of the California CAA of 1988, a number of air districts in California exceeded the CAAQS and NAAQS. At that time, a 1987 deadline to attain NAAQS had come and gone. California enacted the California CAA

New facilities must submit an initial application for an operating permit within 12 months after the source becomes subject to Title V.

in response to the federal government's failure to enact tougher legislation to address non-attainment. The Act is intended to achieve and maintain the CAAQS, with an emphasis for non-attainment areas to achieve and maintain four CAAQS: ozone, CO, NO_X, and SO_2. Many of the strategies in the California CAA of 1988 were adopted two years later in the federal CAA Amendments of 1990.

The California CAA classifies non-attainment areas according to the time it would take to achieve attainment. The Act imposes stringent requirements for stationary sources and expands air district authority to manage mobile and indirect sources. The Act requires that an air district designated non-attainment (whether moderate, serious, severe, or extreme) must prepare and update a district attainment plan (DAP) to demonstrate how the district will attain and maintain the CAAQS by the earliest practicable date. HSC 40910–40926.

DAP = District attainment plan

District Attainment Plan

A DAP sets forth an air district's schedule for adopting rules to ensure attainment with CAAQS by specified dates.

A DAP sets forth an air district's schedule for adopting rules to ensure attainment with CAAQS by specified dates. Air districts implement their DAPs by promulgating new rules that could impact existing, unpermitted stationary sources, as well as by implementing transportation control for mobile sources (discussed later in this chapter).

Basic requirements. The California CAA requires that a DAP achieves a district-wide emissions reduction of five percent per year for each non-attainment pollutant (ozone, CO, NO_X, and SO_2) or its precursors, averaged every three years. The baseline year to measure reductions is 1987. An air district may use an alternative strategy that will achieve less than a five percent reduction of non-attainment pollutants if one of the following is true:

- The alternative is demonstrated to be equal to or more effective than the five percent per year reduction

- The district is unable to achieve the five percent reduction despite use of all feasible measures

In addition, a DAP must include a permitting program designed to achieve a no-net-increase in emissions of non-attainment pollutants or precursors from all permitted new or modified sources. HSC 40914.

Air districts must publish an annual report summarizing progress toward meeting schedules for developing, adopting, and implementing air quality control measures.

Air districts must publish an annual report summarizing progress toward meeting schedules for developing, adopting, and implementing air quality control measures. Triennially, air districts must assess the:

- Overall effectiveness of the air quality program

- Quantity of emissions reductions achieved in preceding three-year period

- Current and projected rates of population, industrial emissions, and vehicular emissions growth

- Validity of assumptions and progress toward goals in the DAP

Elimination of no-net-increase permitting requirements. AB 3319 (HSC 40918.5 *et seq.*) established a procedure for all air districts, except the South Coast Air Quality Management District (SCAQMD), to eliminate their no-net-increase permitting requirements within their DAPs. Although this legislation does not define "no net increase," it does state that air districts may not operate out of compliance with BACT.

SCAQMD = South Coast Air Quality Management District

An air district may petition the California ARB under this procedure if all of the following requirements are met:

- The air district makes an official finding (after a public hearing) that the no-net-increase program is not necessary to achieve ambient air quality standards
- The air district has considered possible emissions growth that would occur in the absence of the no-net-increase program
- The air district has scheduled for adoption all feasible measures to achieve ambient air quality standards

Upwind and downwind districts. Air districts responsible for or affected by emissions transported from one air basin to another must achieve attainment in both upwind and downwind air districts. The upwind districts must, at a minimum, adopt all mitigation measures established by the ARB. The downwind districts must have DAPs that contain sufficient measures to reduce local emissions below levels at which CAAQS violations occur in the absence of the transported emissions.

Non-attainment area requirements. California air districts experiencing non-attainment of the four criteria pollutants regulated by the California CAA are classified by the severity of non-attainment and must meet corresponding requirements. *See* Table 5-7. The requirements are additive—for example, an extreme non-attainment air district for a given pollutant must meet all moderate, serious, and severe requirements. Table 5-8 compares the California CAA and the federal CAA definition of a "major source" of ozone in non-attainment air districts.

District attainment plans manage mobile sources of air pollution, as well as stationary sources.

Market-based incentive programs. Air districts may adopt market-based incentive programs as part of their DAPs. A market-based incentive program for stationary sources can substitute for "command and control" regulations and future air quality measures, but must achieve an equivalent or greater reduction in emissions, at equivalent or less cost. HSC 39616(c).

Local Permitting for Criteria Pollutants

There are generally two types of air quality permits for criteria pollutants under California law—a permit to construct (known as an authority

Table 5-7. Non-attainment Area New Source Review Requirements

| | Non-attainment classification | | | |
	Moderate	Serious	Severe	Extreme
Major source definition for NSR	Potential to emit is 25 TPY	PTE is 15 TPY	PTE is 10 TPY	Local NSR can be triggered by any increase over one lb/day (in the South Coast Air Quality Management District and the San Joaquin Valley Air Pollution Control District)
Control requirements	Reasonably available control technology for existing sources Best available retrofit control technology for existing larger sources (5 tons per day or 250 tons per year)	All moderate non-attainment requirements BARCT for all existing sources	All serious and moderate non-attainment requirements	All severe, serious, and moderate non-attainment requirements NSR permitting program to incorporate no-net-increase requirements
Transportation requirements	Reasonably available transportation control measures for districts with urbanized populations exceeding 50,000 Includes indirect/area source control programs	Measures to achieve the use of a significant number of low-emission motor vehicles by operators of motor vehicle fleets	Measures to achieve average weekday commuter ridership of 1.5 persons by 1999 and no net vehicle emissions after 1997 for districts with populations exceeding 250,000	Any other feasible measures that can be implemented within 10 years after an air quality plan has been adopted
Deadline requirements	Failure to meet requirements by December 31, 1997, triggers serious requirements	Failure to meet requirements by December 31, 1997, triggers severe requirements	Exposure levels must be reduced by at least 50 percent by December 31, 2000	None

Source: HSC 40920 *et seq.*

BARCT = Best available retrofit control technology

to construct or ATC permit) and a permit to operate. These permits are required for a major new or modified source under the NSR permitting program (including non-attainment NSR and PSD). The criteria governing stationary source permitting, and substantive requirements for stationary sources, are detailed in local and regional air district rules and regulations. The definition of stationary source varies depending on the type of air quality permitting program and the local jurisdiction.

Authority to construct. A stationary source, unless exempt, requires an air quality permit before a device or piece of equipment is installed, constructed, or operated. ATC permits and PTOs typically are issued using the same permit application form, which must include detailed information describing the proposed equipment, along with anticipated materials, fuels, and operations. The ATC permit application process is intended to ensure that district requirements are considered before constructing or installing a stationary source, and to allow the applicant to make design changes in the early planning stages. HSC 42301.

Table 5-8. Definition of a "Major Source" of Ozone in Non-attainment Air Districts		
Non-attainment classification	California Clean Air Act definition (PTE in tons per year)	Federal Clean Air Act definition (PTE in tons per year)
Marginal	--	100
Moderate	25	100
Serious	15	50
Severe	10	25
Extreme	0	10

Source: HSC 40910 *et seq.* and 42 USC 7401 *et seq.*

The applicant is responsible for demonstrating compliance with the air district's substantive and procedural requirements.

Each air district describes categories of operations and activities exempt from the ATC permit requirement. Exemptions vary from district to district. Owners of facilities claiming a permit exemption should consider drafting an internal memorandum describing the basis for reliance on the exemption.

ATC permits (as well as PTOs) may be subject to environmental review under the California Environmental Quality Act. *See* chapter 2. Local air districts may serve as either a CEQA lead agency or a CEQA responsible agency. Some air districts have agency-specific CEQA procedures. Many districts in urban areas have adopted air quality thresholds of significance for determining whether an EIR is required, and have established standard mitigation measures to reduce air quality impacts.

EIR = Environmental impact report

Permit to operate. After the district permitting engineer issues an ATC permit and the stationary source has been installed or constructed, air district staff will inspect the stationary source to verify that the equipment meets the performance standards specified in the ATC permit. The air district then will issue a permit to operate, subject to payment of operating fees. The PTO may require the owner or operator to follow one or more operating conditions (*e.g.*, specifying use of a certain fuel type, hours of operation, or use of an abatement device). Depending on the air district, PTOs are valid for one or two years and may be renewed simply by paying renewal fees.

The permit must incorporate conditions that govern specified emission limitations, fuels usage, control devices, and more. Typically, these conditions are identified through the CEQA process, as well as the NSR and air toxics permitting programs.

Air districts issue standardized permits for identical or similar air emission sources that require the same or similar information for monitoring and permit conditions. Typically, air districts maintain a list of pre-certified equipment subject

Air districts issue standardized permits for identical or similar air emission sources that require the same or similar information for monitoring and permit conditions.

to expedited permitting, such as portable internal combustion units, which require registration instead of a permit. HSC 42320 *et seq.*

A single facility may include several types of equipment that generate criteria pollutants and air toxics. As a result, a facility may have a number of source-specific air quality requirements. For example, typical large facilities that may require several PTOs include bulk petroleum operations, refineries, large-scale manufacturing, and power plants. Typical small businesses that may require only one PTO include dry cleaners, auto body shops, and printers.

Local New
Source Review

Federal non-attainment NSR programs and federal PSD programs are typically incorporated into local NSR programs; however, the emissions thresholds that require application of local BACT or offsets are considerably lower than the federal standards.

Federal versus local programs. Federal non-attainment NSR programs and federal PSD programs are typically incorporated into local NSR programs; however, the emissions thresholds that require application of local BACT (equivalent to federal LAER) or offsets are considerably lower than the federal standards. As a result, a source with emissions too small to be a major source under the federal non-attainment NSR may be subject to the local NSR program. EPA refers to the local NSR programs in California as the minor or state NSR programs. The requirements of the California CAA non-attainment NSR program are also incorporated into local rules by air districts.

Local emission control requirements. Local emission control requirements vary among air districts. Typically, the local non-attainment NSR programs apply to sources of air emissions that are subject to ATC permit and PTO requirements, and that exceed specified emission thresholds that trigger the need to comply with emissions control (*e.g.*, local BACT) and offsets. It is important to note that the California definition for BACT is the same as LAER under the federal non-attainment NSR program.

Local emission offset requirements. Local emission offset requirements (like local emission control requirements) vary among air districts. Some air districts allow emissions banking, as described above for federal offsets. Local air district banking rules include administrative procedures that certify offsets. Typically, the rules include an application procedure and also specify which types of emissions do not qualify as offsets.

Local District Rules

Structure of local air district rules. Although local air district rules vary from district to district, each rule typically follows the structure shown in Table 5-9.

Local air districts establish RACT to address specified stationary sources that may not require permits.

Local prohibitory rules. Local air districts establish RACT to address specified stationary sources that may not require permits. These rules, known as prohibitory rules, regulate inorganic and organic sources of emissions. Typical air district prohibitory rules regulate open burning, nuisance emissions, particulate matter emissions, organic pollutant emissions, inorganic gaseous pollutants, and hazardous air pollutants.

Open burning. The ARB has special programs regulating agricultural burning (HSC 41580 *et seq*.) and nonagricultural burning (HSC 41800 *et seq*.). ARB establishes guidelines for agricultural burning control in air basins and determines days on which agricultural burning is prohibited.

Nuisance emissions. Industrial facilities in full compliance with federal, state, and local permits and requirements may still be in violation of California's nuisance rule. California sets forth a "catchall" nuisance prohibition (HSC 41700) that is often used as a tool by the public to further control air emissions. For example, a paint manufacturer in full compliance with its PTO could be required to install additional controls to manage the olfactory emissions. Local air districts typically promulgate nuisance provisions similar or identical to the state nuisance rule, which reads:

> [N]o person shall discharge from any source whatsoever such quantities of air contaminants or other material which cause injury, detriment, nuisance, or annoyance to any considerable number of persons or to the public, or which endanger the comfort, repose, health, or safety of any such persons or the public, or which cause, or have a natural tendency to cause, injury or damage to business or property.

Visible emissions. California has regulatory programs for visible emissions. HSC 41701. Local air districts typically adopt California regulations into local air district rules. For example, local air district rules typically state that a person may not emit any air pollutant into the atmosphere for more than three minutes during any one hour if the emissions are dark or darker in shade or opacity as designated by No. 2 on the Ringelmann Chart, as published by the United States Bureau of Mines. HSC 41701(a).

Stratospheric Ozone Protection

Title VI of the 1990 federal CAA Amendments (42 USC 7661 *et seq*.) was designed to implement the Montreal Protocol, which is an international treaty directing the phase-out of substances that deplete the ozone layer. These substances (known as ozone-depleting chemicals) include well-known

Table 5-9. Typical Structure of a Local Air District Rule

Section	Content
General Provisions	Scope and applicability, including rule-specific exemptions
Definitions	Definitions specific to the particular rule; the same term defined in a particular rule may be defined differently in another rule
Substantive Standards	Permitting (authority to construct permits, permits to operate, and exemptions)
	Non-attainment new source review
	Prevention of significant deterioration
	New source performance standards (federally delegated)
	Operating permit program (federally delegated)
	Air toxics
	Prohibitory rules (equivalent to federal reasonably available control technology)
Administrative Procedures	Application procedures, timeframes, methodologies, and other administrative requirements
Monitoring and Recordkeeping	Type and frequency of monitoring and recordkeeping
Manual of Procedures	Permitting procedures and policies, CEQA review, sample and source testing, monitoring emissions, and emission credits for mobile sources

Title VI of the 1990 federal CAA Amendments was designed to implement the Montreal Protocol, an international treaty directing the phase-out of substances that deplete the ozone layer.

refrigerants such as freons, chlorofluorocarbons (CFCs), and other halogenated compounds that aggressively react with ozone molecules in the upper stratosphere (approximately seven miles above the ground).

The program prohibits the production (with some exceptions) of carbon tetrachloride, methyl chloroform, and Class I substances (that include CFCs and halons). Production of Class II chemicals (that consist of 33 hydrochlorofluorocarbons or HCFCs) must be frozen at baseline year levels (1993) beginning January 1, 2015. After January 1, 2015, Class II substances cannot be introduced into interstate commerce unless one of the following is true:

- The substance has been used, recovered, or recycled
- The substance is used and entirely consumed in the production of other chemicals
- The substance is used as a refrigerant in an appliance manufactured before January 1, 2020

By January 1, 2030, there will be a ban on production of Class II substances.

The 1990 federal CAA Amendments (42 USC 7401 *et seq.*) authorize the trading or production and consumption allowances between two or more persons under specified circumstances. Also, standards exist for the use and disposal of Class I and II substances during the service, repair, or disposal of industrial process refrigeration. 42 USC 7671g(b).

Greenhouse Gases

Federal Program

In Massachusetts v. EPA (2007) 549 U.S. 1438, the U.S. Supreme Court ruled that EPA does have authority to set GHG emission standards for motor vehicles.

Prior to 2007, it was unclear whether the EPA possessed authority under the CAA to regulate GHG emissions. In *Massachusetts v. EPA* (2007) 549 U.S. 1438, the U.S. Supreme Court ruled that EPA does have authority to set GHG emission standards for motor vehicles. However, as of Spring 2008, neither Congress nor EPA had established a comprehensive strategy for managing the emissions.

State Program

The California Global Warming Solutions Act of 2006 is a pioneering state program creating a framework comprehensively limiting GHG emissions.

California's climate change programs are established both by Executive Order S-03-05 adopted prior to AB 32, and by AB 32. The California Global Warming Solutions Act of 2006 (AB 32, HSC 38500 *et seq.*) is a pioneering state program creating a framework comprehensively limiting GHG emissions. The provisions of the Act are expected to achieve a 25 percent reduction in GHG emissions in 2020, compared to 2006 levels. The Act and its forthcoming regulations are expected to regulate utilities and a wide variety of other private and public sources of GHG emissions, including refineries, cement kilns, landfills, and agriculture. The Act defines GHGs as carbon dioxide, methane, nitrous oxide, hydrofluorocarbons, perfluorocarbons, and sulfur hexafluoride. It limits GHG emissions expressed in tons of "carbon dioxide equivalent;" the impact of other greenhouse gas is converted to the equivalent heat-trapping impact of carbon dioxide. HSC 38505(c), (g).

Emissions Reporting

Under the Act, entities that voluntarily participated in the emissions reporting program of the California Climate Action Registry by December 31, 2006 will not be required to "significantly alter" their program when the ARB adopts new requirements. (The Registry is a nonprofit public/private partnership that serves as a voluntary GHG registry to promote early efforts to reduce GHG emissions.) Also, these participants will receive "early action" credit after specific emission reduction regulations are implemented. HSC 38530 *et seq.*

In late 2007, ARB adopted regulations for reporting and verifying GHG emissions. HSC 95100 *et seq.* Industrial facilities emitting 25,000 metric tons or more of CO_2 annually from stationary combustion, along with power generation and cogeneration facilities, will be required to monitor and report their GHG emissions by April 1 each year. The Act requires ARB to incorporate the Registry's standards and protocols to the maximum extent possible. HSC 38530 *et seq.*

CO_2 = Carbon dioxide

Emissions Limitations

The Act required ARB to determine California's statewide GHG emission level in 1990, and to approve that level as the statewide limit to be achieved by 2020; ARB approved the 1990 emissions level and 2020 emissions limits in late 2007. Executive Order S-03-05 sets additional GHG emission reductions targets of 2000 levels by 2010, and 80 percent below 1990 levels by 2050.

For individual sources, the Act required ARB to publish a list of "early action" GHG emission reduction measures that can be implemented within three years. These include development of a low carbon fuel standard designed to reduce the GHG intensity of transportation fuels 10 percent by 2020; a ban on auto air conditioning recharge kits with HFC-134a; and additional controls on landfill GHG emissions (ARB 2007. Expanded List of Early Action Measures). Formal, enforceable regulations adopting the early action measures must be adopted by January 1, 2010. HSC 38550 *et seq.*, 38560, 38560.5.

State Scoping Plan

The Act requires ARB to develop a scoping plan by January 1, 2009. The plan must achieve the maximum technologically feasible and cost-effective reductions in GHG emissions from specific sources by 2020. To develop the plan, ARB must consult with agencies having authority over GHG emissions, hold public workshops, and consider costs and benefits of proposed programs. Also, ARB must convene two committees–an Environmental Justice Advisory Committee and an Economic and Technology Advancement Advisory Committee–to assist in plan development and implementation. HSC 38561.

After the plan is published, the Act requires ARB to implement the emissions reduction measures identified in the plan through regulations adopted by January 1, 2011–the regulations become effective one year later. The governor is allowed to suspend emission reduction measures for one year in the event of "extraordinary circumstances, catastrophic events or the threat of extreme economic disruption." HSC 38562.

Market-Based Mechanisms

The Act allows the 2011 regulations to include market-based compliance mechanisms, such as a cap-and-trade-program, to achieve required levels of emission reduction.

The Act allows the 2011 regulations to include market-based compliance mechanisms, such as a cap-and-trade-program, to achieve required levels of emission reduction. Any market-based program proposed in the regulations must not increase emissions of criteria air pollutants, and must consider localized and cumulative impacts of emissions. HSC 38570.

In 2006, Governor Schwarzenegger issued a controversial Executive Order (S-20-06) that advances the schedule for implementing market-based mechanisms ahead of the AB 32 timetable established in the Act, without detailed standards governing the public process. The EO required the Cal/EPA Secretary to convene a "Market Advisory Committee" comprised of national and international experts to make program recommendations. Executive Order S-20-06 establishes a goal to create a market-based program that will allow trading, not only among California companies, but also with the European Union and with nine northeastern states participating in a regional initiative.

Acid Rain

Federal Program

The goal of the federal acid rain program is to reduce emissions of the two primary causes of acid rain: sulfur dioxide (SO_2) and nitrogen oxides (NO_X). Authorized by Title IV of the 1990 federal CAA Amendments (42 USC 7651 *et seq.*), the federal program reduces SO_2 and NO_X emissions in a number of ways.

First, the CAA Amendments established an SO_2 allowance trading program primarily affecting large coal-fired power plants. Under Phase I of this program, EPA issued SO_2 allowances to mostly coal-burning electric utility plants for each ton of SO_2 emitted. Allowances are transferable, allowing a utility to buy, sell, or bank its allowances as necessary. At the end of the year, the utility must have enough allowances to cover its SO_2 emissions. However, if the utility comes up short, the source will be deemed non-compliant and subject to monetary penalties. 42 USC 7651e. Phase II of this allowance trading program began in 2000. Phase II applies to all fossil-fuel-fired utility plants and implements a permanent, collective cap of 8.95 million tons per year.

Second, in addition to limiting SO_2 emissions, the CAA Amendments also established a NO_X reduction program, with the goal of reducing annual NO_X

emissions by two million tons from 1980 levels. Unlike the SO_2 program, the NO_X program focuses on emission rates rather than allowances and emission ceilings. Utility boilers may opt into the NO_X program by complying with individual emission rates or by using emission averaging, whereby utilities may average emission rates over two or more unit sources.

State Program

The state has established a program to control acid rain, called the Atmospheric Acidity Protection Act of 1988 (HSC 39900 *et seq.*). The program compiles data about the impact of acid rain on public health and on aquatic and terrestrial ecosystems to assess California's current and future air pollution control measures.

The state has established a program to control acid rain, called the Atmospheric Acidity Protection Act of 1988.

Air Toxics

Federal Program

National Emission Standards for Hazardous Air Pollutants Program. Historically, Congress and EPA emphasized control of the six federal criteria pollutants. These high volume pollutants, emitted largely from sources involving combustion, were better understood than air toxics at the time of the 1970 CAA and its major amendments in 1977.

Prior to the enactment of the 1990 federal CAA Amendments, the EPA regulated only eight hazardous air pollutants pursuant to the National Emission Standards for Hazardous Air Pollutants program. Title III of the 1990 federal CAA Amendments dramatically expanded EPA's authority to regulate routine HAP emissions and accidental releases. Congress greatly increased the number of HAPs subject to regulation to include 189 chemicals or chemical compounds. The current list includes only 188 chemicals or chemical compounds because mercapton was since removed.

Prior to the enactment of the 1990 federal CAA Amendments, the EPA regulated only eight hazardous air pollutants pursuant to the National Emission Standards for Hazardous Air Pollutants program.

Program applicability. The NESHAP program regulates two types of stationary sources of HAPs–major sources and area sources. A major source is defined as an industrial facility or contiguous group of stationary sources under common control with a PTE of 10 TPY or more of any single HAP or 25 TPY of any combination of HAPs. Major sources of HAPS must comply with the maximum achievable control technology (MACT) standards. Area sources (sources too small to qualify as major sources) must comply with generally achievable control technology (GACT).

GACT = Generally available control technology

MACT = Maximum achievable control technology

Maximum achievable control technology. Unlike NSR programs that are premised on meeting and attaining the NAAQS, the NESHAP program does not establish ambient air quality standards for HAPs. Instead, the program requires major new or modified major sources of HAPs to comply with maximum achievable control technology. As of 2006, EPA regulations established industry-specific MACT standards for 85 industrial categories. The NESHAP program allows

EPA to later promulgate more stringent MACT for individual industrial categories that, based on health risk assessment, warrant increased control. 40 CFR 63.

MACT represents technology-based standards that require the maximum degree of emissions reduction of HAPs that EPA, after considering costs and other environmental impacts, determines is achievable. 42 USC 7412(d). MACT standards are more stringent for new sources compared to existing sources within a given industrial category. For new stationary sources, MACT is as stringent as the control achieved in practice by the best controlled similar sources; for existing sources, MACT is the average emissions reduction of the top 12 percent of sources or the top five similar sources.

MACT standards include control equipment, process changes, material substitutions, work practices, operator trainings and certifications, and more. Some MACT standards control fugitive emissions (*e.g.*, emissions from flanges, pumps, seals, valves, and compressors), while others capture and treat emissions.

MACT is required for major new sources of HAPs or modifications to existing major sources that exceed de minimis thresholds of HAPs. As a practical matter, MACT typically reduces emissions of air toxics by about 95–99 percent. MACT is not required for new or modified sources that fully offset their net emission increases of HAPs below these major threshold amounts. Four major provisions govern the schedule for MACT implementation (42 USC 7412(i)):

- New sources must comply with standards when beginning operations that emit HAPs.

- Sources constructed or reconstructed after issuance of draft MACT rules, but before final MACT rules, may comply with the draft rules if the final rules are more stringent.

- After MACT rules are finalized, existing sources must comply no more than three years after the rule is finalized.

- A qualifying facility may be granted compliance deferment under the Early Reductions Program if the facility reduces its HAP emissions by 90 percent before MACT standards are proposed.

Area sources. Generally available control technology is required for area sources. The aggregate emissions of area sources account for 90 percent of HAP emissions that pose the greatest public health risk in the majority of urban areas. In 1999, the EPA created the Urban Air Toxics Strategy to establish and prioritize the unequal risks that HAPs in urban areas have on the public health and the environment. The strategy establishes GACT standards for dry cleaners, gas stations, municipal landfills, and paint stripping operations, to name a few.

Accidental release program. The 1990 federal CAA Amendments (section 112(r)) also establishes a program to prevent the accidental release of "highly hazardous chemicals" such as anhydrous ammonia and chlorine. 42 USC 7412. Facilities that manufacture, process, use, store, or handle highly hazardous chemicals exceeding threshold quantities of flammable and toxic compounds must complete hazard assessments and, in some cases, risk management plans (RMPs). These regulations apply to, among other facilities, cold storage facilities (using ammonia as a refrigerant), public drinking water systems (using chlorine gas), manufacturers, propane retailers, some wholesalers, and some service industries. RMPs may require inclusion of (40 CFR 68 *et seq.*):

- A hazard assessment, including a modeled off-site consequence analysis
- A prevention plan, including a description of the management system used to manage the risk posed by the hazard assessment
- An emergency response plan

The RMP program consists of three program tiers. Program 1 consists of an abbreviated RMP. Program 2 applies if the facility is not subject to Program 1 or 3. Finally, Program 3 requires developing and implementing an RMP with the complete set of RMP program features. Program 3 RMPs apply to processes in specific industrial facilities such as pulp mills, petroleum refineries, and petrochemical manufacturing. Program 3 RMPS are similar to a federal worker safety program that manages potential, catastrophic chemical releases in the workplace (under the OSHA process safety management (PSM) standard). 29 CFR 1910.119.

ATCM	= Airborne toxic control measure
OEHHA	= Office of Environmental Health Hazard Assessment
PSM	= Process safety management
RMP	= Risk management plan

State Program

Toxic air contaminants. Prior to the 1990 federal CAA Amendments, which significantly revamped the original NESHAP program, California already had established a rigorous air toxics program (HSC 39650 *et seq.*), often referred to as AB 1807. This program requires the Office of Environmental Health Hazard Assessment (OEHHA) to study, on an ongoing basis, the health effects of potentially harmful chemicals.

After extensive review, OEHHA is authorized to identify toxic air contaminants. Once a TAC is identified or "listed," the ARB has authority to control the TAC using airborne toxic control measures (ATCMs), which control emissions to the lowest achievable level. If it is possible to measure a specified TAC threshold level, the ATCM is designed to reduce emissions at or below that threshold. Local air districts implement ATCMs through promulgation of rules.

The ARB has identified approximately 20 TACs and promulgated ATCMs for many of these chemicals. Perhaps the most common ATCM is the Phase II vapor recovery used at retail gasoline stations to control benzene (a TAC) emissions during fueling operations. The 188 HAPs are California TACs (HSC 39650 *et seq.*), so the ARB can impose ATCMs for federal HAPs. There are now more than 200 TACs.

Toxic hot spots. The California Air Toxic "Hot Spots" Information and Assessment Act (HSC 44300 *et seq.*) is a unique procedural and substantive law designed to identify hot spots of exposure and risk and, in some cases, control them. The program applies to facilities that manufacture, formulate, use, or release one or more regulated toxic substances and emit or have the potential to emit specified amounts of the following criteria pollutants: toxic organic gases (*e.g.*, VOCs including methane), PM, NO_X, and SO_X. Emission inventory submittal dates vary for facilities emitting or having the potential to emit over 25 TPY, between 10–25 TPY, and less than 10 TPY. Appendix E of ARB's "Emission Inventory Criteria and Guidelines Report" lists classes of facilities emitting less than 10 TPY of criteria pollutants (such as wastewater treatment facilities) that are subject to the Act's requirements. In some cases, facilities are subject to the Act because they historically appeared on local air district air toxics inventories.

Regulated facilities must inventory their routine air toxic emissions every four years. In some instances, air toxics emissions must be quantified, while in other cases only reporting of the production or other presence of chemicals is required. The air emissions inventory data must be submitted to the local air district with jurisdiction over the facility. The air district performs an assessment of the air toxics emissions inventory and determines whether the facility poses a potentially "high" health risk to the surrounding community. HSC 44360 *et seq.*

Those facilities deemed to be a high risk are required to perform a health risk assessment. If the assessment concludes that the facility poses a significant health risk, the facility must notify exposed persons of this risk. As a practical matter, shortly after the Act became effective, some businesses substituted regulated toxic substances to avoid the need to perform the risk assessments that could require notification of neighbors of a significant health exposure.

Additionally, facilities that pose a significant risk must adopt an airborne risk reduction program within six months of the risk assessment. The airborne risk reduction program must reduce risks below the significance threshold discussed in the health risk assessment within five years. If risk reduction measures are technically feasible and economically practicable, the five-year timetable can be shortened. HSC 44390 *et seq.*

CalARP = California Accidental Release Prevention Program

California Accidental Release Prevention Program. The California Accidental Release Prevention Program (CalARP, 19 CCR 2735 *et seq.*) is administered by the Governor's Office of Emergency Services. The goal of the program is to reduce and eliminate the accidental release of potentially harmful substances into the environment. The CalARP implements the federal Risk Management Program. However, compared with the RMP, CalARP has additional requirements under the California Health and Safety Code, such as a more inclusive list of toxic chemicals, smaller chemical threshold quantities, performance of external event analysis (such as seismic analysis), and development of a risk management plan. California's legislative intent was that compliance by a regulated business or agency with CalARP would satisfy requirements of the federal accidental release prevention program. HSC Chapter 6.95, Article 2.

Air emissions from solid waste disposal sites. California legislation requires air quality and water quality testing at solid waste disposal sites (at active sites and, in some cases, inactive sites), as well as the reporting of results. HSC 41805(a). The ARB has issued guidelines for this testing program. HSC 41805.5.

Transportation Controls

The California CAA requires air districts to implement transportation control measures to attain SIP requirements. HSC 40716 *et seq.* Transportation control measures are strategies to reduce vehicle trips, vehicle use, and vehicle miles traveled, such as employee trip reduction programs. For example, under the federal CAA, states such as California must require employers of 100 or more persons located in severe and extreme ozone non-attainment areas to increase average vehicle ridership by at least 25 percent by certain dates.

Transportation control measures are strategies to reduce vehicle trips, vehicle use, and vehicle miles traveled.

Recognizing that transportation control measures can be controversial, the Legislature has established detailed conditions that must be met before an air district may impose a trip reduction program to assure the requirement is legally necessary, is not duplicative, is feasible, and is cost-effective. HSC 40717.5, 40919. Air districts generally may not impose transportation control measures that reduce shopping trips, or on event centers such as sports arenas that meet certain average vehicle ridership. The Legislature has enacted specific restrictions on the ability of the South Coast AQMD to impose employee trip reduction programs. HSC 40454 *et seq.*

Transportation Conformity Process

Regional planning agencies or Caltrans, and ultimately the U.S. Department of Transportation (DOT), are required to show that transportation plans and projects conform to the SIP. 40 CFR 93.105. The process is designed to assure that new transportation investments do not create a new air quality violation, increase the frequency or severity of an existing air quality violation, or delay timely attainment of NAAQS. The conformity requirement applies to regional transportation plans, the state transportation improvement plan (TIP), and transportation projects funded or approved by DOT.

DOT = U.S. Department of Transportation
TIP = Transportation improvement plan

To show SIP conformity, the estimated emissions produced by transportation activities may not exceed the SIP motor vehicle emissions budget. Project-level, hot-spot analysis also is required for carbon monoxide and particulates.

Air Quality Benefits from Land Use Activities

Many California communities and development projects are implementing the principles of smart growth, intending to create pedestrian and transit-friendly development that reduces vehicle-miles traveled. *See* chapter 3. Air quality reductions derived from these land use activities can be accounted for in one of three ways (EPA 2001):

- The reductions can be included in the initial forecast of future emissions in the SIP
- The reductions can be included as control strategies in the SIP
- The reductions can be included in a conformity determination without inclusion in the SIP

Land use strategies that provide air quality benefits include the following:

- Transit-oriented development
- Neotraditional pedestrian-oriented development
- Infill development
- Brownfield redevelopment
- Mixed-use development
- Concentrated high-density activity centers
- Strengthened downtowns
- Improved jobs–housing balance

Mobile Source Regulation

The federal CAA establishes control strategies for motor vehicle fuel additives and motor vehicle emissions. ARB is primarily responsible for statewide programs and strategies to reduce the emission of smog-forming pollutants and air toxics by mobile sources and, in many cases, has created more stringent mandatory or voluntary control strategies. Mobile sources include both on- and off-road sources such as passenger cars, motorcycles, trucks, buses, heavy-duty construction equipment, recreational vehicles, marine vessels, lawn and garden equipment, and small utility engines.

Vehicle fuels. ARB was required, no later than January 1, 1992, to take whatever actions were necessary, cost-effective, and technologically feasible to achieve by December 31, 2000 an emissions reduction of (HSC 43018(b)):

- Reactive organic gases of at least 55 percent
- NO_X from motor vehicles of at least 15 percent
- Particulate matter, CO, and TACs from vehicular sources, to the maximum feasible extent

Federal and state laws regulate motor vehicle fuels and tailpipe emissions.

MTBE = Methyl tertiary butyl ether

ARB's fuels effort is made up of several components that broadly fall into two categories: adopting and enforcing fuel specifications, and controlling emissions from marketing and distributing fuels in California.

Beginning in 1992, California required clean-burning, reformulated gasoline to be sold in the state, to reduce emissions of VOCs and toxics. Also in 1992, California prohibited lead as a gasoline additive; MTBE then became a widely used additive in California's reformulated gasoline. However, in the late

1990s, the Legislature became concerned that MTBE was appearing in drinking water, surface water, and groundwater. In 1999, Governor Davis issued an Executive Order (D-5-99) requiring that MTBE be phased out as a gasoline additive.

ARB also regulates specifications for diesel fuel to make it cleaner burning, and has implemented an alternative diesel fuels program. In addition, in response primarily to diesel-particulate concerns, 2003 legislation (HSC 40720 *et seq.*) required each marine terminal in the state to reduce truck idling during loading and unloading to no more than 30 minutes.

Pursuant to the California AB 1807 air toxics program (HSC 39666), local air districts regulate emissions from the distribution of gasoline. Service station vapor recovery nozzles have been required in California since the late 1970s. Vapor recovery systems also are required for cargo tanks used to haul gasoline.

Low carbon fuel standard. The LCFS program was created by Executive Order S-01-07, which sets a target of reducing the carbon intensity of California's transportation fuels by a least 10 percent by 2020. (Carbon intensity is GHG emissions per unit of motive power.) In addition to setting the 2020 target, the EO instructed Cal/EPA to coordinate activities among the University of California, the California Energy Commission, and other state agencies to develop and propose a draft compliance schedule to meet the 2020 target. It also directed ARB to consider initiating regulatory proceedings to establish and implement the LCFS.

In response, ARB identified the LCFS as an AB 32 early action item, with a regulation to be adopted and implemented by 2010. ARB 2007. The LCFS will be measured on a lifecycle basis to capture all emissions from upstream processes as well as fuel consumption. Low carbon fuels include biofuels such as ethanol and biodiesel, as well as hydrogen, electricity, compressed natural gas, liquefied petroleum gas, and biogas.

Emissions standards and the clean fuels vehicle program. The CAA regulates tailpipe emissions by requiring motor vehicle manufacturers to achieve certain reductions in exhaust emissions, and California has a parallel and in many cases more stringent program. EPA has established emissions standards for NO_X, CO, hydrocarbons, particulates, diesel smoke, and formaldehyde.

The CAA regulates tailpipe emissions by requiring motor vehicle manufacturers to achieve certain reductions in exhaust emissions, and California has a parallel and in many cases more stringent program.

Although Section 209 of the CAA preempts the authority of states to regulate emissions from new motor vehicles, the CAA allows EPA waivers from preemption for specific standards enacted by California. For example, ARB has adopted separate low emission vehicle (LEV) emissions standards, and requirements for manufacturers to sell a certain percentage of zero emission vehicles (ZEVs); ARB proposed major revisions to the ZEV program in early 2008.

LEV = Low emissions vehicle
ZEV = Zero emissions vehicle

In the absence of such an EPA waiver, state emissions standards can be preempted. For example, in *Engine Manufacturers Assn. v. South Coast AQMD* (2004) 124 S. Ct. 1756, the U.S. Supreme Court held that SCAQMD regulations controlling emissions from vehicle fleets were at least partially preempted by federal law.

Only new motor vehicles covered by an EPA certification of conformity may be sold or distributed in the U.S.

Only new motor vehicles covered by an EPA certification of conformity may be sold or distributed in the U.S. EPA enforces the emissions standards through durability testing at the time of certification, confirmatory testing, emission control system warrant and recall, and tampering provisions. The state emissions standards cover all these topics, require state certification of new motor vehicles, and include an inspection (smog check) program. The CAA also created a clean fuels vehicle program. A pilot project required that 300,000 clean fuel vehicles be sold in California annually beginning in 1999; however, many more than the stipulated 300,000 clean fuel vehicles were sold. Clean fuel vehicles include those that use electric, hybrid electric, alternative fuel, fuel cell, or "cleanest gas" technology.

Assembly Bill 1493 of 2002 required California to establish new standards for motor vehicle GHG emissions beginning in the model year 2009.

Motor vehicle GHG emissions standards. Assembly Bill 1493 of 2002 required California to establish new standards for motor vehicle GHG emissions beginning in the model year 2009. HSC 42823, 43018.5. AB 1493 mandates a 30 percent reduction in motor vehicle GHG emissions by 2016. ARB adopted implementing regulations in 2005. 13 CCR 1900, 1961, 1961.1. In December 2005, ARB requested from EPA a waiver of federal preemption to implement the GHG emissions standards. As of November 2007, EPA had not responded to the waiver request, so California filed a lawsuit in the U.S. District Court for the District of Columbia to force EPA to respond.

In December 2007, the President signed into law the Energy Independence and Security Act of 2007 (EISA, PL 110-140). EISA sets a target of 35 miles per gallon for the combined fleet of cars and light trucks by 2020; however, California's GHG emissions standards would achieve higher standards sooner. Shortly thereafter, the EPA Administrator denied California's waiver request, in part because EPA believed that the EISA mileage standards preempted the California mileage standards. In January 2008, California filed a petition with the Ninth Circuit Court of Appeals challenging EPA's denial.

A separate set of legal proceedings has upheld California's GHG emissions standards from an automobile industry challenge that the standards are preempted by federal fuel economy law.

A separate set of legal proceedings has upheld California's GHG emissions standards from an automobile industry challenge that the standards are preempted by federal fuel economy law. In December 2007, California's authority to regulate GHG emissions from motor vehicles was upheld in *Central Valley Chrysler Jeep, Inc. v. Goldstone* (2007) 529 F. Supp. 2d 1151. The case is similar to a September 2007 case ruling that Vermont's adoption of the California GHG emissions standards was not preempted by federal fuel economy law (*Green Mountain Chrysler Plymouth et al. v. Crombie,* 508 F. Supp. 2d 295). These cases were influenced by the Supreme Court's landmark ruling in *Massachusetts v. EPA* (2007) 549 US 1438, in which the Court confirmed that EPA has authority under the Clean Air Act to issue GHG emission regulations more stringent than the Department of Transportation's fuel economy standards. However, a year after the decision, EPA had not determined whether to regulate GHGs under the CAA; the California Attorney General, joined by 17 other states and several environmental groups, filed suit in the District of Columbia Court of Appeals in April 2008, asking the court to order EPA to release its determination within 60 days.

Enforcement

Federal Enforcement

EPA has concurrent authority, with the states, to enforce CAA permit conditions and SIP provisions. Citizen suits can be filed to force EPA or the states to enforce clean air laws, and citizen suits also can be filed against violating sources. Enforcement options include abatement orders, civil penalties, and criminal penalties. EPA can seek a monetary fine (up to $25,000 per day per violation) or an injunction against a non-complying source. EPA is alternatively authorized to pursue an administrative action without going through the Department of Justice and a trial court. CAA Section 113(d), 42 USC 7413(d).

EPA has concurrent authority, with the states, to enforce CAA permit conditions and SIP provisions.

A Field Citation Program allows EPA to impose monetary fines of up to $5,000 per day per violation for minor violations. Alleged violators under this program can pay the fine or request an informal, administrative hearing at a place "reasonably close" to the place of business receiving the citation. 42 USC 7413(d)(B)(3). The field citation program streamlines EPA's ability to enforce noncompliance enforcement without having to bring every violation to court.

Civil penalties. The maximum total civil penalty for violations under the CAA is $200,000 unless the EPA administrator and U.S. Attorney General agree that this amount is insufficient. 42 USC 7413(d). EPA may place a violating company on a list of those ineligible for federal contracts.

The maximum total civil penalty for violations under the CAA is $200,000 unless the EPA administrator and U.S. Attorney General agree that this amount is insufficient.

Citizen suits may seek civil penalties against the EPA or a private party for violating the CAA. 42 USC 7604(a). Also, EPA may pay $10,000 for information that leads to a criminal conviction or judicial, administrative, or civil penalty. Financial penalties from successful damage awards may be earmarked for air quality compliance activities or mitigation projects. The self-reporting obligations under the federal Title V CAM rule make compliance data available to the public, which increases the potential for EPA enforcement and citizen suits.

Criminal penalties. Felony-level sanctions or imprisonment of up to five years are authorized for individuals committing a first-time offense. Knowingly releasing any listed hazardous pollutant or substance, with knowledge that the release places another person in imminent danger, is punishable by a fine and/or imprisonment of no more than 15 years. Any organization that knowingly commits a violation under the CAA is subject to criminal fines of up to $1 million, plus imprisonment of up to 15 years. 42 USC 7413(5)(A)(c). Penalties are determined based on business size, economic impact of the penalty, compliance history, violation duration, good faith efforts to comply, payment of penalties previously assessed for the same violation, economic benefit of noncompliance, and violation

Knowingly releasing any listed hazardous pollutant or substance, with knowledge that the release places another person in imminent danger, is punishable by a fine and/or imprisonment of no more than 15 years.

seriousness. A person can be imprisoned for up to two years for knowingly committing any of these reporting and monitoring violations:

- Omission of material information
- Destruction, alteration, concealment, or failure to maintain documents necessary for compliance
- Failure to install, or tampering with, monitoring devices

State Enforcement

California law establishes an enforcement program that includes administrative, civil, and criminal penalties, as well as injunctive relief. The California CAA does not allow citizen suits. Civil penalties can be brought against violators who engage in negligent, willful, or intentional acts. The more willful the violation, the higher the potential civil penalty.

Civil penalties. The negligent emission of an air contaminant can result in a fine of up to $25,000; if great bodily injury or death occurs, the fine can be up to $100,000. Each day of a violation is a separate offense. HSC 42402.1. The willful and intentional emission of an air contaminant can result in a fine of up to $75,000; if an unreasonable risk of great bodily injury or death occurs, the fine can be up to $125,000, and if great bodily injury or death occurs, the fine can be up to $250,000. Corporations are subject to different fines. HSC 42402.3. An air district may impose an administrative civil penalty of up to $500 per violation. HSC 42402.5. An administrative penalty cannot exceed the amount of a civil penalty or $10,000 per day of violation or a maximum of $100,000 per penalty. HSC 42410(a).

Criminal penalties. The filing of a criminal complaint requires the dismissal of any earlier civil action brought for the same offense. If civil penalties are recovered for the same offense, criminal prosecution is precluded. HSC 42400.4(c).

Persons who violate the California air quality statutes, an air quality permit, or a rule or regulation are subject to a $1,000 fine or imprisonment in county jail for up to six months or both.

Persons who violate the California air quality statutes, an air quality permit, or a rule or regulation are subject to a $1,000 fine or imprisonment in county jail for up to six months or both. HSC 42400(a). As with the civil penalty structure, the more willful the criminal violation, the higher the financial penalty (ranging from $25,000 to $75,000 per violation per day). Similarly, negligent emissions that cause great bodily injury or death result in fines of $100,000. Willful and intentional emissions resulting in great bodily injury or death are punishable with a fine of up to $250,000. In addition, the more willful the air quality violation, the more time a defendant can serve in jail (from nine months in county jail to up to three years in state prison). HSC 41500-42708.

California law establishes a variance procedure for sources seeking temporary relief from permit conditions or other air district rules and regulations.

Variances. California law establishes a procedure for sources seeking temporary relief from permit conditions or other air district rules and regulations. The procedure includes public notice and hearing, specific findings, and a compliance deadline. A variance provides protection from state enforcement actions, but must have EPA approval as a SIP revision to provide protection from EPA enforcement.

For more information...

Publications

Air Resources Board. 2007. Expanded List of Early Action Measures to Reduce Greenhouse Gas Emissions in California Recommended for Board Consideration

Air Resources Board. 2006. Emission Inventory Criteria and Guidelines Report: For the Air Toxics "Hot Spots" Programs

Curtis, M.H., and S.F. Sawyer. 2003. NFPA 1 Uniform Fire Code Handbook. Quincy, Mass.

Denney, R.J., J.C. Mueller, and P.W. Dennis, eds. 1999. California Environmental Law Handbook. 11th ed. Maryland: Government Institutes

Environmental Protection Agency. 1990. United States Environmental Protection Agency, Office of Air Quality. New Source Review Workshop Manual. North Carolina: United States EPA

Environmental Protection Agency. 2001. EPA Guidance: Improving Air Quality Through Land Use Activities. EPA Report 420-R-01-001

Goldsteen, J.B. 2003. The ABCs of Environmental Regulation, 2nd ed., chapter 6. Government Institutes

Hsiao and Black (eds.). 2004. Chapter II of California Environmental Law and Natural Resources Handbook. Government Institutes

Manaster, K.A. and D.P. Selmi (eds). ND. California Environmental Law and Land Use Practice, Chapter 40-43. Matthew Bender, San Francisco, Calif.

March, J.G. 2000. Transportation Law in California. Solano Press. Point Arena, Calif.

Wooley and Morss (eds.). 2001. Clean Air Act Handbook, 11th ed. West Group. St. Paul, Minn.

Websites

Air Resources Board
www.arb.ca.gov/homepage.htm

Air Resources Board, 2006
Top 25 Emissions Report
www.arb.ca.gov/ap/emsinv/t25cat/cat_top25.php

Air Resources Board, Air Quality Links
(includes links to local air district websites)
www.arb.ca.gov/html/links.htm

Air Resources Board,
Ambient Air Quality Standards
www.arb.ca.gov/aqs/aaqs2.pdf

Air Resources Board, California
Air Pollution Control Laws
www.arb.ca.gov/bluebook/bluebook.htm

Air Resources Board,
California Air Toxics Program
www.arb.ca.gov/toxics/toxics.htm

Air Resources Board, Clean
Fuels Vehicle Program
www.driveclean.ca.gov/en/gv/home/index.asp

Air Resources Board,
Consumer Products Program
www.arb.ca.gov/consprod/consprod.htm

Air Resources Board, Fact Sheets
www.arb.ca.gov/html/fslist.htm

Air Resources Board,
Laws and Regulations
www.arb.ca.gov/html/lawsregs.htm

Air Resources Board, Local Air District
Rules and Rulemaking Databases
www.arb.ca.gov/drdb/drdb.htm

Air Resources Board, Permits,
Certifications, Exemptions, and Registrations
www.arb.ca.gov/permits/permits.htm

Bay Area Air Quality
Management District, General
www.baaqmd.gov

California Climate Action Registry
www.climateregistry.org

California Energy Commission,
Climate Change Program
www.energy.ca.gov/global_climate_change/index.html

California EPA
www.calepa.ca.gov

Environmental Protection Agency, Air Data
www.epa.gov/air/data/nonat.html?us~USA~United%20States

Environmental Protection Agency,
Air Toxics Strategy: Overview
www.epa.gov/ttn/atw/urban/urbanpg.html

Environmental Protection Agency,
Nonattainment Areas
www.epa.gov/oar/oaqps/greenbk/mappm25.html

Environmental Protection Agency,
Ozone Depletion, General
www.epa.gov/Ozone/index.html

Environmental Protection Agency,
Plain English Guide to the Clean Air Act
www.epa.gov/air/oaqps/peg_caa/pegcaain.html

Environmental Protection
Agency, Region IX, Air Programs
www.epa.gov/region09/air

Environmental Protection Agency,
Region IX, Delegation of NSPS and
NESHAP to California air districts
http://yosemite.epa.gov/r9/r9nsps.nsf/ViewAgencies?ReadForm&State=CA

Environmental Protection Agency, Region IX,
Office of Transportation and Air Quality
www.epa.gov/otaq/oms-def.htm

Environmental Protection Agency, Terms of
Environment: Glossary, Abbreviations and Acronyms
www.epa.gov/OCEPAterms

South Coast Air Quality Management District
www.aqmd.gov

State and Territorial Air Pollution Program
Administrators and the Association
of Local Air Pollution Control Officials
(STAPPA/ALAPCO), General
www.4cleanair.org

Noise

This chapter reviews –

- Key laws and agencies involved in regulating environmental noise
- Federal and state noise standards
- Local noise regulatory programs
- Enforcement of noise regulations

Glossary

CNEL (community noise equivalent level)—same as Ldn, except 5 dB is added to noise levels between 7 pm and 10 pm.

dB (decibel)—the unit of measurement describing the amplitude of sound.

dbA (A-weighted decibel)—a decibel scale approximating the sensitivity of the human ear.

L10—the A-weighted noise level that is exceeded 10 percent of the time.

Ldn (day–night average level)—the average equivalent A-weighted noise level during a 24-hour day, obtained by adding 10 decibels to noise levels between 10 pm and 7 am.

Leq (equivalent energy level)—the average acoustic energy content of noise during the time it lasts.

Noise contour—a line drawn about a noise source indicating equal levels of noise exposure.

CHAPTER 6

Noise

Introduction

Major sources of environmental noise include motor vehicles, aircraft, equipment, and machinery. California state and local governments have the primary responsibility for controlling noise sources. However, federal legislation has been enacted to provide a uniform approach to noise control among states. For an overview of federal noise standards, *see* Bearden (2003).

This chapter reviews key laws and agencies involved in noise regulation, federal and state noise standards, and local noise regulatory programs and their enforcement.

Key Laws and Agencies

Federal Laws and Agencies

Noise Control Act of 1972. This Act (42 USC 4901 *et seq.*) authorizes federal noise emission standards for products distributed in commerce. State or local governments may not set different limits on noise emissions once a federal standard has been established.

To implement the Act, the Environmental Protection Agency (EPA) has established noise emission standards for interstate rail carriers (40 CFR 201), motor carriers engaged in interstate commerce (40 CFR 202), construction equipment (40 CFR 204), and transportation equipment (40 CFR 205). Manufacturers of noise-producing products must warrant to purchasers that their products operate at noise levels at or below the EPA noise standards. The Act also requires EPA to establish labels rating the effectiveness of hearing protection products.

Major sources of environmental noise include motor vehicles, aircraft, equipment, and machinery.

CFR = Code of Federal Regulations
EPA = U.S. Environmental
     Protection Agency
USC = United States Code

Aircraft noise legislation. Federal controls on aircraft noise are established by other laws, such as:

- **Aircraft Noise Abatement Act.** Requires the Federal Aviation Administration (FAA) to establish noise standards through consultation with the EPA and apply standards in connection with issuance of civil aircraft certificates. 49 USC 44715

- **Airport and Airway Improvement Act.** Establishes the Airport Improvement Program to provide federal assistance for airport construction projects and to award noise mitigation grants. 49 USC 47101 *et seq.*

- **Airport Noise and Capacity Act.** Phased out the noisiest classes of aircraft in 1999. 49 USC 47521 *et seq.*

Occupational Safety and Health Act of 1970. This Act requires the Occupational Safety and Health Administration (OSHA) to develop and enforce health and safety standards, including noise exposure, for workplace activities. 26 USC 65.

Environmental Protection Agency. In the past, the EPA coordinated all federal noise control activities through its Office of Noise Abatement and Control. However, in 1981, the Administration concluded that noise issues were best handled at the state or local government level. As a result, the EPA phased out the office's funding in 1982. Although EPA no longer plays an important role in regulating noise, its previously adopted standards and regulations remain in effect.

Federal Aviation Administration. In addition to setting aircraft noise standards as required by the Aircraft Noise Abatement Act, the FAA also has adopted regulations for controlling the planning of aviation noise containability on and around airports. 14 CFR 150.

State and Local Laws and Agencies

The California Noise Control Act of 1973 is the main state law controlling noise; the Act establishes coordination of federal, state, and local noise regulation.

California Noise Control Act. The California Noise Control Act of 1973 (HSC 46000 *et seq.*) is the main state law controlling noise; the Act establishes coordination of federal, state, and local noise regulation. Noise control enforcement is largely the responsibility of local governments. The Act established an Office of Noise Control (ONC) within the Department of Public Health (DPH)–formerly the Department of Health Services (DHS)–to oversee the state's noise program. However, the ONC no longer exists.

In addition to the California Noise Control Act, California has adopted regulations establishing noise standards for categories of sources such as aircraft (CCR 5000 *et seq.*) and motor vehicles (Vehicle Code 27200 *et seq.*).

Caltrans Division of Aeronautics and airport land use commissions. The Division of Aeronautics oversees public airport planning and operation. As part of its duties, the Division administers the State Aeronautics Act (PUC 21670 *et seq.*), which fosters compatible land use around airports and is implemented by county airport land use commissions (ALUCs).

Noise Standards

Noise Terminology

Environmental noise has a unique lexicon. The decibel (dB) is the basic unit of noise measurement. The A-weighted decibel (dbA) is a decibel scale approximating the sensitivity of the human ear. Typical noise levels are as follows:

CNEL	= Community noise equivalent level
dB	= Decibel
dbA	= A-weighted decibel
FHWA	= Federal Highway Administration
HUD	= U.S. Department of Housing and Urban Development

- 5 dbA: threshold of hearing
- 45 dbA: auto at low speed
- 65 dbA: conversation
- 85 dbA: busy street
- 110 dbA: rock band
- 125 dbA: DC-10 aircraft
- 130 dbA: threshold of pain

Other common noise terms are as follows:

- **Leq (equivalent energy level).** The average acoustic energy content of noise during the time it lasts
- **Ldn (day–night average level).** The average equivalent A-weighted noise level during a 24-hour day, obtained by adding 10 decibels to noise levels between 10 pm and 7 am
- **L10.** The A-weighted noise level that is exceeded 10 percent of the time
- **CNEL (community noise equivalent level).** Same as Ldn, except 5 dB is added to noise levels between 7 pm and 10 pm

Transportation Project Noise

The Federal Highway Administration (FHWA) has established noise standards for federally funded transportation projects and local projects requiring FHWA or Caltrans review. 23 CFR 772 *et seq.* These standards are shown in Table 6-1.

The FHWA has established noise standards for federally funded transportation projects and local projects requiring FHWA or Caltrans review.

The FHWA regulations specify that in determining and abating traffic noise impacts, primary consideration is to be given to exterior areas. Abatement usually will be necessary only where frequent human use occurs and a lowered noise level would be of benefit. In those situations where there are no exterior activities to be affected by the traffic noise, or where the exterior activities are far from or physically shielded from the roadway, the interior criterion is used to determine noise impacts.

Exterior Noise Levels

The U.S. Department of Housing and Urban Development (HUD) has established standards for exterior noise levels for HUD-supported or HUD-assisted housing projects, as follows (24 CFR 51.100 *et seq.*):

Table 6-1. Design Noise Levels of the Federal Highway Administration

Activity category	Category description	Design noise levels*	
		Leq (dbA)	L10 (dbA)
A	Lands on which serenity and quiet are of extraordinary significance, such as natural parks and wildlife habitat	57 (exterior)	60 (exterior)
B	Sensitive receptors, such as residences, recreation areas, schools, and hospitals	67 (exterior)	70 (exterior)
C	Developed lands or activities not included in categories A or B	72 (exterior)	75 (exterior)
D	Undeveloped lands	—	—
E	Sensitive receptors, such as residences, recreation areas, schools, and hospitals	52 (interior)	55 (interior)

*Either Leq or L10 may be used on a project, but not both.   Source: Federal Highway Administration 1995

- **65 dbA Ldn**. An acceptable zone where all projects could be approved
- **65–75 dbA Ldn**. A normally acceptable zone where project-specific mitigation measures would be required
- **75 dbA Ldn**. An unacceptable zone in which projects normally would not be approved

California noise regulations (24 CCR Part 2) establish a standard of 45 CNEL or 45 dbA for residences, schools, and other sensitive receptors. A similar set of noise standards is also within California's Uniform Building Code (Appendix chapter 12). California noise standards are shown in Table 6-2.

The regulations require that acoustical studies be prepared whenever a residential building or structure is proposed to be located near an existing or adopted freeway route, expressway, parkway, major street, thoroughfare, rail line, rapid transit line, or industrial noise source, where this source creates an exterior CNEL of 60 dbA or greater. The acoustical analysis must demonstrate that the residence has been designed to limit interior noise CNEL to 45 dbA.

Aircraft Noise

The FAA has set national standards for aircraft noise. For Stage 3 aircraft (encompassing most modern aircraft currently flying), separate standards are established for runway takeoffs, landings, and sidelines; these standards range from 89–106 dbA depending on the aircraft's weight and number of engines. FAA 2001, 14 CFR 36.

California has adopted the federal noise standards (Gov. Code 65302), as well as regulations to implement those standards, requiring the airport owner, aircraft operator, local governments, and FAA to work cooperatively to reduce noise problems. The regulations' intent is to reduce the noise impacts on communities

Table 6-2. California Interior and Exterior Noise Levels

Land use category	Land use	Interior*	Exterior**
Residential	Single and multifamily, duplex	45	65
	Mobile homes	––	65
Commercial	Hotel, motel, transient housing	45	––
	Commercial retail, bank, restaurant	55	––
	Office, research and development	50	––
	Amphitheater, concert hall, auditorium, movie theater	45	––
	Gymnasium (multipurpose)	50	––
	Sports club	55	––
	Manufacturing, warehousing, wholesale, utilities	65	––
Institutional/Public	Hospital, school classroom or playground	45	65
	Church, library	45	––
Open space	Parks	––	65

* CNEL (dbA). Indoor environment excludes bathrooms, kitchens, toilets, closets, and corridors.

** CNEL (dbA). Outdoor environment limited to private yard of single-family dwellings, multiple-family private patios or balconies accessed from within the dwelling, mobile home parks, park picnic areas, school playgrounds, and hospital patios.

Source: 24 CCR Part 2

in the vicinity of airports. 21 CCR 5000 *et seq.* Local governments and individual airports may enact stricter requirements, unless prohibited by federal law.

Railroad Noise

EPA has established railroad noise standards (40 CFR 201) that are enforced by the Federal Railroad Administration (FRA). The standards do not apply to horns, whistles, or bells used as warning devices. The standards are as follows:

FRA = Federal Railroad Administration

- Locomotives built in 1979 and earlier: 73 dbA in stationary operations and idle speeds, 96 dbA at cruising speeds
- Locomotives built after 1979: 70 dbA in stationary operations and idle speeds, 90 dbA at cruising speeds
- Railway cars: 88 dbA at 45 miles per hour or less, 93 dbA at 45 miles per hour or more
- Car coupling activities at railway stations: 92 dbA

Motor Vehicle Noise

Interstate motor carriers. EPA has established noise standards for motor carriers engaged in interstate commerce; FHWA enforces the standards. 42 USC 4917, 49 CFR 325. Commercial vehicles over 10,000 pounds are subject to standards for highway travel and stationary operation, but horns or sirens are not subject to standards. Highway travel standards range from 81–93 dbA, depending on vehicle speed and distance from the vehicle. Stationary standards range from 83–91 dbA, depending on distance from the vehicle.

California has established noise standards for motor vehicles that are broadly defined to include any self-propelled vehicle.

California motor vehicle standards. California has established noise standards for motor vehicles that are broadly defined to include any self-propelled vehicle. The application of these standards, which are as strict or stricter than corresponding federal standards, varies depending on the motor vehicle category, speed, age, and weight. Vehicle Code 27200 *et seq.* Also, every vehicle subject to registration in California, as well as off-highway vehicles and motorized recreational vessels, must be equipped at all times with an adequate and continually operating muffler.

Workplace Noise

OSHA has established standards for the duration of time employees can be exposed to specific noise levels.

OSHA has established standards for the duration of time employees can be exposed to specific noise levels. 29 CFR 1910.95. Constant exposure may not exceed 90 dbA over 8 hours. Exposure to levels higher than 115 dbA must be limited to 15 minutes within an 8-hour period. Instantaneous exposure (*e.g.*, impact noise) may not exceed 140 dbA. If noise levels exceed these standards, employers must provide hearing protection to reduce sound levels below the standards.

Other Federally Regulated Sources of Noise

Pursuant to the Noise Control Act, EPA has established the following noise standards for other sources not mentioned above (40 CFR 204, 205):

- Motorcycles manufactured after 1982: 80–86 dbA depending on model year and whether the motorcycle is designed for street or off-road use
- Mopeds: 70 dbA
- Trucks over 10,000 pounds manufactured after 1978: 80–83 dbA depending on model year (these standards are in addition to the standards for interstate motor carriers)

Local Noise Regulatory Programs

Noise Element

Appendix C of the General Plan Guidelines (Governor's Office of Planning and Research) sets forth recommended procedures and contents for the general plan noise element. The goals of the noise element are to:

- Provide sufficient information about the community noise environment so that noise may be effectively considered in the land use planning process
- Develop strategies for abating excessive noise exposure
- Protect existing noise-sensitive areas
- Provide for local compliance for the state noise insulation standards

The noise element guidelines set forth a four-phased process for noise element preparation:

- Phase A: Noise environment definition
- Phase B: Noise-compatible land use planning
- Phase C: Noise mitigation measures
- Phase D: Enforcement

The local noise element must analyze noise levels from transportation facilities, railroads, aircraft, industrial plants, and other ground stationary sources. Gov. Code 65302(f). Noise contours must be shown for these sources and stated in terms of either CNEL or Ldn. These contours are to guide land use planning, using guidelines for acceptable noise exposure for different land use categories.

The local noise element must analyze noise levels from transportation facilities, railroads, aircraft, industrial plants, and other ground stationary sources.

Figure 6-1 shows land use compatibility for noise exposure. Established by DHS, these guidelines are used to develop noise element recommendations. For each land use, noise levels are classified as normally acceptable, conditionally acceptable, normally unacceptable, and clearly unacceptable.

Airport Noise

Airport land use commissions. For aircraft noise, the State Aeronautics Act (PUC 21670 *et seq.*) requires the establishment of ALUCs, which are responsible for developing airport land use compatibility plans (ALUPs) for noise-compatible land uses in the immediate proximity of a commercial or public airport. The *Airport Land Use Planning Handbook* (Caltrans 2002) establishes guidance for airport land use compatibility planning. Local agencies preparing noise elements must coordinate with the appropriate county ALUC. The purposes of an ALUC are to ensure orderly expansion of public airports and to minimize land use, noise, and safety conflicts with adjacent land uses. ALUCs have two major roles:

Comprehensive airport land use plans regulate development near airports.

ALUC = Airport land use commission
ALUP = Airport land use plan

- Preparation and adoption of airport land use compatibility plans, which address policies for both noise and safety
- Review of certain local government land use actions and airport plans for consistency with the land use compatibility plan

The ALUP is the major tool for ALUC land use regulation. The ALUP typically includes (PUC 21675(a)):

- Height restrictions within the airport influence area
- Permissible and conditional land uses
- Soundproofing and other building standards

Local governments within the ALUP planning boundaries must refer certain proposed land use changes (*e.g.*, general plan amendments, specific plans, zoning ordinances) to the ALUC for a determination of consistency

Figure 6-1
Community Noise Exposure Guidelines

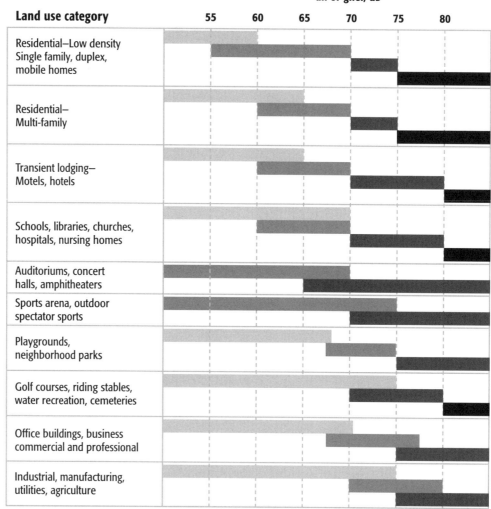

INTERPRETATION

NORMALLY ACCEPTABLE
Specified land use is satisfactory, based on the assumption that any buildings involved are of normal conventional construction, without any special noise insulation requirements.

CONDITIONALLY ACCEPTABLE
New construction or development should be undertaken only after a detailed analysis of the noise reduction requirements is made and needed noise insulation features included in the design. Conventional construction, but with closed windows and fresh air supply systems or air conditioning, will normally suffice.

NORMALLY UNACCEPTABLE
New construction or development should generally be discouraged. If new construction or development does proceed, a detailed analysis of the noise reduction requirements must be made and the needed noise insulation features included in the design.

CLEARLY UNACCEPTABLE
New construction or development should generally not be undertaken.

Source: Governor's Office of Planning and Research. General Plan Guidelines, Appendix C

with the ALUP. If the ALUC determines the proposed action is inconsistent with the ALUP, the local government may still override this determination and approve the land use change by making certain findings. If the ALUC has not adopted an ALUP, no consistency determination can be made, but the ALUC may nevertheless approve or disapprove the land use change if substantial progress is being made toward completion of the ALUP. PUC 21675.1(c), 21676.

Local governments. Cities and counties have two additional procedures for coordinating land use decisions with aircraft noise. First, a plan for airport expansion must be submitted for approval to the applicable city or county before acquisition of property for the expansion. PUC 21661.6(a). Second, cities and counties may adopt airport approach zones for either public or private airports, and may establish special zoning restrictions in approach zones to prevent airport hazards, including excessive noise. Gov. Code 50485.

Enforcement

Federal Noise Control Act

Willful or knowing violations of many provisions of the federal Noise Control Act are subject to a criminal fine of up to $25,000 per day of violation, by imprisonment of up to one year, or both. 42 USC 4910(a)(1). These violations also may be punished civilly by fines of up to $10,000 per day of violation. Also, citizens may file civil actions against anyone alleged to be in violation of any federal noise control requirement. 42 USC 4911(f).

Local Noise Ordinances

Most cities and counties have adopted a noise ordinance to implement their noise elements and to provide a process for resolving noise complaints. For example, the City of Los Angeles noise ordinance (Los Angeles Municipal Code 116.01) provides that officers should consider the following factors, in addition to the noise level violating noise standards, in determining whether an activity violates the noise ordinance:

- Nature of the noise (usual or unusual)
- Origin of the noise (natural or unnatural)
- Level and intensity of any background noise
- Proximity of the noise to sleeping facilities
- Nature and zoning of the area
- Density of inhabitation in the area
- Time of day or night the noise occurs
- Duration of the noise
- Whether the noise is recurrent, intermittent, or constant
- Whether the noise is produced by commercial or non-commercial activity

A violation of the city's noise ordinance is a misdemeanor. Officers responding to a complaint regarding a violation of the noise ordinance may:

- Advise the concerned parties of the violation
- Seek to gain voluntary compliance
- Direct parties to other enforcement entities when appropriate
- Complete a crime report
- Accept a lawful citizen's arrest
- Prepare a complaint application when the violator is a business entity

For more information...

Publications

Bearden, D.A. 2003. Noise Abatement and Control: An Overview of Federal Standards and Regulations. Congressional Research Service, Order Code RS20531

Caltrans, Division of Aeronautics. 2002. Airport Land Use Planning Handbook

Federal Aviation Administration. 2001. Noise levels for U.S. Certificated and Foreign Aircraft. Advisory Circular 36-1H

Federal Highway Administration. 1995. Highway Traffic Noise Analysis and Abatement: Policy and Guidance

Governor's Office of Planning and Research. General Plan Guidelines, Appendix C (Noise Element Guidelines)

Manaster, K.A. and D.P. Selmi (eds.). ND. Chapter 83 of California Environmental Law and Land Use Practice. Matthew Bender. San Francisco, Calif.

Websites

Caltrans Division of Aeronautics
www.dot.ca.gov/hq/planning/aeronaut/htmlfile/index

Caltrans Standard Environmental Reference, Noise chapter
www.dot.ca.gov/ser/vol1/sec3/physical/ch12noise/chap12noise.htm#laws

Federal Highway Administration, "Noise Central"
www.noisecentral.com/fhwa_noisestand.htm

Noise Pollution Clearinghouse
http://nonoise.org

U.S. Department of Housing and Urban Development, Noise Standards
www.hudnoise.com

CHAPTER 7

Hazardous Materials
and Toxic Substances

This chapter reviews—

- Key laws and agencies involved in regulating hazardous materials and toxic substances

- Hazard communication programs

- Community right-to-know programs

- Chemical handling and storage

- Hazardous material transportation

- Underground storage tank regulation

- Other hazardous materials programs (Toxic Substances Control Act, asbestos, lead, PCBs, toxic mold, Proposition 65, health tracking, chemical bans)

- Pesticide programs

- Federal enforcement

- California enforcement

Related Solano Press titles—

Guide to Hazardous Materials and Waste Management: Risk, Regulation, Responsibility. Jon W. Kindschy *et al.* 1997

Glossary

Asbestos-containing material–any material that contains more than one percent asbestos by weight.

Asbestos management plan*–a plan detailing the strategy to manage the discovery of asbestos.

Brominated flame retardants–also known as polybrominated diphenyl ethers or PBDEs. Found in plastic housing of electronics, computers, and textiles used in furniture.

Cathodic protection–a technique used to prevent corrosion of a metal surface by making it the cathode of an electrochemical cell.

Combustible liquid–any liquid having a flashpoint at or above 100°F. Combustible liquids are divided into two classes.

Compressed gas–a gas or mixture of gases at a high pressure that can be used as a propellant.

Corrosive chemicals–chemicals that are either highly acidic or caustic and react with other substances and "burn" the other substances chemically.

Designated UST operator–one or more individuals designated by an owner of an underground storage tank facility having responsibility for training employees and conducting monthly visual inspections.

Existing underground storage tank–an underground storage tank installed after 1988 (under federal law) or 1984 (under California law) that was required to be upgraded to meet specified technology standards or removed by December 22, 1998.

Flammable liquid–any liquid having a flashpoint below 100°F.

Flashpoint–the minimum temperature at which a liquid gives off vapor within a test vessel in sufficient concentration to form an ignitable mixture with air near the surface of the liquid.

Handler–any business that has contact with a hazardous material.

Hazardous chemical–"[a]ny chemical which is a physical hazard or health hazard," as defined under federal OSHA.

Hazardous material–a substance or waste that, because of its physical, chemical, or other characteristics, may pose a risk of endangering human health or safety or of degrading the environment.

Hazardous materials business plan*– a plan that includes an inventory of hazardous materials stored, handled, or used; emergency response plans; procedures for mitigating harm in the event of a release; evacuation plans; and employee training.

New underground storage tank– underground storage tank installed after 1988 (under federal law) or 1984 (under California law) that must have been permitted and must now be equipped with specified equipment such as secondary containment and overflow protection.

Operator–any person in control of, or having responsibility for, the daily operation of an underground storage tank system.

Owner–the owner of an underground storage tank.

Personal protective equipment– clothing and equipment to protect the employee from work hazards.

Primary containment–the first level of containment in an underground storage tank, such as the inner surface that comes into immediate contact with the hazardous substance being contained.

Proposition 65–requires regulated businesses to notify the public and employees of their potential exposure to chemicals that cause cancer and reproductive harm.

Regulated substances–"hazardous substances" and petroleum, under the federal underground storage tank program.

Reportable quantity–a quantity of a hazardous substance that triggers reporting under CERCLA. If the substance exceeds its reportable quantity, then the release must be reported to the National Response Center, SERC, and community emergency coordinators for areas likely to be affected.

Secondary containment–the level of containment external to, and separate from, the primary containment in an underground storage tank.

Toxic material–a material that has a lethal dose concentration based on one of three categories–a chemical with a median lethal dose of more than 50 milligrams per kilograms (mg/kg) but not more than 500 mg/kg of the body weight of albino rats weighing between 200 and 300 grams each; a chemical with a median lethal dose of more than 200 mg/kg but not more than 1,000 mg/kg of the body weight of albino rabbits weighing two to three kg, that is administered continuously for 24 hours; a chemical with a median lethal concentration in air of more than 200 parts per million but not more than 2,000 parts per million by volume of gas or vapor, or more than two mg/liter but not more than 20 mg/liter of mist.

Toxic release inventory*–a publicly available EPA database that contains information on toxic chemical releases and other waste management activities reported annually by regulated industry groups as well as federal facilities.

Underground storage tank–one or a combination of tanks, including associated piping used to contain industrial solvents, petroleum products, and other hazardous substances. The tank is totally or substantially (10 percent) beneath the surface of the ground.

* equals permits and approvals

CHAPTER 7

Hazardous Materials and Toxic Substances

Introduction

Hazardous materials (sometimes referred to as HAZMATs, hazardous products, or hazardous chemicals) are regulated under a number of state, federal, and local environmental, health, and safety regulatory programs. Generally, hazardous materials are divided into the following categories:

Hazardous materials are regulated under a number of state, federal, and local environmental, health, and safety regulatory programs.

- **Flammables** (gasoline, paints, adhesives, and solvents, etc.)

- **Combustibles** (lubricating oil and diesel fuel, etc.)

- **Corrosives** (battery acid, chlorine, and alkaline cleaners, etc.)

- **Compressed gases** (acetylene, nitrogen, oxygen, helium, and argon, etc.)

- **Reactives** (organic peroxides, cyanides, and lithium, etc.)

- **Toxics** (isocyanates, benzene, lead, and methyl ethyl ketone (MEK), etc.)

This chapter reviews laws and agencies involved in hazardous materials and toxic substances regulation; programs for hazard communication, community right-to-know, chemical handling and storage, hazardous material transportation, underground storage tanks, pesticides, and other hazardous materials and toxic substances; and enforcement of hazardous materials and toxic substances regulations.

MEK = Methyl ethyl ketone
USC = United States Code

Key Laws and Agencies

Federal Laws and Agencies

Occupational Safety and Health Act. This Act (29 USC 651 *et seq,*. 29 CFR 1900 *et seq.*), enacted in 1970, is intended to create a safe workplace. This program establishes procedures and standards for the safe handling and storage of hazardous chemicals. 29 CFR 1910.1200(c) *et seq.* In addition, a material safety data sheet

AHERA = Asbestos Hazard
Emergency Response Act

CFR = Code of Federal Regulations

EPA = U.S. Environmental
Protection Agency

EPCRA = Emergency Planning and
Community Right-to-Know Act

FIFRA = Federal Insecticide, Fungicide,
and Rodenticide Act

HMTA = Hazardous Materials
Transportation Act

LEPC = Local emergency
planning centers

MSDS = Material safety data sheet

RCRA = Resource Conservation
and Recovery Act

SARA = Superfund Amendments and
Reauthorization Act of 1986

SERC = State Emergency
Response Center

UST = Underground storage tanks

TSCA = Toxic Substances Control Act

The Toxic Substances Control Act enables the U.S. Environmental Protection Agency to track industrial chemicals produced or imported into the United States.

(MSDS) containing specified information must be provided to customers, making them aware of chemical hazards to which they may be exposed.

Emergency Planning and Community Right-to-Know Act. The Emergency Planning and Community Right-to-Know Act, (EPCRA, 42 USC 116 *et seq.*, 40 CFR 350 *et seq.*) also is referred to as the Superfund Amendments and Reauthorization Act of 1986, or SARA Title III. EPCRA requires facilities that store or use hazardous chemicals to submit a specified plan with copies of MSDSs to the State Emergency Response Center (SERC) and the local emergency planning center (LEPC). Additionally, facilities must submit an annual inventory list with details on the amount, location, and storage method of regulated chemicals present at the facility. 40 CFR 370.20 *et seq.*

Resource Conservation and Recovery Act, Subtitle I. To protect groundwater, the Resource Conservation and Recovery Act (RCRA), Subtitle I, establishes design, construction, and operational standards to prevent chemical releases from underground storage tanks (USTs) that are 10 percent or more beneath the ground. 42 USC 6991 *et seq.*, 40 CFR 280 *et seq.*

Hazardous Materials Transportation Act. The Hazardous Materials Transportation Act (HMTA) regulates any transporter of hazardous materials or any person who manufactures, marks, repairs, or tests a package that was certified, sold, or marked for use in the transportation of hazardous materials. 49 CFR 100 *et seq.*

Toxic Substances Control Act. The Toxic Substances Control Act (TSCA, 15 USC 2601 *et seq.*, 40 CFR 700 *et seq.*) enables the U.S. Environmental Protection Agency (EPA) to track industrial chemicals produced or imported into the United States. EPA screens the chemicals and can require testing to determine if any pose an environmental or human-health hazard. Any chemical that poses an unreasonable risk then can be regulated or banned from manufacturing or importation.

Asbestos Hazard Emergency Response Act. AHERA regulates asbestos material in school buildings, requiring schools to maintain an asbestos inventory, implement a management plan and conduct periodic inspections of the premises. 15 USC 2651 *et seq.*, 40 CFR 763 *et seq.*

Residential Lead-Based Paint Hazard Reduction Act. This Act (42 USC 4851 *et seq.*, 40 CFR 745.100) requires that sellers and landlords disclose known lead-based paint or lead-based paint hazards to buyers and tenants of dwelling units. The seller or landlord must provide the buyer or tenant pamphlets providing information on the hazards associated with lead and provide 10 days to inspect the premises for lead-based paint hazards.

Federal Insecticide, Fungicide, and Rodenticide Act and the Federal Food, Drug, and Cosmetic Act. The use of pesticides is regulated by the EPA under the Federal Insecticide, Fungicide, and Rodenticide Act and the Federal Food, Drug, and Cosmetic Act (FIFRA, 7 USC 136 *et seq.*), which creates the foundation for regulation, sale, distribution, and use of pesticides in the United States. EPA is authorized to review and register pesticides for particular uses. Additionally, EPA is authorized to suspend or cancel the registration of a pesticide if research shows the continued use would create an unreasonable risk. The Federal Food, Drug, and Cosmetic Act (FFDCA) gives EPA the authority to mandate maximum residue levels or tolerances for pesticides used in or on foods, or in animal feed. 21 USC 301 *et seq.*, 21 CFR 5.

Environmental Protection Agency. EPA has extensive authority under several federal environmental statutory programs discussed in this chapter, including EPCRA, RCRA Subtitle I, AHERA, TSCA, NESHAP, and FIFRA. EPA regulates the use of asbestos-containing materials (ACMs), and hazardous materials and substances, under TSCA to reduce the risk of exposure to humans and the environment. Under the Act, EPA has the ability to track production and importation of industrial chemicals into commerce in the United States. Based on a chemical screening process, EPA can ban specific chemicals it finds that pose an unreasonable risk to humans or the environment.

FIFRA establishes federal control over the use, sale, and distribution of pesticides. FIFRA gives EPA authority to require pesticide testing to determine potential environmental and health effects, while also requiring pesticide users to register their purchased products.

EPCRA, also known as Title III of SARA, requires businesses using potentially hazardous chemical substances to notify EPA and state and local emergency planning groups of their inventory and of releases, whether accidental or planned.

RCRA, Subtitle I is a program designed to regulate underground storage tanks containing hazardous substances or petroleum. EPA sets standards governing tank construction based on whether the tank is new or whether an existing tank is upgraded. EPA also imposes operation and maintenance procedures for UST owners and operators, and establishes reporting requirements from regulated tanks that release substances into the environment.

Section 112 of the Clean Air Act requires EPA to set air toxics standards for regulating the emissions of hazardous air pollutants. *See* chapter 5.

United States Department of Labor, Occupational Safety and Health Administration. The Occupational Safety and Health Administration (OSHA) administers and enforces the federal Occupational Safety and Health Act (also referred to as OSHA). For purposes of this chapter, OSHA implements the laws governing the Hazard Communication program and the safe handling of hazardous chemicals and products.

Department of Transportation. The Department of Transportation (DOT) administers the HMTA and governs the transportation of hazardous materials in commerce, including those who manufacture, mark, repair, or test packaging that was certified, sold, or marked for use in the transportation of hazardous materials.

ACM = Asbestos-containing material
FFDCA = Federal Food, Drug, and Cosmetic Act
NESHAP = National Emissions Standards for Hazardous Air Pollutants
OSHA = Occupational Safety and Health Act

EPA has extensive authority under several federal environmental statutory programs, including EPCRA, RCRA Subtitle I, AHERA, TSCA, NESHAP, and FIFRA.

CCR = California Code of Regulations

CUPA = Certified unified program agency

DOT = U.S. Department of Transportation

HMBP = Hazardous materials business plan

HSC = Health and Safety Code

HSITA = Hazardous Substances Information and Training Act

HUD = U.S. Department of Housing and Urban Development

Department of Housing and Urban Development. Effective in 1996, Congress directed the U.S. Department of Housing and Urban Development (HUD) and EPA to promulgate joint lead-based paint hazard regulations for sales and leases of older housing. While HUD is primarily responsible for enforcing the residential lead-based paint disclosure program, EPA has established hazard standards for paint, dust, and soil in most "target" housing (housing constructed pre-1978, except elderly housing or zero-bedroom housing) and child-occupied facilities.

State Laws and Agencies

California Hazardous Substances Information and Training Act. The Hazardous Substances Information and Training Act (HSITA, California Labor Code 360 *et seq.*) requires manufacturers and importers of hazardous substances to assess the hazards posed by the products they introduce into commerce. They, along with distributors, are required to capture this information into MSDSs that must be supplied to purchasers. Also, employers must train their staff on the safe use of hazardous products in the workplace.

California Hazardous Materials Release Response Plans and Inventory Law. Under this law (HSC 25500 *et seq.*), a handler of hazardous material is required to submit a hazardous materials business plan (HMBP) to the local emergency planning center, the certified unified program agency (CUPA), or the local authorized administrating agency. Hazardous materials handlers must review the HMBP at least once every three years after submission. The HMBP must include an inventory of hazardous materials stored, handled, or used; emergency response plans; procedures for mitigating harm in the event of a release; evacuation plans; and employee training. HSC 25503.5 *et seq.*, 19 CCR 2729–2732.

California became the first state to regulate USTs. California law requires a permit to operate a UST system that stores hazardous substances.

California underground storage tank law. California became the first state to regulate USTs. California law (HSC 25280 *et seq.*, 22 CCR 2630) requires a permit to operate a UST system that stores hazardous substances. Owners or operators of USTs must meet specific construction, design, and monitoring requirements, along with periodic testing and recordkeeping responsibilities.

California Asbestos Notification Act. This Act (HSC 25915 *et seq.*) requires owners who know their pre-1979 buildings contain asbestos to give written notice to employees working in the building. The notice must provide the specific location of asbestos-containing construction materials; the general procedures and handling restrictions necessary to limit or prevent release or exposure to the asbestos; a summary of sample analyses; and the potential health risks associated with asbestos exposure.

Lead programs. Under the Lead Hazard Reduction Enforcement Act (HSC 105250–105257), if a building contains lead hazards that are likely to endanger the health of the public or building occupants, the building owner will be in violation of the state housing law or the Health and Safety Code. The Occupational Lead Poisoning Prevention Act (HSC 105185 *et seq.*) creates a lead poisoning program to register and monitor laboratory reports of adult lead toxicity cases; to conduct investigation of take-home exposure cases (*i.e.,* when lead is carried home on the worker's body, clothes, shoes, or personal vehicle); and to train employees and health experts regarding the program.

Toxic Mold Protection Act of 2001. This Act (HSC 26100 *et seq.*) requires sellers and landlords to disclose the presence of mold to buyers and tenants. Commercial and industrial landlords, under certain circumstances, must assess the condition of property other than real property.

Proposition 65. Proposition 65 (HSC 25249.5 *et seq.*, 22 CCR 12000 *et seq.*), also known as the Safe Drinking Water and Toxic Enforcement Act of 1986, requires that regulated businesses not expose persons to significant concentrations of carcinogens or reproductive toxicants without providing a "clear and reasonable" warning. Additionally, regulated businesses must not discharge or release any listed carcinogens or reproductive toxicants that potentially may contact a source or potential source of drinking water.

Mercury Reduction Act of 2001. In 2001, the California Legislature pioneered a trend-setting law–the Mercury Reduction Act–which bans the manufacture, sale, or supply of mercury fever thermometers and other mercury-containing products. PRC 15025 *et seq.* The Act prohibits schools from purchasing devices or materials containing mercury for use in classrooms; bans the sale of mercury thermometers; bans the sale of vehicles (built on or after January 1, 2005) having mercury light switches; and prohibits the sale in California of novelty items containing mercury.

In 2001, the California Legislature pioneered a trend-setting law–the Mercury Reduction Act–that bans the manufacture, sale, or supply of mercury fever thermometers and other mercury-containing products.

Brominated Flame Retardant regulation. California law prohibits manufacturing, processing, or distributing in commerce a product or a flame-retardant part of a product that contains brominated flame retardants (BFRs), otherwise known as polybrominated diphenyl ethers (PBDEs). HSC 108920 *et seq.*

BFR	= Brominated flame retardants
Cal/EPA	= California Environmental Protection Agency
DPH	= Department of Public Health
EHSS	= Environmental Health Surveillance System
PBDE	= Polybrominated diphenyl ether

Toxics in Packaging Prevention Act. This Act (HSC 25214.11 *et seq.*) prohibits manufacturers and importers from selling packaging that includes lead, cadmium, mercury, or hexavalent chromium. Manufacturers and importers must also furnish to their purchasers a certification indicating that the package and packaging materials they offer meet the conditions of the Act.

Health Tracking Act of 2003. The Act established the California Environmental Health Surveillance System (EHSS), a collaborative research program led by the California Department of Public Health (DPH) (formerly Department of Health Services), the California Environmental Protection Agency (Cal/EPA), and the University of California to evaluate the potential nexus between chemicals present in the environment and chronic diseases. HSC 104324.25.

Cal/OSHA = California Occupational
    Safety and Health
    Administration
DPR = Department of
    Pesticide Regulation
DTSC = Department of Toxic
    Substances Control
OEHHA = Office of Environmental
    Health Hazard Assessment
PEL = Permissible exposure limit
SWRCB = State Water Resources
    Control Board

*The DTSC is the main agency that over-
sees compliance and enforcement of rules
governing hazardous waste in California.*

Pesticide regulation. California pesticide law is designed to control pesticide usage and mitigate damage incurred by pesticide usage; to protect the environment; and to protect workers who come in contact with pesticides. California law establishes product labeling standards and requires the most efficient and effective approach to pest management. The California Department of Pesticide Regulation (DPR) is the authorized agency to implement and enforce these laws and regulations. Food and Agricultural Code 12751 *et seq.*

State Water Resources Control Board. The State Water Resources Control Board (SWRCB) is principally responsible for administering the UST program. The State of California delegated day-to-day implementation and enforcement of this program to the CUPAs.

Department of Toxic Substances Control. The Department of Toxic Substances Control (DTSC) is the main agency that oversees compliance and enforcement of rules governing hazardous waste in California.

Department of Pesticide Regulation. DPR is principally responsible for implementing and enforcing the pesticide program in California. It manages pesticide registration, pesticide use restrictions, and licensing of pesticide applicators.

California Occupational Safety and Health Administration. The California Occupational Safety and Health Administration (Cal/OSHA) administers and enforces the state's occupational safety and health program, including setting permissible exposure levels (PELs) for asbestos, as well as regulating employee exposure to and management of hazardous materials.

Department of Public Health. DPH (formerly Department of Health Services) administers the lead poisoning program, adopts PELs for mold in indoor environments, and develops standards to identify and remediate mold infestations.

California Governor's Office of Emergency Services. The Office of Emergency Services (OES) serves as the SERC under EPCRA and receives notifications of chemical spills and releases.

Office of Environmental Health Hazard Assessment and the Attorney General. The Office of Environmental Health Hazard Assessment (OEHHA) administers the Proposition 65 program and evaluates all scientific information on substances considered for placement on the Proposition 65 list. While OEHHA administers the law, the Attorney General enforces Proposition 65.

Certified unified program agencies. CUPAs administer a number of environmental regulatory programs that the state of California delegated to certified local agencies. Typically, city or county fire or health departments serve as CUPAs. CUPAs serve as the LEPC under EPCRA with authority to administer and enforce the HMBP program. CUPAs also are delegated authority to implement and enforce the UST program; the hazardous waste generator program (including the regulation of PCBs with concentrations between 5 and 50 ppm);

the on-site hazardous waste tiered treatment permitting program (*see* chapter 8); the spill prevention control and countermeasure program (*see* chapter 10); and the California Accidental Release Prevention Program (CalARP) (*see* chapter 5).

CalARP	=	California Accidental Release Prevention Program
HAZCOM	=	Hazard communication
PCB	=	Polychlorinated biphenyl

Hazard Communication

The federal and state governments have enacted several programs designed to inform customers and employees about the potential hazards of chemicals used in commerce and the workplace.

Federal Occupational Safety and Health Act

Material safety data sheet. The federal OSHA requires manufacturers, importers, and employers to inform customers about the potential hazards of their chemical products. This information is contained in a material safety data sheet. Each MSDS includes, among other things, information on:

The federal OSHA requires manufacturers, importers, and employers to inform customers about the potential hazards of their chemical products.

- Chemical ingredient characteristics
- Hazards
- Recommended personal protective equipment (such as specified gloves, respirator, and safety glasses)
- Fire risk management
- Disposal instructions

OSHA requires MSDSs for materials that meet OSHA's definition of hazardous chemical and are "known to be present in the workplace where employees may be exposed under normal conditions or in a foreseeable emergency." 29 CFR 1910.1200(b)–(h). A hazardous chemical, under Federal OSHA, is defined as "any chemical which is a physical hazard or health hazard."

Employee communication. OSHA requires that employers communicate to their employees the hazards posed by the chemicals used in the workplace. Employers must have a written hazard communication (HAZCOM) program designed to provide information on chemical hazards to employees. The requirements for an employer are based on whether the employer manufactures, imports, or uses chemicals.

OSHA requires that employers communicate to their employees the hazards posed by the chemicals used in the workplace.

Hazard communication training. Personnel who store, handle, or use hazardous materials must receive HAZCOM training that addresses routine management procedures, emergency response, and how to read an MSDS. Further, employees must have access to information (hard copy or electronic) on the chemicals they use in the workplace.

Container labels. Employers must display hazards on chemical containers, except on portable containers under employee control and immediate use. Employers may use any type of labeling as long as it conveys the chemical name, the responsible party (*e.g.,* manufacturer, importer) name and address,

Figure 7-1
NFPA Label

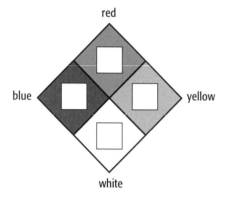

and the hazard warnings. Permissible labeling systems include the National Fire Protection Association (NFPA) system or the Hazardous Material Identification System (HMIS) established by the National Paint and Coatings Association. *See* Figure 7-1 for an NFPA label.

The NFPA diamond label shows the potential severity of the hazardous chemical, using five hazard levels (0 through 4) in relation to four color-coded hazards: health hazard (blue), fire hazard (red), reactive hazard (yellow), and specific hazard (white). *See* Table 7-1 for NFPA severity ratings.

California Hazardous Substances Information and Training Act

HSITA (Calif. Labor Code 6360 *et seq.*) largely mimics federal OSHA regulations governing hazard communication. Like the federal program, the HSITA requires manufacturers and importers of hazardous substances to evaluate the hazards posed by the products they introduce into commerce. They must label their products to identify hazards and must prepare MSDSs that explain the hazards. Distributors, along with manufacturers and importers, must supply MSDSs to purchasers. Finally, employers must train their staff on the safe use of hazardous products used in the workplace.

The HSITA regulates the same hazardous substances regulated under the federal OSHA. CLC 6382(d). Manufacturers, importers, and employees must develop written procedures describing how to assess hazardous substances. These procedures may be included in the employer's written hazard communication program. 8 CCR 5194(d)(2).

Employers must keep an updated inventory of MSDSs for each hazardous substance used. These MSDSs must be readily accessible to employees in their work areas. CLC 6398(a); 8 CCR 5194(g)(1), (8). If a manufacturer does not provide the employer with MSDS or other required information, California law states that the employer must request in writing within seven days that the manufacturer send a complete MSDS. 8 CCR 5194(g)(12).

The state program is more stringent than federal requirements with regard to training. In California, training must be provided to any employee who receives a new or revised MSDS within 30 days of receipt of the MSDS. 8 CCR 5194(h).

Community Right-to-Know Programs

Federal Inventory and Right-to-Know Requirements

Requirements for facilities. EPCRA (42 USC 11001 *et seq.*) requires regulated "facilities" (defined below) that store or use any extremely hazardous

Table 7-1. Severity Ratings of the National Fire Protection Association

Hazard Levels	Health Hazard (Blue)	Fire Hazard (Red)	Reactive Hazard (Yellow)	Specific Hazard (White)
4	Deadly	Very flammable	May detonate	Oxidizer (OXY)
3	Extreme danger	Readily ignitable	Shock and heat may detonate	Acid (ACID)
2	Hazardous	Ignited with heat	Violent chemical change	Alkali (ALK)
1	Slightly hazardous	Combustible	Unstable if heated	Corrosive (COR)
0	Normal material	Will not burn	Stable	Use no water (W)

Source: Compiled from information available on the University of Wisconsin--Platteville Chemistry Department website

substance (EHS, defined at 40 CFR 355.20) exceeding certain thresholds to comply with community right-to-know reporting requirements. One of the primary objectives of EPCRA is to support emergency planning at the state and local levels of government.

"Facilities" include stationary structures located on a single site, or located on adjacent or contiguous sites and owned or operated by the same person. These facilities must:

- Notify the CUPA of the on-site presence of EHSs in quantities equal to or exceeding specified amounts (known as threshold planning quantities or TPQs). 40 CFR 355.30
- Provide information to the SERC and the LEPC
- Submit to the SERC and LEPC annual chemical inventories of listed hazardous chemicals produced at or shipped to the facility. 42 USC 11022; 40 CFR 370, 370.25

Toxic release inventory. Manufacturers (including importers) and processors within certain industries with at least 10 full-time employees, and who manufacture or process a minimum of 25,000 pounds of chemicals, or use 10,000 pounds/year, must submit an annual toxic chemical release form summarizing the environmental fate of chemical releases. This program is known as the Toxic Release Inventory (TRI). 42 USC 11023(f), 40 CFR 372. These facilities must complete a Form R, which includes technical information and the amounts of chemicals released to the air, water, land, underground injection wells, and off-site transfers to publicly owned treatment works. Facilities must also report to EPA information on off-site transfers for disposal, waste treatment, recycling, and energy recovery, as well as pollution prevention data addressing source reduction, recycling, and waste management activities. 42 USC 13106. *See* the sidebar for general guidance on release reporting.

Guidance on Release Reporting

Unless legal counsel advises otherwise, it is prudent to "over notify" when in doubt. The principal agencies that require notification include the Governor's Office of Emergency Services (OES), the National Response Center (NRC), and the relevant CUPA. OES typically will make courtesy notifications to all other state agencies, such as the DTSC and the RWQCB. Similarly, the NRC makes courtesy notifications to the appropriate federal agencies. Nonetheless, it is advisable to follow up and provide individual notifications to each agency for which a reportable quantity of a regulated chemical has been released. Failure to comply with these obligations can result in fines of several thousand dollars per day. ▪

EHS = Extremely hazardous substance
NRC = National Response Center
OES = Office of Emergency Services
TPQ = Threshold planning quantities
TRI = Toxic release inventory

33/50 Program. EPA created the 33/50 Program to target 17 specific chemicals companies reported to the TRI. This program received its name based on the goal of achieving a 33 percent national reduction in releases and transfers by 1992 and a 50 percent reduction by 1995, using the 1988 TRI information as a baseline. The 17 chemicals were chosen based on the following three criteria: if the chemical posed an environmental and health concern; if it was a high-volume industrial chemical; or if chemical reduction through pollution prevention was possible.

Hazardous material inventory. Other facilities that manufacture, process, use, or store hazardous chemicals but are not required to complete a Form R must submit a hazardous material inventory report to the LEPC annually. 42 USC 11022. The hazardous material inventory report must detail the location, amount, and storage method for chemicals at the facility.

State Inventory and Right-to-Know Requirements

Requirements for businesses. All businesses that store, handle, or use "hazardous materials" (defined below) in the quantities specified below must submit a HMBP to the local administering agency (typically the CUPA) annually. HSC 25500 *et seq.,* 19 CCR 2729–2732. The threshold quantities, which are much lower than those required under EPCRA, are as follows:

- 55 gallons of a liquid
- 500 pounds of a solid
- 200 cubic feet of a gas at standard temperature (68°F) and pressure
- Radioactive materials in quantities for which an emergency response plan is required under federal or state regulations

Exemptions from HMBP requirements include:

- Hazardous materials that are in transit or that are temporarily maintained in a fixed facility for less than 30 days during transportation (*e.g.,* hazardous material contained in any railcar or marine vessel)
- Oxygen and nitrous oxide stored at medical offices
- Less than 55 gallons of lubricating oil (excluding used oil) when the total volume of lubricating oil handled at the facility does not exceed 275 gallons at any one time
- Farms meeting specified conditions

Businesses required to submit HMBPs are referred to as handlers. A handler is defined as "any business that handles a hazardous material." HSC 25501(n). A hazardous material is defined as a substance or waste that, because of its physical, chemical, or other characteristics, may pose a risk of endangering human health or safety or of degrading the environment, and the definition includes hazardous wastes. HSC 25260(d).

HMBP handlers must also submit the following HMBP components to the CUPA:

- Hazardous material inventory (also meets EPCRA's inventory requirements)
- List of emergency contacts
- Site plan with chemical locations

Handlers must also report to the CUPA any changes in the quantities of chemicals stored at a facility.

Individual CUPAs may require submission of additional HMBP components, including the facility's internal emergency response plan and its internal training plan. Businesses on leased property that already are required to develop and implement an HMBP must meet specified notification requirements. HSC 25503.6, 25505.

Individual CUPAs may require submission of additional HMBP components, including the facility's internal emergency response plan and its internal training plan.

Toxic release inventory. In 2006, EPA raised the federal threshold for reporting chemical releases that trigger TRI reporting from 500 pounds per year to 2,000 pounds. By raising the threshold, millions of pounds of toxic chemicals will not be reported and made available to the public. In response, the California Legislature enacted the California Toxic Release Inventory Program of 2007 (effective on January 1, 2009), which requires facilities to submit a toxic chemical release form to DTSC if the facility is not required to submit a form containing the same information under EPCRA. HSC 25546 *et seq.* Also, in November 2007, the California Attorney General, along with 11 other states, challenged EPA's changes to the TRI in the U.S. District Court for the Southern District of New York.

Release reporting. Under California law, handlers must immediately report the release of any material where there is "a reasonable basis for believing that it would be injurious to the health and safety of persons or harmful to the environment if released into the workplace or the environment." HSC 25507 19, CCR 2703. Handlers must decide on a case-by-case basis whether to report; miscalculating whether a release meets the reporting criteria could result in significant penalties. Unlike the vast number of release reporting laws, this release reporting law imposes no minimum numeric reportable quantity.

If a chemical spills into the environment, a number of other federal, state, and local reporting obligations must be met, including notifying various agencies within specified timeframes. For the most part, other California reporting requirements follow the federal scheme involving a specified list of chemical substances that must be reported when a hazardous substance threshold or "reportable quantity" has been exceeded.

A reportable quantity (RQ) is a quantity expressed in pounds. If a release over a 24-hour period meets or exceeds the RQ, then the notification requirements apply. Specific RQs are identified for extremely hazardous substances under CERCLA, the Comprehensive Environmental Response, Compensation, and Liability

CERCLA = Comprehensive Environmental Response, Compensation, and Liability Act

RQ = Reportable quantity

Act. The RQ for EHSs is one pound. For substances that are CERCLA hazardous substances, or are a combination of an EHS and a CERCLA hazardous substance, the RQ is listed in 40 CFR 302.4. RQs range from one pound to 5,000 pounds. RQs for releases impacting water quality have different thresholds.

Each regulatory reporting requirement is independent for compliance purposes (*i.e.*, reporting under one law does not necessarily relieve a party from reporting under another law). For this reason, if a spill or release occurs, it is advisable to examine all federal and state release reporting requirements as applicable under one or more of the programs described above and in chapters 8 and 10. For guidance on release reporting, *see* the sidebar on page 157.

Chemical Handling and Storage

Overview of Federal OSHA Requirements

Federal OSHA (29 CFR 1910.1200 *et seq.*) regulates all employers (with some exceptions, such as self-employed persons and farmers who employ family members). OSHA addresses all facets of worker safety, ranging from managing electrical hazards, confined spaces, fall hazards, and chemical handling, among many other areas. This discussion only addresses those OSHA standards governing hazardous chemicals. These standards essentially codify good management housekeeping practices to prevent chemical spills, reactions, and exposures. As a general rule, OSHA standards specify where and how to store different categories of hazardous materials and hazardous waste. For example, hazardous materials and waste must be labeled to indicate chemical content, along with hazard warnings.

The federal OSHA rules specify prescriptive chemical storage standards for the following general categories of hazardous materials:

- Flammable and combustible liquids

- Corrosives

- Reactive chemicals, including compressed gases

- Toxic materials

This section addresses the "front end" risks posed by these chemicals; the "back end" risks are discussed in chapter 8, which addresses RCRA Subtitle C.

Flammable and Combustible Liquids

A flammable liquid is defined as any liquid having a flashpoint below 100°F, while a combustible liquid includes any liquid having a flashpoint at or above 100°F.

Definitions. Federal OSHA rules distinguish between flammable and combustible liquids. A flammable liquid is defined as any liquid having a flashpoint below 100° Fahrenheit, while a combustible liquid includes any liquid having a flashpoint at or above 100° Fahrenheit. 29 CFR 1910.106(a)(19). Flammable

Table 7-2. Ignitable, Flammable, and Combustible Chemical Regulatory Classifications

Environmental Protection Agency	Federal Occupational Safety and Health Administration	U.S. Department of Transportation
D001 Ignitable hazardous waste Flashpoint <140°F	Class IA flammable liquid Flashpoint ≤73°F Boiling point <100°F	Packaging group II Flashpoint <73°F
	Class IB flammable liquid Flashpoint ≤73°F Boiling point ≥100°F	
	Class IC flammable liquid Flashpoint >73°F and <100° F	Packaging group III Flashpoint ≥73°F and ≤141°F
	Class II combustible liquid Flashpoint ≥100°F and <140°F	
Nonhazardous waste Flashpoint >140°F	Class IIIA combustible liquid Flashpoint ≥140°F and <200°F	Combustible liquids for bulk packaging only Flashpoint >141°F and <200°F
	Class IIIB combustible liquid Flashpoint ≥200°F	Not regulated by the U.S. DOT Liquids with flashpoint ≥200°F

Source: 40 CFR 261, 29 CFR 1910.106(a)(18), 49 CFR 171, 173

liquids and combustible liquids are subdivided into hazard classes as illustrated in Table 7-2, which also describes the regulatory programs and terminology used to characterize "ignitable" hazardous wastes and "flammable" and "combustible" materials. The flashpoint for a given hazardous material is listed on an MSDS; the handler can then determine whether the hazardous material is flammable or combustible, and what class it is.

Flammable storage standards. The NFPA codes and standards were created to address industrial and large storage facilities that maintain large quantities of hazardous materials used for processing, manufacturing, and storage. Chapter 66 of the Uniform Fire Code (UFC) establishes performance standards for flammable and combustible liquids in containers, tanks, and buildings, including:

UFC = Uniform Fire Code

- Design, installation, and construction of tanks and piping systems that store and transport flammable and combustible liquids
- Creation and construction of containers and portable tanks for storing such liquids

UFC Chapter 67 discusses the requirements for storing, using, and handling flammable solids. UFC Chapter 70 addresses the general storage, use, and handling of oxidizers and organic peroxides. Section 71.1 of the UFC deals with the proper outdoor storage and handling of pyrophoric solids and liquids.

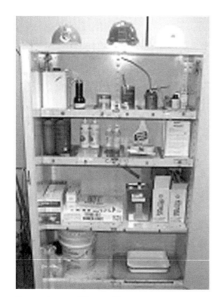

Proper storage of flammable and combustible materials

Whether the flammable and combustible materials are stored in a flammable cabinet or inside a storage room or building, the chemicals must meet specified storage standards.

Federal OSHA standards specify requirements for flammable and combustible liquids. 29 CFR 1910.106(d)(3) *et seq.* Storage of more than 25 gallons must be in fire-rated cabinets meeting certain specifications, including secondary containment to capture spills. No more than 60 gallons of Class I or Class II liquids, and no more than 120 gallons of Class III liquids, may be stored in a flammable cabinet. Chemical containers too large to fit within a flammable cabinet, with a size of more than 60 gallons of Class I or Class II liquids, or more than 120 gallons of Class III liquids, must be stored in specially equipped rooms or buildings meeting certain specifications.

The UFC also contains provisions on the capacity, construction, and design of storage cabinets for Class I, II, and IIA liquids that vary depending on the occupancy of the building. UFC Section 66.4.3. Additionally, the UFC addresses environmental concerns associated with hazardous materials storage lockers, as well as design features necessary to meet applicable local, state, and federal regulations. UFC Section 66.4.6.

Whether the flammable and combustible materials are stored in a flammable cabinet or inside a storage room or building, the chemicals must meet specified storage standards. Hazardous materials must be segregated from incompatible chemicals. For example, acid cleaners (which are corrosive) must be isolated from flammable chemicals such as gasoline. In addition, flammables such as solvent-based paint must be separated from oxidizers such as lithium batteries. Further guidance on chemical compatibility may be found on the chemical's MSDS.

Individual flammable and combustible containers must be kept closed, except when adding or entering contents. In addition, the containers must display the chemical hazard warnings reflected on the MSDS as more fully discussed in Hazard Communication, above.

UFC Chapter 43 establishes recommended or mandatory operating procedures for spraying, dipping, and coating using flammable or combustible materials, for example, performance requirements for each spray area. The UFC also addresses requirements for storing, handling, and mixing flammable and combustible liquids.

Corrosives

Corrosive chemicals (such as strong acids and bases) can cause damage to human tissues, causing serious burns and irritation to skin and eyes. Safety showers and eye wash stations must be located near corrosive storage and activities to allow quick drenching or flushing of the eyes and body. 29 CFR 1910.151(c). *See* sidebar on facing page for further information on corrosives.

Reactive Chemicals, Including Compressed Gases

Gases stored under pressure pose fire and explosion hazards. Federal OSHA rules require that compressed gases be stored securely to prevent tipping. Incompatible compressed gas fuel cylinders (such as propane and oxygen) must be stored separately at least 20 feet apart. The rules also establish smoking restrictions near storage areas. 29 CFR 1910.101, 1910.106(d)(7).

Toxic Materials

Toxic materials can cause chronic and acute harm, ranging from organ damage to cancer. To avoid occupational exposures, personnel should consult MSDSs to learn what types of PPE to apply. UFC Chapter 68 addresses the storage, use, and handling of toxic solids and liquids, and establishes standards for indoor and outdoor storage of toxic materials.

Hazardous Materials Transportation Act

The HMTA protects against risks to life and property from transporting hazardous materials in commerce. 49 CFR 105 *et seq.* The Act regulates any transporter of hazardous materials or any person who manufactures, marks, repairs, or tests a package that was certified, sold, or marked for use in the transportation of hazardous materials. Any person requesting transportation of hazardous materials must maintain shipping papers describing the substances to be shipped. Each person providing shipping papers must retain copies or keep an electronic image at their principal place of business for specified time periods.

Underground Storage Tank Regulation

Federal Program

Overview. Following the pioneering policies of California, the Congress enacted RCRA Subtitle I (42 USC 6991 *et seq.*) in 1988 to regulate and manage underground storage tank risks. EPA regulations (40 CFR 280.20 *et seq.*) govern the design, permitting, operation, and closure of USTs to prevent releases of specified chemicals to the environment.

The federal program is designed to be implemented by the states, which must submit their UST programs to EPA for

Corrosive Chemicals

It is advisable to consult an MSDS to determine what type of personal protective equipment (PPE) to use when handling corrosive chemicals. Corrosive chemicals should not be stored in metal drums or containers because the chemicals can corrode and compromise the container. For common acids and bases requiring special management, *see* the table below.

Common Acids and Bases

Acids (pH 0–6)	Bases (pH 8–14)
Hydrochloric acid	Sodium hydroxide (lye)
Hydrofluoric acid	Sodium hypochlorite (bleach)
Nitric acid	Aqueous ammonia
Phosphoric acid	Potassium hydroxide (potash)
Chromic acid	Ammonium hydroxide

PPE = Personal protective equipment

EPA regulations govern the design, permitting, operation, and closure of USTs to prevent releases of specified chemicals to the environment.

approval. California has not sought EPA approval yet, though the Legislature has expressed this intent. *See* HSC 25299.7. Until the California program is approved, both federal and state requirements apply to USTs.

Applicability. RCRA Subtitle I establishes performance standards governing "UST systems" that store a "regulated substance." A "regulated substance" includes "hazardous substances" and petroleum. 40 CFR 280.12. "A hazardous substance" is a broadly defined term that includes all chemicals regulated under CERCLA (*see* chapter 8) with the exception of "hazardous waste" (which is defined under RCRA Subtitle C). "Petroleum" includes crude oil and fractions, such as motor fuels, jet fuels, distillate fuel oils, lubricants, petroleum solvents, and used oils. A "UST system" includes tanks that are 10 percent or more beneath the surface, plus underground piping, that stores a regulated substance. A regulated UST system must be constructed of nonearthen materials, such as wood, concrete, steel, and plastic. 40 CFR 280.20.

Federal rules impose a number of performance requirements for new USTs and upgrades to existing USTs.

New and upgraded underground storage tanks. Federal rules impose a number of performance requirements for new USTs and upgrades to existing USTs. 40 CFR 280.20. New USTs installed after 1988 must have been permitted and be equipped with specified secondary containment, including associated piping. For single-walled USTs, secondary containment capacity must be at least 100 percent of the primary tank. For tank systems with more than one tank, the secondary containment capacity must be at least 150 percent of the largest primary tank or 10 percent of the aggregate of all tanks (whichever is greater). For tanks with secondary containment structures exposed to rainfall, the containment capacity must be able to accommodate 24 hours of precipitation for a 25-year storm.

New USTs also must be equipped to monitor for releases into secondary containment. Specifically, UST monitoring must be able to detect releases into the interstitial space that separates the primary from the secondary tank. 23 CCR 2611. In addition, USTs must be equipped with spill and overfill controls (*e.g.*, automatic shutoff at 95 percent capacity and alarms) to prevent releases. Corrosion protection (*e.g.*, cathodic protection) may be required for UST systems comprised of metal to protect the integrity of the tank. 40 CFR 280.20, 280.30, 280.31. For those tanks not constructed with metal, the following construction materials must be used:

- Fiberglass-reinforced plastic
- Steel with cathodic protection
- Steel fiberglass-reinforced plastic composite

Owners and operators of UST systems must monitor to ensure that regulated substances are neither released from the primary to the secondary tank nor from the secondary tank to the environment.

Owners and operators of UST systems must monitor to ensure that regulated substances are neither released from the primary to the secondary tank nor from the secondary tank to the environment. Monitoring procedures must be described in a written routine monitoring program. 40 CFR 280.34, 280.45.

Owners and operators must submit monthly reports and annual reports showing that data is within allowable variations. Also, owners and operators must develop and implement a response plan to address the possibility of an unauthorized release. 40 CFR 280.66.

Retrofit and upgrade of "existing" underground storage tanks. UST systems in place prior to December 22, 1998, were considered to be "existing" tanks and were required to meet specified retrofit and upgrade standards by December 22, 1998, or be shut down. These requirements included retrofitting the tank with an interior lining, installing cathodic protection for the tank and piping, installing secondary containment (with some exceptions), and installing spill and overfill prevention equipment.

View of underground storage tank from surface

Operating permits. UST systems must operate pursuant to a UST permit, which lasts for five years. UST system owners and operators must maintain records documenting any change in service, repairs, leak detection, monitoring, inspections, corrosion protections, agency notifications, and closure information. Each record must be maintained for a specified period of time.

Closure. UST systems that are taken out of service temporarily or permanently must meet specified closure requirements. Different requirements apply for temporary closures of fewer than 12 consecutive months, and permanent closures of more than 12 months. 40 CFR 280.70(b)(c). An application for closure must be submitted within 30 days prior to removal from use. 40 CFR 280.71(a).

State Program

Applicability. California led the nation with its groundbreaking underground storage tank policies in 1984. This program was later adopted by Congress, EPA, and other states. An underground tank system includes the tank and the underground piping that stores a "hazardous substance," is substantially or totally beneath the surface, and is constructed of nonearthen materials (*e.g.*, wood, concrete, steel, and plastic). A "hazardous substance" is defined broadly to include hazardous wastes (as defined under California law; *see* chapter 8) and "petroleum," which includes crude oil and fractions (*e.g.*, motor fuels, jet fuels, distillate fuel oils, lubricants, petroleum solvents, and used oils). HSC 25280 *et seq.*, 23 CCR 2611 *et seq.* A master list of hazardous substances can be obtained from DTSC. HSC 25282.

For each UST system, owners and operators must operate pursuant to a permit issued by the CUPA. If there is no CUPA, the agency responsible for implementing the UST program is the local agency

California led the nation with its groundbreaking underground storage tank policies in 1984. This program was later adopted by Congress, EPA, and other states.

designated by the Secretary for Environmental Protection. HSC 25281(i), (j), (k); 25283(a), (b); 25404.3(f).

USTs may be operated only by designated operators that meet certain training and certification requirements. 23 CCR 2715. Also, owners and operators of USTs that store petroleum products must meet specified financial assurance requirements. 23 CCR 2805 *et seq.*

Exemptions. The California UST program exempts specific containers from regulation under the statute. For example, the following USTs are exempt: tanks with 1,100 gallons or less capacity that are located on a farm and used for storing motor vehicle fuel that is used primarily for agricultural purposes, or tanks storing home heating oil for consumptive use. Other exemptions apply to structures such as sumps, storm drains, catch basins, evaporation ponds, lagoons, and tanks holding hydraulic fluid for a closed loop mechanical system using compressed air or hydraulic fluid to operate lifts or other similar devices. HSC 25281(y)(1)(A).

New and upgraded underground storage tanks. The performance standards for new USTs are similar to federal standards; however, for tanks storing hazardous substances, the California standards apply to tanks installed after 1984, whereas the federal standards apply to tanks installed after 1988. Like the federal program, secondary containment for new USTs is required. The minimum volume requirements for secondary containment are the same as the federal requirements. The SWRCB offers grants of up to $15,000 to small businesses to assist in complying with testing and leak detection equipment, meeting interstitial space requirements, and integrity testing. HSC 25290.1(c)(4), (5); HSC 25290.2 (c)(4), (5); 23 CCR 2631.

All new UST systems must be made of or lined with materials that are compatible with the substance being stored. Secondary containment systems must be tested every 36 months after initial testing. UST owners or operators must annually test the spill containment structure to show that it is capable of containing the substance if an overfilling event occurs. Owners or operators of UST systems are also required to prevent releases from overfilling during product delivery. 23 CCR 2631.1(a), 2637(a), 2712(k); HSC 25284.2. For an illustration of some required performance standards, see Figure 7-2.

Since the deadline to upgrade or close USTs expired in 1998 (*see* below), owners and operators of USTs in California have been confronted with new state rules calling for additional performance standards. 23 CCR 2662 *et seq.*

Underground storage tank systems installed after July 1, 2004. These tanks must be designed and constructed with a continuous monitoring system capable of detecting entry of liquid or vapor into the secondary containment from the primary containment, or detecting water intrusion. These tanks must be double-contained, with the primary and secondary containment designed to be "product

USTs installed after July 1, 2004 must be designed and constructed with a continuous monitoring system capable of detecting entry of liquid or vapor into the secondary containment from the primary containment, or detecting water intrusion.

tight" (impervious to liquid and vapor of the contained substance). Secondary containment must be constructed to prevent water intrusion into the UST system by precipitation, infiltration, or surface runoff. HSC 25281(o), 25290.1, 25290.2 *et seq.* Interstitial space of USTs must be maintained under constant vacuum or pressure to detect a breach in the primary or secondary containment before liquid or vapor is released to the environment. HSC 25290.1 *et seq.*

All secondary containment, including under-dispenser containment (*e.g.*, gasoline dispenser), must be equipped with a continuous monitoring system that either activates an alarm or stops the flow of the product when it detects a leak. Automatic line leak detectors that restrict or shut off the flow of product through the piping must be installed on all underground pressurized piping. 23 CCR 2636(f)(1) and (2).

Vent lines, vapor recovery lines, and fill pipes that are beneath the surface of the ground must have secondary containment. Underground pressurized piping must be equipped with an automatic line leak detector and must be tightness tested annually. HSC 25290.

Installation requirements. Owners and operators of UST systems must certify that the UST and piping was installed by certified UST installers and that that the CUPA approved the installation. All secondary containment systems, including piping, must comply with specified construction and performance standards similar to the federal UST program, and all secondary containment systems are required to be periodically tested. All tank and piping integrity tests must be performed or supervised by a licensed tank tester with a valid tank testing license. Finally, owners or operators of UST systems are required to notify the CUPA at least 48 hours before installing, repairing, replacing, calibrating, or certifying monitoring equipment. HSC 25284.4; 23 CCR 2635 *et seq.*.

Retrofit and upgrade of "existing" underground storage tanks. "Existing" underground storage tanks were required to have been upgraded to meet specific technology standards or removed by December 22, 1998.

Figure 7-2
UST Performance Standards for Leak Detection

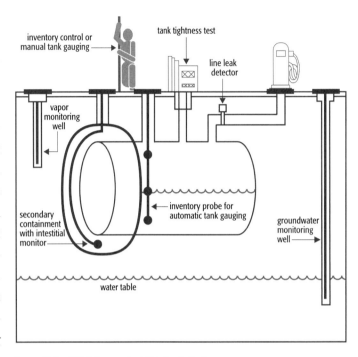

Source: National Work Group on Leak Detection Evaluations

Owners and operators of UST systems must certify that the UST and piping was installed by certified UST installers and that the CUPA approved the installation.

Monitoring, recordkeeping, and release reporting. The day-to-day operation of the UST system must follow a CUPA-approved monitoring and response program. A copy of the permit and monitoring plan must be retained either at the facility or off-site at a readily available location. The site must maintain certain records; requirements are similar to the federal standards. HSC 25286, 25293; 23 CCR 2632–2634, 2636, 2711, 2712.

Unauthorized releases of hazardous substances from the secondary or primary containment (where no secondary containment exists) must be reported to the CUPA within 24 hours. UST owners or operators responsible for the unauthorized release must submit a written report to the local agency within five days. The report must describe the nature and volume of the release along with the corrective actions that were taken. Water Code 13271, 13272.

Closure and cleanup. Owners or operators of USTs must notify the CUPA and receive approval before temporarily or permanently closing USTs. Owners or operators also must meet specified requirements for temporarily closed USTs and permanently closed USTs and must demonstrate that no unauthorized release occurred. 23 CCR 2670–2672.

Created in 1989, the UST cleanup fund was enacted to help petroleum UST owners and operators pay for cleanup of contaminated soil and groundwater caused by leaks. HSC 25299.10 *et seq.* The funds can be used for repair, replacement, upgrade, or removal of petroleum USTs. The program is financed by a fee paid by UST owners and operators. To be eligible for cleanup funds, UST owners and operators must demonstrate that contamination resulted from a UST leak, and cleanup work must have been performed after 1987. The claimant also must be in compliance with UST permitting requirements and cleanup orders. The maximum reimbursement per occurrence is no more than $1.5 million.

A site-specific variance is a state-approved departure from the regulations for a particular UST system based on site-specific circumstances.

Variances. A site-specific variance is a state-approved departure from the regulations for a particular UST system based on site-specific circumstances. Permit holders and permit applicants may apply to the appropriate Regional Water Quality Control Board. HSC 25299.4.

Other Hazardous Materials Programs

In addition to the regulatory programs previously reviewed, there are a variety of additional federal and state programs regulating some aspect of hazardous materials ands toxic substances. These miscellaneous programs are reviewed below.

Toxic Substances Control Act

Enacted in 1976, TSCA (15 USC 2601 *et seq.*, 40 CFR 700 *et seq.*) protects human health and the environment by regulating chemical substances that are manufactured, processed, distributed, or used for commercial purposes. TSCA authorizes

EPA to screen new chemicals before they are introduced into commerce for their potential health or environmental effects. The Act also allows EPA to screen existing chemicals if they pose an unreasonable risk of harm to human health or the environment. Currently, as a direct result of this screening process, more than 500 chemicals are subject to regulatory controls.

PAIR = Preliminary Assessment Information Rule

PMN = Premanufacture notice

Section 5(a) premanufacture notice. TSCA requires manufacturers, processors, or importers to notify EPA before they produce or introduce a non-exempt chemical product into the country. 15 USC 2604(a). The notice is called a pre-manufacture notice (PMN) and must be submitted at least 90 days prior to the activity. Upon notification, EPA then has 45 days to determine the chemical's potential risk to human health or the environment, if any. 40 CFR 720 *et seq.*

TSCA (15 USC 2604(h)) grants some exemptions to the PMN requirement. Specifically, upon application, manufacturers, processors, or importers of non-exempt new chemicals for test marketing purposes are exempt from submittal of a PMN. Similarly, small quantities of chemicals solely for research and development are exempt. 40 CFR 720.36, 720.38.

Section 8(a) general reporting and recordkeeping requirements. Manufacturers, processors, and importers of listed chemical substances and mixtures must comply with various reporting and recordkeeping requirements. The Preliminary Assessment Information Rule (PAIR) requires manufacturers and importers to report site-specific information for each plant site at which they manufactured or imported the listed chemical. The information must include:

- The quantity of the imported or manufactured chemical
- The amount routinely lost to the environment during manufacture or importation
- The quantity of enclosed, controlled, and open releases of the chemical
- Worker exposure information

Some companies are exempt from this reporting requirement. 40 CFR 712.20, 712.25(a)–(c). Most chemical products manufactured for export are excluded from TSCA requirements, except for Section 8's general reporting and recordkeeping requirements. 15 USC 2607(a), TSCA Section 12 (b), 40 CFR 707.60(b).

Section 8(c) allegations of significant adverse reactions rule. Producers, processors, and distributors of regulated chemical substances must maintain a file of allegations of significant adverse reactions (to human health or the environment) and report those allegations to the EPA. Companies must keep these files for five years at their headquarters or at a centrally located site near the company's chemical operations. Not all allegations are subject to this rule. Exemptions include accusations alleging "known human effects," anonymous accusations, and any allegations directly attributable to an environmental contamination incident that has been reported to the federal government. 15 USC 2607(c), 40 CFR 717.12(b), (d).

Producers, processors, and distributors of regulated chemical substances must maintain a file of allegations of significant adverse reactions to human health or the environment and report those allegations to the EPA.

Section 8(e) substantial risk information requirement. Companies have a duty to report to EPA within 30 calendar days any new information they have that reasonably shows that a substance or mixture they manufacture, import, process, or distribute presents a substantial risk to human health or the environment. These notices generally include, among other things, toxicity and exposure data, and any ongoing actions that reduce potential risks to human health or the environment. EPA 2003, *see also* 15 USC 2607(e).

Title II asbestos regulation. The Asbestos Hazard Emergency Response Act became law in 1986 as Title II of TSCA. 15 USC 2641 *et seq.* The Act regulates asbestos–a naturally occurring mineral substance that has been used widely for insulation (*e.g.*, for boilers) and fireproofing (*e.g.*, pipe lagging, floor tiles, roof shingles, and gaskets). Generally, asbestos is not a hazard unless it is inhaled.

ACBM = Asbestos-containing building material

ASHARA = Asbestos School Hazard Abatement Reauthorization Act

AHERA governs the control and abatement of asbestos hazards in school buildings and requires school agencies to develop an inventory of friable (capable of being pulverized under hand pressure) and non-friable asbestos-containing materials. The schools must implement management plans that detail abatement actions they can undertake. In addition, school officials must label building materials that contain asbestos and periodically conduct facility inspections. The local school district must ensure that all staff members who work in an area with asbestos-containing building material (ACBM) will have at least two hours of training. 15 USC 2643 *et seq.*, 40 CFR 763.92 (a).

AHERA was amended in 1990 by the Asbestos School Hazard Abatement Reauthorization Act (ASHARA). 15 USC 2641, 40 CFR 763 *et seq.* ASHARA requires personnel inspecting ACM in schools and commercial and public buildings to be trained on the proper methods for handling ACM.

Asbestos Regulation

Occupational Safety and Health Act general industry standards. OSHA's general industry standards most typically apply to asbestos manufacturers and businesses involved in brake and clutch repairs. Specific monitoring, operational practices, and notification rules govern the construction industry for ACM demolition and removal and installation, repair, maintenance, or renovation of structures containing asbestos. 29 CFR 1926.1101(d).

National Emissions Standards for Hazardous Air Pollutants. Section 112 of the Clean Air Act created the National Emissions Standards for Hazardous Air Pollutants with the goal of protecting the public from known hazardous pollutants. The NESHAP program (more fully described in chapter 5), among other things, regulates the release of asbestos during the demolition or renovation of all facilities, excluding residential structures with four or fewer dwelling units. Building owners and contractors must notify the local pollution control district before any processing, handling, or disposal of ACM from buildings exceeds threshold amounts. The notification must contain information such as a description of the work to be conducted, the name and location of the waste disposal site, and an estimate of the amount of regulated asbestos-containing material (RACM) to be removed. Most removed RACM must be disposed of in either a Class II landfill that can accept "designated" wastes (*see* chapter 9) or a Class I hazardous waste landfill (*see* chapter 8). 40 CFR 61.145 *et seq.*

RACM = Regulated asbestos-containing material

California asbestos program. The California Asbestos Notification Act (HSC 25915 *et seq.*) requires that the owner of any building constructed before 1979, who knows that the building contains asbestos, must provide written notice to employees working in the building of the following:

- Specific locations within the building of asbestos-containing construction materials
- General procedures and handling restrictions to limit, prevent release of, or prevent exposure to asbestos
- A summary of the results of any bulk sample analysis, or air monitoring, conducted for or by the owner, or within the owner's control
- Potential health risks associated with asbestos exposure

Notice must be given within 15 days of the owner receiving information identifying the presence of ACM. Subsequently, the owner must provide annual written notice to all employees.

New employees must receive notice within 15 days of beginning work in the building. Contractors expected to do work on the building must make copies of the ACM notice and distribute the notice to all employees working within the building. The owner must post a clean and conspicuous warning notice addressing any construction, maintenance, or remodeling in an area where there is a potential for employees to come in contact with ACM.

Cal/OSHA also imposes occupational permissible exposure limits for asbestos.

Lead Regulation

Federal lead program. Lead-based paint has been extensively applied on surfaces for decades. Lead-based paint was banned from residential use in 1978, under the Residential Lead-Based Hazard Reduction Act of 1992. 42 USC 4851 *et seq.*, 24 CFR 35 Subpart A.

Lead-based paint was banned from residential use in 1978, under the Residential Lead-Based Hazard Reduction Act of 1992.

The Act, also known as Title X, requires sellers and landlords of residential property built before 1978 (also known as target housing) to provide the following to property buyers and renters:

- Specified disclosures about lead
- A lead-based paint hazard pamphlet developed by the EPA, the Department of Housing and Urban Development, and the Consumer Product Safety Commission (CPSC)

CPSC = Consumer Product Safety Commission

Exemptions from the Act include houses built after 1978, structures with zero-bedroom units (*e.g.* dormitories, studio apartments), leases for less than 100 days, housing for the elderly or handicapped, rental housing found by a certified inspector to be lead-free, and foreclosure sales. 42 USC 4851 *et seq.*, 24 CFR 35 Subpart A, 40 CFR 745.100 *et seq.*

Under the Act, sellers must allow the buyer a 10-day period to conduct a lead-based paint inspection or risk assessment, at the buyer's expense. The seller's contract must contain language of notification and disclosure about any known lead-based paint or lead-based paint hazards in the dwelling unit. Additionally, with any renovation of target housing, the renovator must provide the owner and occupant pamphlets on lead hazards before beginning such activities. 42 USC 4852(d), 40 CFR 745.85.

California lead program. The Lead Hazard Reduction Enforcement Act (HSC 105250–105257) makes it a crime to own a residential or public building that contains lead hazards that are likely to endanger the health or the public or occupants, or to engage in an activity that creates a lead hazard. Lead hazard is defined as "deteriorated lead-based paint, lead contaminated dust, lead contaminated soil, disturbing lead-based paint or presumed lead-based paint without containment, or any other nuisance which may result in persistent and quantifiable lead exposure." 17 CCR 35037.

The Occupational Lead Poisoning Prevention Act (HSC 105185 *et seq.*) establishes an occupational lead poisoning prevention program, to register and monitor laboratory reports of adult lead toxicity cases, to identify sources of lead poisoning through monitoring, to conduct investigations of take-home exposure cases, to train employees and health experts on prevention measures, and to recommend methods for lead poisoning prevention.

Polychlorinated Biphenyl Regulation

Polychlorinated biphenyls are a family of over 200 aromatic chemicals that have been used pervasively due to their effective insulating properties and the fact that they are nonflammable.

Polychlorinated biphenyls are a family of over 200 aromatic chemicals that have been used pervasively due to their effective insulating properties and the fact that they are nonflammable. PCBs have been used extensively as coolants in electrical equipment (*e.g.*, PCB-containing insulating oils in transformers and capacitors), fluorescent light ballasts, and building materials (*e.g.*, adhesives, tile and tar coatings, caulking, paints, and inks).

PCBs contain dioxin, a probable carcinogen that also poses potentially significant health risks, including liver damage, neurological disorders, and skin hazards. PCBs are highly persistent chemicals that have a long life in the environment.

Manufacturing ban. TSCA Section 6 (15 USC 2601 *et seq.*) allows EPA to regulate chemicals presenting unreasonable risk. Due to the significant health and environmental hazards posed by PCBs, EPA banned PCB production in 1979.

TSCA prohibits the manufacturing and use of PCBs, with some exceptions. PCBs may be used in existing equipment (such as transformers and capacitors) and in small quantities for research and development. 40 CFR 761 *et seq.*

Cradle-to-grave requirements. TSCA regulates PCB manufacturing and use, as well as storage, disposal, import, export, and spills. TSCA established a cradle-to-grave program governing the management of PCBs from the time the PCB becomes a waste to its ultimate disposal. This federal program is administered by the EPA and regulates only PCB oils and other PCB-containing equipment with concentrations above 50 parts per million (ppm). The following items, containing between 50 and 500 ppm PCB, are regulated and are subject to specified marking and labeling requirements:

TSCA established a cradle-to-grave program governing the management of PCBs from the time the PCB becomes a waste to its ultimate disposal.

- PCB capacitors
- PCB-contaminated electrical equipment
- PCB-contaminated transformers
- PCB articles (*i.e.,* a manufactured item that contains PCBs and where the surface has been in direct contact with PCBs, such as capacitors, transformers, and electric motors)
- PCB containers (*e.g.,* packages, cans, bottles, drums, tanks, or other package that contains PCBs, or PCB articles or equipment where the surface has been in direct contact with PCBs)
- PCB-containing light ballasts

PCB transformers that contain greater than 500 ppm PCB must be inspected once every three months. 40 CFR 761.30 (a)(1)(ix).

Key aspects of the PCB program include maintaining an annual PCB inventory and properly equipping long-term storage facilities, similar to 90-day hazardous waste storage facilities (*see* chapter 8). The primary difference between a 90-day hazardous waste storage facility and a PCB long-term storage facility is that the PCB bulk product waste may be stored only if the waste is piled in a manner to control dissemination by wind or any means other than water. Also, the waste must not generate leachate through decomposition or any other reaction. 40 CFR 761.65(4)(b)(1).

A one-year time limit exists for disposal of PCBs with concentrations of 50 ppm or more. PCB handlers must annually complete by July 1 of each year a log that must include an inventory of PCB items, including information on the PCB content. The PCB waste must be disposed of within one year from the date the handler determines it to be a waste and decides to dispose of it. 40 CFR 761.65. TSCA regulations specify disposal options that range from a TSCA-approved incinerator, a TSCA-approved chemical waste landfill, or a high-efficiency boiler.

A one-year time limit exists for disposal of PCBs with concentrations of 50 ppm or more.

Certain PCB items may be stored temporarily for up to 30 days from the date of their removal from service. These items include:

- Non-leaking PCB articles and equipment
- Leaking PCB articles and equipment if placed in non-leaking PCB containers
- PCB containers containing non-liquid PCBs
- PCB containers with PCB liquid concentrations of 50 ppm or more

Temporary storage is allowed only if a spill prevention, control, and countermeasure plan has been prepared, and if the waste is packed according to DOT hazardous materials regulations.

Temporary storage is allowed only if a spill prevention, control, and countermeasure plan (*see* chapter 10) has been prepared, and if the waste is packed according to DOT hazardous materials regulations.

Similar to the hazardous waste manifest program (*see* chapter 8), PCB shipments are tracked by a PCB manifest, with copies for the PCB generator, the initial transporter, and the owner or operator of the disposal facility. Like the hazardous waste program, the generator must ensure that a signed copy of the manifest is received within 35 days of the date the PCB was accepted by the initial transporter. If the signed copy does not arrive by the 35th day, the generator immediately must contact the transporter or owner or operator of the "designated facility" to determine the status of the PCB waste. The generator must file an exception report with the EPA if the paperwork is not returned within 45 days of the date the waste was accepted by the initial transporter. Disposal facilities

COD = Certificate of Disposal

are required to issue a Certificate of Disposal (COD) for each shipment of manifested PCB accepted. 40 CFR 761.3, 761.215.

California requirements. As discussed more fully in chapter 8, PCB wastes between 5 and 50 ppm must be managed as a California-only hazardous waste. It may be necessary to manage PCB wastes with concentrations less than 5 ppm as "designated" wastes (more fully discussed in chapter 10).

Toxic Mold Protection Act of 2001

This Act (HSC 26100 *et seq.*) requires sellers and landlords of residential, commercial, and industrial real property to disclose mold presence to buyers and tenants. Specifically, when the seller or landlord knows of mold presence that exceeds the PEL or poses a health threat, he or she must provide a written disclosure to the prospective or current buyers or tenants. Residential landlords must disclose before tenants enter into a rental agreement. These obligations only will apply after DPH sets PELs and other health standards for mold. Commercial and industrial landlords also have an affirmative duty to assess the condition of mold if they know or have notice that the mold is present on property other than real property (such as heating, ventilation, and air conditioning systems).

Proposition 65

The Safe Drinking Water and Toxic Enforcement Act of 1986 is a unique California law designed to minimize the public's exposure to known human carcinogens and reproductive toxicants.

The Safe Drinking Water and Toxic Enforcement Act of 1986 (known as Proposition 65) is a unique California law designed to minimize the public's exposure to known human carcinogens and reproductive toxicants. HSC 25249.5–25249.13. Citizens can bring actions to enforce the law when prosecutors (*i.e.,* the Attorney General, district attorney, or city attorney) fail to sue an alleged violator after receiving a 60-day notice of the alleged violation. The law lays out an elaborate scheme designed to ensure that only cases with merit are pursued, and that settlements between private citizens and alleged violators are brought into the open.

Proposition 65 imposes two principal requirements upon businesses (local, state, and federal government entities are exempt) that have more than 10 employees. First, regulated businesses must not expose persons to listed carcinogens and reproductive toxicants without providing a "clear and reasonable" warning (known as the warning requirement). Second, regulated businesses are prohibited from discharging or releasing any listed carcinogens and reproductive toxicants (22 CCR 12000 *et seq.*) that may potentially contact a source or potential source of drinking water (known as the prohibition of discharge). The list of regulated chemicals is adopted by the OEHHA.

Businesses are exempt from Proposition 65 if the exposures or discharges do not cause a significant amount of chemical to enter any drinking water source, and the exposures or discharges conform to all applicable regulations, permits, requirements, and orders. A business is exempt from the warning requirement if the exposure is not significant (known as a no-significant-risk-level or NSRL). For listed carcinogens, significant amount is defined as a lifetime exposure to the listed chemical resulting in an incremental cancer risk of more than one in 100,000. The significance threshold for reproductive toxicants is defined as a risk 1,000 times lower than the "no observable effect level." Significance levels may be determined by performing a quantitative risk assessment. 22 CCR 12803; 12805(a), (c). In addition, significance levels have been established for many listed chemicals by regulation.

Private or "citizen" Proposition 65 actions may not be undertaken without a certificate of merit. The plaintiff's attorney must demonstrate good cause before filing notice to sue, based on expert consultation and factual evidence.

Health Tracking Act

Under the Health Tracking Act of 2003, the California Environmental Health Surveillance System pulls together the collective research and surveillance strengths of DPH, Cal/EPA, and University of California to explore possible links between chemicals in the environment and chronic diseases. Ultimately, this program requires these organizations to fashion exposure prevention strategies. HSC 104324.25.

WARNING

ALL AREAS OF THIS DEALERSHIP CONTAIN CHEMICALS KNOWN TO THE STATE OF CALIFORNIA TO CAUSE CANCER AND BIRTH DEFECTS OR OTHER REPRODUCTIVE HARM. THESE CHEMICALS ARE CONTAINED IN VEHICLES AND PARTS AND ACCESSORIES OFFERED FOR SALE AND IN SOME OF THE PRODUCTS AND MATERIALS USED TO MAINTAIN THE PROPERTY, AND IN EMISSIONS, FUMES, AND SMOKE FROM BUSINESS OPERATIONS, EMPLOYEE AND GUEST ACTIVITIES, INCLUDING, BUT NOT LIMITED TO, THE OPERATION AND SERVICING OF MOTOR VEHICLES, AND THE USE OF TOBACCO PRODUCTS.

(POSTED IN ACCORDANCE WITH PROPOSITION 65, CALIFORNIA HEALTH AND SAFETY CODE §25249.5 *ET SEQ.*)

Under Proposition 65, regulated businesses must provide a clear and reasonable warning before exposing persons to listed carcinogens and toxicants.

NSRL = No significant risk level

California Chemical Bans

California law bans the manufacture and sale of specified hazardous materials. The Mercury Reduction Act of 2001 bans the manufacture, sale, or supply of mercury fever thermometers and other mercury-containing products. PRC 15025 *et seq.* California law also bans another class of chemicals, known as brominated flame retardants (BFRs), which contain polybrominated diphenyl ethers (PBDEs). BFRs are alleged endocrine disruptors and are found in plastic housing of electronics, computers, and textiles used in furniture. Manufacturing, processing, or distributing products, or a flame-retardant part of a product, containing one-tenth of one percent pentaBDE or octaBDE is prohibited by January 1, 2008. HSC 108920 *et seq.* Manufacturers are required to mark BFRs with warnings, as well as distribution and disposal instructions, and to pay a fee for BFR sales.

Manufacturers, importers, agents, and suppliers are prohibited from offering for sale for promotional purposes a package or packaging component that includes a regulated metal. Regulated metals include lead, cadmium, mercury, and hexavalent chromium. Each manufacturer, importer, agent, and supplier must furnish a certificate of compliance to the purchaser of a package or packaging component. HSC 25214.11 *et seq.* California law also prohibits the use of phthalates (plastic softeners) in children's toys and baby products and requires that manufacturers use the least toxic alternative instead. HSC 108935 *et seq.*

Pesticide Programs

Federal Pesticide Programs

FIFRA is the foundation for regulation, sale, distribution, and usage of pesticides in the U.S. EPA has been delegated the duty to review and register the use of pesticides.

FIFRA (7 USC 136 *et seq.*) is the foundation for regulation, sale, distribution, and usage of pesticides in the U.S. EPA has been delegated the duty to review and register the use of pesticides. Without registration with EPA's Office of Pesticide Programs, a pesticide cannot be used legally. Also, EPA is authorized to suspend or cancel the registration of a pesticide when research shows that continued use would create an unreasonable risk. EPA 2006.

During the pesticide registration process, EPA must examine the product ingredients, the location or item on which the pesticide will be used, the quantity and frequency of application, and the containment and disposal procedures. In this process, EPA determines if the pesticide will have an "unreasonable adverse effect on humans, the environment and non-target species." EPA 2006. After much debate and legal proceedings, the case of *EDF v. Ruckelshaus* (1971) 439 F. 2d 584 confirmed EPA's authority to cancel pesticide registrations. In that case, EPA canceled the pesticide registration for DDT. FIFRA allows EPA to suspend pesticide registration to thwart an imminent hazard or when there is inadequate data necessary to support re-registration. 7 USC 136d. EPA must review pesticide registrations every 15 years. 7 USC 136a (g)(1)(A); 40 CFR 160, 172; 7 CFR 110.

Generally, there are two types of pesticides—restricted and unrestricted. Unrestricted pesticides must be used in accordance with labeling information. Because restricted use pesticides pose public health, worker, or environmental risks, these pesticides are subject to rigorous possession and use standards. Persons who use or supervise the use of any restricted pesticide must receive a pesticide applicator certification. 40 CFR 171.11.

The Federal Food, Drug, and Cosmetic Act also gives EPA the authority to mandate maximum residue levels or tolerances for pesticides used in or on foods, or in animal feed. 21 USC 301 *et seq.*

Unrestricted pesticides must be used in accordance with labeling information. Because restricted use pesticides pose public health, worker, or environmental risks, these pesticides are subject to rigorous possession and use standards.

State Pesticide Programs

All pesticides must be registered by the DPR. The Director is authorized to deny registration for pesticides having a significant adverse and unavoidable impact unless the benefit clearly outweighs the risks. 3 CCR 6158.

People in the pest control business must hold a pest control license issued by DPR and must be registered with the county agricultural commissioner. Applicators of some restricted use pesticides also may require a permit from the county agricultural commissioner. Food and Agricultural Code 14004 *et seq.*

Employers with personnel who handle pesticides must comply with a hazard communication training and information program addressing specific risks posed by pesticide use. 3 CCR 6723 *et seq.* For guidance on storing pesticide containers and managing empty containers, see the Chemical Handling and Storage discussion above, as well as chapter 8.

Federal Enforcement

Emergency Planning and Community Right-to-Know Act

EPA may order a facility owner or operator to comply with its obligation to notify OES that the facility has an excess of listed extremely hazardous substances or to provide an emergency plan. Violation of the order may result in a civil penalty of up to $25,000 per violation per day. Any person may commence a civil suit against a facility owner or operator, or against EPA for failing to comply with the statute. Any person who knowingly and willfully fails to provide notice can be fined not more than $25,000 or imprisoned for no longer than two years. 42 USC 11045 *et seq.*

EPA may order a facility owner or operator to comply with its obligation to notify OES that the facility has an excess of listed extremely hazardous substances or to provide an emergency plan.

Occupational Safety and Health Act

Any employer who willfully or repeatedly violates OSHA may face civil penalties of up to $70,000 per violation and not less than $5,000 per willful violation. An employer with either a serious violation citation or a non-serious violation citation can receive a civil penalty of up to $7,000 per violation. Employers who fail to correct a violation within the permitted period may receive a civil penalty of no more than $7,000 per day if the violation remains uncorrected. Any willful violation that results in death to any employee can result in fines of up to $10,000 or imprisonment for no more than 6 months. Convictions for violations committed after a first conviction can result in a fine of up to $20,000 or imprisonment for up to one year. 29 USC 651 *et seq.*, 29 CFR 1910 *et seq.*

Resource Conservation and Recovery Act Subtitle I

Any owner of a regulated UST who knowingly fails to notify EPA or submits false information is subject to a civil penalty of up to $10,000 per violation.

Any owner of a regulated UST who knowingly fails to notify EPA or submits false information is subject to a civil penalty of up to $10,000 per violation. Additionally, EPA can issue an order against a UST owner or operator to comply with requirements within a reasonable time. Failure to comply with the order within the specified time can result in a civil penalty of up to $25,000 per day of noncompliance. 42 USC 6991(e), 40 CFR 280 *et seq.*

Hazardous Materials Transportation Act

A person violating the HMTA is liable for a civil penalty of up to $25,000 per day or may be imprisoned for up to five years. 49 USC 1501 *et seq.*, 49 CFR 100 *et seq.*

Toxic Substances Control Act

Any person who violates TSCA can be liable for civil and criminal penalties of up to $25,000 per day per violation, or imprisonment for up to one year. 15 USC 2615, 2616(b).

Asbestos Hazard Emergency Response Act

AHERA authorizes citizen suits against EPA or the relevant state government in which the ACM-containing school building is located. Any local educational agency that fails to create management plans, fails to inspect, or submits false information can be held civilly liable for up to $5,000 per day of violation. 15 USC 2647(a).

Contractors are civilly liable for up to $5,000 per day of violation if they fail to obtain accreditation pursuant to AHERA and then inspect for ACM, or design or conduct response actions for friable ACM in a school, public, or commercial building. Federal employees are exempt from liability. 15 USC 2647(g).

Residential Lead-Based Paint Hazard Reduction Act

Any person who knowingly violates the Act by failing to disclose lead information upon transfer of residential property is subject to a civil penalty not to exceed $11,000 per violation. Persons who knowingly violate Subpart F are subject to joint and several liability to the property buyer or tenant for three times the amount of damages incurred by the buyer or tenant. 42 USC 4852d(b)(1); 42 USC 3545; 15 USC 2615(a), (b); 24 CFR 30.60(a), (b); 40 CFR 745.87.

Federal Insecticide, Fungicide, and Rodenticide Act

EPA may assess a civil penalty against registrants, commercial applicators, wholesalers, dealers, retailers, or other distributors who violate any FIFRA provision. These parties are subject to up to a $50,000 criminal fine or imprisonment for up to one year for knowingly violating any FIFRA provision. Other fines apply to commercial and private applicators of restricted use pesticides who distribute or sell pesticides or who knowingly violate any FIFRA provision. 7 USC 1361 (a)(1)(A), (B).

EPA may assess a civil penalty against registrants, commercial applicators, wholesalers, dealers, retailers, or other distributors who violate any FIFRA provision.

State Enforcement

California Hazardous Materials Business Plan for Inventory Reporting

Businesses that violate HMBP provisions may be administratively or civilly liable for up to $2,000 per day of violation. If the violation results in or significantly contributes to an emergency, including a fire, the business also is responsible for the full cost of emergency response, as well as the cost of cleaning up and disposing of the hazardous materials. Any business that knowingly violates HMBP provisions after reasonable notification is subject to a civil penalty not to exceed $5,000 and is guilty of a misdemeanor upon conviction. HSC 25514(a), (b).

California Occupational Safety and Health Act Penalties

Any employer convicted of certain violations is subject to a maximum civil penalty of $7,000 per violation. In certain circumstances, good faith, history, and size can be considered in determining the fine amount. 8 CCR 334(a).

Any employer who violates any standard or order that Cal/OSHA considers a serious violation (meaning that substantial probability of death or serious physical injury could occur) is subject to a civil penalty of up to $25,000 per violation. 8 CCR 334(c), 336.

Any employer who knowingly or negligently violates any standard under Labor Code 6423–6436 may face a penalty of up to six months in county jail or a $5,000 fine or both. More stringent penalties exist for repeat violators. Labor Code 6423 *et seq.*

Any employer convicted of a willful violation that causes death or prolonged injury to an employee will result in a fine of up to $250,000 or imprisonment for up to three years or both. Anyone convicted of making a false statement or certification on record is subject to a fine of up to $70,000 or six months imprisonment or both. Labor Code 6425.

California Underground Storage Tank Law

Operators of UST systems are liable for a civil penalty of not less than $500 or more than $5,000 per UST per day of violation for any of the following:

- Operating a tank without a permit
- Violating permit requirements or conditions
- Failing to comply with monitoring, recordkeeping, reporting, or closure requirements

Owners or operators who intentionally fail to notify the SWRCB or local agency when required to do so, or who submit false information in a permit application or amendment, are liable for a civil penalty of up to $5,000 per UST.

Owners or operators who intentionally fail to notify the SWRCB or local agency when required to do so, or who submit false information in a permit application or amendment, are liable for a civil penalty of up to $5,000 per UST. Owners or operators who falsify required monitoring records or who knowingly fail to report an unauthorized release, or who intentionally disable or tamper with an automatic leak detection system, are subject to a fine of not less than $5,000 or more than $10,000, or may be imprisoned in county jail for up to one year. Owners and operators of petroleum USTs who fail to comply with financial responsibility or corrective action requirements are subject to a civil penalty of up to $10,000 per UST per day of violation. HSC 25299.76, 25299(a)–(h).

Proposition 65

All settlements must be reported to the Attorney General. Private parties seeking a settlement must submit a specified report to the Attorney General that includes a summary of the settlement report and the final disposition of the case.

Proposition 65's enforcement provisions are unique due to the law's bounty hunter provision. This provision allows private parties to bring an enforcement action against an alleged violator on behalf of the general public if the government fails to take action after receiving a 60-day notice. Penalties include fines of up to $2,500 per day per violation, and private enforcers may receive up to 25 percent of the penalties assessed. HSC 25249.7. In addition, private enforcers may be able to collect their attorney's fees.

Mercury Reduction Act of 2001

Any person who manufactures, offers for final sale or use, or distributes for promotional purposes a mercury-added novelty, and knows or should know that the product contains mercury, is guilty of a misdemeanor punishable by a fine of up to $1,000 and imprisonment for up to one year. PRC 15027(b).

Brominated Flame Retardants

Persons who manufacture, process, or distribute in commerce a prohibited flame-retardant product can be civilly liable for a fine of up to $5,000 per day per violation. A second offense or an offense committed with the intent to mislead or defraud, or where tableware is primarily used or marketed for children, is subject to a fine of up to $10,000 or imprisonment for up to one year or both. HSC 108900(a)–(h).

Persons who manufacture, process, or distribute in commerce a prohibited flame-retardant product can be civilly liable for a fine of up to $5,000 per day per violation.

Lead Hazard Reduction Enforcement Act

Violations of this Act generally are punishable by a fine of up to $1,000 or imprisonment for not more than six months or both. Violations of the Act include:

- Engaging in lead construction work without a certificate
- Submitting false information to DPH
- Creating a lead hazard while performing lead-related construction work

Additionally, if DPH determines that a condition or activity is creating a lead hazard in a building, then DPH may order the owner to abate the lead hazard and may order the person whose activity is creating or created the hazard to cease and desist. Failure to obey such an order is illegal, and violations are subject to a civil penalty not to exceed $1,000. HSC 105250–105257.

Occupational Lead Poisoning Prevention Act

There are no penalties established under this Act. HSC 105185–105197. The Act establishes a program whereby employers of specific regulated industries pay an annual fee ranging from $195 to $2,232, depending on business size. The state annually allocates $100,000 to the Division of Occupational Safety and Health for the division's costs to enforce employer compliance with training and certification requirements. 17 CCR 35001 *et seq.*

Pesticide Regulation

Pesticides are regulated under 3 CCR 6000 *et seq.* Violations of pesticide requirements are designated as Class A, Class B, and Class C. 3 CCR 6130(a)(A)–(C). Class A violations create an actual health or environmental hazard, are violations of a lawful order of the commissioner, or are violations that are repeat Class B violations. The fines for Class A violations range from $700 to $5,000. Class B violations pose a reasonable possibility of creating a health or environmental effect or are violations that are repeat Class C violations. The civil fines for Class B violations range from $250 to $1,000. Class C violations are violations that do not fit under either Class A or Class B. The civil fines for Class C violations range from $50 to $400.

California Asbestos
Notification Act

Any owner who knowingly or intentionally fails to comply with this Act, or who knowingly or intentionally submits false or misleading information to employees or other owners, is guilty of a misdemeanor punishable by a fine of up to $1,000 or imprisonment of not more than one year in county jail or both. HSC 25919.7.

For more information...

Publications

Curtis, M.H., and S.F. Sawyer (eds.). 2003. NFPA 1 Uniform Fire Code Handbook. Quincy, Mass.

Environmental Protection Agency. 2006. Registering Pesticides (www.epa.gov/pesticides/regulating/registering/laws.htm)

Environmental Protection Agency. June 3, 2003. TSCA Section 8(e) Notification of Substantial Risk: Policy Clarification and Reporting Guidance. 68 FR 33129

Kindschy, J. *et al.* 1997. Guide to Hazardous Materials and Waste Management. Solano Press. Point Arena, Calif.

Manaster, K.A. and D.P. Selmi (eds). ND. California Environmental Law and Land Use Practice, Chapter 58. Matthew Bender. San Francisco, Calif.

Websites

Asbestos Hazard Emergency Response Act
www.epa.gov/region2/ahera/ahera.htm

California Department of Health Services
www.dhs.ca.gov

California Department of Health Services, Occupational Lead Poisoning Prevention Program
www.dhs.ca.gov/childlead/html/GENregs.html

California Department of Pesticide Regulation
www.cdpr.ca.gov

California Department of Toxic Substances Control
www.dtsc.ca.gov

California Department of Toxic Substances Control, Managing Hazardous Waste
www.dtsc.ca.gov/HazardousWaste/index.cfm

California Division of Occupational Safety and Health
www.dir.ca.gov/DOSH/dosh1.html#CalOSHA

California Division of Occupational Safety and Health, Asbestos Programs
www.dir.ca.gov/dosh/Asbestos.html

California EPA
www.calepa.ca.gov

California Governor's Office of Emergency Services
www.oes.ca.gov/Operational/OESHome.nsf/1?OpenForm

California Governor's Office of Emergency Services, Hazardous Materials
www.oes.ca.gov/Operational/OESHome.nsf/LevelTwoWithNav?OpenForm&Key=Hazardous+Materials

California Governor's Office of Emergency Services, Hazardous Materials Business Plan Program
www.oes.ca.gov/Operational/OESHome.nsf/Content/4D1BF55BB0BDBE4888256C2C0076E65F?OpenDocument

California Health and Safety Code
http://caselaw.lp.findlaw.com/cacodes/hsc.html

ChemAlliance.org Regulatory Handbook
www.chemalliance.org/Handbook/background/index.asp

Environmental Protection Agency
www.epa.gov

Environmental Protection Agency, Emergency Planning and Community Right-to-Know Act
www.epa.gov/region5/defs/html/epcra.htm

Environmental Protection Agency, Polychlorinated Biphenyls Program
www.epa.gov/pcb

Environmental Protection Agency, PCB Laws and Regulations Database
www.epa.gov/pcb/pubs/laws.html

Environmental Protection Agency, PCB Question and Answer Manual
www.epa.gov/pcb/pubs/qacombined.pdf

Environmental Protection Agency, Pesticide Registration
www.epa.gov/opp00001/regulating/registering/index.htm

Environmental Protection Agency, Pesticide Regulations
www.epa.gov/pesticides/regulating/laws.htm

Environmental Protection Agency, Region IX, Lead Program
www.epa.gov/region09/toxic/lead/index.html

Websites *continued*

Environmental Protection Agency,
Region IX, PCB Program
www.epa.gov/region09/toxic/pcb

Environmental Protection Agency,
Regulations and Standards Related
to Underground Storage Tanks
www.epa.gov/OUST/fedlaws/cfr.htm

National Fire Protection
Association, Label Information
www.nmsu.edu/~safety/programs/
chem_safety/hazcom_NFPA_labels.htm

Occupational Safety and
Health Administration
www.osha.gov

Occupational Safety and Health
Administration, Hazard Communication
www.osha.gov/SLTC/
hazardcommunications/index.htm

Occupational Safety and Health
Administration, Laws, Regulations,
and Interpretations
www.osha.gov/comp-links.html

Office of Environmental
Health Hazard Assessment
www.oehha.ca.gov

Office of Environmental Health
Hazard Assessment, Proposition 65
www.oehha.ca.gov/prop65.html

State Water Resources
Control Board
www.swrcb.ca.gov/index.html

State Water Resources
Control Board, Underground
Storage Tank Program
www.swrcb.ca.gov/ust

Toxic Substances Control Act
www.epa.gov/region5/defs/html/tsca.htm

Unidocs (Local and State
Hazardous Materials/
Waste Compliance Assistance)
www.unidocs.org

United States Department of
Housing and Urban Development,
Lead-Based Paint Disclosure Rule
www.hud.gov/offices/lead/
disclosurerule/index.cfm

Hazardous Wastes

This chapter reviews—

- Key laws and agencies involved in hazardous waste regulation and cleanup

- Major hazardous waste regulations

- Other hazardous waste regulations

- Enforcement

- Federal cleanup programs

- State cleanup programs

Related Solano Press titles—

Guide to Hazardous Materials and Waste Management: Risk, Regulation, Responsibility. Jon W. Kindschy *et al.* 1997

Glossary

Acutely hazardous waste—a waste that EPA has determined to be very dangerous, even in minute quantities.

Applicable or relevant and appropriate requirement—a promulgated or legally enforceable federal or state requirement used to govern investigation and remedial actions throughout the RI/FS process. These requirements also influence the cleanup standard (*i.e.,* how clean is clean).

Biennial Report*—all large quantity generators of hazardous waste must annually report (by March 1 of each even-numbered year) summarizing waste shipments for a two-year period.

Border zone property—a property located within 2,000 feet of a hazardous waste deposit designated by DTSC and which may not be used for human habitation, a hospital, a school, or a day care center.

Brownfield—a "real property" whose development may be complicated by the potential presence of a hazardous substance, pollutant, or contaminant (except property subject to a planned or ongoing CERCLA removal action, listed or proposed for the NPL, or subject to specified orders and consent decrees under CERCLA).

California-only hazardous waste—a non-RCRA hazardous waste that meets California's more stringent hazardous waste definition.

Characteristic waste—a waste that has one or more of the following characteristics—ignitability, corrosivity, reactivity, or toxicity.

Conditional authorization*—a type of "permit by rule" authorizing on-site treatment of "California-only," non-RCRA hazardous wastes. Hazardous waste generators of low concentrations of hazardous waste are authorized to use specified treatment technologies.

Conditionally exempt small quantity generator—a person or facility that generates 100 kilograms or less per month of hazardous waste, or one kilogram or less per month of acutely hazardous waste.

Contained-in policy—a policy that requires that soil, sediment, and other environmental media must be managed as hazardous wastes so long as the mixture contains listed hazardous wastes or exhibits a characteristic of hazardous wastes.

Corrosive hazardous waste—a waste that dissolves metals and other materials or burns the skin or eye on contact. A waste is corrosive if it fails any one of a number of tests such as aqueous wastes with a pH equal to or less than 2.0 or greater than 12.5.

County hazardous waste management plan conformity*—applicants for an off-site hazardous waste treatment, storage, or disposal facility must demonstrate that the facility will be located in accordance with siting criteria specified in a County HWMP. For example, a facility may not be located in a flood plain or a seismically unsafe zone.

Derived-from rule—a rule that classifies solid waste generated from the treatment of a hazardous waste as a hazardous waste.

Empty container—under federal rules, a container with no residual hazardous waste (*e.g.,* no more than one inch remaining in a particular-sized container).

EPA identification number*—a number assigned to a facility that generates hazardous waste, a business that transports hazardous waste, or a business that operates a facility that recycles, treats, stores, or disposes of hazardous waste.

Extremely hazardous waste—a waste that exceeds specified toxicity levels expressed as either a lethal dose or a lethal concentration, or if the chemical appears on a list of pesticides or heavy metals, or is a PCB that exceeds a specified concentration in milligrams per kilogram.

F-listed hazardous waste—a type of process waste (*i.e.,* generated from industrial activity) that is non-industry-specific and is hazardous. Examples include spent solvents, wastewater treatment sludges, and spent plating solutions.

Feasibility study—an analysis of the practicability of a proposal; a description and analysis of potential cleanup alternatives for a contaminated property appearing on the National Priorities List. The feasibility study is used to inform decision-makers on cost-effective cleanup alternatives. The feasibility study usually starts as soon as the remedial investigation is underway; together, they commonly are referred to as the RI/FS.

Hazardous waste generator—a person or facility whose processes and actions create hazardous waste.

Hazardous substance—broadly defined for CERCLA purposes to include all regulated chemicals, except for petroleum and natural gas, under the major federal statutes.

Ignitable hazardous waste—a waste that is easily combustible or flammable. Ignitable hazardous waste includes a liquid with a flashpoint equal to or less than 140°F; a non-liquid capable under standard temperature and pressure of causing fire by means of friction, absorption, moisture, or spontaneous chemical changes and that when ignited burns so vigorously and persistently that it creates a hazard; an ignitable compressed gas, as defined in the Department of Transportation (DOT) regulations; or an oxidizer, as defined in DOT regulations.

K-listed hazardous waste—a type of process waste (*i.e.,* generated from industrial activity) that is industry-specific (*e.g.,* refineries, metal smelting) and is hazardous. Examples include industry-specific waste streams such as slop oil emulsion solids from the refining industry (*e.g.,* K-049).

Large quantity generator—a person or facility that generates more than 2,200 pounds of hazardous waste and one kg (*i.e.,* 2.2. pounds) per month of acutely hazardous waste.

Large quantity handler—a person or facility that accumulates more than 5,000 kg of universal waste.

Listed hazardous waste—a process waste (*i.e.,* generated from an industrial process) or a non-process waste (includes unused commercial chemicals, container residues, pill residues, and expired chemicals).

Manifest–a shipping document that tracks hazardous waste from the time it leaves its place of origin until it reaches an off-site treatment, storage, and disposal facility (TSDF).

Mixed hazardous waste–a waste that results from the combination of a nonhazardous waste and a hazardous waste and that exhibits a hazardous waste characteristic. There are exceptions to this definition, such as when a characteristic hazardous waste is mixed with a nonhazardous waste and the resulting mixture is diluted enough to pass the test for ignitability, corrosivity, or reactivity. However, a mixed hazardous waste that exhibits the toxicity characteristic must be managed as a hazardous waste regardless of the concentration of the toxic constituent.

National Priorities List–a list of highly contaminated sites that EPA prioritizes for cleanup and access to Superfund monies.

P-listed hazardous waste–a type of non-process waste that is non-industry-specific and is acutely hazardous.

Permit by rule*–a permit in which the applicant submits a notice of intent to comply with pre-set permit conditions that are not site-specific.

Potentially responsible party–any individual or business–including owners, operators, transporters, or generators–potentially responsible for, or contributing to, a spill or other contamination at a Superfund site. Whenever possible, through administrative and legal actions, EPA requires cleanup of hazardous sites by potentially responsible parties.

RCRA Part B TSDF permit*–"Part B" is the portion of a hazardous waste TSDF permit application (known as the "operations plan") that provides details governing operation of the TSDF along with a detailed contingency plan in the event of an accidental release of hazardous waste.

Reactive hazardous waste–a waste that is unstable or that undergoes rapid or violent chemical reactions, such as exploding, catching fire, or giving off fumes (when exposed to or mixed with water, air, or other materials).

Record of Decision*–a public document that explains the cleanup alternative(s) to be followed.

Recyclable waste–material that is removed or separated from other residential, commercial, or industrial garbage for the purpose of reuse or reprocessing.

Release–broadly defined under RCRA to include any spill, leaking, pouring, emitting, emptying, discharging, injecting, pumping, escaping, leaching, dumping, or disposing of hazardous waste or constituents into the environment.

Remedial action–the actual construction or implementation phase of a Superfund site cleanup that follows remedial design.

Remedial action plan*–a state plan to restore or clean up a site.

Remedial investigation–an in-depth study to gather data needed to determine the nature and extent of contamination at a Superfund site, to establish site cleanup criteria, to identify preliminary alternatives for remedial action, and to support technical and cost analyses of alternatives. The remedial investigation is usually done with the feasibility study. Together they commonly are referred to as the RI/FS.

Removal action–a straightforward cleanup effort requiring immediate attention to stabilize the release or threat of a release of a hazardous substance (*e.g.,* controlling surface water runoff, pumping leaking ponds, or removing bulk containers of hazardous substances).

Restricted waste–a hazardous waste that must meet special requirements before being disposed of in land-based disposal facilities.

Satellite accumulation point–a location where hazardous waste is accumulated at the point

of generation. No more than 55 gallons of a hazardous waste, or one quart of an acutely hazardous or extremely hazardous waste, may be accumulated at each SAP.

Small quantity generator–a person or facility that generates between 220–2,200 pounds per month of hazardous waste and no more than one kg (*i.e.,* 2.2 pounds) per month of acutely hazardous waste.

Small quantity handler–a person or facility that accumulates no more than 5,000 kg (or 11,000 pounds) of universal waste at any time.

Solid waste–garbage, refuse, sludge and other discarded material including solid, liquid, semisolid or contained gaseous material resulting from industrial, commercial, mining and agricultural operations and from community activity.

Special waste–items such as auto shredder waste, bag house and scrubber waste, cement kiln dust, dewatered sludge from industrial process water treatment, sand from sand-blasting, foundry casting, and coal gasification.

Standardized permit*–in the context of hazardous waste regulation, governs treatment and storage of "California-only," non-RCRA hazardous wastes.

Superfund–the program operated under the legislative authority of CERCLA and SARA that funds and carries out EPA solid waste emergency and long-term removal and remedial activities. These activities include establishing the National Priorities List, investigating sites for inclusion on the list, determining their priority, and conducting and/or supervising cleanup and other remedial actions.

Surface impoundment–a ditch constructed primarily of earthen materials used for treating, storing, or diluting liquid hazardous waste.

Tiered permit*–a permit program based on regulatory requirements matched against the risks associated with a facility's activities.

Toxic hazardous waste–a waste that appears on a list that exceeds a specified regulatory level.

Glossary *continued*

Treatment, storage, and disposal facility— a regulated facility that treats, stores, or disposes of hazardous wastes.

U-listed hazardous waste—a type of non-process waste that is non-industry-specific and is hazardous.

Underground storage tank—one or a combination of tanks, including associated piping used to contain industrial solvents, petroleum products, and other hazardous substances. The tank is totally or substantially (10 percent) beneath the surface of the ground.

Universal waste—a hazardous waste that is not fully regulated as a hazardous waste. Examples include batteries, thermostats, lamps, cathode ray tube material, aerosol cans, mercury-containing motor vehicle and non-automotive light switches, dental amalgam wastes, mercury-containing pressure or vacuum gauges, mercury counterweights and dampers, mercury dilators and weighted tubing, mercury-containing rubber flooring, mercury-added novelties, and mercury gas flow regulators.

Waste discharge requirements*—permit issued by a RWQCB for discharge of waste into waters of the state.

Waste management unit—containers, tanks, landfills, surface impoundments, land treatment facilities, waste piles, incineration units, and miscellaneous units used for hazardous waste treatment.

* equals permits and approvals

CHAPTER 8

Hazardous Wastes

Introduction

Manufacturing and even household activities generate a considerable amount of hazardous waste each year. In 1981, a few years after the United State Environmental Protection Agency (EPA) implemented the federal hazardous waste program, each American was producing one ton of hazardous waste each year. Since then, that number has grown dramatically.

Historically, hazardous wastes were not well managed, resulting in a legacy of over 30,000 highly contaminated properties costing billions per year to clean up. Today, hazardous wastes are subject to specific requirements governing their generation, transportation, treatment, storage, and disposal. This chapter reviews these hazardous waste regulatory programs, as well as federal and state programs for cleanup of hazardous waste sites.

Key Laws and Agencies

Federal Laws and Agencies

Resource Conservation and Recovery Act. The Solid Waste Disposal Act, enacted in 1965, was designed to manage municipal solid wastes. Today, these wastes are governed by the Resource Conservation and Recovery Act (RCRA) Subtitle D and 40 CFR 257 and 258 (*see* chapter 9 for more on solid waste management). Congress enacted RCRA Subtitle C in 1976 (Subtitle C 42 USC 6901 *et seq.*) in an effort to proactively manage hazardous waste and to minimize and avoid hazardous waste contamination that today is regulated pursuant to the Comprehensive Environmental Response, Compensation, and Liability Act (CERCLA).

CCR = California Code of Regulations
CERCLA = Comprehensive Environmental Response, Compensation, and Liability Act
CFR = Code of Federal Regulations
EPA = U.S. Environmental Protection Agency
RCRA = Resource Conservation and Recovery Act
USC = United States Code

Congress enacted RCRA Subtitle C in an effort to proactively manage hazardous waste and minimize and avoid hazardous waste contamination that today is regulated pursuant to CERCLA.

189

Unregulated hazardous waste disposal

The Hazardous Materials Transportation Act of 1990 clarifies the maze of conflicting state, local, and federal regulations by encouraging uniformity among various state and local highway regulations.

DOT = U.S. Department of Transportation
HMTA = Hazardous Materials Transportation Act
HMTUSA = Hazardous Materials Transportation Uniform Safety Act
HSC = Health and Safety Code
HSWA = Hazardous and Solid Waste Amendments
HWCL = Hazardous Waste Control Law

RCRA Subtitle C addresses hazardous waste from cradle-to-grave, regulating the generation, transport, storage, treatment, and disposal of hazardous waste. RCRA, Subtitle I, the Hazardous and Solid Waste Amendments (HSWA) of 1984, expanded and clarified RCRA Subtitle C. The EPA administers RCRA Subtitle C pursuant to regulations found at 40 CFR 260 *et seq.* (primarily Parts 260–273 and Part 279) and has delegated RCRA Subtitle C implementation and enforcement within California to the state.

Hazardous Materials Transportation Act. The Hazardous Materials Transportation Act (HMTA) regulates transport of hazardous materials on water, rail, highways, airplanes, and pipelines, in intrastate, interstate, and foreign commerce. 49 USC 1801 *et seq.* The Department of Transportation (DOT) administers the Act, pursuant to 49 CFR 100 *et seq.* The Hazardous Materials Transportation Uniform Safety Act (HMTUSA) of 1990 clarifies the maze of conflicting state, local, and federal regulations by encouraging uniformity among various state and local highway regulations regarding (49 USC 5101 *et seq.*, 49 CFR 171 *et seq.*):

- Criteria for issuance of permits to hazardous materials carriers
- Transport of radioactive materials

Comprehensive Environmental Response, Compensation, and Liability Act. CERCLA, also known as Superfund, establishes procedures to identify and clean up chemically contaminated sites posing a significant environmental health threat. 42 USC 9601 *et seq.* The program also establishes an elaborate and heavily litigated liability process that governs which party or parties are responsible for the enormous costs of cleanup. Under CERCLA, the EPA is authorized to clean up hazardous waste sites and seek reimbursement from liable individuals for expenses incurred during the cleanup process. 42 USC 9606(a). EPA administers CERCLA. 40 CFR 300 *et seq.*

Environmental Protection Agency. RCRA authorizes the EPA to develop regulations identifying certain hazardous wastes and to issue permits for facilities that treat, store, and dispose of hazardous waste. Additionally, RCRA authorizes EPA to bring suit against any individual who contributes to an "imminent and substantial endangerment to health or the environment." 42 USC 6973(a).

State Laws and Agencies

Hazardous Waste Control Law. The Hazardous Waste Control Law (HWCL) is the principal state law regulating hazardous waste. HSC 25100 *et seq.*, 22 CCR 66260 *et seq.* The state regulations, sometimes referred to as "Title 22" follow a numerical order that aligns regulatory sections with their federal counterpart sections–however, the state sections are preceded by "66." For example, 40 CFR 262 corresponds to 22 California Code of Regulations (CCR) 66262. In many cases, the state statutes and regulations are more stringent than the federal rules.

Carpenter–Presley–Tanner Hazardous Substance Account Act. The Carpenter–Presley–Tanner Hazardous Substance Account Act (HSAA) establishes a state Superfund program to clean up contaminated sites not listed on the National Priorities List (NPL). The HSAA authorizes the Department of Toxic Substance Control (DTSC) to initiate remedial and removal actions, and to enter into enforceable agreements with potentially responsible parties to investigate and remediate contamination. HSC 25300 *et seq.*

California corrective action program. This program (22 CCR 66264.550 *et seq.*) establishes a Superfund-like program governing the cleanup of hazardous waste releases from solid waste management units.

Porter–Cologne Water Quality Control Act. This Act (Water Code 13000 *et seq.*) authorizes the regional water quality control boards (RWQCBs) to order cleanup of chemical contamination not classified as hazardous.

Department of Toxic Substances Control. EPA delegates authority to implement and enforce the law to DTSC; however, EPA retains oversight authority. DTSC administers both RCRA Subtitle C and the HWCL (22 CCR 66260 *et seq.*). DTSC often serves as the lead agency overseeing hazardous waste contamination under specified circumstances. DTSC can order responsible parties to conduct short-term cleanup efforts and can require an owner of a solid waste management unit to clean up hazardous wastes releases from such units.

Certified unified program agencies. State authority to regulate the management of hazardous waste generators is delegated primarily to city and county departments of health and fire. These local agencies are collectively referred to as certified unified program agencies (CUPAs). HSC 25404 *et seq.*, 27 CCR 15100 *et seq.* CUPAs apply statewide standards governing hazardous waste generation on behalf of DTSC. DTSC retains primary oversight over permitted treatment, storage, and disposal facilities.

State Water Resources Control Board. The State Water Resources Control Board (SWRCB) governs the cleanup and abatement of discharges of groundwater containment zones.

Regional water quality control boards. Regional water quality control boards can issue cleanup and abatement orders (CAOs) to parties who have discharged wastes into waters of the state. RWQCBs are the lead agency overseeing contaminated property where the source of contamination is leaking underground storage tanks (LUSTs), agricultural operations, or inactive mines. In addition,

CAO = Cleanup and abatement order
CUPA = Certified unified program agency
DTSC = Department of Toxic Substances Control
HSAA = Hazardous Substances Account Act
NPL = National Priorities List
RWQCB = Regional water quality control board
SWRCB = State Water Resources Control Board

State authority to regulate management of hazardous waste generators is delegated primarily to city and county departments of health and fire.

Table 8-1. Overview of State and Federal Regulations

Brief description	State regulation	Federal regulation
Definitions	22 CCR 66260	40 CFR 260
Defines hazardous waste	22 CCR 66261	40 CFR 260
Describes standards governing generators of hazardous waste	22 CCR 66262	40 CFR 262
Contains standards applicable to transporters of hazardous waste	22 CCR 66263	40 CFR 263
Includes requirements governing facilities that treat, store, or dispose of hazardous wastes	22 CCR 66264	40 CFR 264
Includes requirements for interim status facilities known as treatment, storage, and disposal facilities (TSDFs)	22 CCR 66265	40 CFR 265
Addresses standards applicable to recycling hazardous waste and waste managed in boilers and industrial furnaces (BIFs)	22 CCR 66266.1 *et seq.*	40 CFR 266
Sets forth treatment standards for waste that is to be sent to land disposal units (land disposal requirements or LDRs)	22 CCR 66268	40 CFR 268
Sets forth the issuance and administration requirements for hazardous waste permits	22 CCR 66270	40 CFR 270
Presents a set of more relaxed management requirements for a subset of hazardous wastes known as universal wastes	22 CCR 66273	40 CFR 273
Describes requirements governing the characterization, storage, recycling, and disposal of used oil	Primarily California HSC 25250 *et seq.*, as well as 22 CCR 66279	40 CFR 279

Source: 22 CCR 66260 *et seq.*, 40 CFR 260 *et seq.*

BIF = Boiler and industrial furnace
LUST = Leaking underground storage tank
TSDF = Treatment, storage, and disposal facility

RWQCBs become the lead agency when the contamination:

- Primarily affects surface water
- Is from a non-RCRA surface impoundment
- Is from a landfill not regulated by DTSC

Major Hazardous Waste Regulations

Overview of State and Federal Regulations

An overview of state and federal regulations that govern hazardous waste is presented in Table 8-1.

Defining Hazardous Waste

Generators of waste must determine whether their wastes meet the definition of hazardous waste. A determination may be made by one of the following:

- Using knowledge of the chemicals and processes involved (a strategy known as process knowledge)
- Laboratory testing of representative samples of routine, predictable waste streams

Using process knowledge is typically more practical for evaluating routine, predictable waste streams; laboratory testing is more suited for complex waste streams.

The generator must first determine if the waste material meets the federal definition of "solid waste," which includes solids, semi-solids, liquids, and gases. A material is considered a waste if it is abandoned, recycled, or inherently waste-like. The primary criterion is whether the material is discarded. Examples of solid wastes include abandoned materials such as waste paint or spent solvents (spent material is no longer fit for use, as a result of contamination, without being regenerated, reclaimed, or otherwise processed). Waste also can include materials kept in storage that are no longer useable and cannot be reclaimed or recycled, such as a drum of solvent that has degraded and is unsuitable for its intended purpose.

Once a waste is determined to be a solid waste, the next step is to determine whether it is a "hazardous waste," first under federal law and then under California law. The waste generator must determine whether the waste appears on a specified list of hazardous wastes or whether it meets one or more of the following hazardous characteristics: ignitable, corrosive, reactive, or toxic. If a waste is on one or more lists or fails one or more of the characteristic tests, the waste is considered to be a hazardous waste. Hazardous waste generators must identify each hazardous listing and each hazardous characteristic that causes the waste to be hazardous. Figure 8-1 illustrates the process of making a hazardous

Once a waste is determined to be a solid waste, the next step is to determine whether it is a "hazardous waste," first under federal law and then under California law.

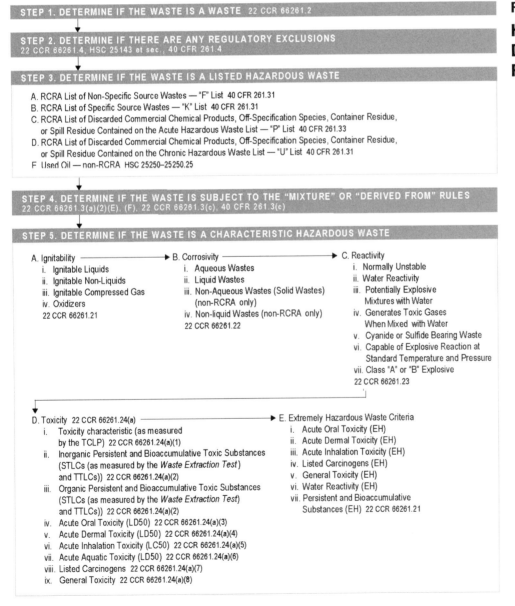

STEP 1. DETERMINE IF THE WASTE IS A WASTE 22 CCR 66261.2

STEP 2. DETERMINE IF THERE ARE ANY REGULATORY EXCLUSIONS
22 CCR 66261.4, HSC 25143 et sec., 40 CFR 261.4

STEP 3. DETERMINE IF THE WASTE IS A LISTED HAZARDOUS WASTE

    A. RCRA List of Non-Specific Source Wastes — "F" List 40 CFR 261.31
    B. RCRA List of Specific Source Wastes — "K" List 40 CFR 261.31
    C. RCRA List of Discarded Commercial Chemical Products, Off-Specification Species, Container Residue,
       or Spill Residue Contained on the Acute Hazardous Waste List — "P" List 40 CFR 261.33
    D. RCRA List of Discarded Commercial Chemical Products, Off-Specification Species, Container Residue,
       or Spill Residue Contained on the Chronic Hazardous Waste List — "U" List 40 CFR 261.31
    F. Used Oil — non-RCRA HSC 25250–25250.25

STEP 4. DETERMINE IF THE WASTE IS SUBJECT TO THE "MIXTURE" OR "DERIVED FROM" RULES
22 CCR 66261.3(a)(2)(E), (F), 22 CCR 66261.3(c), 40 CFR 261.3(c)

STEP 5. DETERMINE IF THE WASTE IS A CHARACTERISTIC HAZARDOUS WASTE

A. Ignitability   →   B. Corrosivity   →   C. Reactivity
  i. Ignitable Liquids   i. Aqueous Wastes   i. Normally Unstable
  ii. Ignitable Non-Liquids   ii. Liquid Wastes   ii. Water Reactivity
  iii. Ignitable Compressed Gas   iii. Non-Aqueous Wastes (Solid Wastes)   iii. Potentially Explosive
  iv. Oxidizers   (non-RCRA only)   Mixtures with Water
  22 CCR 66261.21   iv. Non-liquid Wastes (non-RCRA only)   iv. Generates Toxic Gases
                 22 CCR 66261.22   When Mixed with Water
                               v. Cyanide or Sulfide Bearing Waste
                             vi. Capable of Explosive Reaction at
                               Standard Temperature and Pressure
                            vii. Class "A" or "B" Explosive
                             22 CCR 66261.23

D. Toxicity 22 CCR 66261.24(a)   →   E. Extremely Hazardous Waste Criteria
  i. Toxicity characteristic (as measured   i. Acute Oral Toxicity (EH)
    by the TCLP) 22 CCR 66261.24(a)(1)   ii. Acute Dermal Toxicity (EH)
  ii. Inorganic Persistent and Bioaccumulative Toxic Substances   iii. Acute Inhalation Toxicity (EH)
    (STLCs (as measured by the *Waste Extraction Test*)   iv. Listed Carcinogens (EH)
    and TTLCs)) 22 CCR 66261.24(a)(2)   v. General Toxicity (EH)
  iii. Organic Persistent and Bioaccumulative Toxic Substances   vi. Water Reactivity (EH)
    (STLCs (as measured by the *Waste Extraction Test*)   vii. Persistent and Bioaccumulative
    and TTLCs)) 22 CCR 66261.24(a)(2)   Substances (EH) 22 CCR 66261.21
  iv. Acute Oral Toxicity (LD50) 22 CCR 66261.24(a)(3)
  v. Acute Dermal Toxicity (LD50) 22 CCR 66261.24(a)(4)
  vi. Acute Inhalation Toxicity (LC50) 22 CCR 66261.24(a)(5)
  vii. Acute Aquatic Toxicity (LD50) 22 CCR 66261.24(a)(6)
  viii. Listed Carcinogens 22 CCR 66261.24(a)(7)
  ix. General Toxicity 22 CCR 66261.24(a)(8)

Figure 8-1

Hazardous Waste Determination Flow Chart

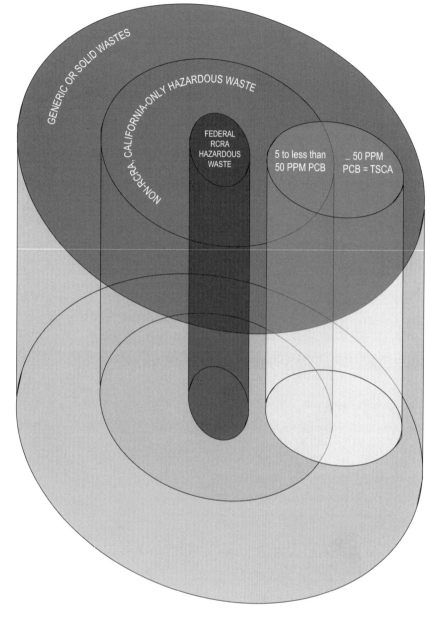

GENERIC OR SOLID WASTES

NON-RCRA, CALIFORNIA-ONLY HAZARDOUS WASTE

FEDERAL
RCRA
HAZARDOUS
WASTE

5 to less than
50 PPM PCB

≥ 50 PPM
PCB = TSCA

Figure 8-2
California and Federal
Hazardous Wastes Compared

NPDES = National Pollutant Discharge Elimination System

waste determination under federal and California law.

The definition of hazardous waste in California is very complex (HSC 25141 *et seq.*, 66261.20 *et seq.*) and subject to detailed exemptions. Hazardous waste in California includes all wastes considered hazardous waste under federal law (RCRA Subtitle C), as well as additional materials known as non-RCRA (or California-only) hazardous wastes. In many instances a solid waste will pass the federal test, but fail the more rigorous California definition.

Figure 8-2 illustrates the relationship between federal and California hazardous wastes. The outer rim represents the universe of all wastes including nonhazardous wastes. The inner circle captures the subset of all wastes that meet the federal definition. The middle ring depicts wastes that would pass the federal definition of hazardous waste (and thus not be considered hazardous waste under federal law) but which would be considered hazardous waste under the broader California definition.

Exemptions. Some materials that are solid waste are exempt from regulation as a hazardous waste. For example, materials exempt from regulation include household hazardous waste, as well as industrial waste discharged pursuant to a National Pollutant Discharge Elimination System (NPDES) surface water permit. *See* chapter 10. If a waste is exempt, it may still be managed either as a nonhazardous municipal solid waste (*see* chapter 9), a biohazardous waste (*see* chapter 9), or a designated waste (*see* chapter 10).

Variances. DTSC may grant a variance from classification of a material as a hazardous waste if the waste is a non-RCRA hazardous waste, poses an insignificant hazard to health or the environment, or is effectively regulated by another agency.

Types of Hazardous Wastes

Listed hazardous wastes. Listed hazardous wastes are either process wastes (*i.e.*, generated from an industrial process) or non-process wastes (wastes that include unused commercial chemicals, container residues, spill residues, and expired chemicals). Both are further sub-divided and described below.

Process wastes are generated from industrial activities. Some are industry-specific (*e.g.*, refineries, metal smelting) and are classified as K-listed hazardous wastes. Examples include industry-specific waste streams such as slop oil emulsion solids from the refining industry (K-049). Non-industry-specific process wastes are classified as F-listed hazardous wastes. Examples include spent solvents, wastewater treatment sludges, and spent plating solutions.

Non-process wastes are not industry-specific. Acutely hazardous non-process wastes are classified as P-listed hazardous wastes. Those that are not acutely hazardous are classified as U-listed hazardous wastes.

The relationship between listed, process, and non-process wastes is illustrated in Table 8-2.

Listed wastes are further categorized as:

- Industry-specific process hazardous wastes: K-listed hazardous wastes
- Non-industry-specific process hazardous wastes: F-listed hazardous waste
- Non-industry-specific, non-process hazardous wastes: U-listed hazardous waste
- Non-industry-specific, non-process, acutely hazardous wastes: P-listed hazardous waste

These four listed hazardous waste categories are divided by four key distinguishing characteristics, as shown in Table 8-3. Additionally, California law

Table 8-2. Relationship Among Listed Wastes, Process Wastes, and Non-process Wastes

Type of waste	Listed waste nomenclature
Process wastes	
Signature waste streams from specified industry categories (*e.g.*, refineries, and metal smelting)	K-listed hazardous waste
Spent solvents	F-listed hazardous waste
Wastewater treatment sludges	F-listed hazardous waste
Spent plating solutions	F-listed hazardous waste
Still bottoms from the recovery or recycling of spent solvents	F-listed hazardous waste
Non-process wastes	
Off-specification products (*i.e.*, a chemical product that remained in stock too long and is no longer efficacious for its intended purpose)	U- or P*-listed hazardous waste
Unused chemical product and container residues	U- or P*-listed hazardous waste
Spilled, unused chemical product	U- or P*-listed hazardous waste

* Refers to acutely hazardous wastes

Source: 40 CFR 261 *et seq.*

Table 8-3. K-, F-, U-, and P-Listed Wastes Compared

Waste classification	Industry-specific waste	Process waste	Non-process waste	Acutely hazardous waste
K	X	X		
F		X		
U			X	
P			X	X

ASTM = American Society for Testing and Material
LDR = Land disposal requirement
MSDS = Material safety data sheet
PCB = Polychlorinated biphenyl
STLC = Soluble threshold limit concentration
TCLP = Toxic characteristic leaching procedure
TTLC = Total threshold limit concentration
WET = Waste extraction test

regulates a somewhat larger category of listed hazardous wastes by including:

- Used oil that exceeds minimum standards set by the American Society for Testing and Materials (ASTM) and specified levels of lead, arsenic, chromium, cadmium, total halogens, and PCBs

- Mercury switches

Characteristic hazardous wastes. If a waste is not listed as a hazardous waste, the generator must determine whether it exhibits a hazardous characteristic (*i.e.*, ignitable, corrosive, reactive, or toxic) by using knowledge of the waste. This can be accomplished by consulting a material safety data sheet (MSDS) and determining, for example, whether the pH fails the corrosivity standard or whether the flashpoint for a liquid is below the ignitability threshold. Alternatively, the generator can determine if the waste exhibits one or more characteristics by performing specified laboratory tests using a California-certified environmental testing laboratory. The California definition for toxicity is considerably more expansive than the federal definition. As a result, a waste that may pass the federal definition for toxicity could fail under one of the many California toxicity tests and thus be characterized as a toxic hazardous waste. *See* sidebar on the facing page for a description of the federal and state hazardous waste characteristics.

Additional waste categories. California law regulates several other categories of hazardous wastes:

- Restricted wastes. These wastes include all hazardous wastes that must meet specified pretreatment standards before being disposed of in land-based disposal facilities (*e.g.*, landfills, surface impoundments, waste piles, injection wells, and land treatment facilities). These requirements, known as land disposal restrictions (LDRs), apply to hazardous waste generators who dispose of (*i.e.*, place) waste on-site to land-based units or ship waste off-site from land-based units.

Ignitable. A waste is ignitable if a representative sample is easily combustible or flammable. Ignitable waste includes:

- A liquid with a flashpoint equal to or less than 140°F
- A non-liquid capable under standard temperature and pressure of causing fire by means of friction, absorption, moisture, or spontaneous chemical changes and that when ignited burns so vigorously and persistently that it creates a hazard
- An ignitable compressed gas, as defined in the Department of Transportation regulations
- An oxidizer, as defined in DOT regulations

An ignitable waste is assigned the EPA Hazardous Waste Number D001. 40 CFR 261.21, 22 CCR 66261.21.

Ignitable is distinguished from combustible and flammable. Combustible refers to a hazardous material (not a hazardous waste) which has a flashpoint above 100°F, while flammable refers to a hazardous material with a flashpoint under 100°F. 29 CFR 1910.106(a)(18).

Corrosive. A waste is corrosive if a representative sample dissolves metals and other materials or burns the skin or eye on contact. A waste is corrosive if:

- It is aqueous (*i.e.,* contains water) and has a pH equal to or less than 2.0 or greater than 12.5.
- It is a liquid and corrodes steel (SAE 1020) at a rate greater than 6.35 mm (0.250 inch) per year at a test temperature of 55°C (130°F).
- It is not aqueous (typically a solid) and, when mixed with an equivalent weight of water, produces a solution having a pH less than or equal to 2 or greater than or equal to 12.5.
- It is not a liquid and, when mixed with an equivalent weight of water, produces a liquid that corrodes steel (SAE 1020) at a rate

greater than 6.25 mm (0.25 inch) per year at a test temperature of 55°C (130°F).

- California has a corrosive test for solids (*e.g.,* powder NaOH).

A corrosive waste is assigned the EPA Hazardous Waste Number D002. 40 CFR 261.22, 22 CCR 66261.22.

Reactive. A waste is a reactive hazardous waste if it is unstable or undergoes rapid or violent chemical reactions, such as exploding, catching fire, or giving off fumes (when exposed to or mixed with water, air or other materials). A reactive waste meets one of the following criteria:

- Is normally unstable and readily undergoes violent change without detonating
- Reacts violently with water
- Forms potentially explosive mixtures with water
- When mixed with water, generates toxic gases, vapors or fumes in a quantity sufficient to present a danger to human health or the environment
- Is a cyanide or a sulfide which, when exposed to pH conditions between 2 and 12.5, can generate toxic gases
- Is capable of detonation or explosive reaction if it is subject to a strong initiating source or if heated under confinement
- Is readily capable of detonation or explosive decomposition or reaction at standard temperature and pressure
- Is a forbidden explosive per DOT regulations (40 CFR 173.51). *See* 40 CFR 261.23, 22 CCR 66261.23.

A reactive waste is assigned the EPA Hazardous Waste Number D003. 40 CFR 261.23, 22 CCR 66261.23.

Toxic. A waste is toxic if it is on a list of toxic substances (22 CCR 66261.24) and exceeds a specified regulatory level. If the waste is on the list, or the toxicity thresholds for the waste are unknown, generators must use

their knowledge of the waste or test the waste to determine if it exceeds the total threshold limit concentration (TTLC).

- If the waste does exceed the TTLC, then the waste is a California Hazardous Waste.
- If the waste does not exceed the TTLC, then do the following:
  – If the TTLC value for the waste is 10 times the soluble threshold limit concentration (STLC, known as the Waste Extraction Test or WET test), then determine if it exceeds STLC limits. If so, the waste is a California Hazardous Waste.
  – If the TTLC value is 20 times the federal toxic characteristic leaching procedure (TCLP), then analyze the waste using TCLP (40 CFR 261.24) to determine if the waste is a federally regulated hazardous waste under RCRA Subtitle C. If limits are exceeded, the waste is a federal hazardous waste.
  – If the waste is not subject to the TCLP test (*i.e.,* it is not listed in 22 CCR 66261.24) and does not exceed the listed regulatory level, then conduct an aquatic bioassay test. If the waste fails this test, it is a California Hazardous Waste. If it does not fail the test, the waste is nonhazardous unless it fails specified acute oral, dermal, and inhalation toxicity tests (40 CFR 261.24, 22 CCR 66261.24).

The federal and state solubility tests (*i.e.,* TCLP and STLC) expose a representative sample of waste to a weak acid and then measure the amount of regulated constituent that leaches out. If the leachate exceeds specified regulatory thresholds, the waste is a hazardous waste for the characteristic of toxicity. The TTLC test completely digests the representative sample to determine the total amount of regulated substance bound within the sample. As a result, the TTLC results in a higher yield of regulated substance than the TCLP or the STLC, for the same sample. ▪

- **Extremely hazardous wastes.** These wastes pose an extreme hazard to public health. A waste is considered to be an extremely hazardous waste if it exceeds specified toxicity levels expressed as either a lethal dose or a lethal concentration, or if the chemical appears on a list of pesticides or heavy metals, or is a PCB that exceeds a specified concentration in milligrams per kilogram.

- **Universal wastes.** Federal and state regulations relax requirements for a subset of hazardous wastes that are universally generated in society regardless of whether they come from industrial or commercial facilities. The California universal waste program includes batteries, pesticides (suspended, canceled, or unused), thermostats, cathode ray tubes (from computers or televisions), mercury-containing lamps (*e.g.*, fluorescent bulbs), mercury-containing thermostats, and aerosol cans. There are two types of generators of universal wastes: small quantity handlers (SQH) and large quantity handlers (LQH). SQHs do not accumulate more than 5,000 kg (or 11,000 pounds) of universal waste at any time while LQHs accumulate more than 5,000 kg at any time.

- **Special wastes.** These wastes include, among other things, auto shredder waste, bag house and scrubber waste, cement kiln dust, dewatered sludge from industrial process water treatment, sand from sandblasting, foundry casting, and coal gasification. These wastes may be disposed of in nonhazardous waste Class II facilities (accepting designated wastes) or Class III facilities (accepting nonhazardous, municipal solid wastes).

- **Recyclable wastes.** These wastes (*e.g.*, batteries and used oil filters) must be handled as hazardous wastes unless recycled and managed consistent with certain standards (HSC 25143.2), unless they are subject to a variance. Materials recycled consistent with these standards are excluded from the definition of hazardous waste.

- **Banned, unregistered, or outdated agricultural wastes.** This category is defined as a hazardous waste, including extremely hazardous waste, containing a pesticide for which EPA or the California Director of Pesticide Regulation has canceled or suspended its registration. This waste must be prepackaged according to the DOT and include the appropriate shipping papers. HSC 25207.1(a), 25207.6.

When hazardous wastes are mixed with nonhazardous wastes, the entire mixture must be managed as a hazardous waste, subject to some exceptions.

Mixed hazardous waste. When hazardous wastes are mixed with nonhazardous wastes, the entire mixture must be managed as a hazardous waste, subject to some exceptions. An exception is made when a characteristic hazardous waste is mixed with a nonhazardous waste and the resulting mixture is diluted enough to pass the test for ignitability, corrosivity, or reactivity. However, a mixed hazardous waste that exhibits the toxicity characteristic must be managed as a hazardous waste regardless of the concentration of the toxic constituent. Deliberately diluting a mixed hazardous waste is not permitted.

Even if a mixed hazardous waste satisfies the exemption criteria, the waste must be pretreated before being disposed to a land management unit. The generator must consult land disposal requirement standards that specify pre-treatment for the underlying hazardous constituents.

State law offers a conditional exemption from the mixture rule for contaminated textile materials (*e.g.*, solvent-soaked rags), which are made reusable by laundering or other cleaning. Laundry facilities seeking the conditional exemption must meet specified management procedures to ensure that the materials are appropriately managed. HSC 25144.6.

The hazardous waste debris rule offers relief from the hazardous waste mixture rule for hazardous debris (defined as a solid material exceeding 60 mm or 2.5 inches in particle size). A mixture of listed hazardous waste and hazardous debris is not considered mixed hazardous waste as long as it meets the pretreatment LDR standards. Hazardous debris that is treated and that no longer exhibits a hazardous characteristic after treatment is not a hazardous waste and does not need to be managed as such. However, if the debris exhibits a hazardous characteristic after treatment, it must be regulated as hazardous waste. Furthermore, any residuals from the treatment must be separated from the treated debris and managed as hazardous waste.

Empty containers. Completely empty containers (such as a 55-gallon drum) are not considered hazardous wastes. However, containers with residual hazardous waste, in specified amounts, are hazardous waste and thus must be managed in accordance with hazardous waste generator requirements discussed below. Under federal rules, small containers (with a capacity of 110 gallons or less) are considered empty only if no more than one inch or 3 percent of the total weight of the container's contents remain in the container. Additionally, under DTSC regulations, it must not be possible for any hazardous waste residue to be removed by scraping, chipping, or pouring. Aerosol cans and compressed gas cylinders are not empty unless the container has reached atmospheric pressure.

Completely empty containers are not considered hazardous wastes. However, containers with residual hazardous waste, in specified amounts, are hazardous waste.

Empty containers no longer intended for use on-site must be sent to be reclaimed for scrap value (for metal recovery), reconditioned, or remanufactured. Empty containers with a capacity of five gallons or less also may be disposed of at an appropriate, permitted solid waste facility. Before choosing to dispose of empty containers, generators should consider potential liability under CERCLA (discussed below).

Contained-in policy. A generator who manages contaminated environmental media (such as groundwater, soil, water, or solid sediments) may be subject to hazardous waste requirements. DTSC has authority to regulate environmental media that contain hazardous waste pursuant to EPA's "contained-in" policy. Under this policy, soil and other environmental media must be managed as hazardous wastes so long as they contain listed hazardous waste or exhibit a characteristic of hazardous waste. The contained-in policy was upheld by the D.C. Circuit Court of Appeals in *Chemical Waste Management v. EPA* (1989) 869 F. 2d 1526.

Contaminated environmental media are no longer considered to be hazardous waste once the hazardous constituents are removed by treatment, or when DTSC determines by risk assessment that the waste no longer poses a threat to human health and the environment. A contaminated medium that contains a hazardous waste listed solely for a characteristic would no longer need to be managed as hazardous waste when it no longer exhibits that characteristic.

Residues derived from the treatment, storage, or disposal of hazardous waste are considered to be hazardous waste.

Derived-from rule. Residues derived from the treatment, storage, or disposal of hazardous waste are considered to be hazardous waste. These residues include sludge, spill residue, ash, emission control dust, and leachate. These highly concentrated wastes are considered hazardous unless the waste does not exhibit a characteristic of hazardous waste, or if the waste is delisted. 40 CFR 261.3(c)(2).

Hazardous Waste Generator and Storage Requirements

The hazardous waste generator has the primary responsibility for determining whether material generated is classified as a hazardous waste.

Overview. The HWCL imposes a number of rigorous responsibilities, referred to as the generator requirements, on hazardous waste generators. The hazardous waste generator has the primary responsibility for determining whether material generated is classified as a hazardous waste.

Generators of hazardous waste fall into one of three categories, depending on the amount of hazardous waste generated by weight. These weight thresholds are based on monthly values and the cumulative quantity (by weight) stored at any one time. Criteria for the various types of generators, and federal and state requirements for each, are compared below in Table 8-4.

Table 8-5 shows separate requirements for the different types of hazardous waste generators under federal and state law.

SAP = Satellite accumulation point

Hazardous waste accumulation. Determining how long wastes can be stored on-site is complex. There are two categories of hazardous waste accumulation: satellite accumulation points (SAPs) and long-term storage.

SAPs initially accumulate hazardous wastes at or near the point of generation, and are under the control of the generator. These initial accumulation points are referred to as satellite accumulation points because they are like a satellite orbiting a larger celestial body (*i.e.*, the long-term storage area). Typically, one or more SAPs are in place at industrial and commercial facilities.

For long-term storage, conditionally exempt small quantity generators and small quantity generators may not store hazardous waste for more than 180 days after receipt from the SAP. For large quantity generators, hazardous waste may not be stored for more than 90 days after receipt from the SAP. Generators who store hazardous wastes beyond these time limits must obtain a long-term storage permit. 22 CCR 66270.

A generator may accumulate up to 55 gallons of a specific hazardous waste (or one quart of acutely or extremely hazardous waste) at a SAP. To qualify as

Table 8-4. Types of Hazardous Waste Generators

Type of generator	Applicability criteria	Federal storage limits	California storage limits
Conditionally exempt small quantity generator (CESQG)	No more than 220 pounds (*i.e.*, 100 kg) per month	No accumulation time limit	Same as SQG after collecting first 220 pounds (or 100 kg) except for household generators of hazardous waste
Small quantity generator (SQG)	No more than between 220 pounds (*i.e.*, 100 kg) per month and less than 2,200 pounds (*i.e.*, 1,000 kg) per month No more than 1 kg (*i.e.*, 2.2 pounds) per month of acutely hazardous waste	No more than 180 days or 270 days (if hazardous waste must be transported more than 200 miles to a TSDF) No more than 13,200 pounds (*i.e.*, 6,000 kg) on-site at any time Subject to a DTSC-approved 30-day extension	Same as federal
Large quantity generator (LQG)	2,200 pounds (*i.e.*, 100 kg) or more per month 1 kg (*i.e.*, 2.2 pounds) per month of acutely hazardous waste	No more than 90 days Subject to a 30-day extension approved by the Department of Toxic Substances Control	Same as federal

Source: 40 CFR 261.5, 262.34; 22 CCR 66262.34

a SAP, these hazardous wastes must be stored at or near the point of generation, provided that the waste is within the control of the generator. After 55 gallons of hazardous waste (or one quart of acutely or extremely hazardous waste) are accumulated, the waste must be moved (within three days) to one of the following:

CESQG = Conditionally exempt small quantity generator
LQG   – Large quantity generator
SQG   = Small quantity generator
TSDF   = Treatment, storage, and disposal facility

- On-site to a designated long-storage area (either a 90-day or 180-day storage area depending on whether it is a LQG or SQG)
- To a licensed treatment, storage, and disposal facility (TSDF)

Once the first drop or particle of hazardous waste is accumulated at the SAP, a one-year clock begins. Under California law, the generator must ensure that the hazardous waste is ultimately moved off-site to a permitted TSDF within one year, regardless of whether 55 gallons of hazardous waste (or one quart of acutely or extremely hazardous waste) is accumulated at the SAP. This one-year time limit is more strict than the federal standard, which allows a generator to accumulate hazardous waste at a SAP indefinitely as long as no more than 55 gallons (or one quart of acutely or extremely) hazardous waste is collected. 22 CCR 66262.34(e)(1)(B).

Once the first drop or particle of hazardous waste is accumulated at the SAP, a one-year clock begins.

A hazardous waste generator often affixes labels to containers indicating "full" and "arrival date," to demonstrate compliance with time frames. By using this approach, a hazardous waste generator can demonstrate meeting three different time frames as follows:

A hazardous waste generator often affixes labels to containers indicating "full" and "arrival date," to demonstrate compliance with time frames.

Table 8-5. Hazardous Waste Generator Requirements

Requirement	Federal conditionally exempt small quantity generator (federal CESQG)	Federal small quantity generator (federal SQG)	Federal large quantity generator (federal LQG)	State conditionally exempt small quantity generator (state CESQG)
Waste characterization	X	X	X	X
Obtain EPA identification number		X	X	X
Manifesting		X	X	X
Land disposal requirements notification		X	X	X
Exception reporting		X	X	X
Tank labeling		X	X	X
Personnel training		X	X	X
Personnel training program			X	
Contingency plan			X	
Weekly inspections			X	
Post emergency information		X	X	X
Emergency equipment		X	X	X
Container management		X	X	X
Tank management		X	X	X
Storage facility closure			X	
Biennial report			X	
Short-term waste accumulation limit (*i.e.,* satellite accumulation)*		Up to 55 gallons of hazardous waste and one quart of acutely hazardous waste*	Up to 55 gallons of hazardous waste and one quart of acutely hazardous waste*	Up to 55 gallons of hazardous waste and one quart of acutely or extremely hazardous waste*
Long-term waste accumulation limit*		180 Days	90 Days	180 Days

* California law prohibits storing wastes for more than one year from collection of the first drop or particle at a satellite accumulation area regardless of whether 55 gallons have been accumulated at the SAP.

Source: 40 CFR 262.34, 22 CCR 66262.34

- **Initial accumulation date.** The date that the first drop or particle enters the container at the SAP, which starts the one-year clock for storage.

- **Full date.** The date that the drum at the SAP is full (up to 55 gallons of each type of hazardous waste or one quart of each type of acutely or extremely hazardous waste), which starts the three-day clock for moving wastes from the SAP to the long-term storage area. 22 CCR 66262.34 (e)(3).

- **Arrival date.** The date the full drum arrives at the long-term storage area that starts the 180- or 90-day clock for storing waste after receipt from the SAP.

Although not required at SAPs, it is advisable to store liquid hazardous waste drums or containers within secondary containers, to collect potential spills and prevent releases to the environment.

Containers and labeling. Hazardous waste containers must be labeled with:

- The composition of the waste
- Its physical state (liquid, solid, or gas)
- Its hazardous properties (*e.g.,* reactive, ignitable)
- Contact information of the person producing the waste (*i.e.,* name, address, telephone number, and EPA identification number of the facility)
- The date waste was first placed into the container

Hazardous wastes must be collected in containers compatible with the wastes stored, approved by the U.S. Department of Transportation. Hazardous wastes collected at SAPs also must be segregated from incompatible wastes such as acids and bases or combustibles and acids. Additionally, containers must prevent the release of volatile organic chemicals, such as solvents. Containers must be kept securely closed at all times, except to add or remove wastes.

Requirements for storage areas. Hazardous waste 180-day and 90-day storage areas must be equipped with specified equipment, including a telephone, alarm, portable fire extinguishers, fire control equipment, and spill control and decontamination equipment. The generator must inspect the 90-day hazardous waste accumulation facility weekly to ensure that the containers and tanks are in good condition (free of corrosion and not leaking), that accumulation storage time frames have not been exceeded, and that containers are securely closed.

Hazardous waste 180- and 90-day storage areas must be equipped with specified equipment, including a telephone, alarm, portable fire extinguishers, fire control equipment, and spill control and decontamination equipment.

LQGs must write and implement a hazardous waste contingency plan that, among other things, describes actions to be taken to respond to fires, explosions, or unplanned releases of hazardous waste. Additionally, the contingency plan must describe arrangements the generator has made with local police, fire, hospitals, response contractors, and emergency response teams to manage emergency response scenarios. 22 CCR 66264.51 *et seq.*

Universal waste handler requirements. Universal waste handlers have more relaxed management requirements, including simpler staging requirements. Both LQG and SQH of universal wastes may store the wastes for up to one year, but need not follow requirements associated with satellite accumulation discussed above. Universal waste handlers must store wastes in closed, non-leaking containers to ensure that the wastes are not released to the environment.

Training. LQGs must ensure that employees receive initial training within six months of receiving or changing a job assignment involving the management of hazardous waste. LQGs must ensure that personnel receive training on the handling, storage, and emergency response considerations of managing hazardous waste. LQGs must ensure that personnel receive annual refresher training. Also, LQGs must establish a training program that assigns different levels of hazardous waste training curricula for a range of job categories. Hazardous waste training records must be maintained for at least three years. 22 CCR 66262.34(a)(3),

LQGs must ensure that employees receive initial training within six months of receiving or changing a job assignment involving the management of hazardous waste.

22 CCR 66265.16. SQGs of hazardous waste are subject to reduced training requirements. 22 CCR 66262.34(d)(2).

Handlers of universal waste have reduced training requirements compared to generators of hazardous waste.

Handlers of universal waste have reduced training requirements compared to generators of hazardous waste. SQHs of universal waste must ensure that employees who handle or have responsibility for managing universal wastes are apprised of proper handling and emergency procedures. LQHs must make sure that all employees are thoroughly familiar with proper waste handling and emergency procedures, relative to their responsibilities during normal facility operations and emergencies. 22 CCR 66273.36.

Recordkeeping. Hazardous waste generators and universal waste handlers must retain the following records for at least three years:

- 90-day storage facility inspections on-site (for LQGs)
- Copies of each signed hazardous waste manifest (for LQGs and SQGs)
- Biennial reports (for LQGs)
- Manifest exception reports (for LQGs and SQGs)
- All test results, waste analyses, or other hazardous waste characterization determination data (for LQGs and SQGs)
- Training records (for LQGs)
- Records of each shipment of universal waste received by or sent from their facilities (for LQHs of universal wastes)

Waste Minimization

Pollution Prevention Act of 1990. This federal Act (42 USC 13101 *et seq.*, 40 CFR 370, 372) establishes a national policy to reduce or prevent pollution at the source. Each owner or operator of a facility is required to file (with EPA) an annual toxic chemical release report. This report must describe toxic chemical source reduction and recycling initiatives for the previous calendar year, including the quantity of the chemical entering any waste stream before it is recycled, treated, or disposed of, and the percentage change from the previous year.

Hazardous Waste Source Reduction and Management Review Act. This state Act (commonly known as SB 14 or the Pollution Prevention Act, HSC 25244.12, 22 CCR 67100 *et seq.*) is intended to encourage businesses that generate large quantities of hazardous waste to decrease the amount of waste they produce. Specifically, SB 14 is designed to reduce the generation of hazardous waste at its source, reduce releases to the environment of chemicals that have adverse health or environmental effects, and document hazardous waste management information and make that information available.

SB 14 applies to LQGs who routinely generate more than 12,000 kg (or 26,455 pounds) of hazardous waste or more than 12 kg (or 26.4 pounds) of extremely hazardous waste during a reporting year. For purposes of determining

SB 14 applicability, the law excludes a number of waste streams from the aggregate hazardous waste total, including universal wastes, non-routine wastes, motor vehicle fluids, and household hazardous wastes. HSC 25244.12 *et seq.*

SB 14 provides a framework for companies to evaluate site-specific pollution prevention practices to minimize generation of hazardous waste without mandating specified waste reduction levels. In general, SB 14 requires LQGs to detail their waste generation processes as well as their goals and methods to decrease the amount of hazardous waste generated. Pollution prevention reports must be submitted every four years covering the previous year. *See* DTSC 2006.

Hazardous Waste Transportation

Generators of hazardous waste must use registered haulers of hazardous waste and complete a hazardous waste shipping document known as a manifest. 22 CCR 66263.10 *et seq.* When signing a manifest, the generator certifies that a waste minimization program is in place. Generators of hazardous waste must take steps to ensure that hazardous wastes leaving the facility ultimately arrive at the TSDF. Generators must receive a signed copy of the manifest from the TSDF within 35 days; otherwise, generators must contact the transporter and/or the TSDF owner or operator. If the generator does not receive a copy of the signed manifest within 45 days, the generator must submit an exception report to DTSC explaining its efforts to locate the missing hazardous waste. 22 CCR 66262.42(B).

Generators of hazardous waste must use registered haulers of hazardous waste and complete a hazardous waste shipping document known as a manifest.

If a TSDF rejects a shipment of hazardous waste, the TSDF may use the original manifest to return the hazardous waste load. The generator who receives the rejected shipment may accumulate the rejected hazardous waste on-site for up to 90 days, provided it is labeled indicating that the load was rejected and the date it was received by the generator.

Generators and operators responsible for loading hazardous waste must verify the transporter's class of driver's license and hazardous materials endorsements.

Hazardous waste transporters must:

- Obtain an EPA identification number and DTSC registration
- Submit a disclosure statement and undergo background checks
- Use properly equipped vehicles passing annual inspections by the California Highway Patrol
- Complete hazardous waste manifests
- Comply with Highway Patrol regulations on packaging, labeling, and other matters
- Report to DTSC if hazardous wastes of concern (*e.g.,* explosives, poisons) become missing during transport

Transporters that handle hazardous wastes of concern are required to submit a disclosure statement to DTSC and submit to a background check. In addition, they must contact DTSC within 24 hours and file a report when they discover that hazardous wastes of concern are missing or appear unusual. HSC 25169.5.

Hazardous Waste Facilities

Regulatory requirements. The HWCL imposes a number of particularly rigorous requirements on facilities that own or operate hazardous waste treatment (such as neutralization, incineration, and bioremediation), storage, transfer, recycling, and disposal (such as landfills and surface impoundments) facilities. The rules establish a complex and cumbersome set of requirements for permitting several types of these waste management units (WMUs). WMUs include containers, tanks, landfills, surface impoundments, land treatment, waste piles, incineration units, and miscellaneous units.

In addition to hazardous waste permitting requirements, facilities that dispose of hazardous wastes are also regulated under the Porter–Cologne Water Quality Control Act pursuant to waste discharge requirements (WDRs) (discussed in chapter 10). Class I WDR permits are issued to waste units that collect hazardous wastes. Class II WDR permits govern waste units that collect designated wastes (which include wastes that pass the definition for hazardous wastes but that exceed the beneficial uses for water quality). Finally, Class III permits are required for municipal solid waste landfills, which collect nonhazardous wastes. *See* chapter 9. WMU classification is illustrated in Figure 8-3.

Waste management unit requirements. The HWCL imposes a number of responsibilities on the operation of hazardous waste facilities, including WMU-specific requirements and requirements applicable to all WMUs. Owners or operators of all facilities must (22 CCR 66264 *et seq.*):

- Develop a waste analysis plan to identify testing and sampling methods to be used, among other things

- Meet certain general facility standards, *e.g.*, for worker safety and accident prevention

- Meet emergency preparedness and prevention requirements, including preparation of an emergency contingency plan

- Implement a hazardous waste manifest system and retain records

The HWCL imposes a number of responsibilities on the operation of hazardous waste facilities, including WMU-specific requirements and requirements applicable to all WMUs.

Figure 8-3
WMU Classification

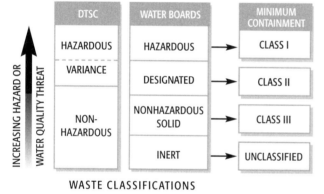

WASTE CLASSIFICATIONS

Source: Jon Marshack. Reprinted with permission

WDR = Waste discharge requirement
WMU = Waste management unit

- Implement air quality and water quality monitoring programs
- Meet financial responsibility requirements
- Take corrective action in the event of release of hazardous waste from the facility
- Develop and implement a training plan
- Develop and implement a site security plan
- Develop and implement facility inspections
- Notify DTSC when reportable quantities of hazardous wastes of concern (*i.e.,* poisons and explosives) have been released or are missing
- Handle hazardous wastes generated from cleanup activities pursuant to Corrective Action Management Unit (CAMU) regulations

CAMU = Corrective Action Management Unit

- Prepare a facility closure plan and provide post-closure monitoring

Different requirements for Resource Conservation and Recovery Act and California-only hazardous waste. In addition to RCRA facility standards, the HWCL establishes standards for facilities that treat, store, or dispose of non-RCRA, California-only hazardous waste. TSDFs are grouped into tiers in descending order of regulatory stringency:

- Tier 1. RCRA Subtitle C-equivalent permits that are required for treatment, storage, and disposal of all RCRA hazardous waste
- Tier 2. Facility permits (known as standardized permits) for off-site facilities that treat and store (but do not dispose) California-only hazardous wastes
- Tier 3. "Permit by rule" governing specified on-site treatment (but facilities do not store or dispose) specified methodologies and specified California-only hazardous waste categories
- Tier 4. Conditional authorization for on-site facilities that treat (but do not store or dispose) other types of waste with low hazardous chemical concentrations
- Tier 5. Conditional exemption for on-site treatment of certain low-risk waste or de minimis amounts of certain waste

Treatment, storage, and disposal facility permit applications. Hazardous waste TSDF permit applications consist of two parts. Part A of the application includes a description of the hazardous waste management processes and facilities and of the hazardous waste itself. Part B of the application is known as the operations plan, and includes detailed contingency plans in case of accidental releases.

The HWCL allows for expedited approval of off-site hazardous waste facilities. The process includes:

- Complying with applicable laws
- Soliciting public comment
- Having an appeal process regarding local agency decisions denying a land use permit for a TSDF
- Requiring counties to develop county hazardous waste management plans to identify locations within the county suitable for building or expanding upon

TSDFs. Cities and counties are required to appoint a local assessment committee with certain specified membership, to advise the local agencies on permit terms and conditions to make the facility acceptable to the community. Health and Safety Code 25199 *et seq.*

Applicants for TSDFs and tiered permits, and applicants seeking authorization to transport hazardous wastes, must issue a disclosure statement to DTSC and undergo background checks. In addition, applicants for TSDFs must provide fingerprint images to DTSC.

Other Hazardous Waste Regulations

Surface impoundments and land treatment. The Toxic Pits Cleanup Act of 1984 (HSC 25208 *et seq.*) regulates the cleanup of surface impoundments containing liquid hazardous waste, where structures once thought to contain hazardous leachates had proved insufficient. This Act mandates that all such impoundments meet specified requirements, such as a double lining and being located a certain distance from drinking water supplies. Discharge of hazardous waste is prohibited into land treatment units that are unequipped with liners, leachate collection and removal systems, a groundwater monitoring system, and a vadose zone monitoring system.

Discharge of hazardous waste is prohibited into land treatment units that are unequipped with liners, leachate collection and removal systems, a groundwater monitoring system, and a vadose zone monitoring system.

TIWCA = Toxic Injection Well Control Act of 1985

More stringent state requirements were enacted under the Toxic Injection Well Control Act of 1985 (TIWCA) (HSC 25159.10–25159.25). TIWCA prohibits injection of hazardous wastes into an underground well unless the following criteria are satisfied:

- The well may not be within 0.5 mile of a source of drinking water.
- No discharge is allowed into or above a formation that contains a source of drinking water.
- The well must be permitted as a hazardous waste facility.

Hazardous waste properties and border zone properties. A hazardous waste property (where a hazardous waste deposit poses a hazard to public health or safety) may not be used for any new use, other than modification of certain existing industrial or manufacturing facilities on the property. A border zone property (a property located within 2,000 feet of a hazardous waste deposit) designated by DTSC (*see* HSC 25220 *et seq.*) may not be used for human habitation, a hospital, a school, or a day care center. Requests for DTSC determination of whether a property is a hazardous waste or border zone property may be made by certain owners, lessors, or lessees, or by cities or counties with jurisdiction over the property.

A hazardous waste property may not be used for any new use, other than modification of certain existing industrial or manufacturing facilities on the property.

Enforcement

DTSC and local authorized health officers may employ a broad range of enforcement mechanisms for violations of California hazardous waste laws. Potential enforcement mechanisms include facility inspections and corrective action orders, permit revocation, injunctions, civil penalties, and criminal fines and imprisonment.

DTSC inspectors may, at any time, enter and inspect facilities where hazardous wastes are stored, handled, processed, disposed of, or treated. Permits may be suspended without a hearing if violations threaten "imminent and substantial danger to the public health or safety of the environment." If orders for corrective action are ignored, DTSC may outsource the enforcement work and bill the violator up to $100,000. HSC 25187.5(b).

DTSC inspectors may, at any time, enter and inspect facilities where hazardous wastes are stored, handled, processed, disposed of, or treated.

Civil penalties depend on the type and severity of the violation. Minor violations are those that (HSC 25117.6):

- Do not present a significant threat to human health or safety
- Do not impede waste being properly disposed of
- Do not cause the release of waste
- Do not impede release detection
- Do not compromise cleanup
- Are not chronic, committed by a recalcitrant violator
- Are not knowing, willful, or intentional

Minor violations do not immediately result in individual civil penalties, but are aggregated and will incur penalties up to $25,000 per day if corrective action orders are ignored. Civil penalties for almost all other violations (known as Class II violations) incur up to $25,000 per day per violation. A select group of knowing, willful, and intentional violations may trigger penalties up to $100,000 per day, or $250,000 per day and imprisonment if violations cause serious bodily injury or death. HSC 25189.5. In addition to civil penalties, violators may be subject to criminal misdemeanor charges, punishable by up to $1,000 in fines and up to 6 months imprisonment. HSC 25190.

Federal Cleanup Programs

Comprehensive Environmental Response Compensation and Liability Act

Overview. CERCLA (42 USC 9601 *et seq.*), known as Superfund, imposes a retroactive, strict liability process assigning responsibility for cleanup of contaminated property. In addition, the law establishes a process for investigation and cleanup of contaminated sites and determination of cleanup levels. 40 CFR 300 *et seq.*

CERCLA imposes a retroactive, strict liability process assigning responsibility for cleanup of contaminated property.

CERCLA governs a release or threat of a release of a "hazardous substance, pollutant, or contaminant" (which is expansively defined to include all regulated chemicals under the major federal statutes except for petroleum and natural gas) into the "environment" (which is also broadly defined), where it may present imminent and substantial danger. The liability process imposes strict, joint, and several retroactive liability at multiparty sites. This means that regardless of the care taken to prevent a spill or release into the environment, a person potentially is liable for cleanup costs if the person is one of the following:

- The current owner or operator of the facility
- The historic owner or operator of the facility, when disposal of the hazardous substance occurred
- The person who "by contract, agreement or otherwise arranged for disposal or treatment" of the hazardous substance (*e.g.*, a hazardous waste generator who made arrangements to send hazardous waste to a licensed TSDF that leaks)
- The person who accepted the hazardous substance for transport, disposal, or treatment

NCP = National Contingency Plan
PRP = Potentially responsible party

These persons are called potentially responsible parties (PRPs). CERCLA broadly defines persons to include individuals, business entities, and state, federal, and local government agencies. Corporate officers and employees who participated actively in the challenged conduct are also considered persons, and can be held liable as PRPs. *United States v. NEPACCO* (1986) 810 F. 2d 726, *cert. denied*, 484 US 848, 1987. EPA is exempt from the person definition when acting in its regulatory or remedial capacity. Lenders may be exempt when they involuntarily acquired a contaminated site through means such as acquisition of security interests.

Potentially responsible party liability. CERCLA imposes liability on a PRP who is responsible for a hazardous substance release even when the party was not negligent or at fault, or the PRP's actions were consistent with standard industry practices at the time. Current owners may be liable even if they have not actively participated in the management of the facility or contributed to the hazardous substance release, while former owners are liable only if disposal occurred at the time of ownership or operation. PRPs may be held jointly and severally (*i.e.*, separately) liable for the government's cleanup costs, and may seek contribution from other responsible parties. If other PRPs cannot be found or cannot pay their proportional liability, the PRP may be responsible for the entire cleanup cost. 42 USC 9607(a).

PRPs may be required to reimburse EPA for response costs (costs associated with cleanup) unless the investigation and cleanup activities are inconsistent with standards in National Contingency Plan (NCP) regulations. 40 CFR 300 *et seq*. PRPs are presumed liable for response costs unless evidence of inconsistency with the NCP standards (defined below) can be demonstrated, effectively contending that the response costs were not cost-effective.

CERCLA liability can be avoided if a PRP did not know and had no reason to know of a hazardous substances disposal at the site prior to acquisition.

Potentially responsible party defenses. CERCLA liability can be avoided if a PRP did not know and had no reason to know of a hazardous substances disposal at the site prior to acquisition. If a PRP engages in "all appropriate inquiries" into the previous use of the property in accordance with specified due diligence standards (such as a phase one or two property assessment), one of three defenses under CERCLA may be asserted—the innocent landowner, bona fide prospective purchaser, and contiguous property defenses.

"All appropriate inquiries" means that a PRP must do the following:

- Interview past and present owners, operators, and occupants
- Review historical sources of information
- Conduct a visual inspection of the facility
- Review government records
- Search for environmental cleanup liens
- Assess any specialized knowledge of the prospective owner
- Assess purchase price in comparison to the fair market value of the property if it was not contaminated
- Obtain commonly known or reasonably ascertainable information

A PRP is exempt from CERCLA liability if less than 110 gallons of liquid or 200 pounds of solid hazardous substance were generated and disposed of before April 1, 2001, and these *de micromis* volumes are the sole reason for liability. Also, municipal waste contributors (*e.g.*, residential property owners, small businesses, and nonprofits) also are exempt from CERCLA liability.

Cleanup process. CERCLA establishes standards for two types of cleanup activities—removal actions and remedial actions. A removal action is a straightforward cleanup effort requiring immediate attention to stabilize the release or threat of a release of a hazardous substance (*e.g.*, controlling surface water runoff, pumping leaking ponds, or removing bulk containers of hazardous substances). A remedial action involves a contaminated property that cannot be readily cleaned up without a lengthy and sophisticated investigation, and which typically requires expensive treatment technologies to remedy the contaminated site.

Tens of thousands of properties are either underutilized or too dangerous to occupy due to contamination. These sites include leaking landfills, Department of Defense installations, operating and abandoned industrial facilities, and more. The NCP guidelines establish criteria for prioritizing which sites are eligible for government cleanup funds (*i.e.*, the Superfund) when one or more PRPs cannot be located or are insolvent. These prioritized sites appear on the National Priorities List and must follow NCP cleanup standards. The NCP is composed of a two step process that includes conducting a remedial investigation (RI) and a feasibility study (FS). This process is illustrated in Figure 8-4.

The RI/FS process is an elaborate set of procedures that determines the nature and extent of contamination and that governs site remediation. Prior to commencing the RI, a preliminary assessment/site investigation (PA/SI) typically is performed to gather information to support an informed risk management decision on the appropriate remedy.

FS   = Feasibility study
PA/SI = Preliminary assessment/
        site investigation
RI   = Remedial investigation

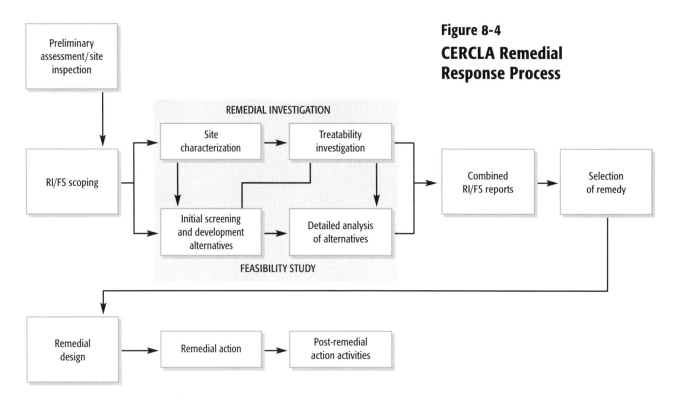

Figure 8-4
CERCLA Remedial
Response Process

ARAR = Applicable or relevant and
          appropriate requirement
IDW = Investigation-derived waste
ROD = Record of Decision

The FS process is informed by a variety of criteria designed to balance the protection of human health and the environment with compliance with "applicable or relevant and appropriate requirements" for environmental health and safety.

The RI characterizes site conditions and identifies the source and extent of contamination to determine whether and to what extent a contaminant plume is migrating. In addition, the RI determines the extent to which human populations and the environment are exposed to the contaminants. The data collected from the RI are used to develop and evaluate remedial alternatives that are considered in the FS stage. Remedial action remedies are adopted at the conclusion of the FS.

The FS process is informed by a variety of criteria designed to balance the protection of human health and the environment (typically based on a risk assessment) with compliance with "applicable or relevant and appropriate requirements" (ARARs) for environmental health and safety. These threshold criteria must be balanced against the long-term effectiveness and permanence of the proposed cleanup remedy, compared with the technical administrative ease and cost-effectiveness of implementing the cleanup remedy. The NCP guidelines show a strong preference for on-site treatment instead of off-site disposal. The ultimate cleanup remedies must be documented in a Record of Decision (ROD), which is available for public comment in the Federal Register.

Throughout the RI/FS process, ARARs govern investigation and remedial activities. ARARs also influence the cleanup standard (*i.e.*, how clean is clean?). ARARs must be met for both remedial actions and, to the extent feasible, for removal actions. Examples of ARARs include RCRA Subtitle C land disposal restrictions and Clean Water Act storm water standards.

During field investigating activities under CERCLA, wastes (known as investigation-derived waste or IDW) are generated that can pose a public or environmental health risk. IDW is created during sampling and investigation to determine the nature and extent of contamination. IDW includes drilled muds, soil cuttings, and purge water from well installation and sample collection. Under EPA guidance, IDW must be disposed of immediately or managed through an interim process. Site managers must choose an option that protects human health and the environment, and complies with or waives ARARs. EPA 1992.

Waste characterization is necessary to determine which ARARs may apply. Characterization determines whether the waste is a RCRA hazardous waste, a regulated waste under other laws, or nonhazardous. For example, characterizing an IDW as an RCRA hazardous waste determines if land disposal restrictions are applicable, whether the waste can be managed on-site, or whether the waste must be disposed of in a TSDF.

Waste characterization is necessary to determine which ARARs may apply. Characterization determines whether the waste is a RCRA hazardous waste, a regulated waste under other laws, or nonhazardous.

Resource Conservation and Recovery Act

RCRA, Subtitle C (40 CFR 264.550 *et seq.*) establishes a program to clean up releases of hazardous waste or hazardous waste constituents from permitted TSDFs. A release is broadly defined to include any spill, leaking, pouring, emitting, emptying, discharging, injecting, pumping, escaping, leaching, dumping, or disposing of hazardous waste or constituents into the environment. The RCRA corrective action program requires TSDF owners and operators to investigate and clean up hazardous waste releases from permitted waste management units (*e.g.*, surface impoundments or landfills). A release from a regulated TSDF sets in motion a prescriptive site assessment and cleanup process similar to the CERCLA RI/FS process; however, the RCRA corrective action program uses different terminology. *See* Table 8-6 for a comparison of terms.

An owner or operator required to implement corrective action has the following responsibilities:

- Ensuring that regulated units are in compliance with groundwater protection standards
- Implementing a program that prevents hazardous constituents from exceeding concentration limits at the compliance point by removing the hazardous waste constituents or treating them in place
- Beginning a corrective action within a reasonable time period after the groundwater protection standard is exceeded
- Establishing and implementing a groundwater monitoring program to show the effectiveness of the corrective action program
- Conducting a corrective action program to remove any hazardous constituents that exceed concentration limits in groundwater
- Continuing corrective action measures during the compliance period to guarantee that groundwater protection standards are not exceeded

- Writing and submitting a semiannual report to EPA describing the effectiveness of the corrective action program
- Submitting a permit modification application within 90 days to make changes to the program, if the corrective action program is no longer applicable

Federal Brownfields Program

The Brownfields Revitalization and Environmental Restoration Act of 2001 authorizes up to $200 million per year to support assessment and cleanup of brownfields.

The Brownfields Revitalization and Environmental Restoration Act of 2001 (42 USC 9604(k)) authorizes up to $200 million per year to support assessment and cleanup of brownfields. A brownfield is real property whose development may be complicated by the potential presence of a hazardous substance, pollutant, or contaminant (except property subject to a planned or ongoing CERCLA removal action, listed or proposed for the NPL, or subject to specified orders and consent decrees under CERCLA). The Act authorizes grants of up to $200,000 per site to investigate and plan for cleanup.

The brownfields law clarifies what actions property owners or operators must undertake to satisfy the "all appropriate inquiries" defense under CERCLA. These inquiry criteria apply to land that is contaminated solely due to a release from a contiguous or similarly situated property owned by someone else, if the owner or operator:

- Did not cause or contribute to the release or threatened release
- Is not potentially liable or affiliated with any other person potentially liable
- Exercises appropriate care regarding the release
- Provides full cooperation, assistance, and access to persons authorized to undertake the response action and natural resource restoration
- Complies with all land use controls and does not impede the performance of any institutional controls
- Conducted all appropriate inquiry at the time of purchase and did not know or have reason to know of the contamination

The Act also exempts from liability "bona fide prospective purchasers," including their tenants. All disposals must have taken place before the purchase, and the person must have made all appropriate inquiries exercising appropriate care with respect to any release.

State Cleanup Programs

California Hazardous Substances Account Act

The California HSAA establishes a state Superfund program to clean up contaminated sites not listed on the NPL.

Overview. The California HSAA establishes a state Superfund program to clean up contaminated sites not listed on the NPL. The California HSAA authorizes DTSC to initiate remedial and removal actions and to enter into enforceable agreements with PRPs to investigate and remediate contamination. HSC 25355.5(a)(1)(C).

Term	CERCLA	RCRA
Process initiation	Release or threat of release of a hazardous substance into the environment or a release of any pollutant or contaminant that may present an imminent and substantial danger to public health or welfare	Hazardous waste treatment, storage, and disposal facility permit action or RCRA enforcement order
Record search	Preliminary assessment (PA)	RCRA facility assessment (RFA) (conducted by EPA/state)
Sampling to confirm or refute	Site inspection (SI)	No direct equivalent However, an optional phase known as Phase I RFI (or release assessment) can be used to determine whether interim/stabilization measures are needed or focus should be on the RFI (Occasionally, sampling occurs during RFA)
Site scoring	Hazard ranking system National Priorities List	No equivalent
Determine nature and extent of contamination	Remedial investigation (RI)	RCRA facility investigation (RFI)
Interim action (can occur at any point in the process)	Time critical removal action (TCRA) or Non-time critical removal action (NTCRA)	Interim stabilization measure (ISM)
Evaluate alternatives	Feasibility study	Corrective measures study (CMS)
Proposed action	Proposed plan	Statement of basis
Decision document	Record of Decision (ROD)	Permit modification
Action implementation	Remedial design/Remedial action (RD/RA)	Corrective measures implementation (CMI)

Source: Adapted from U.S. Army Corps of Engineers. 2001. CERCLA/RCRA Remediation Process Workshop Manual

Differences from the Comprehensive Environmental Response, Compensation, and Liability Act. The state and federal Superfund programs are fundamentally the same, except for terminology and a few substantive differences. Differences include:

- **Retroactive liability.** Unlike CERCLA, the California HSAA does not impose retroactive liability for activities that occurred on or before January 1, 1982.

- **Definition of hazardous substance.** California's HSAA definition of hazardous substance is more expansive than in CERCLA and includes California hazardous waste and extremely hazardous waste (as defined in HSC 25115 and 25117). The California HSAA definition excludes petroleum and natural gas, but includes "non-toxic, non-flammable, non-corrosive storm water runoff drained from underground vaults, chambers, or manholes into gutters or storm sewers."

- **Liability defense.** The California HSAA provides an additional liability defense for special districts, entities, or organizations holding a specified conservation

CMI = Corrective measures implementation
CMS = Corrective measures study
ISM = Interim stabilization measure
NTCRA = Non-time critical removal action
RD/RA = Remedial design/ Remedial action
RFA = RCRA facility assessment
RFI = RCRA facility investigation
RI = Remedial investigation
ROD = Record of Decision
TCRA = Time critical removal action

New and past releases of hazardous substances must be reported to DTSC unless subject to exemption. Any release of a reportable quantity of hazardous substances must be reported to DTSC within 30 days of discovery.

easement for properties acquired on or after January 1, 1995, and where there is no evidence of a hazardous substances release. The California HSAA also offers a defense to "innocent owners" of single-family residences located on five acres or less, and also presumes no liability against owners of common areas within residential common interest developments.

- **Orphan shares.** The California Orphan Share Reimbursement Trust Fund underwrites the investigation and cleanup of listed sites associated with orphan shares (*i.e.,* the portion of liability attributable to defunct or insolvent persons).

Release reporting. New and past releases of hazardous substances must be reported to DTSC unless subject to exemption. Any release of a reportable quantity of hazardous substances must be reported to DTSC within 30 days of discovery. Reportable quantity includes volumes below federal thresholds for reporting if the hazardous substance may pose a significant threat to public health and safety or the environment. Release means "any spilling, leaking, pumping, pouring, emitting, emptying, discharging, injection, escaping, leaching, dumping, or disposing into the environment." HSC 25320.

Cleanup process. DTSC serves as the lead agency for overseeing cleanup of hazardous waste sites where no responsible party is identified. When there is a responsible party, DTSC serves as the lead agency if the site is on the EPA's NPL, or when it is deemed appropriate to expend state Superfund money. Additionally, DTSC becomes the lead agency when the contamination is primarily confined to soil or when a release stems from a TSDF. If the contamination is primarily airborne, DTSC must consult with the appropriate air district.

A responsible party may petition Cal/EPA to designate a particular agency as lead agency under the Unified Agency Review Law. HSC 25262. To prevent developers from choosing a lead agency, Cal/EPA (2005, www.calepa.ca.gov/Brownfields/MOA/MOA3_05.pdf) issued a memorandum of agreement (MOA) among DTSC, the SWRCB, and the nine RWQCBs. The MOA:

- Establishes procedures for determining whether DTSC or a RWQCB will serve as lead agency
- Calls for a single, uniform site assessment procedure to be used by both agencies

All cleanups must address the requirements of both agencies. DTSC and each RWQCB must provide ample opportunity for public involvement in the cleanup decisions. Finally, both must coordinate and communicate on brownfield sites.

Heavy equipment is often used to clean up contaminated soils.

MOA = Memorandum of agreement

DTSC can order responsible parties to conduct removal actions to "prevent, minimize, stabilize, mitigate, or eliminate the release or threat of release" of a hazardous substance. DTSC requires development of a full remedial action plan (RAP) for removal actions unless the total cost is less than $2 million, and DTSC determines that an abbreviated RAP provides equivalent protection of human and environmental health. (A federal ROD is the counterpart to a California RAP.) Typically, responsible parties (or a DTSC contractor) prepare draft RAPs according to the RI/FS process (discussed above). Draft RAPs must be made available for public comment. HSC 25323.

When the remedial action results in residual contamination, DTSC may issue land use restrictions such as easements, covenants, restrictions, servitudes, and other institutional controls.

Also, the Expedited Remedial Action Reform Act is a pilot program that expedites cleanups of hazardous substances while allowing increased flexibility. HSC 25396 *et seq.*

RAP = Remedial action plan
SWMU = Solid waste management unit

California Corrective Action Program

Corrective action may be required if the DTSC or CUPA determines that a hazardous waste facility released hazardous waste into the environment. 22 CCR 66264.550 *et seq.* For facilities required to have a permit, DTSC can seek remedies, such as the issuance of a corrective action order, before seeking legal remedies, with the following exceptions:

- The responsible party voluntarily requests in writing that DTSC issue a corrective action order
- The responsible party is unable to pay for the corrective action
- The responsible party is unwilling to take a corrective action
- The release is part of a regional or multi-site groundwater contamination problem that cannot be addressed fully using available legal remedies
- A corrective action order was issued previously against the responsible person who has agreed to address the required cleanup

Corrective action may be required if the DTSC or CUPA determines that a hazardous waste facility released hazardous waste into the environment.

Under California's Corrective Action Program, the first step is to conduct an RCRA facility assessment, performed by DTSC, to identify solid waste management units (SWMU) located at a given facility while obtaining information on potential releases from those units. Absent any releases, DTSC prepares a memo in lieu of the RFA. If a release is discovered, DTSC issues a corrective action order or permit condition to require the owner or operator to conduct further investigative work; this process is called RCRA facility investigation. When the RFI indicates release levels that threaten the health of humans or the environment, then the owner or operator must conduct a corrective measures study to determine possible remedies to address the SWMU releases.

California Water Quality Cleanup Programs

The RWQCBs can require cleanup of chemical contamination that would not otherwise be classified as hazardous under state or federal hazardous laws.

Regional water quality control board cleanup and abatement orders. The RWQCBs can require cleanup of chemical contamination that would not otherwise be classified as hazardous under state or federal hazardous laws. RWQCBs can issue cleanup and abatement orders to parties who have discharged waste into waters of the state. RWQCBs are the lead agencies overseeing contaminated property where the source of contamination is leaking underground storage tanks, agricultural operations, or inactive mines. In addition, RWQCBs become the lead agency when the contamination:

- Primarily impacts surface water
- Is from a non-RCRA surface impoundment
- Is from a landfill not regulated by DTSC

Containment-zone policy. This SWRCB policy allows certain contaminated sites to be cleaned up at levels higher than background. The policy ensures that when applicable water quality objectives cannot be reasonably achieved due to technological or economic infeasibility, risk-based assessments may be used to guide groundwater cleanup efforts in lieu of traditional, standard-based cleanup goals. Dischargers may petition RWQCBs to designate a containment zone if the zone is limited in size; human health and safety and the environment are protected; and a violation of water quality objectives beyond the containment zone is not expected.

When applicable water quality objectives cannot be reasonably achieved due to technological or economic infeasibility, risk-based assessments may be used to guide groundwater cleanup efforts in lieu of traditional, standard-based cleanup goals.

California Brownfields Programs

Throughout California, thousands of properties have been abandoned or under developed because of contamination. The objective of brownfields programs is to provide incentives to developers, lenders, and prospective property purchasers to rehabilitate properties.

The Private Site Manager Program Act allows a private site manager certified as a Class II environmental assessor to independently supervise a cleanup effort. The private site manager is authorized to undertake a site investigation and submit recommendations to DTSC. If the private site manager recommends a response action, the project proponent may request DTSC to approve a private site management team to administer the response action. The management team must prepare a RAP, and when the remediation effort is completed, must file a request for a certificate of completion.

California law establishes other mechanisms to promote cleanup of brownfields sites, by reducing liability. The California Land Reuse and Revitalization Act of 2004 (HSC 25395.60 *et seq.*) protects innocent landowners, bona fide purchasers, and contiguous property owners by providing immunity from liability for response costs or damage claims under common law and statutory schemes. A property owner can qualify for immunity by meeting the standards of a qualifying property owner (QPO) and by entering into an agency agreement committing the QPO to perform a property site assessment.

DTSC also promotes redevelopment of brownfields in other ways, including the establishment of a prospective purchaser policy, which provides assurances against future liability. DTSC 1996. Prospective purchaser agreements include covenants not to sue, contribution protection, and voluntary cleanup agreements. Broad eligibility criteria includes sites under DTSC's Voluntary Cleanup Program (VCP), described below. The Cleanup Loan and Environmental Assistance to Neighborhoods (CLEAN) account established a now defunct account to provide low interest loans for cleanup of underutilized brownfield properties. RWQCBs and, in some cases local agencies, can serve as the lead agency under the CLEAN loan program. The state also established an environmental insurance program, known as FAIR (Financial Assurance and Insurance for Redevelopment), to provide cleanup loan guarantees for smaller redevelopment programs. HSC 25395.20 *et seq.*

CLEAN = Cleanup Loan and Environmental Assistance to Neighborhoods
CLRRA = California Land Restoration and Reuse Act
FAIR = Financial Assurance and Insurance for Redevelopment
QPO = Qualifying property owner
VCP = Voluntary cleanup program

The California Land Restoration and Reuse Act (CLRRA) authorizes municipalities to compel landowners to complete investigations of brownfields that are less than five acres (including larger contiguous sites under the same ownership that meet specified conditions). Subject to DTSC approval, cities and counties are authorized to start remedial and removal actions for sites on the state Superfund list. HSC 25401 *et seq.*, 25351.2.

The Polanco Redevelopment Act authorizes local redevelopment agencies to remedy or remove a release of hazardous substances on, under, or from property within a redevelopment project. DTSC, a RWQCB, or a local agency must approve the redevelopment agency's RAP before starting cleanup. HSC 33459 *et seq.*

The VCP allows responsible parties, with DTSC oversight, to investigate and remediate contaminated sites that are not on the NPL or the state Superfund list. Program participants agree to pay DTSC's costs for overseeing site characterization and cleanup. DTSC 1995. The VCP allows participants the freedom to conduct the cleanup in accordance with their own schedules. Ultimately, project participants receive "no further action" letters or remedial-action certifications from DTSC that specify acceptable land uses, deed restrictions, and other requirements.

The VCP allows responsible parties, with DTSC oversight, to investigate and remediate contaminated sites that are not on the NPL or the state Superfund list.

DTSC administers another VCP that permits a responsible party to request that cleanup be supervised by a local officer, that is, by a county or city health officer or a county director of an environmental health program. A local officer who has enough staff and resources to supervise the remedial action may enter into a remedial action agreement. This process is not available for state Superfund sites, NPL sites, sites subject to RWQCB cleanup and abatement orders, or hazardous waste facilities subject to a corrective action or corrective action order.

For more information...

Publications

Cooke, S.M. (ed.). 2003. The Law of Hazardous Waste: Management, Cleanup, Liability, and Litigation. Matthew Bender. San Francisco, Calif.

Department of Toxic Substances Control. 1990. OPP 87-14, Development and Implementation of Land Use Covenants

Department of Toxic Substances Control. 1995. EO-95-006-PP, Policy and Procedure for Managing Voluntary Site Mitigation Projects

Department of Toxic Substances Control. 1996. EO-96-005, Prospective Purchaser Policy

Department of Toxic Substances Control. 2006. Guidance Manual for complying with the Hazardous Waste Source Reduction and Management Review Act of 1989

Environmental Protection Agency. 1992. Guide to Management of Investigation-Derived Wastes. Publication 9345.3-03FS

Kindschy, J. *et al.* 1997. Guide to Hazardous Materials and Waste Management: Risk, Regulation, Responsibility. Solano Press. Point Arena, Calif.

Manaster, K.A. and D.P. Selmi (eds). ND. California Environmental Law and Land Use Practice, Chapters 50–57. Matthew Bender. San Francisco, Calif.

Websites

California Department of Health Services
www.dhs.ca.gov

California EPA
www.calepa.ca.gov

California EPA, Memorandum of Agreement Regarding Brownfield Sites
www.calepa.ca.gov/Brownfields/MOA/MOA3_05.pdf

Department of Toxic Substances Control
www.dtsc.ca.gov

Department of Toxic Substances Control, Brownfields Reuse
www.dtsc.ca.gov/SiteCleanup/Brownfields

Department of Toxic Substances Control, Fact Sheet
www.co.eldorado.ca.us/emd/solidwaste/toxic_fact_sheet.html

Department of Toxic Substances Control, Laws, Regulations, and Policies
www.dtsc.ca.gov/LawsRegsPolicies/index.cfm

Department of Toxic Substances Control, Site Cleanup
www.dtsc.ca.gov/SiteCleanup

Environmental Protection Agency
www.epa.gov

Environmental Protection Agency, Generator Summary Chart
www.epa.gov/epaoswer/osw/gen_trans/summary.htm

Environmental Protection Agency, Generators
www.epa.gov/epaoswer/osw/gen_trans/generate.htm

Environmental Protection Agency, Hazardous Waste (General)
www.epa.gov/epaoswer/osw/hazwaste.htm

Environmental Protection Agency, Pollution Prevention Act
www.epa.gov/region5/defs/html/ppa.htm

Environmental Protection Agency, Resource Conservation and Recovery Act
www.epa.gov/rcraonline

Environmental Protection Agency, Superfund
www.epa.gov/superfund/index.htm

Environmental Protection Agency, Terms of Environment
www.epa.gov/OCEPAterms

Environmental Protection Agency, Treatment, Storage, and Disposal of Hazardous Waste
www.epa.gov/epaoswer/osw/tsds.htm#store

Environmental Protection Agency, Universal Waste
www.epa.gov/epaoswer/hazwaste/id/univwast/index.htm

State Water Resources Control Board
www.swrcb.ca.gov/index.html

CHAPTER 9

Solid Wastes

This chapter reviews —

- Key laws and agencies
  involved in managing
  solid and related wastes

- Federal requirements
  for landfills

- California solid waste
  management programs

- Enforcement

Glossary

Biohazardous waste—"laboratory wastes" such as human and animal specimen cultures, human surgery specimens or tissues removed at surgery contaminated with infectious agents, blood, fluid blood products, containers, or equipment containing blood.

Construction and demolition debris facility permit*—a permit governing facilities that receive, store, handle, transfer, or process construction and demolition debris and inert debris such as lumber, wallboard, glass, metal, roofing material, tile, carpeting, and materials.

Household hazardous waste—means any hazardous waste generated incidental to owning or maintaining a place of residence. Household hazardous waste does not include any waste generated in the course of operating a business concern at a residence.

Medical waste—waste that meets both of the following requirements: (1) biohazardous waste or sharps waste, and (2) waste that is generated or produced as a result of the diagnosis, treatment, or immunization of human beings or animals, in research, in the production or testing of biologicals, or in the accumulation of properly contained home-generated sharps waste.

Municipal solid waste landfill unit— a discrete area of land or an excavation that receives household waste and that is not a land application unit, surface impoundment, injection well, or waste pile.

Municipal solid waste transfer station— a solid waste management facility that temporarily stores municipal solid waste before being shipped to a permitted municipal solid waste landfill for disposal.

Report of Disposal Site Information*— a report filed with the LEA if an applicant proposes to handle, process, transport, store, or dispose of solid wastes.

Sharps waste—any device having acute rigid corners, edges, or protuberances capable of cutting or piercing, including, but not limited to, hypodermic needles, broken glass, and any item capable of cutting or piercing that is contaminated with trauma scene waste.

Solid waste—garbage, refuse, sludge and other discarded material including solid, liquid, semisolid or contained gaseous material resulting from industrial, commercial, mining and agricultural operations and from community activity.

Solid waste assessment test— method to to determine the potential risk of a release or discharge from a municipal solid waste landfill. SWATs are designed to evaluate the potential air emissions liberated and water discharged from a municipal solid waste landfill and to potentially mitigate the releases.

Source reduction—any action that causes a net reduction in the generation of solid waste. Source reduction includes, but is not limited to, reducing the use of non-recyclable materials, replacing disposable materials and products with reusable materials and products, reducing packaging, reducing the amount of yard wastes generated, establishing garbage rate structures with incentives to reduce waste tonnage generated, and increasing the efficiency of the use of paper, cardboard, glass, metal, plastic, and other materials.

Source reduction and recycling elements— a municipality's approach to managing solid waste, including all feasible source reduction, recycling, and composting programs while identifying the landfill and transformation capacity necessary for solid waste that cannot be reduced, recycled, or composted.

Transfer station—a permitted facility that receives, handles, separates, converts, or otherwise processes solid waste.

Transformation—incineration, pyrolysis, distillation, or biological conversion other than composting. Transformation does not include composting, gasification, or biomass conversion.

Waste discharge requirements*— permit issued by a RWQCB for discharge of waste into waters of the state.

Waste tire facility permit*—authorizes owners or operators of facilities to store or dispose of tires subject to standards ranging from fire protection and security to vector controls.

* equals permits and approvals

CHAPTER 9

Solid Wastes

Introduction

Not long ago, Californians earned the dubious distinction of being the largest generators of solid waste, per capita, in the country. The Legislature responded by enacting several laws to promote waste reduction and encourage recycling and reuse. Additionally, the Legislature passed other laws to encourage businesses to convert wastes into products. Wastes are broken into the following categories:

Not long ago, Californians earned the dubious distinction of being the largest generators of solid waste, per capita, in the country.

- Nonhazardous "solid waste" (covered in this chapter)
- Hazardous waste (*see* chapter 8)
- Universal waste (*see* chapter 8)
- Used oil (*see* chapter 8)
- Household hazardous waste (covered in this chapter)
- Designated waste (*see* chapter 10)
- Medical waste (covered in this chapter)
- Special waste (*see* chapter 8)
- Tire waste (covered in this chapter)
- Asbestos (*see* chapter 7)

This chapter reviews key laws and agencies involved in solid waste management, federal landfill requirements, California solid waste management programs, and enforcement of solid waste management laws.

SWDA = Solid Waste Disposal Act
USC = United States Code

Key Laws and Agencies

Federal Laws and Agencies

Solid Waste Disposal Act and Resource Conservation and Recovery Act. Congress enacted the Solid Waste Disposal Act (SWDA, 42 USC 6901 *et seq.*) in 1965 to

CCR = California Code of Regulations
CFR = Code of Federal Regulations
CIWMB = California Integrated Waste Management Board
EPA = Environmental Protection Agency
HSC = Health and Safety Code
IWMA = Integrated Waste Management Act
MSWLF = Municipal solid waste landfill
PRC = Public Resources Code
RCRA = Resource Conservation and Recovery Act
RWQCB = Regional water quality control board
SWAT = Solid waste assessment test
WC = Water Code
WTE = Waste to energy

The IWMA establishes a hierarchy of actions that local governments must follow to manage waste, including reducing waste at the source, recycling, composting, transformation, and landfilling.

manage municipal solid wastes. This Act was later amended by the Resource Conservation and Recovery Act (RCRA), Subtitle D. Environmental Protection Agency (EPA) regulations implementing Subtitle D are found at 40 Code of Federal Regulations (CFR) 257 and 258.

Subtitle D led to the promulgation of regulations in Part 258. Subtitle D governs nonhazardous "solid waste, " defined as:

> [A]ny garbage, refuse, sludge from a waste treatment plant, water supply treatment plant, or air pollution control facility and other discarded material including solid, liquid, semisolid or contained gaseous material resulting from industrial, commercial, mining and agricultural operations and from community activity.

Subtitle D establishes provisions governing municipal solid waste landfills (MSWLFs), which collect and dispose of "household wastes." Medical waste, if determined to be hazardous, is regulated by RCRA under Subtitle J.

Environmental Protection Agency. EPA administers RCRA Subtitle D. This program is delegated to the California Integrated Waste Management Board (CIWMB) for implementation and enforcement. 42 USC 6941 *et seq.*

State Laws and Agencies

Integrated Waste Management Act of 1989. The Integrated Waste Management Act (IWMA, Public Resources Code (PRC) 40000 *et seq.*) is the principle state statutory authority governing solid waste planning and management. (IWMA also is known as Assembly Bill 939.) The Act is implemented by regulations found at 14 California Code of Regulations (CCR) Division 7 *et seq.* Among other things, the IWMA establishes a hierarchy of actions that local governments must follow to manage waste, including reducing waste at the source, recycling, composting, transformation, and landfilling. Each city and county must develop plans to divert solid waste from landfills by 50 percent compared to the amount of wastes disposed of in 1990. PRC 41780.

Integrated Solid Waste Management Act of 1989. This Act establishes the permitting program for solid waste facilities, including landfills, transfer stations, and waste to energy (WTE) facilities. PRC 43020, 43021; HSC 4250. It is implemented by regulations found at 14 CCR 17600 *et seq.* and 27 CCR 21600 *et seq.*

Solid Waste Assessment Test Program. This program (HSC 41805.5, Water Code (WC) 13273) requires owners and operators of active or closed landfills to complete a solid waste assessment test (SWAT) program to evaluate the potential risk of a release or discharge from a MSWLF. Regional water quality control boards (RWQCBs) administer this program. SWATs do the following:

- Evaluate the potential air emissions liberated from an MSWLF
- Potentially mitigate the emissions liberated from an MSWLF
- Evaluate the potential release of hazardous wastes from MSWLFs to the soil, surface, or groundwater

California Beverage Container Recycling and Litter Reduction Act. Passed in 1986, this Act establishes recycling rates for certain beverage containers. PRC 14500 *et seq.*

Cell Phone Recycling Act of 2004. Effective July 1, 2006, this Act makes it illegal for retailers to sell cell phones to a consumer unless the retailers implement a system for their collection, reuse, and recycling. PRC 42490 *et seq.*

Electronic Waste Recycling Act of 2003. Effective January 1, 2005, this Act is designed to reduce the amount of hazardous substances used in certain products sold throughout California. PRC 42460 *et seq.* This reduction is accomplished primarily through a funding system to collect and recycle electronic wastes.

The Electronic Waste Recycling Act of 2003 is designed to reduce the amount of hazardous substances used in certain products sold throughout California.

California Lighting Efficiency and Toxics Reduction Act. This Act is designed to promote energy efficient lighting by prohibiting the sale or manufacturing of incandescent and other lighting that contains hazardous substances prohibited by the European Union under the RoHS (Restriction of Hazardous Substances in electrical and electronic equipment) Directive. HSC 25210.9.

California Medical Waste Management Act. This Act established a program governing the cradle-to-grave management of medical wastes. HSC 117600 *et seq.*, 22 CCR 65600 *et seq.* The program sets forth on-site generator, treatment, storage, and disposal requirements administered at the county level.

California Integrated Waste Management Board. EPA delegated authority to implement and enforce RCRA Subtitle D to the CIWMB in September 1993; however, EPA retains oversight authority regarding implementation and enforcement of federal requirements. The CIWMB consists of a six-member board charged with implementing the IWMA. The CIWMB must concur with the issuance of a solid waste facility permit prior to issuance by the local enforcement agency (LEA). Each LEA is responsible for processing solid waste facility permits and for conducting inspections of permitted solid waste facilities. Landfills and transfer/processing stations that accept solid waste also must obtain waste discharge requirement (WDR) permits from RWQCBs governing discharge to a Class III landfill (*see* chapter 10) and permits from local air pollution control districts (APCDs).

APCD = Air pollution control district
LEA = Local enforcement agency
WDR = Waste discharge requirement

California Department of Conservation. This agency implements the Beverage Container Recycling Act through enforcement, audits, education, technical assistance, and certification of recycling centers, curbside programs, and beverage container processors.

Local enforcement agency. Cities and counties serve as LEAs and have primary authority to implement and enforce solid waste facility programs and CIWMB rules. LEAs process solid waste facility permits, together with RWQCBs and local APCDs. Before the LEA may issue a final solid waste facility permit, the CIWMB must have an opportunity to concur or object to the proposed permit. PRC 43101(c).

Air pollution control districts. Local APCDs are authorized to implement the SWAT program and issue air quality permits for solid waste facilities.

Regional water quality control boards. RWQCBs and LEAs jointly review applications for solid waste facilities. In addition, RWQCBs implement the SWAT program and issue WDR permits for solid waste facilities.

Federal Requirements for Landfills

EPA promulgated revised regulations governing MSWLFs in 1993 governing the design, construction, operation, and permitting of landfills and transfer/processing stations accepting municipal solid waste.

EPA promulgated revised regulations governing MSWLFs in 1993 (58 FR 51536; October 9, 1993) under RCRA Subtitle D. These Subtitle D rules govern the design, construction, operation, and permitting of landfills and transfer/processing stations (facilities that temporarily store solid wastes prior to ultimate disposal) accepting municipal solid waste. These regulations apply to approximately 6,000 landfills nationwide. Prior to the Subtitle D regulatory programs, many landfills functioned as unlined open dumps that collected refuse along with household hazardous wastes (such as paints, solvents, pesticides, and other household chemical waste products). Wastes disposed in these landfills could leak into the surrounding soil and groundwater, causing significant contamination. A number of current and former landfills are listed on the National Priorities List of Superfund sites (*see* chapter 8) and are subject to multi-million dollar cleanup efforts.

A MSWLF unit is a discrete area of land or an excavation that receives household waste and that is not a land application unit, surface impoundment, injection well, or waste pile.

A MSWLF unit is a discrete area of land or an excavation that receives household waste and that is not a land application unit, surface impoundment, injection well, or waste pile. 40 CFR 257.2. A MSWLF unit also may receive RCRA Subtitle D wastes, such as commercial solid waste, nonhazardous sludge, conditionally exempt small quantity generator waste, and industrial solid waste.

Criteria exists for the classification of solid waste disposal facilities and practices (40 CFR 257), as well as for MSWLF units (40 CFR 258). New MSWLFs must be located away from hazardous or unsuitable areas, including flood plains, seismic impact zones, wetlands, airports, and unstable areas. Permitted landfills must be equipped with specified liners and leachate collection systems and must meet groundwater monitoring and corrective action requirements. 40 CFR 258.40. Landfill owners and operators must semiannually monitor for 15 heavy metals and 47 volatile organic constituents. If the monitoring results yield statistically significant increases, the owner or operator must monitor for an expanded list of 213 organic and inorganic constituents. 40 CFR 258.40, 258.54.

Landfill owners and operators must commit to specified closure, post-closure, and financial assurance requirements, and also must establish procedures to exclude acceptance of hazardous waste. Additionally, landfills must comply with specific criteria addressing:

- Daily cover requirements
- Disease vector control
- Explosive gases control
- Air criteria
- Access control requirements
- Liquids restrictions
- Run-off and run-on control systems (to prevent storm water flow into and from the landfill)
- Surface water requirements
- Record keeping requirements

In 2002, EPA delegated authority to the states to implement "bioreactor" landfills. These are the next generation of landfilling being promoted by industry. Bioreactor landfills add water in a regulated environment to accelerate decomposition of materials landfilled. Pilot facilities have begun operating in California and may expand to more operations in the future.

Bioreactor landfills add water in a regulated environment to accelerate decomposition of materials landfilled.

California Solid Waste Programs

Solid Waste Planning and Waste Minimization

Source reduction and recycling elements. Prior to enactment of the IWMA in 1989, approximately 90 percent of California solid waste was disposed of in landfills. Approval for new landfills or expanded capacity for existing ones was increasingly difficult to obtain due to the prevalence of the "not in my backyard" attitude. Predictions suggested that landfill space in California would be exhausted by 2000–a mere decade away. With this backdrop, the Legislature approved the IWMA, which was designed to fundamentally shift from landfilling and incinerating municipal solid waste to reducing wastes through source reduction, recycling, and composting. By focusing on reducing waste, the Legislature expected less demand for landfilling and hoped to preserve the remaining landfill capacity.

Largely implemented by cities and counties, the IWMA requires local governments to divert solid waste from landfills by reducing waste at the source (source reduction or reuse), by recycling, by composting, and by implementing environmentally safe transformation and land disposal. Ultimately, municipal solid wastes that are not reduced at their source, recycled, or composted can be either landfilled or incinerated.

The Act required cities and counties to divert 25 percent of all solid waste from landfill or transformation facilities (*i.e.*, environmentally safe incineration that includes "incineration, pyrolysis, or distillation,

California law requires that cities and counties meet source reduction and recycling targets.

or biological conversion other than composting and does not include composting or gasification") by January 1, 1995, through source reduction, recycling, and composting. It required a similar diversion of 50 percent by January 1, 2000. Up to 10 percent of these targets can be met via transformation. PRC 40201.

SRRE = Source reduction and recycling element

Local governments implement the 50 percent diversion target by developing and implementing source reduction and recycling elements (SRREs) that establish, among other things, the waste management hierarchy described above. Each city and county was required to develop and implement its own SRRE by 1991. Each SRRE must have following components:

- **Waste composition.** Analysis of types and quantities generated
- **Source reduction.** Analysis of generator incentives to reduce quantities and increase recyclable and reusable materials and products
- **Recycling.** Analysis of curbside recycling, zoning, rate structures, etc., to encourage recycling
- **Solid waste facility capacity.** Projection of disposal capacity
- **Household hazardous waste.** Description of collection and disposal plan for household hazardous waste
- **Composting.** Development of a program and implementation schedule describing the types of materials to be composted
- **Education and public information.** Description of how the city or county will increase public awareness of, and participation in, source reduction, recycling, and composting
- **Funding.** Description of costs, revenues, and revenue sources used to implement the SRRE
- **Special waste.** Description of existing waste handling and disposal practices and identification of proposed programs

Zero waste and other waste reduction goals. The CIWMB adopted a strategic plan in 2001 that included zero waste as one of its goals to:

> Promote a "zero-waste California" where the public, industry, and government strive to reduce, reuse, or recycle all municipal solid waste materials back into nature or the marketplace in a manner that protects human health and the environment and honors the principles of California's Integrated Waste Management Act.

Many communities are developing sustainability goals and policies and working to reduce greenhouse gases.

In addition, many local governments have adopted Urban Environmental Accords developed by the United Nations for World Environment Day in 2005 in San Francisco. One of the Urban Environmental Accords establishes a zero waste policy by 2040. Many communities are developing sustainability goals and policies and working to reduce greenhouse gases. These communities are now recognizing that landfills are a significant source of greenhouse gas emissions—especially methane.

As part of these efforts, communities that have adopted zero waste as a goal as of 2007 include:

- Berkeley
- Burbank (informally)
- Del Norte County
- Fresno
- Marin County
- Novato
- Oakland
- Palo Alto
- San Diego County
- San Francisco City and County
- San Luis Obispo County
- Santa Cruz County (including separate adoption of the zero waste goal by all of the four cities in the county)
- Sonoma County

Palo Alto and Oakland have also developed comprehensive zero waste plans to guide the implementation of zero waste in their communities. These plans define success to be the diversion of more than 90 percent of their residential and commercial waste streams. Other communities in California have not adopted waste goals, but have adopted higher diversion goals than the state-mandated 50 percent rate, including the following:

- Alameda County established a 75 percent landfill reduction target
- City of Los Angeles established a 75 percent landfill reduction target

Countywide Integrated Waste Management Plans. In addition to submitting an SRRE to the CIWMB, counties must submit an integrated waste management plan (IWMP). The IWMP consists of a household hazardous waste element (HHWE), a city and county non-disposal facility element (NDFE), and a countywide siting element (CSE). These plans, described further below, can be submitted for approval individually or as a package.

CSE = Countywide siting element

HHWE = Household hazardous waste element

IWMP = Integrated waste management plan

NDFE = Non-disposal facility element

The HHWE sets forth the municipality's program to safely collect, recycle, treat, and dispose of hazardous wastes generated from households. The city or county NDFE must describe the current and future facilities available to implement the SRRE. These facilities must be capable of recovering materials for reuse or recycling, but can not include disposal or transformation facilities. The NDFE must describe those recovery facilities located within the municipality and those facilities outside the county that it plans to utilize. PRC 41733, 14 CCR 18753.

To better predict and plan for future municipal solid waste management capacity, each county must develop a CSE. PRC 41700 *et seq.* Each CSE must include:

- The 15-year estimated landfill and transformation capacity
- The capacity currently available
- Identification of areas for new facilities

If existing capacity will be consumed within 15 years, then the CSE must identify new areas for transformation or disposal that are consistent with the city or county general plan. PRC 41701, 14 CCR 18755 *et seq.*

Solid Waste Facilities Regulation

Landfills. In 1967, California completed a study uncovering dangerous conditions that existed at disposal sites throughout the state. The study highlighted the fire and safety hazards as well as the vector, air, and water pollution problems present at these facilities. This study led to the state's current permit programs, which rigorously manage solid waste facilities in California.

Applicants must complete a permit application called a report of disposal site information (RDSI) if they propose to handle, process, transport, store, or dispose of solid wastes (including household garbage, trash, refuse, paper, rubbish, ashes, industrial wastes, construction debris, abandoned vehicles, discarded appliances, manure, and other discarded wastes). Applicants must submit the RDSI to the LEA; it must include:

- Proposed manner of operation
- Types and quantities of wastes to be received
- Capacity
- Life expectancy
- Site location (disposal site standards are in 14 CCR 17600 *et seq.*)

Like a MSWLF under the federal program, solid waste landfills (also known as Class III landfills, as further described in chapter 10) must be located in accordance with the State Water Resources Control Board's (SWRCB's) siting and design criteria. 27 CCR 20260. The applicant also must obtain a WDR permit from the RWQCB (*see* chapter 10) and air quality permits from the APCD (*see* chapter 5). New or expanded solid waste facilities must conform to CSEs. In addition, the California Environmental Quality Act (CEQA) likely will apply to the project.

California is required to ensure that its solid waste permitting program for solid waste disposal facilities are at least as stringent as federal MSWLF standards. EPA is authorized to enforce its MSWLF requirements should California fail to implement these standards. 42 USC 6945(c)(1)(B).

Solid waste assessment tests. MSWLFs have the potential to release dangerous air emissions (*e.g.*, dust, odor, smoke, and gases such as methane and other toxic chemicals) and to discharge water pollution (chemical leachate) to the soil and surface and groundwater. The Legislature responded to this risk by enacting a law, sometimes referred to as the Calderon Act (HSC 41805.5, CWC 13273), that requires owners and operators of active or closed landfills to complete a SWAT to evaluate the potential risk of a release or discharge from the MSWLF.

On or before July 1, 1987, owners and operators of active Class III landfills, referred to as solid waste disposal (SWD) sites, were obligated to complete

In 1967, California completed a study uncovering dangerous conditions that existed at disposal sites throughout the state.

CEQA = California Environmental Quality Act
CWC = California Water Code
RDSI = Report of disposal site information
SWD = Solid waste disposal
SWRCB = State Water Resources Control Board

MSWLFs have the potential to release dangerous air emissions and to discharge water pollution to the soil and surface and groundwater.

an air-SWAT for submission to the local APCD. HSC 41805.5, 23 CCR 2510 *et seq.* On or before November 1, 1986, owners and operators of inactive SWD sites were obligated to complete a preliminary screening questionnaire and submit it to the APCD for review. Based on the results of these submittals, the local APCD is authorized to determine whether the air pollutant releases pose a health risk or an environmental threat to sensitive populations including schools, hospitals, and residences. The APCD has authority to impose mitigation measures to reduce or minimize those impacts that pose a health risk to human beings or a threat to the environment. HSC 41805.5(g).

To evaluate SWD sites for hazardous waste leakage to the subsurface, the SWRCB ranked all SWD sites based on the threat they may pose to water quality. The first 150 SWD operators were to submit water-SWATs by January 1, 1987; the next 150 SWD operators were to submit water-SWATS by July 1, 1988. CWC 13273. If the SWRCB determines that hazardous waste has migrated into the water, it must notify the Department of Toxic Substances Control (DTSC) and the CIWMB and take appropriate remedial action. CWC 13273(3).

DTSC = Department of Toxic Substances Control

Transfer stations. Transfer processing stations are temporary locations for the transfer of materials from smaller collection vehicles onto larger, higher-volume vehicles (*e.g.*, trucks, barges, and trains) for transport to ultimate destinations. The final destination for solid waste is generally a landfill or transformation facility. EPA 2002. California requires permits for the design and operation of transfer stations and has recordkeeping requirements. 14 CCR 17400 *et seq.* Transfer stations also must be permitted by the LEA, RWQCB, and local APCD. Permitting and operations standards differ for small versus large transfer stations. A medium transfer station is one that receives less than 100 tons/day. 14 CCR 17402(a)(11).

Waste-to-energy facilities. Waste-to-energy facilities burn municipal refuse or other waste to produce electricity or steam. These facilities must comply with specified permitting standards for solid waste facilities, air quality standards (*see* chapter 5), and CEQA review requirements (*see* chapter 2). WTE facilities with a generating capacity of 50 megawatts or more must comply with specific permitting requirements under the Warren–Alquist Act (PRC 25500 *et seq.*), which is discussed in chapter 17. 14 CCR 17225.58, HSC 39050.5.

Waste-to-energy facilities burn municipal refuse or other waste to produce electricity or steam.

Waste tire facilities. Owners or operators of facilities that store or dispose of tires must obtain a permit issued by the CIWMB. Each waste tire facility permit establishes specified storage and disposal standards ranging from fire protection and security to vector controls. Solid waste facilities that accept for transfer, or discard up to, 150 tires per day require a waste tire facility permit. People who transport waste tires to tire facilities must operate pursuant to a permit. PRC 42800 *et seq.*

Construction and demolition debris facilities. The LEA also issues permits for facilities that receive, store, handle, transfer, or process construction and demolition debris and inert debris, which includes lumber and wood, gypsum wallboard, glass, metal, roofing material, tile, carpeting and floor coverings, window coverings, plastic pipe concrete, fully cured asphalt, heating ventilation and air conditioning systems and their components, lighting fixtures, appliances, equipment, furnishings, and fixtures. 14 CCR 18223.

California Beverage Container Recycling and Litter Reduction Act

DOC = Department of Conservation

The California Department of Conservation (DOC) is principally responsible for implementing this Act, also known as the California Bottle Bill (PRC 14500 *et seq.*). The Act establishes a redemption value on specific categories of beverage containers (such as beer, wine, coffee, tea, fruit drinks, and soft drinks, in aluminum, glass, plastic, and bi-metal containers). This law is designed to ensure that no less than 65 percent of specified beverage containers are recycled. The redemption value assigned to each regulated beverage container can fluctuate to a higher level whenever the redemption rate drops below 65 percent.

In 2006, the Beverage Container Recycling and Litter Reduction Act resulted in cumulatively recycling 13.2 billion beverage containers, making the state number one in the nation to recycle bottles and cans. DOC 2007. However, California is experiencing a continuing drop in the recovery rate of these products as more and more plastic containers are introduced into the marketplace. The Legislature responded by increasing the redemption value of containers, now $.05 for small bottles and $0.10 for larger beverage containers. PRC 14575.

Cell Phone Recycling Act of 2004

Californians throw away thousands of cell phones each day. Cell phones often contain hazardous amounts of materials such as lead, arsenic, and cadmium. Once in the landfill, the toxins ultimately may be released into groundwater.

The Cell Phone Recycling Act of 2004 requires that cell phone retailers establish, by July 1, 2006, a system to collect, reuse, and recycle cell phones.

The Cell Phone Recycling Act of 2004 (PRC 42490 *et seq.*) requires that cell phone retailers establish, by July 1, 2006, a system to collect, reuse, and recycle cell phones. Retailers must inform consumers about cell phone recycling opportunities, and California agencies that purchase or lease cell phones must require bidders to certify compliance with the provisions described above. Further, the Act requires that DTSC provide online information on cell phone recycling rates by July 1, 2007.

Electronic Waste Recycling Act of 2003

The Electronic Waste Recycling Act of 2003 (PRC 42460 *et seq.*) requires manufacturers to phase-out the use of heavy metals in electronic devices and to increase the use of recycled materials. The Act also imposes a ban on the sale of covered electronic devices (CEDs) if those devices would be prohibited from sale in the European Union due to the presence of heavy metals. The ban conditionally took effect January 1, 2007.

CED = Covered electronic device

The Act also requires that no later than July 1, 2004, retailers of CEDs collect from consumers an electronic waste recycling fee of $6 to $10 depending on the size of the screen. These fees are to be paid to authorized CED recyclers who must provide free and convenient collection, consolidation, and transportation of CED wastes. Exporters of electronic waste to foreign destinations must meet standards adopted by the Organization for Economic Cooperation and Development. The Act also requires CED manufacturers to label equipment with the manufacturer's brand label. Additionally, manufacturers must provide information to consumers describing where and how to return, recycle, and dispose of CEDs. Manufacturers are required to report annually on the:

The Electronic Waste Recycling Act requires that manufacturers provide information to consumers describing where and how to return, recycle, and dispose of CEDs.

- Number of CEDs sold in the state
- Amount of recycled materials used in CED manufacture
- Efforts to design CEDs for recycling
- Goals to increase CED recycling

The CIWMB must annually establish and update statewide electronic waste recycling goals. Cities and counties were required to revise their IWMPs by January 1, 2004, to ensure that the household hazardous waste element articulates actions necessary to promote the collection, consolidation, recovery, and recycling of covered electronic waste.

California Lighting Efficiency and Toxics Reduction Act

The California Lighting Efficiency and Toxic Reductions Act bans (on and after January 1, 2010) the sale or manufacture of incandescent and other lighting that contains hazardous substances prohibited by the European Union pursuant to the RoHS Directive. DTSC and the CIWMB are required to develop a strategy to collect and recycle general purpose lights. HSC 25210.9

Laws Promoting Recycled Product Markets

As millions of tons of materials are diverted from landfills each year, more and more resources are available for other productive uses. California law leverages the enormous marketing power of its procurement system by requiring that the Department of General Services purchases products made with post-consumer materials where fitness and quality are equal. State law promotes development of markets for recycled goods by requiring that state agencies purchase minimum percentages of post-consumer content of the following recycled products: paper, compost, glass, oil, plastic, solvents, paint, and tires. Companies that fail to meet the required minimum post-consumer content are banned ("debarred") from state contracts. Public Contracts Code 12200 *et seq.*

In addition to these procurement policies, commercial printers and publishers must ensure that at least 50 percent of newsprint contains a minimum of 40 percent post-consumer paper fiber. PRC 42760.

California Medical Waste Management Act

The California Medical Waste Management Act significantly reformed the management of medical waste in California.

This Act (HSC 117600 *et seq.*) significantly reformed the management of medical waste in California. Prior to this Act, medical waste was regulated as a California-only, non-RCRA hazardous waste. Medical waste means waste that meets both of the following requirements (HSC 117635, 117690, 117755):

- "Biohazardous waste" (such as blood or infectious agents) or "sharps waste" (such as a syringe)
- Waste that is generated or produced as a result of the diagnosis, treatment, or immunization of human beings or animals, in research or in the production of or testing of vaccines, antigens, and other "biologicals"

The Act imposes a cradle-to-grave program on the generation, treatment, storage, and disposal of medical wastes. The level of program rigor depends on quantities of medical wastes generated. A large quantity generator generates 200 pounds or more per month of medical waste. A small quantity generator generates less than 200 pounds per month.

Generators of medical wastes must meet specified registration and labeling requirements. In addition, they must meet specified hold times and complete a medical waste management plan.

Generators of medical wastes must meet specified registration and labeling requirements. In addition, they must meet specified hold times and complete a medical waste management plan. HSC 117935. Wastes must be labeled with the words "Biohazardous Waste" or the international biohazard symbol, and the word "BIOHAZARD." Sharps waste must be labeled "sharps waste" or the international biohazard symbol, and the word "BIOHAZARD." In addition, on-site accumulation areas must display specified labels.

Bags containing biohazardous wastes must be tied to prevent leakage. HSC 118280(a). Generators of medical wastes are subject to different accumulation and holding requirements that depend on the amount of medical waste generated monthly and whether the waste is refrigerated. HSC 118280. Sharps waste must be stored in rigid containers and taped or closed with a tight lid. HSC 118285.

Medical wastes may be incinerated, steam sterilized, or microwaved. Liquid and semi-liquid medical wastes may be chemically disinfected.

Enforcement

Federal Enforcement

The SWDA authorizes any person including the United States or any other governmental agency to enforce the Act. Additionally, EPA and the CIWMB are authorized to issue formal administrative orders to ensure compliance with the SWDA. SWDA 7002, 40 CFR 254.1.

State and Local Enforcement

LEAs are required to inspect all solid waste facilities and sites at least once each month and, if any violations are found, a notice of violation must be sent to the operator. PRC 43218, 14 CCR 18083.

Facilities with chronic violations of state minimum standards have their names published on the Board's Inventory list. These facilities must develop a compliance schedule to prove they are diligently working to comply with the standards. PRC 44106.

Violation of any LEA order may result in a civil penalty not greater than $5,000 per day of noncompliance. The intentional or negligent violation of a facility's permit may subject the owner or operator to civil penalties of no more than $10,000 per day of violation. PRC 45011 and 45023.

LEAs can:

- Issue cease and desist orders for solid waste facilities that operate without a permit. PRC 44002, 44005
- Issue injunctions and penalties to any person failing to comply. PRC 45014
- Issue an enforcement order requiring a facility or site to comply within a given timeframe
- Suspend or revoke a facility permit

A Superior Court can issue an injunction to any person failing to comply with a final order (PRC 45014), and LEAs are authorized to issue administrative civil penalties to operators who fail to comply by the deadline in a final notice and order. Penalties can range up to $5,000 per day per violation, with no limit on the total fine amount. Owners and operators who intentionally or negligently violate the terms of a solid waste facility permit are subject to civil penalties of up to $10,000 per day of violation. PRC 45023.

If the CIWMB determines a jurisdiction has not implemented its SRRE, the CIWMB may issue an order of compliance with a specific schedule for achieving compliance. If the jurisdiction subsequently fails to meet the compliance schedule, the CIWMB has authority to fine a city or county up to $10,000 per day. PRC 41850.

The CIWMB can issue similar penalties and injunctive relief for violations of the waste tire storage and disposal requirements. PRC 42850 *et seq.*

LEAs are required to inspect all solid waste facilities and sites at least once each month and, if any violations are found, a notice of violation must be sent to the operator.

A Superior Court can issue an injunction to any person failing to comply with a final order, and LEAs are authorized to issue administrative civil penalties to operators who fail to comply by the deadline in a final notice and order.

For more information...

Publications

Department of Conservation. 2007. Biannual Report of Beverage Container Sales, Returns, Redemption, and Recycling Rates

Environmental Protection Agency. 2002. Waste Transfer Stations: A Manual for Decision-Making. United States Environmental Protection Agency, EPA 530-A-02-002, June 2002

Manaster, K.A. and D.P. Selmi (eds.). ND. California Environmental Law and Land Use Practice. Chapters 90–91. Matthew Bender. San Francisco, Calif.

Websites

California EPA
www.calepa.ca.gov

California Integrated Waste Management Board
www.ciwmb.ca.gov

California Integrated Waste Management Board Zero Waste Plan
www.ciwmb.ca.gov/boardinfo/strategicplan/2001/Goals.htm#ZeroWaste

City of Oakland Zero Waste Plan
http://clerkwebsvr1.oaklandnet.com/attachments/14983.pdf

City of Palo Alto Zero Waste Strategic Plan
www.cityofpaloalto.org/zerowaste/graphics/Strategic_Plan_FInal_100405.pdf

Earth Resource Foundation Zero Waste
www.earthresource.org/zerowaste.html

Environmental Protection Agency
www.epa.gov

United Nations World Environment Day 2005
www.wed2005.org/3.0.php?PHPSESSID=7d73899326d54dd704c4ece96f92f64b

Zero Waste International Alliance
www.zwia.org/zwc.html

CHAPTER 10

Water Quality

This chapter reviews –

- Key laws and agencies involved in water quality regulation
- Water quality planning and standards
- Permit programs for point sources and nonpoint sources
- Ocean protection programs
- Oil management programs
- Water quality release reporting
- Enforcement

Glossary

Basin plan–a RWQCB basin plan sets forth WQS for surface and groundwaters within a particular water body or portion thereof and implementation plans to achieve the WQS. Designed to protect water quality within specified hydrological units.

Best available technology economically achievable standard–considers the controls that are technologically and economically achievable, but does not balance the cost of attainability against the potential benefit for ELGs for non-conventional and toxic pollutants.

Best conventional pollutant control technology standard–considers the controls that are technologically and economically achievable in relation to the benefits for ELGs for conventional pollutants.

Best management practices–methods determined to be the most effective, practical means of preventing or reducing pollution from nonpoint sources.

Best practicable control technology–allows industries to emit higher than normal pollution levels with equipment that uses the best practicable means available.

Categorical effluent limitation guidelines and standards–includes ELGs for conventional, non-conventional, and toxic pollutants, as well as new sources and indirect discharges.

Concentrated animal feeding operations–agricultural facilities that house and feed a large number of animals in a confined area.

Construction general permit*–requires development of a storm water pollution prevention plan describing best management practices to prevent storm water pollution associated with construction activities disturbing soil of one acre or more.

Conventional pollutants–typical, higher volume pollutants that include biochemical oxygen demand, total suspended solids, fecal coliform, pH, and oil and grease.

Designated waste–nonhazardous waste that consists of or contains pollutants that, under ambient environmental conditions at the waste, management unit could be released at concentrations exceeding applicable WQOs; designated waste that is hazardous waste is subject to a hazardous waste variance.

Effluent limitations–limitations on discharge in an NPDES permit (the more stringent of either technology-based or water quality-based limitations).

Facility response plan*–a comprehensive spill response and contingency plan designed to prevent the discharge of oil from vessels and land-based oil storage facilities that could reasonably be expected to cause substantial harm to the environment by discharging oil into or on navigable waters or adjoining shorelines.

General industrial permit*–an NPDES permit that regulates storm water discharges associated with ten broadly described industrial activities. Among other things, the permit requires the development of a storm water pollution prevention plan designed to implement best management practices to prevent storm water contamination.

Municipal separate storm sewer system–a conveyance (that can include roads with drainage systems, municipal streets, catch basins, curbs, gutters, ditches, built channels, or storm drains) designed to collect or convey storm water, but is not a combined sewer or part of a POTW.

Municipal storm water permit*–governs storm water discharges from municipalities serving over 100,000 people. The site-specific NPDES permit must incorporate a monitoring program to evaluate runoff and water received.

National Pollutant Discharge Elimination System permit*–a permit that controls water pollution by regulating point sources that discharge pollutants into surface waters defined as "waters of the United States."

New source performance standards–emissions limitations for industrial source categories, adopted by EPA.

Non-conventional pollutants–all pollutants other than conventional and toxic pollutants, and including but not limited to chemical oxygen demand, total organic carbon, nitrogen, phosphorus, ammonia, and sulfide.

Nonhazardous solid waste–municipal solid waste or refuse that has a significant proportion of degradable material or "inert" waste (such as paving fragments and non-degradable construction debris).

Nonpoint source pollution–diffuse sources of pollution (*i.e.,* without a single point of origin or not introduced into a receiving stream from a specific outlet). The pollutants are generally carried off the land by storm water. Common nonpoint sources are agriculture, forestry, urban, mining, construction, dams, channels, land disposal units, saltwater intrusion, and city streets.

Oil–broadly defined to include petroleum, fuel oil, sludge, oil refuse, and oil mixed with wastes other than dredge spoil, including non-petroleum oils such as vegetable oil.

Point source–any discernible, confined, and discrete conveyance, including pipes, ditches, channels, tunnels, conduits, wells, vessels, and more.

Pollutant–dredged spoil, solid waste, incinerator residue, filter backwash, sewage, garbage, sewage sludge, munitions, chemical wastes, biological materials, radioactive materials (except those regulated under the Atomic Energy Act of 1954, as amended (42 USC 2011 *et seq.*)), heat, wrecked or discarded equipment, rock, sand, cellar dirt, and industrial, municipal, and agricultural waste discharged into water.

Pretreatment standards–standards designed to prevent the introduction of pollutants to publicly owned treatment works that would interfere with operations and to prevent pollutants incompatible with the POTW from passing through.

Priority toxic pollutant–129 specified pollutants commonly subdivided into heavy metals, organic compounds, and pesticides.

Sole source aquifer–a principal source area that supplies at least 50 percent of the drinking water consumed in a specific area overlying the aquifer.

Spill prevention control and countermeasure plan*–establishes engineering and management procedures and equipment standards designed to prevent oil from entering surface waters. Each plan must document site-specific spill prevention and control measures to manage facility structures, procedures, and equipment.

Storm water–precipitation that flows over a surface, or urban runoff or melted snow that flows into the storm drain system or otherwise into surface waters.

Storm water pollution prevention plan*– identifies pollution sources that affect the quality of storm water discharges from a site and requires implementation of best management practices to reduce pollutants in storm water discharges.

Supplemental environmental projects– pollution prevention efforts that exceed the existing statutory obligations of dischargers and achieve an environmental benefit.

Technology-based effluent limitation–a minimum level of effluent control that uniformly applies to industry categories, regardless of where the discharge occurs or the quality of the surface water receiving the discharge.

Total maximum daily load–specifies waste load allocations for point and nonpoint sources that discharge into an impaired water body (*i.e.,* a water body that does not meet one or more established beneficial uses specified for that water body).

Underground injection control program– the program, under the federal Safe Drinking Water Act, that regulates the discharge of wastes into underground injection wells.

Waste discharge requirements*– permit issued by a RWQCB for discharge of waste into waters of the state.

Waste management unit–an area of land, or a portion of a waste management facility, at which waste is discharged. The term includes containment features and ancillary features for precipitation and drainage control and for monitoring.

Water quality objective–an area of land, or a portion of a waste management facility, at which waste is discharged. The term includes containment features and ancillary features for precipitation and drainage control and for monitoring.

Water quality standards–composed of two parts: (1) the designated uses of water and (2) criteria to protect those uses. Water quality standards are enforceable limits in the bodies of water for which they have been established.

Water quality-based effluent limitation– an effluent limitation applied to dischargers when technology-based limitations have the potential to cause violations of water quality standards.

Waters of the United States–all waters used or susceptible to use in interstate or foreign commerce, or that could affect interstate or foreign commerce. Waters of the United States include lakes, rivers and coastal waters, as well as all adjacent "other waters" such as wetlands, the use, degradation or destruction of which could affect interstate or foreign commerce.

* equals permits and approvals

CHAPTER 10

Water Quality

Introduction

The industrial fire that erupted on the Cuyahoga River in Cleveland, Ohio in 1969 shined a spotlight on the nation's damaged water systems. Before Congress enacted the federal Clean Water Act (CWA) of 1972, 90 percent of watersheds in the United States were polluted. Adler 1993. The CWA was enacted to restore and maintain water quality levels that protect fish, wildlife, and recreational uses.

This chapter reviews the key laws and agencies involved in water quality regulation, water quality planning and standards, permit programs for point and nonpoint sources, ocean protection programs, oil management programs, water quality release reporting, and enforcement of water quality laws.

Key Laws and Agencies

Federal Laws and Agencies

Clean Water Act of 1972. The CWA (33 USC 1251–1376) protects the water quality of jurisdictional surface waters. The CWA revamped the Federal Water Pollution Control Act (enacted in 1948), to restore and maintain the "chemical, physical, and biological integrity of the Nation's waters."

The CWA created the following programs to achieve and maintain water quality:

- **National Pollutant Discharge Elimination System (NPDES).** To grant permits for point source discharges of industrial and municipal wastewater to waters of the United States (33 USC 1342; 40 CFR 122–125, 403), including specialized requirements for general permits, storm water, concentrated animal feeding operations (CAFOs), and pretreatment

CAFO = Concentrated animal feeding operation

CFR = Code of Federal Regulations

CWA = Clean Water Act

NPDES = National Pollutant Discharge Elimination System

USC = United States Code

The CWA protects the water quality of jurisdictional surface waters.

241

EPA	= Environmental Protection Agency
SDWA	= Safe Drinking Water Act
SPCC	= Spill prevention control and countermeasure
SWRCB	= State Water Resources Control Board
TMDL	= Total maximum daily load
UIC	= Underground injection control
WDR	= Waste discharge requirement

- **Total maximum daily loads (TMDLs).** To specify waste load allocations for both point and nonpoint source discharges for impaired waters (waters that do not meet water quality standards). 33 USC 1313(d)
- **Nonpoint source grants.** To enable states to address nonpoint source pollution via management programs. 33 USC 1329
- **Spill prevention control and countermeasure (SPCC) program.** To regulate the discharge of oil and hazardous substances, and to report releases of oil and "hazardous substances." 33 USC 1321; 40 CFR 116, 177; 40 CFR 112 *et seq.*
- **Permits for discharge of dredged or fill material into waters of the United States.** 33 USC 1344, 40 CFR 230, 232 (*see* chapter 15)
- **Administrative, judicial, and citizen enforcement.** 33 USC 1319, 1365, 1369; 40 CFR 135

Under the CWA, EPA sets national effluent standards based on industry-specific criteria. EPA also approves state receiving water quality standards to protect specific uses of waters of the U.S.

The federal SDWA protects groundwater aquifers by regulating discharges of waste to deep and shallow underground geological formations.

Safe Drinking Water Act. The federal SDWA (42 USC 300(f) *et seq.*) protects groundwater aquifers by regulating discharges of waste to deep and shallow underground geological formations. The Act establishes permitting requirements governing injection of wastes known as the underground injection control (UIC) program. The Act additionally regulates sole source aquifers with the goal of protecting drinking water systems from contaminants that could jeopardize public health. 40 CFR 149. Finally, the Act also regulates drinking water. *See* chapter 11.

Environmental Protection Agency. EPA administers the federal CWA and SDWA programs. EPA also has authority to administer NPDES permits. 33 USC 1251 *et seq.* Authority to administer NPDES permits may be delegated to states and Native American tribal governments.

State Laws and Agencies

The Porter–Cologne Act implements and augments federal protections under the CWA via regulation of the "waters of the state," which include surface, ground, and ocean water as well as point sources and nonpoint sources.

Porter–Cologne Water Quality Control Act. The Porter–Cologne Act (Water Code 13000 *et seq.*) implements and augments federal protections under the CWA via regulation of the "waters of the state," which include surface, ground, and ocean water as well as point sources and nonpoint sources. To protect waters of the state, the Act implements the federal NPDES permitting program and the California Waste Discharge Requirement (WDR) permitting program.

Lempert–Keene Act. This Act (Gov. Code 8670 *et seq.*) establishes spill contingency plans and other programs to protect marine waters from oil spills.

State Water Resources Control Board. The State Water Resources Control Board (SWRCB) is authorized by EPA to implement and enforce the surface water permitting and TMDL programs and has adopted federal regulations under the Porter-Cologne Act. The SWRCB implements and ensures compliance with the Porter-Cologne Act, including the adopted federal standards, and the CWA. The SWRCB is comprised of a board with members who represent a variety of

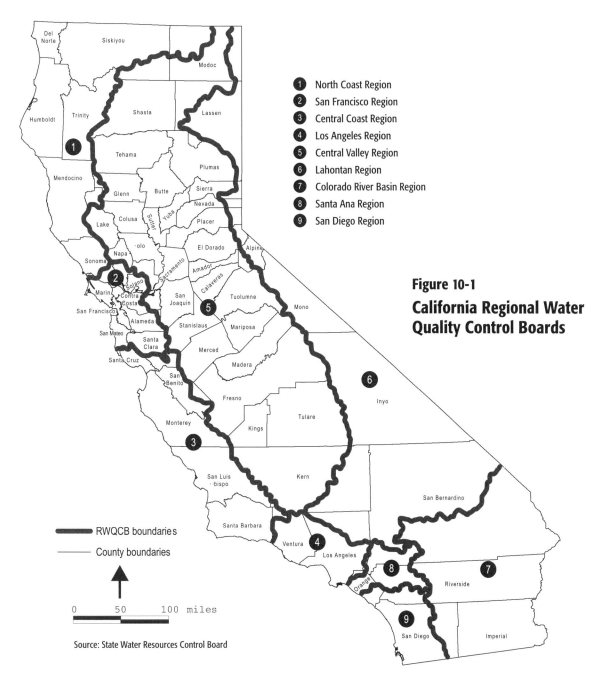

1 North Coast Region
2 San Francisco Region
3 Central Coast Region
4 Los Angeles Region
5 Central Valley Region
6 Lahontan Region
7 Colorado River Basin Region
8 Santa Ana Region
9 San Diego Region

Figure 10-1
California Regional Water Quality Control Boards

RWQCB boundaries
County boundaries

0   50   100 miles

Source: State Water Resources Control Board

water quality and water supply interests and who serve staggered terms. The SWRCB has both administrative rulemaking and adjudicatory powers.

RWQCB = Regional water quality control board

The SWRCB is responsible for creating and implementing a statewide plan that establishes policies to protect waters of the state. It also issues statewide general NPDES permits. The SWRCB also administers the state's water rights program. *See* chapter 13.

Regional water quality control boards. The nine RWQCBs implement state water policy on a regional basis and establish regional water quality standards and policy. Regional boards are established along major drainages within the state, as depicted in Figure 10-1. RWQCBs implement and ensure compliance with the Porter–Cologne Act, including the adopted federal standards, and the CWA. RWQCBs are comprised of a board with members who serve staggered terms. The Boards have both administrative rulemaking and adjudicatory powers.

RWQCBs are responsible for creating and implementing regional water quality control plans, also called basin plans. Regionally, each basin plan is tailored to the unique characteristics of that watershed and provides a scientific and regulatory basis for each regional board's water protection efforts.

The boards issue and enforce WDRs, including NPDES permits. Specifically, RWQCBs issue facility-specific WDR and NPDES permits within their regions, as well as general WDRs and NPDES permits to regulate similar waste discharges within each region. RWQCBs, as well as the SWRCB, implement water quality monitoring and reporting programs and have authority to issue enforceable orders.

Ocean Protection Council. This council is authorized to protect coastal water habitat. The Council is comprised of the Resources Agency, the California Environmental Protection Agency, and the chair of the State Lands Commission. It is required to establish a science advisory team to incorporate the best available science into the council's decisions.

Governor's Office of Emergency Services. This office plans for statewide disasters and receives notifications and reports of chemical spills to the environment.

DOC = Department of Conservation
WQS = Water quality standards

California Department of Conservation. The Department of Conservation's (DOC's) Division of Oil and Gas oversees the federal UIC program for discharge of oil and gas wastes.

Department of Fish and Game. This agency oversees oil contingency plans and other prevention programs to manage oil spills in marine waters.

Water Quality Planning and Standards

Federal Requirements

Water quality standards (WQS) serve to protect the public health or welfare, and also enhance the quality of water. They reflect "the limits or levels of water quality constituents or characteristics which are established for the reasonable protection of beneficial uses of water or the prevention of nuisance within a specific area." 40 CFR 130.2(d), 131.3(i). WQS include two components: beneficial uses of water, and water quality criteria to protect those uses. The CWA mandates that each state specify beneficial uses for each of its water bodies.

State Requirements

The state's water quality planning process consists primarily of developing, adopting, reviewing, and updating a variety of statewide water quality control plans and regional water quality control plans (basin plans). The SWRCB adopts statewide water quality plans, and the RWQCBs adopt basin plans. WQS contained in these plans are translated into effluent limitations written into NPDES permits and WDRs.

The SWRCB has adopted a number of statewide water quality control plans and policies, including:

- Statement of Policy with Respect to Maintaining High Quality of Waters in California (antidegradation plan)
- Ocean Plan
- Enclosed Bays and Estuaries Plan
- Inland Surface Water Plan
- Thermal Plan (temperature control in coastal and interstate waters and in enclosed bays and estuaries)
- Bay-Delta Plan (Sacramento–San Joaquin Delta and Suisun Marsh)
- Lake Tahoe Basin Water Quality Plan
- Sources of drinking water policy

California toxics rule. States are required to adopt numeric water quality criteria for priority toxic pollutants if there is a reasonable chance that the pollutant could interfere with the designated beneficial uses of the state's water. In April 1991, California adopted numeric criteria for priority toxic pollutants. However, two of the state's water control plans (the Inland Surface Water Plan and the Enclosed Bays and Estuaries Plan) were rescinded by a 1994 state court decision, leaving the state without numeric water quality criteria for many toxic pollutants. EPA responded by issuing a final rule known as the California toxics rule (CTR). 33 USC 1313. CTR criteria, along with beneficial use designations in California's basin plans, constitute WQS for priority toxic pollutants in California inland and estuarine surface waters.

CTR = California toxics rule
WQO = Water quality objective

Originally published in 1997, the CTR became effective on May 18, 2000. 65 CFR 31681. The CTR establishes ambient aquatic life criteria for 23 priority toxic pollutants, as well as ambient human health criteria for 57 priority toxic pollutants. The rule also authorizes the state to conditionally issue compliance schedules for new or revised NPDES permit limits based on the federal criteria. Until the state re-adopts its own numeric criteria for toxics, the federal criteria apply to the state's inland surface waters, enclosed bays, and estuaries, in addition to state-adopted water quality standards contained in the basin plans.

Beneficial uses. In its basin plan, each RWQCB identifies desired beneficial uses for specified surface and groundwaters located within that region (*e.g.*, waters for spawning, fishing, recreation). Examples of beneficial uses are presented in Table 10-1.

Water quality objectives. In California, water quality criteria adopted to protect uses of water ("beneficial uses") are called water quality objectives (WQOs).

Table 10-1. Examples of Beneficial Uses	
General category	**Beneficial uses**
Supply	Municipal and domestic supply, agricultural supply, industrial process supply, industrial service supply, groundwater recharge, freshwater replenishment, navigation, hydropower generation, aquaculture, commercial fisheries, shellfish harvesting
Recreation	Water contact recreation, non-contact water recreation, sport fishing
Wildlife protection	Freshwater habitat, saline water habitat, estuarine habitat, marine habitat, wildlife habitat, endangered species habitat, aquatic organism migration, spawning, areas of special biological significance

Basin plans set forth water-quality objectives for beneficial uses such as contact recreation.

MCL = Maximum contaminant level

Basin plans establish WQOs, in numeric and narrative form, for specified water bodies and for particular segments of water bodies. Numeric WQOs serve as the upper receiving water limits for permits for specified pollutants, while narrative WQOs are translated into appropriate numerical permit limits where feasible. Establishing such numerical limits may involve reviewing the maximum contaminant levels (MCLs) under the state or federal Safe Drinking Water Acts (*see* chapter 11) or evaluating ambient water quality criteria, cancer risk estimates, or health advisories. Marshack 2001.

For example, the San Francisco Bay RWQCB's basin plan establishes WQOs for the following constituents and parameters:

- Bacteria
- Bioaccumulation
- Biostimulatory substances
- Color
- Dissolved oxygen
- Floating material
- Metals
- Oil and grease
- Pesticides
- pH
- Radioactivity
- Salinity
- Sediment
- Settleable material
- Suspended material
- Temperature
- Turbidity

Sources of drinking water policy. This policy (SWRCB Resolution No. 88-63) implements the Safe Drinking Water and Toxic Enforcement Act of 1986 (otherwise known as Proposition 65). This policy provides that all surface and groundwater of the state must be protected as existing or potential sources of municipal and domestic supply, unless the water body meets certain conditions.

Antidegradation policy. Another important policy for water quality control is the antidegradation policy (SWRCB Resolution No. 68-16), which is derived from EPA's antidegradation policy (40 CFR 131.12). The antidegradation policy provides that existing high water quality (exceeding water quality standards) can be "degraded" only if it can be demonstrated to the SWRCB or RWQCB that any such change is in the best interest of the people of California. Specifically, the degradation must:

The antidegradation policy provides that existing high water quality can be degraded only if it can be demonstrated to the SWRCB or RWQCB that any such change is in the best interest of the people of California.

- Be consistent with the maximum benefit to the people of the state
- Not unreasonably affect present or probable future beneficial uses of such water
- Not result in water quality less than prescribed in state policies

The antidegradation policy must be considered when arriving at numerical water quality limits in water quality permits.

Point Source and Groundwater Permit Programs

Federal Point Source Programs

Applicability. The CWA prohibits the discharge of any pollutant by any person to waters of the United States, except pursuant to the NPDES permitting program. 40 CFR 122. The NPDES program requires permits for:

The CWA prohibits discharge of any pollutant by any person to waters of the United States, except pursuant to the NPDES permitting program.

- Discharge of "pollutants"
- Discharge from any "point source"
- Discharge into "waters of the United States"

The CWA's definition of "pollutant" (adopted by reference in California) includes:

- Dredged spoil
- Solid waste
- Incinerator residue
- Filter backwash
- Sewage
- Garbage
- Sewage sludge
- Munitions
- Chemical wastes
- Biological materials

- Radioactive materials (except those regulated under the Atomic Energy Act of 1954, as amended (42 USC 2011 *et seq.*))
- Heat
- Wrecked or discarded equipment
- Rock
- Sand
- Cellar dirt
- Industrial, municipal, and agricultural waste discharged into water

Excluded from the CWA definition of pollutant is sewage from vessels, and some water and materials associated with oil or gas production. 40 CFR 122.2.

A "point source" is defined by federal regulations "as any discernible, confined, and discrete conveyance." This includes any pipes, ditches, channels, tunnels, conduits, wells, vessels, and more.

A "point source" is defined by federal regulations "as any discernible, confined, and discrete conveyance." This includes any pipes, ditches, channels, tunnels, conduits, wells, vessels, and more. 40 CFR 122.2. Although federal regulations explicitly exclude agricultural return flows and storm water runoff, agricultural sources are covered under a conditional waiver that allows RWQCBs to waive WDRs for a certain type of discharge based on certain criteria (*see* below). In addition, the Ninth Circuit Court of Appeals has narrowed this exception and found that aerial spraying constitutes a point source that requires an NPDES permit. *League of Wilderness Defenders/Blue Mountain Diversity Project et al. v. Forsgren et al.* (2002) 309 F. 3d 1181.

The term "waters of the United States" is defined to include (40 CFR 122.2):

- Waters used in interstate or foreign commerce
- All interstate waters
- Intrastate waters where use, degradation, or destruction could affect interstate commerce
- Impoundments of any of the above
- Tributaries of any of the above
- The territorial sea
- Wetlands adjacent to any of the above

The courts, mostly in the context of wetlands regulation, have interpreted the term "waters of the United States" extensively. *See* chapter 15 for a discussion of recent judicial interpretations. Groundwater is not a water of the United States unless there is a known direct conduit from the groundwater to surface water.

Key features of the NPDES program are summarized in Table 10-2.

Point source permitting: Technology-based effluent limitations. Effluent limitations are NPDES permit limits on the quality of wastewater that may be discharged from point sources. There are two types of effluent limitations. Technology-based limitations are established industry-by-industry and apply nationwide. Water quality-based limitations are derived for individual water bodies. For an individual NPDES permit, the stricter of the two limitations applies.

Table 10-2. National Pollutant Discharge Elimination System Permitting Summary

Clean Water Act program	Program features	CWA regulatory citation
NPDES permitting	Addresses requirements for standard permits, general permits, and municipal separate storm sewer systems (MS4s)	40 CFR Part 122
State authorization	Outlines EPA procedures for approving, revising, and withdrawing state NPDES programs (California has been delegated authority to implement the NPDES program)	40 CFR Part 123
Permit approval provisions	Establishes procedures to evaluate NPDES permit applications and to issue NPDES permits	40 CFR Part 124
NPDES technology-based treatment requirements	Establishes criteria and standards for technology-based treatment requirements	40 CFR Part 125
Toxic pollutants	Provides toxic "priority pollutant" effluent standards and prohibitions	40 CFR Part 129
Effluent limitation guidelines	Provides technology-based effluent guidelines and standards for existing and new sources based on certain industrial classifications	40 CFR Part 401, 405–499
Water quality standards	Describes requirements and procedures for state development and approval of water quality standards; additional specific requirements are in 40 CFR 131.37	40 CFR Part 131
Pretreatment requirements	Establishes pretreatment standards for pollutants passing through publicly owned treatment works	40 CFR Part 403

Source: 40 CFR 112, 123–125, 129, 131, 401, 405, 499

Technology-based effluent limitations serve as a minimum level of effluent water quality control. These limitations apply uniformly to industry categories, regardless of where the discharge occurs or the quality of the surface water receiving the discharge. For example, the standards for a semiconductor plant may be different than for an electronics manufacturer. Nonetheless, standards will be the same for all semiconductor facilities, whether the facility is in San Francisco discharging into the San Francisco Bay or in New York City discharging into the Hudson River. Similarly, all publicly-owned treatment works (POTWs) are required to provide a minimum of secondary wastewater treatment.

General requirements for technology-based water quality limitations are in 40 CFR 125.3; industry-specific requirements, known as categorical effluent limitation guidelines and standards (ELGs) are in 40 CFR 405–499. These categorical effluent limitations are established for conventional, non-conventional, and toxic pollutants, as well as new sources and indirect discharges.

Conventional pollutants consist of the following typical, higher volume pollutants found in municipal wastewater (40 CFR 401.16):

- Biochemical oxygen demand (BOD)
- Total suspended solids (TSS)
- Fecal coliform
- pH
- Oil and grease (O&G)

BOD = Biochemical oxygen demand
ELG = Effluent limitation guideline
O&G = Oil and grease
POTW = Publicly owned treatment work
TSS = Total suspended solids

Table 10-3. Effluent Limitation Guidelines by Pollutant Source

Pollutant source	Level of treatment
Conventional	BCT/BPT
Non-conventional	BAT/BPT
Toxic	BAT/BPT

BAT = Best available technology economically achievable

BPJ = Best professional judgment

BCT = Best conventional pollutant control technology

BMP = Best management practice

BPT = Best practicable control technology currently available

COD = Chemical oxygen demand

NSPS = New source performance standards

PSES = Pretreatment standards for existing sources

PSNS = Pretreatment standards for new sources

SIC = Standard Industrial Classification

TOC = Total organic carbon

Non-conventional pollutants consist of all pollutants other than conventional and toxic pollutants, and include:

- Chemical oxygen demand (COD)
- Total organic carbon (TOC)
- Nitrogen
- Phosphorus
- Ammonia
- Sulfide

Toxic pollutants consist of 65 specified pollutant categories commonly categorized as heavy metals, organics, and pesticides. 40 CFR 401.15.

The ELGs for each industrial category must meet specific standards for each pollutant type. The ELGs for conventional pollutants are based on a "best conventional pollutant control technology" (BCT) standard, which considers what controls are technologically and economically achievable in relation to the benefits. The ELGs for non-conventional and toxic pollutants are based on a "best available technology economically achievable" (BAT) standard, which considers what controls are technologically and economically achievable but does not balance the cost of attainability against the potential benefit. Additionally, a "best practicable control technology currently available" (BPT) standard may be used where the BCT or BAT standard is equivalent to the BPT (an older standard), or where the BCT or BAT standard has not yet been promulgated. Effluent limitation guidelines by pollutant source are shown in Table 10-3.

The ELGs for new dischargers are the "new source performance standards" (NSPS), which represent state-of-the-art treatment technology. The ELGs for indirect dischargers (into publicly owned treatment works, discussed in further detail below) include "pretreatment standards for existing sources" (PSES) and "pretreatment standards for new sources" (PSNS).

A given industrial source type or category typically shares similar wastewater discharge characteristics, and accordingly is subject to industry-specific ELGs defined by Standard Industrial Classification (SIC) code. Each ELG sets forth the following: applicability criteria, definitions, effluent limitations, process procedures, operating methods, and pretreatment requirements. ELG examples for some industrial categories are shown in Table 10-4.

An applicant for an NPDES permit must, at a minimum, meet the nationwide, industry-specific, technology-based ELG for the conventional, non-conventional, and toxic pollutants they discharge. Where no ELGs are established, a best professional judgment (BPJ) standard must be applied by the permitting authority on a case-by-case basis. 33 USC 1342.

Point source permitting: Water quality-based effluent limitations. Where technology-based ELGs are not sufficient to meet a state or federal water quality standard, EPA or the state is required to establish more stringent water quality-based effluent limitations (WQBELs). WQBELs also may be developed for discharges that are not subject to categorical effluent limitations. WQBELs may be derived from water quality standards or TMDLs, where TMDLs have been established.

NPDES permitting process. The NPDES permit application must be completed and submitted at least 180 days before commencing the discharge. 40 CFR 122.21. Permit applications must include:

- General facility information
- Expected effluent characteristics
- Effluent flow rate
- A proposed treatment system

A final NPDES permit will set forth, among other requirements, effluent limitations, monitoring, and reporting obligations. In addition, NPDES permits often include standard terms and conditions addressing, among other things, proper operation of treatment systems, prohibitions against bypass, and what to do if a treatment system upset occurs. NPDES permits must be renewed every five years. Storm water discharges today are regulated by special NPDES programs (discussed later in this chapter).

National Pollutant Discharge Elimination System monitoring. An essential element of an NPDES permit is the monitoring of discharges and the submittal of discharge monitoring reports (DMRs). Typical NPDES monitoring requirements are in Table 10-5.

Pretreatment permitting. Some industrial facilities do not directly discharge wastewater into surface waters. Rather, they indirectly discharge their wastewater via a sanitary sewer to a POTW. These indirect dischargers,

Table 10-4. Examples of Effluent Limitation Guidelines by Industrial Category

Industry	Effluent limitation guidelines
Battery manufacturing	BPT, BAT, NSPS, PSES, PSNS
Dairy products processing	BPT, BCT, NSPS, PSES, PSNS
Electrical and electronic components	BPT, BCT, BAT, NSPS, PSES, PSNS
Explosives manufacturing	BPT
Inorganic chemicals manufacturing	BPT, BAT, NSPS, PSES, PSNS (limited BCT)
Organic chemicals manufacturing	BPT, BCT, BAT, NSPS, PSES, PSNS
Petroleum refining	BPT, BCT, BAT, NSPS, PSES, PSNS
Pharmaceutical manufacturing	BPT, BCT, BAT, NSPS, PSES, PSNS
Pulp and paper mills	BPT, BCT, BAT, NSPS, PSES, PSNS
Steam electric power plants	BPT, BAT, BCT, NSPS, PSES, PSNS
Timber products processing	BPT, BCT, BAT, NSPS, PSES, PSNS

Source: 40 CFR Part 400 *et seq.*

DMR = Discharge monitoring report
WQBEL = Water quality-based effluent limitation

Table 10-5. Typical Monitoring Requirements of the National Pollutant Discharge Elimination System Program

Parameter/Constituent	Units	Sampling type	Sampling frequency	Reporting frequency
Flow	million gallons per day	N/A	Daily/monthly	Quarterly
Biochemical oxygen demand	lbs/day	24-hour composite	Daily/monthly	Quarterly
Total suspended solids	lbs/day	24-hour composite	Daily/monthly	Quarterly
pH	pH	Grab	Daily/monthly	Quarterly
Settleable material	mL/L	Grab	Daily/monthly	Quarterly
Bioassay	% survival	24-hour composite	Weekly	Quarterly
Temperature	degrees	Grab	Daily	N/A
Metals	mg/L	24-hour composite	Quarterly	Quarterly

both new and existing sources, are subject to specified pretreatment discharge limitations. In this case, the POTW or municipality, in lieu of the RWQCB, serves as the permitting authority for those facilities discharging to its sanitary sewer system. In California, municipalities typically incorporate relevant pretreatment requirements into their ordinances.

Among other things, pretreatment standards are designed to prevent the introduction of pollutants to the POTW that would interfere with operations and to prevent pollutants incompatible with the POTW from passing through. Effluent limitation guidelines for indirect dischargers are based upon requirements in CWA Section 307. 33. USC 1317.

Total maximum daily loads. Section 303(d) of the CWA requires each state to develop a list of impaired water bodies (segments of surface waters that do not meet WQS). The list must be based on "all existing and readily available water quality-related data and information," must identify specific pollutant(s) causing impairment, and must be ranked by priority. 33 USC 1313(d).

TMDL = Total maximum daily load
WLA = Waste load allocation

States must then develop total maximum daily loads (TMDLs) to restore the 303(d)-listed water bodies. TMDLs calculate the maximum amount of a pollutant that a water body can receive from both point and nonpoint sources (its loading capacity) and still attain WQS. TMDLs may include more than one water body and more than one pollutant (for example, see San Francisco Bay RWQCB's TMDL for diazinon and pesticide-related toxicity in Bay Area urban creeks).

Each TMDL uses the loading capacity, in conjunction with a margin of safety, to allocate pollutant loadings among point and nonpoint sources. These allocations are called waste load allocations (WLAs) and load allocations, respectively. If WLAs are more stringent than other water quality-based effluent limitations, or more stringent than technology-based limitations, the WLAs are incorporated into NPDES permits. EPA issued controversial rules that require waste load allocations for nonpoint sources of pollution. 40 CFR 130.

In the 1990s, California, along with other states, failed to submit its list of impaired waters to EPA as required by the CWA. Environmental advocacy groups then compelled California to prepare its list of impaired waters and to prepare TMDLs, resulting in a number of TMDLs driven by consent decrees. In 2002, the SWRCB identified and EPA approved a list of more than 600 impaired stream segments, river segments, lakes, and estuaries (available at www.waterboards.ca.gov/tmdl/303d_lists.html).

Federal Groundwater Programs

Underground injection control wells. The UIC program (40 CFR 144), established under the federal SDWA, protects drinking water in underground aquifers. The program regulates the use of wells to pump waste fluids into the ground (*i.e.*, in soils and porous rock formations above the water table, in groundwater aquifers, in deep geological formations). The UIC program regulates discharges of:

The UIC program, established under the federal SDWA, protects drinking water in underground aquifers.

- Hazardous wastes
- Wastes from oil and gas exploration and production (*i.e.*, the re-injection of briny waters)
- Fluid injection for mineral extraction
- On-site disposal systems that discharge into septic systems and leach fields (known as Class V wells)

Table 10-6 depicts the agencies responsible for managing individual classes of UIC wells.

Sole source aquifer protection program. The EPA defines a sole source aquifer as a "principal source aquifer which supplies at least 50 percent of the drinking water consumed in the area overlying the aquifer." The sole source aquifer protection program is authorized under the SDWA and allows EPA to determine whether an aquifer is the sole or principal source of drinking water for an area. Under the program, EPA reviews federally financed projects that are proposed for an aquifer area and determines whether there is a possibility of source contamination. The sole source aquifer demonstration program creates procedures for developing, implementing, and evaluating demonstrations to protect critical aquifer protection areas (CAPAs). 42 USC 300h-c, 40 CFR 149.

CAPA = Critical aquifer protection area

State Permitting Requirements

Waste discharge requirements. The Porter–Cologne Act governs discharges of waste that could affect the quality of the waters of the state. The Act regulates individual dischargers of both point sources (*e.g.*, an industrial discharge from a

Table 10-6. Underground Injection Control Well Classifications by Agency		
Type of discharge	**UIC well classification**	**Agency**
Deep wells	Class 1	Environmental Protection Agency
Oil and gas injection wells	Class 2	California Department of Conservation
Mining wells	Class 3	Environmental Protection Agency
Shallow hazardous and radioactive injection wells	Class 4	Environmental Protection Agency
Shallow injection wells	Class 5	Environmental Protection Agency

Source: 40 CFR Part 144

pipe to a surface water) and nonpoint sources (*e.g.*, potential releases from landfills). Waters of the state include both surface waters and groundwater in California

Where waste discharges could affect the quality of the waters of the state, the discharger must obtain a WDR. In California, an individual NPDES permit is technically a type of WDR granted by RWQCB order. Therefore, every individual NPDES permit applicant must fill out a state Report of Waste Discharge form (basically, an application form) in addition to the standard NPDES permit application forms. The RWQCB then issues either a combined NPDES permit/ WDR or just a WDR. A WDR sets limits on discharge by specifying effluent limits, receiving water limits, prohibitions, or best management practices, or a combination of these. The SWRCB issues a statewide or general permit for storm water (discussed below). Water Code 13260(a)(1), 13263 (a).

Like NPDES permits, complete WDR applications must be submitted to the RWQCB within 180 days of the proposed discharge. While NPDES permits last for five years, WDRs can last for longer than five years. Complete renewal applications must be submitted within 180 days prior to the expiration date.

Permitting process. The water quality permitting process in California begins with determining whether a pollutant:

- Potentially could threaten a designated beneficial use of water
- Will be released to a surface water (thus requiring an NPDES permit)
- Will be released to groundwater (thus requiring a WDR)
- Will be treated, stored, or disposed of in a waste management unit, thus requiring a WDR (*see* below)

Next, the applicant must determine whether the proposed activity could impair present or probable future beneficial uses by consulting the WQOs for those uses, or whether it could cause nuisance. Finally, the concentrations of the projected constituents must be compared against the narrative and numerical WQOs and antidegradation policies.

Nonpoint Source Permit Programs

Despite a quarter century of rigorous water quality control, as of 2002, approximately 40 percent of surface waters in the United States remained impaired for their beneficial uses (www.epa.gov/waters/305b/index.html). Much of this remaining impairment is due to significant exceptions carved out of the definition of point source. For example, agricultural runoff and irrigation return flows, and most silvicultural activities, were and continue to be outside of the CWA's definition of point source.

Federal Nonpoint Source Programs

Nonpoint sources are managed through a national program established by Section 319 of the CWA (33 USC 1329).

Storm water. Major elements of the storm water program include:

- General permits
- Storm water pollution prevention plan (SWPPP)
- Training
- Monitoring
- Annual reporting

The Clean Water Act regulates urban runoff.

The CWA amendments of 1987 required EPA to develop a regulatory program to manage storm water. 33 USC 1342(p). This program requires large and small municipalities to seek NPDES permits to regulate storm water; it also requires certain industrial facilities and construction sites to obtain NPDES storm water permits. 40 CFR 122.26.

Urban storm water. Urban storm water runoff is a nonpoint source, but becomes a point source when collected in a storm sewer pipe. When discussing storm water discharges, it is useful to distinguish between two types of municipal sewer systems:

SWPPP = Storm water pollution prevention plan

- Sanitary sewer systems, which typically receive domestic sewage and industrial wastewaters that typically route to a POTW
- Municipal separate storm sewer systems (MS4s) that collect storm water precipitation (*e.g.,* from rain, snow, sleet, and freezing rain)

Storm water is discharged in either a separate sanitary sewer system, or in a combined sanitary and storm water sewer system. Figure 10-2 shows the two types of sewer systems and illustrates that storm water in an MS4 is not treated, unlike storm water in a sanitary sewer system.

Industrial storm water. EPA's 1990 storm water regulations require industrial facilities included in one of 11 listed categories to acquire an NPDES storm water permit:

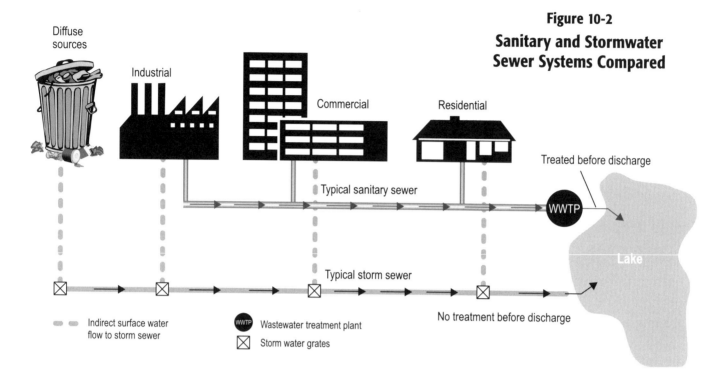

Figure 10-2
Sanitary and Stormwater Sewer Systems Compared

Diffuse sources

Industrial

Commercial

Residential

Treated before discharge

Typical sanitary sewer

WWTP

Lake

Typical storm sewer

No treatment before discharge

Indirect surface water flow to storm sewer

WWTP   Wastewater treatment plant

Storm water grates

- **Category one.** Facilities with effluent limitations
- **Category two.** Manufacturing
- **Category three.** Mineral, metal, oil and gas
- **Category four.** Hazardous waste, treatment, or disposal facilities
- **Category five.** Landfills
- **Category six.** Recycling facilities
- **Category seven.** Steam electric plants
- **Category eight.** Transportation facilities
- **Category nine.** Treatment works
- **Category ten.** Construction activity of one acre or more
- **Category eleven.** Light industrial activity

A discharger may seek a permit exemption for a facility that meets the "no exposure" exclusion. 40 CFR 122.26(g). This exclusion exists for facilities where discharges are composed entirely of storm water, and where there is no exposure of industrial materials and activities to runoff.

Storm water discharges associated with oil and gas exploration, production, or processing are also exempt from NPDES permits under the Energy Policy Act of 2005. 42 USC 13201 *et seq.*

NOI = Notice of intention

To qualify for coverage under California's general storm water permit, a discharger must submit a notice of intention (NOI) to the RWQCB (discussed below). The discharger also must prepare an SWPPP, which is intended to identify potential sources of storm water pollution and to establish a program to minimize or eliminate pollutants that could be discharged during a storm event. When storm water pollution cannot be avoided, treatment may be warranted before discharging the polluted storm water. Typical requirements of an SWPPP include:

- Establishing a pollution prevention team to implement the SWPPP
- Identifying and inventorying significant materials that could come in contact with storm water
- Delineating storm water drainages
- Developing best management practices (BMPs) to minimize or prevent pollution of storm water
- Identifying cross-connections of piping to the storm sewer system, which could result in unpermitted discharges of process or non-process wastewater
- Developing procedures to review and update the SWPPP

BMPs are the heart of SWPPPs. BMPs can include managerial practices (*e.g.*, good housekeeping and inspections) and structural measures (*e.g.*, berming, covers, oil/water separators, grassy swales, rock-lined ditches, and detention ponds). EPA has developed a guidance manual to assist in developing and implementing SWPPPs. EPA 1992.

Municipal storm water. Municipalities serving large populations (over 100,000) are subject to MS4 permits. MS4 storm water discharges are not covered by the statewide general permit and thus require a site-specific NPDES storm water permit. Municipalities must control storm water pollution to the "maximum extent practicable." 33 USC 1342(p). Municipalities must obtain renewed permits from the RWQCB every five years. NPDES regulations require that all MS4 permits incorporate a monitoring program in order to evaluate runoff and water received. The monitoring program creates an evaluation process for environmental risks associated with storm water discharges that include identifying the types and quantity of pollutants, the possible sources of pollutants, and the effectiveness of permit requirements and storm water management plans.

MS4 storm water discharges are not covered by the statewide general permit and thus require a site-specific NPDES storm water permit.

Construction storm water. Construction-related dischargers who disturb one acre or more of soil are required to obtain coverage under the California statewide storm water construction permit. RWQCBs implement and enforce this statewide permit. Construction activities include, among other actions, site clearing, grading, and excavation. Applicants must submit a notice of intention to the SWRCB, pay a filing fee, and develop a site-specific SWPPP that describes BMPs to prevent erosion and the discharge of contaminated storm water. Common BMPs for

BMPs are required for construction activities.

construction activities include silt fences, hay bales, preventive maintenance of construction equipment, and good housekeeping.

Construction-related dischargers who disturb less than one acre of soil, including dischargers subject to TMDL provisions (discussed above), can be required to comply with storm water permitting if the permit authority determines that the discharge significantly contributes to storm water pollution. 40 CFR 122.26(b)(15). Construction discharges in the Lake Tahoe basin and those by Caltrans are not regulated by the SWRCB general NPDES permit, but rather by separate NPDES permits.

State Nonpoint Source Programs

Nonpoint source discharges are not covered under the point source permitting program. Yet, nonpoint discharges could affect waters of the state. These nonpoint source discharges involve, among other activities, irrigated agriculture, mining, oil and gas operations, septic tanks, leach fields, and some percolation ponds.

Nonpoint source management plan. The SWRCB has adopted a statewide plan to manage nonpoint source pollution (www.swrcb.ca.gov/nps/5yrplan.html). The plan more than 60 BMPs and effluent limitations to manage nonpoint source pollution from agriculture, forestry, urban areas, marinas, recreational boats, and hydromodification; it also sets forth protection objectives for wetlands and riparian areas. *See* chapter 16 for a discussion of nonpoint source discharges from forest practices.

Discharges of waste to land: Hazardous waste and nonhazardous solid waste. RWQCBs issue WDRs for indirect discharges of waste to land that have the potential to impair the quality of state waters. One set of regulations (often called Chapter 15 regulations) addresses the indirect discharge of hazardous waste to land; another set governs the treatment, storage, processing, or disposal of nonhazardous "solid waste" (includes refuse and "designated" wastes, nonhazardous solid wastes, and inert wastes) to land.

These regulatory programs set forth standards for locating, constructing, monitoring, closing, and post-closure maintenance of RCRA-type waste management units (WMUs), such as surface impoundments, landfills, and waste piles (*see* chapter 8 for a discussion of WMUs). State law allows alternatives to these standards where an engineering alternative is demonstrated to protect water quality. Water Code 13172, 23 CCR 2510–2601 (dealing with hazardous waste), 27 CCR 20200 (governing nonhazardous waste). The regulatory programs regulate potential nonpoint sources of pollution by managing WMUs to prevent wastes from accidentally or indirectly discharging wastes to waters of the state.

The Department of Toxic Substances Control (DTSC) is authorized to classify wastes as either hazardous waste (*see* chapter 8) or nonhazardous waste (*see* chapter 9). The nonhazardous waste classification is further subdivided into designated waste, nonhazardous solid waste, or inert waste, based on the potential threat to beneficial uses of groundwater and surface water.

Designated waste can be nonhazardous or hazardous waste. Designated waste that is nonhazardous waste consists of or contains pollutants that, under ambient environmental conditions at the WMU, could be released at concentrations exceeding applicable WQOs; designated waste that is hazardous waste is subject to a hazardous waste variance. Nonhazardous solid waste includes municipal solid waste or refuse with a significant proportion of degradable material. Inert waste includes paving fragments and non-degradable construction debris. 23 CCR 2521, 2523, 2524; 27 CCR 20210, 20220, 20230.

Each of the four waste classifications (hazardous, designated, nonhazardous solid, inert) has a corresponding minimum WMU classification, as shown in the preceding Figure 8-3. Important waste and WMU distinctions include:

- **Hazardous wastes.** May be treated, stored or disposed ("discharged") only to Class I WMUs. These heavily regulated units must be equipped with both natural geologic and engineered containment structures to ensure that the wastes will be not released to surface or groundwaters. Hazardous wastes may be "discharged" to a less protective Class II WMU pursuant to a hazardous waste variance granted by DTSC.

- **Designated wastes.** Must be discharged either to a Class II or optionally to a Class I WMU.

- **Nonhazardous solid wastes.** Must be discharged to Class III WMUs (although these waste units do not provide complete containment, but rather are designed to protect beneficial uses of water) or optionally in a Class I or Class II WMU.

- **Inert wastes.** May be discharged to "unclassified units" (which must be in a location and have equipment that prevents wastes from entering drainage courses) or optionally in a Class I, II, or III WMU.

Discharges of waste to land: Underground injection, underground storage tanks, and septic systems. Discharges of waste to land also can occur through USTs and septic systems. Important regulatory program elements for these discharges include:

- California is delegated the authority by EPA to implement and enforce the injection of oil and gas wastes into underground wells. 14 CCR 1724. Discharge of other wastes into UIC wells is largely the domain of the federal SDWA (discussed above). California regulates new and existing USTs that store petroleum products and "hazardous substances." *See* chapter 7.

- California establishes minimum statewide standards that requires DPH, the Coastal Commission, and municipalities to adopt minimum regulations for septic systems. Regulations address the construction, replacement, major repair of systems, and pooling or discharging to the surface. Water Code 13290 *et seq.*

Cal/EPA = California Environmental Protection Agency
HSC = Health and Safety Code
PRC = Public Resources Code
SLC = State Lands Commission
SWAT = Solid waste assessment test

Special landfill requirements. Landfill owners and operators must implement a water quality testing program to determine the water quality impacts of disposal sites. California requires the SWRCB to rank all active and inactive disposal sites based on the threat posed to water quality. Water Code 13273. Current operators must complete a solid waste assessment test (SWAT) to evaluate the threat to groundwater and submit it to the RWQCB. For an operator ranked within the first 150 priority sites, the SWAT was due by July 1, 1987.

Toxic Pits Cleanup Act. The TPCA bans use of new surface impoundments that store or dispose of liquid hazardous wastes within one-half mile of potential sources of drinking water. Preexisting surface impoundments were required to be removed by June 30, 1988. HSC 25208 *et seq.*

Storm water. California's industrial, including construction, and municipal storm water programs are implemented via a general NPDES permit adapted by the SWRCB (*see* previous discussion). Some city and county ordinances prescribe more rigorous storm water management standards.

Under California law, nonpoint agricultural discharges (including irrigation return flows and nonpoint storm water) are not wholly exempt from permitting as they are under the federal CWA.

Agricultural discharges. Under California law, nonpoint agricultural discharges (including irrigation return flows and nonpoint storm water) are not wholly exempt from permitting as they are under the federal CWA. Because the Porter–Cologne Act requires that such discharges be regulated, the various RWQCBs have had to determine whether such discharges qualify for a public conditional waiver of WDRs. For these discharges, as of 2007, the Central Valley, Los Angeles, and Central Coast RWQCBs have granted a conditional waiver, which functions similar to, though less stringently than, a storm water general permit. An RWQCB (Water Code 13269) can:

- Grant a conditional waiver for a class or category of nonpoint sources, as long as specific BMPs are implemented
- Terminate a conditional waiver at any time

Ocean Protection Programs

The Legislature enacted the California Ocean Protection Act (PRC 35500 *et seq.*), in response to several studies, including the Pew Oceans Commission Report (2003), which found the ocean habitat along California's 1,100-mile coastline is in failing health. The Act establishes the Ocean Protection Council, comprised of the Secretaries of the Resources Agency and the California Environmental Protection Agency (Cal/EPA), and the chair of the State Lands Commission (SLC). The Council is authorized to protect the state's coastal waters and ocean ecosystems.

The Act also establishes the California Ocean Protection Trust Fund, which is authorized to issue grants and loans for projects that:

- Eliminate or reduce threats to coastal and ocean ecosystems, habitats, and species

- Foster sustainable fisheries

- Improve coastal water quality

- Allow increased public access to oceans and coastal resources

- Improve management, conservation, and protection of coastal waters and ocean ecosystems

- Provide monitoring and scientific data to improve conservation and protection of ocean resources

Oil Management Programs

Federal Requirements: Spill Prevention Control and Countermeasure Program

Overview. In 1973, EPA issued regulations designed to prevent oils from reaching waters of the United States. 40 CFR 112. These regulations require specified facilities to prepare an SPCC plan. The SPCC plan is intended to minimize a facility's potential for an oil spill and to implement corrective measures to correct the cause of an oil spill. Generally, the SPCC plan establishes engineering and management procedures and equipment standards to prevent oil from entering surface waters. Each plan must document site-specific spill prevention and control measures to manage facility structures, procedures, and equipment.

Applicability to non-transportation-related onshore facilities. "Oil" is broadly defined to include "petroleum, fuel oil, sludge, oil refuse, and oil mixed with wastes other than dredge spoil." Thus, in addition to crude oil, gasoline, and diesel fuel, "oil" includes waste oils and waste fuels, and non-petroleum oils (such as turpentine, animal fats such as tallow and lard, and vegetable oils). "Oil" does not include compressed gases or liquefied natural gas. 33 USC 1321(a)(1), 40 CFR 112.2.

In addition to crude oil, gasoline, and diesel fuel, "oil" includes waste oils and waste fuels, and non-petroleum oils. "Oil" does not include compressed gases or liquefied natural gas.

SPCC plans are required for non-transportation-related onshore and offshore facilities that could reasonably be expected to discharge oil into navigable waters of the United States or adjoining shorelines. These facilities include those that drill, produce, gather, store, use, process, refine, transfer, distribute, or consume oil and oil products. 40 CFR 112.1(b). Non-transportation-related facilities are found in such industries as oil drilling and production, oil refining and storage, agriculture, and oil treatment.

Transportation-related vessels, such as oil tankers, are subject to another set of specific SPCC requirements. This section focuses on non-transportation-related onshore facilities that, due to their locations, could be reasonably expected to discharge harmful quantities of oil into or upon surface waters or adjoining shorelines. 40 CFR 112.1 and 112.2. This "reasonably expected" determination:

Oil tanks are subject to SPCC requirements.

UST = Underground storage tank

- Is based on land features (*e.g.,* topographic contours with respect to drainage) and related factors (*e.g.,* facility proximity to navigable waters or adjoining shorelines)

- Must not consider equipment (*e.g.,* shut-off valves and catchment basins) designed to prevent oil from reaching navigable waters or adjoining shorelines

A non-transportation-related onshore facility is subject to an SPCC plan and related requirements if the facility meets one of the following "oil" volumes:

- The total unburied storage capacity of the facility is greater than 1,320 gallons (only counting containers greater than or equal to 55 gallons). 40 CFR 112.1(d)(2)

- Underground storage tanks (USTs) with combined capacity of greater than 42,000 gallons (except for completely buried tanks meeting UST regulations; *see* chapter 7 for a discussion of UST regulatory requirements)

A stand-alone 2,000-gallon above-ground tank storing oil could trigger SPCC requirements.

Containers and tanks are broadly defined to include:

- Units that are owned and operated, such as units used by tenants.

- Mobile oil units, such as units used for aircraft ground equipment, waste oils (presumed also to be hazardous waste under California law), polychlorinated biphenyl oils (may be inside transformers along with other operational tanks such as manufacturing equipment and hydraulic equipment), and fuel trucks.

Plan requirements. Facilities meeting the SPCC applicability requirements must prepare an SPCC plan within six months of a new operation and fully implement the plan as soon as possible. 40 CFR 112.1(f)(4). The SPCC plan must include, among other things:

- Each container's type of oil and storage capacity. 40 CFR 112.7(a)(3)(i)

- Spill response systems (*e.g.,* emergency coordinator, arrangements with local emergency agencies and local emergency response contractors). 40 CFR 112.7(a)(3)(vi)

- Emergency prevention and response equipment and procedures. 40 CFR 112.7(a)(3)(iii)–(v), 40 CFR 112.7(a)(4)–(5)

- Reasonable potential for equipment failure. (CFR 112.7(b))

- Corrosion protection for buried metallic storage tanks. 40 CFR 112.8(c)(4)

- Written inspection procedures. 40 CFR 112.7(e); 40 CFR 112.8(c), (d)

- Integrity testing of above-ground storage tanks (ASTs) on a regular schedule, and whenever repairs are made. 40 CFR 112.8(c)(6)

- Secondary containment systems or diversionary structures for all tanks, piping, and loading and unloading areas (such as dikes, berms, and curbs). 40 CFR 112.7(a)(3)(iii), (c)

- Security measures (such as fencing and locked gates). 40 CFR 112.7(g)

The SPCC plan, along with technical amendments, must be reviewed by a professional engineer. Unlike most environmental plans, the SPCC plan need not be submitted to EPA or other state or local agencies. 40 CFR 112.3, 112.5(c). Additionally, owners and operators must instruct their staff how to operate and maintain spill control equipment to prevent discharges. Owners and operators also must annually schedule and conduct briefings for staff to ensure familiarity and understanding of the facility's SPCC plan. 40 CFR 112.7(f).

Unlike most environmental plans, the SPCC plan need not be submitted to EPA or other state or local agencies.

The owner or operator of the non-transportation-related onshore facility must amend the SPCC plan within six months of a change in facility design, construction, operation, or maintenance that materially affects the facility's potential for the discharge of oil (*e.g.*, installation of new piping systems or changes in volume of oil). 40 CFR 112.5. The amended plan must be implemented as soon as possible and no later than six months following the amendment. Additionally, the owner or operator must review and evaluate the plan every five years. 40 CFR 112.5(b).

Release reporting. A reportable spill is a discharge greater than 1,000 gallons of oil or two discharges of more than 42 gallons of oil each in any 12-month period. If an owner or operator experiences a reportable spill, the facility must submit specified information to EPA regarding details of the discharge and corrective measures taken. 40 CFR 112.4(a).

A reportable spill is a discharge greater than 1,000 gallons of oil or two discharges of more than 42 gallons of oil each in any 12-month period.

Federal Requirements:
The Oil Pollution Act of 1990

Overview. This Act was passed in response to the 1989 catastrophic release of more than 11 million gallons of oil from the Exxon Valdez, which killed about 500,000 birds, more than 4,000 sea otters, 300 seals, and dozens of killer whales. It has been reported that the Exxon Valdez resulted in the death of more wildlife than any other environmental disaster in U.S. history.

This Act (3 USC 2701 *et seq.*, 40 CFR 112.20):

- Prohibits the discharge of oil into waters of the United States by tank vessels and marine transportation

- Establishes the National Oil Spill Liability Trust Fund

- Requires facilities that "could reasonably be expected to cause substantial harm to the environment by discharging oil into or on the navigable waters or adjoining shorelines" to prepare and submit a facility response plan (FRP)

The 1969 Santa Barbara oil spill had devastating effects on wildlife.

FRP = Facility response plan

Applicability. As noted above, an FRP is required for substantial harm facilities, defined as a non-transportation-related onshore facility that "because of its location, could reasonably be expected to cause substantial harm to the environment by discharging oil into or on navigable waters or adjoining shorelines." 40 CFR 112.20(a). A substantial harm facility must complete an FRP if the facility meets one of the following substantial harm criteria:

AST = Above-ground storage tank

- Has a total oil storage capacity greater than or equal to 42,000 gallons and transfers oil over water to or from vessels

- Has a total oil storage capacity greater than or equal to one million gallons and the facility lacks sufficient secondary containment to contain the amount of oil that could be released from the largest above-ground storage tank (AST) plus sufficient freeboard to allow for precipitation

- Has a total oil storage capacity greater than or equal to one million gallons and, due to the facility's location, a discharge could injure fish and wildlife and sensitive environments

- Has a total oil storage capacity greater than or equal to one million gallons and, due to its location, a discharge would shut down a public drinking water intake (as per 40 CFR 143.2(c))

- Has a total oil storage capacity greater than or equal to one million gallons and the facility has had a reportable oil discharge in an amount greater than or equal to 10,000 gallons within the past five years (40 CFR 112.20(f)(1))

The FRP must document how the facility would respond to a worst-case discharge of oil and to a substantial threat of such a discharge.

The FRP must document how the facility would respond to a worst-case discharge of oil and to a substantial threat of such a discharge. Among other things, the FRP must include a flow diagram and must specify quantity limits and types of locations with potential for substantial harm. 40 CFR 112.20(h).

State Requirements

Aboveground Petroleum Storage Act. In 2008, major revisions to the state's Aboveground Petroleum Storage Act (APSA, HSC 25270 *et seq.*), which was first enacted in 1991, became effective. Responsibility for the implementation, enforcement, and administration of the APSA was transferred from the SWRCB to CUPAs. The Act applies to either tank facilities subject to 40 CFR 112, or to facilities storing petroleum with an aggregate storage capacity of at least 1,320 gallons. These facilities must prepare and implement an SPCC plan in accordance with 40 CFR 11. HSC 25270.3, 25270.5.

Each owner or operator of a tank regulated by the APSA must file an annual tank facility statement with the CUPA specifying the tank facility's name, address, contact person, and total storage capacity.

Each owner or operator of a tank regulated by the APSA must file an annual tank facility statement with the CUPA specifying the tank facility's name, address, contact person, and total storage capacity. The submission of a hazardous materials business plan (*see* chapter 7) to the CUPA satisfies the tank facility statement requirement. For each tank exceeding 10,000 gallons capacity and that holds a substance containing at least five percent petroleum, the statement must contain additional information: the tank's location on the facility, size, age, and contents. HSC 25270.6(a).

Commencing in 2010, each owner and operator of an AST must pay an annual fee to the CUPA. Owners and operators are required to notify the California Governor's Office of Emergency Services and the CUPA when there is a spill or release of at least one barrel (42 gallons) of petroleum. HSC 25270.8.

At least once every three years, the CUPA must inspect each AST, or a representative sample of ASTs, at tank facilities with a storage capacity of at least 10,000 gallons of petroleum. The purpose of the inspection is to determine whether the tank is owner or operator is in compliance with the SPCC plan. HSC 25270.5.

Lempert–Keene Act. The Lempert–Keene Act is designed to prevent and respond to oil spills into marine waters along the California coast. The Department of Fish and Game has developed an oil spill contingency plan describing how to respond to potential oil spills using "best achievable protection" of marine waters and the coast. In addition, operators of vessels, and owners and operators of marine facilities, must develop and implement contingency plans addressing preparation for and response to oil spills. The Act further requires that ports along the California coast develop harbor safety committees and plans for safe navigation of vessels within the port jurisdiction. The Act further governs loading and unloading of oil tankers. Gov. Code 8670.23.1, 8670.29, 8670.31, 8670.56; 14 CCR 851 *et seq.*

The Lempert–Keene Act is designed to prevent and respond to oil spills into marine waters along the California coast.

Water Quality
Release Reporting

The Porter–Cologne Act and CWA (42 USC 311) require agency reporting for releases of specified quantities (*i.e.,* reportable quantities or RQs) of hazardous substances and oil or petroleum products. Not all discharges exceeding the RQ must be reported. Only those discharges that reach or probably will reach surface and groundwaters must be reported. The reportable quantity depends on whether the release is of petroleum or of other hazardous chemicals.

The Porter–Cologne Act and CWA require agency reporting for releases of specified quantities of hazardous substances and oil or petroleum products.

Discharges exceeding the RQ and that could reach or probably reach surface and groundwaters must be reported to State Office of Emergency Services (OES) and to either the SWRCB or the RWQCB "as soon as the discharge is discovered and notification can be provided without substantially impeding cleanup or emergency measures." Immediate notification to the appropriate federal agency complies with California Water Code reporting provisions. 42 USC 311; Water Code 13271, 13272.

OES = Office of Emergency Services
RQ = Reportable quantity

Any person, regardless of intent or negligence, who permits or causes the discharge of sewage or waste in or on waters of the state is required to notify the local health officer or director of environmental health as soon as the person learns of the release, regardless of whether the person has already notified OES. Water Code 13271.

Enforcement

State versus Federal Enforcement

The SWRCB and RWQCBs are the principal state agencies responsible for regulating water quality. Water Code 13001. This role includes enforcing statutes and regulations (including the Porter–Cologne Act and TPCA) to prevent and mitigate impacts to the state's waters. The Boards may exercise their authority via any one or more of the following:

- Cleanup and abatement orders (CAOs)
- Cease and desist orders
- Administrative civil liability (fines)
- Referral to the Attorney General for injunctive or civil action or both

Although EPA's regulations authorize (and require) states with NPDES programs to enforce violations of the CWA, EPA is not precluded from also utilizing its enforcement authority in such cases. In fact, EPA explicitly retains the authority "to commence enforcement actions to the extent that State judgments or settlements provide penalties in amounts which EPA believes to be substantially inadequate." 40 CFR 123.27.

EPA policy dictates that the agency will utilize its enforcement authority to support and strengthen state programs (EPA 1986). EPA policy generally limits "overfiling" to four types of cases–the state has requested EPA action, local enforcement has not been timely or appropriate, important legal or programmatic precedents are involved in the case, or there has been a violation of an EPA order or consent decree.

Violations of the Clean Water Act and Porter–Cologne Act

If the SWRCB determines that there is a continual violation of any CAOs, or if any person fails to achieve compliance, civil enforcement allows for fines of up to $10,000 per day of violation. Water Code 13300 *et seq*. Passed in 1999, the California Clean Water Enforcement Act established mandatory minimum penalties of $3,000 for every "serious" violation–any waste discharge that exceeds permitted levels for a hazardous pollutant by 20 percent or more, or a nonhazardous pollutant by 40 percent or more. These minimum penalties also will be assessed for facilities that commit four or more ongoing violations in a six-month period, including exceeding numeric effluent limitations, failing to file a permit application, filing an incomplete application, exceeding chronic or acute toxicity limitations, violating compliance schedules, or (for a POTW) failing to enforce pretreatment requirements.

In addition to Board enforcement, violations of effluent limitations under the CWA may be enforced by civil "citizen suits." 33 USC 1365(a). Such suits are generally brought by environmental organizations.

Supplemental Environmental Projects

Dischargers may mitigate civil penalties by up to half by agreeing to fund and implement supplemental environmental projects (SEPs). An SEP is a pollution prevention effort that exceeds the existing statutory obligations of the discharger and achieves an environmental benefit. SEPs include anything from wetlands preservation projects to educational efforts. Water Code 13385 (h)(i).

SEP = Supplemental environmental project

For more information...

Publications

Adler, R. *et al.* 1993. The Clean Water Act: 20 Years Later. Island Press. Washington, D.C.

Environmental Protection Agency. 1986. Revised Policy Framework for State/EPA Enforcement Agreements

Environmental Protection Agency. 2005. SPCC Guidance for Regional Inspectors. EPA 550-B-05-001

Environmental Protection Agency. 1992. Storm Water Management for Industrial Activities: Developing Pollution Prevention Plans and Best Management Practices. EPA 832-R-92-006

Manaster, K.A. and D.P. Selmi (eds.). ND. California Environmental Law and Land Use Practice. Chapters 30–33. Matthew Bender. San Francisco, Calif.

Marshack, J.B. November 2001. California's Water Quality Standards and Their Application to Waste Management and Site Cleanup. Regional Water Quality Control Board, Central Valley Region

Pew Oceans Commission. 2003. America's Living Oceans: Charting a Course for Sea Change. A Report to the Nation. Arlington, Va.

Websites

California Environmental Protection Agency
www.calepa.ca.gov

California Integrated Waste Management Board
www.ciwmb.ca.gov

Central Valley Regional Water Board, Synopsis of Conditional Waiver Program
www.waterboards.ca.gov/centralvalley/programs/irrigated_lands/index.html

Environmental Protection Agency
www.epa.gov

Environmental Protection Agency, Sole Source Aquifer Program
www.epa.gov/safewater/swp/ssa.html

MS4 Questions and Answers
www.waterboards.ca.gov/rwqcb9/programs/stormwater/faq.html

Office of Environmental Health Hazard Assessment: Safe Drinking Water and Toxic Enforcement Act of 1986/Proposition 65
www.oehha.ca.gov/prop65/law/P65law72003.html

Pew Oceans Commission
www.pewtrusts.org/pdf/env_pew_oceans_final_report.pdf

State Water Resources Control Board, Site Assessment and Cleanup Policy, including Containment Zone Policy (Resolution No. 9249)
www.waterboards.ca.gov/plnspols/docs/wqplans/res92-49.html

State Water Resources Control Board, General Permit for Industrial Storm Water
www.waterboards.ca.gov/stormwtr/docs/induspmt.pdf

State Water Resources Control Board List of Impaired Waters
www.waterboards.ca.gov/tmdl/303d_lists2006.html

State Water Resources Control Board, Sources of Drinking Water Policy (Resolution No. 88-63)
www.waterboards.ca.gov/plnspols/docs/wqplans/res88-63.html

State Water Resources Control Board, "Statement of Policy with Respect to Maintaining High Quality of Waters in California" (Resolution No. 68-16)
www.waterboards.ca.gov/plnspols/docs/wqplans/res68-16.pdf

State Water Resources Control Board, Storm Water Pollution Prevention Plan and Monitoring Program Review Sheet
www.waterboards.ca.gov/stormwtr/docs/i_swppp.pdf

State Water Resources Control Board, Storm Water Program
www.waterboards.ca.gov/stormwtr/index.html

Drinking Water

This chapter reviews –

- Key laws and agencies involved in drinking water regulation
- Basics of drinking water programs
- California drinking water programs
- Security measures
- Enforcement

Glossary

Consumer confidence report—annual report, written by public water suppliers who serve community water systems, that summarizes information about drinking water sources used (rivers, lakes, reservoirs, aquifers, etc.), detected contaminants, and other educational information. To be delivered to customers by July 1 of each year.

Domestic water supply permit*— a permit issued by DHS for a PWS that supplies domestic water.

Maximum contaminant level goal— a non-enforceable concentration of a drinking water contaminant, set at the level at which no known or anticipated adverse effects on human health occur and that allows a margin of safety. The MCLG is usually the starting point for determining the enforceable maximum contaminant level.

Potable water—tap water that is safe and satisfactory for drinking and cooking.

Primary maximum contaminant level— a mandatory and enforceable standard (federal and state) that is protective of human health.

Public health goal—contaminant level in drinking water that does not pose a significant health risk to consumers and is based solely on scientific and public health considerations without regard to economic considerations.

Public water system—system that provides the public with piped water for human consumption, and has 15 or more service connections or regularly serves 25 individuals daily at least 60 days out of the year.

Secondary maximum contaminant level— a mandatory and enforceable standard (state only) that protects aesthetic qualities of drinking water, such as taste, odor, and color.

Underground injection control program— the program, under the federal Safe Drinking Water Act, that regulates the discharge of wastes into underground injection wells.

Vulnerability assessment—an evaluation conducted by community drinking water systems that service more than 3,300 people, that evaluates vulnerability to attack (*e.g.,* terrorist attack, vandalism, insider sabotage) and identifies actions to reduce the threat risk.

* equals permits and approvals

CHAPTER 11

Drinking Water

Introduction

Californians take for granted that clean water flows from the tap. Waterborne disease used to be the primary killer of babies and young children and still is in some developing countries. Thanks to improved water quality during the 20th century, health and life expectancy have improved dramatically. Chlorination and other drinking water treatments began in the early 1900s and became widespread public health practices, further decreasing the incidence of waterborne diseases. Since 1900, the average lifespan has increased approximately 30 years in the United States, with improved water quality playing a critical role in this advance. Centers for Disease Control and Prevention 1999a, 1999b.

Since 1900, the average lifespan has increased approximately 30 years in the United States, with improved water quality playing a critical role in this advance.

This chapter reviews key laws and agencies involved in drinking water regulation, federal and state drinking water programs, and enforcement.

Key Laws and Agencies

Federal Laws and Agencies

Safe Drinking Water Act. The Safe Drinking Water Act (SDWA) regulates public water systems (PWSs) that supply drinking water. 42 USC 300(f) *et seq.*, 40 CFR 141 *et seq.* The principle objective of the federal SDWA is to ensure that water from the tap is potable (safe and satisfactory for drinking and cooking). The main components of the federal SDWA are to:

CFR = Code of Federal Regulations
PWS = Public water system
SDWA = Safe Drinking Water Act
USC = United States Code

- Ensure that water from the tap is potable
- Prevent contamination of groundwater aquifers that are the main source of drinking water for a community

- Regulate distribution systems that convey treated water to homes, businesses, and factories
- Regulate the discharge of wastes into underground injection wells pursuant to the Underground Injection Control program (*see* 40 CFR 144 and chapter 10)

The Public Health Security and Bioterrorism Preparedness and Response Act of 2002. This Act, also called the Bioterrorism Act (Pub. Law 107-188, 42 USC 300hh, *et seq.*), was enacted in response to September 11, 2001. Title IV of the Act requires a PWS serving more than 3,300 people to perform a vulnerability assessment of its water system. The vulnerability assessment evaluates the risk of a terrorist attack or other intentional acts intended to substantially disrupt the ability of the system to provide a safe and reliable drinking water supply.

Environmental Protection Agency. The United States Environmental Protection Agency (EPA) implements the federal SDWA by:

- Establishing levels of contaminants (*e.g.,* inorganics, organics, pesticides, fecal coliform, and radionuclides) that must not be exceeded in drinking water
- Delegating duties to the states

Public water supply systems must ensure that specified levels of contaminants are not exceeded. PWSs accomplish this via treating, monitoring, and reporting on achievement of drinking water quality standards.

State Laws and Agencies

California Safe Drinking Water Act. The California SDWA (HSC 116270 *et seq.*, 22 CCR 64400 *et seq.*) regulates drinking water more rigorously than the federal law. Like the federal SDWA, California requires that primary and secondary maximum contaminant levels (MCLs) be established for pollutants in drinking water; however, some California MCLs are more protective of health. The Act also requires the Department of Public Health (DPH) (formerly DHS or Department of Health Services) to issue domestic water supply permits to public water systems.

Department of Public Health. DPH (formerly Department of Health Services) enforces the federal and state SDWAs and regulates more than 7,500 public water systems across the state. (Implementation of the federal SDWA is delegated to the state of California.)

DPH's Division of Drinking Water and Environmental Management oversees the state's comprehensive Drinking Water Program (DWP). The DWP consists of three branches: the Northern California Field Operations Branch, the Southern California Field Operations Branch, and the Technical Programs Branch.

Office of Environmental Health Hazard Assessment. The California Environmental Protection Agency's (Cal/EPA's) Office of Environmental Health Hazard Assessment (OEHHA) informs state and local regulatory agencies of important

Cal/EPA = California Environmental
Protection Agency

CCR = California Code of Regulations

DPH = Department of Public Health

DWP = Drinking water program

EPA = Environmental
Protection Agency

HSC = Health and Safety Code

MCL = Maximum contaminant level

OEHHA = Office of Environmental
Health Hazard Assessment

toxicological and medical information relevant to decisions involving public health. OEHHA is primarily responsible for developing procedures and practices for performing health risk assessments to determine healthy levels of exposure to pollutants. These assessments help risk managers to determine California MCLs.

Drinking Water Programs: The Basics

Definition of Public Water System

The key provisions of the federal and state SDWAs apply to PWSs that supply drinking water to the public. A PWS is defined as a system for providing the public with piped water for human consumption that has 15 or more service connections or regularly serves at least 25 individuals daily at least 60 days out of the year. 42 USC 300(f)(4), HSC 116275(h). PWSs collect water either from groundwater or surface water and then treat, store, and distribute the water for use. There are four types of PWSs:

The key provisions of the federal and state SDWAs apply to PWSs that supply drinking water to the public.

- **Community PWS.** A PWS that regularly serves at least 15 service connections to year-round residents or regularly serves at least 25 year-round residents.
- **Non-community PWS.** A PWS that is not a community water system. (This includes all other water systems meeting the PWS definition.)
- **Non-transient, non-community PWS.** A PWS that is not a community water system and regularly serves at least 25 of the same people over six months of the year. (This is aimed at school and workplace water supplies that cause long-term exposure.)
- **Transient, non-community PWS.** A PWS that is not a community system and does not regularly serve at least 25 of the same people over six months of the year. (This includes rest stop areas, campgrounds, restaurants, and motels.)

Drinking Water Standards

Primary drinking water standards. EPA established primary drinking water standards (also known as MCLs) that are mandatory and enforceable health-protective standards. 40 CFR 141 Subparts B, G. EPA establishes a primary MCL for a specified contaminant by:

EPA established primary drinking water standards that are mandatory and enforceable health-protective standards.

- Determining a preliminary level where no adverse health effects appear and including a margin of safety; this figure is known as a maximum contaminant level goal (MCLG). 40 CFR 141 Subpart F
- Setting the MCL as close to the MCLG as possible while taking into account technological feasibility and costs. 42 USC 300(g)(b)(4)(B)

MCLG = Maximum contaminant level goal

Primary MCLs are established for:

- Inorganic contaminants (*e.g.,* metals)
- Organic contaminants (*e.g.,* benzene)

- Synthetic organic contaminants (*e.g.*, pesticides)

- Trihalomethanes (THMs if disinfectant has been added)

- Microbial contaminants (*e.g.*, fecal coliforms, viruses, *giardia*, and *cryptosporidium*)

- Radioactivity

- Corrosivity

- Turbidity (*i.e.*, a measure of the amount of particles in water, and that can be caused by microbial or non-microbial sources)

The greatest public health risk related to drinking water is microbial contamination, causing waterborne disease.

The greatest public health risk related to drinking water is microbial contamination, causing waterborne disease. Potential microbes in water supplies (prior to treatment) include bacteria such as cholera and *salmonella*, viruses such as polio and Norwalk virus, and protozoans such as *cryptosporidium* and *giardia*. Surface waters are filtered to remove most of these pathogens. Groundwater is less vulnerable to these pathogens because the soil acts as a natural filter. All surface water and most groundwater in California is disinfected to reduce microbial risk. Common disinfectants include chlorine, chloramines, and ozone.

A federal MCL for arsenic (10 micrograms/liter) became effective in January 2006. 40 CFR 141.62. Ingestion of arsenic can pose a risk of cancer. Achieving compliance with the arsenic MCL has been difficult because arsenic is commonly found in California drinking water sources. Most of the drinking water systems affected are small and rural, with few regulatory requirements prior to the arsenic MCL.

EPA also established secondary drinking water standards to protect aesthetic qualities (taste, odor, color) that are state enforceable in California.

Secondary drinking water standards. EPA also established secondary drinking water standards (another set of MCLs) that are not federally enforceable, but are state enforceable in California. 22 CCR 64449 *et seq.* Secondary MCLs protect aesthetic qualities (taste, odor, color) of drinking water. 40 CFR 143. Thus far, EPA has issued secondary MCLs for 15 contaminants, including color, odor, pH, total dissolved solids, fluoride, iron, and manganese.

Drinking Water Standards as Benchmarks for Cleanup

Primary and secondary MCLs often are used as benchmarks for acceptable cleanup standards for contaminated groundwater. (*See* chapter 8.)

Monitoring Requirements: Water Quality

Frequency and contaminants. Public water systems must monitor the water quality leaving their water systems to ensure that concentrations do not exceed MCLs. Typically, all contaminants on the MCL list initially are tested at a given PWS. Afterwards, the frequency of monitoring and the contaminants to be monitored are based on (40 CFR 141 Subpart C):

- The contaminant group
- The type of drinking water facility
- The number of people served
- The water source (*i.e.,* groundwater or surface water)
- Whether any MCLs have been exceeded

Municipal water treatment plants assure that drinking water quality standards are met.

Each PWS is also subject to nine-year monitoring cycles, divided into three-year compliance periods, to demonstrate compliance with scores of MCLs. During the initial period, a PWS must monitor contaminants using a state-certified lab to conduct the analyses. Should the PWS exceed one or more MCLs, the PWS must complete more frequent monitoring and commit to corrective measures. 40 CFR 141. During each compliance period, a PWS is obligated to collect samples from groundwater supply systems, as well as surface water supply systems after treatment.

Monitoring plan. A PWS must write a monitoring plan, and DPH must approve the plan. Monitoring programs vary by PWS type and size and include sampling for the following:

- Inorganic contaminants
- Organic contaminants (including synthetic organic contaminants)
- Total trihalomethane
- Radioactivity
- Turbidity
- Chlorinated compounds
- Disinfectant residuals (*e.g.,* chlorine, chloramines)
- Microbial contaminants
- Miscellaneous contaminants (*e.g.,* sulfate, sodium, corrosivity, general minerals, pH)

PWSs must also sample for microbial activity by collecting microbial samples at representative locations throughout the distribution system. The sampling strategy and plan is captured in a written sampling plan that is approved by DPH. The sampling frequency is determined by the population served. If a microbial sample is positive for coliform, DPH must be notified within 24 hours if further testing reveals the presence of fecal coliform or *E. coli.* 40 CFR 141.21, 22 CCR 64421 *et seq.*

PWSs must also sample for microbial activity by collecting microbial samples at representative locations throughout the distribution system.

In October 2006, EPA published a "groundwater rule" that applies to all systems that use groundwater as a source of drinking water. 71 Federal Register 216, November 8, 2006. The purpose of the rule is to reduce disease incidence associated with disease-causing microorganisms in drinking water. The rule establishes a risk-based approach to target groundwater systems that are vulnerable to fecal contamination. Groundwater systems that are identified as being at risk of fecal contamination must take corrective action to reduce potential illness from exposure to microbial pathogens.

Filtration and disinfection are required for PWSs that use surface water or groundwater that is under the influence of surface water. 40 CFR 141 Subpart H. PWSs using surface water supplies must sample for turbidity and disinfectant residuals nearly continuously, typically once every four hours. 40 CFR 141.22. Low turbidity and the presence of a chlorine residual ensure that water does not contain pathogenic microbes such as bacteria, viruses, and protozoans.

Monitoring Requirements: Distribution Systems and Cross-Connections

A PWS must monitor for lead and copper levels at the tap, to ensure that its distribution system does not add unacceptable levels of lead and copper to tap water.

Lead and copper. A PWS must monitor for lead and copper levels at the tap, to ensure that its distribution system does not add unacceptable levels of lead and copper to tap water. 40 CFR 141 Subparts E, I. If a representative lead or copper action level is exceeded (*i.e.*, if at least 10 percent of tap water samples exceed the lead or copper MCL), the PWS must implement a corrosion control program and treat the source water. If the MCL still is exceeded after corrective measures are implemented, then the PWS must replace lead service lines. Pipes, solder, flux, and water coolers installed after June 19, 1986, must be lead-free.

Backflow. No federal programs regulate backflow; however, the state does regulate backflow through the DPH's Office of Drinking Water. 17 CCR 7583–7605, HSC 116800 *et seq.* DPH and local health agencies implement and enforce backflow prevention programs (also known as cross-connection programs).

A PWS owner or operator is required to protect the system from backflow-related contamination by implementing a cross-connection control program. 17 CCR 7584. Backflow prevention devices are designed to ensure that contaminants, especially pathogens, are not back-siphoned into a potable water system. A PWS's program must include, at a minimum, the following elements:

- Operating rules or ordinances to implement a backflow prevention program
- Surveys to identify water-user premises where cross-connections are likely to occur
- Provisions of backflow protection by the water-user at all connections where a cross connection hazard has been identified
- At least one person trained in cross-connection control to carry out the cross-connection program
- A procedure for testing backflow preventers, with a frequency of semiannual to biennial depending on the device (17 CCR 7605)
- Records of locations, tests, and repairs of backflow preventers

Water suppliers (*i.e.*, owners or operators of PWSs) also must evaluate the potential health hazard created by conditions on the water user's premises.

17 CCR 7585. Water users, not water suppliers, are responsible for abatement of cross-connections.

Consumer Confidence Reports

PWSs are required to report annually on the water quality served to their users. 40 CFR 141 Subpart O. Each report must, at a minimum, provide consumers with the following information about their drinking water:

- **Water system information.** Name and phone number of PWS contact person; public meetings and hearings; information for non-English speaking populations (if applicable).
- **Water source.** Type (i.e., groundwater or surface water); common name; location; availability of source water assessment; summary of potential sources of contamination.
- **Definitions.** Key definitions such as MCL and MCLG.
- **Detected contaminants.** Tabular summary of detected regulated and unregulated contaminants that were detected during sampling; known or likely source of each detected contaminant; potential health effects; *cryptosporidium* information (if applicable).
- **Compliance with drinking water regulations.** Explanation of violations; compliance with other drinking water rules.
- **Required educational information.** Explanation of contaminants and their presence in drinking water; information on nitrate, arsenic, lead, and total THM (if applicable); EPA's drinking water hotline number.

Like other federal drinking water regulations, states may set their own regulations for PWS reports. California has established its own requirements for consumer confidence reports that parallel the federal requirements. HSC 116470; 22 CCR 64480 *et seq.* Both EPA and the states can take enforcement action to ensure that consumers' right-to-know is respected by all water suppliers.

Records

Owners or operators of PWSs are also responsible for complying with reporting and recordkeeping requirements. 40 CFR 141 Subpart D, 22 CCR 64453. PWSs must maintain records of:

Owners or operators of PWSs are also responsible for complying with reporting and recordkeeping requirements.

- Bacteriological analyses, for at least five years
- Chemical analyses, for at least ten years (40 CFR 141.33)
- Corrective measures taken for violations of primary drinking water regulations, for at least three years
- Water quality complaints and corrective measures taken, for at least five years (state requirement)

Federal and state law requires timely notification to EPA and DPH, respectively, of failure to meet applicable drinking water standards.

California Drinking Water Programs

Primary and Secondary Maximum Contaminant Levels

MTBE = Methyl tertiary butyl ether
PHG = Public health goal

Although the state adopted the federal primary and secondary MCLs, the state also adopted (22 CCR 64449):

- Some primary MCLs that are lower (more health-protective) than the federal MCLs (*e.g.,* arsenic, perchlorate, and 1,4 dichlorobenzene). 22 CCR 64441–64444, 22 CCR 64670 *et seq.*

- Some primary MCLs for which there are no federal MCLs (*e.g.,* bentazone and perchlorate). The perchlorate MCL of 6 ppb (0.006 mg/l) was adopted in 2007. Perchlorate is a widespread drinking water contaminant, especially in Southern California, derived primarily from rocket fuel propellants.

- Some secondary MCLs that are lower (more health-protective) than the federal MCLs (*e.g.,* methyl tertiary butyl ether or MTBE).

- Some secondary MCLs for which there are no federal MCLs (*e.g.,* manganese and the herbicide thiobencarb). 22 CCR 64449.

A DPH-approved laboratory must analyze samples used to determine MCL compliance in California.

Risk Assessments

OEHHA performs risk assessments that are used to set public health goals. Like the federal MCLGs that serve as a starting point for setting federal MCLs, the PHGs are used by DPH to set California MCLs.

OEHHA performs risk assessments that are used to set public health goals (PHGs). Like the federal MCLGs that serve as a starting point for setting federal MCLs, the PHGs are used by DPH to set California MCLs. PHGs represent levels of contaminants in drinking water that do not pose a significant health risk to consumers. HSC 116365(c). For each contaminant, the risk assessment assumes that an individual consumes contaminated water daily for a lifetime and does not experience a one in one million incremental cancer risk. PHGs are based solely on scientific and public health considerations without regard to economic considerations. On the other hand, the state's primary MCLs must consider economics and technical feasibility and be set as close as feasible to the corresponding PHG while placing primary emphasis on protecting public health. HSC 116365(a).

Domestic Water Supply Permits

No person may operate a PWS without having secured a domestic water supply permit from DPH. As mentioned above, the California SDWA defines a PWS as any entity that serves drinking water to at least 25 persons for at least 60 days out of the year, or that services domestic water to 15 or more service connections. DPH (2004) has issued detailed instructions to applicants for a domestic water supply permit. If a community water system serves at least five but fewer than 15 service connections, it is called a state small water system, and is regulated by the local health department rather than DPH. HSC 116525, 116530, 116540, 116550.

Security Measures

Under the Bioterrorism Act (42 USC 300hh *et seq.*), community drinking water systems that service more than 3,300 people must conduct vulnerability assessments (VAs), assessing their vulnerability to attack (*e.g.*, terrorist attack, vandalism, and insider sabotage). The Act is intended to defend the nation's water supplies and systems against harmful disruptions. EPA and PWSs are the primary entities responsible for ensuring a safe and reliable supply of drinking water, and are charged with developing response measures for potential threats to the nation's water supplies and systems.

Under the Bioterrorism Act, community drinking water systems that service more than 3,300 people must conduct vulnerability assessments, assessing their vulnerability to attack.

Under the Bioterrorism Act, a community water system serving more than 3,300 people must:

- Conduct a vulnerability assessment (VA)

VA = Vulnerability assessment

- Certify and submit a written copy of the VA to the EPA administrator
- Prepare or revise an emergency response plan that incorporates VA results
- Certify to the EPA administrator, within six months of completing the VA, that an emergency response plan has been completed or revised
- Maintain a copy of the emergency response plan for five years

The Bioterrorism Act prohibits states from reviewing PWS VAs. 42 USC 300i-2. Therefore, DPH cannot require a copy of the completed VA. However, DPH (2003) has published Emergency Response Plan guidelines to help PWSs serving more than 1,000 service connections.

Enforcement

Federal Enforcement

Under the federal SDWA, EPA can bring a civil action against a violator, and the court can impose a civil penalty of up to $25,000 per day of violation. 42 USC 300(g) *et seq.*, 42 USC 1414(b). EPA also can collect the following:

Under the federal SDWA, EPA can bring a civil action against a violator, and the court can impose a civil penalty of up to $25,000 per day of violation.

- A maximum penalty of up to $25,000 for violation of an administrative order. 42 USC 1414(g)(3)
- Up to $5,000 per violation per day of an emergency order. 42 USC 1431(b)
- Up to $50,000 for tampering with a PWS. 42 USC 1432(c)
- Up to $20,000 for attempting to or threatening to tamper with a PWS. 42 USC 1432(c)
- Up to $25,000 for failing to keep or make appropriate records. 42 USC 1445(c)

State Enforcement

Civil penalties. Under California law, DPH can assess the following civil penalties:

- $5,000 per day per violation, against any person who knowingly makes a false statement or representation in a record, report, application or other submitted document. HSC 116725.

- $25,000 per day per violation, against any person who violates a schedule of compliance for a primary MCL other than turbidity.

- $5,000 per day per violation, against any person who violates any order under the HSC. (The fine is larger, and prison time can be imposed, if violating the order creates a substantial likelihood of imminent danger to the health of people; *see* paragraph below.)

Criminal penalties. A person may be fined up to $25,000 per day of violation or imprisoned in county jail for up to one year or both, if convicted of knowingly committing any of the following (HSC 116730):

- Making a false representation or statement on any record, report, or application

- Altering any record currently in the individual's possession that is required to be maintained under the Health and Safety Code

- Destroying or concealing any record

- Withholding information about an imminent and substantial danger to the public health or safety, if the information has been requested by DPH

- Violating an order that creates a substantial likelihood of imminent danger to the health of people

- Operating a PWS without a DPH-issued permit

A person may be fined up to $30,000 for tampering with a PWS or imprisoned for three to five years (a felony) or both. HSC 116750.

For more information...

Publications

Centers for Disease Control and Prevention. 1999a. Ten Great Public Health Achievements–United States, 1900–1999. Morbidity and Mortality Weekly Report 48(12): 241–243. April 2, 1999

Centers for Disease Control and Prevention. 1999b. Achievements in Public Health, 1900–1999: Control of Infectious Diseases. Morbidity and Mortality Weekly Report 48(29): 621–629. July 30, 1999

Department of Health Services. 2003. California Emergency Response Plan Guidance

Department of Health Services. 2004. Domestic Water Supply Permit Applicant Instructions

Manaster, K.A. and D.P. Selmi (eds.). ND. California Environmental Law and Land Use Practice, Chapter 33. Matthew Bender, San Francisco, Calif.

Websites

American Water Works Association
www.awwa.org

Department of Public Health
Drinking Water Program
www.cdph.ca.gov/programs/Pages/DWP.aspx

Environmental Protection Agency,
Arsenic MCL Compliance
www.epa.gov/environmentaltechnology/forum/problem/
progressreports/arsenic_compliance-9-22-06.html

Environmental Protection Agency,
Consumer Confidence Reports
www.epa.gov/safewater/ccr/index.html

Environmental Protection Agency,
Groundwater and Drinking Water
www.epa.gov/safewater

Environmental Protection Agency,
Vulnerability Assessment Factsheet
www.epa.gov/safewater/watersecurity/
pubs/va_fact_sheet_12-19.pdf

Office of Environmental Health
Hazard Assessment, Water
www.oehha.ca.gov/water.html

Safe Drinking Water Act
www.epa.gov/safewater/sdwa/index.html

U.S. Food and Drug Administration,
Bioterrorism Act of 2002
www.fda.gov/oc/bioterrorism/bioact.html

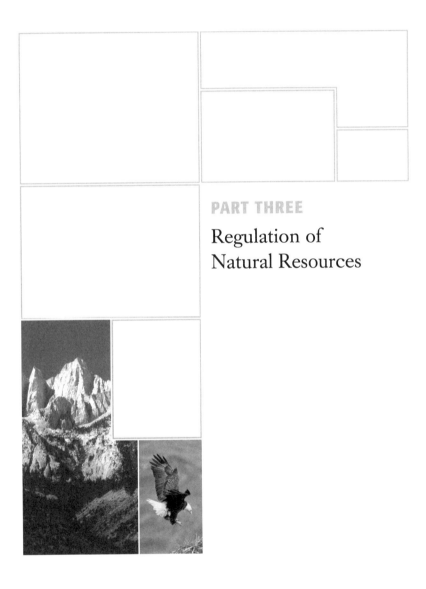

PART THREE

Regulation of
Natural Resources

CHAPTER 12

Agricultural Land

This chapter reviews —

- Key laws and agencies involved in agricultural land preservation

- Role of the California Environmental Quality Act in agricultural land preservation

- Williamson Act

- Conservation and open space easements

- Right-to-farm ordinances

Related Solano Press titles—

Curtin's California Land Use and Planning Law
Cecily T. Talbert. 2008

Glossary

Conservation easement–a recorded deed restriction voluntarily executed by a landowner with the purpose of retaining land predominantly in its natural scenic, historical, agricultural, forested, or open space condition.

Subvention–as used in the Williamson Act, the granting of funds from state government to local governments to partially compensate for foregone property tax revenues when land is placed under contract.

Williamson Act contract*–a voluntary contract entered into between a landowner and a local government in which the landowner receives reduced property tax assessments in return for restricting land to agricultural and open space uses.

* equals permits and approvals

CHAPTER 12

Agricultural Land

Introduction

California is the leading agricultural producer and exporter in the United States. In 2003, the total value of agricultural product sales in California was $27.8 billion. California Department of Food and Agriculture (DFA) 2004.

Agricultural land in California provides other important public benefits, including open space and aesthetics. Urban growth and water supply shortages, however, have been steadily reducing the acreage of California farmland in production. The Legislature has recognized that farmland preservation is in the public interest and has enacted several farmland preservation programs. (Local land use planning and zoning, reviewed in chapter 3, also plays an important role in agricultural land preservation.) This chapter reviews key laws and agencies involved in agricultural land preservation, the role of the California Environmental Quality Act (CEQA), the Williamson Act, conservation and open space easements, and right-to-farm ordinances.

CEQA = California Environmental Quality Act

DFA = California Department of Food and Agriculture

Key Laws and Agencies

Key Laws

Williamson Act. The Williamson Act, also called the California Land Conservation Act (Gov. Code 51200 *et seq.*), is California's oldest agricultural land preservation program, dating back to 1965. The Williamson Act offers agricultural landowners reduced property tax assessments if they contract with counties or cities to voluntarily restrict their land to agricultural and open space uses. In return, restricted parcels are assessed for property taxes at rates consistent with their actual uses, rather than potential market value. Revenue and Taxation Code 423 *et seq.*

The Williamson Act offers agricultural landowners reduced property tax assessments if they contract with counties or cities to voluntarily restrict their land to agricultural and open space uses.

287

Key Agencies

DFA = Department of
Food and Agriculture

DLRP = Division of Land
Resource Protection

DOC = Department of Conservation

FRPP = Farm and Ranch Lands
Protection Program

NRCS = Natural Resources
Conservation Service

USC = United States Code

Natural Resources Conservation Service. The Natural Resources Conservation Service (NRCS), formerly the Soil Conservation Service, is within the United States Department of Agriculture. It operates the Farm and Ranch Lands Protection Program (FRPP), a voluntary conservation easement program authorized by the Farm Security and Rural Investment Act of 2002. 16 United States Code (USC) 3830 *et seq.* NRCS also operates other programs that promote farmland preservation, including programs for technical assistance, environmental improvement, and resource assessments.

California Department of Conservation. Through its Division of Land Resource Protection (DLRP), the Department of Conservation (DOC) operates four programs related to agricultural land preservation: the Farmland Mapping and Monitoring Program, the Resource Conservation District Assistance Program, the Williamson Act Program, and the California Farmland Conservancy Program. The first two programs are described below, and the latter two programs are described in detail later in this chapter.

The Farmland Mapping and Monitoring Program produces maps and statistical data used for analyzing impacts on California's agricultural resources. Agricultural land is rated according to soil quality and irrigation status; the best quality land is called prime farmland. Maps are updated every two years using aerial photographs, a computer mapping system, public review, and field reconnaissance. Between 2000 and 2002, California's urban land expanded by 92,750 acres; prime farmland had a net decrease of 47,172 acres, and was the source of 21 percent of newly urbanized acreage. California Department of Conservation 2004.

DLRP provides support to Resource Conservation Districts (RCDs), which are special districts involved in conservation of both agricultural and non-agricultural land (*see* below). This support includes financial assistance through an RCD grant program and technical assistance.

DFA's mission is "to help the governor and Legislature ensure delivery of safe food and fiber through responsible environmental stewardship in a fair marketplace for all Californians."

California Department of Food and Agriculture. The DFA plays an indirect role in agricultural land preservation by promoting a strong agricultural industry. According to the Department's website, DFA's mission is "to help the governor and Legislature ensure delivery of safe food and fiber through responsible environmental stewardship in a fair marketplace for all Californians." DFA's goals are to:

- Ensure that only safe and quality food reaches the consumer
- Protect against invasion of exotic pests and diseases
- Promote California agriculture and food products both at home and abroad
- Ensure an equitable and orderly marketplace for California's agricultural products
- Build coalitions supporting the state's agricultural infrastructure to meet evolving industry needs

Resource conservation districts. RCDs emerged during the 1930s as a way to prevent the soil erosion problems of the Dust Bowl from recurring. Formed as independent local liaisons between the federal government and landowners, RCDs always have worked closely with NRCS. RCDs are California special districts locally governed by locally appointed or elected boards of directors. PRC 9001 *et seq.* There are currently over 100 RCDs in California implementing agricultural land resource conservation projects and programs, including agricultural land preservation.

LESA = California Agricultural Land Evaluation and Site Assessment
PRC = Public Resources Code
RCD = Resource conservation district

California Environmental Quality Act Role in Agricultural Land Preservation

CEQA Appendix G

CEQA plays an important role in agricultural land preservation. Appendix G of the CEQA Guidelines sets forth an initial study checklist used to determine whether a project's impacts are potentially significant. *See* chapter 2. In 1998, several examples of significant impact that directly address agricultural land were added to Appendix G of the CEQA Guidelines. If these significant impacts would occur, an environmental impact report or a mitigated negative declaration is required.

Under Appendix G, a project would have significant effects on agricultural resources if the project would:

- Convert prime farmland, unique farmland, or farmland of statewide importance, as shown on DLRP maps, to non-agricultural use
- Conflict with existing agricultural zoning or a Williamson Act contract
- Involve other environmental changes that could result in the conversion of farmland to non-agricultural use

Appendix G also states that the California Agricultural Land Evaluation and Site Assessment (LESA) model may be used to assess agricultural land impacts. The LESA model quantifies the relative importance of agricultural land resources based upon specific measurable features. The model evaluates factors such as soil resource quality, water resource availability, amount of surrounding agricultural lands, and amount of surrounding protected resource lands.

Appendix G of the CEQA Guidelines states that the California Agricultural Land Evaluation and Site Assessment model may be used to assess agricultural land impacts.

Conservation easements (*see* below) sometimes are proposed as mitigation measures for significant agricultural land impacts. Their effectiveness and legal standing as mitigation measures are debatable, since they do not result in "no net loss" of agricultural land, but rather seek to preserve existing agricultural land.

Farmland Definitions

DLRP definitions of farmland classifications used in Appendix G are as follows:

- **Prime farmland.** Farmland with the best combination of physical and chemical features able to sustain long-term agricultural production. This land has the soil quality, growing season, and moisture supply needed to produce sustained, high yields. Land must have been used for irrigated agricultural production at some time during the four years prior to the mapping date.

- **Farmland of statewide importance.** Farmland similar to prime farmland but with minor shortcomings, such as greater slopes or less ability to store soil moisture. Land must have been used for irrigated agricultural production at some time during the four years prior to the mapping date.

- **Unique farmland.** Farmland of lesser quality soils used for production of the state's leading agricultural crops. This land usually is irrigated, but may include nonirrigated orchards or vineyards as found in some climatic zones in California. Land must have been cropped at some time during the four years prior to the mapping date.

Williamson Act

Overview

The Williamson Act, also called the California Land Conservation Act (Gov. Code 51200 *et seq.*), is California's oldest agricultural land preservation program, dating back to 1965. The Williamson Act offers agricultural landowners reduced property tax assessments if they contract with counties or cities to voluntarily restrict their land to agricultural and open space uses. In return, restricted parcels are assessed for property taxes at rates consistent with their actual uses, rather than potential market value. Revenue and Taxation Code 423 *et seq.*

The Department of Conservation DLRP is responsible for interpretation and enforcement of the Williamson Act. The Department administers a subvention program to partially reimburse local governments for property tax revenues foregone as a result of Williamson Act participation.

About 17 million of the state's 45 million acres of farm and ranch land currently are protected under the Williamson Act. California DOC 2005. As of 2005, all counties except Del Norte, Los Angeles, San Francisco, Inyo, and Yuba offered Williamson Act contracts.

Term of Contract

A Williamson Act contract has a minimum 10-year rolling term. Unless either party files a notice of nonrenewal, the contract automatically is renewed annually for an additional year. An optional program within the Williamson Act allows landowners of certain lands to petition a county to create a farmland security zone with a 20-year rolling contract. Gov. Code 51244, 51296.

Supreme Court Interprets Williamson Act in Landmark Case

In *Sierra Club v. City of Hayward* (1981) 28 Cal. 3d 840, the Supreme Court firmly established that nonrenewal of a Williamson Act contract is the preferred method of termination. The court ruled that cancellation can occur only in "extraordinary circumstances," when the difficult findings required by the Act can be made by a city or county.

The case dealt with the City of Hayward's cancellation of a 93-acre parcel under Williamson Act contract. The court first held that local government Williamson Act cancellation decisions are judicially reviewable and should be construed narrowly to achieve the purposes of the Act. The court then proceeded to invalidate some of the City of Hayward's cancellation findings as unsupported by substantial evidence. ▪

Agricultural Preserves

Only land within an agricultural preserve is eligible for a Williamson Act contract. This boundary is designated by the city or county, which adopts rules restricting land uses within the preserve to ensure it is maintained for agricultural and open space uses. Gov. Code 51231, 51237.

The Williamson Act establishes certain rules for uses compatible with the agricultural, recreational, or open spaces uses of land in an agricultural preserve. Gov. Code 51238.1. Local compatibility rules may be more restrictive than those required by the Act. The Act discourages public agencies from placing federal, state, or local public improvements or public utility improvements in agricultural preserves; it establishes special procedures that must be followed if public agencies acquire land under Williamson Act contract.

The Williamson Act establishes certain rules for uses compatible with the agricultural, recreational, or open spaces uses of land in an agricultural preserve.

An agricultural preserve must consist of at least 100 acres (with local exceptions possible), in one or more ownerships. Once an agricultural preserve is established, the city or county must file a map and a resolution creating the preserve with the county recorder and must keep this information current. Gov. Code 51237.

Nonrenewal and Cancellation

Nonrenewal, rather than cancellation, is the preferred termination method for Williamson Act contracts. *See* sidebar.

Nonrenewal, rather than cancellation, is the preferred termination method for Williamson Act contracts.

A notice of nonrenewal starts a nine-year nonrenewal period, during which the annual tax assessment gradually increases until the property is taxed at its full market value by the time the contract expires. The goal of this process is to achieve fair taxation as the Williamson Act restriction is eliminated over time. Revenue and Taxation Code 426.

Alternatively, a landowner can petition to cancel a Williamson Act contract if "extraordinary circumstances" exist. Gov. Code 51280. To approve a contract cancellation, a county or city must make findings that the cancellation is consistent with the Williamson Act or in the public interest. An opportunity for another use is not a sufficient reason for cancellation, nor is, by itself, the uneconomic character of an existing agricultural use. Upon cancellation, the landowner must pay a cancellation fee of 12.5 percent of the unrestricted current fair market valuation of the property. Gov. Code 51283.

Enforcement

Williamson Act contracts are binding on successors in interest of the owner, with special provisions for transfers among immediate family members. If a landowner fails to comply with the terms and conditions of a contract, the local government or DOC may seek an injunction to enforce the contract. Structures permitted or built after January 1, 2004, that exceed 2,500 square feet and are not

Williamson Act contracts are binding on successors in interest of the owner, with special provisions for transfers among immediate family members.

permitted by the contract terms are considered material breaches of the contract and may be subject to penalties equal to 25 percent of the value of the affected land and 25 percent of the value of any improvements. Gov. Code 51250(a).

Conservation and Open Space Easements

Conservation Easements

Conservation easements are a major tool to preserve California agricultural land.

CFCP = California Farmland Conservancy Program

A statutory conservation easement is a recorded deed restriction voluntarily executed by a landowner with the purpose of retaining land "predominantly in its natural scenic, historical, agricultural, forested, or open space condition." Civil Code 815.1. Conservation easements may be held by state and local governments authorized to hold real property, by tax-exempt nonprofit organizations, and by California Native American tribes. For a general reference on conservation easements, *see* Byers and Ponte (2005).

Conservation easements "run with the land," meaning they are binding on all current and future owners of the property. Violations may be enforced through injunctions and money damages.

California Farmland Conservancy Program Act. Funding for agricultural conservation easements is available under the California Farmland Conservancy Program (CFCP) Act. PRC 10200 *et seq.* Agricultural conservation easements are created specifically to support agriculture and prevent development on the agricultural parcels subject to the easements. Easements funded by the CFCP must be of a size and nature suitable for viable commercial agriculture. Although other benefits (*e.g.,* scenic) may result from the land not being developed, the primary use of the land under easement must be agricultural. The placement of an agricultural conservation easement on land may provide income, property tax, and estate tax benefits.

Agricultural land easements may be held by land trusts or local governments, which are responsible for enforcing the terms of the easement. The easement may be donated to the easement holder, purchased, or both.

Several nonprofit organizations provide technical assistance for establishing conservation easements. These include the American Farmland Trust and Land Trust Alliance.

Farm and Ranch Lands Protection Program. The Farm and Ranch Lands Protection Program, operated by the NRCS, provides funding for conservation easements, working through state, tribal, or local governments that acquire the easements. Participating landowners agree not to convert their land to non-agricultural uses and to implement a conservation plan for any highly erodible land. To qualify for the FRPP, the land must meet a number of requirements, including the requirements to contain prime, unique, or other productive soil, or historical or archeological resources; and to be included in a pending offer for a state, tribal, or local farmland protection program. 7 CFR 1491.

CFR = Code of Federal Regulations

Open Space Easements

Open space easements authorized by the Open Space Easement Act of 1974 (Gov. Code 510070 *et seq.*) also may be used for agricultural land preservation. Open space easements may be held only by cities, counties, or nonprofit organizations, and must have at least a rolling 10-year term. An open space easement can be approved by a city or county only if preservation of the land as open space is consistent with the general plan and in the best interest of the city or county. Building permits may not be issued if inconsistent with the easement.

Open space easements may be held only by cities, counties, or nonprofit organizations, and must have at least a rolling 10-year term.

An easement can be terminated through nonrenewal, similar to a Williamson Act contract. Alternatively, a landowner may seek abandonment of the easement by filing a petition; the relevant city or county must approve the petition through making certain findings.

Right-to-Farm Ordinances

Right-to-farm ordinances seek to reduce the opposition of urban neighbors to agricultural operations through requiring disclosure of the potential adverse impacts of agricultural operations to purchasers of nearby property. About 40 counties and 50 cities have adopted right-to-farm ordinances. Wacker *et al.* 2001. First enacted in the 1980s, they were encouraged by passage of Civil Code 3482.5, which declares that a farm in operation for more than three years is not considered a nuisance due to changed circumstances, such as urbanization, in the area.

Right-to-farm ordinances seek to reduce the opposition of urban neighbors to agricultural operations through requiring disclosure of the potential adverse impacts of agricultural operations to purchasers of nearby property.

Ordinances typically contain the following provisions (Wacker *et al.* 2001):

- **Statement of purpose.** For example, to preserve agricultural operations as an important part of the local economy, or to promote a good neighbor policy between farm and other landowners

- **Nuisance.** A reference to Civil Code 3482.5, although some ordinances reduce the time of operation from three years to one year

- **Disclosure.** A requirement that potential purchasers or developers of property near farming operations be notified of the potential adverse impacts of agricultural operations

- **Grievance procedure.** A process for resolving complaints against agricultural operations

For more information…

Publications

Byers, E. and K.M. Ponte. 2005. The Conservation Easement Handbook (2nd ed.). Land Trust Alliance and Trust for Public Land. San Francisco, Calif.

California Department of Conservation. 2004. California Farmland Conversion Report, 2000–2002

California Department of Conservation. 2005. Williamson Act Questions and Answers

California Department of Food and Agriculture. 2004. California Agricultural Statistics, 2003

Manaster, K.A. and D.P. Selmi (eds). ND. Chapter 70 of California Environmental Law and Land Use Practice. Matthew Bender. San Francisco, Calif.

Talbert, C.T. 2008. Curtin's California Land Use and Planning Law. Solano Press. Point Arena, Calif.

Wacker, M., A. Sokolow, and R. Elkins. 2001. County Right-to-Farm Ordinances in California: An Assessment of Impact and Effectiveness. University of California Agricultural Issues Center Brief Number 15

Websites

American Farmland Trust
www.farmland.org

California Association of
Resource Conservation Districts
www.carcd.org

California Department of Conservation,
Division of Land Resource Protection
www.consrv.ca.gov/DLRP

California Department
of Food and Agriculture
www.cdfa.ca.gov

California Farm Bureau Federation
www.cfbf.com

California Farmland
Conservancy Program
www.consrv.ca.gov/DLRP/cfcp/overview/index.htm

Land Trust Alliance
www.lta.org

Natural Resources
Conservation Service
www.nrcs.usda.gov/programs

CHAPTER 13

Water Resources

This chapter reviews—

- Key laws and agencies
  involved in California water law
- Water rights law
- Water supply planning
- Wild and scenic rivers
  (federal and state systems)

Related Solano Press titles—

*Water and Land Use: Planning
Wisely for California's Future*
Karen E. Johnson
and Jeff Loux. 2004

California Water II
Arthur L. Littleworth
and Eric L. Garner. 2007

Glossary

Acre-foot—325,851 gallons or enough water to cover an acre of land one foot deep.

Adjudication—the judicial proceeding in which a priority is assigned to appropriations, and a decree is issued defining water rights.

Anadromous fish—a fish species, such as salmon, that migrates from freshwater streams to the ocean and back to complete its cycle.

Appropriative right—a water right based on physical control over water (pre-1914), or based on a permit or license for its beneficial use (post-1914).

Beneficial use—use of an amount of water that is reasonable and appropriate under efficient practices to accomplish, without waste, the purpose for which a diversion is made.

CALFED—a consortium of federal and state agencies overseeing Bay–Delta water management, superseded by the Bay–Delta Authority.

Certificate of approval*—a certificate issued by DWR for construction of certain dams.

Conjunctive use—combined use of surface and groundwater supplies.

Correlative right—in the context of riparian rights, the right to use a portion of the natural flow of water in common with other riparian users. Similar doctrine also applies in the context of groundwater rights, where overlying landowners must share rights to groundwater.

Desalination—treatment of seawater or brackish water to reduce salt levels, making the water useful for potable or non-potable supplies.

FERC license*—a license for a hydroelectric project using navigable waters or federal land.

Firm yield—the dependable annual water supply that could be available in all years, without exceeding specified shortages in agricultural deliveries during droughts.

Groundwater—water that is seeped beneath the earth's surface and is stored underground.

Instream use—the beneficial use of water within a stream, such as for fisheries habitat.

Law of the River—numerous compacts, judicial decisions, contracts, and other instruments, governing the management and operation of the Colorado River.

Long-term transfer*—a transfer of water or water rights lasting more than one year.

Overdraft—a groundwater basin in which the amount of water withdrawn exceeds the amount of water replenishing the basin.

Paper water—water entitlements under water contract that may never be delivered.

Percolating groundwater—all underground water other than underflow or underground streams.

Prescriptive right—a water right obtained by "open, notorious, continuous, and adverse use" (each of these terms is a legal term of art) for the prescriptive period, which in California is five years.

Public trust doctrine—enforceable doctrine by which certain natural resources are held in trust by the government for the use and enjoyment of the public.

Riparian right—a water right based on the ownership of land bordering a river or waterway.

Temporary change*—a short-term (one year or less) water transfer involving a change in point of diversion, place of use, or purpose of use.

Temporary urgency changes*—a short-term (one year or less) water transfer to meet an urgent need involving a change in point of diversion, place of use, or purpose of use.

Underflow—the water in soil, sand, and gravel in the streambed of a stream in its natural state, and essential to its existence.

Underground streams—groundwater that flows in a known and definite channel in a subterranean water course.

Water banking—storage of surface water in groundwater basins in times of surplus, for withdrawal during times of shortage. Can also involve the use of surface water in lieu of groundwater to enable groundwater recharge.

Water right—a legal entitlement authorizing water to be diverted from a specified source and put to beneficial, nonwasteful use. Water rights are property rights, but their holders do not own the water itself—they possess the right to use it.

Water right license*—an SWRCB license issued when a permitted water project is completed, the permit terms have been met, and water is put to beneficial use.

Water right permit*—an SWRCB permit required for a post-1914 appropriative water right.

Water transfer—marketing arrangement that can include the permanent sale or lease of a water right by the water right holder, or the sale or lease of a contractual right to a quantity of water.

Watermaster—a court-appointed person or agency given the authority to regulate the quantity of groundwater to be extracted from a designated basin.

Watershed—the area from which water drains to a single point.

* equals permits and approvals

CHAPTER 13

Water Resources

Introduction

California water law is a very complex field with a long history, and this chapter can do no more than provide a basic outline. For further general reading, the Water Education Foundation's "Layperson's Guides" provide an excellent, easy-to-understand introduction to California water law and policy.

A key to understanding California water law is to understand the various state, federal, and local water projects that have been constructed over the years to solve a fundamental distribution problem: most of the state's water is located in northern California, whereas most of the demand is located in the southern two-thirds of the state. This chapter reviews key agencies involved in California water resources management, California water resources background information, water rights law, water supply planning, and wild and scenic river systems.

Key Laws and Agencies

Federal Laws and Agencies

U.S. Bureau of Reclamation. The federal government has played a major role in developing California's water resources. The U.S. Bureau of Reclamation was created in 1902 to reclaim western lands, mainly for agricultural development. This agency owns and operates two large water supply projects serving California—the Central Valley Project (CVP) and the Colorado River facilities.

Central Valley Project. The CVP was authorized in 1937 and was largely completed in 1951. CVP features include the following (as described on the U.S. Bureau of Reclamation's Mid-Pacific Region web site):

The federal government has played a major role in developing California's water resources.

CVP = Central Valley Project

- Reaches from the Cascade Mountains near Redding in the north some 400 miles to the Tehachapi Mountains near Bakersfield in the south
- Is comprised of 20 dams and reservoirs, 11 power plants, and 500 miles of major canal as well as conduits, tunnels, and related facilities
- Manages some 9 million acre-feet of water
- Delivers about 7 million acre-feet annually for agriculture, urban, and wildlife use
- Provides about 5 million acre-feet for farms, enough to irrigate about 3 million acres or approximately one-third of California agricultural land
- Furnishes about 600,000 acre-feet for municipal and industrial use, enough to supply close to 1 million households with their water needs each year
- Generates 5.6 billion kilowatt hours of electricity annually to meet the needs of about 2 million people
- Dedicates 800,000 acre-feet per year to fish and wildlife and their habitat and 410,000 acre-feet to state and federal wildlife refuges and wetlands pursuant to the Central Valley Project Improvement Act (CVPIA)

CVPIA = Central Valley Project
Improvement Act

FERC = Federal Energy
Regulatory Commission

USACE = U.S. Army Corps of Engineers

USC = United States Code

In 1992, the CVPIA (34 USC 3401 *et seq.*) amended the project's purpose to place fish and wildlife mitigation and restoration on equal footing with water supply, and to place fish and wildlife enhancement on equal footing with power generation. The CVPIA also allows water transfers outside CVP service areas, requires water conservation criteria for water contractors, establishes specific fish restoration objectives, and establishes a land retirement program for drainage-impaired agricultural lands in the San Joaquin Valley.

Colorado River facilities. The Colorado River is a highly regulated river that passes through seven states. California, Arizona, and Nevada are the lower basin states. The U.S. Bureau of Reclamation built a series of major dams, reservoirs, and aqueducts on the lower Colorado River. Facilities serving California include:

- **Colorado River Aqueduct.** Operated by the Metropolitan Water District of Southern California
- **All-American Canal, Imperial Dam, and Yuma Project.** Operated by the Imperial Irrigation District
- **Coachella Project.** Operated by the Coachella Valley Water District
- **San Diego Project.** Operated by the San Diego County Water Authority

The FERC licensing process balances hydropower needs with other objectives such as water supply, recreation, and environmental protection.

Federal Energy Regulatory Commission. Pursuant to the Federal Power Act (16 USC 791 *et seq.*), the Federal Energy Regulatory Commission (FERC) issues licenses for hydroelectric projects using navigable waters or federal land. The FERC licensing process balances hydropower needs with other objectives such as water supply, recreation, and environmental protection. Many public and private multi-purpose water projects are subject to FERC licensing.

U.S. Army Corps of Engineers. The U.S. Army Corps of Engineers (USACE) is the primary federal flood control agency. *See* chapter 4. USACE constructs flood control projects and operates multi-purpose projects that provide water supply, such as New Melones Dam and Reservoir.

State Laws and Agencies

California Department of Water Resources. DWR operates and maintains the State Water Project (SWP), including the California Aqueduct. DWR also provides dam safety and flood control services, assists local water districts in water management and conservation activities, promotes recreational opportunities, and plans for future statewide water needs.

State Water Project. The SWP, authorized in 1960, is the nation's largest state-built water and power development and conveyance system. It includes facilities—pumping plants, power plants, reservoirs, canals, and pipelines—to capture, store, and convey water to 29 water agencies. Major facilities include Oroville Dam and Reservoir, with a storage capacity of 3.5 million acre-feet, and the North Bay, South Bay, and California Aqueducts, serving major urban and agricultural users.

California Bay–Delta Authority and CALFED. The Sacramento–San Joaquin River Delta is the heart of California's water supply system and has been the subject of much water resources management planning and litigation. In the 1990s, federal and state agencies collaborated in an effort known as CALFED to develop actions for ecosystem restoration, water use efficiency, and water supply reliability. CALFED objectives are to:

The Sacramento–San Joaquin River Delta is the heart of California's water supply system and has been the subject of much water resources management planning and litigation.

- Provide good water quality for all beneficial uses
- Improve and increase aquatic and terrestrial habitats and improve ecological functions in the Bay–Delta
- Reduce the mismatch between Bay–Delta water supplies and current and projected beneficial uses dependent on the system
- Reduce the risk to land use, water supply, infrastructure, and the ecosystem from catastrophic breaching of Delta levees

The CALFED program was adopted in 2000 (CALFED 2000) and is being implemented through a programmatic Record of Decision. In 2003, the California Bay–Delta Authority Act (Water Code 79400 *et seq.*) established the California Bay–Delta Authority to oversee the 25 state and federal agencies working cooperatively to implement the CALFED program. The Authority is responsible for providing accountability, ensuring balanced implementation, tracking and assessing program progress, using sound science, assuring public involvement and outreach, and coordinating and integrating related government programs.

State Water Resources Control Board. The mission of the State Water Resources Control Board's (SWRCB's) Division of Water Rights is to establish and maintain a stable system of water rights in California to best develop, conserve, and utilize in the public interest the water resources of the state, while protecting vested rights,

CALFED = Consortium of federal and state agencies overseeing Bay–Delta water management, superseded by the Bay–Delta Authority

DWR = Department of Water Resources

SWP = State Water Project

SWRCB = State Water Resources Control Board

The Water Commission Act of 1914 created the agency that later evolved into the SWRCB, and granted it the authority to administer permits and licenses for California's surface water.

water quality, and the environment. The SWRCB's major water rights responsibility is issuance of permits and licenses for water appropriation. *See* below.

The Water Commission Act of 1914 (Statutes of 1913, Ch. 586) created the agency that later evolved into the SWRCB, and granted it the authority to administer permits and licenses for California's surface water. The Act was the predecessor to today's Water Code provisions (Water Code 1200 *et seq.*) governing appropriation.

In addition to issuing permits and licenses, the SWRCB conducts statutory adjudications; statutory adjudication is a process by which the comprehensive determination of all water rights in a stream system is made. Also, the SWRCB can act as referee or fact-finder in court cases involving water rights.

Colorado River Board of California. This agency's mission is to protect California's rights and interests in the resources provided by the Colorado River and to represent California in discussions and negotiations regarding the Colorado River and its management.

Regional and Local Laws and Agencies

California has thousands of regional and local water agencies with varying responsibilities for the development, contracting of wholesaling, or retailing of water supplies.

California has thousands of regional and local water agencies (including city water departments and various types of special districts) with varying responsibilities for the development, contracting of wholesaling, or retailing of water supplies. Regional and local agencies may be formed through either a general district or a special district act. See Department of Water Resources (1994) for a general comparison of water district acts. Several regional or local water agencies have developed their own large water supply projects, including the City of San Francisco (Hetch Hetchy project), the East Bay Municipal Utility District (Mokelumne River Aqueduct System), the City of Los Angeles (Owens Valley Project), and the Imperial Irrigation District (Colorado River projects).

Background Information on California Water Resources

History

California's water resources management history is long and complex. Table 13-1 presents a summary of important historic water events in California. California's water history can roughly be divided into five eras (Johnson and Loux 2004):

- The early years (1769–1900). Includes local development of water supplies and the Gold Rush
- First importation projects (1900–1930). Includes construction of Los Angeles Aqueduct from Owens Valley
- Era of great importation projects (1930–1970). Includes construction of the CVP, Colorado River project, and SWP

Table 13-1. Important Historic Water Events in California

1769	First permanent Spanish settlement Water rights established	1928	Worst California drought of 20th century begins; ending in 1934, it established benchmark for storage and transfer capacity of all major water projects
1848	Gold discovered on American River		
1848	California ceded from Mexico California republic established	1931	State Water Plan published
1850	California granted statehood; Office of Surveyor General established and charged with planning water projects	1931	County of Origin Law passed, giving counties right to reclaim water from water exporters if ever needed in county of origin; subsequent laws were enacted to give similar protection to "areas" and "watersheds" of origin
1860	Legislature authorizes formation of levee and reclamation districts		
1884	*Woodruff v. North Bloomfield* (18 F. 753) requires termination of hydraulic mining debris discharges into California rivers	1933	Central Valley Project (CVP) Act passed
		1940	Metropolitan Water District's Colorado River Aqueduct completed, with first deliveries in 1941
1888	*Lux v. Haggin* (69 Cal. 255) reaffirms legal pre-eminence of riparian rights	1944	Mexican-American Treaty guarantees Mexico 1.5 (maf/yr) of Colorado River water
1901	First California deliveries from the Colorado River made to Imperial Valley farmland		
		1945	State Water Resources Control Board (SWRCB) created
1902	Reclamation Act creates U.S. Bureau of Reclamation	1951	State authorizes Feather River Project Act (later to become the State Water Project)
1903	*Katz v. Walkinshaw* (141 Cal. 3d 116) establishes the doctrine of correlative rights for groundwater		
		1951	First deliveries from CVP's Shasta Dam to Central Valley
1905	First bond issue for city of Los Angeles' Owens Valley project (second bond issue for construction approved in 1907)	1957	California Water Plan published
		1959	Delta Protection Act enacted to solve issues of legal boundaries, salinity control, and water export
1905	Colorado River flooding diverts river into Imperial valley, forming Salton Sea		
1908	City of San Francisco filing for Hetch Hetchy project approved	1960	Voters ratify Burns-Porter Act, authorizing$1.75 million bond issue to assist statewide water development
1913	Los Angeles Aqueduct begins service		
1920	U.S. Geological Survey proposes statewide plan for water storage and conveyance	1963	*Arizona v. California* (373 U.S. 546) allocates 2.8 maf/yr of Colorado River water to Arizona
		1966	Federal government begins construction of New Melones Dam on Stanislaus River (completed in 1978)
1922	Colorado River Compact of 1922 appropriates 7.5 million acre-feet per year (maf/yr) to basin states		
		1968	Congress authorizes Central Arizona Project, to deliver 1.5 maf/yr of Colorado River water to Arizona
1923	Hetch Hetchy Valley flooded to produce San Francisco water supply		
1928	Congress passes Boulder Canyon Act, authorizing construction of Boulder (Hoover) Dam and other Colorado River facilities	1968	Congress passes Wild and Scenic River Act
		1972	California legislature enacts California Wild and Scenic Rivers Act
1928	Under Rivers and Harbors Act , federal government assumes most costs of Sacramento Valley Flood Control System	1973	First SWP deliveries to Southern California
		1978	SWRCB issues Water Rights Decision 1485 (D-1485), setting Delta water quality standards
1928	California Constitution amended to require that all water use be "reasonable and beneficial"		

Source: Adapted from *Layperson's Guide to California Water.* 2003. Water Education Foundation. Reprinted with permission

Table 13-1. Important Historic Water Events in California *continued*

1980	State-designated wild and scenic rivers placed under federal Wild and Scenic Rivers Act protection		1992	Congress approves landmark CVP Improvement Act, authorizing CVP water transfers and water use for fish and wildlife purposes
1982	Peripheral Canal (isolated Delta conveyance facility) proposition over-whelming defeated in statewide vote		1994	SWRCB amends Los Angeles' water rights licenses for Mono Lake
1982	Reclamation Reform Act raises from 160 to 960 acres the amount of land a farmer can own and still receive low-cost federal water		1995	SWRCB adopts new water quality plan for Delta and begins hearings on water rights
1983	*National Audubon Society v. Superior Court* (33 Cal. 3d 419) rules that public trust doctrine applies to Los Angeles' diversions from Mono Lake tributary streams		2000	CALFED Record of Decision signed by state and federal agencies, implementing 30-year plan to improve water quality, reliability, and Delta ecosystem
1983	Dead and deformed waterfowl discovered in Kesterson Reservoir, indicating problems of selenium-tainted agricultural drainage water in San Joaquin Valley		2001	Legislature enacts SB 601 and SB 221, requiring greater coordination between water supply and land use planning
1983	Legislature enacts first requirements for urban water suppliers to prepare Urban Water Management Plans		2002	Voters approve Proposition 50, authorizing $3.4 billion in bonds to water quality, reliability, and drinking water
1986	"Racanelli decision" (*United States v. State Water Resources Control Board,* 182 Cal. App. 3d 82) directs SWRCB to consider all beneficial uses of Delta water, including instream needs, when setting water quality standards		2002	Quantification Settlement Agreement signed, allocating California's 4.4 maf/yr of Colorado River water among California water agencies
1986	Coordinated Operation Agreement signed to coordinate CVP and SWP operations in Delta		2003	Interior Secretary orders California's allocation of Colorado River water limited to 4.4 maf/yr
1987	SWRCB's Bay-Delta Proceedings begin to revise D-1485 water quality standards		2003	Legislature enacts Salton Sea Restoration Act, requiring DWR to develop a plan for Salton Sea ecosystem restoration
1989	*California Trout v. SWRCB* (207 Cal. App. 3d 585) holds that fish are a public trust resource		2003	Environmental Groups and Department of Water Resources settle suit over 1995 Monterey Agreement, which restructured SWP water supply contracts
1989	MWD and Imperial Irrigation District (IID) agree that MWD will pay for IID water conservation projects and receive the conserved water		2005	DWR adopts California Water Plan Update
1991	Inyo County and City of Los Angeles agree to jointly manage Owens Valley water, ending 19 years of litigation		2006	Legislature and Governor launch development of Delta Vision, a strategy for managing the Sacramento-San Joaquin Delta as a sustainable ecosystem
1991	Legislature enacts first legislation authorizing local agencies to prepare groundwater management plans (further legislation was enacted in 1992 and 2002)		2006	Voters approve $4 billion in flood control bonds and $5.4 in multipurpose water supply and quality bonds

Source: Adapted from *Layperson's Guide to California Water.* 2003. Water Education Foundation. Reprinted with permission

- Environmental transition (1970–1990). Includes passage of major federal and state environmental laws, changing water projects and water use

- Towards collaboration and water management (1990–present). Initiation of regional collaborative water management programs such as CALFED

Major Water Facilities

Figure 13-1 shows the location of major federal, state, and local water project facilities in California.

Water Rights Law

Overview

Water use and supplies in California are controlled and managed under a complex system of common law principles, constitutional provisions, state and federal statutes, court decisions, and water contracts. The below summary of California water rights is derived largely from a description in Volume 4 of the 2005 California Water Plan. DWR 2005.

Water use and supplies in California are controlled and managed under a complex system of common law principles, constitutional provisions, state and federal statutes, court decisions, and water contracts.

General Principles

Principle of reasonable and beneficial use. Article X, Section 2 of the California Constitution requires that all uses of the state's water be reasonable and beneficial. This principle can limit water rights because it prohibits the waste, unreasonable use, unreasonable method of use, or unreasonable diversion of water. This requirement applies to all California water rights, including riparian rights, appropriative rights, and groundwater rights.

Article X, Section 2 of the California Constitution requires that all uses of the state's water be reasonable and beneficial.

Article X, Section 2 requires fact-specific balancing of uses. The meaning of reasonableness changes as conditions change, and the reasonableness of one use is relative to other uses. In determining whether a use is reasonable and beneficial, the following factors are important (*in re Waters of Long Valley Creek Stream System* (1979) 25 Cal. 3d 339, 354):

- Other beneficial uses to be made of the water

- Social, economic, cultural, environmental, and other benefits and costs associated with competing water uses

- Whether there is a "physical solution" available by which the needs of competing users can be met

- The technical, hydrologic, engineering, economic, and environmental feasibility of competing uses

Public trust doctrine. The public trust doctrine imposes responsibilities on state agencies, as trustees, to protect trust resources associated with California's waters, such as navigation, fisheries, recreation, and ecological preservation. *See* chapter 1 for a review of the origins and scope of the public trust doctrine. The importance of the public trust doctrine in guiding state water planning and allocation

LADWP = Los Angeles Department of Water and Power

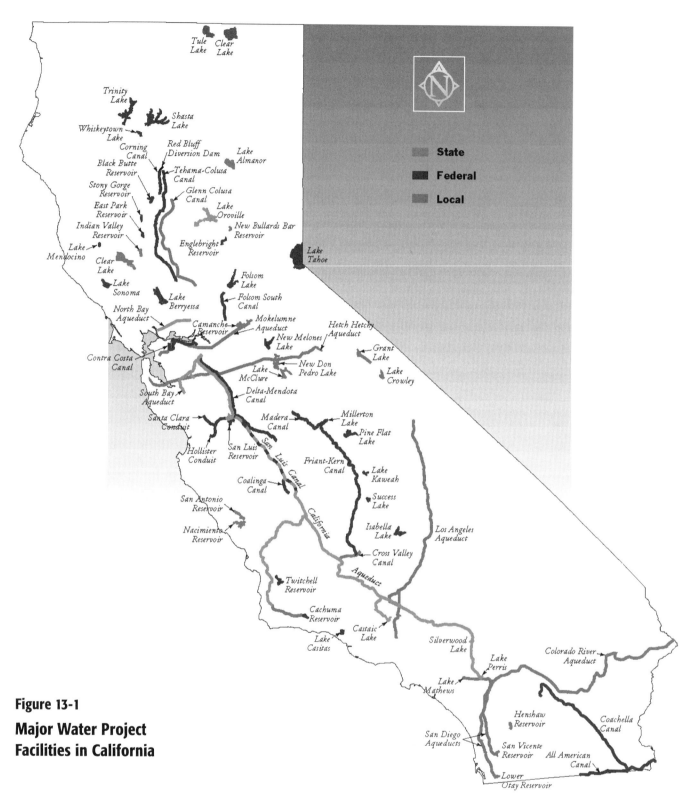

State

Federal

Local

Tule Lake

Clear Lake

Trinity Lake

Shasta Lake

Whiskeytown Lake

Corning Canal

Red Bluff Diversion Dam

Lake Almanor

Black Butte Reservoir

Tehama-Colusa Canal

Stony Gorge Reservoir

Glenn Colusa Canal

Lake Oroville

East Park Reservoir

Indian Valley Reservoir

New Bullards Bar Reservoir

Lake Mendocino

Clear Lake

Englebright Reservoir

Lake Sonoma

Lake Berryessa

Folsom Lake

Folsom South Canal

North Bay Aqueduct

Mokelumne Aqueduct

Camanche Reservoir

Hetch Hetchy Aqueduct

Lake Tahoe

Contra Costa Canal

New Melones Lake

Grant Lake

New Don Pedro Lake

Lake McClure

Lake Crowley

South Bay Aqueduct

Delta-Mendota Canal

Santa Clara Conduit

Madera Canal

Millerton Lake

Hollister Conduit

San Luis Reservoir

Pine Flat Lake

Coalinga Canal

Friant-Kern Canal

Lake Kaweah

San Antonio Reservoir

Success Lake

Nacimiento Reservoir

Isabella Lake

Los Angeles Aqueduct

Cross Valley Canal

Twitchell Reservoir

Cachuma Reservoir

Castaic Lake

Silverwood Lake

Colorado River Aqueduct

Lake Casitas

Lake Perris

Coachella Canal

Lake Mathews

Henshaw Reservoir

San Diego Aqueducts

San Vicente Reservoir

All American Canal

Lower Otay Reservoir

Figure 13-1

Major Water Project Facilities in California

Source: Littleworth and Garner. 2007. California Water II. Solano Press. Reprinted with permission

was affirmed in the landmark case *National Audubon Society v. Superior Court of Alpine County* (1983) 33 Cal. 3d. 419 (*see* sidebar).

The public trust doctrine and water rights law developed independently and, in some ways, are inconsistent. A water right is an estate in real property; water rights holders need to rely on certainty of water rights to make investments and to be economically productive.

To resolve this inherent conflict, the Supreme Court in *National Audubon* announced the principle of accommodation, under which the public trust and private ownership are to be balanced, and the public trust protected where "feasible." Although the Supreme Court did not elaborate on the meaning of feasibility, the concept is generally thought to encompass environmental, economic, legal, technical, and social concerns.

Surface Water Rights

California has a dual system of surface water rights, recognizing both riparian and appropriative rights. Prescriptive rights are a third type of surface water right and are described later in this chapter.

Riparian rights. A riparian right entitles landowners to use a share of the water flowing past their property. Unlike an appropriative right, a riparian right is not quantified. Rather, it is a "correlative right" to use a portion of the natural flow of water in common with other riparian users.

Riparian rights do not require government approval, but they apply only to the water that would naturally flow in the stream. Riparian rights do not entitle a water user to divert water to storage in a reservoir for use in the dry season or to use water on land outside of the watershed. Riparian rights remain with the property when it changes hands, although parcels severed from the adjacent water source generally lose their right to the water.

When riparian land is divided and sold, a parcel that is no longer contiguous to the river may or may not lose its riparian rights. The general rule is that courts examine the intent of the parties under all of the circumstances; one factor may be the nature and purpose of the conveyance. For example, conveyance of an easement or right-of-way typically would not result in a severance of riparian rights.

Appropriative rights. An appropriative water right has certain fundamental characteristics: amount of water claimed, priority of the right, point of diversion, place of use, purpose of use, and season of diversion. Water right priority has long been the central principle in California water law; the more senior right holders take water before junior right holders in times of shortage.

As noted above, a riparian right can be used only on the riparian parcel, generally on the parcel adjacent to the river. The appropriative system

Public Trust Doctrine Limits Water Rights

The public trust doctrine has its origins in ancient Roman law and was introduced to California through federal and state judicial decisions, as well as through the influential writings of Professor Joseph Sax. Sax 1970 (*see* chapter 1). A series of judicial decisions prior to *National Audubon* placed limits on the government's ability to dispose of trust resources, but the issue of whether the public trust doctrine applied to water rights was unresolved.

In *National Audubon Society v. Superior Court of Alpine County* (1983) 33 Cal. 3d 419, the California Supreme Court found that the public trust doctrine applied to the tributary streams of Mono Lake. The court prohibited the Los Angeles Department of Water and Power (LADWP) from exercising its vested right to divert these streams if public trust values would be harmed. Past LADWP diversions had decreased the level of Mono Lake, causing harm to a large breeding colony of California Gulls.

The court recognized that the state may have to approve water appropriations despite foreseeable harm to public trust use. However, the court required the state as a trustee to consider the effect of water appropriations on the public trust, and to avoid or minimize harm to public trust interests if feasible. Further, the court held that even after an appropriation has been approved, the state may reconsider the allocation decision if it failed to adequately weigh and consider public trust uses. ▪

developed to allow the user to convey water for use on non-riparian parcels. Under the "first in time, first in right" principle, the first appropriator had the most senior priority, regardless of whether subsequent users were upstream or downstream of the first appropriator. Subsequent appropriators "lined up" in priority behind the first appropriator based on the same principle. In times of shortage, the most recent (junior) right holder must be the first to discontinue use of water.

The doctrine of progressive development allows a water user to claim an amount greater than could immediately be put to use, to allow for the orderly construction of facilities and growth. The doctrine of progressive development is balanced by the "use it or lose it" doctrine, under which water rights may be forfeited through non-use. The courts or SWRCB may declare a water right forfeited after five years of non-use, assuming that water was available. Water Code 1240 *et seq*.

California recognizes two categories of appropriative surface water rights—those acquired prior to 1914, and those acquired after 1914, the effective date of the Water Commission Act.

Pre-1914 appropriative rights. Before 1872, an appropriative water right could be acquired simply by posting notice and putting the water to beneficial use. In 1872, a provision was added to the Civil Code to require appropriators to record notice with the county clerk. Pre-1914 water rights are subject to the jurisdiction of the courts, but generally not to the jurisdiction of the SWRCB. The SWRCB may, however, exercise jurisdiction over pre-1914 rights if necessary to decide an issue that is within its jurisdiction, to enforce the prohibition against waste and unreasonable use in Article X, Section 2, or to enforce the public trust doctrine.

Also, water users with pre-1914 appropriative rights, as well as riparian rights, are required to file a Statement of Water Diversion and Use with the SWRCB. Water Code 5100 *et seq*. The purpose of filing these statements is to make a public record of all surface diversions not already on file with or known to the SWRCB. Failure to file the statements does not result in penalties, but willful misstatements are subject to misdemeanor prosecution. Water Code 5107, 5108.

Valid pre-1914 rights are senior to post-1914 rights. Riparian rights are generally senior to pre-1914 rights, unless the date of appropriation occurred prior to the date that the riparian owner acquired the patent for the land (for example, *see United States v. State Water Resources Control Board* (1986) 182 Cal. App. 3d 82).

Post-1914 appropriative rights and the State Water Resources Control Board water rights process. The Water Commission Act of 1913 established the current water rights permitting and licensing process, and created the agency that later evolved into the SWRCB. After 1914, only the SWRCB had the authority to issue new appropriative rights for surface water. Water Code 174 *et seq*.

SWRCB water right permits establish the amounts, conditions, and construction timetables for a proposed project. Only unappropriated waters are

The doctrine of progressive development allows a water user to claim an amount greater than could immediately be put to use, to allow for the orderly construction of facilities and growth.

Before 1872, an appropriative water right could be acquired simply by posting notice and putting the water to beneficial use.

CCR = California Code of Regulations

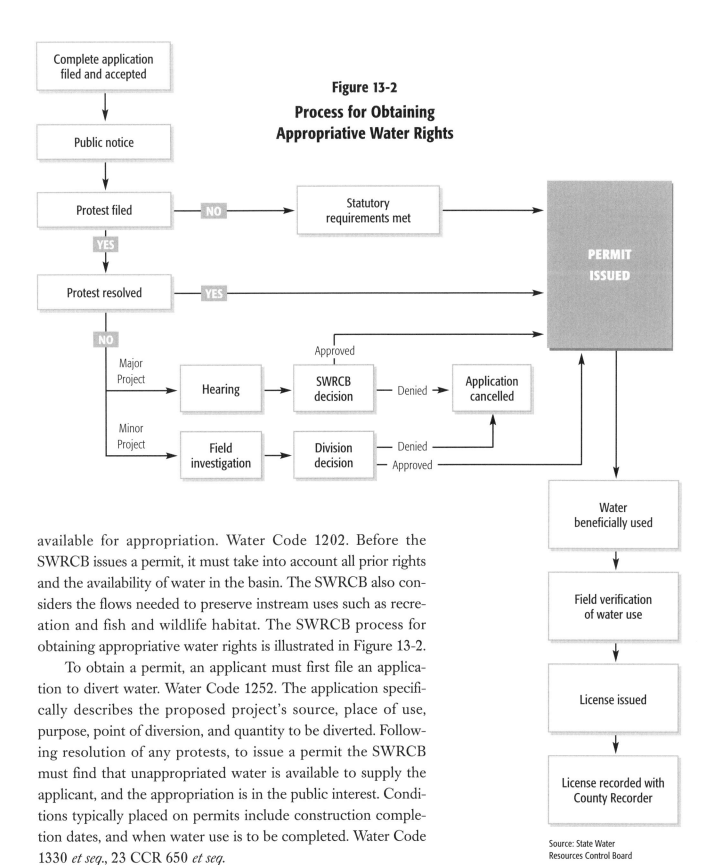

Figure 13-2
Process for Obtaining Appropriative Water Rights

Source: State Water Resources Control Board

available for appropriation. Water Code 1202. Before the SWRCB issues a permit, it must take into account all prior rights and the availability of water in the basin. The SWRCB also considers the flows needed to preserve instream uses such as recreation and fish and wildlife habitat. The SWRCB process for obtaining appropriative water rights is illustrated in Figure 13-2.

To obtain a permit, an applicant must first file an application to divert water. Water Code 1252. The application specifically describes the proposed project's source, place of use, purpose, point of diversion, and quantity to be diverted. Following resolution of any protests, to issue a permit the SWRCB must find that unappropriated water is available to supply the applicant, and the appropriation is in the public interest. Conditions typically placed on permits include construction completion dates, and when water use is to be completed. Water Code 1330 *et seq.*, 23 CCR 650 *et seq.*

When the water project is completed, the terms of the permit have been met, and water under the permit is put to beneficial use, the SWRCB issues a license to the appropriator. The license is the final confirmation of the water right and remains effective as long as its conditions are fulfilled and beneficial use continues. Water Code 1395 *et seq.*

The SWRCB has the authority to enforce the conditions of both permits and licenses, and can revoke them if conditions are not met. Other, less severe enforcement actions, such as cease-and-desist orders, can be taken to ensure compliance with permit terms. 23 CCR 820 *et seq.*

If the appropriation includes construction or enlargement of a dam or reservoir, the applicant also may need to obtain a Certificate of Approval from DWR's Division of Safety of Dams. Water Code 6000 *et seq.* The Division has jurisdiction over dams that are at least 25 feet high or have an impounding capacity of at least 50 acre-feet or more. Any dam shorter than 6 feet, regardless of storage capacity, or that has a storage capacity less than 15 acre-feet regardless of height, is not considered jurisdictional. In addition to approving new dams, the Division also inspects operating dams to ensure they are adequately maintained.

Changes in appropriative rights. The point of diversion, place of use, and purpose of use for a water right may be changed as long as the change does not injure other water right holders, whether junior or senior. For example, a water user with an appropriative right may decide to divert water from a different location on a stream, use water on other lands than originally designated, or change the purpose of use from agricultural to urban.

The method of change and enforcement of the no-injury rule differs between pre-1914 and post-1914 rights. For pre-1914 rights, a user may change any of these variables without notice to others or the state, and any challenges based on injury must be affirmatively filed and are generally heard only by the courts.

For post-1914 rights, a user must file a petition with the SWRCB before undertaking the change. The SWRCB will issue public notice of the request and will evaluate claims of injury to other right holders or public trust values. Typically, a water right holder cannot increase the amount of water claimed (but can progressively develop the amount claimed) or change the season of diversion. 23 CCR 791 *et seq.*

Loss or Severance of Surface Water Rights

Prescriptive rights. Historically, a prescriptive right could be obtained by "open, notorious, continuous, and adverse use" (each term is a legal term of art) for the prescriptive period, which in California is five years. Essentially, a prescriptive right is the right to prevent another water user from objecting to one's own water use. A right held by a public entity, including the federal or state government, may not be lost by prescription. Civil Code 1007. Prescriptive rights today are difficult to establish in the absence of an SWRCB adjudication or court proceeding.

The point of diversion, place of use, and purpose of use for a water right may be changed as long as the change does not injure other water right holders, whether junior or senior.

Historically, a prescriptive right could be obtained by "open, notorious, continuous, and adverse use" for the prescriptive period, which in California is five years.

Abandonment. Appropriative water rights can be permanently lost through abandonment. Abandonment requires both relinquishment of possession and the permanent intent to abandon the water. *See Wood v. Etiwanda Water Company* (1905) 146 Cal. 228.

Forfeiture. An appropriative water right may be lost when water is not put to a reasonable, beneficial use. For post-1914 rights, an appropriative right may be lost by five years of nonuse, after which the water can be appropriated by another user. An SWRCB hearing is required prior to forfeiture. Water Code 1240, 1241.

Groundwater Rights

Correlative rights. In contrast to surface water use, California has limited regulatory authority over groundwater use. In 1903, the California Supreme Court, in *Katz v. Walkinshaw* (1903) 141 Cal. 3d 116, established the doctrine of correlative rights for groundwater, under which every landowner overlying a groundwater basin has a right to extract and use groundwater correlative with the rights of other overlying landowners. An overlying right is analogous to a riparian right. Groundwater cannot be appropriated for use on nonoverlying lands unless it is surplus to the needs of overlying landowners.

In contrast to surface water use, California has limited regulatory authority over groundwater use.

Underground streams and underflow. Water under the ground is classified either as percolating groundwater, as a subterranean stream that flows in a known and definite channel in an underground water course (an underground stream), or as underflow. Percolating groundwater water is subject to groundwater law rather than surface water law. Percolating groundwater is defined as all underground water other than underground streams and underflow. Water Code 1200, 2500. In contrast, underground streams and underflow are subject to surface water law and potentially to SWRCB jurisdiction.

Water under the ground is classified either as percolating groundwater, as a subterranean stream that flows in a known and definite channel in an underground water course, or as underflow.

Proof of the existence of an underground stream is shown through the direction of the flow, confinement within the water course banks, and flow within a defined channel. The underflow of a surface stream consists of the water in the soil, sand, and gravel in the bed of a stream in its natural state and essential to its existence; the underflow may include lateral extensions of the stream on each side of the surface channel if its movement and location can be determined. Water Code 1200.

Groundwater regulation. Despite the importance of groundwater to California's water supplies, California does not have a statewide regulatory program for groundwater use. Groundwater management is generally the responsibility of local agencies; 13 groundwater management agencies have been directly authorized by state legislation. In addition, there are 19 adjudicated groundwater basins in which groundwater is regulated by a judicially appointed watermaster. Many local agencies voluntarily have prepared Assembly Bill 3030 groundwater

Despite the importance of groundwater to California's water supplies, California does not have a statewide regulatory program for groundwater use.

management plans pursuant to state legislation (Water Code 10750 *et seq.*); these are described below in the "Water Supply Planning" section.

Also, several counties have adopted groundwater management ordinances intended to sustain groundwater as a viable local resource and to regulate export of groundwater from the county. These ordinances typically require an export project proponent to show that the project will not cause groundwater depletion, groundwater degradation, or subsidence.

Federal and Tribal Reserved Rights

When the federal government reserved land from the public domain for uses such as Indian reservations, national parks, and national forests, it also reserved sufficient water to fulfill the uses of reservations at the time they were established.

When the federal government reserved land from the public domain for uses such as Indian reservations, national parks, and national forests, it also reserved sufficient water to fulfill the uses of reservations at the time they were established. Federal reserved rights are often senior in priority to water rights established under California law. In *United States v. New Mexico* (1978) 438 U.S. 690, the U.S. Supreme Court ruled that reserved rights apply only to the extent necessary to accomplish the primary purposes for which a land reservation was made, thereby limiting expansion of use.

Colorado River Water Rights: Law of the River

The Law of the River, consisting of numerous compacts, judicial decisions, contracts and other instruments, governs the management and operation of the Colorado River; *Arizona v. California* (1963) 373 U.S. 546 is a seminal case. Under the Law of the River:

MAFY = Million acre-feet per year

- The upper basin and lower basin states are entitled to 7.5 million acre feet per year (MAFY).
- Of this amount, California's apportionment is 4.4 MAFY.
- Mexico must receive 1.5 MAFY.

California's Colorado River water use historically exceeded the 4.4 MAFY apportionment. California's Colorado River water users entered into a Quantification Settlement Agreement in 2002, which established a program to limit water use to achieve the 4.4 MAFY apportionment.

Water Contracts

State Water Project. DWR has entered into long-term water supply contracts with 29 agricultural and urban water districts. Most SWP water goes to urban users. Table A amounts represent the maximum amount of SWP water a contractor can request each year. The combined maximum Table A amount for all 29 water districts is 4.17 MAFY, but SWP facilities to deliver the full amount have never been completed. Department of Water Resources 2002a.

Central Valley Project. The CVP supplies water to more than 250 water contractors under contracts with the U.S. Bureau of Reclamation. Most CVP water goes to agricultural uses. CVP contracts call for a maximum annual delivery of 9.3 MAFY. Contracts allocate both 4.8 MAFY of "project water" and 4.5 MAFY of "settlement water" (water covered in agreements with water rights holders whose diversions existed before the CVP was constructed). In 2005, the CVP delivered 7 MAFY to agricultural users and 600,000 acre-feet per year (AFY) to urban users. U.S. Bureau of Reclamation 2005.

The CVP supplies water to more than 250 water contractors under contracts with the U.S. Bureau of Reclamation. Most CVP water goes to agricultural uses.

AFY = Acre-feet per year

Racanelli decision. The SWRCB has jurisdiction over both water rights and water quality (*see* chapter 6), but the ability of the SWRCB to regulate operation of the CVP and SWP based on water quality objectives was unclear until the Racanelli decision. In *United States v. SWRCB* (1986) 182 Cal. App. 3d 82 (decided by Judge Racanelli), the court held that the SWRCB could impose water-quality based restrictions on both the CVP and the SWP, without regard to their water right priorities. The court ruled that the SWRCB has the power to determine the proper balance between water quality interests and the effects of water diversions in determining whether a water use is "reasonable."

Water Transfers

Water transfers are an increasingly common way to provide flexibility in water use. Usually, transfers are from agricultural to urban uses, and the transfers can substitute for additional surface water diversions by urban water agencies. The Quantification Settlement Agreement and CALFED (through an Environmental Water Account) both place heavy reliance on water transfers to achieve their program objectives.

Water transfers are an increasingly common way to provide flexibility in water use. Usually, transfers are from agricultural to urban uses, and the transfers can substitute for additional surface water diversions by urban water agencies.

For post-1914 water rights, the SWRCB is authorized to approve short-term and long-term water transfers of water or appropriative rights. Most water transfers have been short-term (one year or less). Short-term transfers may be either temporary urgency changes (Water Code 1435) or temporary changes (Water Code 1724 *et seq.*); temporary urgency changes have expedited processing procedures. For long-term transfers–lasting more than one year–the SWRCB must provide an opportunity for a hearing. To approve either a short-term or long-term water transfer, the SWRCB must find that the transfer will not injure any legal user of water and will not unreasonably affect fish, wildlife, or other instream beneficial uses.

Area of Origin Protections

The Legislature, through several statutes, has sought to protect the water rights of areas of origin, watersheds from which water projects obtain water for exporting outside the watershed, so that water will be available to these areas of origin when needed. Protected areas include:

- Certain specified areas of origin, *e.g.,* lands within the Sacramento and San Joaquin River systems, which may not be deprived of water by means of appropriations after 1985. Water Code 1215 *et seq.*

- Northern California counties in which water for the SWP and CVP originates, which may not be deprived of water by means of state-filed applications. Water Code 10505, 10505.5

- Watersheds of origin, which may not be deprived of water through operation of the SWP and CVP. Water Code 11460 *et seq.*

The area of origin laws have seldom been interpreted by the courts, and many uncertainties about the scope of these laws remain. The first meaningful appellate court discussion of these statutes can be found in *SWRCB Cases* (2006) 136 Cal. App.4th 674.

Remedies

A wide variety of remedies is available to enforce water rights. Administrative and statutory procedures are available, but final jurisdiction lies with the courts. *See* Littleworth and Garner, 2007. Remedies include injunctions, "physical solutions" (judicially-developed water allocations), and adjudication of water rights through judicial or statutory procedures.

The SWRCB has exclusive jurisdiction over the issuance of permits and licenses. Claims that the SWRCB has exceeded its authority or acted arbitrarily in denying or issuing a permit or license are subject to judicial review, but such review is rare.

Water Supply Planning

State Water Plan

DWR publishes the California Water Plan and updates its status every five years. The plan provides a statewide overview of water supplies, demands, and management strategies, and provides detailed assessments for each of the state's hydrologic regions. The latest version of the California Water Plan was released in 2005. Department of Water Resources 2005. It uses a scenario-based approach to evaluate water supply and demand in the year 2030, rather than a single set of projections, and provides a roadmap for meeting the state's water demands through the year 2030.

The plan emphasizes both sustainability and reliability of water supplies. To ensure sustainability, the plan calls for California water management to be based on three foundational actions:

The California Water Plan calls for water resources to be managed in ways that protect and restore the environment.

- Use water efficiently
- Protect water quality
- Manage water in ways that protect and restore the environment

To ensure reliability, the plan calls for two initiatives that incorporate these actions:

- Promote and practice integrated regional water management
- Maintain and improve statewide water management systems, the backbone of California water management.

Because development of new surface water supplies is difficult and time-consuming, the State Water Plan encourages use of other water supply management strategies. These strategies can include (*see* Johnson and Loux 2004, chapter 5):

- Demand management, including water conservation and leak detection
- Conjunctive use of surface water and groundwater
- Water purchases, transfers (*see* above discussion), and banking
- Desalination
- Offstream storage and expansion of existing reservoirs
- Use of reclaimed wastewater
- Watershed management for source protection

Urban Water Management Plans

The Urban Water Management Planning Act (Water Code 10610 *et seq.*) calls for large water purveyors (those serving 3,000 acre-feet per year or serving 300 customers) to prepare a UWMP that evaluates water supplies and demands for a 20-year period. UWMPs took on increased importance with the passage of SB 610 and SB 221 of 2001, which rely on these plans for local development project reviews (*see* below).

SB = Senate Bill
UWMP = Urban water management plan

UWMPs must be submitted to DWR for approval every five years. DWR recommends that UWMPs include the following:

- Planning process
- History of local growth and water services, and description of existing facilities
- Past, current, and projected water supply
- Water conservation program
- Water shortage contingency analysis
- Recycled water use

Water Conservation

Global climate change has focused attention on water conservation as a way to save energy, and thus reduce greenhouse gas emissions. Water-related energy use in 2005 used 19 percent of the state's electricity and 30 percent of its natural gas.

CEC 2005. Both the State Water Plan and UWMPs have policies encouraging water conservation. In order for urban water suppliers to be eligible for state water management grants and loans, water conservation measures included in UWMPS must be implemented. PRC 10631.5 *et seq.* Other state legislation also encourages water conservation. For example, in 2007 the Legislature passed bills requiring the following:

- The California Energy Commission (CEC) must set water efficiency standards for household appliances, since appliances that use less water also use less energy. PRC 25402

- CEC must also incorporate water conservation standards for water efficiency and conservation into existing energy efficiency building standards. Health and Safety Code 17921.10

- All toilets sold in California must be low-flush by 2014. Health and Safety Code 17921.3

SB 610 and SB 221

SB 610 of 2001 requires that CEQA documents incorporate water supply assessments for certain large development projects, e.g., residential projects exceeding 500 units.

Senate Bill 610 of 2001 (Water Code 10631, 10656, 10910, 10912, 10915, 10657) requires California Environmental Quality Act (CEQA) documents to incorporate water supply assessments (WSAs) for certain large development projects, *e.g.*, residential projects exceeding 500 units. WSAs are prepared by local water suppliers and can be based on information in the latest applicable UWMP. The WSA must determine whether sufficient water supplies will be available to serve the proposed project in normal, dry, and multiple dry years, after taking into account a 20-year projection of demands from existing and other planned water users.

Senate Bill 221 of 2001 (Gov. Code 66473) creates analogous but stricter requirements for local government approval of subdivision maps for subdivisions over 500 units. Water suppliers must prepare a water supply verification, verifying that a sufficient reliable water supply will be available to serve the proposed project in normal, dry, and multiple dry years, after taking into account a 20-year projection of demands from existing and other planned water users. A final subdivision map may not be approved unless a sufficient reliable water supply is available.

DWR has issued a useful guidebook for implementation of both SB 610 and SB 221. Department of Water Resources 2002b.

CEQA and Water Supply Planning

In the 1990s and 2000s, several CEQA cases considered the adequacy of water supply impact analysis in CEQA documents prepared for development and other water-using projects. For example, *see Santa Clarita Organization for Planning the Environment v. County of Los Angeles* (2003) 106 Cal. App. 4th 715. Courts have insisted that water supply impact analyses for development projects should not rely on "paper water" (*e.g.*, SWP entitlements that may never be delivered).

These cases, mostly decided before implementation of SB 610 and SB 221, have encouraged concurrent land use and water supply planning. SB 610 water supply assessments must now be included in CEQA documents for projects subject to SB 610.

Groundwater Management Plans

Assembly Bill 3030 of 1992 (Water Code 10750 *et seq.*) provides authority for local water agencies to prepare groundwater management plans for groundwater basins not subject to existing management. To be eligible for certain groundwater management funds administered by DWR, groundwater management plans must include the following components (DWR 2003):

- Public involvement in the plan
- Basin management objectives
- Monitoring programs for tracking basin conditions
- Map showing basin and local agency boundaries
- Management of groundwater levels and quality, and of subsidence
- Plan for involving other agencies whose service areas overlie the basin

Wild and Scenic Rivers

Federal Wild and Scenic Rivers Act

This Act (16 USC 1271 *et seq.*) designates, and provides for further designations of, rivers that possess extraordinary scenic, historical, wildlife, geological, or other similar values. It requires designated rivers to be maintained in free-flowing

CEQA Cases on Water Supply Impacts

Stanislaus Natural Heritage v. Stanislaus County (1996) 48 Cal. App. 4th 182. Programmatic Environmental Impact Report prepared for large master-planned community was inadequate because it failed to evaluate water supply impacts, and deferred such evaluation to second-tier EIRs.

County of Amador v. El Dorado County Water Agency (1999) 76 Cal. App. 4th 931. EIR for water supply project was inadequate because it was predicated on population projections in a draft general plan that had not been adopted.

Planning and Conservation League v. Department of Water Resources (2000) 83 Cal. App. 4th 89. Programmatic EIR for an amendment to state water contracts (the Monterey Agreement) was inadequate in part because it failed to properly evaluate a realistic no-project alternative based on realistic SWP deliveries.

Save Our Peninsula Committee v. Monterey County Board of Supervisors (2001) 87 Cal. App. 4th 99. EIR for a residential project was inadequate because the lead agency used a wrong environmental baseline for evaluation of water supply impacts and related mitigation measures.

Napa Citizens for Honest Government v. Napa County Board of Supervisors (2001) 91 Cal. App. 4th 342. EIR for specific plan was inadequate because it failed to describe secondary sources of water supply in the event the primary designated sources were not available.

Friends of the Santa Clara River v. Castaic Lake Water Agency (2002) 95 Cal. App. 4th 1373. EIR prepared for water transfer was inadequate because it tiered from a program EIR that had been de-certified in *Planning and Conservation League v. Department of Water Resources*.

Santa Clarita Organization for Planning and the Environment v. County of Los Angeles (2003) 106 Cal. App. 4th 715. EIR for residential development was inadequate because it did not present an accurate analysis of available water supply to serve the project, relying on SWP entitlements ("paper water") versus realistic SWP deliveries.

California Oak Foundation v. City of Santa Clarita (2005) 133 Cal. App. 4th 1219. EIR for industrial development was inadequate because it tiered from EIRs found to be inadequate and because water supply analysis relied on SWP "paper water."

Vineyard Area Citizens for Responsible Growth v. City of Rancho Cordova (2007) 40 Cal. 4th 412. EIR for specific plan was inadequate because it failed to disclose specific long-term water supplies, and the impacts of developing those supplies.

Santa Clarita Organization for Planning the Environment v. County of Los Angeles (2007) 157 Cal. App. 4th 149. EIR for residential development (previously challenged in 2003 case) was adequate because water supply analysis showed that water supplies were reasonably certain.

In re Bay-Delta Programmatic Environmental Impact Report (2008) 08 CDOS 6822. Program EIR for CALFED Bay-Delta program was upheld. The EIR did not need to evaluate a reduced Delta exports alternative, and did not need to evaluate project-specific impacts of second-tier projects.

The Eel River is a federal- and state-designated wild and scenic river.

The Secretaries of Agriculture and the Interior are directed to carry out suitability studies and recommend to Congress possible additions to the wild and scenic rivers system.

CFR = Code of Federal Regulations

conditions and requires management plans for designated rivers. River segments are classified as "wild," "scenic," and "recreational," with different management objectives for each classification. In California, the federal system designates 18 river segments totaling more than 1,900 miles. Designated rivers are as follows:

- American River (Lower)
- American River, North Fork
- Big Sur River
- Eel River System
- Feather River, Middle Fork
- Kern River, North Fork
- Kern River, South Fork
- Kings River
- Kings River, South Fork
- Kings River, Middle Fork
- Klamath River System
- Merced River
- Merced River, South Fork
- Sespe Creek
- Sisquoc River
- Smith River System
- Trinity River System
- Tuolumne River

Federal agencies are prohibited from licensing or permitting hydroelectric dams or major diversions on designated rivers. In addition, federal agencies are prohibited from assisting any water resource projects that may directly affect designated rivers.

The Secretaries of Agriculture and the Interior are directed to carry out suitability studies and recommend to Congress possible additions to the wild and scenic rivers system. The Act establishes a river corridor averaging about one-quarter mile on each side of the river, and requires federal agencies to manage the public lands in the corridor to protect the river's free-flowing character and outstanding values. In addition, the managing federal agency for federally designated rivers is required to develop and implement a management plan that will ensure the river's protection. 36 CFR 251, 297; 43 CFR 8350.

California Wild and Scenic Rivers Act

This Act (PRC 5093.50 *et seq.*) was passed in 1972 to preserve designated rivers possessing extraordinary scenic, recreation, fishery, or wildlife values. Patterned after the federal act, the state act declares that certain rivers that possess these extraordinary values must be preserved in their free-flowing state, together with their immediate environments. The Act prohibits impoundments and diversions on designated rivers (with a few exceptions), but these prohibitions are not applicable to federal agencies. State-designated rivers are as follows:

- American River
- Carson River
- Eel River
- Klamath River
- McCloud River
- Salmon River
- Scott River
- Smith River
- Trinity River
- Van Duzen River
- West Walker River

The state act is more limited than the federal act in that it does not establish a one-quarter mile corridor or require management plans for state-designated rivers. The state act provides protection only to the first line of permanent riparian vegetation.

The state act is more limited than the federal act in that it does not establish a one-quarter mile corridor or require management plans for state-designated rivers.

The state act requires state and local agencies to exercise their existing powers consistent with the Act's policies and provisions. PRC 5093.61. The Act does not, however, change the land use regulatory powers or authorities of state and local agencies granted by other laws.

For more information...

Publications

CALFED Bay–Delta Program.
2000. Program Summary

Department of Water Resources.
1994. General Comparison of
Water District Acts, Bulletin 155-94

Department of Water Resources.
2002a. The State Water Project
Delivery Reliability Report

Department of Water Resources.
2002b. Guidebook for Implementation of Senate Bill 610
and Senate Bill 221 of 2001

Department of Water Resources.
2003. California's Groundwater.
Bulletin 118

Department of Water Resources.
2005. California Water Plan
Update 2005

Johnson, K. and J. Loux. 2004.
Water and Land Use: Planning
Wisely for California's Future.
Solano Press. Point Arena, Calif.

Littleworth, A. and E. Garner.
2007. California Water II. Solano
Press. Point Arena, Calif.

Sax, J. 1970. The Public Trust Doctrine
in Natural Resource Law: Effective
Judicial Intervention. Volume 68,
Michigan Law Review, 471

Slater, S. 1995. California Water
Law and Policy. Matthew
Bender. San Francisco, Calif.

U.S. Bureau of Reclamation.
2005. Reclamation: Managing
Water in the West, Mid-Pacific
Region Overview

Water Education Foundation.
2000. Layperson's Guide
to California Water

Web sites

California Bay–Delta Authority
http://calwater.ca.gov

California Department of Water
Resources
www.dwr.water.ca.gov

California Department of Water
Resources, Division of Dam Safety
http://damsafety.water.ca.gov

National Wild and
Scenic Rivers System
www.nps.gov/rivers/wildriverslist.html

Quantification
Settlement Agreement
www.crss.water.ca.gov/crqsa/index.cfm

State Water Resources Control
Board, Division of Water Rights
www.waterrights.ca.gov

Water Education Foundation
www.water-ed.org

U.S. Bureau of Reclamation,
Lower Colorado Region
www.usbr.gov/lc

U.S. Bureau of Reclamation,
Mid-Pacific Region
www.usbr.gov/mp

Fish and Wildlife

This chapter reviews –

- Key laws and agencies involved in fish and wildlife protection
- Federal ESA
- State CESA
- Natural Community Conservation Planning Act

Related Solano Press titles–

Curtin's California Land Use and Planning Law
Cecily T. Talbert. 2008

Glossary

Anadromous fish—a fish species, such as salmon, that migrates from freshwater streams to the ocean and back to complete its cycle.

Biological assessment—a document prepared for Section 7 consultation to determine whether a proposed federal major construction activity is likely to adversely affect a listed species, proposed species, or designated critical habitat.

Biological diversity—the variety of life and its processes, including the variety of living organisms, the genetic differences among them, and the communities and ecosystems in which they occur.

Biological opinion*—a document stating the opinion of USFWS or NOAA Fisheries on whether a federal action is likely to jeopardize the continued existence of a listed species or result in destruction or adverse modification of its critical habitat.

California Natural Diversity Database—an inventory of the reported locations of listed species and species of special concern.

Candidate species—a plant or animal species for which enough information is known concerning biological vulnerability and threats to support a proposal to list as endangered or threatened.

Conserve, conserving, and conservation—the use of methods and procedures necessary to bring any listed species to the point at which measures under the ESA are no longer necessary.

Critical habitat—a formally designated specific geographic area that contains those physical or biological features essential to the conservation of a listed species and that may require special management or protection.

Ecosystem—a dynamic and interrelated complex of plant and animal communities, and their associated environment.

Endangered species—a species in danger of extinction throughout all or a significant portion of its range.

Formal consultation—the required process under ESA Section 7 when a proposed federal action is likely to adversely affect a listed species or critical habitat, used to determine in a biological opinion whether the proposed action is likely to jeopardize the continued existence of the species or adversely modify critical habitat.

Fully protected species—a species for which DFG may not issue a take permit, except for scientific purposes.

Habitat—the place or environment where a plant or animal lives naturally.

Habitat conservation plan*—a plan prepared under ESA Section 10(a) that outlines ways of maintaining, enhancing, and protecting a habitat type needed to protect a listed species.

Harass—to intentionally or negligently create the likelihood of injury to wildlife by annoying it to such an extent as to significantly disrupt normal behavior patterns such as breeding, feeding, or sheltering.

Harm—to perform an act that kills or injures wildlife; may include significant habitat modification or degradation when it kills or injures wildlife by significantly impairing essential behavioral patterns such as nesting or reproduction.

Incidental take—take of a listed species that results from, but is not the purpose of, otherwise lawful activity.

Incidental take permit*—a permit issued by USFWS or NOAA Fisheries under the federal ESA Section 10(a), or DFG under CESA Section 2081, authorizing take of a listed species.

Informal consultation—a process under ESA Section 7 prior to or in lieu of formal consultation that includes all interactions between USFWS or NOAA Fisheries and a federal agency or its designated non-federal representative such as an applicant.

Jeopardize—appreciably reducing the likelihood of both the survival and recovery of a listed species in the wild by reducing the reproduction, numbers, or distribution of the species.

Listing—the formal process by which USFWS or NOAA Fisheries under the federal ESA, or the Fish and Game Commission under CESA, adds species to the list of endangered and threatened wildlife and plants.

Migratory birds—birds that migrate across state and national borders.

Natural community conservation plan*—a regional plan prepared under the NCCPA that provides measures necessary to conserve and manage natural biological diversity within the plan area while allowing compatible and appropriate economic development, growth, and other human uses.

No surprises rule—under the federal ESA and the NCCPA, assurances given to incidental take permittees that unforeseen circumstances will not result in additional conservation or funding requirements.

Range—the geographic area a species is known or believed to occupy.

Reasonable and prudent alternative–
a recommended alternative action identified in a biological opinion that is feasible, can be implemented consistent with the purpose of the action, is consistent with the federal agency's legal authority and jurisdiction, and would avoid jeopardy.

Reasonable and prudent measure–
an action necessary to minimize the impacts of incidental take of a listed species that is anticipated to result from implementing a project with a non-jeopardy opinion.

Recovery–the process by which decline of a listed species is stopped or reversed, or threats to its survival neutralized, so that its long-term survival in the wild can be ensured.

Recovery plan–a document serving as the guide for activities to recover or conserve a listed species.

Section 4(d) rule–a regulation that establishes prohibitions on take necessary and advisable to provide for conservation of a threatened species.

Section 7 consultation*–the process by which a federal agency consults with USFWS or NOAA Fisheries under the federal ESA to determine whether any activity authorized, funded, or carried out by the agency may affect a listed species or designated critical habitat.

Section 2081 incidental take permit*–
DFG permit authorizing take of state-listed species incidental to otherwise lawful development projects.

Species of special concern–animals not listed under the federal ESA or CESA, but that nonetheless are declining at a rate that could result in listing, or that historically occurred in low numbers and known threats to their persistence currently exist.

Take–under the federal ESA, to harass, harm, pursue, hunt, shoot, wound, kill, trap, capture, or collect a listed species, or to attempt such conduct; under CESA, to hunt, pursue, catch, capture, or kill a listed species, or to attempt such conduct.

Threatened species–a species likely to become endangered within the foreseeable future throughout all or a significant part of its range.

* equals permits and approvals

CHAPTER 14

Fish and Wildlife

Introduction

This chapter covers federal and state regulation of biological resources, focused on protection of endangered, threatened, and other sensitive species. The federal Endangered Species Act (ESA) is the main regulatory program for protecting these species, but the California Endangered Species Act (CESA) and Natural Communities Conservation Planning Act (NCCPA) also can play major roles.

CESA	= California Endangered Species Act
ESA	= Endangered Species Act
NCCPA	= Natural Community Conservation Planning Act
NOAA	= National Oceanographic and Atmospheric Administration
USC	= United States Code
USFWS	= U.S. Fish and Wildlife Service

Key Laws and Agencies

Federal Laws and Agencies

Endangered Species Act. The federal ESA (16 USC 1531 *et seq.*), reviewed in detail later in this chapter, is considered one of the most comprehensive wildlife conservation laws in the world. Enacted in 1973, the Act is administered by the U.S. Fish and Wildlife Service (USFWS) and the National Oceanographic and Atmospheric Administration (NOAA) Fisheries Service (formerly National Marine Fisheries Service). (In this chapter, when USFWS's ESA responsibilities are mentioned, they are meant to also include NOAA Fisheries' parallel responsibilities for marine species.)

The purpose of the ESA is to conserve and recover endangered and threatened species, and the ecosystems upon which they depend. The ESA requires all federal agencies to protect listed species and preserve their habitats. The law:

The purpose of the ESA is to conserve and recover endangered and threatened species, and the ecosystems upon which they depend.

- Sets forth a process for listing species as endangered or threatened, for designating critical habitat for listed species, and for preparing recovery plans for listed species (Section 4)

- Requires federal agencies to consult with USFWS or NOAA Fisheries to ensure their actions do not jeopardize listed species (Section 7)
- Prohibits the "take" of a listed species (Section 9)
- Allows non-federal entities that prepare a habitat conservation plan (HCP) to obtain an incidental take permit (ITP) allowing development projects to proceed (Section 10)
- Sets forth enforcement and penalty provisions (Section 11)

Regulations for implementing the ESA are found at 50 CFR 17.

Other federal laws protecting fish and wildlife. Other federal laws protecting fish and wildlife include:

- **Fish and Wildlife Coordination Act.** Requires federal agencies, when approving or implementing an action to modify a water body, to consult with USFWS and the relevant state wildlife agency. 16 USC 661 *et seq.*
- **Convention on International Trade on Endangered Species.** Regulates trade in endangered species and is implemented via the ESA. Regulations are found at 50 CFR 23.
- **Marine Mammal Protection Act.** Lists protected marine mammals and establishes a moratorium on taking of listed marine mammals, with some exceptions. 16 USC 1361 *et seq.* Administered by USFWS and NOAA Fisheries. Permits may be issued to authorize take, with the permit process differing depending on whether the species also is listed under the ESA. Regulations are found at 50 CFR 18.
- **Migratory Bird Treaty Act.** Prohibits the taking, killing, or possessing of migratory birds (birds that migrate across state and national borders) (16 USC 703 *et seq.*). Regulations are found at 50 CFR 21.
- **Bald Eagle and Golden Eagle Protection Act.** Prohibits the taking or possession of and commerce in bald and golden eagles, with a few exceptions. 16 USC 668. Regulations are found at 50 CFR 22.
- **Magnuson–Stevens Fishery Conservation and Management Act.** Regulates ocean fishing and allows NOAA Fisheries to designate essential fish habitat (EFH) within coastal rivers and streams. 16 USC 1801 *et seq.* The Act creates eight regional fishery management councils that work in partnership with NOAA Fisheries to manage marine fish stocks. Federal agencies must consult with NOAA Fisheries on activities that may affect EFH. Regulations are found at 50 CFR 600.
- **Lacey Act.** Makes it a federal crime to import, export, transport, sell, receive, acquire, possess, or purchase any fish, wildlife, or plant taken, possessed, transported, or sold in violation of any federal, state, foreign, or Indian tribal law, treaty, or regulation. 16 USC 1855. Regulations are found at 50 CFR 16.

U.S. Fish and Wildlife Service. Under the ESA, USFWS has jurisdiction and permitting authority over terrestrial wildlife, freshwater fish, and some marine species. USFWS also has responsibility for implementing many of the other laws listed above, as well as operating a system of national wildlife refuges. USFWS general permit procedures, covering implementation of many of these laws, are found at 50 CFR 13.

National Oceanographic and Atmospheric Administration Fisheries. Under the ESA, NOAA Fisheries has jurisdiction and permitting authority over marine species, including anadromous fish species such as salmon and steelhead. NOAA Fisheries also has responsibility for implementing the Marine Mammal Protection Act and the Magnuson–Stevens Fishery Conservation and Management Act.

Under the ESA, NOAA Fisheries has jurisdiction and permitting authority over marine species, including anadromous fish species such as salmon and steelhead.

State Laws and Agencies

California Endangered Species Act. CESA (Fish and Game Code 2050 *et seq.*), reviewed in detail later in this chapter, is similar but less comprehensive than the federal ESA. Administered by the Department of Fish and Game (DFG), CESA establishes a state policy to conserve, protect, enhance, and restore endangered and threatened species and their habitat. Like the federal ESA, CESA establishes a state listing process, prohibits unauthorized "take," and provides for incidental take permits.

CEQA = California Environmental
       Quality Act
DFG = Department of Fish and Game
NCCP = Natural community
       conservation plan

CESA emphasizes early consultation to avoid potential impacts to endangered and threatened species, and to develop appropriate mitigation planning to offset impacts to listed species populations and their essential habitats. State and local agencies consult with DFG through the California Environmental Quality Act (CEQA) process, prior to taking actions that may affect listed species; there is no separate consultation process analogous to the federal ESA's Section 7 consultation process.

Natural Community Conservation Planning Act. The NCCPA (Fish and Game Code 2800 *et seq.*), reviewed in detail later in this chapter, was re-enacted in 2003 and replaced an earlier version of the law originally enacted in 1991. The NCCPA's goal is to encourage voluntary, broad-based planning to provide effective wildlife protection and allow appropriate development through preparation of natural community conservation plans (NCCPs). The focus of the initial NCCP effort in the 1990s was to protect the coastal sage scrub habitat of Southern California, home to the California gnatcatcher and approximately 100 other potentially threatened or endangered species. Many NCCPs have now been prepared or are underway statewide.

The NCCPA's goal is to encourage voluntary, broad-based planning to provide effective wildlife protection and allow appropriate development through preparation of NCCPs.

Fully protected species. State law (Fish and Game Code 3511, 4700, 5050, and 5515) designates 37 species of fish and wildlife as "fully protected." DFG may not issue permits authorizing take of fully protected species, except for scientific purposes. Thus project proponents must assure their project will not result in take of a fully protected species. Similarly, DFG is unable to authorize the incidental take of five types of birds listed in Fish and Game Code 3505, or the incidental take of unlisted raptors or the destruction of their nests or eggs. Fish and Game Code 3503.5.

Other state and local laws protecting fish, wildlife, and plants. Other state and local laws protecting fish, wildlife, and plants include the following:

- **Native Plant Protection Act.** Establishes a listing process and protections for "rare" or "endangered" plants. Fish and Game Code 1900 *et seq.* When CESA was enacted in 1984, the list of endangered plants from the Native Plant Protection Act was included in CESA's list of endangered plants. Rare plants receive no CESA protection. Plants are no longer proposed for listing under the Native Plant Protection Act, and the Act today has little regulatory effect compared to CESA.

- **California Desert Native Plants Act.** Regulates the harvesting of certain desert plants in specified counties. Food and Agriculture Code 80001 *et seq.* DFG enforces the Act, but county agricultural commissioners and sheriffs are authorized to issue harvesting permits.

- **Marine Life Protection Act.** Establishes a network of marine protected areas to protect marine life and habitats, marine ecosystems, and marine natural heritage. Fish and Game Code 2850 *et seq.* Marine protected areas include marine reserves, marine parks, and marine conservation areas.

- **Local programs (cities and counties).** Establish policies for protection of fish, wildlife, and plants through the general plan conservation element. In addition, some cities and counties have enacted regulations for the protection of specified resources such as riparian vegetation, wetlands, or heritage trees.

Department of Fish and Game. DFG regulates activities related to fish, wildlife, and plants in California. DFG is responsible for administering CESA and the other state laws mentioned above. DFG also manages the California Natural Diversity Database (CNDDB), an inventory of the reported locations of listed species and species of special concern. CNDDB data are available to the public digitally or as hard copy.

To locally administer fish and wildlife laws, DFG is divided into seven regions: Northern California–North Coast, Sacramento Valley–Central Sierra, Central Coast, San Joaquin Valley–Southern Sierra, South Coast, Eastern Sierra–Inland Deserts, and Marine.

Fish and Game Commission. The Commission is composed of up to five members, appointed by the governor and confirmed by the Senate. The Commission meets at least 11 times each year to publicly discuss various proposed regulations, permits, licenses, management policies, and other subjects within its areas of responsibility. Major Commission responsibilities include making listing decisions under CESA and formulating general policies to administer DFG. The Commission also decides hunting seasons, bag limits, and methods of take for game animals and sport fish.

CNDDB = California Natural Diversity Database

Federal Endangered Species Act

Species Listing

A species is "endangered" when it is in danger of extinction throughout all or a significant portion of its range. 16 USC 1532(6). A species is "threatened" if it is likely to become endangered within the foreseeable future throughout all or a significant part of its range. 16 USC 1532(20). Endangered species are entitled to all the ESA's protections, whereas threatened species may receive less protection from "take," as identified at the time of listing under "a Section 4(d) rule." ESA Section 4(d) (16 USC 1533(d)) authorizes USFWS to define the exact activities constituting take of a threatened species.

A species is "endangered" when it is in danger of extinction throughout all or a significant portion of its range. A species is "threatened" if it is likely to become endangered within the foreseeable future throughout all or a significant part of its range.

All species of plants and animals, except pest insects, may be listed as endangered or threatened. USFWS lists species on the basis of the best scientific and commercial data available, considering solely the species' biological status and threats to their existence. The term "species" is defined broadly to include "subspecies" and, for fish and wildlife, any "distinct population segment" of a vertebrate fish or wildlife species. 16 USC 1532(16).

Listings can be justified by one or more of the following factors (16 USC 1533(a)(1)):

- Present or threatened destruction, modification, or curtailment of the species' habitat or range
- Over-utilization for commercial, recreational, scientific, or educational purposes
- Disease or predation
- Inadequacy of existing regulatory mechanisms
- Other natural or anthropogenic factors affecting the species' survival

USFWS, through a formal rulemaking process lasting 12 months, can list species either independently or in response to a citizen petition. 16 USC 1533(b). A complete catalog of all listed species can be found on the USFWS website (www.fws.gov/endangered/wildlife.html#Species).

USFWS also may de-list species using a process similar to the listing process, if successful recovery efforts warrant this change. 16 USC 1533(c). For example, the bald eagle has been de-listed because nesting pairs of bald eagles have risen nationwide to 7,066, compared to a low of 417 in 1963 when high levels of the insecticide DDT were damaging their eggs. 71 CFR 8238.

The bald eagle was de-listed because recovery efforts were successful.

USFWS must perform status reviews of listed species every five years to determine whether, based on current best available science, each listed species should have its status changed (*i.e.*, either lowered from endangered to threatened or raised from threatened to endangered) or have its status removed because protection is no longer justified. 16 USC 1533(c)(2).

USFWS also maintains a list of "candidate" species. Candidate species are those with enough information to be proposed for listing, but for which USFWS has not yet developed a listing proposal. 50 CFR 424.02(b). Candidate species are not protected by ESA, but they may be protected in HCPs.

Critical Habitat

The ESA requires designation of critical habitat for listed species when prudent and determinable. Critical habitat designation affects federal agencies, but does not directly affect private landowners. Federal agencies, under the Section 7 consultation process, must protect critical habitat when undertaking federal actions. *See* below.

Critical habitat is a formally designated specific geographic area that contains those physical or biological features essential to the conservation of a listed species, and that may require special management or protection.

Critical habitat is a formally designated specific geographic area that contains those physical or biological features essential to the conservation of a listed species, and that may require special management or protection. Critical habitat may include areas not occupied by the species at the time of listing, but essential to conservation of the species. In designating critical habitat, the USFWS must consider the best scientific data available, as well as the probable economic and other impacts of making the designation. Critical habitat may be reduced in acreage if economic effects of designation would be severe. 16 USC 1532, 1533(b).

USFWS is required to designate critical habitat at the time of listing if prudent, but no later than one year after listing. 16 USC 1533(a)(3), (b)(6)(C). Budget and administrative constraints have prevented USFWS from meeting the one-year deadline for many species, leading to lawsuits by environmental groups to force critical habitat designation.

Recovery

The ESA's ultimate goal is to recover species so they no longer need the Act's protection.

The ESA's ultimate goal is to "recover" species so they no longer need the Act's protection. USFWS is required to prepare recovery plans for listed species describing the actions needed to encourage the species' overall health and viability, such that ESA protection is no longer needed. 16 USC 1533(f)(1). Recovery plans are advisory and have no legal effect. The pace of recovery plan preparation has been slowed by lawsuits and competing USFWS priorities.

Section 7 Consultation

The ESA is given teeth mainly by Section 7 consultation and the Section 10 incidental take permit process. *See* below. Section 7 prohibits federal agencies from undertaking actions that are likely to jeopardize the continued existence of a listed species or that result in the destruction or adverse modification of designated critical habitat. 16 USC 1536(a)(2). Federal actions covered include federal funding, permits, leases, or other entitlements issued to private or local and state government applicants. 50 CFR 402.02. However, Section 7 consultation is required only for discretionary federal actions for which there is federal control and responsibility. *National Association of Homebuilders v. Defenders of Wildlife* (2007) 127 S. Ct. 2518.

USFWS and NOAA Fisheries have issued detailed regulations on Section 7 consultation (50 CFR 402), as well as a detailed handbook (USFWS and NOAA Fisheries 1998) explaining the Section 7 consultation process.

Under Section 7, federal agencies must consult with USFWS to ensure that actions they authorize, fund, or carry out will not "jeopardize" listed species; jeopardize means appreciably reducing the likelihood of both the survival and recovery of a listed species in the wild by reducing the reproduction, numbers, or distribution of the species. Federal agencies and applicants may not make any irreversible or irretrievable commitment of resources during the consultation process. 16 USC 1536(a)(2).

Under Section 7, federal agencies must consult with USFWS to ensure that actions they authorize, fund, or carry out will not jeopardize listed species.

The Section 7 process typically starts with "informal consultation," during which the federal agency (or a designated non-federal representative such as an applicant) communicates with USFWS to determine which listed or proposed species and critical habitats are in the federal action area, and whether the action may affect these species or critical habitats. The informal consultation process is illustrated in Figure 14-1.

For "major construction activities," the federal agency must prepare a biological assessment if there may be an effect on a listed species or critical habitat; a major construction activity is an action that significantly affects the quality of the human environment and thus would trigger an environmental impact statement (EIS) under the National Environmental Policy Act (NEPA, 16 USC 1536(c), 50 CFR 402.02).

EIS = Environmental impact statement
NEPA = National Environmental Policy Act

The biological assessment must be based on the best scientific and commercial data available. 50 CFR 402.14(d). It must consider the direct, indirect, and cumulative effects of the federal agency action. After preparation of the biological assessment, USFWS must conclude that the proposed action has one of three effects on listed species and critical habitat: "no effect," "not likely to adversely affect," or "likely to adversely affect." If the latter finding is made, then formal Section 7 consultation is required. USFWS and NOAA Fisheries 1998.

Under formal consultation (*see* Figure 14-2), USFWS determines whether a proposed action will "jeopardize" the species or result in destruction or adverse modification of critical habitat. If it will, then USFWS issues a jeopardy opinion, which offers "reasonable and prudent alternatives" to avoid jeopardy. A federal agency is prohibited (with very narrow exemptions) from implementing the action if it would jeopardize the species or eliminate critical habitat. Following issuance of a jeopardy opinion, the federal agency must notify USFWS of its final decision on the project, and either adopt one of the

Under formal consultation, USFWS determines whether a proposed action will "jeopardize" the species or result in destruction or adverse modification of critical habitat.

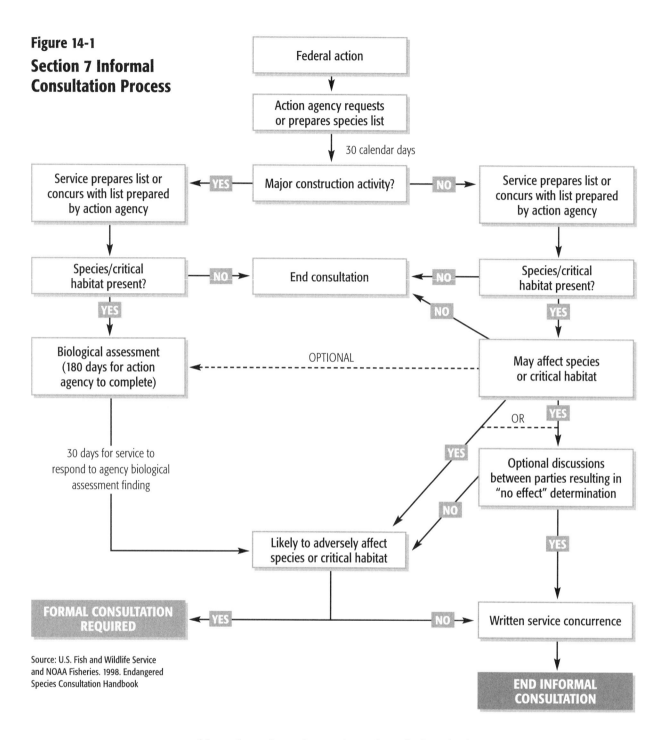

Figure 14-1

Section 7 Informal Consultation Process

Federal action

Action agency requests or prepares species list

30 calendar days

Major construction activity?

YES → Service prepares list or concurs with list prepared by action agency

NO → Service prepares list or concurs with list prepared by action agency

Species/critical habitat present?

NO → End consultation

YES

Biological assessment (180 days for action agency to complete)

Species/critical habitat present?

NO → End consultation

YES

May affect species or critical habitat

OPTIONAL

30 days for service to respond to agency biological assessment finding

OR

YES

NO

YES

Optional discussions between parties resulting in "no effect" determination

YES

Likely to adversely affect species or critical habitat

FORMAL CONSULTATION REQUIRED ← YES

NO → Written service concurrence

END INFORMAL CONSULTATION

Source: U.S. Fish and Wildlife Service and NOAA Fisheries. 1998. Endangered Species Consultation Handbook

reasonable and prudent alternatives identified in the biological opinion, deny the action, or apply for an exemption (the exemption process is highly complex and almost never pursued).

If USFWS issues a non-jeopardy opinion, the opinion often includes an incidental take statement setting forth "reasonable and prudent measures" to minimize the impacts of any incidental take of a listed species. The federal agency must implement these measures as a condition of approval of the action in order to obtain incidental take coverage.

Figure 14-2

Section 7 Formal Consultation Process

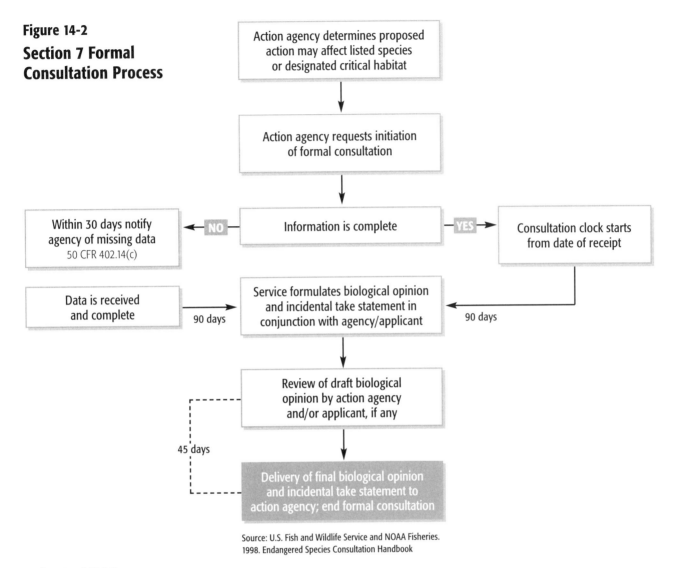

Source: U.S. Fish and Wildlife Service and NOAA Fisheries. 1998. Endangered Species Consultation Handbook

Take Prohibition and Authorization

Prohibition against take. Section 9 of the ESA makes it unlawful for a person to "take" a listed fish or wildlife species, as well as to possess, transport, deliver, or sell a listed species. The take prohibition does not apply to listed plants, which are protected from transport and sale, and from removal, damage, or destruction only on federal lands. 16 USC 1538(a)(1), (2).

"Take" means to "harass, harm, pursue, hunt, shoot, wound, kill, trap, capture, or collect" a listed species, or to attempt such conduct. Controversial USFWS regulations (50 CFR 17.3, 222.102) define the term "harm" as including "significant habitat modification or degradation" if it actually kills or injures wildlife by significantly impairing essential behavioral patterns such as nesting or reproduction. *See* sidebar on page 332.

Take authorizations. Section 10 of the ESA (16 USC 1539) authorizes USFWS to issue several types of take authorizations. These include:

EA = Environmental assessment
NEPA = National Environmental Policy Act

"Take" Includes Significant Habitat Modification

In *Babbit v. Sweet Home Chapter of Communities for a Great Oregon* (1995) 515 US 687, the U.S. Supreme Court upheld the regulatory definition of "harm" (and thus "take") as including significant habitat modification. In *Babbitt*, a group supporting timber harvesting in northern spotted owl old-growth habitat challenged this regulatory definition. The Supreme Court observed that the term "harm" is linked specifically to activities causing death or injury to listed species, and that the USFWS regulation interpreting "harm" to include significant habitat modification leading to death or injury to listed species was reasonable.

However, there must be *some* connection between habitat modification and death or injury to a listed species in order to find a take. Mere modification of suitable habitat may not be sufficient to constitute a take.

In *Arizona Cattle Growers' Association v. USFWS* (2001) 273 F. 3d 1229, the Ninth Circuit in a leading case invalidated, as arbitrary and capricious, incidental take statements in a biological opinion issued pursuant to Section 7 consultation. The biological opinion was issued for proposed federal agency grazing permits, but there was no evidence that the listed fish species of concern was present on the federal lands. USFWS included mitigation measures in the incidental take statements intended to regulate grazing activity because it was possible that listed fish species could return to the federal lands in the future. However, the court held that the ESA was not intended to regulate all parcels of land that are merely capable of supporting a listed species. ▪

- **Scientific take permit.** Allows take for scientific purposes or to enhance the affected species
- **Safe harbor agreement.** Provides incentives for landowners to manage their land to maintain or enhance species. 64 CFR 32717
- **Candidate conservation agreement with assurances.** Promotes the conservation of candidate species, proposed species, or proposed critical habitat. 68 CFR 37170
- **Incidental take permit.** Authorizes incidental take by non-federal entities (*see* below)

Incidental take permits and habitat conservation plans. ITPs were added to Section 10 of the ESA in 1982 as a practical solution for private landowners, state agencies, and local agencies whose activities, even if mitigated, might result in the incidental take of a listed species. "Incidental take" means the take of a listed species that results from, but is not the purpose of, otherwise lawful activity. 16 USC 1539(a)(2). Issuance of a Section 10 incidental take permit requires preparation of both an HCP and a NEPA document.

Habitat conservation plans vary in complexity depending on the number of "covered species" and the number of "covered activities." An HCP is required to address impacts on listed species only. However, many applicants voluntarily include conservation measures for candidate species, to avoid having to amend the HCP if they become listed in the future.

USFWS had approved more than 430 HCPs as of 2004. USFWS 2004b. Useful guidance for HCP preparation includes the USFWS and NOAA Fisheries HCP Manual (USFWS and NOAA Fisheries 1996) as amended by the Five-Point Policy (65 Fed. Reg. 35242), an Institute for Local Self Government guide (Cylinder *et al.* 2004), and USFWS and NOAA Fisheries regulations. 50 CFR 17.22, 17.32. An HCP must include the following information (16 USC 1539(a)(2)(A)):

- Impacts likely to result from the take
- Steps undertaken by the applicant to monitor, minimize, and mitigate these impacts
- Funding assurances to implement conservation measures
- Procedures to address unforeseen circumstances
- Alternatives considered that would not result in take, and why they were not adopted
- Additional measures USFWS identifies as necessary or appropriate

USFWS in the Five-Point Policy (65 Fed. Reg. 35242) recommends that an HCP also include:

- Goals and objectives for covered species
- An adaptive management plan
- A monitoring plan

A controversial aspect of ITPs and HCPs is the "no surprises rule." Under the no surprises rule, incidental take permittees are assured that if "unforeseen circumstances" arise, USFWS will not require the commitment of additional land, water, financial compensation, or additional restrictions on land or water use, beyond that agreed to in the HCP to address "changed circumstances." USFWS will honor these assurances as long as the permittee is implementing the terms and conditions of the HCP and permit in good faith. However, under the "Permit Revocation Rule," an ITP may be revoked if permittee actions would put a species in jeopardy. 50 CFR 17.22(b)(5), 17.32(b)(5), 222.307(g).

The ITP process is illustrated in Figure 14-3. An applicant is responsible for deciding whether to pursue an ITP. The applicant is responsible for submitting a completed permit application, an HCP, an implementation agreement (if required), and a draft NEPA analysis. While processing the permit application, USFWS completes the NEPA analysis and also writes a biological opinion under an "internal" ESA Section 7 consultation.

The time period for USFWS to process a permit application depends on the NEPA document required (USFWS and NOAA Fisheries 1996):

- **"Low effect" HCPs with only "minor or negligible" effects on species.** Requires only a categorical exclusion and has a target processing time of 3 months
- **HCPs requiring an Environmental Assessment (EA).** Target processing time is 4–6 months
- **HCPs requiring an EIS.** Target processing time is up to 12 months

These time periods include a minimum 60-day public comment period on an HCP application, which runs concurrently with any NEPA-required public comment period.

Enforcement and Penalties

Section 11 of the ESA (16 USC 1540) sets forth civil and criminal penalties and authorizes injunctions for violations of any portion of the Act. Lawsuits typically are brought by the Law Enforcement Division of USFWS or NOAA Fisheries. The Act also contains a citizen suit provision allowing any person to file a civil lawsuit to enjoin violations of the Act.

Criminal penalties include a fine of up to $50,000 per violation or imprisonment for one year, for knowing violations of the Section 9 "take" prohibition. All other knowing violations are subject to a fine of up to $25,000 per violation or imprisonment up to 6 months. 16 USC 1540(b).

Figure 14-3
ITP Process

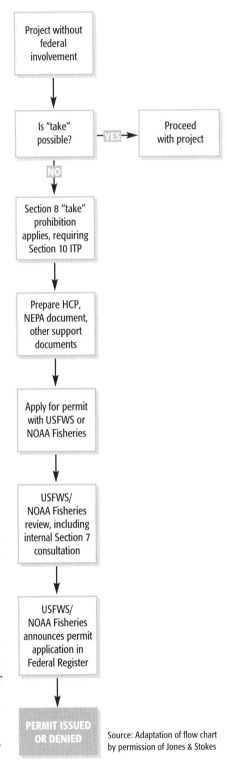

Source: Adaptation of flow chart by permission of Jones & Stokes

In addition to or in lieu of criminal penalties, civil penalties include a fine of up to $25,000 per violation for knowing ESA violations, and a fine of up to $500 per violation for inadvertent violations. 15 USC 1540(a).

California Endangered Species Act

CESA is patterned generally after the federal ESA, but has some notable differences.

CESA is patterned generally after the federal ESA, but has some notable differences. As discussed below, the prohibition against take applies to both endangered and threatened species, and species proposed for listing are afforded greater protection. On the other hand, the state definition of "take" does not include critical habitat modification, and there is no state-level equivalent to recovery plans or the Section 7 consultation process.

Listing

Individuals, organizations, or DFG can submit petitions to the Fish and Game Commission requesting that a species, subspecies, or variety of plant or animal be added to, deleted from, or changed in status on the state lists of rare, threatened, or endangered species. Factors considered in determining the need to list a species include the present or threatened modification or destruction of habitat, competition, predation, disease, overexploitation by collectors, other natural occurrences, or human-related activities. Fish and Game Code 2071 *et seq.*

If the petition is accepted and the species becomes a candidate species, a 12-month review period starts, during which time the candidate species receives the same CESA protection as a listed species. DFG recommends to the Commission whether the species should be listed based on the best scientific information available to DFG. DFG compiles updated lists of state and federally listed species on the agency website. Fish and Game Code 2071 *et seq.*

SSC = Species of special concern

DFG also maintains a list of "species of special concern" (SSC). SSC status applies to animals not listed under the federal ESA or CESA, but which nonetheless are declining at a rate that could result in listing, or which historically occurred in low numbers and known threats to their persistence currently exist. SSC are considered during the CEQA review process and in preparation of conservation plans. Lists of SSC are available at the DFG website.

CESA, unlike the federal ESA, does not require formal designation of critical habitat or preparation of recovery plans (other than a pilot program for the greater sandhill crane) for listed species. Fish and Game Code 2105 *et seq.*

Take Prohibition and Authorization

Prohibition against take. Section 2080 of the Fish and Game Code prohibits "take" of any species that the Commission determines to be an endangered species or a threatened species. Because of an ambiguity in CESA, it is unclear whether the take prohibition applies to listed plants.

Take is defined in Section 86 as "hunt, pursue, catch, capture, or kill, or attempt to hunt, pursue, catch, capture, or kill." Fish and Game Code 86. Unlike the federal ESA, this definition does not encompass harm, harassment, or habitat modification, but rather includes only acts leading to the death of a listed species.

Take is defined in Section 86 as "hunt, pursue, catch, capture, or kill, or attempt to hunt, pursue, catch, capture, or kill."

Incidental take authorization. Fish and Game Code Section 2081 allows for take incidental to otherwise lawful development projects. A flow chart of the Section 2081 permit process is shown in Figure 14-4. Regulations governing incidental take permits (also known as Section 2081 permits) are found at 14 CCR 783 *et seq.*

CCR = California Code of Regulations

A Section 2081 permit is not available to authorize take of fully protected species. The Section 2081 program is a certified regulatory program under CEQA (*see* chapter 2), so DFG does not need to prepare a separate CEQA document when approving a Section 2081 permit. Section 2081 permit CEQA procedures can be found at 14 CCR 783.3.

A Section 2081 permit may be issued if the following criteria are met (Fish and Game Code 2081(b)):

- The authorized take is incidental to an otherwise lawful activity
- The impacts of the authorized take are minimized and fully mitigated
- The measures required to minimize and fully mitigate impacts are roughly proportional to the impact of the taking on the species, maintain the applicant's objectives to the greatest extent possible, and are capable of successful implementation
- Adequate funding is provided to implement the required minimization and mitigation measures and to monitor compliance with and the effectiveness of the measures
- Issuance of the permit will not jeopardize the continued existence of a state-listed species

Measures to minimize the take of species covered by the permit (covered species) and to mitigate the impacts caused by the take are set forth in one or more attachments to the permit. This attachment generally is a mitigation plan (*e.g.*, an HCP) prepared and submitted by the permittee in coordination with DFG staff.

Measures to minimize the take of species covered by the permit (covered species) and to mitigate the impacts caused by the take are set forth in one or more attachments to the permit.

Special streamlining procedures apply if a project will result in take of a species that is both federally and state listed. For such jointly listed species, CESA compliance can be achieved through formal Section 7 consultation or through the Section 10 incidental take process. The applicant must consult with DFG during these federal ESA processes, and DFG must concur with the mitigation measures proposed by USFWS. Fish and Game Code 2080.1.

Scientific collecting permit. Through permits or memoranda of understanding, the DFG also may authorize individuals, public agencies, universities, zoological

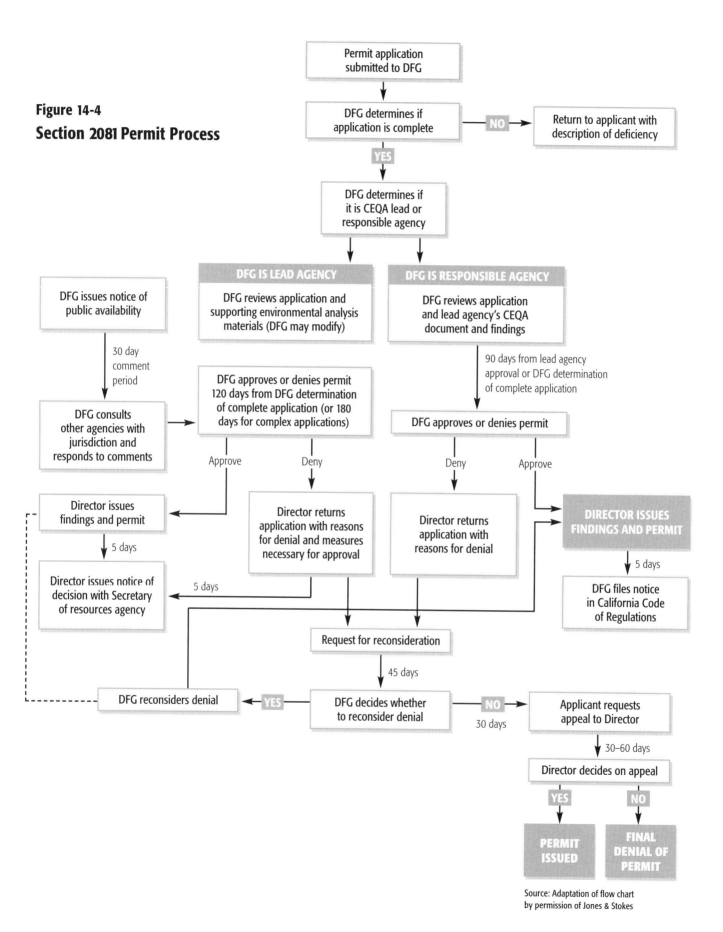

Figure 14-4

Section 2081 Permit Process

Permit application submitted to DFG

DFG determines if application is complete — **NO** → Return to applicant with description of deficiency

YES

DFG determines if it is CEQA lead or responsible agency

DFG IS LEAD AGENCY
DFG reviews application and supporting environmental analysis materials (DFG may modify)

DFG IS RESPONSIBLE AGENCY
DFG reviews application and lead agency's CEQA document and findings

DFG issues notice of public availability

30 day comment period

DFG consults other agencies with jurisdiction and responds to comments

DFG approves or denies permit 120 days from DFG determination of complete application (or 180 days for complex applications)

90 days from lead agency approval or DFG determination of complete application

DFG approves or denies permit

Approve

Deny

Deny

Approve

Director issues findings and permit

5 days

Director issues notice of decision with Secretary of resources agency

Director returns application with reasons for denial and measures necessary for approval

Director returns application with reasons for denial

DIRECTOR ISSUES FINDINGS AND PERMIT

5 days

DFG files notice in California Code of Regulations

5 days

Request for reconsideration

45 days

DFG reconsiders denial ← **YES** — DFG decides whether to reconsider denial — **NO** → Applicant requests appeal to Director

30 days

30–60 days

Director decides on appeal

YES

NO

PERMIT ISSUED

FINAL DENIAL OF PERMIT

Source: Adaptation of flow chart by permission of Jones & Stokes

gardens, and scientific or educational institutions to import, export, take, or possess any endangered species, threatened species, or candidate species of plants and animals for scientific, educational, or management purposes. Fish and Game Code 1002.

Agricultural activities. CESA allows DFG to authorize local voluntary programs for routine and ongoing agricultural activities on farms and ranches that encourage habitat for candidate and listed species and wildlife in general; implementing regulations are found at 14 CCR 786.0 *et seq.* Activities performed under these approved programs are exempt from the prohibition on take. Fish and Game Code 2086 *et seq.*

CESA allows DFG to authorize local voluntary programs for routine and ongoing agricultural activities on farms and ranches that encourage habitat for candidate and listed species and wildlife in general.

Enforcement

CESA states that an intentional taking of a listed species is prosecuted as a misdemeanor. Fish and Game Code 12002, 12003.1. Also, the Penal Code 653(o) *et seq.* prohibits importing or selling the dead bodies of certain listed species. For Penal Code violations, maximum criminal penalties are $5,000 per violation or one year imprisonment; maximum civil penalties are $10,000 per violation. Fish and Game Code 2582, 2583, 12008.

Natural Community Conservation Planning Act

The NCCPA (Fish and Game Code 2800 *et seq.*) establishes a voluntary comprehensive planning approach that balances fish and wildlife protection with community development. NCCPs prepared pursuant to the Act are often combined with HCPs to provide coverage for both state and federally listed and sensitive species.

The NCCPA establishes a voluntary comprehensive planning approach that balances fish and wildlife protection with community development.

The NCCP process begins with a planning agreement signed by DFG and plan participants. The planning agreement outlines the geographic planning area, species, and natural communities to be addressed, processes for scientific and public input, and an interim process for project review. Fish and Game Code 2810.

To approve an NCCP, DFG must find that the NCCP (Fish and Game Code 2815):

- Protects habitat, natural communities, and species diversity on a landscape or ecosystem level
- Includes a reserve system and conservation measures meeting certain ecological requirements
- Identifies activities allowed within reserves
- Includes specific conservation measures for covered species
- Includes monitoring and adaptive management programs
- Includes an implementation schedule and funding provisions

California Gnatcatcher habitat encroachment prompted the state's first NCCP.

An NCCP Implementation Agreement must be prepared. The Implementation Agreement is a binding contract describing the roles and responsibilities of all parties, including plan oversight, establishment of reserves or other conservation measures, monitoring and adaptive management, and funding. Fish and Game Code 2821.

Once an NCCP and associated CEQA documents have been approved, DFG may provide take authorization for all of the NCCP's covered species. Covered species include both CESA-listed and CESA-non-listed species conserved under the NCCP. The NCCP is thus an efficient alternative to obtaining individual Section 2081 incidental take permits for each state-listed species affected by a proposed plan or project. Fish and Game Code 2835.

Similar to the federal ESA "no surprises rule," an NCCP also may include "long term assurances" that unforeseen circumstances will not trigger additional conservation or funding requirements. DFG must suspend or revoke take authorization if the continued take of the species would jeopardize the species continued existence. Fish and Game Code 2820(f), 2835.

For more information...

Publications

Cylinder, P., K. Bogdan, and D. Zippen. 2004. Understanding the Habitat Conservation Planning Process in California. Institute for Local Self Government

Department of Fish and Game. 2005. The Status of Rare, Threatened, and Endangered Plants and Animals of California: 2000–2004

Manaster, K.A. and D.P. Selmi (eds). ND. Chapter 81 of California Environmental Law and Land Use Practice. Matthew Bender. San Francisco, Calif.

Talbert, C.T. 2008. Curtin's California Land Use and Planning Law. Solano Press. Point Arena, Calif.

U.S. Fish and Wildlife Service and National Oceanographic and Atmospheric Administration Fisheries. 1996. Habitat Conservation Planning and ITP Processing Handbook

U.S. Fish and Wildlife Service and National Oceanographic and Atmospheric Administration Fisheries. 1998. Endangered Species Act Consultation Handbook

U.S. Fish and Wildlife Service. 2003. Permits for Native Species Under the Endangered Species Act

U.S. Fish and Wildlife Service. 2004a. ESA Basics: 30 years of Protecting Endangered Species

U.S. Fish and Wildlife Service. 2004b. Habitat Conservation Plans: Section 10 of the Endangered Species Act

Websites

California Native Plant Society
www.cnps.org

California Natural Diversity Database
www.dfg.ca.gov/whdab/html/cnddb.html

Department of Fish and Game
www.dfg.ca.gov

Department of Fish and Game, Species of Special Concern
www.dfg.ca.gov/hcpb/species/ssc/ssc.shtml

Department of Fish and Game, Threatened and Endangered Species
www.dfg.ca.gov/hcpb/species/t_e_spp/tespp.shtml

National Oceanographic and Atmospheric Administration Fisheries
www.nmfs.noaa.gov

U.S. Fish and Wildlife Service
www.fws.gov

U.S. Fish and Wildlife Service, Endangered Species Program
www.fws.gov/endangered

U.S. Fish and Wildlife Service, Endangered and Threatened Species Information
www.fws.gov/endangered/wildlife.html#Species

Wetlands

This chapter reviews—

- Key laws and agencies involved in wetlands regulation
- Clean Water Act Section 404 permit program
- State and regional wetlands regulation programs

Related Solano Press titles—

Wetlands, Streams, and Other Waters: Regulation, Conservation, and Mitigation Planning
Paul D. Cylinder, Kenneth M. Bogdan, April I. Zohn, and Joel B. Butterworth. 2004

Curtin's California Land Use and Planning Law
Cecily T. Talbert. 2008

Glossary

Adjacent wetlands–wetlands that are bordering, contiguous, or neighboring to other waters of the United States.

Compensatory mitigation–mitigation to offset wetlands impacts that cannot be offset through avoidance or minimization.

Delineation–the identification and mapping of wetlands and other waters of the United States.

Dredged material–material removed from waters of the United States.

Fill material–any material used for the primary purpose of replacing an aquatic area with dry land or changing the bottom elevation of a water body.

General permit*–a Section 404 permit for a class of activities precluding the need for a project-specific Section 404 permit.

Headwaters–the point on a nontidal stream above which the average annual flow is less than 5 cubic feet per second (cfs).

Hydrophytic vegetation–plants that can grow in wetland conditions.

Individual permit*–a project-specific Section 404 permit.

Isolated waters–nontidal waters not part of a surface tributary system to interstate or navigable waters of the United States, and not adjacent to such tributaries.

Jurisdictional determination–the final USACE decision on its jurisdiction over a site under Section 404.

Lake or Streambed Alteration Agreement*–an agreement negotiated between DFG and an applicant for activities involving alteration of a lake or stream zone.

Letter of permission*–a Section 404 permit issued through an abbreviated process that includes agency coordination and public interest review, but not public notice.

Mean high water–the average position of the high water mark.

Mitigation banking–use of a site via a credit system for enhancement, restoration, or creation of wetlands, for mitigation of impacts on wetlands at other sites.

Mudflats–periodically inundated and exposed unvegetated areas such as tidal coastal areas and the edges of inland lakes, ponds, and rivers.

Nationwide permit*–a type of general permit that applies nationally.

Navigable waters–waters that are, could be, or were used to transport interstate or foreign commerce.

Ordinary high water mark–the line on the shore established by fluctuations of water and indicated by physical characteristics such as a clear natural line impressed in the bank.

Pre-construction notification–notification made to USACE of an intent to perform fill activities authorized by a nationwide permit.

Programmatic general permit*–permit issued by a USACE district or division where another agency's program provides equivalent protection to the Section 404 program.

Public interest review–USACE evaluation of whether a Section 404 permit is in the public interest, using specific criteria.

Regional general permit*–a Section 404 permit issued by a USACE district or division authorizing a class of activities within a geographic region that has minimal environmental impacts.

Riffle and pool complexes–high quality fish and wildlife habitat where a rapid current flowing over a coarse substrate results in turbulence (riffles) and a slower moving current in deeper areas results in smooth flow (pools).

Section 10 permit*–USACE permit issued pursuant to the Rivers and Harbors Act for activities that involve obstruction of, excavation in, or filling of navigable waters.

Section 401 certification*–RWQCB or SWRCB certification that a Section 404 permit is consistent with state water quality standards.

Section 404 permit*–a USACE permit issued pursuant to the Clean Water Act for the discharge of dredged or fill materials into waters the U.S.

Section 404(b)(1) alternatives analysis–an analysis prepared consistent with the Section 404(b)(1) Guidelines to determine whether a practicable alternative to a proposed discharge exists that has less adverse effect on the aquatic ecosystem.

Special aquatic sites–specific types of waters of the United States for which mitigation requirements are more stringent under Section 404(b)(1) Guidelines.

Standard permit*–in the context of wetlands regulation, a project-specific permit (either a general permit or letter of permission) issued after the formal Section 404 permit review process.

Vegetated shallows–periodically inundated sites with rooted, submerged vegetation.

Waste discharge requirements*–permit issued by a RWQCB for discharge of waste into waters of the state.

Waters of the United States–all waters used or susceptible to use in interstate or foreign commerce, or that could affect interstate or foreign commerce. Waters of the United States include lakes, rivers and coastal waters, as well as all adjacent "other waters" such as wetlands, the use, degradation or destruction of which could affect interstate or foreign commerce.

Wetlands–under the Section 404 program definition, those areas that are inundated or saturated by surface or groundwater at a frequency and duration sufficient to support, and that under normal circumstances do support, a prevalence of vegetation typically adapted for life in saturated soil conditions.

* equals permits and approvals

CHAPTER 15

Wetlands

Introduction

Wetlands are areas of land that are wet seasonally or permanently, and support special types of adapted vegetation. Wetlands were once thought of as useless swamps requiring draining and filling, but are now recognized as providing flood control, fish and wildlife, and water quality benefits.

Wetlands are areas of land that are wet seasonally or permanently, and support special types of adapted vegetation.

The heightened societal awareness of wetlands values, and significant long-term declines in wetland acreage, have caused federal, state, and local governments to implement programs to regulate and protect wetlands. This chapter reviews key laws and agencies involved in wetlands regulation, and federal, state, and regional wetlands regulation programs. It also covers regulation of activities in non-wetlands waters of the state under Fish and Game Code 1600 *et seq*.

Key Laws and Agencies

Federal Laws and Agencies

Clean Water Act. Section 404 of the federal Clean Water Act (CWA, 33 USC 1244) requires private and governmental entities to obtain a USACE permit prior to discharge of dredged or fill material into waters of the United States, which include adjacent wetlands. (This chapter focuses on Section 404 permitting for wetlands fills, but it should be noted throughout that the same permitting requirements apply to all waters of the United States, as defined below.) Section 404 authorizes the U.S. Army Corps of Engineers (USACE) permit program, requires the Environmental Protection Agency (EPA) together with USACE to issue guidelines governing the permit program, and authorizes EPA to veto permits.

CWA = Clean Water Act
EPA   = U.S. Environmental
         Protection Agency
USACE = U.S. Army Corps
         of Engineers
USC   = United States Code

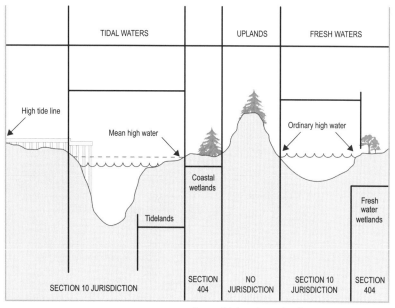

Source: U.S. Army Corps of Engineers, Sacramento District

Figure 15-1
Lateral Extent of Jurisdiction under Section 404 and Section 10

CFR = Code of Federal Regulations

As explained in detail below, the Section 404 program has evolved into a highly complex and pervasive regulatory scheme.

Rivers and Harbors Act of 1899. This Act (33 USC 4501 *et seq.*) is the legislative origin of the Section 404 program. Section 10 permits under the Rivers and Harbors Act are required for any obstruction or alteration of any navigable water of the United States, including placement of structures in, dredging of, or disposal of dredged material into navigable waters.

USACE regulatory authority under the Rivers and Harbors Act is limited to traditional "navigable waters." Traditional "navigable waters" regulated by Section 10 are waters that are, could be, or were once used to transport interstate or foreign commerce. In contrast, "waters of the United States" regulated under Section 404 also include "other waters" such as wetlands that could affect interstate commerce. 33 CFR 328.3. The lateral extent of jurisdiction under Section 10 and Section 404 is shown in Figure 15-1.

In practice, USACE regulatory authority under the Rivers and Harbors Act has been integrated with regulatory authority under the CWA, and USACE uses one permit application for both types of permits.

U.S. Army Corps of Engineers. USACE is primarily responsible for implementing the Section 404 program. USACE is organized geographically into eight divisions and 41 subordinate districts. Three district offices are responsible for administering California's Section 404 program–San Francisco, Sacramento, and Los Angeles. They are all located within the USACE South Pacific Division.

USACE regulations implementing the Section 404 program are found at 33 CFR 320 *et seq.* Other important sources of Section

404 requirements include Regulatory Guidance Letters (RGLs) issued by the Chief of Engineers and published District-specific policies.

Environmental Protection Agency. EPA is responsible for Section 404 program oversight. EPA and USACE have issued several memoranda of agreement (MOAs), including one that defines each agency's roles more specifically. USACE and EPA 1989.

Other federal agencies. U.S. Fish and Wildlife Service (USFWS) and National Oceanographic and Atmospheric Administration (NOAA) Fisheries Service review and comment on Section 404 applications, and USACE must give full consideration to comments of those agencies and the Department of Fish and Game (DFG). If a Section 404 permit may affect a listed threatened or endangered species, then consultation under Section 7 of the Endangered Species Act (ESA) is required (*see* chapter 14).

State Laws and Agencies

State Water Resources Control Board and regional water quality control boards. Section 401 of the CWA requires applicants for a federal permit resulting in a discharge to jurisdictional waters, such as a USACE 404 permit, to provide the USACE with a state certification stating the discharge will comply with the state's water quality plan and standards. The State Water Resources Control Board (SWRCB) and regional water quality control boards (RWQCBs) are responsible for issuing Section 401 certifications for Section 404 permits. RWQCBs are also responsible for issued waste discharge requirements (WDRs) for certain "isolated" wetlands not regulated by the 404 program.

Department of Fish and Game. DFG enters into lake or streambed alteration agreements pursuant to Fish and Game Code 1600 *et seq.* These agreements regulate activities in lakes and the beds, channels, and banks of rivers and streams.

Section 404 Permit Program

Regulated Waters and Activities

Definition of Waters of the United States. Section 404 jurisdiction extends to all waters of the United States, which are defined expansively to include all waters used or susceptible to use in interstate or foreign commerce, or that could affect interstate or foreign commerce. Waters of the United States include lakes, rivers, and coastal waters, as well as all adjacent wetlands. 40 CFR 328.3.

Wetlands are defined as those areas inundated or saturated by surface water or groundwater at a frequency to support, and that under normal circumstances do support, a prevalence of vegetation adapted to saturated soil conditions. "Adjacent" wetlands subject to Section 404 jurisdiction are those that are bordering, contiguous, or neighboring to other waters of the United States. 33 CFR 328.3(b).

DFG	= Department of Fish and Game
ESA	= Endangered Species Act
MOA	= Memorandum of agreement
NOAA	= National Oceanographic and Atmospheric Administration
RGL	= Regulatory guidance letter
RWQCB	= Regional water quality control board
SWRCB	= State Water Resources Control Board
USFWS	= U.S. Fish and Wildlife Service
WDRs	= Waste discharge requirements

Section 404 jurisdiction extends to all waters of the United States, defined expansively to include all waters used or susceptible to use in interstate or foreign commerce, or that could affect interstate or foreign commerce.

Section 404 jurisdiction extends to all waters of the United States, which are defined expansively.

SWANCC = Solid Waste Agency
of Northern Cook County

Section 404 jurisdiction applies to intrastate wetlands if their use, degradation, or destruction could affect interstate or foreign commerce; it does not apply to "isolated" intrastate waters and wetlands. In the controversial *SWANCC* decision (*Solid Waste Agency of Northern Cook County v. U.S. Army Corps of Engineers* (2001) 531 U.S. 159), the U.S. Supreme Court held that Section 404 jurisdiction does not extend to non-navigable, isolated waters, at least when based solely on the fact that these waters are used as habitat by migratory birds (the rejected "Migratory Bird Rule" was part of the preamble to USACE Section 404 regulations, 51 Fed. Reg. 41217).

The Supreme Court again took up the regulation of isolated wetlands in its opinion on two consolidated appeals in *Rapanos v. United States* (2006) 126 S. Ct. 2208. In a highly divided opinion, the controlling test was articulated by Justice Kennedy in a concurring opinion. Under this test, waters of the United States include tributaries to, and wetlands adjacent to, navigable waters, if there is a "significant nexus" to waters that are or were navigable in fact. *See* sidebar.

Methods for determining jurisdictional wetlands and other waters. Project applicants are typically responsible for delineation of jurisdictional wetlands and other waters in the U.S. on their property. USACE is then responsible for verifying the applicant's delineation.

Wetlands are delineated using the 1987 USACE Wetlands Delineation Manual (USACE 1987), together with applicable regional supplements. The 1987 manual uses a three-parameter test–if a site has positive indicators of hydrophytic (water-loving) vegetation, hydric soils, and wetlands vegetation, it is normally considered a jurisdictional wetland. In "disturbed" or "abnormal" circumstances (*e.g.*, when wetland vegetation has been artificially removed from a wetland), all three factors need not be present. This approach addresses situations where an applicant attempts to eliminate the need for a Section 404 permit by intentionally destroying hydrophytic vegetation.

Because of the *SWANCC* and *Rapanos* cases, wetlands delineations also should document hydrologic connections between the wetland and waters of the United States. Also, "special aquatic sites" that receive special protection during the Section 404 permitting process should be identified in delineations. In addition to wetlands, special aquatic sites include sanctuaries and refuges, mudflats, vegetated shallows, coral reefs, and riffle and pool complexes. 40 CFR 230.40 *et seq.*

USACE and EPA have issued guidance on wetlands delineations to implement the requirements of the *Rapanos* case. USACE and EPA

2007a. The guidance identifies categories of waters that are either normally jurisdictional, normally nonjurisdictional, or require fact-specific analysis to determine whether a significant nexus to traditional navigable waters exists. Under this guidance, intermittent ditches draining uplands, swales, and erosional features are normally considered nonjurisdictional. USACE and EPA (2007b) have also issued a memorandum on coordinating jurisdictional determinations in light of both the *SWANCC* and *Rapanos* decisions.

In the absence of wetlands, USACE regulations establish definitions for determining the jurisdictional boundaries of territorial seas, tidal waters, and nontidal waters. 33 CFR 328.4.

Definition of discharge of dredged or fill material. A Section 404 permit is required for the "discharge" of "dredged or fill material" into waters of the United States. Under the CWA, discharge of a pollutant is the addition of any pollutant to waters of the United States from any point source (*see* chapter 6 for further discussion of the CWA). "Dredged material" means materials that were removed from waters of the United States, typically during dredging. "Fill material" are materials such as dirt and rock that replace an aquatic area with dry land or raise its elevation. 33 USC 1344(a), 1362.

The application of Section 404 permits to certain types of activities affecting wetlands has been particularly controversial:

- Dredging or excavation activities per se are not regulated under Section 404, even if they cause "incidental fallback" into waters of the United States, but they are regulated under Section 404 if the redeposit is more than incidental fallback. *National Mining Association v. Army Corps of Engineers* (1998) 145 F. 3d 1399; 40 CFR 232.3

- Tractors conducting deep ripping of agricultural land are regulated under Section 404. *Borden Ranch Partnership v. USACE* (2001) 261 F. 3d 810

- Draining wetlands is not regulated under Section 404 unless there is a discharge of dredged or fill material, or unless the draining is part of land clearing for land use conversion. *Avoyelles Sportsmen's League, Inc. v. Marsh* (1983) 715 F. 2d 897

Supreme Court Interprets "Waters of the United States"

In *Solid Waste Agency of Northern Cook County v. U.S. Army Corps of Engineers* (2001, 531 U.S. 159) (*SWANCC*), a solid waste agency proposed to develop a waste disposal facility on a 533-acre site that was an abandoned sand and gravel mine. About 17 acres of the site was covered by permanent and seasonal ponds created by former excavations. USACE determined that it had jurisdiction over these ponds under the "Migratory Bird Rule" because migratory birds used them, even though the ponds were isolated and not adjacent to any navigable waters. The Supreme Court held that isolated seasonal ponds do not fall under the definition of waters of the United States subject to Section 404 jurisdiction merely because they serve as habitat for isolated birds. The case also has been interpreted to stand for the broader proposition that no other Commerce Clause connection (*e.g.,* use by interstate or foreign travelers) can justify regulation of intrastate isolated waters.

The *SWANCC* case created uncertainty about how to determine whether wetlands are "adjacent" or "isolated." In 2003, USACE and EPA issued complex guidance interpreting the *SWANCC* decision. 68 Fed. Reg. 1991, January 10, 2003. Following this guidance, the USACE generally continued to establish jurisdiction over isolated waters by using factors in its Section 404 regulations other than habitat for migratory birds.

The Supreme Court again took up the regulation of isolated wetland in its opinion on two consolidated appeals in *Rapanos v. United States* (2006) 126 S. Ct. 2208. In a highly divided opinion, the controlling test was articulated by Justice Kennedy in a concurring opinion. Under this test, waters of the United States include tributaries to, and wetlands adjacent to, navigable waters, if there is a "significant nexus" to waters that are or were navigable in fact. A "significant nexus" is established when the tributaries or wetlands significantly affect the chemical, physical, and biological integrity of waters that are or were navigable in fact. USACE and EPA (2007a) again issued guidelines on implementing the *Rapanos* decision (*see* text). ▪

- The placement of pilings is regulated under Section 404 when it would have the effect of a discharge, *e.g.,* when pilings are placed so closely together that they increase sedimentation. 33 CFR 323.2(d)(1)

Exemptions. The following activities are exempt from Section 404 regulation (33 USC 1344(f)(1)):

- "Normal" farming, silviculture (forestry), and ranching that was currently in use as of December 23, 1985

- Constructing or maintaining stock or farm ponds and irrigation ditches, or maintaining drainage ditches

- Constructing or maintaining farm, forest, or mining roads, or temporary roads for moving mining equipment

- Maintaining or reconstructing structures that are currently serviceable

- Construction of temporary construction sedimentation basins

- Activities regulated by an approved best management practices program authorized by Section 208(b)(4) of the CWA

EIS = Environmental impact statement
NEPA = National Environmental Policy Act
NWP = Nationwide permit

These exemptions are subject to a "recapture" provision, and are not exempt under certain circumstances. They are not exempt if the activity would violate toxic effluent standards or if the activity has the purpose of bringing an area within jurisdictional waters into a new use that impairs the flow, circulation, or reach of waters. USACE often applies this recapture provision when agricultural land is converted to a different use such as urban development. 33 USC 1344(f)(2).

Also, a narrow Section 404(r) exemption exists for specific congressionally authorized construction projects invoking that exemption. Before authorizing funding, the federal agency must prepare an environmental impact statement (EIS) pursuant to the National Environmental Policy Act (NEPA) that includes consideration of EPA's Section 404(b)(1) Guidelines. *See* below. 33 USC 1344(r).

Section 404 Permit Process: Overview

There are two broad types of Section 404 permits. "Standard" permits include individual permits, and when applicable, letters of permission. *See* below. "General" permits include nationwide permits (NWPs), regional general permits, and programmatic general permits. General permits are intended to authorize activities that USACE has determined would have minimal adverse effects on aquatic resources (individually or cumulatively), and that would require minimal USACE review time.

Individual permits and NWPs are the two most common types of Section 404 permits.

Individual permits and NWPs are the two most common types of Section 404 permits. The individual permit process is summarized in Figure 15-2, and the NWP process is summarized in Figure 15-3.

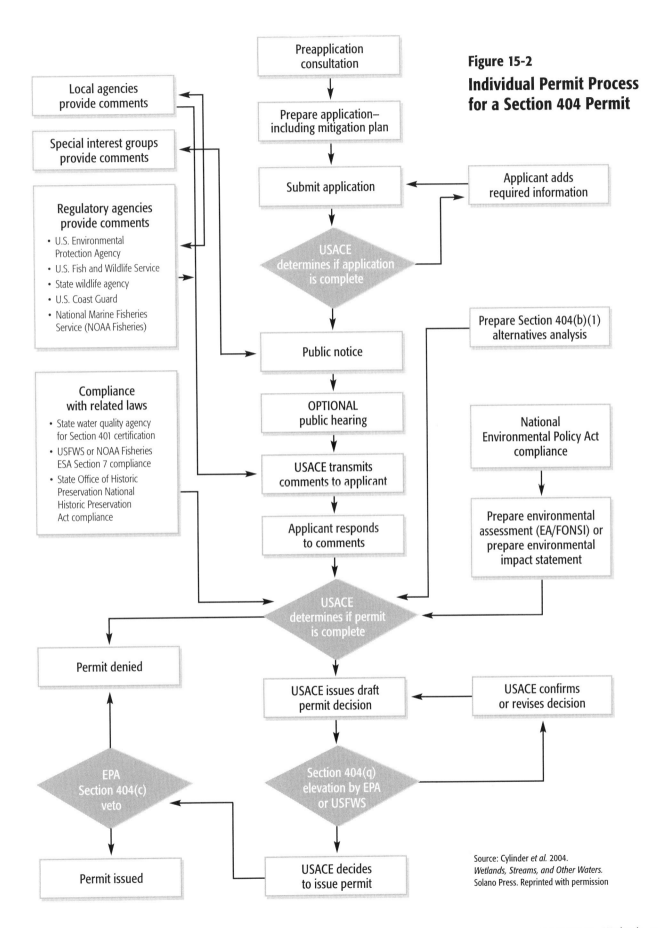

Figure 15-2

Individual Permit Process for a Section 404 Permit

Preapplication consultation

Prepare application–including mitigation plan

Submit application

Applicant adds required information

USACE determines if application is complete

Local agencies provide comments

Special interest groups provide comments

Regulatory agencies provide comments
- U.S. Environmental Protection Agency
- U.S. Fish and Wildlife Service
- State wildlife agency
- U.S. Coast Guard
- National Marine Fisheries Service (NOAA Fisheries)

Compliance with related laws
- State water quality agency for Section 401 certification
- USFWS or NOAA Fisheries ESA Section 7 compliance
- State Office of Historic Preservation National Historic Preservation Act compliance

Public notice

Prepare Section 404(b)(1) alternatives analysis

OPTIONAL public hearing

National Environmental Policy Act compliance

USACE transmits comments to applicant

Prepare environmental assessment (EA/FONSI) or prepare environmental impact statement

Applicant responds to comments

USACE determines if permit is complete

Permit denied

USACE issues draft permit decision

USACE confirms or revises decision

EPA Section 404(c) veto

Section 404(q) elevation by EPA or USFWS

Permit issued

USACE decides to issue permit

Source: Cylinder *et al.* 2004.
Wetlands, Streams, and Other Waters.
Solano Press. Reprinted with permission

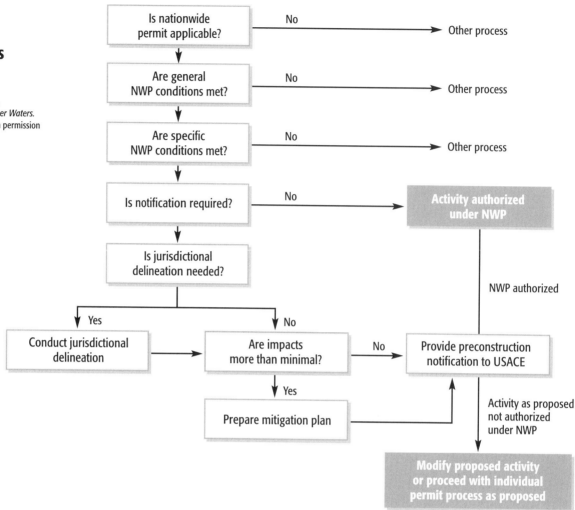

Figure 15-3
Nationwide Permit Process

Source: Cylinder *et al.* 2004.
Wetlands, Streams, and Other Waters.
Solano Press. Reprinted with permission

The permit process typically is initiated by a jurisdictional determination that the proposed activity would occur in wetlands or other waters of the United States. The project applicant typically prepares a wetlands delineation report that documents the extent of jurisdictional waters, and sends the report to USACE, requesting verification. USACE then sends the applicant a verification of jurisdictional boundaries. The verification letter is valid for five years. 33 CFR 320.1(a).

Individual Permits

The individual permit process is shown in the preceding Figure 15-2. Individual permits typically are issued before a discharge occurs, but USACE can also issue "after-the-fact" permits allowing fill to remain in place if certain conditions are met. The individual permit process is supposed to take 60–120 days once a permit application is submitted, but in practice usually takes longer. 33 CFR 325.2(a), 326.3(e).

Pre-application process. The pre-application process includes USACE verification of jurisdictional waters, and a pre-application meeting or meetings.

Relevant agencies such as USFWS are invited to the pre-application meeting to share their views about the proposed project.

Permit application. Individual permit applications must include (33 CFR 325.1), among other things:

- The project description, purpose, and need
- The purpose of activities involving discharge of dredged or fill materials, and type and quantity of material to be discharged
- Acreage of wetlands or other waters to be filled
- Drawings or plans sufficient for public notice
- Federal, state, and local authorizations required for the work

In addition, applicants often include a Section 404(b)(1) alternatives analysis and a mitigation plan together with the permit application. These documents, described below, can speed the permit process when submitted with the permit application.

Following submittal of the permit application, USACE issues a public notice of the permit application and solicits comments during a 30-day review period. A public hearing is sometimes held, if requested. Public comments are submitted to the applicant for response. 33 CFR 25(a)(2).

404(b)(1) Guidelines. The USACE permit decision is based on whether the proposed activity complies with EPA's Section 404(b)(1) Guidelines, and whether issuance of a permit is in the public interest. The Guidelines (40 CFR 230 *et seq.*) state that USACE may not issue a permit if there is a less environmentally damaging practicable alternative to the proposed discharge that would have less effect on the aquatic ecosystem, and not have other significant adverse environmental consequences. The Guidelines also restrict permitting of activities that (40 CFR 230.10(b), (c)):

The USACE permit decision is based on whether the proposed activity complies with EPA's Section 404(b)(1) Guidelines, and whether issuance of a permit is in the public interest.

- Violate water quality or toxic effluent standards
- Jeopardize the continued existence of a species listed under the Endangered Species Act
- Violate marine sanctuary protections
- Cause "significant degradation" to waters of the United States

When a proposed activity that is not "water dependent" involves discharge into a special aquatic site such as wetlands, the Guidelines presume other practicable alternatives are available that do not involve discharge into special aquatic sites, unless it can be clearly demonstrated otherwise. An activity is water dependent if it could not meet the basic project purpose unless located in a special aquatic site; a marina is an example of a water dependent activity. 40 CFR 230.10(a).

Also, the Guidelines require the applicant to prepare a mitigation plan that mitigates the effects of the discharge, and compensates for wetlands impacts that cannot be avoided or minimized. Under the USACE/EPA mitigation policy, mitigation is to be sequenced, with avoidance and minimization of wetlands impacts preferred, and compensation considered only if avoidance and minimization are not feasible (*see* the discussion of mitigation below). 40 CFR 230.10(d).

The project applicant is typically responsible for preparing the Section 404(b)(1) alternatives analysis, which is often submitted as part of the permit application.

If a permit meets the Section 404(b)(1) Guidelines, USACE may still deny the permit if it is determined to be contrary to the public interest.

Public interest review. If a permit meets the Section 404(b)(1) Guidelines, USACE may still deny the permit if it is determined to be contrary to the public interest. The public interest review balances the project benefits against its reasonably foreseeable detriments. Factors considered in the public interest review include conservation, economics, aesthetics, environmental quality, historic values, fish and wildlife values, flood control, land use, navigation, recreation, water supply and quality, energy needs, safety, and food production. A presumption exists that an activity is not in the public interest if it involves a discharge into wetlands performing functions important to the public interest, such as wetlands providing flood control benefits. 33 CFR 320.4(a), (b)(4).

Compliance with related environmental laws. To issue a Section 404 permit, USACE must demonstrate compliance with:

- CWA Section 401 certification (*see* discussion later in this chapter)
- NEPA (*see* chapter 2)
- ESA Section 7 (*see* chapter 14)
- Section 106 of the National Historic Preservation Act (*see* chapter 3)

Elevation and veto of permit decisions. Under CWA Section 404(q) (33 USC 1344(q)), USACE has entered into MOAs with EPA, USFWS, and NOAA Fisheries to elevate disputes with USACE districts, and resolve these disputes expeditiously. To be elevated, permit decisions must involve discharges that have a substantial and unacceptable impact on aquatic resources of national importance.

LOP = Letter of permission

Under CWA Section 404(c) (33 USC 13444(c)), EPA may veto a Section 404 permit issued by USACE if it determines that the discharge would have unacceptable adverse impacts on water supplies or fishing, wildlife, or recreation areas. EPA seldom exercises this veto authority, but the threat of EPA veto may cause changes in proposed projects.

Letter of Permission

The LOP process is an expedited individual permit process not requiring a public notice.

The LOP process is an expedited individual permit process not requiring a public notice. An LOP still requires agency coordination and compliance with the Section 404(b)(1) Guidelines, and compliance with related environmental laws such as the ESA. Activities eligible for an LOP (*e.g.*, habitat restoration) typically have the purpose of benefiting environmental resources. 33 CFR 325.5(b)(2).

Each USACE district lists categories of activities proposed to be authorized under LOP procedures. The district must provide public notice and an opportunity to comment on its proposed list of activities.

General Permits

General permits are intended to streamline the Section 404 permitting process for certain types of activities. General permits apply to categories of activities that are similar in nature and will cause only minimal individual and cumulative adverse environmental effects. Activities meeting conditions of a general permit may proceed without the need for an individual permit, though many require pre-construction notification (PCN) to USACE. USACE reviews general permits every five years, and may reissue, modify, or revoke a general permit following this review. 33 USC 1344(e)(1). Types of general permits include regional general permits, programmatic general permits, and the most common type, nationwide permits.

General permits apply to categories of activities that are similar in nature and will cause only minimal individual and cumulative adverse environmental effects.

NHPA = National Historic Preservation Act

PCN = Pre-construction notification

SHPO = State Historic Preservation Officer

Regional and programmatic general permits. Regional general permits are issued by a USACE district or division, for a specific geographic region. They cover activities for similar projects within that region that have minimal impacts, and are not covered by another general permit. To adopt a regional general permit, USACE must provide a public notice and comment period, and coordinate with resource agencies. To be authorized by a general permit, a proposed activity must fit within the general permit's defined activities, and meet all general permit conditions, which may require PCN. 33 CFR 325.2(e)(2).

Programmatic general permits are issued by a USACE district or division, for federal, state, or local wetlands protection programs that meet or exceed the objectives of the Section 404 program. The agency holding the permit may become the permitting authority, with USACE no longer involved in reviewing each use of the permit. 33 CFR 325.5(c)(3).

Programmatic general permits are issued by a USACE district or division, for federal, state, or local wetlands protection programs that meet or exceed the objectives of the Section 404 program.

Nationwide permits. NWPs are the most common type of general permit. They must be reissued every five years. The current categories of NWPs, listed in the sidebar on page 354, were adopted in March 2007. The full text of the NWPs, and any conditions, should be consulted for complete descriptions. Full descriptions of the NWPs may be found in 72 Fed. Reg. 11092.

USACE regulations (33 CFR 330.5) set forth detailed requirements for the issuance, modification, suspension, and revocation of both NWPs and USACE written authorizations to proceed under NWPs. NWPs offer project applicants a streamlined and time-saving approach to Section 404 compliance for qualifying activities. Commonly used NWPs include those for small fills associated with residential development, minor road crossings, outfall structures, bank stabilization, wetland restoration, and utility line activities.

List of Nationwide Permits

#	Permit	#	Permit
1	Aids to Navigation	28	Modifications of Existing Marinas
2	Structures in Artificial Canals	29	Residential Developments
3	Maintenance	30	Moist Soil Management for Wildlife
4	Fish and Wildlife Harvesting, Enhancement, and Attraction Devices and Activities	31	Maintenance of Existing Flood Control Facilities
5	Scientific Measurement Devices	32	Completed Enforcement Actions
6	Survey Activities	33	Temporary Construction, Access, and Dewatering
7	Outfall Structures and Maintenance	34	Cranberry Production Activities
8	Oil and Gas Structures on the Outer Continental Shelf	35	Maintenance Dredging of Existing Basins
9	Structures in Fleeting and Anchorage Areas	36	Boat Ramps
10	Mooring Buoys	37	Emergency Watershed Protection and Rehabilitation
11	Temporary Recreational Structures	38	Cleanup of Hazardous and Toxic Waste
12	Utility Line Activities	39	Commercial and Institutional Developments
13	Bank Stabilization	40	Agricultural Activities
14	Linear Transportation Projects	41	Reshaping Existing Drainage Ditches
15	U.S. Coast Guard Approved Bridges	42	Recreational Facilities
16	Return Water from Upland Contained Disposal Areas	43	Stormwater Management Facilities
17	Hydropower Projects	44	Mining Activities
18	Minor Discharges	45	Repair of Uplands Damaged by Discrete Activities
19	Minor Dredging	46	Discharges in Ditches
20	Oil Spill Cleanup	47	Pipeline Safety Program Designated Time Sensitive Inspections and Repairs
21	Surface Coal Mining Activities	48	Existing Commercial Shellfish Aquaculture Activities
22	Removal of Vessels	49	Coal Remining Activities
23	Approved Categorical Exclusions	50	Underground Coal Mining Activities
24	Indian Tribe or State Administered Section 404 Programs		
25	Structural Discharges		
26	Reserved		
27	Aquatic Habitat Restoration, Establishment, and Enhancement Activities		

Source: 72 Fed. Reg.11092

All NWPs are subject to general national conditions, which include compliance with the ESA, the National Historic Preservation Act (NHPA), and state water quality standards (*see* Section 401 certification below). NWP permits require mitigation of wetlands impacts following USACE/EPA guidelines (*see* below). USACE districts are authorized to add regional conditions and modify, suspend, or revoke an NWP. 33 CFR 330.1(d).

The NWP process is shown in the preceding Figure 15-3. Many of the NWPs require a PCN prior to undertaking an activity. Once an applicant submits a PCN, USACE has 30 days to determine whether the notification is complete. If a project requiring a PCN results in loss of more than one-half acre of waters of the United States, USACE must immediately provide the PCN to EPA, USFWS, NOAA Fisheries, SWRCB, and the State Historic Preservation Officer (SHPO). Within 45 days of receipt of a complete PCN, USACE must notify the applicant that the activity is authorized under the NWP or requires an individual permit. When a PCN is required, USACE may add conditions to its authorization to ensure the activity complies with the NWP terms and conditions, and results in only minimal individual and cumulative impacts on the aquatic environment. 33 CFR 330.1(e).

Mitigation of Wetlands Impacts

Overview. USACE and EPA have a national goal of no net loss of wetlands, to be applied to each permit decision. In measuring no net loss, USACE primarily will consider loss of wetlands values and functions. USACE and EPA have issued detailed guidance on methods for mitigating impacts to wetlands and other waters of the United States. Mitigation following this guidance is required for both individual and general permits. Mitigation guidance may be found in the USACE and EPA 1990 MOA (USACE and EPA 1990) and Regulatory Guidance Letter 02-2 (USACE 2002), and more recently in USACE and EPA 2008 regulations for compensatory mitigation. 73 Fed. Reg. 19594.

The USACE and EPA 1990 MOA establishes the basic mitigation sequencing framework. Wetlands impacts can be mitigated through avoidance, minimization, or compensation. Avoidance through selecting a non-wetlands site, and minimization of impacts through project modifications and permit conditions, should be implemented prior to compensation.

Compensatory mitigation prior to 2008 regulations. The 1990 MOA and Regulatory Guidance Letter 02-2 provide additional guidance for compensation. To achieve the goal of no net loss of wetlands, replacement acreage often may be greater than the acreage lost. Replacement acreage is determined based on functional values of the area being affected, on temporal loss of habitat that will occur, and on an adequate acreage margin to reflect the expected success of the mitigation plan. In the absence of more definitive information about wetlands functions, one-to-one acreage replacement may be used.

The purpose of compensatory mitigation is to develop long-term self-sustaining wetlands that are not dependent on human intervention after the wetlands become established. Compensatory mitigation may include wetlands preservation, restoration, or creation. USACE and EPA have developed the following compensatory mitigation guidelines:

The purpose of compensatory mitigation is to develop long-term self-sustaining wetlands that are not dependent on human intervention after the wetlands become established.

*   On-site mitigation is preferred to off-site mitigation

*   Off-site mitigation should be close to and in the same watershed as the discharge site

*   In-kind mitigation (the same wetlands type) is preferred to out-of-kind

Compensatory mitigation regulations. USACE and EPA issued comprehensive regulations governing compensatory mitigation in 2008 (73 Fed. Reg. 19594), in response to studies showing that the compensatory mitigation program needs improvement. *See, e.g.*, National Research Council 2001. The regulations establish performance standards and criteria for compensatory mitigation and mitigation banks. They account for regional variations in aquatic resource types, and include a watershed approach to compensatory mitigation. The regulations phase-out in lieu fee programs, in which applicants pay mitigation fees instead of directly implementing mitigation.

The regulations emphasize the use of wetlands mitigation banks under appropriate circumstances, and simplify the process for establishment of mitigation banks. Mitigation banks are a unique form of compensatory mitigation, in which off-site wetlands are enhanced, created, or restored to mitigate impacts on wetlands resources affected by individual projects. A credit system is used to purchase compensation credits. Each credit is a unit of restored or created wetlands that can be withdrawn to offset impacts of an individual project.

Enforcement

Clean Water Act Enforcement

EPA and USACE share authority for enforcing Section 404. Also, under Section 505 of the CWA (33 USC 1365), citizen suits can be filed against alleged violators of Section 404, or against USACE or EPA for failing to perform nondiscretionary duties under the CWA.

EPA and USACE enforcement responsibilities are defined in a 1989 MOA (USACE and EPA 1989). In most cases, USACE conducts initial investigations and uses its enforcement authority. Enforcement techniques include administrative orders and referrals for judicial enforcement.

Administrative orders may require compliance with Section 404 permit conditions, or take the form of cease-and-desist orders for unauthorized discharges.

Administrative orders may require compliance with Section 404 permit conditions, or take the form of cease-and-desist orders for unauthorized discharges. USACE and EPA have the authority to assess administrative penalties for violations of Section 404 permit conditions and for unpermitted discharges of dredged or fill material, respectively. Maximum fines range from $27,500 to $125,000, with a daily maximum of $11,000. 33 CFR 326.6, 40 CFR 19.

For judicial enforcement, referrals are made to the Justice Department, which files the lawsuits.

For judicial enforcement, referrals are made to the Justice Department, which files the lawsuits. USACE and EPA may recommend criminal or civil actions to obtain penalties for violations, compliance with administrative orders, and other relief. Negligent violations can result in misdemeanor penalties of $2,500 to $25,000 per day, and imprisonment for up to one year. Knowing violations can result in felony penalties of $5,000 to $50,000 per day, and imprisonment for up to three years. 33 USC 1319(c)(1), (2).

Regulatory Takings

Permit denials may be subject to takings claims under the Fifth Amendment to the U.S. Constitution, which prohibits the taking of private property without just compensation. An applicant whose permit is denied and who has a takings claim of $10,000 or more must file suit in the U.S. Court of Federal Claims to determine whether a regulatory taking has occurred and just compensation should be awarded. 28 USC 1295(a)(3).

State and Regional Programs

State Regulatory Programs

Lake or streambed alteration agreements. Fish and Game Code 1600 *et seq.* requires any person, state or local government agency, or public utility to notify DFG before beginning any activity that will:

- Substantially obstruct or divert the natural flow of a river, stream, or lake
- Substantially change or use any material from the bed, channel, or bank of a river, stream, or lake (a "bank" is defined by the outer edge of riparian vegetation)
- Deposit or dispose of debris, waste, or other material containing crumbled, flaked, or ground pavement where it may pass into a river, stream, or lake

DFG regulation applies to all perennial, intermittent, and ephemeral rivers and streams in the state, but not wetlands. DFG has not promulgated regulations to implement Fish and Game Code 1600 *et seq.*, so all program requirements are found in statute.

A DFG streambed alteration agreement is needed to alter the bed or banks of rivers.

After receiving a complete notification package, DFG will determine whether a Lake or Streambed Alteration Agreement is needed for the activity. An agreement will be required if the activity could substantially adversely affect an existing fish and wildlife resource. If an agreement is required, DFG will conduct an on-site inspection if necessary, and within 60 days submit a draft agreement to the applicant. If DFG fails to submit the draft agreement within 60 days of receiving a complete application, the agreement is automatically approved. DFG has the authority to impose appropriate mitigation measures for fish and wildlife impacts, including off-site mitigation measures, as conditions to the agreement. The applicant then negotiates a final agreement, using an arbitration panel if necessary. Fish and Game Code 1603.

DFG signs the final agreement when it receives the appropriate notification fee and after it complies with the California Environmental Quality Act (CEQA). Usually, DFG is a CEQA responsible agency for lake or streambed alternation agreements, with a state or local government agency serving as lead agency.

CEQA = California Environmental Quality Act

DFG may suspend or revoke the agreement at any time if it finds the applicant is in noncompliance. Violations of Section 1600 *et seq.* may be corrected through administrative order, and are subject to civil penalties of up to $25,000 per violation. Fish and Game Code 1612, 1615. For certain limited types of emergency work in streams or lakes, no agreement is required, but DFG notification is required 14 days before beginning work. Fish and Game Code 1610.

Agreements typically have a duration of five years or less; otherwise, they are called "long-term agreements." A "master agreement" is a seldom-used type of long-term agreement that may be used to streamline compliance for a project with multiple components that takes more than five years to construct. 14 CCR 669.5(a)(1)(G). For example, a master agreement may be signed for a large-scale development proposal composed of multiple projects for which specific, detailed design plans have not been prepared. The master agreement specifies a notification process to be followed before each component begins, and identifies mitigation measures the applicant must incorporate as part of each component.

A "master agreement" is a seldom-used type of long-term agreement that may be used to streamline compliance for a project with multiple components that takes more than five years to construct.

California Responds to the *SWANCC* and *Rapanos* Decisions

After *SWANCC,* as described by SWRCB guidance (SWRCB 2004), the USACE has disclaimed jurisdiction over many water bodies that are still considered waters of the state. In response to *SWANCC,* the SWRCB has:

- Issued a January 25, 2001, legal memorandum asserting the authority and responsibility of the SWRCB and RWQCBs to regulate discharges to isolated waters

- Coordinated with USACE to ensure that SWRCB and RWQCBs receive copies of all USACE jurisdictional disclaimer letters

- Submitted to the Legislature in April 2003 a report on *Regulatory Steps Needed to Protect and Conserve Wetlands Not Subject to the Clean Water Act*

- Adopted general WDRs in May 2004 for certain discharges to non-federal waters

In 2007, the SWRCB began work to develop a statewide wetland and riparian area protection policy. This policy is intended to clarify the state regulatory framework for wetlands and riparian areas, and establish consistent definitions of these areas and associated beneficial uses.

In 2008, the SWRCB (Resolution No. 2008-0026) defined a specific process for development of wetlands and riparian area policies. Phase 1, a policy to protect the state's wetlands from dredge-and-fill activities, is scheduled for completion in mid-2009. ▪

Section 401 certification. CWA Section 401 requires applicants for Section 404 permits in California to obtain certification from the SWRCB or RWQCB that the discharge will not violate state water quality standards. 40 CFR 230.10(b)(1). Generally, the RWQCB issues Section 401 certifications, but RWQCB decisions may be appealed to the SWRCB, which has ultimate authority over Section 401 certifications. The SWRCB must certify hydropower projects requiring a Federal Energy Regulatory Commission permit, and projects that must secure a state water right permit.

The RWQCB or SWRCB may deny certification, issue certification without conditions, or issue certification with conditions to ensure compliance with water quality standards. 23 CCR 3855 *et seq.* The SWRCB has denied certification to several NWPs, preventing the use of these NWPs in California. Also, the RWQCB or SWRCB may issue "general certifications," which certify a class of activities without the need to obtain a project-specific Section 401 certification. Section 401 certifications are discretionary projects under CEQA, and the RWQCB or SWRCB typically serves as a responsible agency (www.waterboards.ca.gov/rwqcb9/programs/401cert/NWP%20certification.pdf).

For activities undertaken pursuant to an NWP, the SWRCB has pre-certified several NWPs if those activities comply with conditions in the certification; in some cases, pre-discharge notification to the RWQCB or SWRCB is still required. For NWPs that are not pre-certified, project-specific 401 certifications are required (*see* www.waterboards.ca.gov/rwqcb9/programs/401cert/NWP%20certification.pdf).

Coastal Zone Management Act certification. To issue a Section 404 permit, the applicant must certify that the proposed activity complies with the state's Coastal Zone Management Program, and the Coastal Commission must concur with the certification or waive its right to do so. 33 CFR 325.2(b)(2).

State regulation of isolated waters. RWQCBs may regulate wetlands under waste discharge requirements issued pursuant to the Porter-Cologne Act (*see* chapter 10), if dredging, filling, or excavation activities affect the quality of waters of the state, which include wetlands. The SWRCB has taken particular interest in prioritizing WDRs for activities affecting isolated waters no longer subject to federal regulation after the *SWANCC* decision. SWRCB 2004. *See* sidebar.

SWRCB has adopted general WDRs for certain discharges to non-federal waters. Activities authorized are limited to discharges not greater than one-fifth of an acre and 400 linear feet (for fill and excavation) or 50 cubic yards (for dredging). Applicants must submit a notice of intention, a mitigation plan to avoid and minimize impacts, and a compensation plan for unavoidable permanent impacts to wetlands and headwater streams. If a proposed discharge does not qualify for the general WDRs, then project-specific WDRs may be required. SWRCB 2004.

Conservation/mitigation banks. The Resources Agency and DFG distinguish between conservation banks (for mitigated impacts to endangered species) and mitigation banks (for impacts to wetlands), and have developed similar policies for both. DFG recognizes that conservation/mitigation banks are a viable alternative to requiring piecemeal mitigation for individual project impacts, and that conservation/mitigation banks provide incentives to private landowners to practice conservation. Additionally, landowners using conservation/mitigation banks can take advantage of economies of scale otherwise unavailable for individual mitigation projects.

In 1995, Cal/EPA and the Resources Agency published the state's official policy on conservation banks, which provides formal policy guidance on appropriate locations, mechanisms for permanent protection of the habitat, and basic elements needed for DFG to approve a conservation/mitigation bank. Cal/EPA and Resources Agency 1995. In 1996, DFG and USFWS developed a joint policy memorandum as a supplemental policy regarding conservation/mitigation banks within the natural community conservation planning area of southern California. DFG and USFWS 1996. Also, DFG has issued guidance (available online) for lands not appropriate for mitigation banking, and developed a checklist for preparing conservation/mitigation bank legal agreements (available at www.dfg.ca.gov/hcpb/conplan/mitbank/mitbank.shtml).

Statutory treatment of mitigation banking is limited. The Sacramento–San Joaquin Valley Wetlands Mitigation Banking Act (Fish and Game Code 1775) authorized DFG to adopt regulations to qualify Central Valley sites as wetlands mitigation banks. DFG also is required to maintain a database on wetlands mitigation banks and provide status reports to the Legislature. Fish and Game Code 1851.

State Programs for Protecting the Coastal Zone and Suisun Marsh Wetlands

Coastal Act. Under the Coastal Act (*see* chapter 4), wetlands are defined as "lands within the coastal zone which may be covered periodically or permanently with shallow water and include saltwater marshes, fresh water marshes, open or closed brackish water marshes, swamps, mudflats, and fens." PRC 30121. This definition includes isolated wetlands not regulated under Section 404.

Local coastal programs and coastal development permits must comply with wetlands policies of the Coastal Act, and with the Coastal Commission's interpretive guidelines for wetlands. In general, these policies allow wetlands to be filled only for water-dependent activities when no feasible upland alternatives

PRC = Public Resources Code

Local coastal programs and coastal development permits must comply with wetlands policies of the Coastal Act, and with the Coastal Commission's interpretive guidelines for wetlands.

exist. They also require wetland impacts to be avoided or minimized. California Coastal Commission 1994.

Suisun Marsh. Suisun Marsh is a unique and valuable wetlands area subject to special state and regional regulation. The Suisun Marsh comprises approximately 85,000 acres of tidal marsh, managed wetlands, and waterways in southern Solano County. Suisan Marsh is the largest remaining wetland near San Francisco Bay, and includes more than 10 percent of California's remaining wetland area. The Marsh is also a wildlife habitat of nationwide importance.

The Legislature directed BCDC and the DFG to prepare a Suisun Marsh Protection Plan "to preserve the integrity and assure continued wildlife use" of the Suisun Marsh. The Suisun Marsh Preservation Act (PRC 2900 *et seq.*) was enacted in 1977 to incorporate the findings and policies contained in the plan into state law. The Act creates a primary management area that includes all wetlands in the marsh, and a secondary management area (or buffer zone) that includes most of the adjacent agricultural upland areas surrounding the marsh. The Act requires local governments to develop protection plans for both the wetland and upland areas to further ensure the integrity of the marsh.

BCDC = San Francisco Bay Conservation and Development Commission

For more information...

Publications

Cal/EPA and Resources Agency, 1995. Official Policy on Conservation Banks

California Coastal Commission. 1994. Procedural Guidance for the Review of Wetland Projects in the California Coastal Zone

Cylinder, P.D., K.M. Bogdan, April I. Zohn, and Joel B. Butterworth. 2004. Wetlands, Streams, and Other Waters: Regulation, Conservation, and Mitigation Planning. Solano Press. Point Arena, Calif.

Department of Fish and Game and U.S. Fish and Wildlife Service. 1996. Supplemental Policy Regarding Conservation Banks Within the NCCP Area of Southern California

Environmental Protection Agency, U.S. Army Corps of Engineers, U.S. Fish and Wildlife Service, National Oceanographic and Atmospheric Administration Fisheries, and Natural Resources Conservation Service. 1995. Federal Guidance on the Establishment, Use, and Operation of Mitigation Banks

Manaster, K.A. and D.P. Selmi (eds). ND. California Environmental Law and Land Use Practice, Chapter 69. Matthew Bender. San Francisco, Calif.

National Research Council. 2001. Compensation for Wetland Losses under the Clean Water Act

State Water Resources Control Board. 2004. Guidance for Regulation of Discharges to "Isolated" Waters

Talbert, C.T. 2008. Curtin's California Land Use and Planning Law. Solano Press. Point Arena, Calif.

U.S. Army Corps of Engineers. 1987. Corps of Engineers Wetlands Delineation Manual. Technical Report Y-87-1

U.S. Army Corps of Engineers. 2002. Regulatory Guidance Letter 02-2. Guidance on Compensatory Mitigation Projects for Aquatic Resource Impacts under the Corps Regulatory Program

U.S. Army Corps of Engineers and Environmental Protection Agency. 1989, as amended in 1993. MOA Between the Department of The Army and the Environmental Protection Agency Concerning Determination of the Geographic Jurisdiction of the Section 404 Program and the Application of Exemptions Under Section 404(f) of the CWA

U.S. Army Corps of Engineers and Environmental Protection Agency. 1990. MOA Between the Department of the Army and the Environmental Protection Agency Concerning the Determination of Mitigation Under the Clean Water Act Section 404(b)(1) Guidelines

U.S. Army Corps of Engineers and Environmental Protection Agency. 2007a. Clean Water Act Jurisdiction Following the U.S. Supreme Court's Decision in *Rapanos v. United States* and *Carabell v. United States*

U.S. Army Corps of Engineers and Environmental Protection Agency. 2007b. Memorandum: Coordination on Jurisdictional Determinations under Clean Water Act Section 404 in Light of the *SWANCC* and *Rapanos* Supreme Court Decisions

Websites

Department of Fish and Game, Conservation and Mitigation Banks
www.dfg.ca.gov/hcpb/conplan/mitbank/mitbank.shtml

Department of Fish and Game, Streambed Alteration Agreements
www.dfg.ca.gov/1600/index.html

State Water Resources Control Board, 401 Certification
www.waterboards.ca.gov

U.S. Army Corps of Engineers, Los Angeles District Regulatory Program
www.spl.usace.army.mil/regulatory

U.S. Army Corps of Engineers, Regulatory Guidance Letters
www.usace.army.mil/inet/functions/cw/cecwo/reg/rglsindx.htm

U.S. Army Corps of Engineers, Regulatory Program
www.usace.army.mil/inet/functions/cw/cecwo/reg

U.S. Army Corps of Engineers, Sacramento District Regulatory Program
www.spk.usace.army.mil/organizations/cespk-co/regulatory/index.html

U.S. Army Corps of Engineers, San Francisco District Regulatory Program
www.spn.usace.army.mil/regulatory

CHAPTER 16

Forestry

This chapter reviews —

- Key laws and agencies involved in forestry regulation
- Timber harvest regulation
- Enforcement

Related Solano Press titles–

Guide to the California Forest Practice Act and Related Laws
Sharon E. Duggan and
Tara Mueller. 2005

Glossary

Long-term sustained yield–the average growth sustainable by an inventory predicted at the end of a 100-year planning period.

Nonindustrial tree farmer–owner of timberland less than 2,500 acres not primarily engaged in the manufacture of forest products.

Program timber environmental impact report–an environmental impact report prepared for a program timber harvest plan.

Program timber harvest plan* –a timber harvest plan prepared for single or multiple ownerships in which CEQA compliance is achieved through a program timber environmental impact report.

Rangeland–land used primarily for livestock grazing and occupied by a few tree species usually not harvested for lumber products.

Silvicultural system–a planned program of forest stand treatments during the life of a stand.

Special treatment area–an area designation by the Coastal Commission according to Coastal Act criteria, such as scenic view corridors, wetlands, and significant habitats.

State responsibility area–an area where fire protection is primarily a state responsibility.

Sustained yield–the yield of commercial wood that an area of commercial timberland can provide continuously at a given intensity of management consistent with required environmental protection, and that is professionally planned to achieve a balance between growth and removal.

Sustained yield plan–a plan to achieve sustainable levels of timber harvest; supplements the THP process by addressing long-term issues and cumulative effects of timber operations in defined management units.

Timber harvest plan* –under the FPA, a plan prepared by a registered professional forester (RPF) for any proposed timber harvest on non-federal land. Among other contents, the THP describes the site to be harvested, the silviculture methods to be applied, reforestation methods, road building, and mitigation measures to avoid soil erosion and other environmental damage.

Timber operation–under the FPA, an operation that includes cutting of timber for commercial purposes or for incidental work, such as construction and maintenance of roads, fuel breaks, stream crossings, skid trails, fire hazard abatement, and site preparation.

Timberland–under the FPA, non-federal land available for and capable of growing a crop of trees of any commercial species used to produce lumber and other forest products.

Timberland conversion permit* –a permit issued by the Forestry Board authorizing conversion of timberland to non-timber uses.

Woodlands–forest lands composed mostly of hardwood species such as oak.

* equals permits and approvals

CHAPTER 16

Forestry

Introduction

This chapter reviews California law related to forestry regulation. The discussion of forestry regulation focuses on commercial timber harvesting on private forest lands, as opposed to public lands, given the intensity of regulation of timber harvesting on private land.

Key Laws and Agencies

Federal Laws and Agencies

U.S. Forest Service and U.S. Bureau of Land Management. The U.S. Forest Service and U.S. Bureau of Land Management manage extensive forests on federal lands in California. The agencies manage federal forests to achieve multiple use objectives pursuant to the National Forest Management Act (16 USC 471(a) *et seq.*), the Multiple-Use Sustained-Yield Act of 1960 (16 USC 528 *et seq.*), the Forest and Rangeland Renewable Resources Planning Act of 1974 (16 USC 1600 *et seq.*), and regulations implementing these laws. Management of federal forests is coordinated with state and local policies for adjacent lands.

FPA = Forest Practice Act
PRC = Public Resources Code
USC = United States Code

State Laws and Agencies

Z'berg–Njedly Forest Practice Act of 1973 and Forest Practice Rules. The Forest Practice Act (FPA, PRC 4511 *et seq.*) governs harvesting of non-federal timberland in California. The Act's goals are to restore, enhance, and maintain timberland productivity and to achieve the maximum sustained production of high quality timber products while giving consideration to other environmental and economic values.

To implement the FPA, the Board of Forestry and Fire Protection has adopted specific forest practice rules (14 CCR 906 *et seq.*) for three districts: the Coast Forest District, the Northern Forest District, and the Southern Forest District. Within each district, the Forestry Board has created subdistricts and special treatment areas subject to more specific rules. The Forestry Board also has passed rules for Coastal Commission Special Treatment Areas and for five individual counties: Monterey, Santa Cruz, San Mateo, Santa Clara, and Marin. 14 CCR 921 *et seq.*, 924 *et seq.*

CCR = California Code of Regulations
TPZ = Timberland production zone

Forest practice rules cover the following topics (14 CCR 895.1):

- Silvicultural systems (planned programs of forest stand treatments during the life of a stand) and regeneration areas
- Harvesting practices and erosion control
- Site preparation
- Watercourse and lake protection
- Hazard reduction
- Insect and disease protection
- Bird and nesting site protection
- Logging roads and landings
- Archeological and historical resource preservation
- Sensitive species classification
- Sensitive watersheds
- Late succession forest stands

California Forest Legacy Program Act. This Act (PRC 12200 *et seq.*) allows owners of private forest lands or woodlands (forest lands composed mostly of hardwood species such as oak) meeting certain criteria to voluntarily protect significant forest resources by selling or donating conservation easements. Easements may be held by federal, state, or local agencies, or by nonprofit land trusts.

The Timberland Productivity Act implements a state policy to keep timberlands in production, rather than converted to other uses.

Timberland Productivity Act. This Act (Gov. Code 51100 *et seq.*) implements a state policy to keep timberlands in production, rather than converted to other uses. Similar to the Williamson Act, the Timberland Productivity Act provides that if land is placed within a timberland production zone (TPZ), property assessments must be based on the value of the land when restricted to timber growing. Uses of land within TPZs are limited to those compatible with timberland production, as defined by local ordinance. TPZ zoning lasts for a rolling 10-year period, and if rezoning is proposed prior to the end of 10 years, increased taxes and a tax recoupment fee must be paid.

Board of Forestry and Fire Protection. The Forestry Board is responsible for developing forest practice rules and regulations to implement the FPA.

The Forestry Board has the following general powers (PRC 730(a)):

- Developing an adequate state forest policy
- Representing state interest in federal forestry issues
- Setting policy for the California Department of Forestry and Fire Protection (CDF)
- Overseeing forest management information and research

The Forestry Board has the following specific powers (PRC 760, 4516 *et seq.*):

- Overseeing CDF's fire protection system
- Setting minimum standards for firesafe development in state responsibility areas (areas in which the financial responsibility of preventing and suppressing wildfires is primarily the responsibility of the state)
- Licensing of professional foresters
- Setting regulations for forest practices, state forest management, insect and disease control, and forest improvement and vegetation management projects

California Department of Forestry and Fire Protection. CDF oversees enforcement of California's forest practice regulations that guide timber harvesting on private lands. PRC 4570 *et seq.* CDF reviews an average 600 timber harvest plans (THPs) and conducts over 6,500 site inspections each year. CDF also conducts major firefighting activities statewide, including providing emergency services in state responsibility areas (SRAs) in 36 counties through contracts with local governments. Also, CDF conducts the Forest and Resource Assessment Program, which periodically assesses the status and trends of the state's forests and rangelands. Lastly, CDF implements the California Forest Legacy Program by acquiring conservation easements from owners of private forest land to protect forest resources. PRC 12200 *et seq.*

Counties. The FPA generally prohibits counties from requiring permits for conducting timber harvest operations. Counties, however, may recommend to the Forestry Board additional rules and regulations governing timber operations that address local needs. A county also may request a public hearing on a THP at a location within the county.

Timber Harvest Regulation

Activities Regulated

The FPA applies to "timber operations" on "timberland." Timber operations include cutting of timber for commercial purposes or for incidental work, such as construction and maintenance of roads, fuel breaks, stream crossings, skid trails, fire hazard abatement, and site preparation. Timberland is defined as non-federal land available for and capable of growing a crop of trees of any commercial species used to produce lumber and other forest products. Exemptions for emergencies and for minor harvesting operations are available, including a one-time conversion of less than three acres of timberland to non-timber use,

CDF = California Department of Forestry and Fire Protection
SRA = State responsibility area
THP = Timber harvest plan

CDF oversees enforcement of California's forest practice regulations that guide timber harvesting on private lands.

Timber operations include cutting of timber for commercial purposes or for incidental work, such as construction and maintenance of roads, fuel breaks, stream crossings, skid trails, fire hazard abatement, and site preparation.

and harvesting of Christmas trees. Also exempt is the cutting or removal of trees within 150 feet of structures in order to reduce flammable materials and maintain a fuel break. PRC 4584.

Timber operator licenses from the Forestry Board are required for any person engaging in timber operations. PRC 4571(a).

Resource Conservation Standards

To ensure an adequate cover of trees is maintained or established after timber operations, the FPA establishes resource conservation standards for minimum stocking, soil erosion control, and stream protection.

To ensure an adequate cover of trees is maintained or established after timber operations, the FPA establishes resource conservation standards for minimum stocking, soil erosion control, and stream protection. PRC 4561 *et seq.* Minimum stocking standards are met if, within five years after timber operations, certain minimum tree counts or densities are met. Soil erosion standards specify permissible levels of soil loss in timber operations. Stream protection standards prevent unreasonable effects on beneficial uses of waters of the state by regulating activities such as construction of logging roads and stream crossings, and removal of riparian vegetation.

Timber Harvest Plan

A THP must be prepared by a registered professional forester (RPF) for any proposed timber harvest on non-federal land. Among other contents, the THP describes the site to be harvested, the silviculture methods to be applied, reforestation methods, road building, and mitigation measures to avoid soil erosion and other environmental damage. PRC 4582.

THP process. Figure 16-1 illustrates the THP review process. Upon receipt of a THP, the following process is followed (14 CCR 1037 *et seq.*):

Timber harvest plans must be prepared for timber harvest on non-federal land.

- Copies are distributed to all state and federal reviewing agencies.

- A notice of intention is sent to the landowners within 300 feet of the THP, to the office of the county clerk within the THP county, and to the local CDF unit headquarters.

- A first review of the THP is done by a multi-agency team that includes the CDF, the Department of Fish and Game (DFG), the Regional Water Quality Control Board (RWQCB), the California Geological Survey, and other agencies as needed. This first review assesses whether the THP is complete. Incomplete applications are returned for revision to the RPF who prepared the THP.

- Once all review team concerns are clarified and the THP is deemed complete, it is officially "filed," and a notice of filing is issued. The public may submit to CDF comments on a filed THP.

DFG = Department of Fish and Game
EPA = Environmental Protection Agency
PHI = Pre-harvest inspection
RPF = Registered professional forester
RWQCB = Regional water quality control board
SWRCB = State Water Resources Control Board

Within 10 days of the notice of filing, the review team may conduct a pre-harvest inspection (PHI) to examine the proposed logging site. 14 CCR 1037.5(g) (2). Almost all plans receive a PHI. Within 20 days of the PHI, the review team meets to discuss the PHI reports and to finalize any changes needed for the THP.

The public comment period ends 30 days after the PHI. The public comment period may be extended to allow time for agencies involved in the THP process to complete their reviews, or for additional study of a specific THP issue. 14 CCR 1037.3(c).

The review team's final recommendations are sent to the RPF for response. After the RPF's response is received and the public comment period closes, the THP goes to the CDF director, or the director's representative, who has 15 working days to approve or deny the THP. The director considers all Forestry Board rules, the review team's recommendations, and any public comments that were submitted concerning the proposed timber operation before making a decision to approve or deny the THP. PRC 4582.7(a).

If the THP is denied, the applicant may appeal by requesting a public hearing before the Forestry Board. If the THP is approved, the SWRCB and DFG may appeal the approval to the Forestry Board if they participated in an on-site inspection with CDF and in multidisciplinary reviews of the THP. PRC 4582.7(c), 4582.9.

A THP is effective for a maximum of three years, unless extended by an amendment. Once a THP is approved, CDF inspectors periodically will inspect the logging operation to ensure compliance with the approved THP and applicable regulations. When a THP operation has been completed, the timber owner has the responsibility for submitting a completion report to CDF. CDF then inspects the area to certify that all rules were followed. The landowner must restock the area to meet minimum standards. A stocking report must be filed with CDF to certify that these requirements were met. 14 CCR 1037.5, PRC 4585(a).

Water quality regulation. Timber operations under the FPA are exempt from RWQCB waste discharge requirements (WDRs) if certain conditions are met. However, this exemption currently is not in effect because one condition has not

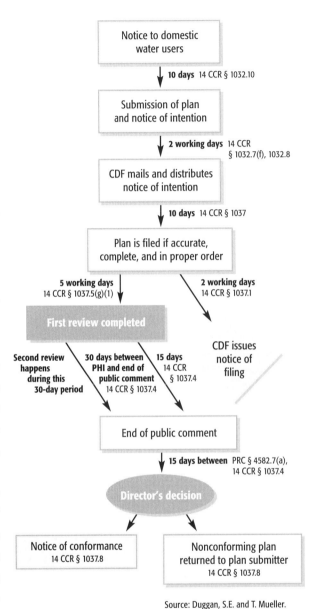

Figure 16-1

Review Process for Timber Harvest Plan

Source: Duggan, S.E. and T. Mueller. 2005. *Guide to the Forest Practice Act and Related Laws*, p. 113. Solano Press. Reprinted with permission

CEQA = California Environmental Quality Act
EIR   = Environmental impact report
NTMP = Nonindustrial timber management plan
PTEIR = Program timber environmental impact report
PTHP   = Program timber harvest plan
SYP   = Sustained yield plan
WDR   = Waste discharge requirement

been met–the Environmental Protection Agency (EPA) and SWRCB must first certify that provisions of the FPA constitute best management practices for silvicultural nonpoint source discharges. Should the EPA and SWRCB in the future make this certification, then the FPA's WDR exemption would become effective unless one of the following occurs (PRC 4514.3):

- The Forestry Board requests issuance of WDRs
- The SWRCB finds that the Forestry Board's water quality regulatory process does not constitute best management practices
- The SWRCB finds that compliance with best management practices would result in less water quality protection than required by the relevant basin plan

Although the RWQCBs have the authority to issue WDRs for timber operations, the North Coast, Central Valley, and Lahontan RWQCBs have adopted waivers of the WDR requirement, provided certain conditions protecting water quality are met. Duggan and Mueller 2005. Further, water quality is protected by 2003 legislation giving the RWQCBs veto authority over THP approval if the timber operations cause a discharge to a water body that is classified as "impaired" due to sediment, and the discharge will contribute to a violation of the regional water quality control plan. PRC 4582.71.

Once a THP is approved, the RWQCB still has the authority to impose water quality monitoring requirements if it believes the THP's water quality monitoring program is not adequate. *Pacific Lumber Company v. SWRCB* (2006) 37 Cal. 4th 574. Although the FPA is intended to streamline permitting and regulation of timber operations, it has a "savings clause" stating that the FPA does not limit the authority of other resource agencies to administer or enforce their laws.

California Environmental Quality Act and THPs. The application of CEQA to THP approval was affirmed in *Natural Resources Defense Council, Inc. v. Arcata Nat. Corp.* (1976) 59 Cal. App. 3d 959. In response, the timber harvest planning process and Forestry Board rulemaking process became certified regulatory programs under CEQA. CEQA's policies and substantive requirements apply to these programs, but the programs are exempt from the requirement to prepare CEQA documents such as environmental impact reports (EIRs). *See* chapter 2.

The application of CEQA to the THP process has been the subject of extensive CEQA litigation, much of which has been related to either logging of old-growth redwood forests, cumulative impacts of forestry operations, or effects of forestry operations on endangered species. In fact, the THP process has by far been the most litigated CEQA certified regulatory program. *See* sidebar.

Other Programs Established by the Forest Practice Act

Program Timber Harvest Plan. A program timber harvest plan (PTHP) may be prepared for ownerships in which a program timber environmental impact report (PTEIR) has been prepared. 14 CCR 1092 *et seq.* The PTEIR and PTHP provide an alternative to the functional equivalent process normally associated with THPs. A PTEIR analyzes significant impacts and identifies mitigation measures as required by CEQA for timber operations within one or multiple ownerships. The PTHP must be within the scope of the analysis contained in the PTEIR. The PTHP must be limited to areas with reasonably similar environmental characteristics that constitute a logical harvesting unit.

Sustained yield plan. An SYP is a plan to achieve sustainable levels of timber harvest. SYPs supplement the THP process by addressing long-term issues and cumulative effects of timber operations in defined management units. In an SYP, the landowner selects sustainable harvest yields that support the production of high-quality timber products. CDF evaluates the SYP and approves a defined level of "long-term sustained yield" that must conform to the Forest Practice Rules. PRC 4513(b); 15 CCR 913.11, 933.11, 953.11.

"Sustained yield" is defined as the yield of commercial wood that an area of commercial timberland can provide continuously at a given intensity of management consistent with required environmental protection, and which is professionally planned to achieve a balance between growth and removal. "Long-term sustained yield" is defined as the average growth sustainable by an inventory predicted at the end of a 100-year planning period. 14 CCR 895.1, 1091.14.

SYPs have a maximum duration of 10 years and are subject to a continuous monitoring process. Individual THPs rely on SYP analyses of sustained timber production, watershed impacts, and fish and wildlife issues. Each THP submitted for an area covered by an SYP must demonstrate consistency with the SYP and must include mitigation measures included in the SYP. 14 CCR 1091.2, 1091.3.

Nonindustrial timber management plan. Nonindustrial tree farmers (owners of timberland less than 2,500 acres not primarily engaged in the manufacture of forest products) may file a NTMP. The NTMP has the objectives of a managed, uneven-aged timber stand and sustained yield. PRC 4593 *et seq.*

Timberland conversion. The FPA requires an owner of timberland intending a "conversion" to non-timber uses to apply to the Forestry Board for a timberland conversion permit. PRC 4621(a). For lands within a TPZ, any immediate rezoning (*i.e.*, rezoning prior to the expiration of the rolling 10-year period for reduced property taxes) is considered a conversion. For TPZ land, the Forestry Board may approve the application if (PRC 4621.2):

- The conversion is in the public interest.

- The conversion would not have a substantial and unmitigated effect on other timberland.

- Soils, slopes, and watershed conditions would be suitable for the proposed new uses.

Removal of trees for subdivision development is exempt from this requirement if a local government has approved a tentative subdivision map and issued a subdivision use permit. The exemption must be consistent with FPA purposes and is not applicable to lands designated within a TPZ. PRC 4628.

Enforcement

Enforcement of timber harvesting regulations starts with a CDF inspection report describing violations observed and corrections needed. If corrections are not made, CDF may take corrective action and charge costs to the responsible person. Failure to make corrections may result in warnings, civil actions, suspension or revocation of timber operator licenses, or misdemeanor prosecutions.

Violation of most FPA procedural rules or regulations generally is punishable as an infraction with a fine of up to $250 per violation; infraction penalties are not applicable if environmental damage is caused or if requirements for THP submission or licensing are violated. PRC 4601.5(a). Knowing or negligent violations of the FPA can result in a civil penalty of up to $10,000 per violation. PRC 4601.1(a)(1). Criminal penalties for violations include misdemeanor fines of up to $5,000 or imprisonment for six months. PRC 4601.

For more information...

Publications

Duggan, S.E. and T. Mueller. 2005. Guide to the California Forest Practice Act and Related Laws. Solano Press. Point Arena, Calif.

Manaster, K.A. and D.P. Selmi (eds.). ND. Chapter 80 of California Environmental Law and Land Use Practice. Matthew Bender. San Francisco, Calif.

Websites

Board of Forestry and Fire Protection
www.bof.fire.ca.gov

California Department of Forestry and Fire Protection
www.fire.ca.gov/php/index.php

California Department of Forestry and Fire Protection, Fire and Resource Assessment Program
http://frap.cdf.ca.gov

California Department of Forestry and Fire Protection, Timber Harvest Plan Process
www.fire.ca.gov/php/rsrc-mgt_forestpractice_thpreviewprocess.php

Surface Mining

This chapter reviews–

- Key laws and agencies involved in surface mining regulation
- Mineral conservation
- Surface mine reclamation
- Enforcement

Related Solano Press titles–

California Surface Mining Law.
In Press. Derek F. Cole. 2008

Glossary

Auger mining—removal of minerals from the walls of mined-out strips using special machines.

Mined land—the surface, subsurface, and groundwater of an area where a surface mining operation is conducted.

Open-pit mining—mining of mineral deposits located at or near the earth's surface from surface openings.

Overburden—soil, rock, or other minerals that lie above a natural mineral deposit or in between mineral deposits before or after their removal by surface mining operations.

Reclamation—process of land treatment that minimizes adverse environmental effects of surface mining operations, so that mined lands are reclaimed to a usable condition that is readily adaptable to alternative land uses and creates no danger to public health and safety.

Reclamation plan*—a plan filed by a surface mining operator that, together with financial assurances, must be approved by a lead agency before mining activities commence.

Surface mining operation—mining of minerals on mined lands by removing overburden and mining directly from the mineral deposits; open-pit mining of naturally exposed minerals; auger mining; dredging and quarrying; or surface work incident to an underground mine. Surface mining operations include exploratory activities, and production and disposal of mining waste.

* equals permits and approvals

CHAPTER 17

Surface Mining

This chapter reviews California law related to surface mining. The discussion of mining focuses on environmental regulation of mining operations under the Surface Mining and Reclamation Act (SMARA). State Water Resources Control Board (SWRCB) regulation of mining wastes is addressed in chapter 10. This chapter does not address regulation of oil and gas mining.

Because of California's growing demand for minerals, the state ranks second among all states in non-fuel mineral production. From more than 820 active mines, California mineral production in 2005 was worth $3.7 billion. Most was for materials needed for construction: sand and gravel production was worth $1.3 billion, and Portland cement production was worth $1.1 billion. Kohler 2005.

PRC	= Public Resources Code
SMARA	= Surface Mining and Reclamation Act
SMGB	= State Mining and Geology Board
SWRCB	= State Water Resources Control Board

Key Laws and Agencies

Key Laws

Surface Mining and Reclamation Act. SMARA (PRC 2710) recognizes the importance of mineral extraction to the California economy and that reclamation of mined lands is needed to protect the environment, and public health and safety. Administered by the State Mining and Geology Board (SMGB), the Act's goals are to:

- Prevent or minimize environmental effects

- Ensure that mined lands are reclaimed to a useable condition adaptable for various uses

- Encourage the production and conservation of minerals, while considering environmental values

- Eliminate residual hazards to public health and safety

SMARA recognizes the importance of mineral extraction to the California economy and that reclamation of mined lands is needed to protect the environment, and public health and safety.

SMARA has two main regulatory programs: mineral conservation and surface mine reclamation. It also requires every operator to obtain a city or county permit, typically a conditional use permit, before conducting surface mining operations. Regulations implementing the Act are found at 14 CCR 3500 *et seq.*

Key Agencies

State Mining and Geology Board. The SMGB serves as a regulatory, policy, and appeals body representing the state's interests in geology, geologic and seismologic hazards, and conservation of mineral resources and reclamation of lands following surface mining activities. SMARA requires SMGB to set state policy for reclaiming mined lands. The Board operates within the Department of Conservation (DOC).

Office of Mine Reclamation. This office, also within DOC, is responsible for administering SMARA implementation. It also includes an Abandoned Mines Land Unit to address research and policy on abandoned mines issues.

California Geological Survey. The California Geological Survey provides staff to the state geologist and is also within DOC. It provides the public with information and advice to protect life and property from natural hazards, and to promote a better understanding of the state's geologic environment. CGS is responsible for classifying the state's mineral resources and inventorying the state's non-fuel mineral resources.

Lead agencies. Under SMARA, cities and counties are designated as lead agencies, and given the responsibility for administering and enforcing SMARA.

Mineral Conservation

Although SMARA is mostly known for its regulation of surface mine regulation, it also plays an important role in preventing mineral resources from being lost through incompatible urban development.

Although SMARA is mostly known for its regulation of surface mine regulation, it also plays an important role in preventing mineral resources from being lost through incompatible urban development. The Act requires the DOC, using input from CGS, to classify those areas of the state that contain "significant mineral deposits" that are subject to urban expansion or other irreversible land uses that would preclude mineral extraction. The SMGB may designate certain of these areas as either significant regional or statewide resources, for which SMARA provides additional protection. PRC 2761(a), (b) (2), 2790.

Classification and Designation of Significant Mineral Deposits

Classification and designation process. CGS classifies mineral deposits as "significant" using marketability and economic criteria (DOC ND). The SMGB may further designate mineral deposits as areas of regional significance (of prime importance in meeting future regional minerals needs) or statewide significance (of prime importance in meeting future state minerals needs). These designations must be preceded by a public hearing, and must me made by regulation. PRC 2726, 2727, 2790.

General plan policies. Cities and counties must adopt mineral resource management policies when they receive a mineral classification report or when SMGB designates land within their boundaries as an area of regional or statewide significance. Local agencies must include these polices in their general plans and submit then to SMGB for review. The policies must recognize mineral classifications, assist in managing land uses affecting areas of regional or statewide significance, and emphasize the conservation and development of mineral deposits identified by the classification process. PRC 2762(a).

Cities and counties must adopt mineral resource management policies when they receive a mineral classification report or when SMGB designates land within their boundaries as an area of regional or statewide significance.

To protect classified or designated areas, cities and counties must implement at least one of the following measures (14 CCR 3676(c)(3)):

- Placing these areas into special or overlay zoning districts

- Recording presence of identified mineral deposits on property titles

- Adopting general plan policies mitigating land use incompatibilities between mining and development

Project-level requirements. SMARA also imposes project-level requirements when cities and counties review an individual project that "threatens the potential to extract minerals" from classified or designated areas. Typically, these projects include projects proposed on mineral lands, as well as projects adjacent to these lands. A city or county proposing to approve such a project must prepare a statement of reasons, include the statement in California Environmental Quality Act (CEQA) documents, and submit the statement to the State Geologist and SMGB. PRC 2762, 2763.

CEQA = California Environmental Quality Act

SMARA places further requirements on cities and counties for a project "involving" lands designated as significant mineral resources. These projects include mining projects as well as development projects. SMARA requires that a decision to approve such a project must be consistent with the city or county mineral resource management policies, and must balance mineral values against alternative land uses. PRC 2763. Also, for lands designated as significant mineral resources, SMGB may hear appeals of city or county decisions approving or denying mining permits. PRC 2775.

Surface Mine Reclamation

SMARA Applicability

Surface mining operations. SMARA generally applies to all surface mining operations. "Surface mining operations" involve the mining of minerals on mined lands by any of these methods (PRC 2735):

- Mining of minerals on mined lands by removing overburden and mining directly from the mineral deposits
- Open-pit mining of naturally exposed minerals
- Auger mining, dredging, and quarrying
- Surface work incident to an underground mine

Surface mining operations include exploratory activities, and production and disposal of mining waste. PRC 2735.

Open-pit mining is the most common surface mining method. It is used for sand and gravel operations and rock quarries. Excavations are usually opened by the removal of overburden (noneconomic material), followed by excavation in step-like layers (termed benching).

Large gravel mines eventually require reclamation under SMARA.

Mined lands. Mined lands subject to SMARA's reclamation requirements are defined broadly as "the surface, subsurface, and ground water of an area in which surface mining operations will be, are being, or have been conducted." Reclamation requirements may also extend to "affected lands" surrounding mined lands. PRC 2729, 2733.

Operators. A mining project operator is a person or entity that directly conducts surface mining operations, or who contracts with others to conduct mining on their behalf. Once a reclamation plan is approved, it is binding on successor operators. PRC 2731, 2779.

Exemptions. Activities exempt from SMARA's reclamation requirements include the following (PRC 2714):

- Excavation and earth-moving activities that are an integral and necessary part of a construction project
- Extraction of less than 1000 cubic yards of material
- Operations that exclusively process mined material
- Earthmoving activities in oil and gas fields necessary for ongoing oil or gas extraction

State Policy and Permit Procedures

SMARA was enacted to prevent the historic practice of mining operators abandoning mines and leaving them in a dangerous and unsightly condition. SMARA requires mining operators to restore mines to a productive land use following mining in a process called reclamation.

SMARA requires SMGB to set state policy for mining operations that includes measures to be used by lead agencies in specifying grading, backfilling, resoiling, revegetation, soil compaction, and other reclamation requirements, as well as for soil erosion control, water quality and watershed control, waste disposal, and flood control. PRC 2756.

The SMGB has established procedures for review and approval of reclamation plans by lead agencies (local agencies responsible for reviewing and approving surface mining operations and reclamation plans). The SMGB has developed a model SMARA ordinance (State Mining and Geology Board 1996) as an example for lead agencies. Lead agencies must adopt ordinances for land use permitting and reclamation procedures to provide the regulatory framework for conducting local mining and reclamation activities. *See* sidebar.

The SMGB reviews lead agency ordinances to determine whether each ordinance meets or exceeds SMARA requirements. If SMGB determines that a lead agency is not in compliance with SMARA, it has the authority to exercise any powers of that lead agency with respect to surface mining and reclamation, except for permitting. PRC 2774.3.

Reclamation Plans and Financial Assurances

Reclamation plan content. Before surface mining operations are conducted, the lead agency must grant a permit, approve a reclamation plan, and approve financial assurances for the reclamation. PRC 2770, 2774. The purposes of a reclamation plan are to restore the mined lands to a useable condition amenable to alternative land uses, minimize adverse impacts on the environment, and protect public health and safety. PRC 2711(a), 2712(a).

The reclamation plan must be applicable to a specific property and must be based on the character of the surrounding area and property, including overburden type, soil stability, topography, geology, climate, streams, and mineral commodities; specific content requirements are found at PRC 2772 and 14 CCR 3502(b). *See* sidebar. The final step in this process is often topsoil replacement and revegetation with suitable plant species.

The reclamation plan must establish site-specific criteria for evaluating plan compliance, usually based on performance standards adopted by SMGB. PRC 2773. A lead agency may allow an exception to SMGB performance standards if necessary based on the approved end use, and only if the alternative standard is not less stringent than the SMGB standard. 14 CCR 3700(b).

Reclamation plan process. Each lead agency must adopt a surface mining ordinance that establishes the process for reclamation plan approval. The hearing and approval process for reclamation plans is integrated into the lead agency's general processes for land use entitlements and CEQA compliance. The lead agency must approve amendments to the reclamation plan if activities substantially deviate from the approved plan. 14 CCR 3502(d). Special reclamation plan approval process requirements apply to

Surface Mining and Reclamation Act Model Ordinance—Sections

1. Purpose and Intent
2. Definitions
3. Incorporation by Reference
4. Scope
5. Vested Rights
6. Process
7. Standards for Reclamation
8. Statement of Responsibility
9. Findings for Approval
10. Financial Assurances
11. Interim Management Plans
12. Annual Report Requirements
13. Inspections
14. Violations and Penalties
15. Appeals
16. Fees
17. Mineral Resource Protection
18. Severability
19. Effective Date

Source: State Mining and Geology Board. 1996. Model SMARA Ordinance

surface mining within the boundaries of the San Gabriel Basin Water Authority and to metallic mineral mining within one mile of certain Native American sacred sites. PRC 2772.5, 2772.6.

Before approving a reclamation plan, the lead agency must submit the reclamation plan and financial assurances to the director of DOC. The director may prepare written comments, and the lead agency must prepare a written response describing the disposition of significant issues raised. PRC 2774(d). Also, operators may appeal actions or inactions of the lead agency under SMARA to SMGB. PRC 2770(e).

Financial assurances. Surface mining operators must provide financial assurances that reclamation will be performed consistent with the reclamation plan. The SMGB has established guidelines for establishing these financial assurances. SMGB 2004.

The amount of the financial assurance must be sufficient to complete reclamation under the proposed reclamation plan, as well as agency administrative costs for overseeing reclamation. Assurance may include bonds, irrevocable letters of credit, or trust funds, and must stay in effect until reclamation is complete. PRC 2770(d), 2773.1(a).

The financial assurance must be payable to both the lead agency and DOC. It must remain in effect for the duration of the mining operation and until reclamation is completed. PRC 2773.1(a).

Enforcement

Operators must file annual reports on the status of mining and reclamation activities. The lead agency must inspect a surface mining operation within six months of receiving the surface mining operator's report, to determine whether the operation complies with SMARA. Thereafter, the lead agency must conduct annual inspections. PRC 2207, 2774(b).

SMARA establishes a comprehensive administrative framework for determining whether a SMARA violation has occurred and for imposing fines. PRC 2774. Remedies for a SMARA violation include a compliance order or a cease-and-desist order, with administrative penalties of up to $5,000 per day if an order is violated. PRC 2774.1. Also, the director of DOC has standing to file a lawsuit alleging illegal or inadequate reclamation plans and financial assurances for surface mining operations. *People ex rel. Dept. of Conservation v. El Dorado County* (2005) 36 Cal. 4th 971.

Lead agencies are responsible for enforcing SMARA, but under certain circumstances, SMGB may take over the lead agency's enforcement powers. For example, SMGB may take over these powers when it finds that the lead agency has approved reclamation plans that do not comply with SMARA, or has failed to take appropriate enforcement actions. PRC 2774.4(a).

For more information...

Publications

Cole, D.F. 2008. In Press. California Surface Mining Law. Solano Press. Point Arena, Calif.

Department of Conservation. ND. Guidelines for Classification and Designation of Mineral Lands

Kohler, S.L. 2005. California Non-Fuel Mineral Production. California Geological Survey

Manaster, K.A. and D.P. Selmi (eds.). ND. Chapter 82 of California Environmental Law and Land Use Practice. Matthew Bender. San Francisco, Calif.

State Mining and Geology Board. 1996. Model SMARA Ordinance

State Mining and Geology Board. 2004. SMARA Financial Assurance Guidelines

Websites

California Geological Survey
www.consrv.ca.gov/CGS

Office of Mine Reclamation
www.consrv.ca.gov/OMR

State Mining and Geology Board
www.consrv.ca.gov/smgb

PART FOUR

Permitting and Environmental Compliance Auditing Guides

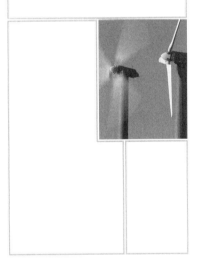

Permitting Guide

This chapter reviews —

- Permitting fundamentals
- Comprehensive permitting laws
- Recommended permitting strategies
- Major permit requirements identified in previous chapters of the book

Glossary

Discretionary permit–requires an agency to exercise a higher level of deliberation and a higher level of analysis before issuing a permit.

Ministerial permit–involves a straight-forward decision judging against standardized, objective criteria.

Permit–for purposes of this chapter, all environmental approvals, including certifications, licenses, and plan and specification approvals.

Permit by rule–a permit in which the applicant submits a notice of intent to comply with pre-set permit conditions that are not site-specific.

CHAPTER 18

Permitting Guide

Introduction

The preceding chapters provided an overview of California environmental law and reviewed specific regulatory programs for different resources and environmental media. How does a project applicant navigate this regulatory maze successfully? The purpose of this chapter is to describe comprehensive approaches to obtaining multiple environmental permits.

A useful though somewhat dated supplement to this chapter is the 2002 California Permit Handbook (California Technology, Trade, and Commerce Agency (CTTCA) 2002), which provides an overview of local, state, and federal environmental permitting requirements. The permit handbook was authored by the CTTCA's Office of Permit Assistance (OPA), which formerly was also available to assist individual applicants with the permit process. However, the OPA no longer exists, and many specifics of the regulatory programs described in the handbook (*e.g.,* agency contact names, application fees) have changed.

CTTCA = California Technology, Trade, and Commerce Agency

OPA = Office of Permit Assistance

Permitting Fundamentals

What Is a Permit?

Environmental permits are required for projects involving new construction or changes to existing facilities. For purposes of this chapter, the term permit is used to mean all environmental approvals, including certifications, licenses, and plan and specification approvals. As the name implies, a permit reflects a privilege to engage in a regulated activity. To obtain a permit, the applicant must demonstrate, through a permit application, compliance with the permitting agency's substantive and procedural requirements.

Environmental permits are required for projects involving new construction or changes to existing facilities.

Some permits are required before project construction commences (such as a building permit, a storm water construction permit, or an authority to construct air quality permit). Other permits are required as a condition of operation (such as an air quality permit to operate and a storm water industrial permit).

Typically, permits last for a limited period of time. Before a permit lapses, the permit owner or operator must renew the permit or obtain a new permit to continue the regulated activity. Also, permits are sometimes subject to modification before they expire as a result of new information, an operational change, or regulatory requirements.

Types of Permits

Discretionary versus ministerial. Permits may be characterized as discretionary or ministerial. A discretionary permit, such as an air quality or water quality permit, requires an agency to exercise deliberation and analysis before issuing a permit. A ministerial permit, such as a typical building permit, involves a straightforward decision judging against standardized, objective criteria, and is not subject to California Environmental Quality Act (CEQA) requirements.

CEQA = California Environmental Quality Act

Site-specific versus permit by rule. Some permits require submission of a detailed and prescriptive site-specific application. In this instance an individualized permit may be issued governing operations at a particular facility address with specified permit conditions and limitations. In other situations, a permit application is more generalized. In this situation, the permit applicant submits a notice of intent to comply with pre-set permit conditions that are not site-specific. This type of permit is known as a permit by rule.

Comprehensive Permitting Laws

Laws Reviewed in Previous Chapters

The Legislature has enacted several laws designed to integrate and streamline environmental permitting requirements.

The Legislature has enacted several laws designed to integrate and streamline environmental permitting requirements. Many of these are reviewed in earlier chapters:

- CEQA (*see* chapter 2) is designed to streamline the permitting process by encouraging all permitting agencies to use a single CEQA document for their project approvals.

- The Permit Streamlining Act (*see* chapter 3) requires local and state agencies to follow standardized time limits and procedures for certain types of land use decisions.

- The Warren–Alquist State Energy Resources Conservation and Development Act (*see* chapter 4) establishes a "one-stop" certification process for new or modified power plants with generating capacity of 50 megawatts or more.

- Assembly Bill 2948 (the Tanner Bill, *see* chapter 8) coordinates the issuance of multiple permits, licenses, land use approvals, and other authorizations in support of an off-site hazardous waste treatment, storage, or disposal facility.

Permit Reform Act

The Environmental Protection Permit Reform Act of 1993 (Permit Reform Act, PRC 71000 *et seq.*) is an additional law occasionally used to expedite the environmental permitting process where more than one permitting authority is involved. Through consolidated permitting, the program is intended to reduce the number of agencies directly involved in the permitting process and to reduce confusing and redundant layers of agency requirements.

The Environmental Protection Permit Reform Act of 1993 is an additional law occasionally used to expedite the environmental permitting process where more than one permitting authority is involved.

To initiate a request for a consolidated permit, an applicant must first complete a consolidated permit notification that, among other things, describes the activities being permitted at the facility, lists the environmental permits anticipated, and identifies the lead permitting agency for purposes of the Permit Streamlining Act and CEQA. The consolidated permit notification also allows the applicant to identify the agency believed to have the "greatest overall jurisdiction" for the project and to name the agency it wants to be the consolidated permit agency. PRC 71021.

The program requires that the California Environmental Protection Agency (Cal/EPA) designate a consolidated permit agency (CPA) to coordinate permitting for a project within 30 days of receipt of the notification. First and second preference is given to lead agencies under CEQA and lead agencies pursuant to the Permit Streamlining Act, respectively. Where the first and second priority agencies do not apply, Cal/EPA must use specified criteria to determine the agency with the greatest overall jurisdiction. PRC 71020(b). CPAs facilitate and coordinate the multimedia permitting effort. Their duties include (PRC 71022):

Cal/EPA = California Environmental Protection Agency
CPA = Consolidated permit agency
PRC = Public Resources Code

- Contact the applicant and all environmental permit agencies identified by the applicant
- Inform the applicant and participating permit agencies of the time, date, and location of the pre-application meeting to determine the environmental permits required for the project and to review the permit application forms and scheduling
- Provide all information necessary for the applicant to submit appropriate permit applications, including provisions of relevant guidance documents, permit applications, and schedules for technical review
- Coordinate the review of all participating agency permits
- Ensure that permit decisions made by the participating permit agencies are made in a timely manner
- Assist in promptly resolving any conflicts
- Compile all participating agency permits into one consolidated permit

Under the Permit Reform Act, participating agencies retain their respective authority to issue permits. Participating agencies are responsible for technical review of their permit renewals and permit modifications. PRC 71020(d).

Permitting Strategies

The California environmental permitting process can be complex and often frustrating. The following strategies should be used to facilitate the permitting process. Project applicants should consider retaining qualified environmental consultants or attorneys to develop and implement these strategies. This section presents strategies from the perspective of a private project applicant, although most strategies can be used by a public agency applicant as well.

Prepare Permit Inventory and Conduct Preliminary Site Evaluation

When undertaking a development project that requires one or more environmental permits before construction or operation, it is essential to determine which permits and approvals federal, state, and local agencies will require.

When undertaking a development project that requires one or more environmental permits before construction or operation, it is essential to determine which permits and approvals federal, state, and local agencies will require. This book can serve as a useful starting point for developing a comprehensive permit inventory. Table 18-2, presented at the end of this chapter, summarizes common environmental permits and approvals. In addition, since most projects require some type of local permit, local governments typically should be contacted first–they often can preliminarily identify other permits required for a proposed project.

When developing the permit inventory, the applicant should consider:

- The location of the proposed project, *e.g.*, city, county, and coastal zone boundaries
- Resources affected by the proposed project, *e.g.*, agricultural lands, waters of the United States
- Construction and operation activities associated with the proposed project
- The specific federal, state, regional, and local agencies with potential regulatory authority over the proposed project

The applicant should conduct a preliminary site evaluation and constraints analysis to identify potential permits and possible project redesigns to avoid or streamline permitting requirements.

The applicant should conduct a preliminary site evaluation and constraints analysis to identify potential permits and possible project redesigns to avoid or streamline permitting requirements. Reconnaissance-level investigations are usually adequate at this step in the permitting process. The investigations should focus on the presence of regulatory triggers such as wetlands and waters of the United States, endangered species, cultural resources, air quality nonattainment status, and hazardous waste and toxic substances.

Prepare Permitting Strategy Plan

PSP = Permitting strategy plan

The primary goal of a permitting strategy plan (PSP) is to define the regulatory approval processes for a proposed project, develop preliminary compliance approaches, and identify any potential inconsistent permitting requirements or other fatal flaws that could jeopardize permit approval.

The PSP may include descriptions of some or all of the following:

- The proposed project's construction and operation features that could trigger an environmental permit
- Relevant permitting agencies and their jurisdiction and permitting issues
- Possible lead agencies for CEQA and National Environmental Policy Act (NEPA) documents
- Specific permits and approvals required for construction and operation
- Applicable design, operational, and pollution control standards
- Application process for each permit
- Fees and financial obligations (*e.g.,* surety bonds) required for each permit
- Baseline studies (*e.g.,* seismic, soils, air quality monitoring, screening health risk assessment, wetland delineation, endangered species surveys) required by each permit
- Common technical studies or permitting steps among multiple agencies, and methods to facilitate consolidated permit processing
- Comprehensive schedules for the permitting process, permitting milestones, pre-application studies, application preparation, and agency decisionmaking
- Prioritization of permitting activities based on their importance or critical path schedule
- Potential permitting hurdles and strategies to address them
- A comprehensive contacts list that identifies individuals on the project applicant team and in permitting agencies responsible for each permitting task, together with their contact information
- An integrated public involvement or community relations plan

Complex projects such as wind farms can benefit from preparation of a permitting strategy plan.

EIR = Environmental impact report
NEPA = National Environmental Policy Act

Use CEQA and NEPA Documents as the Umbrella Processes for Permitting Decisions

Many environmental regulatory programs require state or local agencies to prepare CEQA documents, and federal permitting agencies to prepare NEPA documents. CEQA and NEPA both strongly encourage the integration of related federal, state, and local environmental review and consultation requirements into CEQA and NEPA documents. For example, CEQA requires that the environmental impact report (EIR) project description include a list of related environmental reviews and consultations required by federal, state, or local laws,

Table 18-1. Integrating Selected Environmental Review Requirements with CEQA and NEPA

Requirement	Scoping process	Draft document	Final document	Decisionmaking
NEPA	Notice of intent	Draft EIS	Final EIS	Lead agency decision and Record of Decision
CEQA	Notice of preparation	Draft EIR	Final EIR	Lead agency decision and notice of decision
Endangered Species Act, Section 7	Request species list	Biological assessment	Biological opinion	
Clean Water Act, Section 404 (individual permit)	Define objectives, screen alternatives, submit permit application	Draft Section 404(b)(1) analysis	Final Section 404(b)(1) analysis	USACE issues Section 404 permit (after Section 401 certification or waiver)
National Historic Preservation Act, Section 106	Identify and evaluate historic and archaeological properties	Draft effects assessment	Memorandum of agreement	
Clean Air Act Conformity (non-transportation project)	Determine whether conformity requirement applies	Preliminary analysis (comparison to de minimis levels)	Detailed modeling analysis if necessary	Federal agency issues conformity determination
Public involvement	Scoping meetings	Public comment, public hearing	Public comment	Public hearing

Source: Bass, R.E. et al. 1999. *CEQA Deskbook.*
Solano Press. Reprinted with permission

A CEQA or CEQA/NEPA joint document prepared for a local government land use entitlement often serves as the umbrella document for other permits and approvals needed for a project.

CCR   = California Code of Regulations
DFG   = Department of Fish and Game
EIS   = Environmental impact statement
MOA = Memorandum of agreement
MOU = Memorandum of understanding
USACE = U.S. Army Corps of Engineers

regulations, or policies. CEQA also requires the lead agency, to the fullest extent possible, to integrate CEQA review with these related environmental requirements. 14 CCR 15124(d).

Project applicants should strive to achieve the goal of "one project/one document." A CEQA or CEQA/NEPA joint document prepared for a local government land use entitlement often serves as the umbrella document for other permits and approvals needed for a project. When possible, technical studies supporting CEQA and NEPA documents should be prepared to satisfy the needs of multiple permitting agencies. For example, a wetlands technical study for a land development project should satisfy the information requirements not just of the local CEQA lead agency, but also the U.S. Army Corps of Engineers (USACE) Section 404 regulatory program and Department of Fish and Game (DFG) streambed alteration agreement program.

Using CEQA and NEPA documents as "umbrellas" for related environmental review and consultation requirements reduces the potential for multiple duplicative or inconsistent environmental reviews for individual permits. Table 18-1 illustrates a simplified model approach to integrating selected environmental review requirements with CEQA and NEPA. As shown by this table, to reduce the potential for inconsistent public and agency comments, schedules should be coordinated for public and agency review of draft environmental and permitting documents.

Integrated environmental review sometimes is guided by interagency programmatic memoranda of understanding or agreement (MOUs or MOAs) that already have been adopted, and also may be guided by project-specific MOUs/MOAs. For example, local agency transportation project applicants may take advantage of a programmatic agreement among Caltrans, the Federal Highway

Administration (FHWA)/Federal Transit Administration (FTA), and the Environmental Protection Agency (EPA) (FHWA *et al.* 1994) integrating the requirements of Section 404 permitting and NEPA for projects funded by the FHWA or FTA. The project applicant should identify any programmatic MOUs/MOAs that may apply to the proposed project, and should assist in the development of project-specific MOUs/MOAs.

EPA = U.S. Environmental Protection Agency
FHWA = Federal Highway Administration
FTA = Federal Transit Administration

Prepare Complete Permit Applications and Use Pre-application Consultation

The project design and project description should be substantially complete and final before applications are prepared and filed. The applicant should consider building environmental protection or mitigation measures into the project description to increase the chances for exemptions, variances, or other permit streamlining processes. Applications should be prepared with strict adherence to the agency guidelines. Complete and legally adequate applications will minimize delays caused by return of incomplete or deficient applications. Significantly deficient applications or frequent post-application project description design changes could result in significant delays in obtaining permits as well as increased costs associated with permitting.

The project design and project description should be substantially complete and final before applications are prepared and filed.

Pre-application meetings with each relevant regulatory agency are essential, especially because federal, state, and local agencies do not always talk to each other. These meetings will enable the applicant to build personal relationships with agency staff, identify agency concerns, procedures, and schedules early on, and allow an opportunity to adjust permitting strategies accordingly. During the pre-application process, the applicant can seek permitting agency input on project design and mitigation approaches, and when appropriate can incorporate these agency suggestions into the project description to facilitate the permitting process.

Pre-application meetings with each relevant regulatory agency are essential, especially because federal, state, and local agencies do not always talk to each other.

Before the pre-application meeting, the applicant should research the range of possible permitting actions the agency might take, and how the agency has addressed previous similar projects. For example, when seeking an exemption, variance, or other streamlined permit approach, it is helpful for the applicant to identify similar projects the agency has treated the same way.

Proactively Manage the Permitting Process

Project applicants should communicate openly and continuously with regulatory agency staff throughout the permitting process. Meetings should be scheduled with permitting agencies at key milestones (*e.g.*, completion of baseline studies, submittal of administrative draft documents for review) or if the project description changes. Project changes are sometimes needed, but should be minimized when possible, as they often result in significant delays in the permitting process.

Project applicants should communicate openly and continuously with regulatory agency staff throughout the permitting process.

Frequent agency staff turnover is a fact of life. For that reason, it is essential for project applicants to maintain detailed written documentation of discussions and decisions at every step of the permitting process. When new agency staff is assigned to a project, the applicant should schedule a meeting with the new staff and review the record of previous permitting discussions and decisions. Orienting new permitting staff in this way will reduce the chances for the new staff to reverse previous permitting decisions.

Treat Permitting Staff with Respect and Courtesy

Maintaining good relationships with permitting staff at all times (or retaining consultants or attorneys with these relationships) increases the probability of an expedited permitting process and favorable permitting decisions.

Project applicants often get frustrated with the time, cost, and inefficiencies of the environmental permitting process in California. Regulatory agency staff typically are stretched very thin, staff turnover is common, and agencies sometimes change their permitting policies and procedures when the permitting process is well underway. However, maintaining good relationships with permitting staff at all times (or retaining consultants or attorneys with these relationships) increases the probability of an expedited permitting process and favorable permitting decisions.

Applicants should remember that permitting agency staff view there mission as from regulatory objectives, which typically are not the same as the applicant's objectives. A "win–win" approach to permitting, in which agencies achieve some of their objectives through mitigation or project conditions, is generally more likely to succeed than a "win–lose" approach, in which the agency is pressured to do what the applicant wants while ignoring regulatory objectives.

When faced with a non-responsive or difficult regulator, applicants sometimes go directly to an agency head or an elected official's office to overrule the regulator and get their needs met. While this political approach is sometimes necessary and sometimes successful, it should be used judiciously because it can not only fail, but actually backfire and result in even more onerous demands by the regulator for the applicant's current and subsequent projects.

Applicant assistance is sometimes available if agencies have insufficient staff for permit processing. Some agencies' policies allow applicants to fund staff positions. In the absence of such opportunities, applicants can still volunteer to assist agencies by preparing administrative drafts of regulatory notices and documents.

Comprehensive Permit List

Table 18-2 lists common federal, state, regional, and local environmental permits and other approvals in California. This table can be used as a starting point to prepare a comprehensive permit inventory. The table shows the name of the permit, the activity triggering the permit, the permitting agency, and the chapter in this book where the permit is described in further detail. Because many specialized permits are not included in this book or table, applicants may need to conduct project-specific research to identify additional specialized permits.

Table 18-2. Summary of Environmental Permits and Other Approvals

Topic	Permit or approval	Activity triggering permit or approval	Regulatory agency	Chapter no.
California Environmental Quality Act and National Environmental Policy Act	Environmental impact report	Project that may have a significant environmental impact	State or local lead and responsible agencies	2
	Environmental impact statement	Project that may have a significant environmental impact	Federal lead and cooperating agencies	2
	Finding of no significant impact	Project with no significant environmental impact	Federal lead and cooperating agencies	2
	Negative declaration	Project with no significant environmental impact	State or local lead and responsible agencies	2
Local Land Use and Planning Regulation	Annexation	Incorporating land into existing city or special district boundaries	Local agency formation commission	3
	Conditional use permit	Proposed use not routinely allowed by zoning of a project site	City or county	3
	Dedication	Offering of private land for public use as a condition of project approval	City or county	3
	Development agreement	Developer concessions in return for an agreement that future changes in land use regulations will not apply to proposed project	City or county	3
	Exaction	Offering of fees or dedications as a condition of project approval	City or county	3
	Final subdivision map	Satisfaction of conditions imposed on tentative subdivision map	City or county	3
	General plan amendment	Proposed project-specific change in general plan text or land use diagram	City or county	3
	Impact fee	Offering of monetary exaction to defray costs of public facilities impacts of proposed project	City or county	3
	Planned unit development	Proposed development standards specific to a proposed project	City or county	3
	Specific plan	Proposed land use and infrastructure for a portion of a community	City or county	3
	Tentative subdivision map	Subdivision of land into five or more lots	City or county	3
	Variance	Proposed project-specific waiver of development standards in a zoning ordinance	City or county	3
	Zoning amendment	Proposed project-specific change in land use zones and allowable uses	City or county	3
State and Regional Land Use Controls	Application for certification	Power plant with 50 megawatts or more of generating capacity	California Energy Commission	4
	Certificate of Public Convenience and Necessity	Construction of certain energy facilities by a regulated public utility	Public Utilities Commission	4
	Coastal development permit	Development in coastal zone	Local coastal agencies or Coastal Commission	4
	Land use lease	Use of state-owned Sovereign Lands	State Lands Commission	4
Air Quality	Air toxics inventory	Activity involving the manufacture, use, or release of specified air toxics and specified criteria pollutants	Local air pollution control district (APCD)	5
	Authority to construct	Proposed stationary activity with potential to emit air emissions	Local APCD	5

Topic	Permit or approval	Activity triggering permit or approval	Regulatory agency	Chapter no.
Air Quality *continued*	Non-attainment new source review	Activity with the potential to release major volumes of non-attainment pollutants in a non-attainment area	Local APCD	5
	Permit by rule or prohibitory rule	Activities involving releases of organic or inorganic chemicals, particulate matter, and visible emissions	Local APCD	5
	Permit to operate	Constructed stationary activity with potential to emit air emissions	Local APCD	5
	Prevention of significant deterioration permit	Activity with the potential to release major volumes of attainment pollutants in an attainment area	Local APCD	5
	Risk management plan	Storage or use of highly hazardous and flammable chemicals	Office of Emergency Services or certified unified program agency (CUPA)	5
	Title V operating permit	"Major sources" defined by the Clean Air Act	Local APCD	5
Hazardous Materials and Toxic Substances	Asbestos aanagement plan	Public schools and non-profit private schools (collectively called local educational agencies)	Environmental Protection Agency (EPA)	7
	Hazardous materials business plan	Storage of specified volumes of hazardous materials	CUPA or local administering agency	7
	Prop. 65 compliance	Businesses that expose employees and the public to known carcinogens and reproductive toxins	Office of Environmental Health hazard assessment	7
	Pre-manufacture notice	Manufacturers, processors, or importers who produce or introduce a chemical product into commerce	EPA	7
	Toxic release inventory	Those who manufacture or process 25,000 pounds of chemicals annually or store or use 10,000 pounds of chemicals each year	CUPA or local administering agency	7
	Underground storage tank permit	Storage of petroleum and other hazardous substances in an underground storage tank	CUPA or local administering agency	7
Hazardous Wastes	Biennial report	Generating large quantities of hazardous waste	Department of Toxic Substances Control (DTSC)	8
	Conditionally authorized	On-site treatment of "California-only" hazardous waste using specified treatment methodologies on specified wastes	CUPA	8
	Conditionally exempt	On-site treatment of "California-only" hazardous waste using specified treatment methodologies on specified wastes	CUPA	8
	County hazardous waste management plan conformity	Applicant for an off-site hazardous waste treatment, storage, or disposal facility	City or county and DTSC	8
	EPA's generator identification number	Generating, transporting, treating, storing, or disposing of hazardous waste	DTSC	8
	Hazardous Materials Transportation Act	Shipping or receiving hazardous material or hazardous waste on public roads	U.S. Department of Transportation	8
	Permit by rule	On-site treatment of "California-only" hazardous waste using specified treatment methodologies on specified wastes	CUPA	8
	Resource Conservation and Recovery Act Part B treatment, storage, and disposal facility permit	On- or off-site facilities that treat, store, or dispose of hazardous waste	DTSC	8
	Standardized permit (Class I)	On-site treatment of "California-only" hazardous waste	DTSC	8

Topic	Permit or approval	Activity triggering permit or approval	Regulatory agency	Chapter no.
Solid Wastes	Waste discharge requirements for municipal solid waste landfill (Class III)	Owning or operating a Class III landfill disposing of solid, non-hazardous waste	Regional water quality control board (RWQCB)	9
	Construction/demolition and debris facility permit	Storing or disposing of construction debris	RWQCB	9
	Municipal solid waste transfer station permit	Owning or operating a temporarily stored solid, non-hazardous waste	Local enforcement agency and RWQCB	9
	Waste tire facility permit	Owning or operating a facility that stores or disposes of tires	California integrated waste management board	9
Water Quality	General storm water construction permit	Disturbing at least one acre of soil	RWQCB	10
	General storm water industrial permit	Industrial activity with materials potentially exposed to storm water	RWQCB	10
	General storm water municipal permit	Operators of municipal separate storm sewer systems serving over 100,000 people	State Water Resource Control Board (SWRCB)	10
	Storm water pollution prevention plan	Discharge of construction, municipal, or industrial storm water	SWRCB and RWQCB	10
	National Pollutant Discharge Elimination System permit	Discharges of pollutants to navigable waters from a point source	EPA and RWQCB	10
	Spill prevention control and countermeasure plan	Storing at least 1,320 gallons of oil in vessels of 55 gallons or more	CUPA and EPA	10
	Waste discharge requirements	Discharges of waste that could affect the quality of the waters of the state	RWQCB	10
	Facility response plan	Facilities that could cause "substantial harm" to environment by discharging oil	EPA	10
	Spill control and countermeasure plan	Non-transportation facilities that could discharge oil into navigable waters	EPA	10
Drinking Water	Consumer confidence report	Public water system operators supplying potable water	Public water system operators supplying potable water	11
	Drinking water permit	Operating a domestic water supply	Department of Public Health	11
Agriculture	Conservation easement	Retention of land in agricultural or open space use	City or county	12
	Williamson Act Contract	Reduced property tax assessment in return for keeping land in agricultural or open space use	City or county	12
Water Resources	Certificate of approval	Dam construction	Department of Water Resources	13
	Long-term water rransfer	Transfer of water or water rights lasting more than one year	SWRCB	13
	Temporary change	Water transfer lasting one year or less involving a change in point of diversion, place of use, or purpose of use	SWRCB	13
	Temporary urgency change	Water transfer lasting one year or less to meet an urgent need involving a change in point of diversion, place of use, or purpose of use	SWRCB	13
	Water right permit	Obtaining post-1914 appropriative water right	SWRCB	13
	Water right license	Completion of project with water right permit	SWRCB	13

Topic	Permit or approval	Activity triggering permit or approval	Regulatory agency	Chapter no.
Fish and Wildlife	Biological opinion	Completion of Endangered Species Act (ESA) Section 7 formal consultation	U.S. Fish and Wildlife Service (USFWS) or National Oceanographic and Atmospheric Administration (NOAA) Fisheries	14
	Habitat conservation plan	Proposed plan to conserve habitat needed to obtain ESA incidental take permit	USFWS or NOAA Fisheries	14
	Incidental take permit	Take of ESA-listed species that is incidental to otherwise lawful activities	USFWS or NOAA Fisheries	14
	Natural community conservation plan	Proposed plan to conserve a natural community that authorizes take of California Endangered Species Act (CESA)-listed species	Department of Fish and Game (DFG)	14
	Section 7 consultation	Activity authorized, funded, or carried out by federal agency that may affect an ESA-listed species or critical habitat	USFWS or NOAA Fisheries	14
	Section 2081 incidental take permit	Take of CESA-listed species that is incidental to otherwise lawful activities	DFG	14
Wetlands	General Section 404 permit	Class of activities requiring Section 404 permit	U.S. Army Corps of Engineers (USACE)	15
	Lake or streambed alteration agreement	Activities involving alteration of a lake or stream zone	Department of Fish and Game	15
	Nationwide Section 404 permit	Activities falling within one of the nationwide permit categories	USACE	15
	Pre-construction notification	Intent to perform fill activities authorized by a nationwide permit	USACE	15
	Section 10 permit	Activities involving construction of, excavation in, or filling of navigable waters	USACE	15
	Section 401 certification	Federal activities affecting waters of the state	RWQCB and SWRCB	15
	Section 404 Permit	Discharge of dredged or fill materials into waters of the United States	USACE	15
	Standard Section 404 permit	Individual activities requiring formal Section 404 permit review	USACE	15
Forestry	Professional forester license	Engaging in timber harvest activities or preparing a timber harvest plan (THP)	Board of Forestry	16
	Program timber harvest plan	THP prepared after completing a program timber environmental impact report	Calif. Department of Forestry and Fire Protection (CDF)	16
	Timber harvesting plan	Timber harvesting on non-federal land	CDF	16
	Timberland conversion permit	Converting timberland to non-timber uses	Board of Forestry	16
Surface Mining	Reclamation plan	Commencing surface mining activities	Local lead agencies	17

For more information...

Publications

California Technology, Trade, and Commerce Agency. 2002. California Permit Handbook. Sacramento, Calif.

Federal Highway Administration, Federal Transit Administration, U.S. Army Corps of Engineers, and U.S. Environmental Protection Agency. 1994. Memorandum of Understanding, National Environmental Policy Act and Clean Water Act Section 404 Integration Process for Surface Transportation Projects in Arizona, California, and Nevada

Websites

California Permit Handbook
http://commerce.ca.gov/ttca/pdfs/
detail/dsti/CAPermitHandbook.pdf

Environmental Compliance Auditing

This chapter reviews –

- Key laws involved in the audit process
- Reasons to conduct audits
- Types of audits
- Auditing process
- Audit protections and privileges

Glossary

Best management practices—methods determined to be the most effective, practical means for preventing or reducing pollution from nonpoint sources.

Compliance-focused environmental management system—models from which environmental management system requirements are based. CFEMS must clearly illustrate management's commitment to comply with relevant federal, state and local statutes and regulations, while continuing to make improvements regarding environmental programs.

Due diligence—a regulated entity's systematic efforts, appropriate to the size and nature of the business, to prevent, detect, disclose, and correct violations through various efforts and mechanisms.

Environmental management system—procedures allowing an organization to decrease its environmental impact and increase its operating efficiencies.

International Organization for Standardization—the world's largest developer of technical standards, ISO is a non-governmental organization and consists of a network of the national standards institutes of 157 countries. ISO standards contribute to enabling the manufacture and development of products more efficiently and also provide a safeguard for consumers.

Standard operating procedure—a set of written instructions that document a routine or repetitive activity followed by an organization.

Supplemental environmental projects—pollution prevention efforts that exceed the existing statutory obligations of dischargers and achieve an environmental benefit.

CHAPTER 19

Environmental Compliance Auditing*

Introduction

This chapter ties together the substantive and procedural requirements of the environmental regulatory programs discussed in this book by describing how compliance audits can be used to manage environmental liability. Audits actively help manage the risk of noncompliance with environmental standards. Specifically, an environmental audit is an independent assessment of facility performance against environmental regulatory standards or requirements.

Key Laws

Environmental Protection Agency Audit Privilege

The federal EPA audit privilege is a self-disclosure policy designed to encourage regulated entities to voluntarily discover, promptly notify the EPA, and correct violations of federal environmental requirements. To take advantage of policy benefits (penalty reduction), entities must disclose their violations within 21 days of discovery and correct them within 60 days.

California Environmental Protection Agency Audit Privilege

The California Environmental Protection Agency (Cal/EPA) adopted a more stringent version of the federal EPA audit privilege with more comprehensive policies for penalty reduction, criminal referrals, and fee-for-service certification. Similar to the EPA audit privilege, the Cal/EPA audit privilege allows regulated facilities that meet all nine conditions to be eligible for 100 percent mitigation

Cal/EPA = California Environmental
        Protection Agency
EPA   = U.S. Environmental
        Protection Agency

* This chapter is excerpted from the environmental auditing chapter of Matthew Bender and Company's *California Environmental Law and Land Use Practice* treatise, written by Gary A. Lucks. Reproduced with permission.

of gravity-based penalties. For more information, *see* the Cal/EPA website (www.calepa.ca.gov/Enforcement/policy).

Sarbanes-Oxley Act of 2002

The Sarbanes-Oxley Act of 2002 (SOX) (PL 107-204, 116 Stat. 745) requires publicly traded companies to provide individual audit reports detailing their internal operations. Chief executive officers (CEOs) and chief financial officers (CFOs) must personally certify that the company's financial report does not contain false information on material facts and that it accurately identifies the financial condition of the company.

International Organization for Standardization 14001

The International Organization for Standardization (ISO) 14001 standards govern the creation of Environmental Management Systems (EMSs). An EMS is a set of management processes and procedures that allows an organization to analyze, control, and reduce the environmental impacts of its activities, products, and services, and to operate with greater efficiency and control. Facilities must conduct EMS internal audits to determine whether the EMS conforms to ISO standards. EMSs often commit an organization to conducting environmental audits to demonstrate compliance.

Reasons to Conduct Audits

Audits help a facility's environmental manager identify and correct deficiencies before they result in agency enforcement actions.

Audits primarily help a facility's environmental manager identify and correct deficiencies before they result in agency enforcement actions. Additionally, audits can serve as management tools to help managers more effectively administer compliance programs and implement best management practices (BMPs) that are not required but can optimize environmental compliance. However, audit programs are not limited to regulatory requirements and BMPs. They can evaluate compliance against a variety of standards ranging from the full panoply of federal, state, regional, and local environmental regulations to the prescriptions of the ISO 14001 standards governing the implementation of environmental management systems.

Compliance Management

The primary incentive to develop and implement an environmental compliance audit program is to avoid administrative, civil, or criminal fines, penalties, or injunctions.

The primary incentive to develop and implement an environmental compliance audit program is to avoid administrative, civil, or criminal fines, penalties, or injunctions. Particularly in California, a state known for rigorous environmental compliance standards, an audit is a tool that provides an independent, third-party review of a facility's environmental regulatory programs. The mission of the auditor is to investigate gaps and deficiencies in a facility's compliance programs and correct them before receiving an announced or unannounced inspection from a

BMP = Best management practice
CEO = Chief executive officer
CFO = Chief financial officer
EMS = Environmental management system
ISO = International Organization for Standardization
PL = Public Law
SOX = Sarbanes-Oxley Act

regulatory agency. This not only helps the environmental manager assess the health of the facility's programs, but also assists in deploying limited resources to the weakest programs presenting the largest exposure. Audits additionally provide assurance to corporate officers concerning the status of environmental compliance.

Enforcement Discretion

The existence of an audit program can be a mitigating factor influencing whether and how to prosecute a violator (U.S. Department of Justice 1991) and the ultimate criminal penalties assessed.

Supplemental Environmental Projects

Agencies have authority to offset a portion of the penalty assessed to violators and to allow implementation of an SEP–which can include an audit, a compliance-focused EMS (CFEMS) and a standard EMS. An SEP is more focused on "beyond compliance"–improved environmental performance that in many cases exceeds environmental regulatory requirements. This type of EMS is modeled after ISO 14001, which defines an EMS as:

> [T]hat part of the overall management system which includes organizational structure, planning activities, responsibilities, practices, procedures, processes and resources for developing, implementing, archiving, reviewing, and maintaining [the organization's] environmental policy.

CFEMS = Compliance-focused environmental management system

GAAP = Generally accepted accounting principles

GAGAS = Generally accepted government auditing standards

SEP = Supplemental environmental project

SEPs are offered by the EPA, Cal/EPA, and local agencies. For more information, *see* http://cfpub.epa.gov/compliance/resources/policies/civil/seps and www.calepa.ca.gov/Enforcement/Policy/SEPGuide.pdf. Federal and state SEPs include an "Other Types of Projects" category that allows violating companies to examine their operations for pollution prevention opportunities and to determine if they can reduce the use, production, or generation of hazardous materials and other wastes. These audits go well beyond standard business practices.

Types of Audits

Government Audit

Governments engage in the audit process and base their standards on generally accepted government auditing standards (GAGAS) to foster competency, integrity, and objectivity in their reporting work. These standards are the foundation for using fieldwork and reporting standards to perform quality work.

Governments engage in the audit process and base their standards on generally accepted government auditing standards to foster competency, integrity, and objectivity in their reporting work.

Governmental audits include financial and performance audits, and attestation engagement. Financial audits mainly provide reasonable assurance about whether financial statements are presented accurately in conformity with generally accepted accounting principles (GAAP) or another comprehensive basis for accounting. Performance audits are objective, systematic, and independent evaluations of material to independently examine program performance and management versus objective criteria; they also potentially focus on or summarize BMPs or multidimensional issues. The main goals of performance audits are to improve a facility's operation, to encourage corrective action, and to improve public accountability. Attestation engagement entails examining or performing agreed-upon procedures about a topic, or involves making an assertion about a topic and then reporting the results.

Environmental Compliance Audit

Facilities may benefit from engaging a third-party audit team staffed with individuals from a sister company or division or by using a third-party consultant or accounting firm.

Facilities may benefit from engaging a third-party audit team staffed with individuals from a sister company or division (*see* below) or by using a third-party consultant or accounting firm. Such an "external" audit has the advantage of taking the viewpoint of an environmental agency inspector. Typically, external third-party audit programs conduct an audit every two to five years at individual facilities, buildings, or programs–those that perform well can be scheduled for longer intervals between external audits, while those showing significant weaknesses or gaps may be scheduled more frequently. External audits need not comprehensively review all relevant environmental areas; instead, external audits can focus on the weakest environmental areas (*e.g.*, air quality and hazardous wastes).

Compliance-Focused
Environmental Management System

To proactively manage environmental compliance, facility managers should build on their audit programs by developing and implementing CFEMSs.

Compliance audits are important tools for managing a facility's compliance risks. However, a facility could repeat the same compliance-based finding at the next audit, unless the root cause behind the finding is addressed. To proactively manage environmental compliance, facility managers should build on their audit programs by developing and implementing CFEMSs. Because compliance assurance can be heavily dependent on the individual rather than the position, the CFEMS includes uniform, clear, and consistent schedules and standards. As a result, a CFEMS helps provide a reliable platform for ensuring more accurate compliance performance.

SOP = Standard operating procedure

A CFEMS can help ensure ongoing compliance with environmental laws by clearly documenting responsibilities and establishing standard operating procedures (SOPs). SOPs establish staff accountability by laying out roles and expectations. In addition, a CFEMS helps a facility to manage change and to preserve institutional knowledge and continuity with environmental programs and responsibilities. A CFEMS also establishes an environmental awareness and regulatory training program (including scheduled regulatory and legislative updates).

The CFEMS should include a tickler system to forecast and plan for upcoming deadlines to submit required agency reports, permit and license renewals, and other submittals. The tickler system helps management and staff to better anticipate and respond to regulatory obligations and to manage priorities more effectively. Finally, the CFEMS should include a robust self-inspection program to address compliance gaps between third-party audit intervals.

Environmental Management System Audit

An EMS represents a management framework that assists businesses and government agencies in improving environmental performance and shrinking their "environmental footprint." Some facility managers choose to develop EMSs to decrease costs and environmental impacts (*e.g.*, pollution) associated with energy and raw materials usage and waste, while increasing operational efficiency. In many cases, the EMS goes "beyond compliance" and exceeds environmental regulatory requirements. Additionally, the EMS can be a tool to enhance compliance management. Thus, an EMS can turn environmental management from a perceived "cost center" into an integrated strategic advantage.

An EMS represents a management framework that assists businesses and government agencies in improving environmental performance and shrinking their "environmental footprint."

A facility that develops and implements an EMS can qualify for the EPA Performance Track Program. This program offers participants recognition as environmental leaders, lowers EPA inspection priority, and relaxes specified compliance requirements. More information on the Performance Track Program can be found at the EPA website (www.epa.gov/performancetrack).

Some businesses and facilities choose to develop and implement an EMS in accordance with ISO 14001, as described above. For others, having a certified EMS is a condition of doing business. For example, Ford Motor Company requires ISO 14001 certification from all of its suppliers with manufacturing facilities. All manufacturing facilities shipping products to Ford were required to receive certification by July 1, 2003. For further information, *see* the Ford Press release of October 4, 1999 (http://media.ford.com/newsroom/release_display.cfm?release=2936).

Auditing Process

When performing a multimedia environmental compliance audit, federal, state, regional, and local regulatory requirements are typically evaluated for the following topics:

- Air quality and climate change
- Wastewater and storm water
- Drinking water
- Spill prevention
- Tanks (above and underground)
- Hazardous waste management
- Hazardous materials management
- Chemical transport
- Toxics (polychlorinated biphenyls, asbestos, lead, and radon)

Inspections of oil tanks during environmental audits can prevent later problems.

- Historic and cultural resources
- Solid waste
- Pesticides
- Pollution prevention
- Brownfields and hazardous substances cleanup
- Internal policies and procedures

The principle objective of a regulatory compliance audit, a CFMES, or an EMS conformity audit is to obtain an accurate assessment of site conditions and compliance status at a given facility. An auditor's ability to gather relevant information hinges on proper planning, facility cooperation, qualified auditors, and involvement of senior management. Senior management participation helps ensure that relevant staff attends audit meetings and participates as needed throughout the data-gathering phase as well as in later phases to ensure that corrective actions are implemented expeditiously. Senior management also can assist by directing resources to respond to findings and observations.

An audit consists of three phases: pre-audit activities, on-site audit, and post-audit activities. Each phase is discussed below and further illustrated in Figure 19-1.

Pre-Audit Activities

The audit team leader begins the process by sending a commitment letter to the environmental manager. The commitment letter is intended to commit the facility to specified dates and audit milestones, as well as to provide knowledgeable escorts and logistical support for the audit team.

Before scheduling the audit and deploying the audit team, the audit team leader should obtain as much information as possible about the size of the facility, the number and types of regulated emissions sources and units, and the types of permits, plans, and other regulated environmental programs applicable to the facility. This usually is accomplished by submitting a pre-audit checklist or questionnaire to be completed by the on-site environmental manager with the assistance of staff. The pre-audit questionnaire is designed to clarify the number and type of emission units and the applicability of regulatory programs. It also identifies the records to be reviewed. Typically, the pre-audit questionnaire should be submitted a few months prior to the scheduled on-site audit and completed at least a month before the scheduled visit.

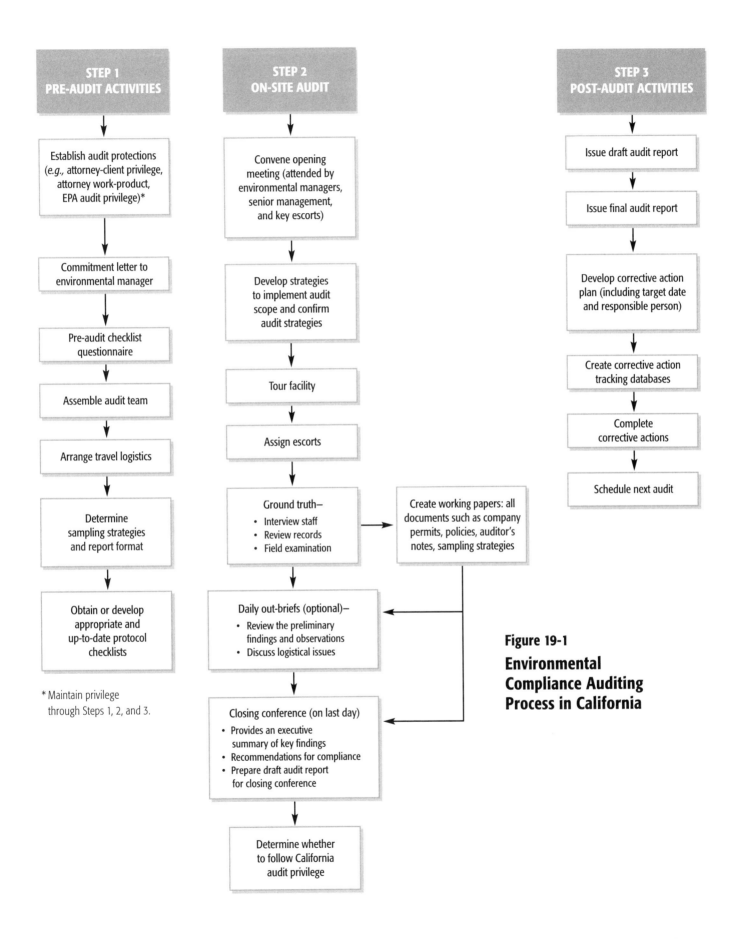

STEP 1
PRE-AUDIT ACTIVITIES

Establish audit protections (*e.g.,* attorney-client privilege, attorney work-product, EPA audit privilege)*

Commitment letter to environmental manager

Pre-audit checklist questionnaire

Assemble audit team

Arrange travel logistics

Determine sampling strategies and report format

Obtain or develop appropriate and up-to-date protocol checklists

* Maintain privilege through Steps 1, 2, and 3.

STEP 2
ON-SITE AUDIT

Convene opening meeting (attended by environmental managers, senior management, and key escorts)

Develop strategies to implement audit scope and confirm audit strategies

Tour facility

Assign escorts

Ground truth—
• Interview staff
• Review records
• Field examination

Create working papers: all documents such as company permits, policies, auditor's notes, sampling strategies

Daily out-briefs (optional)—
• Review the preliminary findings and observations
• Discuss logistical issues

Closing conference (on last day)
• Provides an executive summary of key findings
• Recommendations for compliance
• Prepare draft audit report for closing conference

Determine whether to follow California audit privilege

STEP 3
POST-AUDIT ACTIVITIES

Issue draft audit report

Issue final audit report

Develop corrective action plan (including target date and responsible person)

Create corrective action tracking databases

Complete corrective actions

Schedule next audit

Figure 19-1

Environmental Compliance Auditing Process in California

A completed pre-audit questionnaire assists the audit team leader in visualizing the level of effort necessary to complete the on-site audit, by knowing the scope of the regulated programs.

A completed pre-audit questionnaire assists the audit team leader in visualizing the level of effort necessary to complete the on-site audit, by knowing the scope of the regulated programs. The team leader will be in a position to:

- Determine the "fence line" of the facility (*i.e.*, which physical aspects of the facility or programs are subject to the audit).

- Determine where and how to deploy resources to address relevant environmental programs.

- Craft an appropriate sampling strategy.

- Assemble appropriate regulatory checklists and protocols for use by auditors on-site.

- Assess what personal protective equipment to bring.

- Assemble a team of subject matter experts to review relevant environmental programs. Audit teams should include subject matter experts from all applicable areas: air quality, climate change, water quality, hazardous waste, hazardous materials, oil management, tank management, chemical transport, and toxic materials (*e.g.*, polychlorinated biphenyls, lead, and asbestos) management.

On-Site Audit

On-site data-gathering represents the heart of the audit. The on-site phase typically begins with a scheduled opening meeting attended by the environmental manager, senior management, and key escorts.

On-site data-gathering represents the heart of the audit. The on-site phase typically begins with a scheduled opening meeting attended by the environmental manager, senior management (*e.g.*, Vice President for Environmental Affairs), and key escorts. The opening meeting lays out the objectives of the audit, the expectations of participants, the logistical considerations, and the schedule for on-site and post-audit activities. This meeting usually is followed by a facility tour to familiarize the auditors with the nature and extent of environmental activities and existing programs.

Facility escorts are paired with auditors either before or after the facility tour. After completing the facility tour, the audit team begins to collect the "ground truth," by conducting staff interviews, reviewing records, and examining field conditions (*e.g.*, viewing regulated equipment and emissions units, walking the site). The results of the ground truth are included in the auditor's "working papers," which serve as the evidentiary basis for drafting findings and observations. Working papers include all documents such as company permits, policies, the auditor's rough notes, and sampling strategies.

Depending on the schedule for on-site activities, a schedule for daily meetings or "out-briefs" may be helpful to review preliminary findings and observations and to discuss logistical issues. A final, closing conference, attended by facility management, escorts, and the audit team is held on the last day. This meeting provides an executive summary of key findings, along with strategic recommendations to enable the facility to come into compliance.

Typically, compliance audits focus on assessing facility operations to determine compliance with:

- Prescriptive multimedia environmental regulatory requirements
- Specific permit conditions (*e.g.,* air quality permits, emissions limitations, or maintaining chemical usage logs)
- Environmental plans and inventories (*e.g.,* spill prevention control and countermeasure plans, hazardous materials business plans, storm water pollution prevention plans, and air toxic hotspots)
- Training requirements (*e.g.,* mandatory annual hazardous waste generator and hazardous communication trainings)
- Inspection obligations (*e.g.,* weekly inspections for hazardous waste satellite accumulation points)
- Reporting obligations (*e.g.,* Title V Operating Permit annual compliance certifications, National Pollutant Discharge Elimination System daily monitoring reports and permits, and release reporting obligations)
- Emergency response procedures
- Corporate or divisional policies and procedures
- Facility-specific standard operating procedures or BMPs

The scope of a compliance audit often includes assessing equipment calibration to demonstrate that emissions controls, treatment devices, and other mechanical equipment are functioning properly. In addition, audits typically evaluate preventive maintenance schedules for emissions controls, alarms, and tank integrity testing.

The scope of a compliance audit often includes assessing equipment calibration to demonstrate that emissions controls, treatment devices, and other mechanical equipment are functioning properly.

Post-Audit Activities

When facility operations do not meet environmental standards, the auditor documents the noncompliant issue and characterizes it as either a "finding" or "observation." A finding represents an exceedance or violation of a regulatory standard, whereas an observation may include either an exemplary activity (*i.e.,* a positive observation) or a condition that violates a non-regulated, internal policy or a recommended good or best management practice (GMP or BMP). In addition, an observation can identify a condition representing prospective noncompliance (*e.g.,* a regulated emissions unit such as an underground storage tank is subject to a forthcoming schedule of compliance requiring an equipment retrofit or upgrade); the observation then can allow the facility to begin corrective action before the condition becomes a true regulatory finding. Observations can enhance the value of the audit by bringing other non-regulated but salient issues to the attention of management. Positive observations highlight effective programs that can be shared with other facilities. Findings and observations can be hand-written on a form or entered into a database. Later, the findings and observations are captured in a written report, verbal closing conference, or both.

GMP = Good management practice

To provide more meaning to the audit results, it is advisable to develop a prioritization scheme for findings and observations.

To provide more meaning to the audit results, it is advisable to develop a prioritization scheme for findings and observations. With a prioritization scheme, the audit team leader can advise the facility management and its legal representative on the most efficient way to deploy resources to respond.

There are several approaches to assigning priorities to findings and observations. One type of scheme labels findings as significant, major, or minor, while characterizing observations as positive (for exemplary performance) or negative. Another example of a prioritization scheme is:

NOV = Notice of violation

- **Priority 1.** Should be remedied immediately, due to actual or likely substantial endangerment to the environment or serious violation of federal, state, or local law

- **Priority 2.** Should be remedied as soon as practicable (*e.g.,* 30 days), due to reasonable likelihood of endangerment to the environment or possibility of a future notice of violation (NOV) of law or company policy

- **Priority 3.** Should be remedied within 30 to 180 days, due to reasonable likelihood of endangerment to the environment or possibility of a future NOV of law or company policy

- **Priority 4.** Should be documented and referred for corrective action, but is not driven by a regulatory or company policy

Regardless of the prioritization scheme, the auditor can further characterize findings as repeat findings, carryover findings, and new findings. A repeat finding is one from an earlier audit observed again in a later audit. A carryover finding is one from an earlier audit not corrected prior to the subsequent audit. Finally, a new finding is one not previously observed.

Findings and observations may be summarized in a draft report that describes the conditions observed, along with documentary evidence consisting of photographs or other written evidence.

Findings and observations may be summarized in a draft report that describes the conditions observed, along with documentary evidence consisting of photographs or other written evidence. The draft audit report can be as minimal as a table depicting each regulatory requirement, supporting citation, finding description, and recommended corrective action, or it may include narrative text describing these same elements. It may be advisable to protect the audit report with a confidentiality tool described below.

The report may document which facility activities were assessed (*e.g.,* 10 of 25 hazardous waste satellite accumulation areas and all manifests for the past two years). In addition to describing the basis for the findings and observations, the report should recommend corrective actions along with a suggested time frame for each. An audit report optionally can include the root cause or causes of the findings.

If the facility plans to take advantage of the audit privileges discussed below, the timing of the corrective actions and agency notifications will be affected. The facility manager then will be responsible for tracking and closing findings and observations.

Facility management is given an opportunity to review a draft of the audit report. The facility manager has discretion to assess the compliance risk of each finding and prioritize individual corrective actions. The facility manager ultimately is responsible for developing corrective actions and tracking progress.

Audit Protections and Privileges

Establishing confidentiality is crucial in the audit process. Because audits uncover potential regulatory violations, this information could be used against the facility if obtained by a regulatory agency or other parties. Establishing confidentiality also protects proprietary information, involving industrial processes or other sensitive corporate information, from disclosure to competitors. Facilities therefore should plan for and make resources available to remedy non-compliance findings. If such findings remain uncorrected, a facility risks involuntary disclosure, which could prompt administrative, civil, or criminal liability.

Establishing confidentiality is crucial. Because audits uncover potential regulatory violations, this information could be used against the facility if obtained by a regulatory agency or other parties.

Audit reports prepared without establishing confidentiality cannot retroactively gain protection. The methods described below are designed to protect disclosure of sensitive information identified during an audit. However, these methods cannot prevent disclosure of evidence when employees knowingly violated regulations.

Attorney-Client Privilege

Attorney-client privilege (Calif. Code of Evid. 952 *et seq.*) promotes complete and full disclosure of information between an attorney and client, by relieving the parties from having statements used against them or the company. If clients knew that sensitive information conveyed to their attorney could be disclosed, they may be less willing to communicate such information to counsel.

Attorney-client privilege promotes complete and full disclosure of information between an attorney and client, by relieving the parties from having statements used against them or the company.

Under the attorney-client privilege, the courts protect information from disclosure if all of the following are met:

- The information is communicated to obtain or render legal services.
- The information is confidential.
- The attorney or client asserts the attorney-client privilege.

The attorney-client privilege protects only information communicated between the parties for the purpose of rendering or obtaining legal advice. Because the underlying facts associated with the privileged communication are not protected, adversaries independently may uncover the same information.

Documents and reports required by public agencies as part of the permitting or compliance process (*e.g.*, self-monitoring reports, incident reports) cannot be protected because they are a matter of public record.

If information is intentionally or inadvertently disclosed to individuals or organizations without an appropriate confidentiality agreement, then the privilege is waived, and evidence can be discovered through agency disclosure or civil discovery. For example, the privilege can be inadvertently waived by disclosing the audit report to prospective lenders or purchasers.

Today, more executives are turning to in-house counsel for legal advice. In this situation, defining and maintaining the attorney-client privilege becomes tricky, and often involves risks and difficulties that would not arise with outside counsel. In California, the state courts and Ninth Circuit Court of Appeals have held that the attorney-client privilege applies to communications between a client and in-house counsel just as it applies to communications between a client and outside counsel. *See State Farm Fire and Casualty Co. v. Superior Court* (1997) 54 Cal. App. 4th 625; *U.S. v. Rowe* (1996) 96 F. 3d 1294. Though the privilege applies to confidential communications relating strictly to legal advice, the privilege is lost when communications are made for business purposes.

Attorney Work-Product Doctrine

The work-product doctrine protects information prepared by an attorney or his representative in anticipation of litigation. The purpose of the protection is to withhold from a client's adversaries materials prepared for the defense of that client.

The work-product doctrine protects information prepared by an attorney or his representative in anticipation of litigation. The purpose of the protection is to withhold from a client's adversaries materials prepared for the defense of that client. Protected materials under the work-product doctrine are more diverse than those under the attorney-client privilege. Protected materials may include lawyer's notes, interviews, witness statements, memoranda, photographs, drawings, and computer-generated data. Furthermore, protected materials include those generated by persons working under the direction of the attorney (*e.g.*, consultants).

To invoke the work-product doctrine, a three-part test must be met. First, the protected materials must be collected and prepared in anticipation of litigation. While litigation need not have commenced, it must be more than a remote prospect. In other words, materials likely will be protected if litigation is "fairly obvious," "probable," or "imminent." Second, disclosure of materials may be required if the adversary can show sufficient need and the prospect of suffering undue hardship in obtaining the information through other means. Finally, the greatest protection under the doctrine pertains to the attorney's "opinion" work. In California, the doctrine is defined broadly and protects "any writing that reflects an attorney's impressions, conclusions, opinions, or legal research or theories" used by the lawyer in anticipation of litigation.

Environmental Protection Agency Audit Privilege

The EPA Audit Policy encourages regulated entities to voluntarily discover, promptly disclose to EPA, and expeditiously correct violations of federal environmental requirements.

The EPA Audit Policy encourages regulated entities to voluntarily discover, promptly disclose to EPA, and expeditiously correct violations of federal environmental requirements. This self-disclosure policy encourages regulated entities to audit their facilities with an expectation that violations will be identified and corrected. EPA 2000. In addition, the policy states that EPA will refrain from routine requests for voluntary audit reports.

In exchange for prompt notification and correction of environmental violations, an entity can eliminate or substantially reduce gravity-based civil penalties and avoid criminal prosecution. A gravity-based penalty reflects the economic advantage an entity gains as a result of noncompliance. To take advantage of policy benefits, regulated entities must disclose violations within 21 days of discovery and correct them within 60 days. More specifically, a regulated entity is eligible for 100 percent mitigation of gravity-based penalties if it meets all nine of the policy's conditions described below, and is eligible for a 75 percent reduction if it meets all nine of the policy's conditions except for detecting the violation through a systematic discovery process.

EPA reserves the right to collect any economic benefit that resulted from noncompliance, even when the entity meets all other policy conditions. EPA generally will not recommend criminal prosecution if entities meet all nine conditions except for the systematic discovery process. This "no recommendation for criminal prosecution" incentive is available unless EPA determines there was culpable behavior. The nine conditions necessary to receive penalty mitigation include the following (EPA 2000):

EPA reserves the right to collect any economic benefit that resulted from noncompliance, even when the entity meets all other policy conditions.

- The entity must realize the violation through a systematic discovery process, such as an environmental audit or a compliance management system (*e.g.,* a CFEMS), that reflects due diligence in preventing, detecting, and correcting violations

- The entity cannot discover the violation through legally required monitoring, sampling, or auditing

- The entity must disclose the violation in writing to EPA within 21 days of discovery or such shorter time as may be required by law

- The entity must independently discover and disclose the violation before EPA or another regulator likely would identify the violation through its own investigation or through third-party information

- The entity must correct and remediate the violation within 60 calendar days from the date of discovery and must certify that the violation was corrected

- The entity must prevent recurrence of the violation, through such possible steps as improving environmental auditing efforts or compliance management systems

- Repeat violations are ineligible

- Certain types of violations are ineligible, including violations that result in serious actual harm to the environment or that may have presented imminent and substantial endangerment to the public health or environment

- The entity must cooperate

California Environmental
Protection Agency Audit Privilege

Cal/EPA adopted a self-disclosure audit policy more comprehensive than the federal EPA policy. The Cal/EPA policy is referred to as the Cal/EPA Recommended Guidance on Incentives for Voluntary Disclosure (Cal/EPA 2003), available on the Cal/EPA website (www.calepa.ca.gov/Enforcement/policy). As with EPA's policy, the same nine conditions must be met for a regulated entity to enjoy reduction or elimination of state gravity-based penalties.

Cal/EPA's policy is more comprehensive than the federal policy in three major areas: penalty reduction, criminal referrals, and fee-for-service certification.

Cal/EPA's policy is more comprehensive than the federal policy in three major areas: penalty reduction, criminal referrals, and fee-for-service certification. Like the penalty reduction provisions of the EPA Audit Policy, by fulfilling all nine conditions, regulated entities are relieved of all gravity-based penalties. Similarly, if an entity meets all conditions except the first, gravity-based penalties will be reduced by 75 percent. However, under the California audit policy, gravity-based penalties may be reduced by an additional 15 percent for entities that invest in pollution prevention programs for up to a combined 90 percent reduction in gravity-based fees.

Like the EPA Audit Policy, Cal/EPA will not recommend criminal prosecution if all nine conditions are met.

Although EPA encourages businesses to initiate self-audit or due diligence programs, its policy provides minimal guidance as to the types of procedures that qualify.

Although EPA encourages businesses to initiate self-audit or due diligence programs, its policy provides minimal guidance as to the types of procedures that qualify. The Cal/EPA policy attempts to provide regulated entities with greater certainty by waiving a portion of penalties for violations discovered through due diligence or environmental audits. Cal/EPA defines "due diligence" to mean a "regulated entity's systematic efforts, appropriate to the size and nature of the business, to prevent, detect, disclose, and correct violations" through various efforts and mechanisms. Entities that have implemented an audit or due diligence program will be able to receive certification from Cal/EPA prior to any reporting of a violation discovered through the audit or due diligence. Businesses with audit programs can, for a fee, invite Cal/EPA to certify the adequacy of their audit programs. Certification does not guarantee immunity from an enforcement action, but will likely result in businesses receiving the full advantage of the policy.

For more information...

Publications

The Air Pollution Consultant. 1993. Keeping Environmental Audit Documents Confidential. The Air Pollution Consultant, January/February 1993

Cal/EPA. October 2003. Recommended Guidance on Incentives for Voluntary Disclosure

Environmental Protection Agency. April 11, 2000. Final Policy Statement: Incentives for Self-Policing: Discovery, Disclosure, Correction and Prevention of Violations

Environmental Protection Agency. January 2001. Beyond Compliance: Supplemental Environmental Projects. Office of Enforcement and Compliance Assurance

Environmental Protection Agency. August 2004. Achieving Environmental Excellence: An Environmental Management Systems (EMS) Handbook for Wastewater Utilities

Manaster, K.A. and D.P. Selmi (eds). ND. Sections 54.13(2) and 56.20(2) of California Environmental Law and Land Use Practice. Matthew Bender. San Francisco, Calif.

Ryan, J.E., Jr. 1992. Self-Defense: How to Keep Your Environmental Audit Documents from Killing You. For presentation at the 85th Annual Air and Waste Management Association Meeting and Exhibition, June 21–26, 1992

Schrey, S.G., J.M. Tanenbaum, and T.M. Rudolph. February 24, 2005. Risk and Reward: Avoiding Pitfalls When Conducting Compliance Audits (www.nixonpeabody.com/publications_detail3.asp?Type=P&PAID=2&ID=910)

U.S. Department of Justice. July 1, 1991. Factors in Decisions on Criminal Prosecutions For Environmental Violations in the Context of Significant Voluntary Compliance or Disclosure Efforts by the Violator

Websites

California EPA, Recommended Enforcement Guidance
www.calepa.ca.gov/Enforcement/policy

California EPA, SEP Guide
www.calepa.ca.gov/Enforcement/Policy/SEPGuide.pdf

Ecological Footprint Overview
www.footprintnetwork.org/gfn_sub.php?content=footprint_overview

Environmental Protection Agency, SEP Policy and Guidance
http://cfpub.epa.gov/compliance/resources/policies/civil/seps/

U.S. Government Accountability Office
www.gao.gov/govaud/yb/2003/html/TOC.html

Glossary*

Acid rain–a category of air emissions involving two criteria pollutants (NO_X and SO_X) that chemically react with moisture in the atmosphere to create nitric acid and sulfuric acid. Most acid rain is produced from the burning of high sulfur coal (generating SO_X) and boiler systems (generating NO_X).

Acre-foot–325,851 gallons, or enough water to cover an acre of land one foot deep.

Acutely hazardous waste–a waste that EPA has determined to be very dangerous, even in minute quantities.

Adjacent wetlands–wetlands that are bordering, contiguous, or neighboring to other waters of the United States.

Adjudication–the judicial proceeding in which a priority is assigned to appropriations, and a decree is issued defining water rights.

Affordable housing–housing capable of being purchased or rented by a household with very low, low, or moderate income.

Air Pollution Control District–a local agency responsible for monitoring air pollution.

Air Quality Management District–a multi-county area that administers guidelines on state and federal Clean Air Acts.

Air toxics inventory*–a "comprehensive characterization of the full range of hazardous materials that are released, or that may be released to the surrounding air from" a regulated facility.

Ambient air quality standards–allowable concentrations of atmospheric pollutants. Federal standards

* equals permits and approvals

are adopted by EPA; state standards are adopted by ARB.

Anadromous fish–a fish species, such as salmon, that migrates from freshwater streams to the ocean and back to complete its cycle.

Annexation–incorporating land into an existing city or special district.

Applicable or relevant and appropriate requirement–a promulgated or legally enforceable federal or state requirement used to govern investigation and remedial actions throughout the RI/FS process. These requirements also influence the cleanup standard (*i.e.,* how clean is clean).

Application for certification*–an application filed by an energy facility developer seeking CEC certification of a proposed project with 50 MW or more of generating capacity.

Appropriative right–a water right based on physical control over water (pre-1914), or based on a permit or license for its beneficial use (post-1914).

Asbestos-containing material–any material containing more than one percent asbestos by weight.

Asbestos management plan*–A plan detailing the strategy to manage the discovery of asbestos.

Auger mining–removal of minerals from the walls of mined-out strips using special machines.

Authority to Construct Permit*–permit to construct a new or modified stationary source of air pollution, issued by a local air pollution control district or an air quality management district and guided by new source review rules.

Baseline–the starting point for determining a proposed project's significant effects, normally the same as the existing environmental setting.

Basin plan–a RWQCB basin plan sets forth WQS for surface and groundwaters within a particular water body or portion thereof and implementation plans to achieve the WQS. Designed to protect water quality within specified hydrological units.

Beneficial use–use of an amount of water that is reasonable and appropriate under efficient practices to accomplish, without waste, the purpose for which a diversion is made.

Best available control technology–an emissions limitation based on the maximum degree of reduction for each pollutant on a case-by-case basis, taking into account energy, environmental, and economic impacts and other costs.

Best available technology economically achievable standard–considers controls that are technologically and economically achievable but does not balance the cost of attainability against the potential benefit for ELGs for non-conventional and toxic pollutants.

Best conventional pollutant control technology standard–considers controls that are technologically and economically achievable in relation to the benefits for ELGs for conventional pollutants.

Best demonstrated available control technology–an emissions reduction applicable to industrial source categories based on emission standards or operational standards (where numerical limitations are infeasible) that considers cost, environmental impacts, and energy requirements.

421

Glossary

Best management practices–methods determined to be the most effective, practical means of preventing or reducing pollution from nonpoint sources.

Best practicable control technology–allows industries to emit higher than normal pollution levels by using equipment that uses the best practicable means available.

Biennial report*–all large quantity generators of hazardous waste must annually report (by March 1 of each even-numbered year) summarizing waste shipments for a two year period.

Biohazardous waste–"laboratory wastes" such as human and animal specimen cultures, human surgery specimens or tissues removed at surgery contaminated with infectious agents, blood, fluid blood products, containers, or equipment containing blood.

Biological assessment–a document prepared for Section 7 consultation to determine whether a proposed federal major construction activity is likely to adversely affect a listed species, proposed species, or designated critical habitat.

Biological diversity–the variety of life and its processes, including the variety of living organisms, the genetic differences among them, and the communities and ecosystems in which they occur.

Biological opinion*–a document stating the opinion of USFWS or NOAA Fisheries on whether a federal action is likely to jeopardize the continued existence of a listed species or result in destruction or adverse modification of its critical habitat.

Blight–physical and economic conditions within an area that causes a reduction of, or lack of, proper utilization of that area.

Border zone property–a property located within 2,000 feet of a hazardous waste deposit designated by DTSC and which may not be used for human habitation, a hospital, a school, or a day care center.

Brominated flame retardants–also known as polybrominated diphenyl ethers or PBDEs. Found in plastic housing of electronics, computers, and textiles used in furniture.

Brownfield–a "real property" whose development may be complicated by the potential presence of a hazardous substance, pollutant, or contaminant (except property subject to a planned or ongoing CERCLA removal action, listed or proposed for the NPL, or subject to specified orders and consent decrees under CERCLA).

CAL/FED–a consortium of federal and state agencies overseeing Bay–Delta water management, superseded by the Bay–Delta Authority.

California ambient air quality standards– ambient standards for criteria pollutants that generally are health-based. CAAQS are often more strict than national ambient air quality standards.

California Natural Diversity Database–an inventory of the reported locations of listed species and species of special concern.

California Register of Historic Places–a register of historic places meeting criteria established by state law.

California-only hazardous waste–a non-RCRA hazardous waste that meets California's more stringent hazardous waste definition.

CAM rule–requires that properly designed and adequate control measures for emission limitations are implemented, properly operated, and maintained.

Candidate species–a plant or animal species for which enough information is known concerning biological vulnerability and threats to support a proposal to list as endangered or threatened.

Categorical effluent limitation guidelines and standards–includes ELGs for conventional, nonconventional, and toxic pollutants, as well as new sources and indirect discharges.

Categorical exemption–CEQA exemptions for classes of projects that the Resources Agency has determined have no significant environmental effect.

Cathodic protection–a technique used to prevent corrosion of a metal surface by making it the cathode of an electrochemical cell.

Certificate of approval*–a certificate issued by DWR for construction of certain dams.

Certificate of Public Convenience and Necessity*–a certificate issued by the PUC to a public utility for construction of electricity facilities such as power plants and transmission lines.

Characteristic waste–a waste that has one or more of the following characteristics–ignitability, corrosivity, reactivity, or toxicity.

Charter city–a city that has been incorporated under its own charter rather than under the general laws of the state.

CNEL (community noise equivalent level)–same as Ldn, except 5 dB is added to noise levels between 7 pm and 10 pm.

Coastal development permit*–a permit for development in the coastal zone issued by a local government or the Coastal Commission.

Coastal zone–an area extending seaward to the state's outer limit of jurisdiction and inland to boundaries designated by the Legislature.

Combustible liquid–any liquid having a flashpoint at or above 100°F (37.8°C). Combustible liquids are divided into two classes.

Common law–system of law derived from judges' decisions, rather than statutes or constitutions.

Compensatory mitigation–mitigation to offset wetlands impacts that cannot be offset through avoidance or minimization.

Compliance-focused environmental management system–models from which environmental management system requirements are based. CFEMS must clearly illustrate management's commitment to comply with relevant federal, state, and local statutes and regulations, while continuing to make improvements regarding environmental programs.

Compressed gas—a gas or mixture of gases at a high pressure that can be used as a propellant.

Concentrated animal feeding operations—agricultural facilities that house and feed a large number of animals in a confined area.

Conditional authorization*—a type of "permit by rule" authorizing on-site treatment of "California-only," non-RCRA hazardous wastes. Hazardous waste generators of low concentrations of hazardous waste are authorized to use specified treatment technologies.

Conditional use permit*—pursuant to a zoning ordinance, this permit authorizes uses not routinely allowed on a particular site.

Conditionally exempt small quantity generator—a person or facility that generates 100 kilograms or less per month of hazardous waste, or one kilogram or less per month of acutely hazardous waste.

Conformity process*—the process by which transportation agencies show that their activities conform to the SIP.

Conjunctive use—combined use of surface and groundwater supplies.

Conservation easement—a recorded deed restriction voluntarily executed by a landowner with the purpose of retaining land predominantly in its natural scenic, historical, agricultural, forested, or open space condition.

Conserve, conserving, and conservation—the use of methods and procedures necessary to bring any listed species to the point at which measures under the ESA are no longer necessary.

Construction Demolition and Debris Facility Permit*—a permit governing facilities that receive, store, handle, transfer, or process construction and demolition debris and inert debris such as lumber, wallboard, glass, metal, roofing material, tile, carpeting, and materials.

Construction general permit*—requires development of a storm water pollution prevention plan describing best management practices to prevent storm water pollution associated with construction activities disturbing soil of one acre or more.

Consumer confidence report—annual report, written by public water suppliers who serve community water systems, that summarizes information about drinking water sources used (e.g., rivers, lakes, reservoirs, or aquifers), detected contaminants, and other educational information. To be delivered to customers by July 1st of each year.

Contained-in policy—a policy that requires that soil, sediment, and other environmental media must be managed as hazardous wastes so long as the mixture contains listed hazardous wastes or exhibits a characteristic of hazardous wastes.

Conventional pollutants—typical, higher volume pollutants that include biochemical oxygen demand (BOD), total suspended solids (TSS), fecal coliform, pH, and oil and grease (O&G).

Correlative right—in the context of riparian rights, the right to use a portion of the natural flow of water in common with other riparian users. Similar doctrine also applies in the context of groundwater rights, where overlying landowners must share rights to groundwater.

Corrosive—chemicals that are either highly acidic or caustic and react with other substances and "burn" the other substances chemically.

Corrosive hazardous waste—a waste that dissolves metals and other materials or burns the skin or eye on contact. A waste is corrosive if it fails any one of a number of tests such as aqueous wastes with a pH equal to or less than 2.0 or greater than 12.5.

County HWMP conformity*—applicants for an off-site hazardous waste treatment, storage, or disposal facility must demonstrate that the facility will be located in accordance with siting criteria specified in a County HWMP. For example, a facility may not be located in a flood plain or a seismically unsafe zone.

Criteria pollutant—a category of pollutant for which ambient air quality standards have been established based on the effect upon health and property.

Critical habitat—a formally designated specific geographic area contains those physical or biological features essential to the conservation of a listed species and that may require special management or protection.

Cumulative impacts—two or more individual impacts that, when considered together, are considerable or that compound other environmental impacts.

dB (decibel)—the unit of measurement describing the amplitude of sound.

dbA (A-weighted decibel)—a decibel scale approximating the sensitivity of the human ear.

Dedication*—offering by an applicant, and acceptance by the government, of private land for public use, typically imposed as a condition of development approval.

Delineation—the identification and mapping of wetlands and other waters of the United States.

Density bonus—permission to increase a project's housing density, typically in return for production of low income housing units.

Derived-from rule—a rule that classifies solid waste generated from the treatment of a hazardous waste as a hazardous waste.

Desalination—treatment of seawater or brackish water to reduce salt levels, making the water useful for potable or non-potable supplies.

Designated UST operator—one or more individuals designated by an owner of an underground storage

Glossary

tank facility having responsibility for training employees and conducting monthly visual inspections.

Designated waste—nonhazardous waste that consists of or contains pollutants that, under ambient environmental conditions at the WMU, could be released at concentrations exceeding applicable WQOs; designated waste that is hazardous waste is subject to a hazardous waste variance.

Development agreement*—a legally binding agreement between a city or county and a developer that typically prevents future changes in land use regulations from affecting a given project, in return for developer concessions.

Discretionary permit—requires an agency to exercise a higher level of deliberation and a higher level of analysis before issuing a permit.

District attainment plan—contains a discussion of CAAQS data and trends; a baseline emissions inventory; future-year projection of emissions, which include growth projections and adopted air emission control measures; a comprehensive control strategy of additional measures needed to reach attainment; an attainment demonstration, which generally involves complex modeling; and contingency measures.

Domestic water supply permit*—a permit issued by DHS for a PWS that supplies domestic water.

Dredged material—material removed from waters of the United States.

Due diligence—a regulated entity's systematic efforts, appropriate to the size and nature of the business, to prevent, detect, disclose, and correct violations through various efforts and mechanisms.

Easement—the right to use property owned by another for specific purposes.

Ecosystem—a dynamic and interrelated complex of plant and animal communities, and their associated environment.

Effluent limitations—limitations on discharge in an NPDES permit (the more stringent of either water quality-based or technology-based limitations).

Eminent domain—the taking of private property by a government unit for public use.

Emissions offsets—the reduction of emissions from other sources to mitigate the effect of emissions from a proposed new or modified source.

Empty container—under federal rules, a container with no residual hazardous waste (*e.g.,* no more than one inch remaining in a particular-sized container).

Endangered species—a species in danger of extinction throughout all or a significant portion of its range.

Environmental assessment*—brief preliminary analysis by a federal lead agency to determine whether an EIS should be prepared.

Environmental impact report*—a detailed statement prepared by a state or local lead agency describing a proposed project, its significant environmental effects, mitigation measures, and alternatives.

Environmental impact statement*—a detailed statement prepared by a federal lead agency describing a proposed project, its significant environmental effects, mitigation measures, and alternatives.

Environmental indicator—an objective measure of environmental quality used to assess the effectiveness of environmental programs.

Environmental justice—a program to ensure that environmental programs and enforcement fairly treat people of all races, cultures, and incomes, especially minority and low-income populations.

Environmental management system—procedures allowing an organization to decrease its environmental impact and increase its operating efficiencies.

Environmental setting—the physical environmental conditions in the project vicinity.

EPA identification number*—a number assigned to a facility that generates hazardous waste, a business that transports hazardous waste, or a business that operates a facility that recycles, treats, stores, or disposes of hazardous waste.

Exaction*—land dedication or impact fee required as a condition of development approval or construction.

Existing underground storage tank—an underground tank installed after 1988 (under federal law) or 1984 (under California law) that was required to be upgraded to meet specified technology standards or removed by December 22, 1998.

Extremely hazardous waste—a waste that exceeds specified toxicity levels expressed as either a lethal dose or a lethal concentration, or if the chemical appears on a list of pesticides or heavy metals, or is a PCB that exceeds a specified concentration in milligrams per kilogram.

F-listed hazardous waste—a type of process waste (*i.e.,* generated from industrial activity) that is non-industry-specific and is hazardous. Examples include spent solvents, wastewater treatment sludges, and spent plating solutions.

Facility response plan*—a comprehensive spill response and contingency plan designed to prevent the discharge of oil from vessels and land-based oil storage facilities that could reasonably be expected to cause substantial harm to the environment by discharging oil into or on navigable waters or adjoining shorelines.

Fault trace—the line formed by the intersection of a fault and the earth's surface.

Feasibility study—an analysis of the practicability of a proposal; a description and analysis of potential cleanup alternatives for a contaminated property appearing on the National Priorities List. The feasibility study is used to inform decision makers on cost-effective cleanup alternatives. The feasibility study usually starts as soon as the remedial investigation is underway; together, they commonly are referred to as the RI/FS.

Feasible—capable of being accomplished successfully within a reasonable period of time, taking into account economic, environmental, legal, social, and technological factors.

Federal implementation plan—a plan to achieve attainment of air quality standards, used when a state is unable to develop an adequate plan.

FERC license*—a license for a hydroelectric project using navigable waters or federal land.

Fill material—any material used for the primary purpose of replacing an aquatic area with dry land or changing the bottom elevation of a water body.

Final subdivision map*—map of an approved subdivision filed in the county recorder's office.

Findings—written conclusions prepared by a lead agency at the end of the EIR process explaining the disposition of each significant environmental effect.

Firm yield—the dependable annual water supply that could be available in all years, without exceeding specified shortages in agricultural deliveries during droughts.

Flammable liquid—any liquid having a flashpoint below 100°F.

Flashpoint—the minimum temperature at which a liquid gives off vapor within a test vessel in sufficient concentration to form an ignitable mixture with air near the surface of the liquid.

Formal consultation—the required process under ESA Section 7 when a proposed federal action is likely to adversely affect a listed species or critical habitat, used to determine in a biological opinion whether the proposed action is likely to jeopardize the continued existence of the species or adversely modify critical habitat.

Fully protected species—a species for which DFG may not issue a take permit, except for scientific purposes.

General industrial permit*—an NPDES permit that regulates storm water discharges associated with ten broadly described industrial activities. Among other things, the permit requires the development of a storm water pollution prevention plan designed to implement best management practices to prevent storm water contamination.

General permit*—a Section 404 permit for a class of activities precluding the need for a project-specific Section 404 permit.

General plan—a statement of development policies, including diagrams and text, setting forth objectives, principles, standards, and plan proposals, for the future development of a city or county.

Generally available control technology—imposed on sources that are too small to qualify as major sources.

Greenhouse gas—a gas, principally carbon dioxide, that allows sunlight to enter the atmosphere freely. When sunlight strikes the earth's surface, some of it is reflected back toward space as infrared radiation (heat). Greenhouse gases absorb this infrared radiation and trap the heat in the atmosphere.

Ground shaking—ground movement resulting from the transmission of seismic waves during an earthquake.

Groundwater—water that is seeped beneath the earth's surface and is stored underground.

Growth management—local government use of a variety of measures to influence the amount, type, and location of growth.

Guidelines—state CEQA Guidelines.

Habitat—the place or environment where a plant or animal lives naturally.

Habitat conservation plan*—a plan prepared under ESA Section 10(a) that outlines ways of maintaining, enhancing, and protecting a habitat type needed to protect a listed species.

Handler—any business that has contact with a hazardous material.

Harass—to intentionally or negligently create the likelihood of injury to wildlife by annoying it to such an extent as to significantly disrupt normal behavior patterns such as breeding, feeding, or sheltering.

Harm—to perform an act that kills or injures wildlife; may include significant habitat modification or degradation when it kills or injures wildlife by significantly impairing essential behavioral patterns such as nesting or reproduction.

Hazardous air pollutant—an air pollutant that poses an adverse effect and threat to human health or the environment.

Hazardous chemical—"[a]ny chemical which is a physical hazard or health hazard," as defined under federal OSHA.

Hazardous material—a substance or waste that, because of its physical, chemical, or other characteristics, may pose a risk of endangering human health or safety or of degrading the environment.

Hazardous materials business plan*—a plan that includes an inventory of hazardous materials stored, handled, or used; emergency response plans; procedures for mitigating harm in the event of a release; evacuation plans; and employee training.

Hazardous substance—broadly defined for CERCLA purposes to include all regulated chemicals, except for petroleum and natural gas, under the major federal statutes.

Hazardous waste generator—a person or facility whose processes and actions create hazardous waste.

Headwaters—the point on a nontidal stream above which the average annual flow is less than 5 cubic feet per second (cfs).

Household hazardous waste—any hazardous waste generated incidental to owning or maintaining a

Glossary

place of residence. Household hazardous waste does not include any waste generated in the course of operating a business concern at a residence.

Hydrophytic vegetation–plants that can grow in wetland conditions.

Ignitable hazardous waste–a waste that is easily combustible or flammable. Ignitable hazardous waste includes a liquid with a flashpoint equal to or less than 140°F; a non-liquid capable under standard temperature and pressure of causing fire by means of friction, absorption, moisture, or spontaneous chemical changes and that when ignited burns so vigorously and persistently that it creates a hazard; an ignitable compressed gas, as defined in the Department of Transportation (DOT) regulations; or an oxidizer, as defined in DOT regulations.

Impact fee*–also known as a development fee, a monetary exaction to defray costs of public facilities related to a development project.

Incidental take–take of a listed species that results from, but is not the purpose of, otherwise lawful activity.

Incidental take permit*–a permit issued by USFWS or NOAA Fisheries under the federal ESA Section 10(a), or DFG under CESA Section 2081, authorizing take of a listed species.

Individual permit–a project-specific Section 404 permit.

Informal consultation–a process under ESA Section 7 prior to or in lieu of formal consultation that includes all interactions between USFWS or NOAA Fisheries and a federal agency or its designated non-federal representative such as an applicant.

Initial study*–preliminary analysis to determine whether to prepare a negative declaration or EIR.

Initiative–a legislative measure that has been placed on the election ballot as a result of voter signatures.

Instream use–the beneficial use of water within a stream, such as for fisheries habitat.

International Organization for Standardization–the world's largest developer of technical standards, ISO is a non-governmental organization and consists of a network of the national standards institutes of 157 counties. ISO standards contribute to enabling the manufacture and development of products more efficiently and also provide a safeguard for consumers.

Isolated waters–nontidal waters not part of a surface tributary system to interstate or navigable waters of the United States, and not adjacent to such tributaries.

Jeopardize–appreciably reducing the likelihood of both the survival and recovery of a listed species in the wild by reducing the reproduction, numbers, or distribution of the species.

Jurisdictional determination–the final USACE decision on its jurisdiction over a site under Section 404.

K-listed hazardous waste–a type of process waste (*i.e.,* generated from industrial activity) that is industry specific (*e.g.,* refineries, metal smelting) and is hazardous. Examples include industry-specific waste streams such as slop oil emulsion solids from the refining industry (*e.g.,* K-049).

L10–the A-weighted noise level that is exceeded 10 percent of the time.

Lake or Streambed Alteration Agreement*–an agreement negotiated between DFG and an applicant for activities involving alteration of a lake or stream zone.

Land use lease*–a State Lands Commission lease to use state-owned sovereign lands.

Large quantity generator–a person or facility that generates more than 2,200 pounds of hazardous waste and 1 kg (*i.e.,* 2.2. pounds) per month of acutely hazardous waste.

Large quantity handler–a person or facility that accumulates more than 5,000 kg of universal waste at any time.

Law of the River–numerous compacts, judicial decisions, contracts, and other instruments governing management and operation of the Colorado River.

Ldn (day–night average level)–the average equivalent A-weighted noise level during a 24-hour day, obtained by adding 10 decibels to noise levels between 10 pm and 7 am.

Lead agency–public agency having the principal responsibility for carrying out or approving a project.

Leq (equivalent energy level)–the average acoustic energy content of noise during the time it lasts.

Letter of permission*–a Section 404 permit issued through an abbreviated process that includes agency coordination and public interest review, but not public notice.

Liquefaction–a process by which water-saturated granular solids transform from a solid to a liquid state during strong ground shaking.

Listed hazardous waste–a process waste (*i.e.,* generated from an industrial process) or a non-process waste (includes unused commercial chemicals, container residues, pill residues, and expired chemicals).

Listing–the formal process by which USFWS or NOAA Fisheries under the federal ESA, or the Fish and Game Commission under CESA, adds species to the list of endangered and threatened wildlife and plants.

Local agency formation commission–a county-wide commission that reviews and approves city and special district boundary changes.

Local coastal program–a combination of a local government's land use plans, zoning ordinances, and other implementing actions that meet the requirements of the California Coastal Act.

Long-term sustained yield–the average growth sustainable by an inventory predicted at the end of a 100-year planning period.

Long-term transfer*–a transfer of water or water rights lasting more than one year.

Lowest achievable emission rate–a technology-forcing standard that may not be less stringent than any applicable NSPS. LAER is an emissions rate specific to each type of emissions unit, including fugitive emissions sources.

Major modification–a change to a major stationary source of emissions with respect to Prevention of Significant Deterioration and New Source Review under the Clean Air Act.

Manifest–a shipping document that tracks hazardous waste from the time it leaves its place of origin until it reaches an off-site TSDF.

Maximum achievable control technology–a technology-based standard that requires the maximum degree of reduction in emissions of HAPs, and that EPA determines is achievable or not, after considering costs and other environmental impacts.

Maximum contaminant level goal–non-enforceable concentration of a drinking water contaminant, set at the level at which no known or anticipated adverse effects on human health occur and that allows a margin of safety. The MCLG is usually the starting point for determining the enforceable maximum contaminant level.

Mean high water–the average position of the high water mark.

Medical waste–waste that meets both of the following requirements–(1) biohazardous waste or sharps waste, and (2) waste that is generated or produced as a result of the diagnosis, treatment, or immunization of human beings or animals, in research, in the production or testing of biologicals, or in the accumulation of properly contained home-generated sharps waste.

Methyl tertiary butyl ether–a chemical compound produced by a chemical reaction between methanol and isobutylene.

Migratory birds–birds that migrate across state and national borders.

Mined land–the surface, subsurface, and groundwater of an area where a surface mining operation is conducted.

Ministerial permit–involves a straightforward decision judging against standardized, objective criteria.

Mitigated negative declaration*–brief written statement prepared by a state or local lead agency explaining why a proposed project will not have a significant environmental effect, and therefore will not require an EIR, because the project's significant environmental effects have been mitigated.

Mitigation banking–use of a site via a credit system for enhancement, restoration, or creation of wetlands, for mitigation of impacts on wetlands at other sites.

Mitigation measure–avoiding, minimizing, rectifying, reducing, or compensating for an environmental impact.

Mixed hazardous waste–a waste resulting from the combination of a nonhazardous waste and a hazardous waste that exhibits a hazardous waste characteristic. There are exceptions to this definition, such as when a characteristic hazardous waste is mixed with a nonhazardous waste and the resulting mixture is diluted enough to pass the test for ignitability, corrosivity, or reactivity. However, a mixed hazardous waste that exhibits the toxicity characteristic must be managed as a hazardous waste regardless of the concentration of the toxic constituent.

Mobile source–any non-stationary source of air pollution, such as an automobile or locomotive.

Modification–any physical or operational change in an existing facility that would increase emission of any air pollutant.

Mudflats–periodically inundated and exposed unvegetated areas such as tidal coastal areas and the edges of inland lakes, ponds, and rivers.

Municipal separate storm sewer system–a conveyance (can include roads with drainage systems, municipal streets, catch basins, curbs, gutters, ditches, built channels, or storm drains) that has been designed for collecting or conveying storm water, and also is not a combined sewer or part of a POTW.

Municipal solid waste landfill unit–a discrete area of land or an excavation that receives household waste and is not a land application unit, surface impoundment, injection well, or waste pile.

Municipal solid waste transfer/processing station–solid waste management facility that temporarily stores municipal solid waste before shipping to a permitted municipal solid waste landfill for disposal.

Municipal Storm Water Permit*–governs storm water discharges from municipalities serving more than 100,000 people. The site-specific NPDES permit must incorporate a monitoring program to evaluate runoff and water received.

National ambient air quality standards–ambient standards for six criteria pollutants that are widespread and considered harmful to public health and the environment.

National Pollutant Discharge Elimination System permit*–a permit that controls water pollution by regulating point sources that discharge pollutants into surface waters defined as "waters of the United States."

National Priorities List–a list of highly contaminated sites that EPA prioritizes for cleanup and access to Superfund monies.

National Register of Historic Places–historic properties meeting eligibility criteria established by the Advisory Council on Historic Preservation.

Nationwide permit*–a type of general permit that applies nationally.

Natural Community Conservation Plan*–a regional plan prepared under the NCCPA that provides measures necessary to conserve and manage

Glossary

natural biological diversity within the plan area while allowing compatible and appropriate economic development, growth, and other human uses.

Navigable waters–waters that are, could be, or were used to transport interstate or foreign commerce.

Negative declaration*–brief written statement prepared by a state or local lead agency explaining why a proposed project will not have a significant environmental effect, and therefore will not require an EIR.

Negligence–the failure to exercise the degree of care considered reasonable, resulting in unintended injury to another party.

New source performance standards–emissions limitations for industrial source categories, adopted by EPA.

New source review rules–rules guiding authority-to-construct permits, requiring application of BACT and emissions offsets to new or modified major sources.

New underground storage tank–underground storage tanks installed after 1988 (under federal law) or 1984 (under California law) that must have been permitted and must now be equipped with specified equipment such as secondary containment and overflow protection.

New Urbanism–closely related to smart growth, a planning doctrine that emphasizes restoration of existing urban centers within coherent metropolitan regions, reconfiguration of sprawling suburbs into communities of real neighborhoods, conservation of natural environments, and preservation of the built environment.

Nexus–for purposes of this chapter, a reasonable relationship between a land use regulation and the impacts of a proposed action.

No surprises rule–under the federal ESA and the NCCPA, assurances given to incidental take permittees that unforeseen circumstances will not result in additional conservation or funding requirements.

Noise contour–a line drawn about a noise source indicating equal levels of noise exposure.

Non-attainment area–a geographic area in which the level of an air pollutant is higher than an AAQS.

Non-attainment area plan–a local air district plan for attainment and maintenance of AAQS.

Non-attainment new source review–requires stationary sources of air pollution to obtain permits before they start construction. NSR also is referred to as construction permitting or pre-construction permitting.

Non-conventional pollutant–all pollutants other than conventional and toxic pollutants, and including but not limited to chemical oxygen demand (COD), total organic carbon (TOC), nitrogen, phosphorus, ammonia, and sulfide.

Nonconforming use–land use that was lawful before a zoning ordinance was adopted, but does not conform to the new zoning ordinance.

Nonhazardous solid waste–municipal solid waste or refuse that has a significant proportion of degradable material or "inert" waste (such as paving fragments and non-degradable construction debris).

Nonindustrial tree farmer–owner of timberland less than 2,500 acres not primarily engaged in the manufacture of forest products.

Nonpoint source pollution–diffuse sources of pollution (i.e., without a single point of origin or not introduced into a receiving stream from a specific outlet). The pollutants are generally carried off the land by storm water. Common nonpoint sources are agriculture, forestry, urban, mining, construction, dams, channels, land disposal, saltwater intrusion, and city streets.

Notice of determination–notice filed after project approval, once a negative declaration or EIR has been prepared.

Notice of exemption–optional notice filed after project approval, indicating a CEQA exemption applies.

Notice of preparation–brief notice indicating a lead agency intends to prepare an EIR.

Nuisance–a condition or activity interfering with the free use and enjoyment of property or the exercise of certain public rights.

Oil–broadly defined to include "petroleum, fuel oil, sludge, oil refuse, and oil mixed with wastes other than dredge spoil."

Open-pit mining–mining of mineral deposits located at or near the earth's surface from surface openings.

Operator–any person in control of, or having responsibility for, the daily operation of an underground storage tank system.

Ordinary high water mark–the line on the shore established by fluctuations of water and indicated by physical characteristics such as a clear natural line impressed in the bank.

Overburden–soil, rock, or other minerals that lie above a natural mineral deposit or in between mineral deposits before or after their removal by surface mining operations.

Overdraft–groundwater basin in which the amount of water withdrawn exceeds the amount of water replenishing the basin.

Overlay zone–a set of zoning requirements that is superimposed on a base zone, e.g., an historic preservation district.

Owner–the owner of an underground storage tank.

Ozone-depleting chemical–a chemical that aggressively reacts and destroys ozone molecules in the upper stratosphere. Examples include freons, chlorofluorocarbons (CFCs), and other halogenated compounds.

P-listed hazardous waste–a type of non-process waste that is non-industry-specific and is acutely hazardous.

Paper water–water entitlements under water contract that may never be delivered.

Particulate matter–a mixture of extremely small particles and liquid droplets that can include acids (such as nitrates and sulfates), organic chemicals, metals, and soil or dust particles. Also known as particle pollution. The size of particles is linked directly to the potential for causing health problems.

Percolating waters–all underground waters other than underflow or underground streams.

Permit–for purposes of this book, all environmental approvals, including certifications, licenses, and plan and specification approvals.

Permit by rule*–a permit in which the applicant submits a notice of intent to comply with pre-set permit conditions that are not site-specific.

Permit to operate*–an operational permit issued by an air district to a stationary air emissions source.

Personal protective equipment–clothing and equipment to protect the employee from work hazards.

Planned unit development*–a master-planned development within a zoning district that allows multiple uses (*e.g.,* residential, commercial, industrial).

Point source–any discernible, confined, and discrete conveyance, including pipes, ditches, channels, tunnels, conduits, wells, vessels, and more.

Police power–the power of state and local governments to enact legislation to protect public health, safety, and welfare.

Pollutant–dredged spoil, solid waste, incinerator residue, filter backwash, sewage, garbage, sewage sludge, munitions, chemical wastes, biological materials, radioactive materials (except those regulated under the Atomic Energy Act of 1954, as amended (42 USC 2011 *et seq.*)), heat, wrecked or discarded equipment, rock, sand, cellar dirt, and industrial, municipal, and agricultural waste discharged into water.

Potable water–tap water that is safe and satisfactory for drinking and cooking.

Potential to emit–maximum amount of a specific pollutant capable of being released into the air that must be considered in equipment design.

Potentially responsible party–any individual or business–including owners, operators, transporters, or generators–potentially responsible for, or contributing to, a spill or other contamination at a Superfund site. Whenever possible, through administrative and legal actions, EPA requires clean up of hazardous sites by potentially responsible parties.

Pre-construction notification*–notification made to USACE of an intent to perform fill activities authorized by a nationwide permit.

Prescriptive right–a water right obtained by "open, notorious, continuous, and adverse use" (each of these terms is a legal term of art) for the prescriptive period that in California is five years.

Pretreatment standards–standards designed to prevent the introduction of pollutants to publicly owned treatment works (POTW) that would interfere with operations and to prevent pollutants incompatible with the POTW from passing through.

Prevention of significant deterioration permit*–a permit for a major source of a criteria pollutant, to assure that clean air areas meeting national ambient air quality standards remain clean.

Primary containment–the first level of containment in an underground storage tank, such as the inner surface that comes into immediate contact with the hazardous substance being contained.

Primary maximum contaminant level–a mandatory and enforceable standard (federal and state) that is protective of human health.

Priority toxic pollutant–129 specified pollutants commonly subdivided into heavy metals, organics, and pesticides.

Program timber environmental impact report–an Environmental Impact Report prepared for a Program Timber Harvest Plan.

Program timber harvest plan*–a timber harvest plan prepared for single or multiple ownerships in which CEQA compliance is achieved through a Program Timber Environmental Impact Report.

Programmatic general permit*–permit issued by a USACE district or division where another agency's program provides equivalent protection to the Section 404 program.

Project–the whole of an action with the potential for a direct or indirect physical environmental impact.

Proposition 65–requires regulated businesses to notify the public and employees of their potential exposure to chemicals that cause cancer and reproductive harm.

Public health goal–contaminant level in drinking water that does not pose a significant health risk to consumers and is based solely on scientific and public health considerations without regard to economic considerations.

Public interest review–USACE evaluation to determine if a Section 404 permit is in the public interest, using specific criteria.

Public trust doctrine–enforceable doctrine by which certain natural resources are held in trust by the government for the use and enjoyment of the public.

Public water system–system that provides the public with piped water for human consumption, and has 15 or more service connections or regularly serves 25 individuals daily at least 60 days out of the year.

Quasi-judicial decision–a quasi-judicial decision is one that applies policy based on factual determinations, rather than sets policy.

Range–the geographic area a species is known or believed to occupy.

Rangeland–land used primarily for livestock grazing and occupied by a few tree species usually not harvested for lumber products.

Glossary

RCRA Part B TSDF Permit*–"Part B" is the portion of a hazardous waste TSDF permit application (known as the "operations plan") that provides details governing operation of the TSDF along with a detailed contingency plan in the event of an accidental release of hazardous waste.

Reactive hazardous waste–a waste that is unstable or that undergoes rapid or violent chemical reactions, such as exploding, catching fire, or giving off fumes (when exposed to or mixed with water, air, or other materials).

Reasonable and prudent alternative–a recommended alternative action identified in a biological opinion that is feasible, can be implemented consistent with the purpose of the action, is consistent with the federal agency's legal authority and jurisdiction, and would avoid jeopardy.

Reasonable and prudent measure–an action necessary to minimize the impacts of incidental take of a listed species that is anticipated to result from implementing a project with a non-jeopardy opinion.

Reasonably available control technology–the lowest emissions limit that a particular existing source is capable of meeting by applying control technology that is reasonably available and technologically and economically feasible.

Reclamation–process of land treatment that minimizes adverse environmental effects of surface mining operations, so that mined lands are reclaimed to a usable condition that is readily adaptable to alternative land uses and creates no danger to public health and safety.

Reclamation plan*–a plan filed by a surface mining operator that, together with financial assurances, must be approved by a lead agency before mining activities commence.

Reconstruction–involves replacement of one or more components where the cost of the new component(s) exceeds 50 percent of the cost of constructing a comparable new facility.

Record of Decision*–a public document that explains the cleanup alternative(s) that will be followed.

Recovery–the process by which decline of a listed species is stopped or reversed, or threats to its survival neutralized, so that its long-term survival in the wild can be ensured.

Recovery plan–a document serving as the guide for activities to recover or conserve a listed species.

Recyclable waste–material that is removed or separated from other residential, commercial, or industrial garbage for the purpose of reuse or reprocessing.

Redevelopment–the legally authorized process of rehabilitating or rebuilding a deteriorated section of a city.

Redevelopment plan–legal framework for revitalization activities in a redevelopment project area.

Referendum–a ballot measure challenging a legislative action of a city or county.

Reformulated gasoline–specially refined gasoline with low levels of smog-forming volatile organic compounds and low levels of hazardous air pollutants.

Regional general permit*–a Section 404 permit issued by a USACE district or division authorizing a class of activities within a geographic region that has minimal environmental impacts.

Regulated substances–"hazardous substances" and petroleum, under the federal underground storage tank program.

Release–broadly defined under RCRA to include any spill, leaking, pouring, emitting, emptying, discharging, injecting, pumping, escaping, leaching, dumping, or disposing of hazardous waste or constituents into the environment.

Remedial action–the actual construction or implementation phase of a Superfund site cleanup that follows remedial design.

Remedial action plan*–a state plan to restore or clean up a site.

Remedial investigation–an in-depth study to gather data needed to determine the nature and extent of contamination at a Superfund site, to establish site cleanup criteria, to identify preliminary alternatives for remedial action, and to support technical and cost analyses of alternatives. The remedial investigation is usually done with the feasibility study. Together they commonly are referred to as the RI/FS.

Removal action–a straightforward cleanup effort requiring immediate attention to stabilize the release or threat of a release of a hazardous substance (e.g., controlling surface water runoff, pumping leaking ponds, or removing bulk containers of hazardous substances).

Report of Disposal Site Information–a report filed with the LEA if an applicant proposes to handle, process, transport, store, or dispose of solid wastes.

Reportable quantity–a quantity of a hazardous substance that triggers reporting under CERCLA. If the substance exceeds its reportable quantity, then the release must be reported to the National Response Center, SERC, and community emergency coordinators for areas likely to be affected.

Responsible agency–public agency that uses a lead agency environmental document to carry out or approve a project.

Restricted waste–a hazardous waste that must meet special requirements before being disposed of in land-based disposal facilities.

Riffle and pool complexes–high quality fish and wildlife habitat where a rapid current flowing over a coarse substrate results in turbulence (riffles) and a slower moving current in deeper areas results in smooth flow (pools).

Riparian right–a water right based on the ownership of land bordering a river or waterway.

Risk management plan*–facilities that manufacture, process, use, store, or handle "highly hazardous chemicals" in excess of threshold quantities may be required to develop a plan that evaluates the risk of an unplanned chemical release. The RMP may be required to include a hazard assessment, an off-site consequence analysis, a prevention plan, and an emergency response plan.

Satellite accumulation point–a location where hazardous waste is accumulated at the point of generation. No more than 55 gallons of a hazardous waste, or one quart of an acutely hazardous or extremely hazardous waste, may be accumulated at each SAP.

Secondary containment–the level of containment external to, and separate from, the primary containment in an underground storage tank.

Secondary maximum contaminant level–a mandatory and enforceable standard (state only) that protects aesthetic qualities of drinking water, such as taste, odor, and color.

Section 4(d) rule–a regulation establishing prohibitions on take necessary and advisable to provide for conservation of a threatened species.

Section 7 consultation*–the process by which a federal agency consults with USFWS or NOAA Fisheries under the federal ESA to determine whether any activity authorized, funded, or carried out by the agency may affect a listed species or designated critical habitat.

Section 10 permit*–USACE permit issued pursuant to the Rivers and Harbors Act for activities that involve obstruction of, excavation in, or filling of navigable waters.

Section 401 certification*–RWQCB or SWRCB certification that a Section 404 permit is consistent with state water quality standards.

Section 404 permit*–a USACE permit issued pursuant to the Clean Water Act for the discharge of dredged or fill materials into waters the U.S.

Section 404(b)(1) alternatives analysis–an analysis prepared consistent with the Section 404(b)(1) Guidelines to determine whether a practicable alternative to a proposed discharge exists that has less adverse effect on the aquatic ecosystem.

Section 2081 incidental take permit*–DFG permit authorizing take of state-listed species incidental to otherwise lawful development projects.

Sharps waste–any device having acute rigid corners, edges, or protuberances capable of cutting or piercing, including, but not limited to, hypodermic needles, broken glass, and any item capable of cutting or piercing that is contaminated with trauma scene waste.

Significant effect–a substantial or potentially substantial change in the physical environment.

Silvicultural system–a planned program of forest stand treatments during the life of a stand.

Small quantity generator–a person or facility that generates between 220–2,200 pounds per month of hazardous waste and no more than 1 kg (i.e., 2.2 pounds) per month of acute hazardous waste.

Small quantity handler–a person or facility that accumulates no more than 5,000 kg (or 11,000 pounds) of universal waste at any time.

Smart growth–closely related to new urbanism, a planning doctrine that discourages urban sprawl and emphasizes compact, transit-accessible, pedestrian-oriented, mixed use development patterns, and land reuse.

Sole source aquifer–a principal source area that supplies at least 50 percent of the drinking water consumed in a specific area overlying the aquifer.

Solid waste–garbage, refuse, sludge and other discarded material including solid, liquid, semisolid or contained gaseous material resulting from industrial, commercial, mining and agricultural operations and from community activity.

Solid waste assessment test–method to determine the potential risk of a release or discharge from a municipal solid waste landfill. SWATs are designed to evaluate the potential air emissions liberated and water discharged from a municipal solid waste landfill and to potentially mitigate the releases.

Source reduction–any action that causes a net reduction in the generation of solid waste. Source reduction includes, but is not limited to, reducing the use of non-recyclable materials, replacing disposable materials and products with reusable materials and products, reducing packaging, reducing the amount of yard wastes generated, establishing garbage rate structures with incentives to reduce waste tonnage generated, and increasing the efficiency of the use of paper, cardboard, glass, metal, plastic, and other materials.

Source reduction and recycling elements–a municipality's approach to managing solid waste, including all feasible source reduction, recycling, and composting programs while identifying the landfill and transformation capacity necessary for solid waste that cannot be reduced, recycled, or composted.

Sovereign lands–submerged lands, tidelands, and the beds of navigable rivers.

Special aquatic sites–specific types of waters of the United States for which mitigation requirements are more stringent under Section 404(b)(1) Guidelines.

Special treatment area–an area designation by the Coastal Commission according to Coastal Act criteria, such as scenic view corridors, wetlands, and significant habitats.

Special waste–items such as auto shredder waste, bag house and scrubber waste, cement kiln dust, dewatered sludge from industrial process water treatment, sand from sandblasting, foundry casting, and coal gasification.

Species of special concern–animals not listed under the federal ESA or CESA, but that nonetheless are declining at a rate that could result in listing, or that historically occurred in low numbers and known threats to their persistence currently exist.

Glossary

Specific plan*–a plan addressing land use distribution, open space availability, and infrastructure for a portion of a community.

Sphere of influence–the physical boundary and service area that a local government is expected to ultimately serve, as adopted by the LAFCO.

Spill prevention control and countermeasure plan*–establishes engineering and management procedures and equipment standards designed to prevent oil from entering surface waters. Each plan must document site-specific spill prevention and control measures to manage facility structures, procedures, and equipment.

Standard operating procedure–a set of written instructions that document a routine or repetitive activity followed by an organization.

Standard permit*–in the context of wetlands regulation, a project-specific permit (either a general permit or letter of permission) issued after the formal Section 404 permit review process.

Standardized permit–in the context of hazardous waste regulation, governs treatment and storage of "California-only," non-RCRA hazardous wastes.

State implementation plan–a detailed plan prepared by ARB that describes the program the state will use to attain national ambient air quality standards (NAAQS). A SIP is required by the federal CAA for areas with unhealthy levels of ozone, carbon monoxide, nitrogen dioxide, sulfur dioxide, and inhalable particulate matter.

State responsibility area–an area where fire protection is primarily a state responsibility.

Statement of overriding considerations–written explanation prepared at the end of the EIR process explaining why a lead agency approved a project notwithstanding its significant environmental effects.

Stationary source–any building, structure, facility, or installation that emits or may emit any air pollutant subject to regulation under the Clean Air Act.

Statute of limitations–time limit for filing a lawsuit.

Statutory exemption–an exemption created by the state Legislature.

Storm water–precipitation that flows over a surface, or urban runoff or melted snow that flows into the storm drain system or otherwise into surface waters.

Storm water pollution prevention plan*–identifies pollution sources that affect the quality of storm water discharges from a site and requires implementation of best management practices to reduce pollutants in storm water discharges.

Strict liability–for certain activities (*e.g.*, ultrahazardous activities) a defendant is liable even if the activity is carried out with all reasonable care.

Subdivision–the process of dividing a larger parcel of land into smaller lots.

Submerged lands–includes state-owned lands between the tidelands and the three-mile limit of offshore waters subject to state jurisdiction, as well as lands underlying navigable waters.

Substantial evidence–enough relevant information and inferences that a fair argument can be made to support a conclusion. Includes facts and reasonable assumptions and expert opinion supported by facts.

Subvention–as used in the Williamson Act, the granting of funds from state government to local governments to partially compensate for foregone property tax revenues when land is placed under contract.

Superfund–the program operated under the legislative authority of CERCLA and SARA that funds and carries out EPA solid waste emergency and long-term removal and remedial activities. These activities include establishing the National Priorities List, investigating sites for inclusion on the list, determining their priority, and conducting and/or supervising cleanup and other remedial actions.

Supplemental environmental projects–pollution prevention efforts that exceed the existing statutory obligations of dischargers and achieve an environmental benefit.

Surface impoundment–a ditch constructed primarily of earthen materials used for treating, storing, or diluting liquid hazardous waste.

Surface mining operation–mining minerals on lands by removing overburden and mining directly from mineral deposits; open-pit mining of naturally exposed minerals; auger mining; dredging and quarrying; or surface work incident to an underground mine. Surface mining operations include exploratory activities and production and disposal of mining waste.

Sustained yield–yield of commercial wood that an area of commercial timberland can provide continuously at a given intensity of management consistent with required environmental protection, and that is professionally planned to achieve a balance between growth and removal.

Sustained yield plan–a plan to achieve sustainable levels of timber harvest; supplements the THP process by addressing long-term issues and cumulative effects of timber operations in defined management units.

Take–under the federal ESA, to harass, harm, pursue, hunt, shoot, wound, kill, trap, capture, or collect a listed species, or to attempt such conduct; under CESA, to hunt, pursue, catch, capture, or kill a listed species, or to attempt such conduct.

Taking–the appropriation by government of private land for public use, requiring just compensation under the U.S. Constitution.

Technology-based effluent limitation–a minimum level of effluent control that uniformly applies to industry categories, regardless of where the discharge occurs or the quality of the surface water receiving the discharge.

Temporary change*–a short-term (one year or less) water transfer involving a change in point of diversion, place of use, or purpose of use.

Temporary urgency changes*–a short-term (one year or less) water transfer to meet an urgent need involving a change in point of diversion, place of use, or purpose of use.

Tentative subdivision map*–a map illustrating a subdivision proposal. A subdivision is complete only when conditions imposed on the tentative map have been satisfied and a final map has been certified and recorded.

Threatened species–a species likely to become endangered within the foreseeable future throughout all or a significant part of its range.

Tidelands–lands over which the tide ebbs and flows.

Tiered permit–a permit program based on regulatory requirements matched against the risks associated with a facility's activities.

Tiering–coverage of general matters in broader environmental documents and project-specific matters in subsequent project-specific environmental documents.

Timber harvest plan*–under the FPA, a plan prepared by a registered professional forester for any proposed timber harvest on non-federal land. Among other contents, the THP describes the site to be harvested, the silviculture methods to be applied, reforestation methods, road building, and mitigation measures to avoid soil erosion and other environmental damage.

Timber operation–under the FPA, an operation that includes cutting of timber for commercial purposes or for incidental work, such as construction and maintenance of roads, fuel breaks, stream crossings, skid trails, fire hazard abatement, and site preparation.

Timberland–under the FPA, non-federal land available for and capable of growing a crop of trees of any commercial species used to produce lumber and other forest products.

Timberland Conversion Permit*–a permit issued by the Forestry Board authorizing conversion of timberland to non-timber uses.

Title V operating permit*–all encompassing permit including relevant conditions for all regulated stationary source permits at a "major facility." The permit is effective for five years. Permit holders must submit compliance reports every six months that must be certified by a responsible official.

Total maximum daily load–specifies waste load allocations for point and nonpoint sources that discharge into an impaired water body (*i.e.,* a water body that does not meet one or more established beneficial uses specified for that water body).

Toxic air contaminant–an air pollutant that may cause or contribute to an increase in mortality or in serious illness, or that may pose a present or potential hazard to human health. TACs include substances listed as hazardous air pollutants.

Toxic hazardous waste–a waste that appears on a list that exceeds a specified regulatory level.

Toxic material–a material that has a lethal dose concentration based on one of three categories–a chemical with a median lethal dose of more than 50 milligrams per kilograms (mg/kg) but not more than 500 mg/kg of the body weight of albino rats weighing between 200 and 300 grams each; a chemical with a median lethal dose of more than 200 mg/kg but not more than 1,000 mg/kg of the body weight of albino rabbits weighing two to three kg, that is administered continuously for 24 hours; a chemical with a median lethal concentration in air of more than 200 parts per million but not more than 2,000 parts per million by volume of gas or vapor, or more than two mg/liter but not more than 20 mg/ liter of mist.

Toxic release inventory*–a publicly available EPA database that contains information on toxic chemical releases and other waste management activities reported annually by regulated industry groups as well as federal facilities.

Transfer station–a permitted facility that receives, handles, separates, converts, or otherwise processes solid waste.

Transformation–incineration, pyrolysis, distillation, or biological conversion other than composting. Transformation does not include composting, gasification, or biomass conversion.

Transportation control measures–strategies to reduce vehicle trips, use, and miles traveled.

Transportation improvement plan–a program for transportation projects for a specific period of time, developed by a metropolitan planning organization in conjunction with a state.

Treatment, storage, and disposal facility–a regulated facility that treats, stores, or disposes of hazardous wastes.

Trespass–an unauthorized and wrongful entry or intrusion onto land.

Trustee agency–agency with jurisdiction over natural resources held in trust for the people of the state.

U-listed hazardous waste–a type of non-process waste that is non-industry-specific and is hazardous.

Underflow–the water in soil, sand, and gravel in the streambed of a stream in its natural state, and essential to its existence.

Underground Injection Control program–the program, under the federal Safe Drinking Water Act, that regulates the discharge of wastes into underground injection wells.

Underground storage tank–one or a combination of tanks, including associated piping used to contain industrial solvents, petroleum products, and other hazardous substances. The tank is totally or substantially (10 percent) beneath the surface of the ground.

Underground streams–groundwater that flows in a known and definite channel in a subterranean water course.

Universal waste–a hazardous waste that is not fully regulated as a hazardous waste. Examples include batteries, thermostats, lamps, cathode ray

Glossary

tube material, aerosol cans, mercury-containing motor vehicle and non-automotive light switches, dental amalgam wastes, mercury-containing pressure or vacuum gauges, mercury counterweights and dampers, mercury dilators and weighted tubing, mercury-containing rubber flooring, mercury-added novelties, and mercury gas flow regulators.

Variance*–a limited waiver from the property development standards of a zoning ordinance.

Vegetated shallows–periodically inundated sites with rooted, submerged vegetation.

Vested right–a right to develop that cannot be changed by subsequent changes in regulations.

Volatile organic compound–any organic compound reacting with atmospheric photochemicals except those designated by the Environmental Protection Agency as having a small photochemical reactivity. Examples include gasoline, dry cleaning solvents, and paint solvents.

Vulnerability assessment–an evaluation conducted by community drinking water systems that service more than 3,300 people, that evaluates vulnerability to attack (*e.g.,* terrorist attack, vandalism, insider sabotage) and identifies actions to reduce the threat risk.

Waste discharge requirements*–permit issued by a RWQCB for discharge of waste into waters of the state. A Report of Waste Discharge must be filed with the appropriate RWQCB.

Waste management unit–an area of land, or a portion of a waste management facility, at which waste is discharged. The term includes containment features and ancillary features for precipitation and drainage control and for monitoring.

Waste tire facility permit*–authorizes owners or operators of facilities to store or dispose of tires subject to standards ranging from fire protection and security to vector controls.

Water banking–storage of surface water in groundwater basins in times of surplus, for withdrawal during times of shortage. Can also involve the use of surface water in lieu of groundwater to enable groundwater recharge.

Water quality objective–narrative and numerical objectives for specified water bodies and for particular segments of water bodies. Numeric WQOs serve as the upper limits for permits for specified pollutants, while narrative WQOs are translated into appropriate numerical permit limits where feasible.

Water quality standards–composed of two parts: (1) the designated uses of water and (2) criteria to protect those uses. Water quality standards are enforceable limits in the bodies of water for which they have been established.

Water quality-based effluent limitation–an effluent limitation applied to dischargers when technology-based limitations have the potential to cause violations of water quality standards.

Water right–a legal entitlement authorizing water to be diverted from a specified source and put to beneficial, nonwasteful use. Water rights are property rights, but their holders do not own the water itself–they possess the right to use it.

Water right license*–an SWRCB license issued when a permitted water project is completed, the permit terms have been met, and water is put to beneficial use.

Water right permit*–an SWRCB permit required for a post-1914 appropriative water right.

Water transfer–marketing arrangement that can include the permanent sale or lease of a water right by the water right holder, or the sale or lease of a contractual right to a quantity of water.

Watermaster–a court-appointed person or agency given authority to regulate the quantity of groundwater to be extracted from a designated basin.

Waters of the United States–all waters used or susceptible to use in interstate or foreign commerce, or that could affect interstate or foreign commerce. Waters of the United States include lakes, rivers and coastal waters, as well as all adjacent "other waters" such as wetlands, the use, degradation or destruction of which could affect interstate or foreign commerce.

Watershed–the area from which water drains to a single point.

Wetlands–under the Section 404 program definition, those areas that are inundated or saturated by surface or groundwater at a frequency and duration sufficient to support, and that under normal circumstances do support, a prevalence of vegetation typically adapted for life in saturated soil conditions.

Williamson Act contract*–a voluntary contract entered into between a landowner and a local government in which the landowner receives reduced property tax assessments in return for restricting land to agricultural and open space uses.

Woodlands–forest lands composed mostly of hardwood species such as oak.

Writ of mandamus–a judicial command to an official to perform a ministerial act that the law recognizes as an absolute duty and not discretionary.

Zoning*–a local code dividing a city or county into land use zones and specifying allowable uses in each zone.

List of Acronyms

ACBM = Asbestos-containing building material

ACHP = Advisory Council on Historic Preservation

ACM = Asbestos-containing material

AFC = Application for certification

AFY = Acre-feet per year

AHERA = Asbestos Hazard Emergency Response Act

ALUC = Airport Land Use Commission

ALUP = Airport Land Use Compatibility Plan

APCD = Air Pollution Control District

AQIA = Air quality analysis

AQMD = Air Quality Management District

ARAR = Applicable or relevant and appropriate requirement

ARB = Air Resources Board

ASHARA = Asbestos School Hazard Abatement Reauthorization Act

AST = Above ground storage tank

ASTM = American Society for Testing and Material

ATC = Authority to construct

ATCM = Airborne toxic control measure

BA = Biological assessment

BACT = Best available control technology

BARCT = Best available retrofit control technology

BAT = Best available technology economically achievable

BCDC = Bay Conservation and Development Commission

BCT = Best conventional pollutant control technology

BDACT = Best demonstrated available control technology

BFR = Brominated flame retardants

BIF = Boiler and industrial furnace

BMP = Best management practice

BOD = Biochemical oxygen demand

BPJ = Best professional judgment

BPT = Best practicable control technology

CAA = Clean Air Act

CAAQS = California ambient air quality standards

CAFO = Concentrated animal feeding operation

Cal/EPA = California Environmental Protection Agency

Cal/OSHA = California Occupational Safety and Health Administration

CalARP = California Accidental Release Prevention Program

CAM = Compliance assurance monitoring

CAMU = Corrective action management unit

CAO = Cleanup and abatement order

CAPA = Critical aquifer protection area

CCR = California Code of Regulations

CDF = California Department of Forestry and Fire Protection

CEC = California Energy Commission

CED = Covered electronic device

CEO = Chief executive officer

CEQ = Council on Environmental Quality

CEQA = California Environmental Quality Act

CERCLA = Comprehensive Environmental Response, Compensation, and Liability Act

CERES = California Environmental Resource Evaluation System

CESA = California Endangered Species Act

CESQG = Conditionally exempt small quantity generator

CFC = Chlorofluorocarbons

CFCP = California Farmland Conservancy Program

CFEMS = Compliance-Focused Environmental Management System

CFO = Chief financial officer

CFR = Code of Federal Regulations

CGS = California Geological Survey

CIWMB = California Integrated Waste Management Board

CLEAN = Cleanup Loan and Environmental Assistance to Neighborhoods

CLERRA = California Land Environmental Restoration and Reuse Act

CMI = Corrective measures implementation

CMS = Corrective measures study

CNDDB = California Natural Diversity Database

CNEL = Community noise equivalent level

CO = Carbon monoxide

CO_2 = Carbon dioxide

COC = Condition of certification

COD = Certificate of Disposal

COD = Chemical oxygen demand

COG = Council of Governments

CPA = Consolidated permit agency

CPSC = Consumer Product Safety Commission

CSE = Countywide siting element

CTR = California toxics rule

CTTCA = California Technology, Trade, and Commerce Agency

CUPA = Certified unified program agency

CVP = Central Valley Project

CVPIA = Central Valley Project Improvement Act

CWA = Clean Water Act

CWC = California Water Code

CZMA = Coastal Zone Management Act

DAP = District attainment plan

dB = Decibel

dbA = A-weighted decibel

DFA = Department of Food and Agriculture

DFG = Department of Fish and Game

DHS = Department of Health Services

DLRP = Division of Land Resource Protection

DMR = Discharge monitoring report

DOC = Department of Conservation

DOE = Department of Energy

DOT = Department of Transportation

DPC = Delta Protection Commission

DPH = Department of Public Health

List of Acronyms

DPR = Department of Pesticide Regulation
DTSC = Department of Toxic Substances Control
DWP = Drinking water program
DWR = Department of Water Resources
EA = Environmental assessment
EFH = Essential fish habitat
EHS = Extremely hazardous substance
EHSS = Environmental Health Surveillance System
EIR = Environmental impact report
EIS = Environmental impact statement
ELG = Effluent limitation guideline
EMS = Environmental management system
EPA = Environmental Protection Agency
EPCRA = Emergency Planning and Community Right-to-Know Act
ERC = Emission reduction credit
ESA = Endangered Species Act
FAA = Federal Aviation Administration
FAIR = Financial Assurance and Insurance for Redevelopment
FEMA = Federal Emergency Management Agency
FERC = Federal Energy Regulatory Commission
FFDCA = Federal Food, Drug, and Cosmetic Act
FHWA = Federal Highway Administration
FIFRA = Federal Insecticide, Fungicide, and Rodenticide Act
FIP = Federal implementation plan
FONSI = Finding of no significant impact
FPA = Forest Practice Act
FRA = Federal Railroad Administration
FRP = Facility response plan
FRPP = Farm and Ranch Lands Protection Program
FS = Feasibility study
FTA = Federal Transit Administration
GAAP = Generally accepted accounting principles

GACT = Generally available control technology
GAGAS = Generally accepted government auditing standards
GHG = Greenhouse gas
GMP = Good management practice
HAP = Hazardous air pollutant
HAZCOM = Hazard communication
HCD = Department of Housing and Community Development
HCFC = Hydrochlorofluorocarbon
HCP = Habitat conservation plan
HHWE = Household hazardous waste element
HMBP = Hazardous materials business plan
HMIS = Hazardous Material Identification System
HMTA = Hazardous Materials Transportation Act
HSAA = Hazardous Substances Account Act
HSC = Health and Safety Code
HSITA = Hazardous Substances Information and Training Act
HSWA = Hazardous and Solid Waste Amendments
HUD = U.S. Department of Housing and Urban Development
HWCL = Hazardous Waste Control Law
IDW = Investigation-derived waste
ISO = International Organization for Standardization
ITP = Incidental take permit
IWMA = Integrated Waste Management Act
IWMP = Integrated Waste Management Plan
LADWP = Los Angeles Department of Water and Power
LAER = Lowest achievable emission rate
LAFCO = Local agency formation commission
LCP = Local coastal program
LDR = Land disposal requirement
LEA = Local enforcement agency

LEPC = Local emergency planning centers
LESA = Land evaluation and site assessment
LEV = Low emissions vehicle
LNG = Liquefied natural gas
LOP = Letter of permission
LORS = Laws, ordinances, regulations, and standards
LQG = Long quantity generator
LQH = Large quantity handler
LUST = Leaking underground storage tank
MACT = Maximum achievable control technology
MAFY = Million acre-feet per year
MCL = Maximum contaminant level
MCLG = Maximum contaminant level goal
MEK = Methyl ethyl ketone
MOA = Memorandum of agreement
MOU = Memorandum of understanding
MSDS = Material safety data sheet
MSWLF = Municipal solid waste landfill
MTBE = Methyl tertiary butyl ether
MW = Megawatt
NAAQS = National ambient air quality standards
NCCP = Natural Community Conservation Plan
NCCPA = Natural Community Conservation Planning Act
NCP = National contingency plan
ND = Negative declaration
NDFE = Non-disposal facility element
NEPA = National Environmental Policy Act
NESHAP = National Emission Standards for Hazardous Air Pollutants
NFIP = National Flood Insurance Program
NFPA = National Fire Protection Association
NOAA = National Oceanographic and Atmospheric Administration
NOD = Notice of determination
NOE = Notice of exemption

List of Acronyms

NOI = Notice of intention

NOP = Notice of preparation

NOV = Notice of violation

NO_X = Oxides of nitrogen

NPDES = National Pollutant Discharge Elimination System

NPL = National Priorities List

NRCS = Natural Resources Conservation Service

NSPS = New source performance standards

NSR = New source review

NTCRA = Non-time critical removal action

NTMP = Nonindustrial timber management plan

NWP = Nationwide permit

O&G = Oil and grease

ODC = Ozone-depleting chemical

OEHHA = Office of Environmental Health Hazard Assessment

OES = Office of Emergency Services

ONC = Office of Noise Control

OPA = Office of Permit Assistance

OPR = Office of Planning and Research

OSHA = Occupational Safety and Health Administration

PA/SI = Preliminary assessment/ site investigation

PAIR = Preliminary assessment information rule

PBDE = Polybrominated diphenyl ether

PCB = Polychlorinated biphenyl

PCN = Pre-construction notification

PEL = Permissible exposure limit

PHG = Public health goal

PHI = Pre-harvest inspection

PIC = Products of incomplete combustion

PM = Particulate matter

PMN = Premanufacture notice

POTW = Publicly owned treatment work

PPE = Personal protective equipment

PRC = Public Resources Code

PRP = Potentially responsible party

PSA = Permit Streamlining Act

PSD = Prevention of significant deterioration

PSES = Pretreatment standards for existing sources

PSM = Process safety management

PSNS = Pretreatment standards for new sources

PSP = Permitting strategy plan

PTE = Potential to emit

PTEIR = Program timber environmental impact report

PTHP = Program timber harvest plan

PTO = Permit to operate

PUC = Public Utilities Code

PUC = Public Utilities Commission

PUD = Planned unit development

PWS = Public water system

QPO = Qualifying property owner

RACM = Regulated asbestos-containing materials

RACT = Reasonably available control technology

RAP = Remedial action plan

RCD = Resource Conservation District

RCRA = Resource Conservation and Recovery Act

RD/RA = Remedial design/remedial action

RDSI = Report of disposal site information

RFA = RCRA facility assessment

RFI = RCRA facility investigation

RGL = Regulatory guidance letter

RI = Remedial investigation

RLUIPA = Religious Land Use and Institutionalized Persons Act of 2000

RMP = Risk management plan

ROD = Record of Decision

RPF = Registered professional forester

RPS = Renewable portfolio standard

RQ = Reportable quantity

RWQCB = Regional Water Quality Control Board

SAA = Satellite accumulation area

SARA = Superfund Amendments and Reauthorization Act of 1986

SB = Senate Bill

SCAQMD = South Coast Air Quality Management District

SDWA = Safe Drinking Water Act

SEP = Supplemental environmental project

SERC = State Emergency Response Center

SHPO = State Historic Preservation Officer

SIC = Standard Industrial Classification

SIP = State implementation plan

SLC = State Lands Commission

SMARA = Surface Mining and Reclamation Act

SMGB = State Mining and Geology Board

SNEI = Significant net emissions increase

SOP = Standard operating procedure

SO_X = Oxides of sulfur

SOX = Sarbanes-Oxley Act

SPCC = Spill prevention control and countermeasure

SPPE = Small power plant exemption

SQG = Small quantity generator

SQH = Small quantity handler

SRA = State responsibility area

SRRE = Source reduction and recycling element

SSC = Species of special concern

STLC = Soluble threshold limit concentration

SWANCC = Solid Waste Agency of Northern Cook County

SWAT = Solid waste assessment test

SWD = Solid waste disposal

SWDA = Solid Waste Disposal Act

SWMU = Solid waste management unit

SWP = State Water Project

SWPPP = Storm Water Pollution Prevention Plan

SWRCB = State Water Resources Control Board

List of Acronyms

SYP	= Sustained yield plan		UPA	= Unified program agency	
TAC	= Toxic air contaminant		USACE	= U.S. Army Corps of Engineers	
TCLP	= Toxic characteristic leaching procedure		USC	= United States Code	
TCRA	= Time critical removal action		USEPA	= U.S. Environmental Protection Agency	
THP	= Timber harvest plan		USFWS	= U.S. Fish and Wildlife Service	
TIP	= Transportation improvement plan		UST	= Underground storage tank	
TIWCA	= Toxic Injection Well Control Act of 1985		UWMP	= Urban water management plan	
TMDL	= Total maximum daily load		VA	= Vulnerability assessment	
TOC	= Total organic carbon		VCP	= Voluntary cleanup program	
TPQ	= Threshold planning quantities		VMT	= Vehicle miles travelled	
TPY	= Tons per year		VOC	= Volatile organic compound	
TPZ	= Timberland production zone		WC	= Water Code	
TRI	= Toxic release inventory		WDR	= Waste discharge requirement	
TRPA	= Tahoe Regional Planning Agency		WET	= Waste extraction test	
TSCA	= Toxic Substances Control Act		WLA	= Waste load allocation	
TSDF	= Treatment, storage, and disposal facility		WMU	= Waste management unit	
			WQBEL	= Water quality-based effluent limitation	
TSS	= Total suspended solids		WQO	= Water quality objective	
TTLC	= Total threshold limit concentration		WQS	= Water quality standards	
			WSA	= Water supply assessment	
UIC	= Underground injection control		WTE	= Waste to energy	

Author and Title Index

Index

A

AAQS. *See* ambient air quality standards
AB 32 (Global Warming Solutions
    Act), 40, 68, 120–121
    early action item, 129
AB 70, 78
AB 156, 78
AB 162, 55, 78
AB 939
    See Integrated Waste
    Management Act of 1989
AB 1493, 130
AB 1807, 125, 129
AB 2020. *See* California Beverage Container
    Recycling and Litter Reduction Act
AB 2948. *See* California Hazardous
    Waste Control Act
AB 3030, 315
AB 3319, 115
Aboveground Petroleum
    Storage Act, 264–265
ACBM. *See under* asbestos
acetylene, as compressed gas, 149
ACHP. *See* Advisory Council
    on Historic Preservation
acid rain
    described, 92
    discussed, 99
    federal program (CAA Amendment,
        Title IV), 112, 122–96, 123
        NO_X reduction program, 122–123
        SO_2 allowance trading program, 122
    HSC and, 96
    state program, 123
        Atmospheric Acidity
        Protection Act of 1988, 123
ACM. *See under* asbestos
adhesives, as flammable
    hazardous material, 149
Administrative Procedures Act, 6, 9
adult businesses, zoning ordinances and, 61
Advisory Council on Historic
    Preservation (ACHP), 50, 64

aerial spraying
    as point source requiring
        NPDES permit, 248
aerosol cans, 199
    as universal waste, 188, 198
aesthetics, 287
    NAAQS consideration of, 101
AFC. *See* application for certification
agriculture, 291, 399
    See also silviculture; water
        supply; Williamson Act
    in California, 287
    concentrated animal feeding
        operations (CAFOs), 241
        defined, 238
    general plan and, 53
    HMBP exemption, 158
    incidental take under CESA, 336
    noise exposure guidelines, 144
    as nonpoint source
        of pollution, 238, 255
        regulation of, 258, 260
    Right-to-Farm Ordinances, 293
    RWQCBs and contamination
        from, 191, 218
    as source of GHGs, 120
    SPCC plan requirement, 261
    not subject to Section 404, 348
    UST exemption, 166
    water supply as "beneficial
        use" of water, 246
agricultural burning, 119
agricultural commissioners, 326
agricultural land, 77, 287–293, 298, 399
    agricultural preserves, 291
    California Coastal Act and, 73
    CEQA
        Appendix G, 289
        farmland definitions, 289–290
    conservation/open space
        easements, 292–293, 399
    conversion, 287–289
    in Delta, DPC jurisdiction over, 86
    farmland protection programs, 293

agricultural land *continued*
    farmland of statewide importance, 289
        defined, 290
    introduction, 287
    key laws and agencies, 287–289
        Department of Conservation, 19, 288
        Department of Food
        and Agriculture, 288
        Natural Resources
        Conservation Service, 288
        Williamson Act, 287
    loss of, 287
    prime farmland, 288–289
        defined, 289–290
    rangeland, 367
        defined, 364
    resource conservation districts, 288–289
    Right-to-Farm Ordinances, 293
    San Joaquin Valley, CVPIA
        land retirement program, 298
    State Coastal Conservancy and, 74
    unique farmland, 289
        defined, 290
agricultural return flows
    regulation of, 248, 260
agricultural waste, 198
    discharged into water as
        pollutant under CWA, 238, 248
Agua Tibia Wilderness, as Class I area, 109
AHERA. *See* Asbestos Hazard
    Emergency Response Act
air basin, attainment/non-attainment
    designation, 96
airborne toxic control
    measures (ATCM), 125
aircraft
    noise regulation, 138
        discussed, 140–141
    as noise sources, 137
Aircraft Noise Abatement Act, 138
air districts. *See also* air pollution
    control districts; air quality
    management districts
    AAQS and, 101

attainment/non-attainment *continued*
    CAA
        non-attainment area
            classifications, 102, 114
        non-attainment area deadlines, 101
    California CAA
        attainment/non-attainment
            air districts, 102
        non-attainment area
            classifications, 102, 114
    demonstration, 102
    district attainment plans, 102
        defined, 92
        local air districts and, 97
    non-attainment, 102
attainment area, 104, 398
    See also district attainment plan
    Class I areas, 107
    Class I areas in California, 109
    Class II areas, 107
    Class III area, 107
    increments, 107
    non-attainment area, 101, 104, 398
        classifications, under
            CAA, 102, 114
        classifications, under
            California CAA, 102
        DAP requirements, 115
        defined, 93
    PSD program and, 105–108
attorney-client privilege, 411, 415–416
    in-house counsel and, 416
attorney's fees, Proposition 65
    enforcement and, 180
attorney work-product doctrine, 416
auditoriums, noise exposure guidelines, 144
authority to construct (ATC) permits, 397
    CEQA and, 117
    defined, 92
    discussed, 116–117
    exemptions, 117
    new source review
        local new source review and, 118–119
        rules, 92
auto air conditioning recharge kits, 121
auto body shops, 118
automobiles
    asbestos regulation brake
        and clutch repair, 170
    as mobile sources of
        air pollution, 95, 128
A-weighted decibel. *See under* decibel

B

BAAQMD. *See* Bay Area Air
    Quality Management District
BACT. *See* best available control technology
Bakersfield, 298
Bald Eagle and Golden Eagle
    Protection Act, 324
Baldwin Hills Conservancy, 20
baseline, 39, 157
    See also environmental
        setting; significant effects
    baseline studies, 393
    baseline year
        for district attainment plans, 114
        ozone protection, 120
    defined, 26

batteries
    as universal waste, 188, 198
    manufacturing of effluent
        limitation guidelines, 251
battery acid as corrosive
    hazardous material, 149
Bay Area Air Quality Management
    District (BAAQMD), 97–98
    website, 133
Bay-Delta Plan, 245
BCDC. *See* San Francisco
    Bay Conservation and
    Development Commission
BDACT. *See* best demonstrated
    available control technology
bentazone, state MCLs, 278
benzene
    ATCM for, 125
    as toxic hazardous material, 149
    as VOC, 99
Berkeley, zero waste goal, 229
best available control
    technology (BACT), 115
    defined, 92
    as equivalent to LAER, 118
    local new source review and, 118
    PSD program and, 106–107
    types of, 107
best available retrofit control technology
    (BARCT), non-attainment
    NSR requirements and, 116
best demonstrated available
    control technology (BDACT)
    defined, 92
    stationary industrial sources and, 104
best management practices, 406, 413
    defined, 403
beverage containers
    recycling of, 19, 225, 232
bicycle path, dedication for
    as regulatory taking, 66
big-box development, CEQA review
    of ordinance held unnecessary, 38
Big Sur River as federal
    "wild and scenic river," 316
billboards, zoning ordinances and, 61
biofuels as low carbon fuels, 129
biogas as low carbon fuel, 129
biological diversity, defined, 320
biological materials as
    pollutants under CWA, 238, 247
birds, 325, 366
    California gnatcatcher, 325, 338
    California gulls, 305
    eagles
        bald, 324, 327
        golden, 324
    greater sandhill cranes, 334
    migratory birds, 346–347
        defined, 320
    raptors, 326
bleach. *See* sodium hypochlorite
blight
    defined, 50, 57
    eminent domain and, 57
    redevelopment plans and, 57–58
    urban blight/decay,
        EIR consideration of, 38
boats, recreational, as nonpoint
    sources of pollution, 258

boiler systems
    acid rain role in
        creation of, 92, 99
    regulation of, 123
bonds for public improvements,
    CUPs and, 59
Boulder Canyon Act, 301
Boulder (Hoover) Dam, 301
brominated flame retardants
    (polybrominated diphenyl
    ethers/PBDEs)
    defined, 148
    enforcement, 181
    prohibition of, 153, 176
Brown, Jerry, 40
brownfields, 216
    See also National Priorities List
    compliance audits, 410
    defined, 186, 214
    discussed, 214
    liability, 214
    state programs, 218–219
Brownfields Revitalization
    and Environmental
    Restoration Act of 2001, 214
buildings
    lead paint and,
        regulation of, 171–172
    ACM notification, 171
    unreinforced masonry buildings
        and seismic hazards, 79
Burbank, zero waste goal, 229
Bureau of Automotive Repair, 103
Burns-Porter Act, 301
buses as mobile sources
    of air pollution, 128
Business, Transportation and
    Housing Agency,
    Climate Action Team, 97
Butte Air District, 98

C

CAA. *See* Clean Air Act
CAAQS. *See* California ambient
    air quality standards
cadmium
    in cell phones, 232
    as hazardous waste, 196
    in packaging, regulation
        of, 153, 176
CalARP. *See* California Accidental
    Release Prevention Program
Calaveras Air District, 98
Calderon Act, 230
Cal/EPA. *See* California Environmental
    Protection Agency
Cal/EPA Organization, 16
CALFED, 299, 303
    Bay-Delta Program, 19
        EIR upheld, 315
    defined, 4, 297
    Environmental Water Account, 311
    Record of Decision, 302
    water transfers and, 311
California Accidental Release
    Prevention Program
    (CalARP), 126, 155
California Air Toxic "Hot Spots"
    Information and
    Assessment Act, 125–126

explosives
    manufacturing of, effluent
        limitation guidelines, 251
    use of in residential areas, as
        ultrahazardous activity, 13
extremely hazardous substances (EHSs)
    See under hazardous substances
Exxon Valdez, 263

F

FAA. *See* Federal Aviation
    Administration
facilities with effluent limitations,
    NPDES industrial storm
    water permit requirement, 256
facility manager, 413–414
"fair argument" standard
    CEQA challenges and, 45
    compared to "substantial
        evidence" standard, 45
    EIRs and, 33, 45
farmland. *See* agricultural land
farms, farming. *See* agriculture
Farm Security and Rural
    Investment Act of 2002, 288
fault trace. *See also* seismologic
    hazard, defined, 72
feasible. *See also* alternatives;
    mitigation measures
    defined, 26
    feasibility of alternatives, 40–41
    feasibility of mitigation
        measures, 40–41
feasibility study, 211–212, 215
    See also remedial
        investigation/feasibility study
    applicable or relevant appropriate
        requirements (ARARs), 186, 212
    of hazardous waste
        cleanup, defined, 186
Feather River, as federal "wild
    and scenic river," 316
Feather River Air District, 98
Feather River Project Act, 301
fecal coliform
    as conventional pollutant, 238, 249
    in drinking water
        EPA regulation of, 272, 274
        monitoring, 275
Federal Aviation Administration
    (FAA), aircraft noise
    regulation, 138, 140
Federal Emergency Management
    Agency (FEMA)
    flood control and, 77
        floodplain maps, 55
    hazard mitigation program, 77
    National Flood Insurance
        Program discussed, 77
    website, 87
    Region IX website, 87
Federal Energy Regulatory
    Commission (FERC), 80, 150
    hydroelectric licensing, 298, 358
    license, defined, 296
    website, 87
Federal Food, Drug, and Cosmetic Act
    (FFDCA), pesticide regulation,
    150–151, 177

Federal Highway Administration
    (FHWA), 394
    delegation of NEPA
        implementation to Caltrans, 44
    Design Noise Levels of the
        Federal Highway Administration, 140
    "Noise Central," website, 146
    noise standards
        interstate motor carriers, 141–142
        transportation projects, 139–140
federal implementation plan (FIP)
    defined, 92
    discussed, 103
Federal Insecticide, Fungicide,
    and Rodenticide Act
    (FIFRA), 150–151, 176
    enforcement, 179
federal law, 5–6
    citizen suit provisions, 10, 131
    executive orders, 6
    federal constitution, 5–6
    federal regulations, 6
    federal statutes, 6
    judicial decisions, 6
    precedence over state law, 5
Federal Power Act, 298
Federal Railroad Administration, 141
Federal Register
    EIS filing, 44
    incidental take permit filing, 333
    Record of Decision for
        cleanup remedies, 212
    SIP publication, 103
Federal Transit Administration, 395
fees, 62, 393, 397
    See also exactions
    DFG environmental review, 35, 37
    electronic waste recycling fee, 233
    impact fees (development
        fees), 50, 66–67, 397
        defined, 50
        school fees, limits on, 42, 67
    in lieu fees, for wetlands
        mitigation, 355
    oil tank facility fees, 265
    PTO permits and, 117
    SLC fees for use of state lands, 80
    timberland production zones
        tax recoupment fee, 366
    UST cleanup fund, 168
    Williamson Act contract
        cancellation, 291
FEMA. *See* Federal Emergency
    Management Agency
FERC. *See* Federal Energy
    Regulatory Commission
FFDCA. *See* Federal Food,
    Drug, and Cosmetic Act
FIFRA. *See* Federal Insecticide,
    Fungicide, and Rodenticide Act
filter backwash, as pollutant
    under CWA, 238, 247
findings
    in CEC certification process, 83
    in CEQA process, 30
        mandatory findings
            of significance, 33–34
        project approval, 37
    in compliance audits, 413
    defined, 26

findings *continued*
    disapproval of affordable
        housing projects, 60
    eminent domain, 57
    flood management in
        Central Valley and, 55
    negative declaration, 34
    in NEPA process
        finding of no significant
            impact (FONSI), 44, 397
        record of decision, 44
    no-net-increase permitting
        requirements elimination of, 115
    open space easement
        abandonment, 293
    Section 2081 Incidental
        Take Permit process, 336
    substantial evidence and, 37
    variances, from air
        quality regulation, 132
    Williamson Act contract
        cancellation, 291
fine particulate matter
    See under particulate matter
FIP. *See* federal implementation plan
fire departments
    as CUPAs
        regulation of hazardous
            waste generators, 154, 191
fires and fire protection
    See also forestry
    Forest Practice Act
        exemptions, 368
    general plan and, 53
        safety element and, 76
    state responsibility areas, 79, 367
Fish and Game Commission
    CESA responsibilities, 326
        endangered/threatened/rare
            species listing, 320, 326, 334
fishing and fisheries, 261
    as "beneficial use" of water, 246
        instream use, defined, 296
    DFG regulation of, 19
    general plan and, 53
    public trust protection of, 14, 303
fish and wildlife, 19, 263, 298, 400
    anadromous fish, 325
        defined, 296, 320
    CWA protection of, 241
    enhancement, 298
    essential fish habitat, 324
    federal laws and agencies
        Endangered Species Act,
            323–324, 327–334
        NOAA Fisheries, 325
        other federal laws, 324
        U.S. Fish and Wildlife
            Service, 324–325
    general plan and, 53
    habitat
        recreation areas, noise
            level standards and, 140
        reduction of, as mandatory
            finding of significance, 34
    marine mammals, 324
    mitigation, 298
    old-growth dependent species, 370
    public trust protection of, 15
    as public trust resource, 302

fish and wildlife *continued*
    refuges, 298, 325
        as "special aquatic sites," 346
    salmon, 297, 320, 325
    sanctuaries, 298, 325
        marine sanctuaries, 351
        as "special aquatic sites," 346
    "species," defined, 327
        "distinct population segment," 327
    "species of special concern," 334
    state laws and agencies
        CESA, 325, 334–337
        DFG, 326
        Fish and Game Commission, 326
        fully protected species, 325–326
        NCCPA, 325
        other laws, 326
    steelhead, 325
Fish and Wildlife
    Coordination Act, 324
flammable liquids
    defined, 148, 160–161
    storage standards, 161–162
flashpoint, 160–161
    defined, 148
    ignitable hazardous waste, 186, 197
flood control, 19, 77–78, 302, 352
    2007 legislation, 78
    Central Valley flood
        management, 77–78
    Colbey-Alquist Floodplain
        Management Act, 77–78
    general plan and, 53
        discussed, 55–56
        safety element and, 76
    key laws and agencies, 77
    National Flood
        Insurance Program, 77
    surface mine reclamation, 380
flood hazard zones, 55
flood insurance, National Flood
    Insurance Program, 77
floodplain management ordinances, 77
floodplains, 77
    overlay zones and, 58
floodway, dedication for
    as regulatory taking, 66
flouride, EPA MCL for, 274
FORA. *See* Fort Ord Reuse Authority
Ford Motor Company, 409
    ISO 14001 press release, website, 409
Forest Practice Act
    See Z'berg–Njedly
        Forest Practice Act of 1973
Forest and Rangeland Renewable
    Resources Planning Act
    of 1974, 365
forestry, 400
    See also fires and fire protection
    enforcement, 372
    federal laws and agencies, 365
    nonindustrial tree
        farmer, defined, 364
    as nonpoint source of pollution, 238
        regulation of, 258
    Program Timber Environmental
        Impact Report, 371
        defined, 364
    Program Timber Harvest
        Plan, 364, 371, 400

forestry *continued*
    silviculture
        not point source of
            pollution under CWA, 255
        not subject to Section 404, 348
        silvicultural systems, 364, 366
    state laws and agencies, 365–367
        California Department of
            Forestry and Fire Protection, 367
        California Forest Legacy
            Program Act, 366
        counties, 367
        State Board of Forestry and
            Fire Protection, 366–367
        Timberland Productivity Act, 366
        Z'berg–Njedly Forest Practice
            Act of 1973, 365–367
    sustained yield
        defined, 364, 371
        long-term sustained yield, 364, 371
        sustained yield plan, 364, 371
    timber harvest regulation, 367–372
        activities regulated, 367–368
        CEQA and THPs, 370
        exemptions, 367–368
        other programs, 371–372
        pre-harvest inspection, 369
        timber harvest plan review
            process, 368–369
        timber harvest plans,
            364, 367–370, 400
        resource conservation
            standards, 368
        water quality regulation, 369–370
    timberland, 365
        defined, 364, 367
    timberland conversion
        permit, 371–372
        defined, 364
    timberland production zone, 366
    timber operation
        defined, 364, 367
        THP held inadequate, 370
    timber operator licenses, 368
    timber processing, effluent
        limitation guidelines, 251
forests/timber general plan and, 53
    hardwoods, 364
    late succession forest stands, 366
    old growth, 370
    woodlands, 366
        defined, 364
formaldehyde, EPA regulation
    of tailpipe emissions, 129
Fort Ord, 43
Fort Ord Reuse Authority (FORA), 43
fossil fuel burning sources
    boilers, PTE threshold, 107
    electric steam-fired facilities,
        PTE threshold, 107
    as industrial facilities under CAA, 104
fossil fuels, global warming and, 101
FPA. *See* Z'berg–Njedly Forest
    Practice Act of 1973
freons. *See also* chlorofluorocarbons;
    halogenated compounds
    HFC-134a, 121
    as ozone-depleting
        chemicals, 93, 101, 120
Fresno, zero waste goal, 229

fuel. *See also* diesel; fossil fuels; gasoline
    ARB regulation of, 128–129
    biofuels, as low carbon fuels, 129
    EPA regulation of
        emissions from, 96, 103
    fossil fuels and global warming, 101
        low carbon transportation
            fuel standard, 121, 129
    jet fuels
        as "petroleum" under
            RCRA Subtitle 1, 164
        as "petroleum" under state, 165
    low carbon fuels, 129
    as mobile source of air pollution, 96
    motor fuels
        as "petroleum" under
            RCRA Subtitle 1, 164
        as "petroleum" under state law, 165
    rocket fuel propellants, 278
    waste fuels, as "oil," 261
fuel cell vehicles, 130
fuel conversion plants, PTE threshold, 107

G

GACT. *See* generally achievable
    control technology
garbage/refuse
    as pollutant under CWA, 238, 247
    as solid waste, 187
gasoline. *See also* oil
    "cleanest gas" technology, 130
    as criteria pollutant, 99
    as flammable hazardous material, 149
    as "oil," 261
    reformulated gasoline, 93, 128
    as VOC, 93, 128
gas pipeline. *See under* oil and
    gas energy development
gas stations. *See also* service station
    vapor recovery
    benzene ATCM, 125
    GACT standards, 124
general law cities, application
    of Planning and
    Zoning Law to, 58
generally achievable control
    technology (GACT), 123–124
general plan, 52–56
    See also community/
    area plan; specific plan
    additional elements, 53
    adoption/amendment process, 54–55
        CEQA and, 54
        comments, 54
        consultation with
            Native Americans, 55
    amendments/updates, 56
    challenges, 56
    circulation element, 52–53
    conservation element, 52–53
        fish and wildlife protection, 326
        groundwater recharge, 55
        storm water management, 55
    consistency of land use decisions, 54
    county-wide siting element, 230
    deference to city/
        county decisions, 54
    deficiency, 53
    defined, 50
    diagrams and text, 50, 52, 54, 397

hydroelectric projects
　　FERC licenses, 296, 358
　　wild and scenic rivers and, 316
hydrofluoric acid, 163
　　plants, PTE threshold, 107
hydrogen, as low carbon fuel, 129
hydrogen sulfide, state AAQS, 100
hydromodification, as nonpoint
　　　　source of pollution,
　　　　regulation of, 258
hydropower
　　generation, as "beneficial
　　　　use" of water, 246
　　projects, FERC licensing of, 80, 358
HWCL. *See* Hazardous Waste Control Law

I

impact fees. *See under* fees
Imperial Air District, 98
Imperial Irrigation District, 302
　　All-American Canal, 298
　　Colorado River projects, 300
　　Imperial Dam, 298
　　Yuma Project, 298
Imperial Valley, 301
incineration units, as WMUs, 206
incinerators
　　municipal incinerators
　　　　PTE threshold, 107
　　residue, as pollutant
　　　　under CWA, 238, 247
incorporations, LAFCOs and, 68
industrial development, EIR
　　　　held inadequate, 315
industrial facilities
　　CAA regulation of, 104
　　California general storm water
　　　　permit application process, 256–257
　　federal storm water permits, 255–257
　　　　EPA categories, 256
　　　　"no exposure" exclusion, 256
　　GHG emissions, reporting of, 121
　　light industrial facilities, NPDES
　　　　industrial storm water
　　　　permit requirement, 256
　　noise exposure guidelines, 144
　　as stationary sources
　　　　of air pollution, 95
industrial solvents, as hazardous
　　　　substances, 148
industrial uses, general plan and, 53
industrial waste, discharged
　　　　into water, as pollutant
　　　　under CWA, 238, 248
industrial water supply, as
　　　　"beneficial use" of water, 246
information, new
　　draft EIR and, 36
　　supplemental/
　　　　subsequent EIR and, 38
initial study, 30, 44
　　See also significant effect
　　by CEC for SPPE, 82
　　checklist, 33, 289
　　defined, 26
　　discussed, 33
initiative
　　defined, 50
　　discussed, 9
　　zoning ordinances and, 58

inorganic chemicals, 398
　　manufacturing of, effluent
　　　　limitation guidelines, 251
inorganics, in drinking water
　　EPA regulation of, 272–273
　　monitoring, 275
insects, pest, cannot be
　　　　endangered/threatened, 327
inspections, regulatory
　　　　compliance and, 23
institutional land use, noise levels, 141
Integrated Solid Waste
　　　　Management Act of 1989, 224
Integrated Waste Management
　　　　Act (IWMA) of 1989,
　　　　224, 227–228
Integrated Waste
　　　　Management Board, 16
integrated waste management
　　plans (IWMPs), 229–230
　　county-wide siting element, 229
　　general plan and, 230
　　household hazardous
　　　　waste element, 229, 233
　　non-disposal facility element, 229
International Organization for
　　　　Standardization (ISO)
　　described, 403
　　environmental management
　　　　systems, 406–407
　　　　audit, 409
　　　　compliance-focused
　　　　　　environmental management
　　　　　　system, 403, 407–409
　　　　defined, 403, 407
　　　　standard operating
　　　　　　procedure, 404, 408, 413
　　ISO 14001 standards,
　　　　406–407, 409
interstate rail carriers, EPA
　　　　noise standards for, 137
Inyo County, 290, 302
iron, EPA MCL for, 274
iron and steel mill plants,
　　　　PTE threshold, 107
irrigation, runoff
　　　　not point source pollution
　　　　under CWA, 255
　　use of water for, 298
ISO. *See* International Organization
　　for Standardization
isocyanates, as toxic
　　　　hazardous materials, 149
IWMA. *See* Integrated Waste
　　Management Act
IWMPs. *See* integrated waste
　　management plans

J

jobs, consideration of versus
　　　　environmental impacts, 37
John Muir Wilderness,
　　　　as Class I area, 109
Joint Powers Act, 84
Joshua Tree National Monument
　　as Class I area, 109
judicial review
　　CEC certification, 83
　　CEQA challenges, 45
　　　　barriers to judicial review, 46

judicial review *continued*
　　citizen suits
　　　　AHERA, 178
　　　　California CAA, 132
　　　　Proposition 65 and, 174–175
　　damages, 11–12
　　deference of courts to cities/
　　　　counties in land use decisions, 54
　　delayed discovery rule, 13
　　EIR adequacy, 43
　　federal courts, 6
　　injunctive relief, 11–12
　　　　air quality regulations and, 131–132
　　standards of review
　　　　arbitrary and capricious, 56
　　　　general plan challenges, 56
　　　　rule of reason, 43
　　　　substantial evidence, defined, 26
　　　　substantial harm, 11
　　　　unreasonable use of property, 11
　　state courts, 9–10
　　SWRCB permitting/licensing, 312

K

Kaiser Wilderness
　　as Class I area, 109
Kelo decision, 58
Kennedy, Anthony, 346–347
Kern Air District, 98
Kern River
　　North Fork, as federal
　　　　"wild and scenic river," 316
　　South Fork, as federal
　　　　"wild and scenic river," 316
Kesterson Reservoir, 302
Kings Canyon National Park,
　　　　as Class I area, 109
Kings River, as federal
　　　　"wild and scenic river," 316
　　Middle Fork, as federal
　　　　"wild and scenic river," 316
　　South Fork, as federal
　　　　"wild and scenic river," 316
Klamath River
　　as state "wild and scenic river," 317
　　System, as federal
　　　　"wild and scenic river," 316
Kraft pulp mill, PTE threshold, 107

L

L10, 140
　　defined, 136
Lacey Act, 324
LAER. *See* lowest achievable
　　emissions rate
LAFCOs. *See* local agency
　　formation commissions
Lahontan Regional Water
　　　　Quality Control Board, 243
　　timber harvest plan
　　　　WDR waiver, 370
Lake Air District, 98
lakes, 270, 366
　　as "Waters of the United
　　　　States," 239, 342, 345
Lake Tahoe, 101
　　Basin, 86
　　　　construction discharge
　　　　　　permitting, 258

Occupational Safety and Health
Administration (OSHA)
hazardous material
regulation, 149–151
Hazard Communication
program, 151
Hazard Communication
program website, 184
Ignitable, Flammable, and
Combustible Chemical
Regulatory Classifications, 161
Laws, Regulations, and
Interpretations website, 184
material safety data sheet, 149–150
noise regulation, 138, 142
OSHA Process Safety
Management standard, 125
website, 184
odor, as nuisance, 11
OEHHA. *See* Office of Environmental
Health Hazard Assessment
OES. *See* Governor's Office
of Emergency Services
off-highway motor vehicles, 19
Office of Administrative Law, 9, 24
website, 24
office buildings, noise
exposure guidelines, 144
Office of Environmental Health
Hazard Assessment (OEHHA), 16
drinking water and, 272–273, 278
risk assessments, 278
EPIC program, 16–17
Proposition 65
administration, 154, 175, 398
website, 184, 268
Safe Drinking Water and
Toxic Enforcement Act
of 1986 website, 268
toxic air contaminants and, 125
Water, website, 281
website, 184
Office of Historic Preservation
USACE Section 404
permit review, 349
pre-construction notification, 354
website, 70
Office of Surveyor General, 301
oil
crude oil, 261
as "petroleum" under
RCRA Subtitle 1, 164
as "petroleum" under state law, 165
definition for SPCC purposes, 238, 261
distillate fuel oil
as "petroleum" under
RCRA Subtitle 1, 164
as "petroleum" under state law, 165
fuel oil, 261
lubricating oil
HMBP exemption, 158
oil and gas exploration/production
waste state regulation of
underground injection, 254, 259
recycled oil, purchase of,
by state agencies, 233
sludge, 261
used oil
as "petroleum" under
RCRA Subtitle 1, 164

oil
used oil *continued*
as "petroleum" under state law, 165
regulated as hazardous waste, 192, 196
waste oils, as "oil," 261
oil and gas energy facilities
bulk petroleum facilities,
multiple permits and, 118
gas pipelines, permitting, 80
interstate natural gas
facilities, FERC approval of, 80
leases on sovereign lands, 80
liquefied natural gas (LNG),
siting of LNG facilities, 80
as nonpoint sources of pollution, 258
NPDES industrial storm
water permit requirement, 256
exemption, 256
offshore leases, special
consideration of under
California Coastal Act, 76
oil tanks, regulation of, 261–265
compliance audits, 409, 412
owner/operator
responsibilities, 264–265
petroleum storage and
transfer units PTE threshold, 107
SMARA exemption, 380
SPCC plan requirement, 261–263
oil management plans
Aboveground Petroleum
Storage Act, 264–265
facility response plan, 399
defined, 238
federal requirements, 261–264
Lempert-Keene Act, 242, 265
oil contingency plans, 244
Oil Pollution Act of 1990, 263–264
applicability, 264
facility report plan, 263–264
overview, 263
substantial harm
facilities, defined, 264
release reporting, 263, 265, 413
reportable quantities, 265
"reasonably expected"
determination, 261–264
spill prevention control and
countermeasure (SPCC)
plan, 155, 242, 261–263, 399
amendment/review, 263
compliance audits, 409, 413
defined, 239
engineer review, 262
non-transportation-related
onshore facilities, 261–262
overview, 261–262
plan requirements, 262–263
state requirements, 264–265
Oil Pollution Act of 1990, 263–264
applicability, 264
National Oil Spill Liability Fund, 263
overview, 263
substantial harm facilities, defined, 264
oil refineries
as industrial facilities under CAA, 104
multiple permits and, 118
petroleum refineries
Program 3 RMPs and, 125
PTE threshold, 107

oil spills, 242, 244
oil tankers, 265
open burning, 119
open space, 20, 291, 399
noise levels, 141
specific plan and, 50
zoning, 58
Open Space Easement Act, 293
open space easements
See under easements
open space element. *See* general plan
Operating Permits programs, 22
OPR. *See* Governor's Office of
Planning and Research
orchards, 290
organic chemicals
as air toxics, 99, 398
manufacturing of effluent
limitation guidelines, 251
organic peroxides, 161
as reactive chemicals, 149
organics
in drinking water, EPA regulation
of, 272–273
monitoring, 275
Organization for Economic Cooperation
and Development, 233
Oroville Dam and Reservoir, 299
OSHA. *See* Occupational Safety and
Health Administration
Outer Continental Shelf Lands Act, 76
overlay zone. *See* zoning
Owens Valley, 300, 302
Owens Valley Project, 300
oxidizers, 161, 186
as ignitable hazardous waste, 197
oxygen, 97
as compressed gas, 149, 163
HMBP exemption, 158
ozone, 93, 127
CAAQS and, 114
DAPs and, 114
Definition of a "Major Source" of
Ozone in Non-attainment
Air Districts, 117
as drinking water disinfectant, 274
federal AAQS, 100–101
ground-level ozone, 99
major source definition
CAA, 117
California CAA, 117
non-attainment and, 102
as non-attainment pollutant, 114
precursors, NSR permits and, 108
significant net emission rate, 108
SIPs and, 93
SNEI thresholds, 111
state AAQS, 100–101
stratospheric ozone protection,
119–120
ozone-depleting chemicals
Class I substances,
regulation of, 120
Class II substances,
regulation of, 120
defined, 93
discussed, 101, 119–120
EPA and, 96
health hazards of, 101
HSC and, 96

P

packaging
  regulation of, 153, 176
    certificate of compliance, 176
    U.S. Dept. of Transportation
      classifications, 161
paints
  as flammable hazardous material, 149
  as household hazardous waste, 226
  lead based paints
    disclosure of, 150, 171–172
    regulation of, 152, 171–172
  recycled paints, purchase
    of, by state agencies, 233
  as solid waste, 192–193
paint solvents, as VOCs, 93
paint stripping operations,
  GACT standards, 124
Palo Alto, zero waste goal, 229
  website, 236
paper
  manufacturing of effluent
    limitation guidelines, 251
  recycled paper
    purchase of, by state agencies, 233
    use of in newspapers, 234
parks, 19
  noise exposure guidelines, 144
Parks and Recreation Commission
  responsibilities, 19
particle pollution. *See* particulate matter
particulate matter (PM), 126, 398
  ARB fuel regulation and, 128
  as criteria pollutant, 99
  defined, 93
  diesel PM, 99, 129
    as air toxic, 99
  discussed, 99
  EPA regulation of
    tailpipe emissions, 129
  fine particulate matter, federal
    and state AAQS, 100–101
  inhalable particulate matter
    SIPs and, 93
    federal and state AAQS, 100–101
  non-attainment and, 102
  prohibitory rules, 118, 398
  PSD increments, PM_{10}, 107–108
  significant net emission rate, 108
    PM_{10}, 107
  SIP conformity and, 127
  SNEI thresholds, PM_{10}, 111
  suspended particulate
    matter state AAQS, 101
PA/SI. *See* preliminary assessment/
  site investigation
PBDEs. *See* brominated flame retardants
PCBs. *See* polychlorinated biphenyls
PELs. *See* permissible exposure levels
perchlorates, state MCLs, 278
percolation ponds, as nonpoint
  sources of pollution, 258
perfluorocarbons, defined
  as GHG under AB 32, 120
Peripheral Canal, 302
permanent nuisance. *See* nuisance
permissible exposure levels (PELs)
  asbestos, 154
  mold, 154

permit to operate, 104, 119, 390, 398
  CEQA and, 116
  defined, 93
  as discretionary permits, 390
  discussed, 116–118
  local new source review and, 118
  program, 111–112
Permit Reform Act
  See Environmental Protection
    Permit Reform Act of 1993
permit by rule, 398
  defined, 93, 388, 390
  in hazardous waste
    regulation, 187, 398
  hazardous waste treatment, 186, 207
permits and permitting
  See also Permit Streamlining Act
  air quality permits, 397–398, 413
    authority to construct permits,
      92, 116–117, 119, 390, 397
    as discretionary permits, 390
    local permitting for criteria
      pollutants, 115–118
    non-attainment NSR
      permits, 104, 108, 398
    permit to operate, 93, 104,
      111–112, 116–119, 390, 398
    permit by rule,
      93, 186–187, 207, 388, 390, 398
    post-construction permitting
      program U.S. EPA and, 96
    PSD permits, 93, 96, 104–108, 398
    stationary industrial sources and, 104
    stationary source permit, 93
    Title V operating
      permit, 93, 111–113, 398
  building permits, 390
    as ministerial permits, 390
  coastal development permits, 72, 74, 397
    activities requiring permits, 75
    CEQA and, 75
    emergency permits, 75
    exemptions, 75
    discussed, 75–76
    wetlands regulations, 359–360
  conditional use permit (CUP)/
    special use permit, 397
    defined, 50
    discussed, 59
    for surface mining, 378
  construction general permit, 238
  defined, 388–389
  discretionary permit, 390
    defined, 388
  Environmental Protection
    Permit Reform Act of 1993, 391–392
    consolidated permits, 391
  fish and wildlife
    DFG scientific
      collecting permit, 335, 337
    DFG Section 2081
      permit, 320, 335–336, 400
    Incidental Take Permit,
      320, 324, 328, 332, 400
  hazardous waste treatment
    standardized permit, 187, 207, 398
    tiered permit, defined, 188, 207
    TSDF permits, 187, 207, 215, 398
    waste discharge
      requirements permits, 188

permits and permitting *continued*
  introduction, 389
  ministerial permit, 390
    defined, 388
    not subject to CEQA, 390
  no-net-increase
    permitting program, 114, 116
  permitting laws, 390–392
  regulatory compliance and, 23
  San Francisco Bay
    development permits, 85
  solid waste facilities, 399
    construction and demolition
      debris facility permit, 222, 399
    municipal solid waste
      transfer station permits, 399
    transfer stations, 231, 399
    waste tire facility
      permit, 222, 231, 399
    WDR permits, 258–259
    WDR permits, Class III,
      198, 206, 399
    WTEs, 231
  strategies, 392–396
    CEQA/NEPA documents as
      umbrella processes, 393–395
    complete applications/
      pre-application
      consultation, 395
    Integrating Selected Environmental
      Review Requirements with
      CEQA and NEPA, 394
    MOUs/MOAs, 394–395
    permit inventory/site evaluation, 392
    proactive management, 395–396
    relations with permitting staff, 396
    strategy plan, 392–393
  Suisun Marsh development permits, 85
  Summary of Environmental Per-
    mits/Other Approvals, 397–400
  types, 390
    discretionary versus ministerial, 390
    site specific versus
      permit by rule, 390
  UST operating permits, 165
  water quality permits, 244
    in California, 254
    as discretionary permits, 390
    domestic water supply
      permits, 270, 272, 278–279, 399
    dredged/fill material discharge
      permits, 242, 342–343,
      347–348, 351, 400
    NPDES general industrial
      permit, 238, 241
    NPDES municipal storm water
      permit, 238, 241, 255, 257, 399
    NPDES surface water
      permit, 193, 241, 399
    storm water construction
      permit, 256, 390, 399
    storm water industrial
      permit, 390, 399
  water right permits,
    296, 306–308, 399
  wetlands permits, 400
    general permit, 342, 400
    individual permit, 342, 394, 400
    letter of permission,
      342, 348, 352–353

reactive chemicals, 149, 163
   organic gases, ARB
      fuel regulation and, 128
reasonable relationship, 66–67
   See also nexus; rough proportionality
reasonably available control
      technology (RACT)
   defined, 93
   local air district rules and, 118
   NSR program and, 108, 116
Reclamation Act, 301
reclamation districts, 301
Reclamation Reform Act, 302
reconstruction, defined, 93
Record of Decision
   CALFED, 302
   CERCLA/Superfund, 187, 212, 215
   in NEPA process, 44, 394
recordkeeping, 119
   regulatory compliance and, 23
recreation, 291, 307
   California Coastal Act and, 74
   CEC consideration of, 83
   CWA protection of, 241
   general plan and, 53
   public trust protection of, 14, 303
   State Coastal Conservancy and, 74
   water contact/non-water
      contact recreation as
      "beneficial use" of water, 246
recreational vehicles, as mobile
      sources of air pollution, 128
recreation areas, noise
      level standards and, 140
recycling, 227–228
   beverage containers, 19, 225, 232
   cell phones, 225, 232
   covered electronic devices, 233
   lights, 233
   recycled product markets, 233–234
Redding, 298
redevelopment, defined, 50
redevelopment agency, 57
   brownfields development and, 219
   legal requirements
      concerning eminent domain, 57
redevelopment plans, 50
   contents, 57
   discussed, 57
   eminent domain and, 57–58
   must be consistent
      with general plan, 57
redevelopment project area, 57
Redwood National Park,
      as Class I area, 109
redwoods
   old-growth redwoods, timber
      harvest plan held inadequate, 370
   timber harvest plan did
      not consider all impacts, 370
referendum
   defined, 50
   discussed, 9
   zoning ordinances and, 58
refineries. *See also* oil refineries
   as sources of GHGs, 120
   as stationary sources of air pollution, 95
reformulated gasoline, defined, 93
refrigerants, 120
   as ozone-depleting chemicals, 101

regional planning agencies (RPAs), 84–86
   COGs, 84
   Delta Protection Commission, 86
   San Francisco Bay Conservation
      and Development Commission, 84–85
   Tahoe Regional
      Planning Agency, 85–86
   transportation plans
      and the California SIP, 127
regional water quality control
      boards (RWQCBs),
      16, 157, 231, 243–244
   California Regional Water
      Quality Control Boards, 243
   chemical contamination
      cleanup and, 191
      leaking USTs, 191
   CWA and, 244
   hazardous waste cleanup, 216, 218
      cleanup and abatement
         orders, 191, 218, 266
      containment-zone policy, 218
      RWQCBs as lead agencies, 218
   monitoring and reporting, 244
   oil spill/release reporting, 265–266
   Porter-Cologne Act implementation, 244
regional water quality
      control plans, 244–245
   Section 401 certification, 342, 345,
      349, 352, 354, 358, 394, 400
      RWQCBs as responsible
         agencies, 358
      waiver, 394
      website, 358
   storm water permits
      general permits, 256–257, 399
      MS4s, 257
   SWAT administration, 224, 226, 260
   timber harvest plan review, 368
   UST regulation variances, 168
   waste discharge requirements
      permits, 225–226,
         244–245, 258–259, 399
      agricultural discharge
         conditional waivers, 260
      Chapter 15 regulations, 258
      for Class III landfills, 230, 399
      construction and demolition
         debris facility permit, 399
      defined, 188, 239, 342
      "isolated" wetlands, 345, 358–359
      municipal solid waste
         transfer station permits, 399
      NPDES permits, 244–245, 254
      Report of Waste Discharge, 239
      timber harvest plan exemption,
         discussed, 369–370
   water quality enforcement, 266
registered professional foresters
      (RPFs), 364, 367–368, 400
regulated asbestos containing material
      (RACM). *See under* asbestos
"regulated substance," 148
   defined, 164
regulatory taking. *See under* taking
Religious Land Use and Institutionalized
      Persons Act of 2000 (RLUIPA), 61
   "substantial burden," 61
religious land uses,
      zoning ordinances and, 61

remedial investigation, 215
   defined, 186
   discussed, 212
remedial investigation/feasibility
      study (RI/FS) process, 186
   discussed, 211–213
   scoping, 212
Renewable Portfolio Standard
      (RPS) program, 82
reportable quantity (RQ), 157
   defined, 148
   discussed, 159–160
   water quality
      release reporting, 265
reproductive toxicants, 398
   significance levels, 175
   warnings under Prop. 65,
      153, 174–175
reservoirs, 270, 298, 313
   construction/enlargement, DWR
      Certificate of Approval, 308, 399
residences
   noise level standards and, 140
      low density, 144
      multi-family, 144
residential development
   EIR found to be adequate, 315
   EIR held inadequate, 315
residential land use, noise levels, 141
Residential Lead-Based Paint
      Hazard Reduction Act
      (Title X), 150, 171–172
   enforcement, 178–179
      Subpart F, 179
   exemptions, 172
residential project, EIR
      held inadequate, 315
resolution of necessity, 57
Resource Conservation
      and Recovery Act (RCRA)
   Comparison of Terms Between
      CERCLA and RCRA, 215
   corrective measures
      implementation, 215
   corrective measures study, 215
   discussed, 189
   facility assessment, 215, 217
   facility investigation, 215
   interim/stabilization
      measure release, defined, 187
   Subtitle C, 164, 189–191, 193
      as ARAR, 212
      hazardous waste
         cleanup and, 213–214
   Subtitle D, 189, 224–227
      solid waste, defined, 224
   Subtitle J, 224
   Subtitle I (Hazardous and
      Solid Waste Amendments
      of 1984) (HSWA),
      150–151, 163–164, 190
   TSDF permit, 215
      RCRA Part B, 187, 398
      RCRA Part C, 207
   U.S. EPA website, 220
respirable particulate matter
   See under particulate matter
respiratory illnesses
   ground-level ozone as cause of, 99
   particulate matter as cause of, 99

Credits

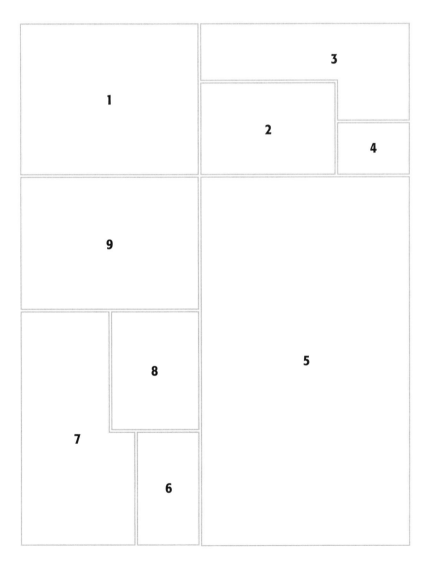

Front cover

1. Mono Lake, courtesy BigStockPhoto.com
2. Smoke stacks, courtesy BigStockPhoto.com
3. Tank farm, courtesy U.S. Dept. of Energy
4. Girl, courtesy BigStockPhoto.com
5. Anza-Borrego Desert, courtesy Albert I. Herson
6. Bald eagle, courtesy Calif. Dept. of Fish and Game
7. Mt. Whitney, courtesy Calif. Dept. of Water Resources
8. Wind farm, courtesy Calif. Dept. of Water Resources
9. Death Valley, courtesy Albert I. Herson

Back cover and spine

Gravel mine, courtesy BigStockPhoto.com
Poppies, courtesy Calif. Dept. of Water Resources
Refinery, courtesy U.S. Dept. of Energy

Interior

Pages 56, 64, 74, 78, 81, 85, 99, 175, 246, 257, 312, 346, 357, courtesy Albert I. Herson
Pages 13, 15, 31, 42, 103, 115, 128, 143, 227, 380, 393, courtesy BigStockPhoto.com
Pages 162, 165, 262, courtesy Gary A. Lucks
Page 190, 216, 263, 410, courtesy U.S. EPA
Page 255, courtesy Rebecca Fricke
Page 316, courtesy U.S. Forest Service Region 5
Page 327, courtesy Calif. Dept. of Fish and Game
Page 338, courtesy U.S. Fish and Wildlife Service
Page 368, courtesy Calif. Dept. of Forestry and Fire Protection

Other Guides and References

PLANNING . LAND USE . URBAN AFFAIRS . ENVIRONMENTAL ANALYSIS . REAL ESTATE DEVELOPMENT

Curtin's California Land Use and Planning Law

Well-known, heavily quoted, definitive summary of California's planning laws with expert commentary on the latest statutes and case law. Includes practice tips, graphics, a table of authorities, and an index. Cited by the California Courts, including the California Supreme Court, as an Authoritative Source.

Cecily T. Talbert
Revised annually

Guide to California Planning

All-new edition describes how planning really works in California, how cities, counties, developers, and citizen groups all interact with each other to shape California communities and the California landscape, for better and for worse. Recipient of the California Chapter APA Award for Planning Education.

William Fulton and Paul Shigley
2005 (third) edition

The Planning Commissioner and the California Dream

An easily readable reference and set of guidelines directed to the on-the-job needs of California's city and county planning commissioners. With interviews, case studies, tips on how to do the job well, photos, illustrations, and a glossary of common terms.

Marjorie W. Macris, FAICP • 2004

Ballot Box Navigator

The authoritative resource on securing a ballot title, qualifying an initiative or referendum for the ballot, and submitting a measure for an election. With short articles, practice tips, drawings, an index, glossary, and a table of authorities.

Michael Patrick Durkee et al. • 2003

California School Facilities Planning

A single-source reference that offers a thorough discussion of laws and regulations that govern planning, funding, siting, design, and construction of educational facilities. The book will guide the reader through every stage of the planning process— from initial conception through construction.

Maureen F. Gorsen et al. • 2005

California Transportation Law

First complete collection of the most important laws and regulations affecting transportation planning in California. Includes ISTEA provisions, Title VI guidelines for mass transit, STIP Guidelines, provisions relating to air quality and equal employment opportunity, civil rights laws, a checklist for mandatory requirements for public outreach, and a glossary.

Jeremy G. March • 2000

California Water II

Comprehensive guide to historical, legal, and policy issues affecting water use in California. This ALL-NEW edition discusses the historic Bay-Delta Accord, the crisis in the Delta, settlement of critical Colorado River issues, global warming, and the emergence of new supplies such as water transfers, conservation, recycling, and the conjunctive use of groundwater.

Littleworth and Garner • 2008 (second) edition

CALL TOLL-FREE
(800) 931-9373 OR FAX (707) 884-4109

Solano Press Books

Eminent Domain

Explains the processes California public agencies must follow to acquire private property for public purposes through eminent domain. Includes case law, legal references, tips, a table of authorities, sample letters and forms, a glossary, and an index.

Richard G. Rypinski • 2002 (second) edition

Guide to the California Environmental Quality Act (CEQA)

The professionals' guide to the California Environmental Quality Act presents an understandable, in-depth description of CEQA's requirements for adequate review and careful preparation of environmental impact reports and other environmental review documents. Includes extensive analyses of statutes, provisions of the CEQA Guidelines, and voluminous case law.

Remy, Thomas, Moose, and Manley • 2006 (eleventh) edition

Guide to the California Forest Practice Act

A comprehensive treatise on state and federal legislation that regulates timber harvesting on private lands in California. Includes short articles, charts, graphs, appendices, a table of authorities, and an index to help understand complex regulatory processes and how they interrelate.

Sharon E. Duggan and Tara Mueller • 2005

The NEPA Book

Practitioner's handbook that takes you through the critical steps, basic requirements, and most important decision points of the National Environmental Policy Act. With short articles, practice tips, tables, illustrations, charts, and sources of additional information.

Ronald E. Bass et al. • 2001 (second) edition

CALL TOLL-FREE
(800) 931-9373 OR FAX (707) 884-4109

Planning for Child Care in California

Presents basic child care information and guidelines for municipal, county, and school district planners, and for child care professionals and their advocates. Includes numerous examples of real child care projects, designs, and partnerships, along with sources of funding and other implementation strategies.

Kristen M. Anderson • 2006

Redevelopment in California

Definitive guide to both the law and practice of redevelopment in California cities and counties, together with codes, case law, and commentary. Contains short articles, notes, photographs, charts, graphs, and illustrative time schedules.

David F. Beatty et al. • 2004 (third) edition

Subdivision Map Act Manual

A comprehensive reference containing information needed to understand Subdivision Map Act legal provisions, recent court-made law, and the review and approval processes. With the full text of the Map Act, practice tips, a table of authorities, and an index.

Daniel J. Curtin, Jr. and Robert E. Merritt • 2003 edition

Telecommunications

Detailed summary and analysis of federal and state laws governing the location and regulation of physical facilities including cable, telephone, and wireless systems (cellular, paging, and Internet), satellite dishes, and antennas. With practice tips, photos, a glossary, table of authorities, and an index.

Paul Valle-Riestra • 2002

Water and Land Use

First complete guide to address the link between land use planning in California and the availability of water. Summarizes key statutes, policies and requirements, and current practices. With illustrations and photos, tables, flow charts, case studies, sample documents, practice tips, a glossary, references, and an index.

Karen E. Johnson and Jeff Loux • 2004

Wetlands, Streams, and Other Waters

A practical guide to federal and state wetland identification, regulation, and permitting processes. Provides detailed information, commentary, and practice tips for those who work with federal and state laws and are engaged in wetland conservation planning.

Paul D. Cylinder et al. • 2004 edition

Solano Press Books

Solano

Press

Books

www.solano.com

spbooks@solano.com

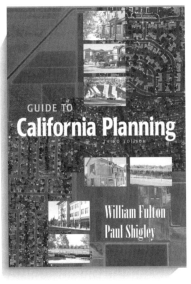

Guide to California Planning

*by William Fulton
and Paul Shigley*

Since the book was first published in 1991, *Guide to California Planning* has served as the authoritative textbook on city and county planning practice. It is used in virtually every college- and graduate-level planning program in California.

In this revised, expanded third edition, the authors lay out planning laws and processes in detail, describing how planning really works—how cities and counties and developers and citizen groups all interact on a daily basis to shape California communities and the California landscape, for better and for worse. Easy to read and understand, *Guide to California Planning* is far more than a textbook. It's also an ideal tool for members of allied professions in the planning and development fields as well as citizen activists.

The Planning Commissioner and the California Dream
Plan It Again, Sam

by Marjorie W. Macris, FAICP

Tackling a serious subject with whimsy and humor, as well as seriousness of purpose, the book offers specific guidelines on how to function as an effective planning commissioner in the face of complex issues, special interests, committed advocates, and intricate planning and environmental laws.

Describing their roles and responsibilities, and how to make sure things go smoothly, *The Planning Commissioner and the California Dream* includes interviews with a variety of commissioners, a glossary of common terms, and tips on how to do the job well. Peppered with amusing references to selected motion pictures that convey the significance of California and its unique environment.

Solano
Press
Books

www.solano.com

spbooks@solano.com

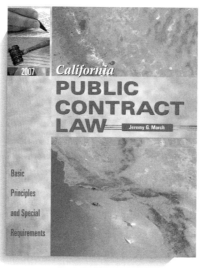

California Public Contract Law
Basic Principles and Special Requirements

by Jeremy G. March

California Public Contract Law is an easy-to-use, concise reference on the laws governing the public contracting processes used by federal, state, regional, and local agencies in California. The book reviews key requirements, suggests model provisions, and provides extensive references for relevant statutes and regulations. An important resource for agency administrators, contractors, and bidders involved in public contracting law.

Includes a list of useful legal research sites on the Internet, a summary of frequently used provisions of the Public Utilities Code and the Public Contract Code, as well as a table of authorities, a list of acronyms, and an index.

Ballot Box Navigator
A Practical and Tactical Guide to Land Use Initiatives and Referenda in California

by Michael Patrick Durkee, Jeffrey A. Walter, David H. Blackwell, and Thomas F. Carey

Ballot Box Navigator focuses on the tools available in California for the regulation of land uses and the control of new development through ballot measures known as initiatives and referenda. The authors provide a comprehensive perspective on the subject, as well as a complete summary of the law and the process.

This book explains how to secure a ballot title, qualify an initiative or referendum for the ballot, and submit a measure for an election. With short articles, practice tips, drawings, an index, glossary, and a table of authorities.

California Water II

*by Arthur L. Littleworth
and Eric L. Garner*

This all-new second edition of *California Water* is the first book since Wells Hutchins' 1956 "bible," *California Law of Water Rights,* to serve as a comprehensive guide to historical, legal, and policy issues that affect the use of water in California.

The book is a major resource for local officials—in water districts, cities, and counties—as well as for lawyers, judges, engineers, planners, community leaders, environmentalists, developers, and farmers. *California Water II* addresses the question, "Do we have enough water?" and covers key developments in water law: the implementation of the historic Bay-Delta Accord, the crisis in the Delta, settlement of critical issues on the Colorado River, global warming, and the emergence of new water supplies such as water transfers, conservation, recycling, and the conjunctive use of groundwater.

Water and Land Use
Planning Wisely for California's Future

*by Karen E. Johnson
and Jeff Loux*

This is the first complete guide to address the increasingly important link between land use planning in California and the availability of water. *Water and Land Use* summarizes key statutes, governmental policies and requirements, and current practices. In addition, the book presents methods for evaluating water demand, supply, reliability, and quality, and for meeting legislative requirements for linking water supplies and land use decisions.

A valuable "how to" handbook for environmental and land use planners, engineers, water resource planners, government officials, and attorneys. With illustrations and photographs, tables, flow charts, case studies, sample documents, practice tips, a glossary, references, and an index.

PLANNING

LAND USE

URBAN AFFAIRS

ENVIRONMENTAL ANALYSIS

REAL ESTATE DEVELOPMENT

CALL TOLL-FREE
(800) 931-9373
OR FAX (707) 884-4109

Solano

Press

Books

www.solano.com

spbooks@solano.com

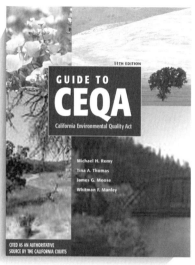

Guide to CEQA

*by Michael H. Remy,
Tina A. Thomas, James G. Moose,
and Whitman F. Manley*

This non-legal and legal professionals' guide to the California Environmental Quality Act includes extensive analyses of the statutes, CEQA Guidelines provisions, and voluminous case law. *Guide to CEQA* presents an understandable, in-depth description of CEQA's requirements for adequate review and careful preparation of environmental impact reports and other environmental review documents.

Of particular significance is the authors' interpretation of the Court of Appeal decision entitled *Communities for a Better Environment v. California Resources Agency.* Attention is given to day-to-day CEQA practice, such as regulatory standards and significant thresholds, as well as the requirement that water supply issues be addressed in EIRs.

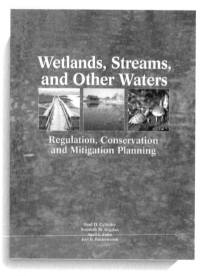

Wetlands, Streams, and Other Waters
Regulation, Conservation, and Mitigation Planning

by Paul D. Cylinder, Kenneth M. Bogdan, April I. Zohn, and Joel B. Butterworth

This book explains the complex laws and regulations that govern our nation's waters. Written in clear, understandable language, *Wetlands, Streams, and Other Waters* guides the reader through the intricacy of federal and state permitting requirements, discussing conservation plans and suggesting strategies to plan and protect resources.

The authors not only exhaustively dissect Section 404 of the Clean Water Act and Section 10 of the Rivers and Harbors Act, but introduce other related federal laws and comprehensively summarize regulations in all 50 states. The book is an invaluable resource for permit applicants, public agencies, environmental organizations, and attorneys confronting these issues.

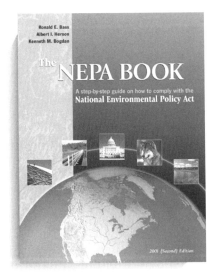

The NEPA Book
A Step-by-Step Guide on How to Comply with the National Environmental Policy Act

by Ronald E. Bass, Albert I. Herson, and Kenneth M. Bogdan

A practitioner's handbook that takes you through the basic requirements and most important decision points of the National Environmental Policy Act. The book will help you determine if a particular action is subject to NEPA, decide whether an environmental assessment or a FONSI is appropriate, prepare legally-adequate environmental documents, write effective mitigation measures, and understand the relationship between NEPA and other environmental laws.

Ideal for environmental specialists, agency reviewers and decisionmakers, attorneys, consultants, students, and citizens who want to effectively influence the environmental decisions that shape their communities.

Guide to the California Forest Practice Act and Related Laws

by Sharon E. Duggan and Tara Mueller

A comprehensive treatise on legislation that regulates timber harvesting on private lands in California, covering state and federal statutory and regulatory requirements, case law, and agency policies. *Guide to the California Forest Practice Act* includes an in-depth discussion of the California Environmental Quality Act; regulation of pesticides; restrictions on streambed alteration; timber harvesting in the coastal zone; common law nuisance and the public trust doctrine; and protection of water quality, endangered and threatened species, and wild and scenic rivers.

Intended as a complete resource for the full range of actors involved, the book includes case studies, short articles, charts, graphs, tables, photos, appendices, a table of authorities, and an index.

PLANNING

LAND USE

URBAN AFFAIRS

ENVIRONMENTAL ANALYSIS

REAL ESTATE DEVELOPMENT

CALL TOLL-FREE
(800) 931-9373
OR FAX (707) 884-4109

Solano Press Books

www.solano.com

spbooks@solano.com

Curtin's California Land Use and Planning Law

by Cecily T. Talbert

Well known, heavily quoted, definitive summary of planning laws, including expert commentary on the latest statutes and case law, this new edition reviews recent CEQA decisions, with particular emphasis on principles governing the adequacy of an EIR's analysis of water supply issues. The book also discusses Corps' and EPA's joint guidance concerning the *Rapanos* decision and federal wetlands jurisdiction, as well as affordable housing case law and legislation, with an extensive review of recent case law concerning density bonus incentives and concessions.

Cited by the California Courts, including the California Supreme Court, as an Authoritative Source. Revised and republished annually in March.

Redevelopment in California

by David F. Beatty, Michael L. F. Buck, Joseph E. Coomes, Jr., T. Brent Hawkins, Edward J. Quinn, Jr., Gerald J. Ramiza, Iris P. Yang, Seth Merewitz, and Ethan Walsh with Calvin E. Hollis and Kathleen H. Head of Keyser Marston Associates

The definitive guide to both the law and practice, this third edition of *Redevelopment in California* is a comprehensive, clearly written reference and practitioner's handbook for policymakers, officials, developers, investors, attorneys, citizens, and students.

The book contains the full text of the law, with legislation adopted through January 1, 2004, including SB 1045, SB 114, SB 966, SB 109, and AB 1731, as well as discussion of recent cases. In addition, the book covers such topics as toxics and military base reuse, plan adoptions, tax-increment financing, affordable housing, and plan implementation. The 2007 Supplement, also available, reflects a number of recent significant changes to the law.

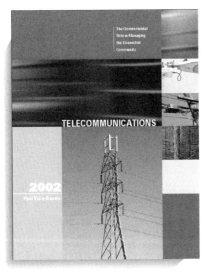

Telecommunications
The Governmental Role in Managing the Connected Community

by Paul Valle-Riestra

Telecommunications explains this dynamic field in straightforward language useful to planners, attorneys, local legislators, cable franchise administrators, and company personnel. The book offers a detailed analysis of federal and state laws governing the location and regulation of physical facilities including cable, traditional telephone systems, wireless systems (cellular, paging, and Internet), satellite dishes, and antennas.

Public policy associated with telecommunications is discussed, along with issues of siting and rights-of-way, current technologies, the future of regulation, and environmental and design standards. Includes practice tips, charts, photographs, a glossary, table of authorities, and an index.

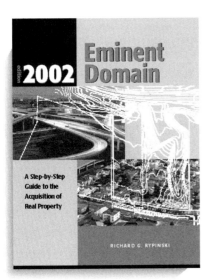

Eminent Domain
A Step-by-Step Guide to the Acquisition of Real Property

by Richard G. Rypinski

This book is a step-by-step guide through the process California public agencies must follow to acquire private property for public purposes through eminent domain. This edition includes recommendations and practice suggestions, the latest legal references, statutory and procedural requirements, and Rules of Court, along with all relevant California case law, a table of authorities, appendices with sample letters and forms, a glossary, and an index.

Eminent Domain is an indispensable reference for public sector attorneys, land acquisition staff and appraisers, and others who need to know how the eminent domain process works.

PLANNING

LAND USE

URBAN AFFAIRS

ENVIRONMENTAL
ANALYSIS

REAL ESTATE
DEVELOPMENT

CALL TOLL-FREE
(800) 931-9373
OR FAX (707) 884-4109

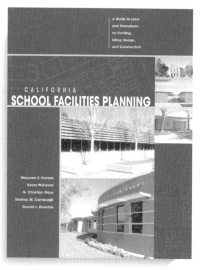

California School Facilities Planning
A Guide to Laws and Procedures for Funding, Siting, Design, and Construction

by Maureen F. Gorsen, Kevin Wilkeson, G. Christian Roux, Thomas M. Cavanagh, and Dennis L. Dunston

A single-source reference that offers a thorough discussion of laws and regulations that govern planning, funding, siting, design, and construction of educational facilities. *School Facilities Planning* will guide the reader chronologically through every stage of the planning process—from initial conception through construction.

Topics covered include the history of school facilities nationwide; funding sources and financing methods; planning and design, both for individual schools and district-wide; school siting issues, including acquisition of property and compliance with land use and environmental laws.

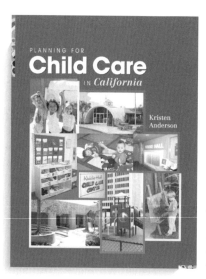

Planning for Child Care in California

by Kristen M. Anderson

Presents basic information and guidelines for municipal, county, and school district planners, and for child care professionals and their advocates. It features strategies for ensuring that child care needs are met locally, with resource material that explains how it is regulated in its various forms through the General Plan and zoning.

Planning for Child Care in California discusses guidelines for incorporating child care goals into the public planning process, with specific attention to the location, planning, and design of housing, centers of employment, and transit-based facilities. Numerous examples of real child care projects, designs, and partnerships are included, along with sources of funding and other implementation strategies.